The International Law of the Sea

Yoshifumi Tanaka
University of Copenhagen, Faculty of Law

CAMBRIDGE
UNIVERSITY PRESS

CAMBRIDGE UNIVERSITY PRESS
Cambridge, New York, Melbourne, Madrid, Cape Town,
Singapore, São Paulo, Delhi, Mexico City

Cambridge University Press
The Edinburgh Building, Cambridge CB2 8RU, UK

Published in the United States of America by Cambridge University Press, New York

www.cambridge.org
Information on this title: www.cambridge.org/9781107009998

First published 2012

Printed in the United Kingdom at the University Press, Cambridge

A catalogue record for this publication is available from the British Library

Library of Congress Cataloguing in Publication data
Tanaka, Yoshifumi.
The international law of the sea / Yoshifumi Tanaka, University of Copenhagen, Faculty of Law.
pages cm
Includes bibliographical references and index.
ISBN 978-1-107-00999-8 (hardback) – ISBN 978-0-521-27952-9 (paperback)
1. Law of the sea. I. Title.
KZA1145.T36 2012
341.4′5–dc23
2011052555

ISBN 978-1-107-00999-8 Hardback
ISBN 978-0-521-27952-9 Paperback

The International Law of the Sea

The law of the sea is a complex and fascinating subject. This textbook explores the subject from the perspective of public international law, covering all the key topics from the legal regimes governing the different jurisdictional zones, to international cooperation for protection of the marine environment. Students interested in international environmental and natural resources law will also find chapters on emerging issues such as the conservation and the protection of natural resources and bio-diversity in the oceans. Combining clarity of expression with engaging academic analysis, this is required reading for all students of the subject.

YOSHIFUMI TANAKA is Associate Professor of International Law at the Faculty of Law, University of Copenhagen. He has taught international law of the sea at several different universities and has also published widely in the field.

Dedicated to my teachers,
Lucius Caflisch, Hugh Thirlway and Tetsuo Sato

Let the heavens rejoice, let the earth be glad;
Let the sea resound, and all that is in it.
Psalm 96:11

Contents

PART II OUR COMMON OCEAN: PROTECTION OF COMMUNITY INTERESTS AT SEA 217

Preface

'The dark oceans were the womb of life: from the protecting oceans life emerged'.[1] As can be seen in the words of Arvid Pardo, the Ambassador for Malta, it would be no exaggeration to say that a sound marine environment provides the foundation for all life. Hence rules of international law governing the oceans are of particular importance in the international community. This book will seek to provide readers with a systematic overview of the international law of the sea as an inseparable part of public international law.

In the present author's view, rules of the international law of the sea must be examined from a dual viewpoint, namely the reconciliation of interests between States and the protection of community interests. This book is thus divided into two parts.

Part I, which consists of Chapters 1 to 6, involves international law governing jurisdictional zones at sea. In the international law of the sea, the oceans are divided into several jurisdictional zones, namely internal waters, territorial sea, archipelagic waters, the contiguous zone, the exclusive economic zone (EEZ), the continental shelf, the high seas and the Area. In principle, the law of the sea regulates human activities in the ocean according to these jurisdictional zones. Thus Part I will examine the rules of international law concerning each jurisdictional zone focusing on the reconciliation of various interests between States. At the same time, limits and delimitation of marine spaces will also be discussed in this part.

Part II, which contains Chapters 7 to 13, deals with international law intended to protect community interests concerning marine affairs. One can no longer deny that the survival of mankind as a whole may be difficult without the protection of community interests, i.e. common interests of the international community as a whole. The protection of community interests is increasingly important in international law in general and the law of the sea is no exception. Thus this part will address the following subjects which may involve the protection of such interests: conservation of marine living resources, protection of the marine environment, conservation of marine

[1] United Nations General Assembly 22nd Session, First Committee, 1515th Meeting, A/C.1/PV.1515, 1 November 1967, p. 2, para. 7.

biological diversity, marine scientific research, maintenance of peace and security at sea, the rights of land-locked States, and peaceful settlement of international disputes.

Because of the ever-expanding nature of the law of the sea, it is highly difficult to make a detailed examination with regard to each and every issue of the law in one book. Thus this book has only the modest aim of examining the principal issues of the law of the sea succinctly. It does not discuss maritime law or admiralty law, which is a distinct body of private law governing maritime questions and offences. Nor does it focus on the municipal law of a particular country or law and policy of particular regions. In essence, this book addresses the laws of peace, not the laws of war.

The manuscript of this book was completed in July 2011 at Copenhagen, Denmark. All websites were current as of that date.

ACKNOWLEDGEMENTS

I would like to express my deep gratitude to three eminent professors of international law: Professor Hugh Thirlway and Professor Lucius Caflisch, both of the Graduate Institute of International Studies, Geneva, and Professor Tetsuo Sato of Hitotsubashi University, Tokyo. They were my supervisors when I was a graduate student in Geneva and Tokyo and I owe much to them. I am also indebted to Professor Kyoji Kawasaki of Hitotsubashi University for his encouragement.

I am grateful to the University of Copenhagen, Faculty of Law, for its support in the completion of this book. My thanks are also due to Sinéad Moloney at Cambridge University Press for her warm and professional assistance.

Finally, I wish to record my deep gratitude to my wife, Akiko, for all her support and prayer throughout my study.

YOSHIFUMI TANAKA

Figures

Figures 1.1, 1.2 and 4.3 are drawn on the basis of T. Kuwahara, *Introduction to the International Law of the Sea* (in Japanese, Tokyo, Sinzansha, 2002) pp. 143–145, with modifications on technical advice from Dr Anne Marie O'Hagan. The author wishes to thank Dr O'Hagan for her technical assistance.

Tables

Abbreviations

AFDI	*Annuaire français de droit international*
AJIL	*American Journal of International Law*
ASDI	*Annuaire suisse de droit international*
BYIL	*British Yearbook of International Law*
CCAMLR	Convention for the Conservation of Antarctic Marine Living Resources
CYIL	*Canadian Yearbook of International Law*
EEZ	exclusive economic sone
EFZ	exclusive fishery zone
EJIL	*European Journal of International Law*
EU	European Union
FAO	Food and Agriculture Organization of the United Nations
GYIL	*German Yearbook of International Law*
ICAO	International Civil Aviation Organization
ICCAT	International Commission for the Conservation of Atlantic Tunas
ICJ	International Court of Justice
ICLQ	*International and Comparative Law Quarterly*
IHO	International Hydrographic Organization
IJMCL	*International Journal of Marine and Coastal Law*
ILC	International Law Commission
ILM	*International Legal Materials*
ILR	*International Law Reports*
IMO	International Maritime Organization
IOC	Intergovernmental Oceanographic Commission
IOTC	Indian Ocean Tuna Commission
ITLOS	International Tribunal for the Law of the Sea
IUCN	International Union for the Conservation of Nature
IUU	illegal, unreported and unregulated fishing
IWC	International Whaling Commission
LOSC	United Nations Convention on Law of the Sea
MARPOL	International Convention for the Prevention of Pollution from Ships

Max Planck Encyclopedia	*Max Planck Encyclopedia of Public International Law* (Oxford University Press, 2008–2011, online edition: www.mpepil.com.)
MPAs	marine protected areas
MSY	maximum sustainable yield
NAFO	Northwest Atlantic Fisheries Organization
NATO	North Atlantic Treaty Organization
NEAFC	North East Atlantic Fisheries Commission
NILR	*Netherlands International Law Review*
ODIL	*Ocean Development and International Law*
OPRC	International Convention on Oil Pollution Preparedness, Response and Cooperation
OSPAR	Convention for the Protection of the Marine Environment of the North-East Atlantic
PSI	Proliferation Security Initiative
PSSA	particularly sensitive sea area
RCADI	*Recueil des cours de l'Académie de droit international*
RECIEL	*Review of European Community and International Environmental Law*
RGDIP	*Revue générale de droit international public*
RIAA	*Reports of International Arbitral Awards*
SOLAS	International Convention for the Safety of Life at Sea
SPLOS	Meeting of States Parties to the United Nations Convention on the Law of the Sea
SUA Convention	Convention for the Suppression of Unlawful Acts against the Safety of Maritime Navigation
TAC	total allowable catch
TSC	Geneva Convention on the Territorial Sea and the Contiguous Zone
UN	United Nations
UNCLOS	United Nations Conference on the Law of the Sea
UNDOALOS	United Nations Division for Ocean Affairs and the Law of the Sea
UNEP	United Nations Environment Programme
UNESCO	United Nations Educational, Scientific and Cultural Organization
UNTS	United Nations Treaty Series
Virginia Commentaries	*United Nations Convention on the Law of the Sea 1982: A Commentary* (The Hague, Nijhoff, 1985–2002), 6 vols.
WMD	weapons of mass destruction
WTO	World Trade Organization
YILC	*Yearbook of International Law Commission*
ZaöRV	*Zeitschrift für ausländisches öffentliches Recht und Völkerrecht*

Table of Cases

Southern Bluefin Tuna Case (New Zealand v. Japan; Australia v. Japan), Provisional Measures (1999), ITLOS, (1999) 38 *ILM* 241–242, 395–396, 412n, 413n, 413–414

Southern Bluefin Tuna Case (Australia and New Zealand v. Japan), Jurisdiction and Admissibility (2000), (2000) 39 *ILM* 400n

S.S. *'Lotus'* Case, PCIJ, 1928 Series A/10 154–155

Tempest Case (1859), Simmonds, *Cases*, Vol. I 79

Tenyu Maru Case, (1910) 4 *Alaska*, Simmonds, *Cases*, Vol. IV 165

Texaco Overseas Petroleum Company/California Asiatic Oil Company v. Libyan Arab Republic, (1978) 17 *ILM* 15

The Twee Gebroeders (1801), Simmonds, *Cases*, Vol. I 85

'Tomimaru' Case (Japan v. Russian Federation), Prompt Release (2007), ITLOS 156, 419

Trail Smelter Case (United States, Canada), (1939) 33 *AJIL*/(1941) 35 *AJIL* 260

Tunisia/Libya Case, ICJ Reports 1982 58, 193, 199, 200, 201, 202n, 204, 205, 206, 207, 210–211, 213–214

United States v. Alaska Case, *Report of the Special Master* 1996, *United States Reports, Cases Adjudged in the Supreme Court at October Term* 1996 70

Wildenhus Case, (1887) 120 *U.S.* 78

Table of Treaties and Instruments

UNITED NATIONS GENERAL ASSEMBLY RESOLUTIONS

UNITED NATIONS SECURTY COUNCIL RESOLUTIONS

NATIONAL LAW

India

Iran

Malaysia

United Republic of Tanzania

Territorial Sea and Exclusive Economic Zone Act (1989) 346
Article 10 (1) (c) 346n

United States

Proclamation by President Truman of 28 September 1945 on Policy of the United States with respect to the Natural Resources of the Subsoil and Sea Bed of the Continental Shelf 15, 22, 132–33, 134

Proclamation by President Truman of 28 September 1945 on Policy of the United States with respect to Coastal Fisheries in Certain Areas of the High Seas 22

PART I

The Divided Oceans: International Law Governing Jurisdictional Zones

OUTLINE OF PART I

1

The Law of the Sea in Perspective

Main Issues

The international law of the sea is one of the oldest branches of public international law. Thus, it must be examined from the perspective of the development of international law in general. Originally the law of the sea consisted of a body of rules of customary law. Later on, these rules were progressively codified. The Third United Nations Conference on the Law of the Sea, which successfully adopted the United Nations Convention on the Law of the Sea (the LOSC) in 1982, is of particular importance in the codification of the law. Furthermore, the international community and the situations that surround the oceans are constantly changing. Accordingly, it is also necessary to examine the evolutionary process of the law after the adoption of the LOSC. As a general introduction, this chapter will address the following issues in particular:

(i) What are the principal functions of the law of the sea?
(ii) What are the sources of the law of the sea?
(iii) What are the principles governing the law of the sea?
(iv) What are the specific procedures of the Third United Nations Conference on the Law of the Sea?
(v) What are the principal features of the LOSC?
(vi) What is the evolutionary process of the LOSC and the law of the sea?

1 INTRODUCTION

1.1 General considerations

Historically, the oceans have been and continue to be fundamental to human life. The ever-increasing use of the oceans necessitates international rules governing various human activities in the oceans. The body of international rules that bind States and other subjects of international law in their marine affairs is called the international law of the sea. Like the international law of armed conflict and the law of diplomacy, the law of the sea is one of the oldest branches of public international law. Furthermore, like international human rights law and international environmental law, the law of the sea is a dynamic field of international law. The law of the sea can be said to mirror both classical and novel aspects of international law. Thus the law of the sea must be studied from the perspective of the development of public international law as a whole.

1.2 Functions of the law of the sea

The law of the sea plays a dual role in international relations.

First, the primary function of international law involves the spatial distribution of jurisdiction of States, and the same applies to the law of the sea. The contemporary international law of the sea divides the ocean into multiple jurisdictional zones, such as internal waters, territorial seas, the contiguous zone, the exclusive economic zone (EEZ), archipelagic waters, the continental shelf, the high seas and the Area. In principle, the law of the sea provides the rights and obligations of a coastal State and third States according to these jurisdictional zones. Consequently, the law seeks to coordinate the interests of individual States. This approach is sometimes called the zonal management approach. Considering that the world is divided into sovereign States, the traditional role of the law of the sea will in no way lose its importance.

Second, given that the ocean is one unit in a physical sense, the proper management of the oceans necessitates international cooperation between States. In general, the spatial scope of man-made jurisdictional zones does not always correspond to marine ecosystems. In fact, several species, such as straddling and highly migratory species, do not respect artificial delimitation lines. The divergence between the law and nature is a serious deficiency in the traditional zonal management approach. International cooperation is thus a prerequisite for conservation of marine living resources as well as biological diversity. Similarly, without international cooperation, the regulation of marine pollution would be less effective because pollution may spread beyond maritime boundaries. Furthermore, a single State's regulation of industrial activities to prevent marine pollution would put that State's economy at a competitive disadvantage. International cooperation is also needed in marine scientific research due to the highly complex nature of the oceans. The law of the sea provides a legal framework for ensuring international cooperation in marine affairs, thereby safeguarding the common interests of the international community as a whole.[1]

These two basic functions – the spatial distribution of national jurisdiction and ensuring international cooperation between States – are not mutually exclusive, but must coexist in the law of the sea. While the first function of the law provides for the

[1] The 'common interest of the international community as a whole' or 'community interests' is an elusive concept and it is difficult, *a priori* to define it in the abstract. As Simma pointedly observed, the identification of common interests does not derive from scientific abstraction but rather flows from the recognition of concrete problems: B. Simma, 'From Bilateralism to Community Interest in International Law' (1994-IV) 250 *RCADI* pp. 235–243. In the law of the sea, one can say that community interests include marine environmental protection, the conservation of marine living resources and biological diversity, the management of the common heritage of mankind, suppression of piracy, and the maintenance of international peace and security at sea For an analysis of the protection of community interests in the law of the sea, see Y. Tanaka, 'Protection of Community Interests in International Law: The Case of the Law of the Sea' (2011) 15 *Max Planck Yearbook of United Nations Law* pp. 329–375. In this book, the term 'common interests of the international community' and 'community interests' will be used interchangeably.

zonal management approach dividing the oceans into multiple jurisdictional zones, the second function requires a holistic or integrated management approach focusing on community interests. Thus the international law of the sea should be considered as a dual legal system comprising both the zonal and the integrated management approaches. Reconciliation between the two different approaches and between division and unity of the oceans should be an essential issue in the law.[2]

2 MARINE SPACES IN THE LAW OF THE SEA

2.1 Scope of the oceans in the law of the sea

The ocean as a subject of the law of the sea is one single unit and is essentially characterised by *the continuity of marine spaces*. In other words, as Gidel pointed out, the marine spaces governed by the law of the sea must communicate freely and naturally with each other all over the world.[3] This means that each marine space must be connected to another sea or the ocean by a narrow outlet, normally a strait. Accordingly, for instance, the law of the sea is not applicable to the Caspian Sea because it is separated from the ocean.[4] Moreover, in order to freely and naturally communicate through the ocean, the water level must essentially be the same. Indeed, it appears to be unreasonable to argue that rules of the law of the sea are applicable to a distinct body of water at an altitude different from sea level, such as a lake located in a mountain several hundred or even thousand metres high. It must be concluded, therefore, that rivers and lakes are part of terrestrial territory and are not governed by the law of the sea.[5] It is also to be noted that under the law of the sea, the ocean is understood to cover three elements, i.e. seabed and the subsoil, adjacent water column and the atmosphere above the sea.

2.2 Typology of marine spaces

As explained earlier, marine spaces are divided into several jurisdictional zones in the contemporary international law of the sea. On the basis of the national jurisdiction of the coastal State, these marine spaces can be divided into two main categories: marine spaces under national jurisdiction and spaces beyond national jurisdiction. The former

[2] The present writer presented the idea in: Y. Tanaka, *A Dual Approach to Ocean Governance: The Cases of Zonal and Integrated Management in International Law of the Sea* (Surrey, England, Ashgate, 2008), in particular pp. 21–25.

[3] G. Gidel, *Le droit international public de la mer: le temps de paix*, vol.1. *Introduction, La haute mer* (reprint, Paris, Duchemin, 1981), p. 40.

[4] *Ibid*. This view is echoed by many writers, including: R. R. Churchill and A. V. Lowe, *Law of the Sea*, 3rd edn (Manchester University Press, 1999), p. 60; Nguyen Quoc Dinh, P. Daillier, M. Forteau and A. Pellet, *Droit International Public*, 8th edn (Paris, L.G.D.J., 2009), p. 1276; P. Vincent, *Droit de la mer* (Brussels, Larcier, 2008), pp. 11–12; L. Caflisch, 'Règles générales du droit des cours d'eau internationaux' (1989-VII) 219 *RCADI* p. 24; S. Vinogradov and P. Wouters, 'The Caspian Sea: Current Legal Problems' (1995) *ZaöRV* pp. 618–619; J.-P. Pancracio, *Droit de la mer* (Paris, Dalloz, 2010), p. 411.

[5] Gidel, *Le droit international public de la mer*, vol.1, pp. 40–42; Churchill and Lowe, *The Law of the Sea*, p. 60.

category contains internal waters, territorial seas, international straits, archipelagic waters, the contiguous zone, the EEZ and the continental shelf, while the latter contains the high seas and the Area, namely the seabed and ocean floor and subsoil thereof beyond the limits of national jurisdiction. Further to this, the present writer proposes to divide the marine spaces under national jurisdiction into two sub-categories.

The first sub-category concerns marine spaces governed by territorial sovereignty. This category of marine spaces contains internal waters, territorial seas, international straits and archipelagic waters. Territorial sovereignty is characterised by completeness and exclusiveness. Territorial sovereignty denotes complete jurisdiction in the sense that it comprises three elements unless international law provides otherwise:

(i) Territorial sovereignty comprises comprehensive jurisdiction, which includes both legislative and enforcement jurisdiction, over the State's territory.
(ii) The State exercises its jurisdiction over all matters within its territory. In other words, territorial sovereignty contains no limit *ratione materiae*.
(iii) The State exercises its jurisdiction over all people regardless of their nationalities. Territorial sovereignty thus contains no limit *ratione personae*.

At the same time, territorial sovereignty is exclusive in the sense that only the State in question may exercise jurisdiction over its territory. In summary, in its territory, the State exercises legislative and enforcement jurisdiction over all matters and all people in an exclusive manner unless international law provides otherwise.

It is important to note that territorial sovereignty is exercisable solely within the territory in question. In this sense, territorial sovereignty is spatial by nature. A jurisdiction that relates to a certain space and can be exercised solely within the space in question may be called 'spatial jurisdiction'.[6] Territorial sovereignty is a typical example of spatial jurisdiction. In light of the comprehensive character of territorial sovereignty, one may call territorial sovereignty the complete spatial jurisdiction. In short, internal waters, territorial seas, international straits and archipelagic waters are marine spaces under territorial sovereignty or complete spatial jurisdiction.

The second sub-category relates to marine spaces beyond territorial sovereignty but under the national jurisdiction of the coastal State. It is clear that the EEZ and the continental shelf are included in this category.[7] Considering that the contiguous zone becomes part of the EEZ where it is established, it may not be unreasonable to put the contiguous zone into the same sub-category as the EEZ.[8]

The coastal State jurisdiction over the EEZ as well as the continental shelf – called sovereign rights – is limited to the matters defined by international law (limitation *ratione materiae*). In this regard, sovereign rights must be distinguished from territorial sovereignty per se, which is comprehensive unless international law provides

[6] It would appear that the concept of territory is not wholly unambiguous in international law. Hence it would seem to be wise to use the term 'spatial' jurisdiction, not 'territorial' jurisdiction. In fact, Gidel used the term 'souveraineté spatiale', not 'souveraineté territoriale'. Gidel, *Le droit international public de la mer*, vol.1, p. 238.
[7] LOSC, Articles 56(1), 77(1). 1833 *UNTS* p. 3.
[8] Where the EEZ is not claimed, however, the contiguous zone forms part of the high seas.

otherwise. Apart from this, however, sovereign rights have commonalities with territorial sovereignty:

(i) Sovereign rights concern a certain space and can be exercised solely within the space in question, that is to say, the EEZ as well as the continental shelf. In this sense, such rights are spatial by nature.
(ii) Concerning matters defined by law, the coastal State may exercise legislative and enforcement jurisdiction in the EEZ as well as the continental shelf.
(iii) The coastal State exercises its jurisdiction over all people regardless of their nationalities within the certain space in question. Thus, sovereign rights contain no limit *ratione personae*. In this respect, jurisdiction over the EEZ as well as the continental shelf should be distinguished from personal jurisdiction.
(iv) Sovereign rights are exclusive in the sense that no one may undertake the exploration and the exploitation of natural resources without the express consent of the coastal State.

The essential point is that, in common with territorial sovereignty, the sovereign rights over the EEZ and the continental shelf are spatially limited by nature. The fact that jurisdiction can be exercised solely within the certain space is the essential element of spatial jurisdiction. The coastal State jurisdiction over the EEZ and the continental shelf is also essentially characterised by the spatial element. Hence, it may be argued that the sovereign rights over the EEZ and the continental shelf can be regarded as a sort of spatial jurisdiction, not as personal or any other type of jurisdiction, although it must be distinguished from territorial sovereignty.[9] Considering that, unlike territorial sovereignty, sovereign rights are limited in their material scope, however, these rights should be called limited spatial jurisdiction.[10]

In summary, spatial jurisdiction comprises both complete spatial jurisdiction (= territorial sovereignty) and limited spatial jurisdiction (= sovereign rights). In either case, it must be stressed that coastal State jurisdiction over marine spaces is spatial by

[9] J. Combacau, *Le droit international de la mer, Que sais-je?* (Paris, PUF, 1985), p. 21. This issue will be discussed in Chapter 4, sections 3.3. and 4.7. Coastal State jurisdiction over the EEZ and the continental shelf is sometimes described as 'functional jurisdiction'. This is not an unreasonable view. However, every jurisdiction is functional in the sense that certain functions are attributed to the jurisdiction. It appears that the functional nature is not an inherent feature of coastal State jurisdiction over the EEZ and the continental shelf.

[10] French writers call such jurisdiction 'la compétence territoriale limitée' or 'la compétence territoriale mineure'. See for instance, C. Rousseau, *Droit international public: les compétences*, vol.3 (Paris, Sirey, 1977), p. 8; S. Bastid, *Droit international public: principes fondamentaux, Les Cours de droit* 1969–1970 (Université de Paris), p. 804; Nguyen Quoc Dinh et al., *Droit international public*, p. 536. In the United Kingdom, Brierly contrasts the fullest rights over territory, namely, territorial sovereignty with 'minor territorial rights'. J. L. Brierly, *The Law of Nations: An Introduction to the International Law of Peace*, 6th edn (Oxford, Clarendon Press, 1963), p. 162. Akehurst also argued that there are lesser rights over territory, that is to say, 'minor rights over territory'. P. Malanczuk, *Akehurst's Modern Introduction to International Law*, 7th rev. edn (London and New York, Routledge, 1997), p. 158. In Japan, Kuwahara categorised marine spaces according to 'la compétence territoriale majeure' and 'la compétence territoriale mineure': T. Kuwahara, *Introduction to International Law of the Sea* (in Japanese) (Tokyo, Shinzansya, 2002), pp. 18–22. In essence, limited spatial jurisdiction is equivalent to 'minor territorial rights' or 'la compétence territoriale limitée'.

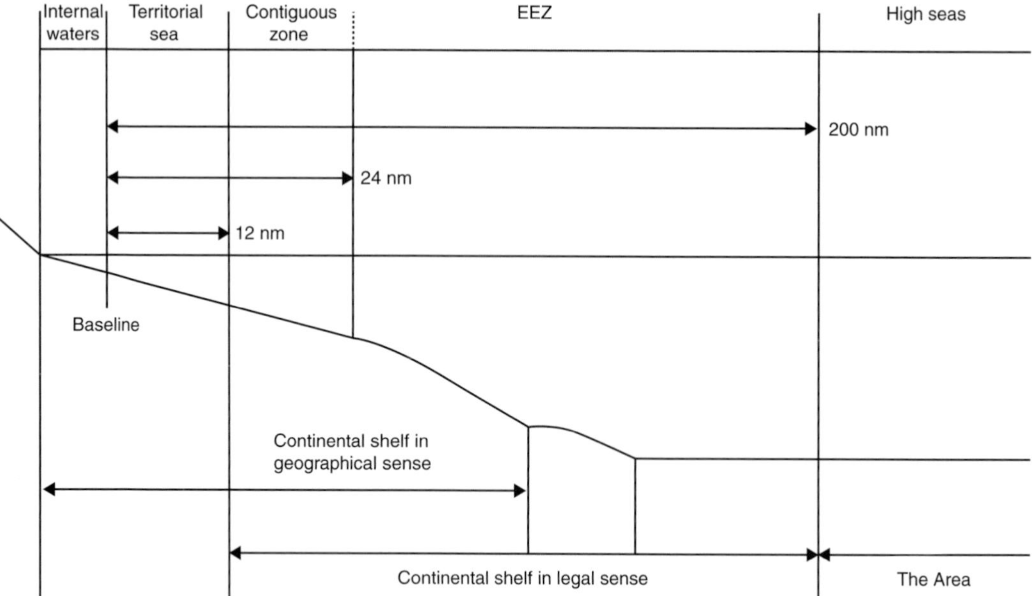

Figure 1.1. The case where the outer edge of the continental shelf does not extend up to 200 nautical miles

nature. It follows from the above discussion that marine spaces in the law of the sea can be categorised as follows (see Figures 1.1 and 1.2):

(a) Marine spaces under national jurisdiction
   (i) Marine spaces under territorial sovereignty (or complete spatial jurisdiction): internal waters, the territorial sea, international straits, and archipelagic waters.
   (ii) Marine spaces under sovereign rights (or limited spatial jurisdiction): the contiguous zone (where the EEZ is established), the EEZ, and the continental shelf.

(b) Marine spaces beyond national jurisdiction
   The high seas and the Area.

Part I of this book will examine rules governing each jurisdictional zone according to this categorisation.

3 SOURCES OF THE INTERNATIONAL LAW OF THE SEA

3.1 Formal sources

As a preliminary consideration, it will be appropriate to briefly examine sources of the international law of the sea. As noted, the law of the sea is an inseparable part of international law in general. Accordingly, the law of the sea is generated from the same sources of international law set out in Article 38(1) of the Statute of the International Court of Justice. Whilst, strictly speaking, Article 38(1) involves only the ICJ, this provision is generally accepted as the statement of sources of

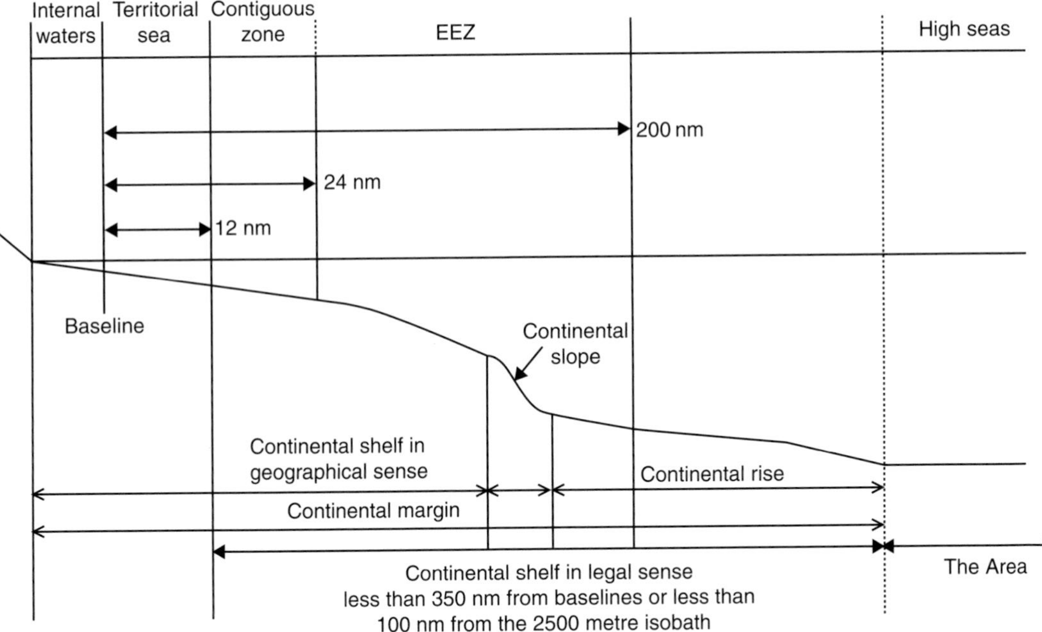

Figure 1.2. The case where the outer edge of the continental margin extends beyond 200 nautical miles from the baselines

international law. Article 38(1) enumerates three formal sources of law, i.e. legal procedures by which a legal rule comes into existence:

(a) international convention, whether general or particular, establishing rules expressly recognised by the contesting States;
(b) international custom, as evidence of a general practice accepted as law;
(c) the general principles of law recognised by civilised nations.

It is conceivable that general principles of law are of limited value in the context of the law of the sea. Thus, the principal focus must be on customary law and treaties.

(a) Customary law

Customary international law can be divided into two categories.

The first category is general customary law. While treaties are binding only upon the parties to them, it is widely accepted that rules of general customary law are binding upon all States in the international community. In this regard, the ICJ, in the *North Sea Continental Shelf* cases, stated that general or customary law rules and obligations 'by their very nature, must have equal force for all members of the international community, and cannot therefore be the subject of any right of unilateral exclusion exercisable at will by any one of them in its own favour'.[11] Thus, rules of general customary

[11] ICJ Reports 1969, pp. 38–39, para. 63.

law are also binding upon newly independent States, even though they did not participate in the formation of these rules concerned. Given that in the context of the law of the sea, there is no treaty to which all States are parties, rules of general customary law continue to be important. Customary law also comes into play in a situation where there is no specific rule in relevant treaties.

The second category involves special or local customary law, which is applicable only within a defined group of States. The well-known example of local customary law may be the practice of diplomatic asylum in Latin America. A special or local customary law may exist between only two States. In this regard, the ICJ in the *Right of Passage over Indian Territory* case held that: 'It is difficult to see why the number of States between which a local custom may be established on the basis of long practice must necessarily be larger than two'.[12]

Orthodox legal theory sees rules of customary law as resulting from the combination of two elements: an objective element of 'extensive and virtually uniform' State practice and the subjective or psychological element known as the *opinio juris*, i.e. a belief that the practice is rendered obligatory by the existence of a rule of law requiring it.[13] A clear statement of the two-element theory can be seen in the *Libya/Malta* judgment, which stated that: 'It is of course axiomatic that the material of customary international law is to be looked for primarily in the actual practice and *opinio juris* of States'.[14]

Concerning the objective element, at least three issues arise. The first issue involves the question of what constitutes State practice. Some writers consider that only physical acts can count as State practice in the making of customary law. However, it appears that this restrictive view is not supported by the ICJ and States. The better view appears to be that, broadly, State practice includes not only physical acts, namely what they do, but also what they say. State practice also includes omissions because some rules of international law prohibit certain conduct by States. Specifically, evidence of State practice can be detected in diplomatic correspondence, policy statements, press releases, official manuals on legal questions, the opinions of official legal advisers, comments by governments on drafts produced by the International Law Commission, State legislation and national judicial decisions, etc.

The second issue involves a degree of uniformity of State practice. Whilst generality cannot be determined in abstract, it is generally recognised that universality is not required to establish a new rule of customary law. According to the ICJ, in order to deduce the existence of customary rules, it is sufficient that the conduct of States should, in general, be consistent with such rules.[15] In this regard, the Court further specified that general State practice includes the practice of States whose interests are specially affected.[16] Historically the practice of maritime States had great influence in

[12] ICJ Reports 1960, p. 39.
[13] ICJ Reports 1969, pp. 42–44, paras. 73–77.
[14] ICJ Reports 1985, p. 29, para. 27.
[15] The *Nicaragua* case (Merits), ICJ Reports 1986, p. 98, para. 186.
[16] ICJ Reports 1969, p. 43, para. 74.

the development of the law of the sea. However, as will be seen, the traditional law of the sea, which was designed to safeguard interests of maritime States only, was strongly criticised by the decolonised new States.

The third issue involves a time element in customary law-making. It can be presumed that normally a long passage of time is needed to formulate rules of customary international law. However, it appears that the ICJ, in the *North Sea Continental Shelf* cases, took a more flexible approach, stating that 'the passage of only a short period of time is not necessarily, or of itself, a bar to the formation of a new rule of customary international law'.[17] The flexible approach may facilitate the formation of rules of customary law which may be suitable for a rapidly changing international society. However, care should be taken that the reduction of the time-element requirement does not directly support the doctrine of 'instant custom'.[18]

The subjective element, i.e, *opinio juris*, has been the subject of extensive debate among legal writers. The well-known paradox of *opinio juris* is that States cannot trust in the existence of a rule of customary law requiring them to act or refrain from acting, before a customary rule is established. At the initial stage of the formation of a rule of customary law, it is illogical to consider that States feel a conviction to comply with a rule of law since there is as yet no legal obligation. In response to this question, it would be sufficient to consider that, at the initial stage, the States concerned regard the practice as conforming to a rule which is a useful and desirable rule and one that should exist.[19] Considering that the formation of customary law is a gradual process, it may be argued that a legal conviction matures gradually.

An obvious difficulty concerning *opinio juris* involves finding the evidence for it. In spite of this difficulty, the majority opinion generally recognises the need for the subjective element in order to make custom as law distinct from custom as a mere fact. In this regard, it is notable that to a certain extent, the process of the formation of customary international law is being more institutionalised under the auspices of international organisations, such as the UN General Assembly. In fact, the ICJ in the *Legality of the Threat or Use of Nuclear Weapons* held that UN General Assembly Resolutions 'provide evidence important for establishing the existence of a rule or the emergence of *opinio juris*'.[20] Hence the difficulty in finding evidence for *opinio juris* would not be a decisive reason to abandon this element.

In relation to this, it is to be noted that the ICJ did not mechanically apply the two-element test to the identification of a rule of customary law. For instance, the Court, in the *North Sea Continental Shelf* cases, rigidly applied the two-element test of customary law to the equidistance method and refused to admit the customary law character of that method. However, the Court did not apply to the equitable principles the rigid

[17] *Ibid.*

[18] It seemed that the ICJ was wary about supporting the doctrine of 'instant custom'. See the *Nicaragua* case (Merits), ICJ Reports 1986, p. 97, para. 184.

[19] H. Thirlway, *International Customary Law and Codification* (Leiden, Sijthoff, 1972), pp. 53–54; by the same writer, 'The Law and Procedure of the International Court of Justice: Part Two' (1990) 62 *BYIL* p. 43.

[20] ICJ Reports 1996, pp. 254–255, para. 70. See also J.-P. Pancracio, *Droit de la mer*, pp. 43–44 and 47.

test of the two elements of custom and regarded the principles as a rule of customary law. While a comprehensive analysis of the ICJ's application of the two-element test is beyond the scope of this chapter, care should be taken in noting that in ICJ case law, the manner of the application of the test may vary on a case-by-case basis.[21]

Furthermore, some mention should be made of the doctrine of the persistent objector. According to the doctrine of the persistent objector, a State which objects consistently to the application of a rule of law while it is still in the process of becoming such a rule may be able to 'opt out' of the application of the rule after it has acquired the status of a rule of general customary law. The origin of the doctrine of the persistent objector is usually traced back to the law of the sea case, i.e. the 1951 *Norwegian Fishery* case. In this case, the United Kingdom disputed the legality of the Norwegian baselines because they were inconsistent with a rule of customary law referred to as the 'ten-mile rule'. Whilst the ICJ did not admit the argument by the United Kingdom, the Court stated that: 'In any event the ten-mile rule would appear to be inapplicable as against Norway inasmuch as she has always opposed any attempt to apply it to the Norwegian coast'.[22] Not a few writers support the doctrine of the persistent objector. However, it appears that the doctrine of the persistent objector is not free from difficulty in theory and practice. Indeed, there is little State or judicial practice to support the doctrine. Furthermore, it appears difficult to explain why the decolonised new States – which had no chance to object to the formation of a customary rule – are automatically bound by a rule of customary law, while persistent objectors could opt out from the customary rule. It should also be noted that persistent objectors could not opt out from a norm of *jus cogens*.

(b) Treaties

Treaties constitute another principal source of the law of the sea According to Paul Reuter, a treaty is 'an expression of concurring wills attributable to two or more subjects of international law and intended to have legal effects under the rules of international law'.[23] At the global and regional levels, various aspects of the law of the sea are currently governed by a considerable number of treaties. Undoubtedly, the LOSC is the most important treaty in this field.[24] Rules of international law governing treaties are codified in the 1969 Vienna Convention on the Law of Treaties. Whilst there will be no need to delve into the law of treaties in this book, two issues call for brief comments.

The first issue involves the interaction between treaties and customary law. A treaty may generate three effects in relation to rules of customary law.[25] First, a treaty may

[21] Cf. P.-M. Dupuy, 'Le juge et la règle générale' (1989) 93 *RGDIP* pp. 569 *et seq.*

[22] ICJ Reports 1951, p. 131.

[23] P. Reuter, *Introduction to the Law of Treaties* (London and New York, Kegan Paul International, 1995), p. 30. See also Article 2(1)(a) of the Vienna Convention on the Law of Treaties.

[24] 1833 *UNTS* p. 3. Entered into force on 16 November 1994. This book uses the abbreviation 'LOSC' to refer to the 1982 UN *Convention* on the Law of the Sea, and 'UNCLOS' to refer to the United Nations *Conference* on the Law of the Sea. In fact, 'UNCLOS' has been used to refer to the UN *Convention* on the Law of the Sea. W. R. Edeson, 'Confusion over the Use of "UNCLOS" and References to Other Recent Agreements' (2000) 15 *IJMCL* pp. 413 *et seq.*

[25] The *North Sea Continental Shelf* cases, ICJ Reports 1969, pp. 38–39, paras. 61–64; the *Nicaragua* case (Merits), ICJ Reports 1986, p. 95, para. 177.

embody already established rules of customary law. This is called the declaratory effect. In the context of the law of the sea, a good example is the Geneva Convention on the High Seas. In fact, the Preamble of the Convention on the High Seas explicitly refers to the codification of the rules of international law relating to the high seas. As we shall discuss later, the LOSC also contains quite a few provisions embodying well-established rules of customary law. Second, where a treaty states rules reflecting State practice prior to the adoption of the treaty, such rules may be ripe for transition from *lex ferenda* to *lex lata*. This is called the crystallising effect. It can be seen in some provisions of the Geneva Convention on the Continental Shelf. In fact, the ICJ, in the *North Sea Continental Shelf* cases, ruled that Articles 1 to 3 of the Convention on the Continental Shelf were regarded as reflecting, or as crystallising, received or at least emergent rules of customary international law relative to the continental shelf.[26] Third, a treaty may generate a new rule of customary law. It is possible that, where after a convention has come into force, States other than the parties to it find it convenient to apply the convention rules in their mutual relations. Such State practice may lead to the development of a new customary rule. This effect is called the generating effect.

A second issue concerns the interrelationship between relevant treaties. The growing number of treaties will necessitate coordination between treaties. Such coordination is required at the interpretation level. For instance, the LOSC makes frequent reference to 'generally accepted international rules and standards'. Such rules and standards are elaborated by specific treaties relating to marine issues. Hence the provisions of the LOSC must be interpreted taking these agreements into account. The provisions of the LOSC must also be read together with the subsequently adopted 1994 Implementation Agreement and the 1995 Fish Stocks Agreement. Further to this, treaty coordination may be needed at the procedural level. In particular, it is important to address the question whether provisions relating to dispute settlement of a treaty should exclude the application of dispute settlement procedures set out under the LOSC.

3.2 Material sources

(a) Judicial decisions and the writings of publicists

Material sources provide evidence of the existence of rules, which, when proved, have the status of legally binding rules of general application. Article 38(1)(d) of the Statute of the ICJ refers to 'judicial decisions and the teaching of the most highly qualified publicists of the various nations, as subsidiary means for the determination of rules of law'. Judicial decisions have had an important influence on the law of the sea and international law in general. Three functions of judicial decisions must, in particular, be highlighted.

First, the existence of rules of law, in particular, rules of customary international law is often a matter for discussion. By applying a specific rule to a particular case or determining the breach of the rule concerned, international courts identify the existence of the rule in positive international law (the identification of rules). Second, it is

[26] ICJ Reports 1969, p. 39, para. 63.

not infrequently that the meaning of rules of international law, customary or conventional, becomes a subject of international disputes. International courts have a valuable role to clarify the meaning and scope of relevant rules through international adjudication (the clarification of rules). Third, judicial decisions may have a formative effect on the development of international law (the formation of rules).

It has been recognised that some writers, such as Grotius, Bynkershoek and Vattel, have had a formative influence on the development of international law. Furthermore, the monumental treatise of Gilbert Gidel, *Le droit international public de la mer* (3 vols., Paris, 1932–34) has been considered as a work of great authority in this field. Some authoritative expert bodies, such as the ILC and the *Institut de droit international*, also furnish important materials analogous to the writings of publicists.

Because of the lack of supreme legislative and judicial authorities in the international community, it is often difficult to identify and interpret rules of customary international law. It is also not uncommon that a treaty provision may allow more than two different interpretations. Thus, even though there is a need for caution, academic writings may have a significant role to play in the identification and interpretation of rules of international law.

(b) Non-binding instruments

Another material source which needs particular notice is non-binding instruments, such as resolutions, declarations and guidelines adopted under the auspices of the United Nations or other international organisations.[27] The non-binding nature of instruments does not mean that they are without legal significance. In fact, non-binding instruments have an influence on the making of international law.

First, some non-binding instruments lead to the conclusion of a new multilateral treaty or specific provisions of the treaty. An example can be seen in the 1970 Declaration of Principles Governing the Deep Seabed. The 1970 Declaration formed the basis for Part XI of the LOSC concerning the Area.[28]

Second, some non-binding instruments may provide guidance on interpretation of a treaty and amplify the terms of a treaty. A good example is the 1970 Declaration on Principles of International Law Concerning Friendly Relations and Co-operation among States in Accordance with the Charter of the United Nations.[29] This Declaration

[27] Non-binding instruments are often called 'soft law'. However, the concept of 'soft law' has more than one meaning. In light of its ambiguity, there appears to be scope to consider the question whether 'soft law' is useful as a concept for analysis. If the term 'soft law' is intended to mean that an instrument is not legally binding, it will be better to use the term 'non-binding instrument'. Furthermore, the 'soft' and 'law' elements are contradictory. The utility of 'soft law' *as a concept for analysis* is questioned by writers, though this does not automatically mean that non-binding instruments have no role to play in international law. This book uses the term 'non-binding instruments'. For a critical analysis of 'soft law', see R. Ida, 'Formation des norms internationales dans un monde en mutation: critique de la notion de soft law', in *Le droit international au service de la paix, de la justice et du développement: Mélanges Michel Virally* (Paris, Pedone, 1991), pp. 333 *et seq.*

[28] UN Resolution 2749 (XXV) adopted on 17 December 1970. The full title is: Declaration of Principles Governing the Seabed and the Ocean Floor, and the Subsoil Thereof, Beyond the Limits of National Jurisdiction. The legal regime of the Area will be examined in Chapter 5, section 3.

[29] UN General Assembly, 2625 (XXV) adopted on 24 October 1970.

further elaborates the meaning of the UN Charter. In the field of the law of the sea, for instance, the 1995 FAO Code of Conduct for Responsible Fisheries amplifies relevant provisions of the LOSC and the 1995 Fish Stocks Agreement.[30] Furthermore, where a non-binding instrument forms 'generally accepted standards established through the competent international organisation', such as the IMO, the instrument must be read together with relevant provisions of the LOSC by rule of reference.

Third, some non-binding instruments confirm existing rules of customary international law. For example, the Arbitral Tribunal, in the 1977 *Texaco Overseas Petroleum Company* case, declared that the UN General Assembly Resolution on Permanent Sovereignty over Natural Resources (1803 (XVII)) reflected 'the state of customary law existing in this field'.[31]

Fourth, non-binding instruments may provide for emergence of new rules of customary international law. By way of example, one may quote the 1960 Declaration on the Granting of Independence to Colonial Countries and Peoples, which seems to have given a strong impetus to the establishment of the right of self-determination as a principle of international law.[32]

(c) Unilateral acts and considerations of humanity

In principle, the unilateral acts of a State cannot result in rights and obligations. An often cited example on this matter is the 1974 *Nuclear Test* case between Australia and France, and between New Zealand and France. In this case, the ICJ ruled that:

> It is well recognized that declarations made by way of unilateral acts, concerning legal or factual situations, may have the effect of creating legal obligations ... When it is the intention of the State making the declaration that it should become bound according to its terms, that intention confers on the declaration the character of a legal undertaking, the State being thenceforth legally required to follow a course of conduct consistent with the declaration.[33]

However, this is an exceptional case, and great caution must be taken if seeking to take any general principles from this judgment. In fact, the Chamber of the ICJ, in the 1986 *Frontier Dispute* case, stated that it had a duty to show even greater caution when it is a question of a unilateral declaration not directed to any particular recipient.[34] In the context of the law of the sea, the unilateral statements of a State have had some formative effect on the development of the law. A case in point is the 1945 Truman Proclamation on the Continental Shelf. As we shall see later, the Truman Proclamation constituted the starting point of the legal regime on the continental shelf.[35]

30 This is a voluntary instrument. The Code of Conduct was unanimously adopted on 31 October 1995 by the FAO Conference: www.fao.org/fi/agreem/codecond/ficonde.asp.

31 *Texaco Overseas Petroleum Company/California Asiatic Oil Company v Libyan Arab Republic* (1978) 17 *ILM* p. 30, para. 87.

32 UN General Assembly Resolution 1514 (XV) adopted on 14 December 1960.

33 The *Nuclear Tests* case (Australia v France), ICJ Reports 1974, p. 267, para. 43.

34 The *Frontier Dispute* case (Burkina Faso v Republic of Mali), ICJ Reports 1986, p. 574, para. 39.

35 See Chapter 4, section 4.

Finally, considerations of humanity in the law of the sea should be mentioned. As human activities in the oceans, including navigation, are not free from risk, elements of humanity must be taken into account in the application of the law of the sea. In judicial decisions, a classical reference to considerations of humanity can be seen in the 1949 *Corfu Channel* judgment. In this case, the Court relied on 'elementary considerations of humanity' as 'general and well-recognized principles'.[36] Likewise, ITLOS, in the *M/V Saiga (No. 2)* case, clearly stated that: 'Considerations of humanity must apply in the law of the sea, as they do in other areas of international law'.[37] Considerations of humanity are embodied in treaties. In 1979, for instance, the International Convention on Maritime Search and Rescue was adopted.[38] It can also be observed that several provisions of the LOSC, such as Articles 18(2), 24(2), 44 and 98, reflect considerations of humanity.

4 PRINCIPLES OF THE INTERNATIONAL LAW OF THE SEA

4.1 Principle of freedom

The international law of the sea is governed by three principles: the principle of freedom, the principle of sovereignty and the principle of the common heritage of mankind. Traditionally the law of the sea was dominated by the principle of freedom and the principle of sovereignty. The French jurist R.-J. Dupuy summarised the essence of the law as follows:

> The sea has always been lashed by two major contrary winds: the wind from the high seas towards the land is the wind of freedom; the wind from the land toward the high seas is the bearer of sovereignties. The law of the sea has always been in the middle between these conflicting forces.[39]

The principle of freedom aims to ensure the freedom of various uses of the oceans, such as navigation, overflight, laying submarine cables and pipelines, construction of artificial islands, fishing and marine scientific research. Historically the freedom of the seas was promoted by England. The policy of Queen Elizabeth I of England may have been the starting point of the principle of the freedom of the seas.[40] This principle

[36] ICJ Reports 1949, p. 22.

[37] (1999) 38 *ILM* p. 1355, para. 155.

[38] 1405 *UNTS* p. 119. Entered into force 22 June 1985.

[39] R.-J. Dupuy, 'The Sea under National Competence', in R.-J. Dupuy and D. Vignes, *A Handbook on the New Law of the Sea*, vol. 1 (Dordrecht, Nijhoff, 1991), p. 247. See also D. P. O'Connell (I. A. Shearer ed.), *The International Law of the Sea*, vol. 1 (Oxford, Clarendon Press, 1982), p. 1.

[40] Gidel, *Le droit international public de la mer*, vol.1, pp. 133–136. Later, the Stuarts, who had replaced the Tudors, turned away from the freedom of the seas and pursued a policy based on the doctrine of *mare clausum*. With the establishment of Britain's naval supremacy, however, the policy of *mare clausum* lost its importance.

may primarily be thought of as aiming to ensure the freedom of navigation in order to advance international trade and commerce across the oceans. In this regard, it is of particular interest to note that in the *Mare Liberum* published in 1609,[41] Grotius upheld the freedom of the seas with a view to vindicating the right of the Dutch East India Company to trade in the Far East against the exclusive claim of Portugal upon the Bull of Pope Alexander IV. In the course of the negotiations for a conclusion of the Dutch war of independence, Spain – supporting Portugal's position – persistently denied Dutch participation in commerce with India. However, this was unacceptable to the Dutch East India Company. Grotius thus prepared the *Mare Liberum* for publication at the request of the Dutch East India Company.[42] Indeed, the primary purpose of the book was to advocate the freedom of commerce on the basis of the freedom of the seas. This episode would seem to demonstrate that the freedom of the sea was essentially characterised by the economic and political interests of maritime States.

Whilst Grotius's argument met with criticism from various writers, such as William Welwood, John Selden, Justo Seraphim de Freitas, Juan Solórzano Pereira, and John Borough, among others, the principle of freedom of the seas has been consolidated through State practice. In particular, England, which established its maritime supremacy, encouraged freedom of the seas for purposes of free commerce and trade across the oceans. In essence, the freedom of the seas was the corollary of the freedom of commerce, which was a prerequisite for expanding capitalism and European domination over the rest of the world.[43]

4.2 Principle of sovereignty

In contrast to the principle of freedom, the principle of sovereignty seeks to safeguard the interests of coastal States. This principle essentially promotes the extension of national jurisdiction into offshore spaces and supports the territorialisation of the oceans. It has been considered that the concept of the modern State was formulated by Vattel.[44] It is

41 H. Grotius, *Mare Liberum* (Leiden, 1609). The first edition of 1609 was published anonymously. For an English translation, along with the Latin text on the basis of the Elzevir edition of 1633, see H. Grotius, *The Freedom of the Seas Or the Right Which Belongs to the Dutch to Take Part in the East Indian Trade* (translated by Ralph Van Deman Magoffin) (originally published by the Carnegie Endowment for International Peace, New York, Oxford University Press, 1916; reprint, New Jersey, Lawbook Exchange, 2001). For another translation, see H. Grotius, *The Free Sea* (translated by R. Hakluyt, edited and with an introduction by D. Armitage) (Indianapolis, Library Fund, 2004). For an analysis of the *Mare Liberum*, see for instance, F. Ito, 'The Thought of Hugo Grotius in the *Mare Liberum*' (1974) 18 *Japanese Annual of International Law* pp. 1 *et seq.*

42 Ito, 'Thought of Hugo Grotius', pp. 1–2; D. Armitage, 'Introduction', in Grotius, *The Free Sea*, p. xii; R. P. Anand, *Origin and Development of the Law of the Sea: History of International Law Revisited* (The Hague, Nijhoff, 1983), p. 79.

43 Nguyen Quoc Dinh *et al.*, *Droit international public*, p. 1334.

44 Albert de Lapradelle argued that Vattel was the first writer who had a clear and complete conception of the modern State. Albert de Lapradelle, 'Introduction' to Emer de Vattel, *Le droit des gens ou principes de la loi naturelle, appliqués à la conduite et aux affaires des Nations et des Souverains* (The Classics of International Law, Washington, Carnegie Institution of Washington, 1916), p. xlvi. For an English translation of Vattel's *Le droit des gens*, see Emmerich de Vattel, *The Law of Nations; or Principles of the Law of Nature, Applied to the Conduct and Affairs of Nations and Sovereigns* (translated by Joseph Chitty, Philadelphia, T. and J. W. Johnson and Co., Law Booksellers, 1853). In this book, Vattel's arguments will be quoted from the English translation to enhance comprehension.

not surprising that the modern concept of the territorial sea was clearly presented by the same writer. In his book published in 1758, Vattel stated that:

> When a nation takes possession of certain parts of the sea, it takes possession of the empire over them, as well as of the domain, on the same principle which we advanced in treating of the land (205). *These parts of the sea are within the jurisdiction of the nation, and a part of its territory*: the sovereign commands there; he makes laws, and may punish those who violate them; in a word, he has the same rights there as on land, and, in general, every right which the laws of the state allow him.[45]

On the other hand, Vattel denied that the high seas could be appropriated by States.[46] Thus, Vattel clearly distinguished the sea under territorial sovereignty from the high seas. At the same time, Vattel accepted the right of innocent passage through the territorial sea and straits.[47] In so doing, the territorial sea is to be connected to the high seas for the purpose of navigation. Vattel's conception represented a prototype of the law of the sea in a modern sense.

Subsequently, a maritime belt adjacent to the coast became increasingly important for coastal States for purposes of neutrality, security, customs control, sanitary regulations, fisheries and economic policy on the basis of the doctrine of mercantilism. The claim over the maritime belt was thus consolidated as the territorial sea through State practice in the nineteenth century. At the international level, the dualism in the oceans which distinguishes the territorial sea from the high seas was clearly confirmed in the *Bering Sea Fur-Seals* case between Great Britain and the United States of America of 1893.[48] A principal issue of this arbitration related to the question whether the United States had any rights of protection in the fur-seals frequenting the islands of the United States in the Bering Sea when such seals are found outside the ordinary three-mile limit. In this case, the Arbitral Tribunal rejected, by a majority of five to two, the right of the United States to the ocean beyond the ordinary three-mile limit with respect to the protection of the fur-seals industry.[49] In so ruling, the Arbitral Tribunal made clear that the coastal State could not exercise jurisdiction over the high seas beyond the three-mile limit. It would seem to follow that the coastal State can exercise jurisdiction over the sea up to the three-mile limit.

[45] Emphasis added. *Ibid.*, section 295. [46] *Ibid.*, section 281.

[47] *Ibid.*, section 288 and section 292.

[48] Fur Seal Arbitration, *Proceedings of the Tribunal of Arbitration convened at Paris under the Treaty between the United States of America and Great Britain, concluded at Washington, February 29, 1882, for the Determination of Questions between the Two Governments Concerning the Jurisdictional Rights of the United States in the Waters of the Bering Sea*, 16 vols. (Washington DC, Government Printing Office, 1895). The Award, together with a summary of facts and arguments in detail, was reproduced in J. B. Moore, *History and Digest of the International Arbitrations to Which the United States Has Been a Party*, vol. 1 (Washington, Government Printing Office, 1898) pp. 75 *et seq*; C. A. R. Robb (ed.), *International Environmental Law Reports*, vol. 1 (Cambridge University Press, 1999) pp. 43 *et seq*.

[49] Moore, *History and Digest*, p. 949.

In summary, on the basis of the principle of freedom and the principle of sovereignty, the ocean has been divided into two categories. The first category relates to marine space adjacent to coasts subject to the national jurisdiction of the coastal State. The second category concerns marine space beyond national jurisdiction where the principle of freedom applies. Until the mid-twentieth century, the scope of the territorial sea was limited to the narrow maritime belt, and the enormous area of the oceans remained the high seas. It could well be said that the oceans were dominated by the principle of freedom at that time. After World War II, however, coastal States increasingly extended their jurisdiction toward the high seas in order to control offshore resources. It may be said that the principle of sovereignty was a catalyst for development of the law of the sea after World War II. In any case, there is little doubt that the coordination of the economic and political interests of maritime States and coastal States has until recently been a central issue in the international law of the sea.

4.3 Principle of the common heritage of mankind

The third principle of the law of the sea is the common heritage of mankind. This principle is enshrined in Part XI of the LOSC. As will be seen in Chapter 5, the principle of the common heritage of mankind emerged as an antithesis against the principle of sovereignty and the principle of freedom. This principle is distinct from the traditional principles in two respects.

First, while the principle of sovereignty and that of freedom aim to safeguard the interests of individual States, the principle of the common heritage of mankind seeks to promote the common interest of mankind as a whole. It may be argued that the term 'mankind' is a transspatial and transtemporal concept. It is transspatial because 'mankind' includes all people on the planet. It is transtemporal because 'mankind' includes both present and future generations.[50] It would seem to follow that the common interest of mankind means the interest of all people in present and future generations.

Second, the principle of the common heritage of mankind focuses on 'mankind' as a novel actor in the law of the sea. 'Mankind' is not a merely abstract concept. As we shall see in Chapter 5, under the LOSC 'mankind' has an operational organ, i.e. the International Seabed Authority, acting on behalf of mankind as a whole. To this extent, it can reasonably be argued that mankind is emerging as a new actor in the law of the sea. In this sense, the principle of the common heritage of mankind introduces a new perspective, which is beyond the State-to-State system, in the law of the sea.

[50] R.-J. Dupuy, 'La notion de patrimoine commun de l'humanité appliquée aux fonds marins', in R.-J. Dupuy, *Dialectiques du droit international: souveraineté des Etats, communauté internationale et droits de l'humanité* (Paris, Pedone, 1999), pp. 189–194.

5 THE CODIFICATION OF THE LAW OF THE SEA

5.1 The Hague Conference for the Codification of International Law (1930)

Originally the law of the sea consisted of a body of rules of customary international law. Such unwritten rules often require further clarification. As rules of customary law are essentially qualified by the times, there is also a need for adaptability. To this end, codification of international law undertaken by a representative body of experts is a notable contribution to the development of the law. This is particularly true of the law of the sea. Initially, attempts to codify the rules of the international law of the sea were undertaken by various non-governmental bodies, such as the International Law Association, *Institut de droit international*, and the Harvard Law School. Later, such attempts were made by intergovernmental conferences.

The first intergovernmental attempt to codify the law of the sea was the 1930 Hague Conference for the Codification of International Law. The Hague Conference was instigated by the League of Nations between 12 March and 12 April 1930, and was attended by forty-seven governments and an observer, i.e. the USSR.[51] The Hague Conference aimed to codify international law concerning three subjects, namely nationality, State responsibility and territorial waters. With regard to territorial waters, two issues, among various issues discussed at the Conference, are of particular interest: the nature of the rights possessed by a State over its territorial sea and the breadth of the territorial sea.

With respect to the nature of the rights of the coastal State to the territorial sea, a clear majority of States, though not unanimously, supported the principle that the coastal State possessed territorial sovereignty over its territorial sea, the airspace above as well as the seabed and subsoil covered by these waters. Thus the Report adopted by the Second Committee at the Hague Conference (hereafter the 1930 Report) stated that: 'it was recognized that international law attributes to each coastal State sovereignty over a belt of sea round its coasts'.[52] At the same time, the right of innocent passage of foreign ships through the territorial sea was generally recognised because of the importance of the freedom of navigation.[53]

On the other hand, the breadth of the territorial sea was the most debatable issue regarding the law of the sea. Although no detailed historical examination can be made here, two different practices should be highlighted.[54]

The first practice relates to the cannon-shot rule. According to the rule, the seaward limit of the territorial sea is determined by the range of cannon shot from the shore. It has been considered that the cannon-shot rule was accepted as a well-established rule in France, most countries in the Mediterranean, and probably in the Netherlands as

[51] For the list of the participating governments, see 'Conference for the Codification of International Law Held at The Hague in March-April, 1930: Final Act' (1930) 24 *AJIL Supplement* p. 169. Documents in the Conference were reproduced in S. Rosenne (ed.), *League of Nations Conference for the Codification of International Law 1930*, 4 vols. (New York, Oceana, 1975).

[52] League of Nations, C.351(b). M. 145(b). Annex V, Report Adopted by the Committee on April 10th 1930, reproduced in Rosenne, *League of Nations* (vol. 4), p. 1411.

[53] Rosenne, *League of Nations* (vol. 4), p. 1412.

[54] W. L. Walker, 'Territorial Waters: The Cannon Shot Rule' (1945) 22 *BYIL* pp. 210 *et seq.*

regards neutrality in wartime.[55] According to the cannon-shot rule, the breadth of the territorial sea is changeable with the development of the range of the cannon shot.

The second practice is the one employed by Scandinavian countries, whereby the limit of the territorial sea is fixed by a distance from the coast. By the middle of the eighteenth century, Denmark and Sweden had advanced a maritime belt extending to four miles' distance from the shore.

Whilst the relationship between the cannon-shot rule and the three-mile rule seems to remain obscure, some States strongly advocated the three-mile rule as the maximum limit of the territorial sea. In 1793, the United States first adopted the three-mile limit as equivalent to the cannon-shot rule for purposes of neutrality on the outbreak of war between Great Britain and France. As typically shown in the *Anna* case of 1805, the three-mile rule was also recognised in Great Britain. The adoption of the three-mile rule by Great Britain was of particular importance due to its considerable naval power. Nonetheless, it would be incorrect to conclude that the three-mile rule had become a universally accepted rule. In fact, the Scandinavian countries continued to claim a four-mile limit. Several countries, such as France and Italy, maintained different limits for different purposes.[56]

The three-mile limit was strongly opposed at the Hague Conference.[57] Whilst maritime powers, such as Great Britain and the United States, claimed that the breadth of the territorial sea belt was three miles, coastal States suggested various breadths beyond three miles, such as four or six miles. The challenge by those States considerably undermined the authority of the traditional three-mile rule, which favoured the interests of strong maritime States. In light of the wide cleavage of opinion between States, no rule was formulated with regard to the breadth of the territorial sea, and the Hague Conference ended without the adoption of a convention on the territorial sea. However, this does not mean that the Conference was without significance. Indeed, the Hague Conference produced valuable statements on important issues regarding the law of the sea. As noted, it must be remembered that the principle of freedom of navigation, territorial sovereignty over the territorial sea and the right of innocent passage through the territorial sea were generally recognised at the Conference.

5.2 The First UN Conference on the Law of the Sea (1958)

Control of offshore natural resources emerged as a central issue as regards the law of the sea after World War II. In particular, the increasing demand for petrol prompted coastal States to extend their jurisdiction over natural resources on the continental shelf. At the same time, in response to the depletion of marine living resources, claims

[55] The role of Bynkershoek was often highlighted in the formation of the cannon-shot rule. According to Walker, however, the cannon-shot rule was already established and well known before the time of Bynkershoek. Thus, Walker has argued that Bynkershoek did not invent the cannon-shot rule, although he was the earliest writer to record the rule. *Ibid.*, p. 230. See also Gidel, *Le droit international public de la mer*, vol. 3, pp. 36–39.

[56] Churchill and Lowe, *Law of the Sea*, p. 78; O'Connell, *International Law of the Sea*, p. 165.

[57] For an analysis in some detail of the Hague Conference, see J. S. Reeves, 'The Codification of the Law of Territorial Waters' (1930) 24 *AJIL* pp. 486 *et seq.*; L. Juda, *International Law and Ocean Use Management: The Evolution of Ocean Governance* (London and New York, Routledge, 1996), pp. 62 *et seq.*

on these resources on the high seas were increasingly advocated by the coastal States. In this context, on 28 September 1945, United States President Truman issued his Proclamations on the Continental Shelf and on Fisheries, respectively.[58] The Truman Proclamations marked the starting point of the new development of the law of the sea.

Against that background, the International Law Commission (ILC) came to wrestle with the codification of the law of the sea. The ILC, established by the UN General Assembly in 1947, aims to promote the progressive development of international law and its codification.[59] The ILC commenced its work on the codification of the law of the sea at its first session in 1949, and J. P. A. François was appointed as the special rapporteur on the regime of the high seas. In its eighth session in 1956, the ILC submitted its final report on 'Articles Concerning the Law of the Sea' to the United Nations. This report provided the basis for the work at the First United Nations Conference on the Law of the Sea (UNCLOS I).

UNCLOS I was convened in Geneva on 24 February 1958, and eighty-six States participated. UNCLOS I successfully adopted four conventions and an optional protocol on dispute settlement:

(i) The Convention on the Territorial Sea and the Contiguous Zone[60]
(ii) The Convention on the High Seas[61]
(iii) The Convention on Fishing and Conservation of the Living Resources of the High Seas[62]
(iv) The Convention on the Continental Shelf[63] and
(v) The Optional Protocol of Signature Concerning the Compulsory Settlement of Disputes.[64]

In addition, UNCLOS I adopted nine resolutions concerning nuclear tests on the high seas, pollution of the high seas by radioactive materials, fishery conservation, cooperation in conservation measures, human killing of marine life, coastal fisheries, historic waters, convening of a Second UN Conference on the Law of the Sea, and a tribute to the ILC.[65]

A remarkable result of this Conference was that the traditional dualism in the oceans was established in the Geneva Conventions as *lex scripta*. Article 1 of the Convention on the High Seas stipulates that:

> The term 'high seas' means all parts of the sea that are not included in the territorial sea or in the internal waters of a State.

[58] The full titles are: Proclamation by President Truman of 28 September 1945 on Policy of the United States with respect to the Natural Resources of the Subsoil and Sea Bed of the Continental Shelf, Proclamation by President Truman of 28 September 1945 on Policy of the United States with respect to Coastal Fisheries in Certain Areas of the High Seas.
[59] Article 1(1) of the Statute of the International Law Commission.
[60] 516 *UNTS* 205. Entered into force 10 September 1964.
[61] 450 *UNTS* 11. Entered into force 30 September 1962.
[62] 559 *UNTS* 285. Entered into force 20 March 1966.
[63] 499 *UNTS* 311. Entered into force 10 June 1964.
[64] 450 *UNTS* 169. Entered into force 30 September 1962.
[65] DOCUMENT A/CONF.13/L.56. United Nations Conference on the Law of the Sea, *Official Records, Vol. II: Plenary Meetings (Geneva, 24 February–27 April 1958)*, pp. 143–145.

It follows that the 1958 Geneva Conventions divided the ocean into three basic categories: internal waters, territorial sea and high seas. Internal waters and the territorial sea are subject to the territorial sovereignty of the coastal States. This was clearly confirmed in Article 1 of the Geneva Convention on the Territorial Sea and the Contiguous Zone (hereafter the TSC):

> The sovereignty of a State extends, beyond its land territory and its internal waters, to a belt of sea adjacent to its coast, described as the territorial sea.

At the same time, the freedom of the high seas, including that of fishing in the high seas, was explicitly laid down in Article 2(2) of the Geneva Convention on the High Seas. In light of its Preamble, this provision can be considered as a codification of customary international law.

Furthermore, the legal institution of the continental shelf was embodied in the Convention on the Continental Shelf. Under Article 1(1) of the Convention, the continental shelf is 'the seabed and subsoil of the submarine areas adjacent to the coast but outside the area of the territorial sea, to a depth of 200 metres or, beyond that limit, to where the depth of the superjacent waters admits of the exploitation of the natural resources of the said areas'. The rights of the coastal State over the continental shelf do not affect the legal status of the superjacent waters as high seas, or that of the airspace above those waters by virtue of Article 3. Accordingly, the continental shelf in the legal sense is part of the seabed and subsoil of the high seas.

It should also be noted that the contiguous zone, which may not extend beyond twelve miles from the baseline, was provided in the TSC. As appears from Article 24(1) of the TSC, '[i]n the zone of the high seas contiguous to its territorial sea', the contiguous zone is part of the high seas.

Despite the valuable contributions at UNCLOS I, two key issues were left open. A first issue concerns the maximum breadth of the territorial sea. As the territorial sea is under the territorial sovereignty of the coastal State, that State can monopolise natural resources there. In light of the increasing demand for marine resources, it was only natural that the breadth of the territorial sea became a serious issue at UNCLOS I. In this regard, all the countries of the Soviet and Arab blocs and most Asian, African and Latin American States favoured the twelve-mile limit of the territorial sea, whilst many maritime States claimed that the three-mile rule was the only rule under international law.[66] In the end, the ILC had to recognise that international practice was not uniform as regards the traditional limitation of the territorial sea to three miles. As a consequence, no rule was adopted with respect to the breadth of the territorial sea.

However, attention should be drawn to Article 24(2) of the TSC, which provides that:

[66] S. Oda, *International Control of Sea Resources* (Dordrecht, Nijhoff, 1989), p. 99.

The contiguous zone may not extend beyond twelve miles from the baseline from which the breadth of the territorial sea is measured.

Given that the contiguous zone lies outside the territorial sea, this provision would seem to signify that the breadth of the territorial sea could not exceed the maximum limit of twelve nautical miles under the TSC. The ILC took the view that international law did not justify an extension of the territorial sea beyond twelve miles,[67] even though the ILC had taken no decision as to the breadth of the territorial sea up to the limit of twelve miles.

A second issue relates to a mechanism for peaceful settlement of international disputes. It is impossible, or at least very difficult, to formulate perfectly clear and detailed rules that do not give rise to disputes as to their interpretation and application. Hence, effective mechanisms for dispute settlement constitute an essential part of a treaty. At UNCLOS I, however, a compulsory mechanism of dispute settlement could be established only as a separate instrument owing to opposition by many States to the mechanism of settlement either by the ICJ or through arbitration. To date, only thirty-eight States have become parties to the Optional Protocol of Signature Concerning the Compulsory Settlement of Disputes.

5.3 The Second UN Conference on the Law of the Sea (1960)

On 17 March 1960, the Second United Nations Conference on the Law of the Sea (UNCLOS II) was convened in Geneva in order to discuss the outer limit of the territorial sea as well as the fishery zone. Eighty-eight States participated in the Conference. In order to break the deadlock on this subject, the United States and Canada put forward a joint proposal which provided for a six-mile territorial sea plus a maximum of six-mile exclusive fishery zone, and for a ten-year moratorium period for historic fishing in the outer six miles.[68] Nonetheless, the joint proposal was defeated by a single vote.[69] Consequently, the efforts to fix the maximum breadth of the territorial sea at UNCLOS II proved once again in vain.

5.4 The Third UN Conference on the Law of the Sea (1973–1982)

(a) General considerations

The legal framework established by the 1958 Geneva Conventions very soon came to encounter serious challenges. Several factors led to review of the Geneva Conventions, but four in particular merit highlighting.

[67] United Nations, (1956-II) *YILC* p. 265.

[68] DOCUMENT A/CONF.19/C.1/L.10. Second United Nations Conference on the Law of the Sea, *Official Records, Summary Records of Plenary Meetings and of Meetings of the Committee of the Whole (Geneva, 17 March–26 April 1960)*, p. 169.

[69] The vote on the proposal ran 54:28:5. *Ibid.*, p. 30. See also Oda, *International Control*, p. 104; Juda, *International Law and Ocean Use Management*, p. 161.

The first factor involves control of offshore natural resources. Growing demand for an augmented supply of marine natural resources led the coastal States to extend national jurisdiction towards the high seas. At that time, some twenty coastal States had already claimed exclusive fisheries jurisdiction beyond twelve nautical miles.[70] It was becoming apparent that the traditional dualism between the narrow territorial sea and the vast high seas was in need of serious reconsideration.

The second factor concerns the development of seabed mining technology. The technological advances made it possible to exploit the immense resources in the seabed. It seemed probable that the development of technology would encourage coastal States to extend their legal continental shelf towards the deep seabed on the basis of the exploitability test set out in Article 1 of the Convention on the Continental Shelf. Thus, a concern was voiced that eventually all seabed in the world would be divided among coastal States. Whilst possible mining of manganese nodules in the deep seabed had attracted growing attention, only developed States possessing the necessary technology as well as financial resources could exploit natural resources in the deep seabed. However, this situation was unacceptable to developing States. Thus, there was a need to formulate a new legal framework for the proper management of natural resources in the deep seabed.

The third factor relates to the protection of the marine environment. Marine environmental protection had attracted little attention at UNCLOS I and II. Nonetheless, the attitude of the international community came to change as a result of a series oil tanker incidents. In particular, the *Torrey Canyon* incident of 1967 had a profound impact on the development of treaties regulating vessel-source pollution. In light of the paucity of rules regulating marine pollution in the 1958 Geneva Conventions, it was necessary to develop new rules at the global level.

Finally, but not least, attention must be drawn to the structural changes of the international community due to the independence of former colonised regions in the 1960s. As many developing States had not gained independence at the time of UNCLOS I and II, the claims of these States had little impact on the 1958 Geneva Conventions. For newly independent States, the existing rules of the law of the sea served only the interests of developed States. It was only natural that newly independent States called for reassessment of the existing rules of the law of the sea as a whole.

Against that background, on 17 August 1967, the Maltese ambassador, Arvid Pardo, tabled a proposal for a Declaration governing the seabed and its natural resources beyond the limits of national jurisdiction.[71] In response to his proposal, UN General Assembly Resolution 2340 (XXII) of 18 December 1967 decided to establish the Ad Hoc Committee on the Peaceful Uses of the Sea-Bed and the Ocean Floor beyond the Limits of National Jurisdiction (the Seabed Committee), consisting of thirty-five members

70 Memorial submitted by the United Kingdom in the *Fishery Jurisdiction* case, 31 July 1973, vol. 1, p. 353, para. 245.

71 *Note Verbale* of 17 August 1967 from Malta to UN Secretary-General, A/6695, 18 August 1967. Reproduced in E. D. Brown, *The International Law of the Sea*, vol. 2 (Aldershot, Dartmouth, 1994), p. 333.

chosen to reflect equitable geographical representation. By UN General Assembly Resolution 2467A (XXIII) of 21 December 1968, this Committee was replaced by the permanent Committee on the Peaceful Uses of the Sea-Bed and Ocean Floor beyond the Limits of National Jurisdiction. The Committee was composed of forty-two Member States. Nonetheless, it became apparent that discussions would not be limited to mineral resources in the deep seabed. Eventually it was acknowledged that there was a great need to review the existing rules of the law of the sea as a whole because marine issues were closely interrelated. Thus, on 17 December 1970, UN General Assembly Resolution 2750C (XXV) decided to convene a conference on the law of the sea in 1973 in order to adopt a comprehensive convention on the law of the sea.

The first session of UNCLOS III was held in New York on 3–15 December 1973, and a total of eleven sessions were convened from 1973 to 1982. Unlike at UNCLOS I and II, the preparatory work was not assigned to the ILC. The primary reason was that in light of the political sensitivity of issues underlying UNCLOS III, the ILC was regarded as inappropriate to deal with these questions. Developing States were also concerned that they were underrepresented in the ILC and that the Commission was too conservative in its approach.[72] Accordingly, the work of the Conference was mainly conducted in three committees.

The First Committee dealt with the legal regime for the deep seabed beyond the limit of national jurisdiction. The Second Committee was charged with the territorial sea, the contiguous zone, the EEZ, the continental shelf, international straits, archipelagic waters, the high seas and land-locked and geographically disadvantaged States. The Third Committee dealt with the protection of the marine environment, marine scientific research and the transfer of technology. Certain issues – such as the Preamble, final clauses, peaceful uses of ocean space, the general principles on dispute settlement, the general provisions and the Final Act – were discussed directly by the Plenary.[73]

(b) Features of UNCLOS III

UNCLOS III was characterised by three principal features.

The first feature is the universality of the participants. The UNCLOS III participants comprised: the members of the United Nations, its specialised agencies and the International Atomic Energy Agency, parties to the Statute of the International Court of Justice, as well as Guinea-Bissau and the Democratic Republic of Vietnam. In addition, the participants in UNCLOS III included a wide range of observers, such as intergovernmental and non-governmental organisations, trust territories, associated States, the United Nations Council for Namibia, and national liberation movements recognised in their region by the Organisation of African Unity or the League of Arab States. It

[72] This does not mean, however, that the role of international lawyers was minor in UNCLOS III. Most of the delegations in UNCLOS III were international lawyers, and they played a key role in formulating acceptable draft rules. A. Shibata, 'International Law-Making Process in the United Nations: Comparative Analysis of UNCED and UNCLOS III' (1993) 24 *California Western International Law Journal* pp. 33–35.

[73] J. Evensen, 'Working Methods and Procedures in the Third United Nations Conference on the Law of the Sea' (1986) 199 *RCADI* p. 454.

could well be said that UNCLOS III was truly universal.[74] This is an important element securing the legitimacy of the process of international law-making.

The second feature concerns the long duration of the Conference. In fact, it took ten years – from 1973 to 1982 – to complete the work. Taking into account the preparatory work of the Seabed Committee, which commenced its work in 1967, it took nearly sixteen years to adopt the LOSC.

The third feature is the enormous task with which the Conference was charged. The task of UNCLOS III was quantitatively enormous because it had to deal with various marine issues in a comprehensive manner. In this regard, UN General Assembly Resolution 3067 (XXVIII) of 16 November 1973 made it clear that 'the mandate of the Conference shall be to adopt a convention dealing with all matters relating to the law of the sea …'.[75] At the same time, the task of the Conference was qualitatively enormous in the sense that it had to formulate a number of provisions reconciling highly complicated interests between States.

(c) Procedures of UNCLOS III

In light of the complexity of its tasks, UNCLOS III adopted some unique and particular procedures for negotiations. Five procedural techniques should be highlighted.

The first remarkable feature of UNCLOS III involves the consensus procedure. The consensus procedure means the method of obtaining the general agreement of all relevant actors in a conference or an organ through negotiations without vote.[76] In light of the economic, political and social differences in the contemporary international community, the majority voting system could run the risk of producing powerful alienated minorities. It seems probable that those minorities would not feel bound by the decisions involved. Thus, in multinational negotiations, there is a need to ensure broad support for decisions despite various divisions between States. The consensus procedure seeks to make every effort to reach agreement with regard to politically sensitive issues.

At UNCLOS III, the consensus procedure was indirectly mentioned in the 'Gentlemen's Agreement' of the Conference as follows:

> The Conference should make every effort to reach agreement on substantive matters by way of consensus and there should be no voting on such matters until all efforts at consensus have been exhausted.[77]

[74] Participants at the sessions of the Conference were listed in the Final Act of the Third United Nations Conference on the Law of the Sea.

[75] Paragraph 3 of the operative part.

[76] The consensus procedure must be distinguished from unanimity. While adoption with unanimity means adoption by voting after all actors involved have agreed, the consensus procedure precludes voting.

[77] Declaration Incorporating the Gentlemen's Agreement made by the President and Endorsed by the Conference at its 19th Meeting on 27 June 1974. Reproduced in (1974) 13 *ILM* p. 1209.

The Rules of Procedure for UNCLOS III made no explicit reference to the consensus procedure. However, paragraph 1 of Rule 37 stated that: 'Before a matter of substance is put to the vote, a determination that all efforts at reaching general agreement have been exhausted shall be made' by the two-thirds majority specified in Rule 39(1).

On the one hand, consensus is a valuable procedure in order to secure the widest possible acceptance of a convention. On the other hand, a text adopted by consensus is likely to be obscure because of the need for compromise. Furthermore, the consensus procedure is inherently slow moving. There is also a concern that consensus may mask opposition and create subsequent opposition or non-participation. In addition, it may be noted that a successful consensus procedure relies on the personal ability of the chairperson because the chairperson is required to take on effective leadership for formulating a consensus by facilitating compromises and, if necessary, generating proposals.

The second procedural technique used at UNCLOS III is the 'package-deal' approach. This is a comprehensive approach by which all key issues are addressed, with reasonable give and take between interested parties and interested groups. Under the package-deal approach, the final treaty is to be accepted in its entirety. On the one hand, it is thus arguable that this approach contributed to the adoption of a comprehensive convention, i.e. the LOSC. On the other hand, it is undeniable that the package-deal approach has complicated the decision-making process at UNCLOS III owing to trade-off tactics by certain States. Furthermore, the pace of the Committees II and III was qualified by the slow progress of Committee I. Arguably, the package-deal approach seems best suited to a conference where the work among committees will progress at roughly the same pace. If this is not the case, the approach may entail slow progress in negotiations.

The third notable feature is that discussions took place in a wide variety of delegation groups with common interests. One may call this the group approach. The Conference realised at an early stage that working groups would be more efficient than plenary meetings owing to the large number of participants and sensitive issues involved. Consequently, negotiations were to a large extent carried out in smaller working or negotiating groups on the basis of interest in a particular issue. Examples include: the group of seventy-seven consisting of developing countries, the coastal States group, the group of archipelagic States, the Oceania group, and the landlocked and geographically disadvantaged States group, the territorialist group, the group of broad-shelf States, the straits States group and the group of maritime States.[78] In particular, the influence of the group of seventy-seven seemed to be strong especially in the First Committee as well as in the Second Committee relating particularly to the EEZ. This situation contrasted with UNCLOS I and II where the participation of developing States was limited.

Fourth, at UNCLOS III, most substantive meetings were informal and without summary records. As a consequence, there is little in the way of formal records of debates and amendments by delegations at UNCLOS III. Some of the most intractable issues of

[78] Concerning various groups, see, in particular, T. B. Koh and S. Jayakumar, 'The Negotiating Process of the Third United Nations Conference on the Law of the Sea', in *Virginia Commentaries*, vol. 1, pp. 68–86.

the Conference were resolved in privately convened negotiating groups, such as the Evensen group and the Castañeda group.[79] It could be said that unofficial negotiations or informality was one of the unique features of UNCLOS III.

Finally, the single text approach should be noted. It has been considered that the only way for the Conference to extricate itself from the proliferation of individual proposals was to formulate a Single Negotiating Treaty Text as the basis for discussion. Therefore, the President of the Conference recommended that the Chairmen of the three Committees should each prepare a single negotiating text concerning the subjects entrusted to his Committee.[80] Arguably, this was an important procedural innovation.

(d) Adoption of the LOSC

After several revisions of the Texts, the Draft Convention on the Law of the Sea was adopted at the resumed tenth session on 28 August 1981. At the eleventh session, a number of changes and amendments were made to the final text of the Convention in order to accommodate the concerns of the United States. Nevertheless, the United States did not support the adoption of the Convention by consensus or without a vote, requesting a recorded vote.[81] Consequently, the consensus procedure was abandoned in the final stage of UNCLOS III. The LOSC was finally adopted on 30 April 1982 by 130 in favour, four against, with eighteen abstentions and eighteen unrecorded.[82] The Convention was opened for signature on 10 December 1982.

The voting record demonstrated that practically all developing countries voted for the Convention. Moreover, Australia, Austria, Canada, France, Greece, Ireland, Japan, Portugal, Switzerland and the five Nordic States voted for the Convention. On the other hand, four States, that is to say, the USA, Israel, Turkey and Venezuela, voted against the Convention. Israel objected to observer status for the PLO. Turkey and Venezuela preferred to resolve maritime boundary disputes with their neighbours before accepting the Convention. The USA voted against the LOSC mainly because the deep seabed regime provided for in Part XI did not meet US objectives. For a similar reason, many Western European countries abstained. Eastern European countries abstained because they were miffed by a technical provision in the Conference resolution on protection of preparatory investments in seabed mining. They felt that this discriminated in favour of United States companies.[83] In any case, it is clear that the adoption of the LOSC marked the beginning of a new era in the international law of the sea.

79 T. B. Koh, 'A Constitution for the Oceans', in United Nations, *The Law of the Sea: United Nations Convention on the Law of the Sea with Index and Final Act of the Third United Nations Conference on the Law of the Sea* (New York, United Nations, 1983), p. xxxvi.

80 UNCLOS III, *Official Records*, vol. 4, p. 26, para. 92. See also, Evensen, 'Working Methods', pp. 462–479.

81 The USA changed its position after the victory by President Reagan in the 1980 presidential election. The new administration decided to re-evaluate the results of UNCLOS III as a whole: *ibid.*, pp. 479–482.

82 For the distribution of the votes, see B. H. Oxman, 'The Third United Nations Conference on the Law of the Sea', in Dupuy and Vignes, *A Handbook*, p. 243. Some documents recorded that seventeen States abstained. However, it would seem that an abstention by Liberia, which was initially unrecorded, was not counted in the abstention number. By including Liberia's abstention, that number should be eighteen. As at 31 May 2011, 162 States have ratified the LOSC.

83 Oxman, 'The Third United Nations Conference', pp. 243–244. See also President's Statement, 9 July 1982, (1982) 82 *Department of State Bulletin*, No. 2065, p. 71.

6 OUTLINE OF THE UN CONVENTION ON THE LAW OF THE SEA

6.1 General considerations

Under Article 308(1) of the LOSC, it 'shall enter into force 12 months after the date of deposit of the sixtieth instrument of ratification or accession'. On 16 November 1993, Guyana deposited the sixtieth instrument of ratification with the UN Secretary-General and, consequently, the LOSC entered into force on 16 November 1994.

The original texts of the LOSC are Arabic, Chinese, English, French, Russian and Spanish, and they are equally authentic under Article 320. This Convention is open for signature by both States and other entities under Article 303(1). Those entities comprise:

(i) Namibia, represented by the United Nations Council for Namibia;
(ii) All self-governing associated States which have chosen that status in an act of self-determination supervised and approved by the United Nations in accordance with General Assembly Resolution 1514 (XV);[84]
(iii) All self-governing associated States which have competence over the matters governed by this Convention;
(iv) All territories which enjoy full internal self-government, recognised as such by the United Nations, but have not attained full independence in accordance with General Assembly Resolution 1514 (XV); and
(v) International organisations, in accordance with Annex IX.[85]

Article 311 contains rules with regard to the relationship between the LOSC and other treaties. Under Article 311(1), the LOSC is to prevail, between States Parties, over the 1958 Geneva Conventions. Furthermore, under Article 311(6), there shall be no amendments to the basic principles relating to the common heritage of mankind set forth in Article 136, and States Parties shall not be party to any agreement in derogation thereof. On the other hand, under Article 311(2), the Convention shall not alter the rights and obligations of States Parties which arise from other agreements compatible with this Convention and which do not affect the enjoyment by other States Parties of their rights or the performance of their obligations under the LOSC. Two or more States Parties may conclude agreements modifying or suspending the operation of provisions of the LOSC, provided that such agreements do not relate to a derogation which is incompatible with the effective execution of the object and purpose of the Convention. Moreover, such agreements shall not affect the application of the basic principles embodied therein, and the provisions of such agreements should not affect the enjoyment by other States Parties of their rights or the performance of their obligations under the Convention pursuant to Article 311(3). States Parties intending to conclude such an agreement are required to notify other States Parties through the depositary of the Convention of their intention to

[84] For an analysis in some detail of associated States, see M. Igarashi, *Associated Statehood in International Law* (The Hague, Kluwer, 2002).

[85] To date, the EEC (EU) is the only international organisation which has signed the LOSC.

conclude the agreement and of the modification or suspension for which it provides by virtue of Article 311(4).

6.2 Principal features of the Convention

Arguably, the LOSC is characterised by four principal features. First, the LOSC, which comprises 320 Articles and nine Annexes, covers marine issues comprehensively. In light of its comprehensiveness, the LOSC is often called 'a constitution for the oceans'. Apart from Annexes, the Convention is divided into seventeen Parts. The first eleven Parts of the Convention provide legal regimes governing each marine space. In this respect, the LOSC divides the ocean into five categories: internal waters, territorial seas, archipelagic waters, the EEZ and the high seas under Article 86. Furthermore, the LOSC provides for the contiguous zone (Part II, section 4), international straits (Part III), the continental shelf (Part VI), and the Area (Part XI). Consequently, it may be said that the spatial structure of the law of the sea was transformed from dualism to multilateralism. Parts XII to XV are devoted to specific issues, that is to say, the protection and preservation of the marine environment (Part XII), marine scientific research (Part XIII), development and transfer of marine technology (Part XIV), and settlement of disputes (Part XV). Parts XVI and XVII deal with general and final provisions, respectively. Reflecting the package-deal approach, the balance of rights and duties as well as overall equitableness are essential elements of the Convention.

Second, an important innovation of the LOSC is that it finally resolved the essential question relating to the breadth of territorial seas. As provided in Article 3 of the LOSC, States had agreed on a maximum seaward limit of the territorial sea of twelve miles. In this respect, it should be noted that the hard issue concerning the breadth of territorial seas could be concluded only by institutionalising a new resource-oriented zone under the coastal State's jurisdiction: the 200-mile EEZ. In other words, States could reach agreement with respect to the breadth of the territorial sea only by diverging from the traditional principle of dualism dividing the sea into the territorial sea and the high seas. Consequently, the division of the sea was further promoted under the LOSC, and the sea was divided into five basic categories: internal waters, the territorial sea, the EEZ, the high seas and archipelagic waters.[86]

Third, unlike the 1958 Geneva Conventions, the LOSC has succeeded in establishing compulsory procedures of dispute settlement.[87] Under Article 286, where no settlement has been reached by means freely chosen by the parties to the dispute, any dispute concerning the interpretation or application of the LOSC must be submitted to the international courts and tribunals having jurisdiction under section 2 of Part XV. This obligation is subject to several exceptions set out in section 3. Despite some limitations,

[86] Where the coastal State has claimed its EEZ, the continental shelf is the seabed and subsoil of the EEZ. If not, the continental shelf is part of the seabed and subsoil of the high seas. As will be seen later, international straits under Part III belong to the territorial sea of the coastal State. See Chapter 3, section 4.3 of this book.

[87] LOSC, Part XV, section 2. The dispute settlement mechanism in the LOSC will be addressed in Chapter 13.

the compulsory procedures entailing binding decisions would seem to have a valuable role in peaceful settlement of international disputes concerning the implementation of the LOSC.

Fourth, the LOSC created three new institutions. The International Seabed Authority is an international organisation governing activities in the Area. The International Tribunal for the Law of the Sea (ITLOS) is the permanent international tribunal for law of the sea disputes. The Commission on the Limits of the Continental Shelf has a principal role to make recommendations with regard to the outer limits of the continental shelf beyond 200 nautical miles. These institutions will be discussed in relevant parts of this book.

Finally, attention must be drawn to the integrity of the Convention. As the LOSC forms an integral whole consisting of a series of compromises, it is not possible for a State to pick what it likes and to disregard what it does not like. This is a corollary of the package-deal approach. Thus Article 309 prohibits reservations, by stating that: 'No reservations or exceptions may be made to this Convention unless expressly permitted by other articles of this Convention.' The prohibition of reservations certainly contributes to secure the integrity of the Convention.

On the other hand, Article 310 of the Convention allows States to make declarations or statements with a view, *inter alia*, to harmonising national laws and regulations with the provisions of the LOSC. In fact, many States made declarations and statements with respect to the LOSC pursuant to Article 310. Article 310 makes clear that such declarations or statements are not intended to exclude or modify the legal effect of the provisions of the LOSC in their application to that State. In fact, the ICJ in the 2009 *Romania/Ukraine* case gave no effect to Romania's declaration to the LOSC.[88] On the other hand, in practice it is at times difficult to make any distinction between a declaration or statement and a reservation prohibited by the Convention. Accordingly, there are growing concerns that some declarations and statements may have the same effect as reservations to the Convention.

7 DEVELOPMENT AFTER UNCLOS III

7.1 General considerations

The establishment of a rule freezes the passage of time at a certain moment. Consequently, the rule stabilises the legal order. However, a society, national or international, is constantly changing. Accordingly, the antithesis between stability and progress becomes a fundamental issue of law,[89] and the law of the sea is no exception. Hence mechanisms of the evolution of the LOSC deserve attentive examination.

[88] ICJ Reports 2009, p. 78, para. 42.

[89] B. N. Cardozo, 'The Paradoxes of Legal Science', reproduced in *Selected Writings of Benjamin Nathan Cardozo: The Choice of Tycho Brahe* (New York, Fallon Publications, 1947), pp. 257–258; M. Virally, *La pensée juridique* (Paris, L.G.D.J., 1960), p. 188.

Amendment is an orthodox method of changing relevant provisions of a multilateral treaty. The amendment procedures of the LOSC are set out in Articles 312–316. Under Article 312, after the expiry of a period of ten years from the date of entry into force of the Convention, a State Party may propose, by written communication to the UN Secretary-General, specific amendments to this Convention, other than those relating to activities in the Area. The Secretary-General is to circulate such communication to all States Parties, and if not less than one-half of the States Parties reply favourably to the request within twelve months, the Secretary-General is to convene the Conference. The Conference should make every effort to reach agreement on any amendments by way of consensus. However adopted, an amendment requires ratification or accession by two-thirds of the States Parties or by sixty States Parties, whichever is greater (Article 316(1)).

The simplified procedure provided for in Article 313 makes it possible to propose an amendment to the Convention without convening a conference. Yet such a proposal can be deterred by only one objection. In light of these difficulties, it is not surprising that so far there has been no attempt to use the amendment procedures. Instead, the LOSC is being developed without referring to the amendment procedures provided for in the Convention. In this regard, three ways of 'change' and 'development' should be highlighted.

7.2 Adoption of two Implementation Agreements

Arguably, the most significant changes of the LOSC were made by two 'implementation' agreements. The first is the 1994 Agreement on the Implementation of Part XI of the Convention adopted by the UN General Assembly on 28 July 1994 (hereafter the 1994 Implementation Agreement).[90] In order to elaborate the regime for the deep seabed beyond the limits of national jurisdiction, the Preparatory Commission for the International Seabed Authority and for the International Tribunal for the Law of the Sea (PREPCOM) had been established by Resolution I annexed to the Final Act of UNCLOS III. The aim of this Commission was to draft the necessary rules and procedures that would enable the Authority to commence its functions and to exercise the powers and functions assigned to it by Resolution II relating to preparatory investment.[91] However, major industrialised States, including the USA, expressed strong opposition to the regime regulating the deep seabed activities, laid down in Part XI of the LOSC, and these States refused to participate in the LOSC.

It was apparent that the fundamental disagreements concerning Part XI prevented the universal participation of industrialised States in the Convention. In order to promote universal ratification of the Convention, the 1994 Implementation Agreement was adopted by the UN General Assembly. As we shall discuss later, this agreement has modified the effect of Part XI of the LOSC.[92] The adoption of the new agreement facilitated the ratification of the LOSC by industrialised States, and major developed States,

[90] 1836 *UNTS* p. 42. Entered into force on 28 July 1996.

[91] Paragraph 5 of Resolution I. [92] See Chapter 5, section 3.7.

including Germany, Japan, France, Italy, the Netherlands and the United Kingdom, ratified the LOSC in the wake of the Implementation Agreement.

The second agreement is the 1995 Fish Stocks Agreement.[93] This Agreement seeks to elaborate provisions concerning the conservation and management of fish stocks provided for in Parts V and VII of the LOSC.

7.3 De facto amendment of the LOSC through Meetings of States Parties

The LOSC, as well as the law of the sea in general, is also developed through international forums. An important forum for this purpose is the Meeting of States Parties (SPLOS). The SPLOS is a forum for the specific tasks attributed to it by the LOSC, namely the election of the members of the International Tribunal for the Law of the Sea (Annex VI, Article 4(4)), determination of the salaries, allowances and compensations as well as retirement pensions of the members and of the Registrar of the Tribunal (Annex VI, Article 18(5), (6) and (7)), decision of the terms and manner concerning the expenses of the Tribunal (Annex VI, Article 19(1)), and the election of the members of the Commission on the Limits of the Continental Shelf (CLCS, Annex II, Article 2(3)). The SPLOS also has a valuable role to play as a forum for information. In fact, ITLOS submits its Annual Reports to the SPLOS. In practice, the Secretary-General of the Authority and the Chairman of the CLCS also make statements concerning their activities during the year at the SPLOS.[94]

Notably, several provisions of the LOSC seemed to have been, de facto, modified through the SPLOS. One amendment concerned the first election of the members of ITLOS. Under Article 4(3) of Annex VI of the LOSC, the first election of ITLOS was to be held within six months of the date of entry into force of the Convention. It followed that the last date set up by this provision was 16 May 1995. In 1994, however, only sixty-three States had ratified the Convention, and most of the parties were developing States. In light of the situation, it appeared difficult to hold the election in accordance with the relevant provisions of the Convention, in particular Articles 2 and 3 of Annex VI, which require to ensure 'the representation of the principal legal systems of the world and equitable geographical distribution' and 'no fewer than three members from each geographical group as established by the General Assembly of the United Nations'. Accordingly, the first SPLOS decided to postpone the first election of ITLOS from that date to 1 August 1996.[95]

Later, two further 'amendments' were made with regard to the outer limits of the continental shelf beyond 200 nautical miles. The first amendment concerned the election of the members of the CLCS. Under Article 2(2) of Annex II to the Convention, the

[93] 2167 *UNTS* p. 88. Entered into force 28 July 1996. The full title is United Nations Agreement for the Implementation of the United Nations Convention on the Law of the Sea of 10 December 1982 relating to the Conservation and Management of Straddling Fish Stocks and Highly Migratory Fish Stocks.

[94] T. Treves, 'The General Assembly and the Meeting of States Parties in the Implementation of the LOS Convention', in A. G. Oude Elferink, *Stability and Change in the Law of the Sea: The Role of the LOS Convention* (Leiden and Boston, Nijhoff, 2005), p. 69.

[95] United Nations Convention on the Law of the Sea, Meeting of States Parties, SPLOS/3, 28 February 1995, p. 7, para. 16(a).

initial election was to be held within eighteen months after the date of entry into force of the Convention, namely before 16 May 1996. Whilst the State Party nominating a member of the Commission shall defray the expenses of that member, developing States were reluctant to defray the expenses at that stage. Furthermore, developed States also expressed their concern that they could not nominate an adequate number of experts to the Commission because of the paucity of ratification of the Convention by developed States. Thus, the SPLOS decided to postpone by a year the date of the first election of the CLCS till March 1997.[96]

In addition, the time limit of ten years provided for in Article 4 of Annex II to the LOSC was also extended. According to this provision, a coastal State intending to establish the outer limits of its continental shelf beyond 200 nautical miles is required to submit particulars of such limits to the CLCS along with supporting data within ten years of the entry into force of the Convention for that State. Yet concerns had been voiced by developing States that many countries would have difficulties complying with the time limit because of the lack of financial and technical resources. The Meeting of the States Parties had expressed general support for the concerns raised and decided that the time limit of ten years should be taken as having commenced on 13 May 1999 for States for which the Convention had entered into force before that date.[97] However, some coastal States, in particular developing countries, continue to face particular challenges in submitting information to the CLCS within the new time frame. Accordingly, SPLOS further decided that the ten-year time period referred to in Article 4 of Annex II to the LOSC may be satisfied by submitted 'preliminary information' including a description of the status of preparation and intended date of making a submission.[98] It is true that the decisions of SPLOS are not formal amendments. Even so, there appears to be scope for considering that these decisions have the practical effect of amending some provisions of the LOSC without using the amendment procedures set out in the Convention.

7.4 Development of the law of the sea through international organisations

The role of international organisations is increasingly important in international law, and the same applies to the law of the sea. Notably, several international organisations, including the UN 'family', make an important contribution to the development of the law of the sea. In this regard, the best example may be the International Maritime Organization (IMO). The IMO has a wide jurisdiction relating to the safety of navigation as well as the protection of the marine environment. To date, many instruments have been adopted under the auspices of the IMO. Those instruments have become more important after the entry into force of the LOSC, since the practice of the States Parties to the Convention shall be conformity to the international standards created through the IMO by virtue of 'rules of reference'.[99] According to the 'rules of reference',

[96] SPLOS/5, 22 February 1996, p. 7, para. 20.

[97] SPLOS/73, 14 June 2001, pp. 11–13, paras. 67–84 (in particular, para. 81). 13 May 1999 is the date of adoption of the Scientific and Technical Guidelines.

[98] SPLOS/183, 20 June 2008, p. 2, para. 1(a).

[99] 'Rules of reference' will be discussed in Chapter 8, section 4.2.

relevant provisions of the LOSC must be implemented in accordance with rules adopted under the auspices of the IMO, to the extent that these rules are 'applicable' or 'generally accepted'. In other words, legal instruments can be incorporated into provisions of the LOSC via the 'rules of reference'. In so doing, IMO instruments can further elaborate provisions of the LOSC.

Another important organisation in the field of law of the sea is the Food and Agriculture Organisation of the United Nations (FAO). The FAO is the only organisation of the UN system that has a global fisheries body, the Committee on Fisheries. The FAO thus has a prime role in the conservation and management of fisheries, including review of world fisheries and assistance to developing countries. At the same time, the FAO serves as the forum for discussion and negotiation of international instruments in this field. The instruments adopted under the auspices of the FAO may affect interpretations and implementation of the LOSC. The 1995 FAO Code of Conduct on Responsible Fishing is a case in point. The Code of Conduct is global in scope, and is directed towards members and non-members of the FAO, fishing entities, subregional, regional and global organisations, whether governmental or non-governmental, and all persons concerned with the conservation of fishery resources and management and development of fisheries pursuant to Article 1.2. Whilst the Code of Conduct is a voluntary instrument relating to fisheries, certain parts of it are based on relevant rules of international law, including those reflected in the LOSC. The Code of Conduct is to be interpreted and applied in conformity with the relevant rules of international law, as reflected in the LOSC. The Code of Conduct is also to be interpreted and applied in conformity with the 1995 UN Fish Stocks Agreement under Article 3. To this extent, in part the Code of Conduct may interpret and amplify relevant provisions of the LOSC as well as the 1995 Fish Stocks Agreement.

Finally, the role of the UN General Assembly in the development of the law of the sea must be mentioned. In light of its universal membership, the UN General Assembly can provide an international forum for discussion and negotiation on the law of the sea, including the LOSC. After the entry into force of the LOSC in 1994, the General Assembly decided 'to undertake an annual review and evaluation of the implementation of the Convention [LOSC] and other developments relating to ocean affairs and the law of the sea'.[100] In relation to this, the General Assembly has requested the UN Secretary-General to prepare annually a comprehensive report on developments relating to the law of the sea.[101] Furthermore, the United Nations Open-ended Informal Consultative Process on Oceans and the Law of the Sea (ICP) was established by the General Assembly Resolution of 24 November 1999.[102] The ICP has met every year since 2002 and has established itself as a useful forum for discussions on marine affairs.[103]

[100] UN General Assembly, *Law of the Sea*, A/RES/49/28, adopted on 6 December 1994, para. 12 of the operative part.

[101] *Ibid.*, para. 15(a) of the operative part.

[102] UN General Assembly, A/RES/54/33, adopted on 24 November 1999, p. 2, para. 2.

[103] However, the General Assembly Resolution of 18 January 2000 made clear that the ICP 'should not pursue legal or juridical coordination among the different legal instruments', *ibid.*, p. 3, para. 3(d).

More generally, it is widely acknowledged that the UN General Assembly makes important contributions to the making of customary international law. Considering that rules of customary law governing the oceans are a matter of interest for all States beyond the circle of the Contracting Parties to the LOSC, the role of the General Assembly in customary law-making in this field will not lose its importance.

8 CONCLUSIONS

The matters considered in this chapter can be summarised as follows:

(i) The law of the sea has a dual function, namely the spatial distribution of State jurisdiction and ensuring international cooperation in marine affairs. Basically, the first function of the law aims to reconcile the various interests of individual States, by dividing the ocean into multiple jurisdictional zones. The second function seeks to protect the common interests of the international community as a whole, by focusing on the unity of the ocean. These two functions are not mutually exclusive, but coexist in the law.

(ii) Like other branches of international law, the principal sources of the law of the sea consist of customary law and treaty law. Further to this, judicial decisions also have an important role to play in the identification, clarification and formation of rules of law. Moreover, non-binding instruments, such as resolutions and guidelines adopted by international organisations, also affect the formulation and interpretation of relevant rules in this legal field. In addition to this, unilateral acts and considerations of humanity have some influence on the development of the law of the sea.

(iii) The law of the sea is essentially governed by three principles, namely the principle of freedom, the principle of sovereignty, and the principle of the common heritage of mankind. Whilst the principle of freedom seeks to ensure various uses of the oceans by States, the principle of sovereignty seeks to promote the interests of coastal States. In essence, the two principles seek to safeguard interests of individual States. However, the principle of the common heritage of mankind seeks to protect the common interest of mankind as a whole. In this sense, it may be said that this principle provides a perspective beyond the traditional State-to-State system in the law.

(iv) The law of the sea was progressively codified through three UN Conferences on the Law of the Sea. In particular, UNCLOS III which adopted the LOSC marked an important landmark in the development of the law of the sea. UNCLOS III was characterised by the universality of the participants, its long duration and the enormity of the task. UNCLOS III introduced five procedures for negotiations, namely, the consensus procedure, the package-deal approach, the group approach, informal negotiations, and the single text approach. These techniques seem to provide an interesting insight into the codification and development of international law through an international conference.

(v) It is beyond serious argument that the LOSC is the most important instrument in the law of the sea. The Convention is characterised by four main features:

- comprehensiveness of issues covered by the Convention,
- determination of the maximum breadth of the territorial sea,
- establishment of compulsory procedures of dispute settlement,
- establishment of three new institutions, namely the International Seabed Authority, ITLOS and the Commission on the Limits of the Continental Shelf.

It must also be remembered that reservations are prohibited with a view to securing the integrity of the Convention.

(vi) The adoption of the LOSC does not mean an end to the history of the law of the sea. After 1982, many binding and non-binding instruments were adopted in the field of the law of the sea. The 1994 Implementation Agreement and the 1995 Fish Stocks Agreement are of particular importance. Furthermore, international organisations, such as the IMO and FAO, make an important contribution to the development of the law of the sea by adopting various treaties and guidelines. Thus particular attention must be paid to the interaction between the LOSC and other binding and non-binding instruments concerning marine affairs.

FURTHER READING

1 General

Among modern textbooks and monographs on the law of the sea, the following books are of particular interest:

E. D. Brown, *The International Law of the Sea*, 2 vols. (Aldershot, Dartmouth, 1994).

R. R. Churchill and A. V. Lowe, *Law of the Sea*, 3rd edn (Manchester University Press, 1999).

C. J. Colombos, *The International Law of the Sea*, 6th edn (London, Longman, 1994).

R.-J. Dupuy and D. Vignes (eds.), *A Handbook on the New Law of the Sea*, 2 vols. (Dordrecht, Nijhoff, 1991).

L. Lucchini and M. Voelckel, *Droit de la mer*, 3 vols. (Paris, Pedone, 1990).

M. S. McDougal and W. T. Burke, *The Public Order of the Oceans* (New Haven, Yale University Press, 1962).

D. P. O'Connell (I. A. Shearer (ed.)), *The International Law of the Sea*, 2 vols. (Oxford, Clarendon Press, 1982 and 1984).

J.-P. Pancracio, *Droit de la mer* (Paris, Dalloz, 2010).

D. Rothwell and T. Stephens, *The International Law of the Sea* (Oxford and Portland, Oregon, Hart Publishing, 2010).

T. Scovazzi, 'The Evolution of International Law of the Sea: New Issues, New Challenges' (2000) 286 *RCADI* pp. 39–243.

L. B. Sohn, K. G. Juras, J. E. Noyes, E. Franckx, *Law of the Sea in a Nutshell*, 2nd edn (St Paul, West, 2010).

T. Treves, 'Codification du droit international et pratique des états dans le droit de la mer' (1990-IV) 223, *RCADI* pp. 9–302.

P. Vincent, *Droit de la mer* (Brussels, Larcier, 2008).

2 Commentary on the UN Convention on the Law of the Sea

The seven-volume commentary on the LOSC was undertaken by the University of Virginia School of Law under the general direction of M. H. Nordquist.

M. H. Nordquist et al., *United Nations Convention on the Law of the Sea 1982: A Commentary*, vol. I (Leiden, Nijhoff, 1985), vol. II (1993), vol. III (1995), vol. IV (1991), vol. V (1989), vol. VI (2002) and vol. VII (2011).

Recently another commentary in English has been published:

A. Prölss, *The United Nations Convention on the Law of the Sea: A Commentary* (Oxford, Hart Publishing, 2011).

3 Anthologies

There are many anthologies on the law of the sea. In particular, the following books provide useful insights into contemporary issues :

H. Caminos, *Law of the Sea* (Aldershot, Ashgate, 2001).

R. Casando Raigón and G. Cataldi (eds.), *L'évolution et l'état actuel du droit international de la mer: Mélanges de droit de la mer offerts à Daniel Vignes* (Brussels, Bruylant, 2009).

P. Ehlers, E. Mann-Borgese and R. Wolfrum (eds.), *Marine Issues* (The Hague, Kluwer, 2002).

E. Franckx and P. Gautier, *The Exercise of Jurisdiction over Vessels: New Developments in the Fields of Pollution, Fisheries, Crimes at Sea and Trafficking of Weapons of Mass Destruction* (Brussels, Bruylant, 2010).

D. Freestone, R. Barnes and D. Ong (eds.), *The Law of the Sea: Progress and Prospects* (Oxford University Press, 2006).

H. Hestermeyer, N. Matz-Lück, A. Seibert-Fohr and S. Vöneky (eds.), *Law of the Sea in Dialogue* (Heidelberg, Springer, 2010).

Norman A. Martínez Gutiérrez (ed.), *Serving the Rule of International Maritime Law: Essays in Honour of Professor David Joseph Attard* (London and New York, Routledge, 2010).

T. M. Ndiaye and R. Wolfrum (eds.), *Law of the Sea, Environmental Law and Settlement of Disputes: Liber Amicorum Judge Thomas A. Mensah* (Leiden and Boston, Nijhoff, 2007).

A. G. Oude Elferink (ed.), *Stability and Change in the Law of the Sea: The Role of the LOS Convention* (Leiden, Nijhoff, 2005).

A. G. Oude Elferink and D. R. Rothwell (eds.), *Oceans Management in the 21st Century* (Leiden, Nijhoff, 2004).

A. Strati, M. Gavoueli and N. Skourtos (eds.), *Unresolved Issues and New Challenges to the Law of the Sea: Time Before and Time After* (Leiden, Nijhoff, 2006).

C. R. Symmons (ed.), *Selected Contemporary Issues in the Law of the Sea* (Leiden, Nijhoff, 2011).

D. Vidas (ed.), *Law, Technology and Science for Oceans in Globalisation: IUU Fishing, Oil Pollution, Bioprospecting, Outer Continental Shelf* (Leiden, Nijhoff, 2010).

4 Codification of the Law of the Sea

Documents on the Hague Conference for the Codification of International Law are reproduced in S. Rosenne (ed.), *League of Nations Conference for the Codification of International Law 1930*, 4 vols. (New York, Oceana, 1975). Concerning the United Nations Conference on the Law of the Sea, see the following documents: *First United Nations Conference on the Law of the Sea, Official Records*, 7 vols. (1958); *Second United Nations Conference on the Law of the Sea, Official Records*, 2 vols. (1960); *Third United Nations Conference on the Law of the Sea, Official Records*, 17 vols. (1973–1982). More comprehensive documents on the UNCLOS III are reproduced in R. Platzöder, *Third United Nations Conference on the Law of the Sea*, 18 vols. (Dobbs Ferry, Oceana, 1982–1988). Documents of the Preparatory Commission are also reproduced in R. Platzöder, *The Law of the Sea (Second Series)*, 15 vols. (Dobbs Ferry, Oceana, 1983–1994). See also S. Oda, *The Law of the Sea in Our Time*, 2 vols. (Leiden, Sijthoff, 1977).

5 Collections of Documents

E. D. Brown, *The International Law of the Sea, Vol. II, Documents, Cases and Tables* (Aldershot, Dartmouth, 1994).

A. V. Lowe and S. A. G. Talmon, *Basic Documents on the Law of the Sea: The Legal Order of the Oceans* (Oxford, Hart Publishing, 2009).

New Directions in the Law of the Sea (Dobbs Ferry, Oceana Publications, 1973–1981, 1983–1995, 1996–1999).

Netherlands Institute for the Law of the Sea, *International Organizations and the Law of the Sea: Documentary Yearbook*, 18 vols. (Dordrecht, Nijhoff, 1985–2002).

S. Oda, *The International Law of the Ocean Development: Basic Documents*, 2 vols. (Leiden, Sijthoff, 1972–1975).

L. B. Sohn and J. E. Noyes, *Cases and Materials on the Law of the Sea* (New York, Transnational Publishers, 2004).

6 Development of the Law of the Sea

R. P. Anand, *Origin and Development of the Law of the Sea* (The Hague, Nijhoff, 1982).

A. Boyle, 'Further Development of the Law of the Sea Convention: Mechanisms for Change' (2005) 54 *ICLQ* pp. 563–584.

A. Boyle and C. Chinkin, 'UNCLOS III and the Process of International Law-Making', in T. M. Ndiaye and R. Wolfrum (eds.), *Law of the Sea, Environmental Law and Settlement of Disputes: Liber Amicorum Judge Thomas A. Mensah* (Leiden and Boston, Nijhoff, 2007), pp. 371–388.

H. Caminos and M. R. Molitor, 'Progressive Development of International Law and the Package Deal' (1985) 79 *AJIL* pp. 871–890.

A. H. Dean, 'The Geneva Conference on the Law of the Sea: What Was Accomplished' (1958) 52 *AJIL* pp. 607–628.

J. Evensen, 'Working Methods and Procedures in the Third United Nations Conference on the Law of the Sea' (1986) 199 *RCADI* pp. 417–519.

A. de Marffy, 'The Pardo Declaration and the Six Years of the Sea-Bed Committee', in R.-J. Dupuy and D. Vignes (eds.), *A Handbook of the New Law of the Sea*, vol. 1, (Dordrecht, Nijhoff, 1991), pp.141–162.

G. Fitzmaurice, 'Some Results of the Geneva Conference on the Law of the Sea' (1959) 8 *ICLQ* pp. 73–121.

T. W. Fulton, *The Sovereignty of the Sea* (Edinburgh and London, William Blackwood and Sons, 1911).

G. Gidel, *Le droit international public de la mer: le temps de paix*, 4 vols. (Paris, Duchemin, 1981).

J. Harrison, *Making the Law of the Sea: A Study in the Development of International Law* (Cambridge University Press, 2011).

P. C. Jessup, *The Law of Territorial Waters and Maritime Jurisdiction* (New York, G. A. Jennings Co., 1927).

L. Juda, *International Law and Ocean Use Management: The Evolution of Ocean Governance* (London and New York, Routledge, 1996).

J.-P. Lévy, *La Conférence des Nations Unies sur le droit de la mer: histoire d'une négotiation singulière* (Paris, Pedone, 1983).

B. H. Oxman, 'The Third United Nations Conference on the Law of the Sea', in R.-J. Dupuy and D. Vignes (eds.), *A Handbook of the New Law of the Sea*, vol. 1, (Dordrecht, Nijhoff, 1991), pp. 163–244.

J. K. Sebenius, *Negotiating the Law of the Sea* (Cambridge, Mass., Harvard University Press, 1984).

United Nations, 'Documents on the Development and Codification of International Law: Historical Survey of Development of International Law and its Codification by International Conferences' (1947) 41 *AJIL Supplement* pp. 80–147.

J. H. W. Verzijl, *International Law in Historical Perspective: Part IV, Stateless Domain* (Leiden, Sijthoff, 1971).

7 Regional Studies

There are many monographs dealing with the regional State practice on the law of the sea. Such monographs published after 1990 include:

J. Crawford and D. R. Rothwell (eds.), *The Law of the Sea in the Asian Pacific Region: Development and Prospects* (Dordrecht, Nijhoff, 1992).

E. C. Farrell, *The Socialist Republic of Vietnam and the Law of the Sea* (The Hague, Nijhoff, 1997).

C. C. Joyner, *Antarctica and the Law of the Sea* (Dordrecht, Nijhoff, 1992).

T. C. Kariotis (ed.), *Greece and the Law of the Sea* (The Hague, Kluwer, 1997).

R. J. Long, *Marine Resource Law* (Dublin, Thomson Round Hall, 2007).

Park Hee Kwon, *The Law of the Sea and Northeast Asia: A Challenge for Cooperation* (The Hague, Kluwer, 2000).

R. C. Raigon (ed)., *Europe and the Sea: Fisheries, Navigation and Marine Environment* (Brussels, Bruylant, 2005).

J. A. Roach and R.W. Smith, *United States Responses to Excessive Maritime Claims*, 2nd edn (The Hague, Nijhoff, 1996).

C. Symmons, *Ireland and the Law of the Sea*, 2nd edn (Dublin, Round Hall Sweet and Maxwell, 2000).

T. Treves and L. Pineschi (eds.), *The Law of the Sea: The European Union and its Member States* (The Hague, Nijhoff, 1997).

Zou Keyuan, *China's Marine Legal System and the Law of the Sea* (Leiden, Nijhoff, 2005).

8 Journals on the Law of the Sea

The following journals are particularly useful for studies on the law of the sea: *Annuaire du droit de la mer, IMO News, International Journal of Marine and Coastal Law, Journal of Maritime Law and Commerce, Law of the Sea Bulletin, Marine Policy, Ocean Development and International Law, Ocean and Coastal Management*, and *Ocean Yearbook*.

R. Wolfrum (ed.), *Max Planck Encyclopedia of Public International Law* (Oxford University Press, 2008–2011; online edition: www.mpepil.com) includes many articles on marine issues.

9 Websites

Food and Agriculture Organization: www.fao.org/
International Court of Justice: www.icj-cij.org/homepage/index.php
International Hydrographic Organization: www.iho-ohi.net/english/home/
International Maritime Organization: www.imo.org/
International Tribunal for the Law of the Sea: www.itlos.org/
Permanent Court of Arbitration: www.pca-cpa.org/showpage.asp?pag_id=363
United Nations Division for Ocean Affairs and the Law of the Sea: www.un.org/Depts/los/index.htm

2

Baselines and Related Issues

Main Issues

A primary task of the law of the sea is to determine the spatial extent of the coastal State jurisdiction over the oceans. The seaward limits of each jurisdictional zone are measured from baselines. Thus rules concerning baselines are of particular importance in the law. In particular, rules governing straight baselines and bays merit serious consideration. Furthermore, attention must be devoted to the legal status of islands and low-tide elevations because the existence of these maritime features may affect the seaward limits of marine spaces under national jurisdiction. Against that background, this chapter will address rules concerning baselines and related issues, focusing mainly on the following questions.

(i) What are the rules governing baselines?
(ii) What are the problems associated with rules with regard to straight baselines?
(iii) What are the rules governing juridical bays in international law?
(iv) What is a historic bay and what are the elements of title to such a bay?
(v) What is the definition of islands?
(vi) What are the differences between islands, rocks and low-tide elevations?

1 INTRODUCTION

In the international law of the sea, the scope of jurisdictional zones under national jurisdiction is to be determined on the basis of distance from the coast.[1] Thus it is important to identify the line from which the outer limits of marine spaces under the national jurisdiction of the coastal State are measured. This line is called the baseline. At the same time, the baseline is the line distinguishing internal waters from the territorial sea. The distinction is important because the legal regime of internal waters differs from that of the territorial sea.[2]

[1] LOSC, Articles 3, 33, 57, 76(1). However, internal waters and archipelagic waters constitute exceptions. The former are located on the landward side of the baseline of the territorial sea under Article 8 of the LOSC, and, under Article 49, the latter consist of the waters enclosed in the archipelagic baselines drawn pursuant to Article 47. Thus the two concepts do not rely on the distance from the baseline.

[2] The most important difference between internal waters and the territorial sea is that a right of innocent passage does not apply to internal waters, whilst the right applies to the territorial sea. The right of innocent passage will be discussed in Chapter 3, section 3.

When considering how international law governs the limits of marine spaces, particular attention should be drawn to the tension between the necessary generality of law and the diversity of coastal configurations. As with all types of law, rules of the law of the sea must have a certain degree of generality in their scope. At the same time, as each coastal configuration differs, there is a need to take particular geographical elements into account. The tension creates a difficult question in the relationship between a general rule and exceptions to the rule. On the one hand, strong emphasis on the generality of law may entail the risk of underestimating special interests of a coastal State in a particular geographical situation. On the other hand, allowance of too many exceptions to a general rule will eventually destroy the rule itself. Noting this question, the present chapter will examine rules of international law governing baselines and related issues.

2 BASELINES

Under the LOSC, four types of baselines are at issue: normal baselines, straight baselines, closing lines across river mouths and bays, and archipelagic baselines.[3]

2.1 Normal baselines

The normal baseline is the low-water line drawn along the coast. In this regard, Article 5 of the LOSC provides as follows:

> Except where otherwise provided in this Convention, the normal baseline for measuring the breadth of the territorial sea is the low-water line along the coast as marked on large-scale charts officially recognized by the coastal State.

The phrase 'except where otherwise provided in this Convention' suggests that the baseline is in principle the low-water line. In relation to this, the ICJ, in the 1951 *Anglo-Norwegian Fisheries* case, stated that:

> [F]or the purpose of measuring the breadth of the territorial sea, it is the low-water mark as opposed to the high-water mark, or the mean between the two tides, which has generally been adopted in the practice of States. This criterion is the most favourable to the coastal State and clearly shows the character of territorial waters as appurtenant to the land territory.[4]

The low-water line is the intersection of the plane of low water with the shore. While States have discretion choosing an appropriate low-water line, normally they will select the low-water line shown on existing charts. In this regard, the ILC stated that 'there is no uniform standard by which States in practice determine this line'.[5] This

[3] Archipelagic baselines will be discussed in Chapter 3, section 5.
[4] ICJ Reports 1951, p. 128. [5] (1956) 2 *YILC* p. 267.

view seems to remain valid. The level of the low-water line relies on the tidal datum.[6] Tidal datum has several definitions and the selection is left to the discretion of each State.[7] Obviously the lower the low-water line selected, the further seaward the normal baseline will lie. However, the impact of a lower-tidal datum will be minimal, unless there is a significant tidal range.[8]

Article 5 of the LOSC contains no further specification with regard to the identification of the low-water line and the scale of 'large-scale charts'. It can therefore be presumed that States exercise some discretion in this matter. According to the United Nations Division for Ocean Affairs and the Law of the Sea (hereafter UNDOALOS), the range of the scale of the chart may lie between 1:50,000 to 1:200,000 where circumstances permit.[9]

The LOSC contains no provision with regard to the normal baseline along polar coasts permanently covered by ice shelves.[10] Nor is it possible to detect consistent State practice on this matter. As a possible solution, it has been submitted that the low-water line along the ice shelf contour could be the baseline. However, the ice foot may seasonally change. A question thus arises as to how it is possible to take into account seasonal variations in the ice shelf contour. Another possibility might be to use the average seasonal maximum or minimum edge of the ice shelf as a baseline. Yet it would seem that this method is untested in practice.

2.2 Straight baselines

Whilst the low-water line is a general rule, its application may be impractical in some situations due to a highly complicated coastal configuration. In such case, the straight baseline system may come into play. Straight baselines can be defined as:

6 A tidal datum may be defined as the reference plane (or surface) to which the height of the predicted tide is referred. The tidal datum is a subset of the vertical datum, which comprises any plane or surface used as a reference to measure vertical distances, such as depths, drying features, heights on shore, etc. Nuno Sérgio Marques Antunes, 'The Importance of the Tidal Datum in the Definition of Maritime Limits and Boundaries', *Maritime Briefing*, vol. 2, no. 7 (Durham, International Boundaries Research Unit, 2000), p. 5.

7 The commonly used tidal datum includes: (i) lowest low water (LLW)/highest high water (HHW); (ii) lowest astronomical tide (LAT)/highest astronomical tide (HAT); (iii) mean lower low-water springs (MLLWS)/mean higher high-water springs (MHHWS); (iv) mean low-water springs (MLWS)/mean high-water springs (MHWS); (v) mean higher low water (MHLW)/mean higher high water (MHHW); (vi) mean low water (MLW)/mean high water (MHW); (vii) mean lower low water (MLLW)/mean lower high water (MLHW); (viii) mean low water neaps (MLWN)/mean high water neaps (MHWN); (ix) mean sea-level (MSL) etc., *ibid.*, pp. 28–29. See also D. P. O'Connell, in I. A. Shearer ed., *The International Law of the Sea*, vol. I (Oxford, Clarendon Press, 1982), pp. 173–174; UNDOALOS, *The Law of the Sea: Baselines: An Examination of the Relevant Provisions of the United Nations Convention on the Law of the Sea* (New York, United Nations, 1989), p. 43.

8 C. Carleton and C. Shofield, 'Developments in the Technical Determination of Maritime Space: Charts, Datums, Baselines, Maritime Zones and Limits', *Maritime Briefing*, vol. 3, no. 3 (Durham, International Boundaries Research Unit, 2001), p. 21.

9 UNDOALOS, *Baselines*, p. 5.

10 Generally on this issue, see T. Scovazzi, 'Baselines', in *Max Planck Encyclopedia*, p. 1, para. 4; UNDOALOS, *Baselines*, p. 5; C. C. Joyner, 'The Status of Ice in International Law', in A. G. Oude Elferink and D. R. Rothwell (eds.), *The Law of the Sea and Polar Maritime Delimitation and Jurisdiction* (The Hague, Kluwer, 2001), pp. 23 *et seq.*; D. R. Rothwell, 'Antarctic Baselines: Flexing the Law of Ice-Covered Coastlines', *ibid.*, pp. 49 *et seq.*

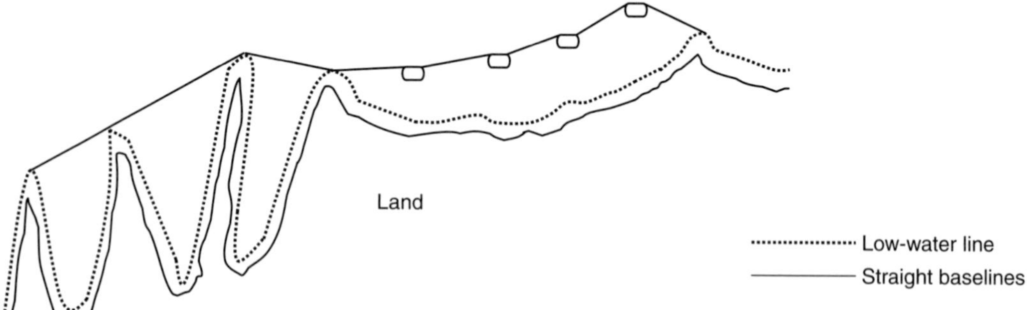

Figure 2.1. Straight baselines (Article 7(1))

> a system of straight lines joining specified or discrete points on the low-water line, usually known as straight baseline turning points, which may be used only in localities where the coastline is deeply indented and cut into, or if there is a fringe of islands along the coast in its immediate vicinity.[11]

The essential difference between the straight baseline system and the normal baseline system is that under the straight baseline system, baselines are drawn *across water*, not along the coast (see Figure 2.1).[12]

Article 7(1) of the LOSC, which followed Article 4 of the Geneva Convention on the Territorial Sea and the Contiguous Zone (hereafter the TSC), provides as follows:

> In localities where the coastline is deeply indented and cut into, or if there is a fringe of islands along the coast in its immediate vicinity, the method of straight baselines joining appropriate points may be employed in drawing the baseline from which the breadth of the territorial sea is measured.

The language of this provision suggests that the use of straight baselines is permissive, and the coastal State can freely determine whether or not to apply the method of straight baselines where a coast meets the conditions set out in Article 7. Whilst Article 7(1) does not specify whether the appropriate points should lie on the charted low-water line, it is generally considered that the basepoints should normally lie on the low-water line rather than further inland. This view is reinforced by Article 7(2), which explicitly refers to the low-water line.[13] Like normal baselines, the landward sides of straight baselines form part of the internal waters of the coastal State. In this

[11] UNDOALOS, *Baselines*, p. 51.

[12] Sir Gerald Fitzmaurice, *The Law and Procedure of the International Court of Justice*, vol. I (Cambridge University Press, 1995), p. 218. See also Figure 2.1.

[13] UNDOALOS, *Baselines*, p. 24 and p. 41. The ICJ, in the 1951 *Anglo-Norwegian Fisheries* case, also specified 'appropriate points on the low-water mark'. ICJ Reports 1951, pp. 129–130.

case, however, a right of innocent passage will still exist in those waters by virtue of Article 8(2).[14]

When considering rules governing straight baselines, the 1951 *Anglo-Norwegian Fisheries* case merits particular attention because it has had a decisive effect on the development of the straight baseline system. The coastal zone concerned in the dispute, which lies north of latitude 66° 28.8'N, is of considerable length, and includes the coast of mainland Norway as well as all the islands, islets, rocks and reefs, known by the name of the *skjærgaard* (literally, rock rampart). The number of islands, large and small, which make up the *skjærgaard*, is estimated by the Norwegian government to be 120,000.[15]

By the Royal Decree of 12 July 1935, the Norwegian government drew straight baselines connecting forty-eight base points selected from extreme points on the mainland, islands or rocks out at sea in order to determine the seaward limit of the exclusive fishery zone off her northern coast. Due to the enforcement of the Decree, a considerable number of British trawlers were arrested. This gave rise to a dispute between the United Kingdom and Norway with regard to the validity of the Norwegian straight baselines laid down by the Royal Decree of 1935. On 28 September 1949, the United Kingdom instituted proceedings against Norway before the ICJ.

In its judgment of 1951, the Court made an important pronouncement on the baseline issue. The Court stated that:

> Where a coast is deeply indented and cut into ... the baseline becomes independent of the low-water mark, and can only be determined by means of a geometrical construction.[16]

The Court further elaborated its view as follows:

> The principle that the belt of territorial waters must follow the general direction of the coast makes it possible to fix certain criteria valid for any delimitation of the territorial sea; these criteria will be elucidated later. The Court will confine itself at this stage to noting that, in order to apply this principle, several States have deemed it necessary to follow the straight base-lines method and that they have not encountered objections of principle by other States. *This method consists of selecting appropriate points on the low-water mark and drawing straight lines between them.*[17]

This passage seems to imply that 'the general direction of the coast' provides the principle governing the baseline; and that the straight baseline method is a result of the application of this principle. This is arguably an innovation of the judgment. In the Court's view, the method of straight lines had been consolidated by a constant and

[14] The right of innocent passage will be discussed in Chapter 3, section 3.

[15] ICJ Reports 1951, p. 127. [16] *Ibid.*, pp. 128–129.

[17] Emphasis added. *Ibid.*, pp. 129–130.

sufficiently long practice and other governments did not consider it to be contrary to international law.[18]

The next issue involves criteria for drawing straight baselines. In this regard, the Court specified three criteria:

(i) The drawing of baselines must not depart to any appreciable extent from the general direction of the coast as it is the land which confers upon the coastal State a right to the waters off its coasts.
(ii) Certain sea areas lying within these lines are sufficiently closely linked to the land domain to be subject to the regime of internal waters.
(iii) Certain economic interests peculiar to a region, the reality and importance of which are clearly evidenced by long usage, should be taken into consideration.[19]

In conclusion, the Court found, by ten votes to two, that the method of straight baselines employed by the Royal Norwegian Decree was not contrary to international law; and, by eight votes to four, that the baselines fixed by the said Decree in application of this method were not contrary to international law.[20]

Later, the formula of the *Fisheries* judgment was incorporated in Article 4 of the TSC as a general rule governing straight baselines. Article 7 of the LOSC followed Article 4 of the TSC almost verbatim. It is clear that the phrase in Article 7(1) of the LOSC, 'where the coastline is deeply indented and cut into', literally follows that in the *Fisheries* judgment. Article 7(3) and (5) also follow the Court's criteria for drawing straight baselines, by providing that:

3. The drawing of straight baselines must not depart to any appreciable extent from the general direction of the coast, and the sea areas lying within the lines must be sufficiently closely linked to the land domain to be subject to the regime of internal waters.
5. Where the method of straight baselines is applicable under paragraph 1, account may be taken, in determining particular baselines, of economic interests peculiar to the region concerned, the reality and the importance of which are clearly evidenced by long usage.

Here one may detect one of the most outstanding instances of judicial impact on the development of international law. On the other hand, these treaty provisions include some elements of obscurity. Two issues must be highlighted.

The first question concerns the interrelationship between the criteria provided in Article 7(1) and (5). The first two criteria concern purely geographical tests, while the third element concerns an economic test. A question that may arise is whether the coastal State can apply the method of straight baselines solely on the basis of the economic element. The intention of the *Fisheries* judgment and Article 7 of the LOSC

[18] *Ibid.*, p. 139. Decrees of Saudi Arabia (1949), Egypt (1951), Ecuador, Yugoslavia (1948), Iran (1934) established straight baselines between outer points of the mainland. M. Whiteman, (1965) 4 *Digest of International Law* p. 148.

[19] ICJ Reports 1951, p. 133. [20] *Ibid.*, p. 143.

would seem to suggest that economic interests alone do not justify the use of straight baselines. In fact, under Article 7(5) of the LOSC, consideration of economic interests is qualified by the condition 'where the method of straight baselines is applicable under paragraph 1'. The ICJ also stated, in the 2001 *Qatar/Bahrain* case (Merits), that:

> Such conditions [of drawing straight baselines] are primarily either that the coastline is deeply indented and cut into, or that there is a fringe of islands along the coast in its immediate vicinity.[21]

A second and more debatable issue relates to the ambiguity of the criteria for drawing straight baselines. There is no objective test that may identify deeply indented coasts. It is also difficult to objectively identify the existence of a 'fringe of islands'. Whilst there must be more than one island in the fringe, the LOSC does not provide any further precision regarding the minimum number of islands. The concept of the coast's 'immediate vicinity' may also depend on subjective appreciation. Furthermore, unlike the cases of bays (Article 10(5)) and archipelagic baselines (Article 47(2)), the LOSC does not specify the maximum length of straight baselines, although arguably length is an important element in assessing the validity of a straight baseline.[22] As a consequence, some States drew excessively long straight baselines. For instance, Burma (Myanmar) established the 222.3-mile long line across the Gulf of Martaban.[23] In so doing, Burma (Myanmar) enclosed about 14,300 sq. miles (equivalent to the size of Denmark) as internal waters.[24] Vietnam drew the 161.3-mile long line between Bay Canh Islet and Hon Hai Islet, and the 161.8-mile long line connecting Hon Hai Islet and Hon Doi Islet.[25] Moreover, there is no objective test which may identify the general direction of the coast. Neither is there any objective test to identify the close linkage between the land domain and the sea area lying within the straight baselines. In addition, 'economic interests peculiar to the region concerned' are also a matter of subjective appreciation.

In short, the rules governing straight baselines are so abstract that the application of the rules to particular coasts is to a large extent subject to the discretion of coastal States. As a consequence, there are many instances where coastal States draw straight baselines too freely.[26]

At present there is a general trend for coastal States to enclose large marine spaces as internal waters by drawing straight baselines. At the same time, the establishment of straight baselines extends the seaward limits of marine spaces under national

[21] The *Qatar/Bahrain* case (Merits), ICJ Reports 2001, p. 103, para. 212.

[22] Fitzmaurice, *Law and Procedure*, p. 239.

[23] US Department of State, *Limits in the Sea*, no. 14 (1970), p. 5. This document, along with a map, is available at: www.state.gov/g/oes/ocns/opa/convention/c16065.htm.

[24] R. R. Churchill and A. V. Lowe, *Law of the Sea*, 3rd edn (Manchester University Press, 1999), p. 39; Roach and Smith, 'Straight Baselines', p. 48.

[25] US Department of State, *Limits in the Sea*, no. 99 (1983), p. 9.

[26] For an analysis in some detail of excessive baseline claims, along with illustrations, see J. A. Roach and R. W. Smith, *United States Responses to Excessive Maritime Claims*, 2nd edn (The Hague, Nijhoff, 1997), pp. 74–146.

jurisdiction towards the high seas. The straight baseline system thus plays a dual role expanding marine spaces under national jurisdiction inside and outside the baselines.

Whilst the coastal States may exercise some discretion in the application of the straight baseline method, this does not mean that the coastal States can make excessive baseline claims, independent of rules of international law. Where a baseline is clearly contrary to rules of international law on this subject, the line will be invalid at least in relation to States that have objected to it.[27] It must be remembered that the ICJ, in the *Norwegian Fisheries* case, stressed that:

> The delimitation of sea areas has always an international aspect; it cannot be dependent merely upon the will of the coastal State as expressed in its municipal law. Although it is true that the act of delimitation is necessarily a unilateral act, because only the coastal State is competent to undertake it, the validity of the delimitation with regard to other States depends upon international law.[28]

The ICJ's view, in the *Qatar/Bahrain* case (Merits), also bears quoting:

> [T]he method of straight baselines, which is an exception to the normal rules for the determination of baselines, may only be applied if a number of conditions are met. This method must be applied restrictively.[29]

A related issue is whether State practice will lead to an agreed interpretation of the LOSC or a new rule of customary international law concerning straight baselines. The answer should be in the negative for two reasons.[30] First, the pattern of non-conforming practice is highly diverse. It appears to be difficult to consider the practice as 'extensive and virtually uniform'. Second, it must be remembered that various States as well as the EU have already protested against extravagant straight baselines. In particular, the USA consistently protests against straight baselines that, in the view of the USA, do not conform to the LOSC. These protests will make it difficult to formulate any *opinio juris* on this matter.

Article 7(2)(4) and (6) of the LOSC further specifies conditions for drawing straight baselines. First, under Article 7(4), straight baselines shall not be drawn to and from low-tide elevations,[31] (i) unless lighthouses or similar installations which are permanently above sea level have been built on them, or (ii) except in instances where the

[27] Where a State has accepted the baseline, however, there may be scope to argue that that State could no longer deny the validity of the baseline because of estoppels. Churchill and Lowe, *Law of the Sea*, p. 57.

[28] ICJ Reports 1951, p. 132.

[29] The *Qatar/Bahrain* case (Merits), ICJ Reports 2001, p. 103, para. 212.

[30] R. Churchill, 'The Impact of State Practice on the Jurisdictional Framework Contained in the LOS Convention', in A. G. Oude Elferink (ed.), *Stability and Change in the Law of the Sea: The Role of the LOS Convention* (Leiden and Boston, Brill, 2005), p. 108.

[31] A low-tide elevation is defined in Article 13(1) of the LOSC, and will be discussed in section 4 of this chapter.

drawing of baselines to and from such elevations has received general international recognition. The first requirement of lighthouses or similar installations serves to benefit navigators because low-tide elevations are, by nature, not visible at all times. The second requirement, which is absent from Article 4(3) of the TSC, reflects the case of Norway where a straight baseline was drawn to and from a low-tide elevation with no lighthouse or similar installation.[32]

Second, the system of straight baselines may not be applied by a State in such a manner as to cut off the territorial sea of another State from the high seas or an exclusive economic zone (Article 7(6)). This provision is based on Article 4(5) of the TSC, which was inspired by a Portuguese proposal, with the additional reference to the EEZ. Article 7(6) seeks to safeguard the access of a coastal State to any open sea area where it enjoys the freedom of navigation. Specifically, this provision deals with exceptional situations, where a smaller territory is embedded in a larger territory, such as Monaco in France, or where small islands belonging to one State lie close to the coast of another State, such as Greek islands lying close to the coast of Turkey. In fact, France established straight baselines in such a manner that they do not cut off the territorial sea of Monaco from the high seas.[33] On the other hand, whilst Croatia took over the Yugoslavian straight baselines, the baselines seem to cut off Bosnia–Herzegovina from the high seas and the EEZ.[34]

Third, Article 7(2) provides a rule concerning an exceptional geographical situation:

> Where, because of the presence of a delta and other natural conditions, the coastline is highly unstable, the appropriate points may be selected along the furthest seaward extent of the low-water line and, notwithstanding subsequent regression of the low-water line, the straight baselines shall remain effective until changed by the coastal State in accordance with this Convention.

This provision was drafted as a result of a Bangladeshi proposal with the specific case of the Ganges/Brahmaputra River delta in mind.[35] Yet the text of Article 7(2) is not wholly unambiguous. For example, the terms 'delta' and 'highly unstable' will need further clarification.[36] A question also arises as to whether only coastlines which satisfy the conditions set out in paragraph 1 of Article 7 will qualify for use of paragraph 2 of the same provision. Considering that originally paragraphs 1 and 2 were set out in one paragraph, it appears to be reasonable to consider that the words in paragraph 2, 'the

[32] *Virginia Commentaries*, vol. II, pp. 102–103; V. Prescott and C. Schofield, *The Maritime Political Boundaries of the World*, 2nd edn (Leiden and Boston, Nijhoff, 2005), p. 160.

[33] Scovazzi, 'Baselines', p. 3, para.16.

[34] In March 1994 and May 1996, the two countries reached an agreement guaranteeing Bosnia–Herzegovina's access to the sea. G. Blake and D. Topalović, 'The Maritime Boundaries of the Adriatic Sea', *Maritime Briefing*, vol. 1, no. 8 (Durham: International Boundaries Research Unit, 1996), pp. 9–12; Prescott and Schofield, *The Maritime Political Boundaries*, p. 161.

[35] UNDOALOS, *Baselines*, p. 24; *Virginia Commentaries*, vol. II, p. 101.

[36] S. McDonald and V. Prescott, 'Baselines along Unstable Coasts: An Interpretation of Article 7(2)' (1990) 8 *Ocean Yearbook* p. 75 and pp. 80–81.

appropriate points', trace back to 'appropriate points' in paragraph 1 of Article 7.[37] It can be said, therefore, that paragraph 2 is subordinate to paragraph 1 of Article 7.[38]

Fourth, some consideration should be given to the obligation of due publicity. In common with the TSC, the LOSC contains no explicit duty to publicise the normal baseline. However, it must be remembered that the normal baseline, namely, the low-water line is to be marked on large-scale charts officially recognised by the coastal State pursuant to Article 5 of the LOSC. Concerning other types of baselines, Article 16 of the LOSC provides that:

1. The baselines for measuring the breadth of the territorial sea determined in accordance with articles 7, 9 and 10, or the limits derived therefrom, and the lines of delimitation drawn in accordance with articles 12 and 15 shall be shown on charts of a scale or scales adequate for ascertaining their position. Alternatively, a list of geographical coordinates of points, specifying the geodetic datum, may be substituted.[39]
2. The coastal State shall give due publicity to such charts or lists of geographical coordinates and shall deposit a copy of each such chart or list with the Secretary-General of the United Nations.

A literal interpretation of Article 16(1) would seem to furnish the two distinct options of either publicising the baselines or the 'limits derived therefrom', presumably without reference to baselines.[40] It appears that the second option is unsatisfactory because the true extent or location of the baselines is unknown to another State. As a consequence, third States cannot properly examine the validity of the baselines concerned. It must also be recalled that a baseline forms the line which distinguishes the territorial sea from internal waters. As the legal regime of internal waters differs from that of the territorial sea, it is important for mariners to know the precise location of jurisdictional zones.[41] Thus, it will be desirable to publicise the geographical location of the baselines.

Finally, a contemporary issue which may arise is the effect of rising sea levels on the limits of marine spaces. Owing to global warming, a substantial sea-level rise may affect coastal configurations. Where an island, rock or a low-tide elevation disappears entirely as a consequence of sea-level rise, it is possible that the extent of marine spaces measured from the marine feature decreases. Where a normal baseline, i.e. a low-water line, shifts landward, it appears to be logical to consider that the outer limits of the territorial sea and the EEZ will also shift landward accordingly. In this case,

[37] *Ibid.*, p. 77. [38] UNDOALOS, *Baselines*, p. 24.

[39] Geodetic datum means a set of parameters specifying the reference surface or the reference coordinate system used for geodetic control in the calculation of coordinates of points on the earth. International Hydrographic Organization (hereafter IHO), *Hydrographic Dictionary, Part I*, vol. I, 5th edn (Monaco, 1994), p. 59.

[40] UNDOALOS, *Baselines*, p. 40, para. 95; C. R. Symmons and M. W. Reed, 'Baseline Publicity and Charting Requirements: An Overlooked Issue in the UN Convention on the Law of the Sea' (2010) 41 *ODIL* p. 89. The second option, namely publication of merely outer limits of the territorial sea, was not provided in Article 4(6) of the TSC.

[41] *Ibid.*, pp. 86–87.

there appears to be good reason to argue that the coastal State should be required to replace the former points submerged under the sea by new ones in conformity with relevant criteria.[42] On the other hand, it is arguable that, notwithstanding the changes in the coastline, the straight baselines drawn under Article 7(2) remain effective.

2.3 Juridical bays

Bays are of particular importance for coastal States because of their intimate connection with land. In this regard, the Arbitral Tribunal, in the 1910 *North Atlantic Coast Fisheries* case, stated that:

> the geographical character of a bay contains conditions which concern the interests of the territorial sovereign to a more intimate and important extent than do those connected with the open coast. Thus conditions of national and territorial integrity, of defence, of commerce and of industry are all vitally concerned with the control of the bays penetrating the national coast line.[43]

Furthermore, where the low-water line rule applies to a bay whose mouth is less than twice of the breadth of the territorial sea, the high seas may be enclosed within the bay. This situation will create inconvenient results for various marine activities. Hence, according to Gidel, it has been recognised that the baseline of bays for measuring the breadth of the territorial sea is not the low-water mark.[44] Indeed, the legal concept of a bay was admitted by the *Institut de droit international* in 1894 and the International Law Association in 1895, respectively.[45] It could be said that customary law has allowed the coastal States to draw a closing line across the entrance of bays, whereby the landward waters from the closing line have become internal waters. In short, the legal concept of bays has emerged as an exception to the normal rule concerning the baseline for measuring the breadth of the territorial sea.[46]

The closing line of bays becomes the baseline for measuring the breadth of the territorial sea. Unlike the territorial sea, the right of innocent passage does not apply to internal waters. Should the waters of a bay be enclosed as internal waters, vessels flying the flag of a foreign State cannot enjoy innocent passage in these waters. The

[42] In practice, the redrawing of baselines is untested.

[43] The *North Atlantic Coast Fisheries* case (Great Britain v United States), 7 September 1910, United Nations, 11 *RIAA* p. 196.

[44] G. Gidel, *Le droit international public de la mer: le temps de paix, Tome III, La mer territoriale et la zone contiguë* (reprinted, Paris, Duchemin, 1981), pp. 537–538.

[45] 'Règles adoptées par l'Institut de Droit international sur la définition et le régime de la mer territoriale (Article 3)', (1904) *Annuaire de l'Institut de Droit International: vingtième volume Session d'Edimbourg Septembre 1904 et tableau décennal de l'organisation, du personnel et des travaux de l'Institut (1894–1904)* p. 342; International Law Association, *Report of the Seventeenth Conference* (1895) p. 109. Whilst the *Institut* took the position that the length of the closing line across a bay would be twelve nautical miles, the ILA took the view that the length of the closing line would be ten nautical miles.

[46] Dissenting Opinion of Judge Oda in *Land, Island and Maritime Frontier Dispute* (El Salvador/Honduras: Nicaragua), ICJ Reports 1992, p. 735, para. 8.

spatial scope of bays thus becomes a matter of important concern for shipping States. In this regard, the question that arises involves the criteria by which a coastal indentation can be recognised as a bay and the maximum length of the closing line across a bay. Concerning the latter, the ten-mile limit rule was applied by comparatively many treaties in the nineteenth and the early twentieth century.

Nonetheless, judicial practice was more cautious about accepting the customary law character of this formula. In the 1910 *North Atlantic Coast Fisheries* case, for instance, the Arbitral Tribunal did not consider the ten-mile formula as 'a principle of international law'.[47] The legal nature of the ten-mile formula was also at issue in the 1951 *Anglo-Norwegian Fisheries* case. Although the United Kingdom asserted that the ten-mile formula could be regarded as a rule of international law, the ICJ refused to admit the customary law character of this formula.[48] Overall it can be observed that customary international law has been vague with regard to the maximum length of closing lines for bays. We must therefore turn to examine treaty law on this subject.

At the global level, the rules governing bays were, for the first time, set out in Article 7 of the TSC, and these rules were echoed essentially verbatim in Article 10 of the LOSC. This provision makes it clear that three classes of bays are outside the scope of its regulations.[49]

First, Article 10 'relates only to bays the coasts of which belong to a single State'. Hence, bays bordered by more than one State are excluded from the scope of Article 10.

Second, historic bays are not regulated by Article 10(6) of the LOSC. As will be seen later, such bays are governed by a special regime.

Third, Article 10(6) provides that this provision does not apply to 'bays' where the system of straight baselines is applied. It is important to note that, legally speaking, the closing line across the mouth of a bay and the straight baseline are regulated by two different rules. In this regard, there is a concern that Article 10(6) can be used as an escape device to avoid rules regulating bays and to draw straight baselines across minor curvatures which are not strictly bays.

Article 10(2) then sets out geographical and geometrical criteria for identifying a bay. Concerning geographical criteria, the first sentence of Article 10(2) provides that:

> For the purposes of this Convention, a bay is a well-marked indentation whose penetration is in such proportion to the width of its mouth as to contain land-locked waters and constitute more than a mere curvature of the coast.

This provision contains two elements. First, a bay must be 'a well-marked indentation' and 'constitute more than a mere curvature of the coast'. Second, the penetration of a bay must be 'in such proportion to the width of its mouth' and contain 'land-locked waters'. It follows that the bay is surrounded on all sides but one.[50]

[47] *Ibid.*, p. 199. [48] ICJ Reports 1951, p. 131.
[49] UNDOALOS, *Baselines*, p. 29. [50] *Ibid.*, p. 29, para. 67.

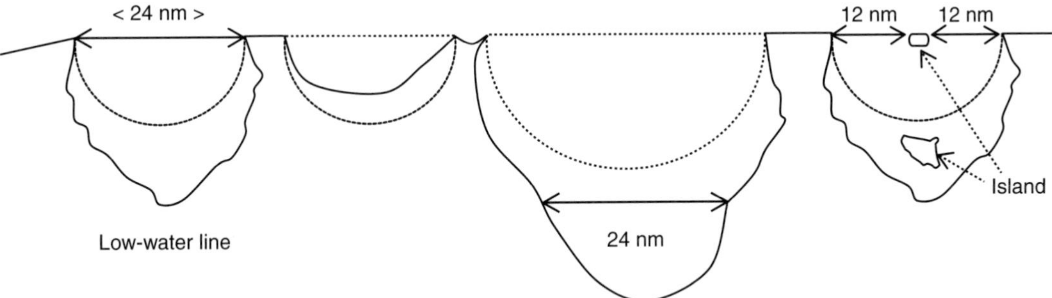

Figure 2.2. Juridical bays (Article 10)

With respect to geometrical criteria, Article 10(2) provides the semi-circle test (see Figure 2.2):

> An indentation shall not, however, be regarded as a bay unless its area is as large as, or larger than, that of the semi-circle whose diameter is a line drawn across the mouth of that indentation.

Article 10(3) further elaborates conditions in the application of the semi-circle test. First, Article 10(3) stipulates that:

> For the purpose of measurement, the area of an indentation is that lying between the low-water mark around the shore of the indentation and a line joining the low-water mark of its natural entrance points.

A point to arise here is that it is not always easy to identify the natural entrance points of a bay. In fact, some bays arguably possess more than one entrance point that can be used. Yet Article 10 contains no criterion for identifying the natural entrance points. In certain circumstances, the low-water line of a bay can be interrupted at the mouths of rivers flowing into the bay. Where the mouth of a river is wide and penetrated by tide, a difficult question arises as to how it is possible to calculate the area of the waters of the bay. This is particularly true in the situation where the area within the bay is very close to the area of the semi-circle.

Second, Article 10(3) provides that:

> Where, because of the presence of islands, an indentation has more than one mouth, the semi-circle shall be drawn on a line as long as the sum total of the lengths of the lines across the different mouths. Islands within an indentation shall be included as if they were part of the water area of the indentation.

Where islands are situated seaward of the entrance of bays, however, the application of the semi-circle test is not free from difficulty.[51]

Third, unlike the method of straight baselines, Article 10(4) and (5) set out a restriction of the maximum length of the closing line of a bay (see Figure 2.2):

> 4. If the distance between the low-water marks of the natural entrance points of a bay does not exceed 24 nautical miles, a closing line may be drawn between these two low-water marks, and the waters enclosed thereby shall be considered as internal waters.
>
> 5. Where the distance between the low-water marks of the natural entrance points of a bay exceeds 24 nautical miles, a straight baseline of 24 nautical miles shall be drawn within the bay in such a manner as to enclose the maximum area of water that is possible with a line of that length.

Obviously the 24-mile limit is based on the double territorial sea limit.

Overall it may be said that general rules determining the bays are currently established in the LOSC. Indeed, the ICJ, in the 1992 *Land, Island and Maritime Frontier Dispute* case, stated that 'these provisions on bays might be found to express general customary law'.[52]

2.4 Historic bays

The TSC and the LOSC contain no definition of historic bays. Historic bays are one of the categories of 'historic waters'. Thus the legal regime of historic bays should be examined in the broad context of historic waters.[53] According to the ICJ, 'historic waters' usually mean 'waters which are treated as internal waters but which would not have that character were it not for the existence of [a] historic title'.[54] By way of example, Judge Oda, in the 1992 *Land, Island and Maritime Frontier Dispute*, defined historic bays as:

> [T]hose bay-like features (in a geographical sense) which, because of their greater width at the mouth or their lack of penetration into the landmass, could not normally be classified legally as bays but can for historical reasons be given the same legal status as 'bays'.[55]

51 *Ibid.*, p. 32; Churchill and Lowe, *Law of the Sea*, pp. 42–43.

52 ICJ Reports 1992, p. 588, para. 383.

53 For an analysis in some detail of legal regime of historic waters, see UN Secretariat, 'Judicial Régime of Historic Waters, Including Historic Bays', Document A/CN.4/143, (1962) 2 *Yearbook of the International Law Commission*. This study sought to present certain *tentative* conclusions on the historic waters by examining the material in the form of known claims to 'historic waters', the literature of international law and previous attempts to formulate the relevant principles on this matter before 1962. *Ibid.*, p. 5, para. 32.

54 The *Anglo-Norwegian Fisheries* case, ICJ Reports 1951, p. 130.

55 Dissenting Opinion of Judge Oda in *Land, Island and Maritime Frontier Dispute* (El Salvador/Honduras: Nicaragua), ICJ Reports 1992, pp. 733–734, para. 4. IHO defines 'historic bays' as 'those over which the coastal state has publicly claimed and exercised jurisdiction and this jurisdiction has been accepted by other states. Historic bays need not match the definition of "bay" contained in the United Nations Convention on the Law of the Sea'. IHO, *Hydrographic Dictionary*, p. 105.

Should the title to a historic bay be established, a coastal State may draw a closing line across the mouth of the bay, and the line forms the baseline. The area inside the closing line constitutes the internal waters of that State.

Traditionally, there were two contrasting views with regard to the legal regime of historic waters, including historic bays. According to the first view, the regime of historic waters could be considered as an exception to the general rules of international law governing the limits of the maritime domain of a coastal State.[56] This view was argued by the United Kingdom in the 1951 *Anglo-Norwegian Fisheries* case.[57] On the second view, the regime of historic waters could not be an exception because there were no general rules of international law regarding the determination of bays.[58] As noted, it is argued that currently general rules concerning the determination of bays are established in the LOSC. Hence there may be room for the view that the regime of historic bays should be considered as an exception to the general rules.

The next issue to be examined involves elements of title to historic bays. As neither the TSC nor the LOSC dealt with historic bays, they are governed by customary international law. Whilst it is difficult to examine the actual State practice concerning historic bays in a comprehensive manner, the study of the UN Secretariat seems to shed some light on this subject. This study enumerated three basic elements for a title to historic waters, including historic bays:

(i) the exercise of authority over the area by the State claiming the historic right,
(ii) the continuity of this exercise of authority, and
(iii) the attitude of foreign States (the acquiescence of foreign States).[59]

According to the view of the UN Secretariat, in order to acquire a historic title to a maritime area, the coastal State must have effectively and continuously exercised sovereignty over the maritime area during a time sufficient to create a usage and have done so under the general toleration of the international community.[60]

In relation to this, a question arises as to whether a claim to historic bays can be justified by a 'vital interest' of the coastal State, such as the requirements of self-defence. At the 1930 Hague Conference for the Codification of International Law, for instance, the Portuguese representative asserted that:

56 Gidel took this view. *Le droit international public de la mer*, pp. 621 *et seq.*
57 Reply submitted by the United Kingdom, vol. II, 28 November 1950, p. 302.
58 Bourquin supported this view. M. Bourquin, 'Les baies historiques', in *Mélanges Georges Sauser-Hall* (Neuchâtel and Paris, Delachaux et Niestlé, 1952), p. 37 *et seq.*
59 UN Secretariat, 'Judicial Régime of Historic Waters', p. 13, para. 80.
60 *Ibid.*, p. 19, para. 132. In the 1951 *Anglo-Norwegian Fisheries* case, the United Kingdom also pointed to two essential elements, namely (i) actual exercise of authority by the claimant State and (ii) acquiescence by the other State. *Reply*, vol. II, p. 303.

> From a variety of circumstances, the State to which the bay belongs finds it necessary to exercise full sovereignty over it without restriction or hindrance. The considerations which justify their claim are the security and defence of the land territory and ports, and the well-being and even the existence of the State.[61]

It would seem that the primary intention of this line of thought is to justify the claim to historic bays ignoring the time or historicity element. Nevertheless, the bypassing of the historicity element is contrary to the concept of *historic* bays. Furthermore, as 'vital interest' is a matter of subjective appreciation, giving States the right to claim 'vital interest' may entail the serious risk of increasing unwarranted claims to historic bays and eventually destroy the rules determining bays in international law.[62] Hence there appears to be good reason to argue that 'vital interest' alone cannot provide a title to a historic bay.

The existence of a title to historic waters, including historic bays, is to a large extent a matter of appreciation depending on specific circumstances. It seems, therefore, that the claim to a historic bay must be evaluated on a case-by-case basis. The ICJ, in the 1982 *Tunisia/Libya* judgment, echoed this view, by stating that:

> It seems clear that the matter continues to be governed by general international law which does not provide for a *single* 'régime' for 'historic waters' or 'historic bays', but only for a particular régime for each of the concrete, recognized cases of 'historic waters' or 'historic bays'.'[63]

In light of the complications in the evaluation, it would be highly difficult to establish a definitive list of historic bays.[64] In reality, claims to historic bays have often evoked protests from foreign States. For instance, the Russian claim to the Peter the Great Bay was protested by many States, such as the USA, Japan, the United Kingdom, France, Canada, Sweden, the Federal Republic of Germany and the Netherlands.[65]

Arguably, the most dramatic instance may be the claim by Libya to the Gulf of Sert (or Sidra).[66] On 10 October 1973, Libya claimed the Gulf as Libyan internal waters and drew a closing line of approximately 300 miles in length across the Gulf. Many States, including Australia, France, the Federal Republic of Germany, Italy, Norway, Spain, the United States, the United Kingdom and the other EC Countries, protested the Libyan claim.[67] On 19 August 1981, the Sixth Fleet of the United States Navy conducted

[61] S. Rosenne (ed.), *League of Nations Conference for the Codification of International Law 1930*, vol. 2 (New York, Oceana, 1975), p. 402.

[62] UN Secretariat, 'Judicial Régime of Historic Waters', p. 20, paras. 135–140.

[63] Emphasis original. ICJ Reports 1982, p. 74, para. 100.

[64] UN Secretariat, 'Judicial Régime of Historic Waters', p. 24, para. 176. A tentative list of historic waters or bays is presented by Scovazzi, 'Baselines', p. 6, para. 30 and C. R. Symmons, *Historic Waters in the Law of the Sea: A Modern Re-Appraisal* (Leiden and Boston, Brill, 2008), pp. 301–304.

[65] Roach and Smith, *United States Responses*, p. 49.

[66] Ahnish indicates that 'Sert' would be the nearest transliteration to the modern Arabic name given to the Gulf and its region. Faraj Abdullah Ahnish, *The International Law of Maritime Boundaries and the Practice of States in the Mediterranean Sea* (Oxford, Clarendon Press, 1993), p. 194, footnote 1.

[67] Roach and Smith, *United States Responses*, p. 45, footnote 23.

military manoeuvres in the proximity of the contested area. This action caused armed conflict and US F-14 fighter aircraft shot down two Libyan Sukhoi-22 fighters above the Gulf of Sidra. On 25 March 1986, air and sea manoeuvres north of the Gulf of Sidra conducted by the US Sixth Fleet created another armed confrontation with Libya, killing twenty-four persons.[68] As illustrated by this episode, claims to historic bays may give rise to a serious international dispute. Under Article 298(1)(a)(i) of the LOSC, however, disputes involving historic bays or titles may be exempted from the compulsory procedure of peaceful settlement of international disputes embodied in Part XV of the Convention.

2.5 Bays bordered by more than one State

Recently the number of bays bordered by more than one State has increased owing to the break-up of existing composite States. The legal regime of such bays thus merits particular attention. In this regard, a question arises as to whether States bordering a bay may draw a closing line across the mouth of the bay. Two different views can be identified.

According to the first view, the coastal States bordering the bay may draw a closing line by agreement.[69] In fact, the 1988 Agreement between Tanzania and Mozambique closed the Ruvuma Bay, by drawing a straight line linking two cross-border points.[70] Article II of the Agreement provides that: 'All waters on the landward side of this line constitute the internal waters of the two countries'. Under the same provision, the internal waters are apportioned by means of a median line.

According to the second view, the normal baseline rule should apply to bays bordered by more than one State because such bays are not regulated by Article 10 of the LOSC or historic bays. In this view, bays bordered by more than one State cannot be closed by a line across the mouth, and the low-water mark around the shores of the bays constitutes the baseline.[71] Legally speaking, the waters of a closing line of a bay are internal waters under territorial sovereignty. As territorial sovereignty is exclusive by nature, the internal waters of one State cannot belong to another State at the same time. Thus, that the idea of a bay bordered by more than one State, the waters of which are internal waters, contains a conceptual contradiction.

In the 1992 *Land, Island and Maritime Frontier Dispute*, the legal status of bays bordered by more than one State – the Gulf of Fonseca – was discussed in connection with historic bays. In this case, the Chamber of the ICJ held that the Gulf was a historic bay

[68] F. Francioni, 'The Status of the Gulf of Sirte in International Law' (1984) 11 *Syracuse Journal of International Law and Commerce* pp. 311 *et seq.*; S. R. Ratner, 'The Gulf of Sidra Incident of 1981: A Study of the Lawfulness of Peacetime Aerial Engagements' (1984–85) 10 *Yale Journal of International Law* pp. 59 *et seq.*; M. M. Marsit, 'Sidra, Gulf of', in *Max Planck Encyclopedia*, pp. 1 *et seq.*

[69] C. R. Symmons, 'The Maritime Border Areas of Ireland, North and South: An Assessment of Present Jurisdictional Ambiguities and International Precedents Relating to Delimitation of "Border Bays"' (2009) 24 *IJMCL* pp. 469–470 and pp. 498–499.

[70] For the text of the Agreement, see C. I. Charney and L. M. Alexander (eds.), *International Maritime Boundaries*, vol. I (Dordrecht, Nijhoff, 1993), pp. 898–902.

[71] Churchill and Lowe, *Law of the Sea*, p. 45; Scovazzi, 'Baselines', p. 6, para. 29.

the waters whereof were held in sovereignty by El Salvador, Honduras and Nicaragua.[72] However, Judge Oda questioned this view and argued that the waters of a historic bay are nothing other than internal waters, and these waters of one State cannot abut the internal waters of another State.[73] The learned Judge took the view that 'there did not and still does not (or, even, cannot) exist any such legal concept as a "pluri-State bay" the waters of which are internal waters'.[74] According to this view, apart from the landward side of the low-water mark, the waters of bays bordered by more than one State fall within the category of the territorial sea, the EEZ or the high seas.

2.6 River mouths

Concerning river mouths, Article 9 of the LOSC stipulates that:

> If a river flows directly into the sea, the baseline shall be a straight line across the mouth of the river between points on the low-water line of its banks.

The language is almost identical to Article 13 of the TSC. This provision calls for four brief comments.

First, concerning the interpretation of the phrase 'directly', the authentic French text of Article 9 reads: '*si un fleuve se jette dans la mer sans former d'estuaire*'. The French text clearly suggests that the phrase 'directly' means 'without forming an estuary'. It follows that a river under Article 9 is a river without an estuary.[75] In reality, it may be difficult to distinguish between a river that flows directly into the sea and one entering the sea via an estuary.

A second issue pertains to the selection of the base points of a straight line across the mouth of the river. Apart from the general requirement that the base points must be on the low-water line of the river bank, there is no further specification in Article 9. However, the mouth of the river can be difficult to locate particularly on a coast with an extensive tidal range.[76]

Third, Article 9 specifies no limitation on the length of the line across the mouth of the river. It may also be noted that the straight line across the mouth of the river shall either be shown on charts or the coordinates of the ends of the lines must be listed pursuant to Article 16 of the LOSC.

Finally, according to one view, Article 9 would appear to apply both to rivers with a single riparian State and to rivers with two riparian States.[77] However, the act of drawing baselines is necessarily a unilateral act. It is debatable whether a coastal State can unilaterally draw a straight line across the mouth of the river from or to a base point located in another coastal State, without the agreement of that State. In practice, the

[72] ICJ Reports 1992, p. 616, para. 432.
[73] Dissenting Opinion of Judge Oda, *ibid.*, p. 746, paras. 24–26.
[74] *Ibid.*, p. 745, para. 24. [75] UNDOALOS, *Baselines*, p. 27.
[76] Churchill and Lowe, *Law of the Sea*, p. 47.
[77] *Ibid.*, p. 46; UNDOALOS, *Baselines*, p. 28.

United States protested the closing line of the Rio de la Plata drawn by Argentina and Uruguay on the ground that Article 13 of the TSC does not apply to rivers whose coasts belong to two or more States.[78]

2.7 Ports

Article 11 of the LOSC provides a rule concerning harbour works:

> For the purpose of delimiting the territorial sea, the outermost permanent harbour works which form an integral part of the harbour system are regarded as forming part of the coast. Off-shore installations and artificial islands shall not be considered as permanent harbour works.

The first sentence of this provision is a replica of Article 8 of the TSC. The second sentence, which was newly added in Article 11 of the LOSC, makes it clear that harbour works must be attached to the coast in order to be used as base points. In relation to this, it is notable that Article 50 of the LOSC allows archipelagic States to draw closing lines for the delimitation of internal waters in accordance with Articles 9, 10 and 11. It would seem to follow that closing lines may be drawn across the entrances to the port.[79]

Neither the LOSC nor the TSC provides a clear meaning for the term 'harbour works which form an integral part of the harbour system'. In this regard, the ICJ, in the 2009 *Romania/Ukraine* case, ruled that these works are 'generally installations which allow ships to be harboured, maintained or repaired and which permit or facilitate the embarkation and disembarkation of passengers and the loading or unloading of goods'.[80]

The admissibility of taking into account the outermost permanent harbour works as part of the coast may be at issue in the context of maritime delimitation. In the 1981 *Dubai/Sharjah Border* arbitration,[81] the harbour works of Dubai were approximately two miles in length and projected approximately one and a half miles seaward, while the harbour works of Sharjah were approximately two miles in length and projected approximately half a mile seaward. The Court of Arbitration ruled that, in light of Article 8 of the TSC and Article 11 of the 1980 Draft Convention on the Law of the Sea, the permanent harbour works of both Dubai and of Sharjah must be treated as a part of the coast for the purpose of drawing the baselines from which the lateral sea boundary between them was constructed.[82]

78 Roach and Smith, *United States Responses*, pp. 143–144.

79 Churchill and Lowe, *Law of the Sea*, p. 47; UNDOALOS, *Baselines*, p. 34.

80 ICJ Reports 2009, p. 106, para. 133. The Technical Aspects of the Law of the Sea Working Group of the IHO defined 'harbour works' as: 'Permanent man-made structures built along the coast which form an integral part of the harbour system such as jetties, moles, quays or other port facilities, coastal terminals, wharves, breakwaters, sea walls, etc.' UNDOALOS, *Baselines*, p. 56.

81 For the text of the award including annexes, see (1993) 91 *ILR* pp. 543–701.

82 *Ibid.*, p. 662.

In the 2009 *Romania/Ukraine* case, a question was raised whether the Sulina dyke – which is a 7.5 km-long dyke out to sea situated on the southern headland of the Musura Bay on Romania's coast – could be regarded as 'permanent harbour works which form an integral part of the harbour system' within the meaning of Article 11 of the LOSC. There was no question relating to the permanent nature of the Sulina dyke. Nonetheless, the Court noted that the functions of a dyke were different from those of a port. According to the Court, the function of the Sulina dyke was to protect shipping destined for the mouth of the Danube and for the ports situated there, and there was no convincing evidence that this dyke served any direct purpose in port activities. Hence the Court ruled that the seaward end of the Sulina dyke was not a proper base point for construction of a provisional equidistance line delimiting the continental shelf and the EEZ.[83]

3 ISLANDS

The presence of islands and low-tide elevations affects the location of the outer limits of marine spaces under national jurisdiction. Hence it will be appropriate to address rules concerning islands and low-tide elevations in this chapter.

3.1 Nature of the problem

Article 121(2) of the LOSC stipulates that:

> Except as provided for in paragraph 3, the territorial sea, the contiguous zone, the exclusive economic zone and the continental shelf of an island are determined in accordance with the provisions of this Convention applicable to other land territory.

As provided in this provision, an island, if so identified, generates vast marine spaces. It is not surprising, therefore, that the question concerning the legal definition of islands is a matter of debate in the law of the sea.

It is said that there are approximately half a million formations of islands in the world, and these formations are extremely diverse. A question thus arises whether all 'islands' should generate an EEZ as well as a continental shelf, regardless of their differences in size, habitability, economic factors, etc. If the answer were in the affirmative, a tiny marine formation could generate a 200-mile EEZ and a continental shelf.[84] On the other hand, this interpretation would further promote the division of the oceans, and diminish the scope of the high seas and the Area, which is the common heritage of mankind.[85] This view would also entail the risk of increasing territorial

[83] ICJ Reports 2009, pp. 106–108, paras. 133–138.
[84] The EEZ and the continental shelf will be discussed in Chapter 4, sections 3 and 4.
[85] B. Kwiatkowska and H. A. Soons, 'Entitlement to Maritime Areas of Rocks Which Cannot Sustain Human Habitation or Economic Life of their Own' (1990) 21 *NYIL* p. 144.

disputes where there are potential natural resources in the maritime area around these islands.[86]

In this regard, at UNCLOS III, a sharp opposition emerged between the group of States (Fiji, New Zealand, Tonga, Western Samoa and Greece) advocating the equal treatment of all islands or island-related formations and the group of States (Romania, Turkey and a group of African States) proposing to limit the maritime zones of islands depending on their conditions. Article 121 was drafted as a compromise between these two opposed groups of States.[87] Owing to the ambiguous language, as will be seen below, this provision raises considerable difficulty with regard to its interpretation.

3.2 Geological elements of islands

The definition of islands is provided in Article 121(1) of the LOSC:

> An island is a naturally-formed area of land, surrounded by water, which is above water at high tide.

This provision, which follows Article 10(1) of the TSC, contains four criteria that call for comments.

First, an 'island' in the legal sense must constitute an 'area of land'. This criterion contains two requirements: (i) that an insular feature must be attached to the seabed; and (ii) that it must have the nature of terra firma.[88] In accordance with these requirements, floating formations, such as icebergs, cannot be regarded as islands.[89] There is no size criterion with regard to the 'area of land' in Article 121. In fact, the ICJ, in the 2001 *Qatar/Bahrain* case (Merits), stated that: 'In accordance with Article 121, paragraph 2, of the 1982 Convention on the Law of the Sea, which reflects customary international law, islands, *regardless of their size*, in this respect enjoy the same status, and therefore generate the same maritime rights, as other land territory.'[90] In some cases, opinions may be divided with regard to the nature of terra firma of a marine formation. Concerning the legal status of Qit'at Jaradah – a maritime feature belonging to Bahrain – for instance, Judges Bedjaoui, Ranjeva and Koroma, in the 2001 *Qatar/Bahrain* case (Merits), took the view that geomorphological characteristics of Qit'at Jaradah did not make it an island because it was not terra firma.[91] Nonetheless, the majority opinion considered Qit'at Jaradah as an island.[92]

[86] R. Kolb, 'L'interprétation de l'article 121, paragraph 3, de la Convention de Montego Bay sur le droit de la mer. Les "roches qui ne se prêtent pas à l'habitation humaine ou à une vie économique propre ..."' (1994) 40 *AFDI* pp. 878–879.

[87] Kwiatkowska and Soons, 'Entitlement to Maritime Areas', pp. 140–142; W. van Overbeek, 'Article 121(3) LOSC in Mexican State Practice in the Pacific' (1989) 4 *International Journal of Estuarine and Coastal Law* pp. 258–261.

[88] Cf. Dissenting Opinion of Judges Bedjaoui, Ranjeva and Koroma, ICJ Reports 2001, pp. 209–210, para. 200.

[89] C. Symmons, *The Maritime Zones of Islands in International Law* (The Hague, Nijhoff, 1979), pp. 21–24.

[90] Emphasis added. ICJ Reports 2001, p. 97, para. 185.

[91] Dissenting Opinion of Judges Bedjaoui, Ranjeva and Koroma, ICJ Reports 2001, p. 209, para. 199.

[92] Judgment, *ibid.*, p. 99, para. 195.

Second, an 'island' must be a 'naturally formed' creation. This requirement means that the composition of the island must be 'natural', not 'artificial'; and that the island must be formed without human intervention in its formation process. Consequently, an artificial island and installation, such as a lighthouse, beacon, oil platform, or defence tower, is not an 'island' under Article 121 of the LOSC. It is arguable that lighthouses built on low-tide elevations or permanently submerged seabed formations do not acquire the juridical status of an 'island'.[93] Unlike islands, artificial islands have no territorial sea of their own, and cannot be used as a base point measuring the territorial sea. This is clear from Article 60(8) of the LOSC.

Third, an 'island' must be 'surrounded by water'. Accordingly, if a marine formation is connected by a sandbar to the mainland which dries out at low tide, the formation cannot be regarded as an island in the legal sense. Similarly, if a marine formation is connected by a causeway to the mainland, the formation would seem to lose its insular status.[94]

Fourth, an 'island' must be 'above water at high tide'. According to this requirement, an island is distinct from low-tide elevations, which are submerged at high tide.[95] However, the meaning of 'above water at high tide' is not uniform in State practice. In borderline cases, the distinction between an island and a low-tide elevation is rather fine.

3.3 Socio-economic elements of islands

With regard to the legal status of islands, the most debatable issue is whether the legal status of islands should be qualified by socio-economic factors. In this regard, Article 121(3) of the LOSC stipulates that:[96]

> Rocks which cannot sustain human habitation or economic life of their own shall have no exclusive economic zone or continental shelf.

It follows that rocks only have the territorial sea and the contiguous zone.[97] However, it must be noted that Article 121(3) does not apply where a rock forms part of a baseline from which marine spaces under national jurisdiction, namely the territorial sea, the EEZ and the continental shelf, are measured. It is clear that the objective of Article 121(3) is to prevent excessive claims over the EEZ and continental shelf by restricting the capacity of 'rocks' to generate these marine spaces. In this sense, it may be said that the function of Article 121(3) is preventive by nature.

[93] Symmons, *The Maritime Zones*, pp. 32–34.
[94] *Ibid.*, pp. 41–42.
[95] Low-tide elevations will be discussed in part 4 of this chapter.
[96] This is a new provision which was not contained in the TSC.
[97] *Virginia Commentaries*, vol. III, p. 338; J. I. Charney, 'Rocks That Cannot Sustain Human Habitation', (1999) 93 *AJIL* p. 864; J. L. Jesus, 'Rocks, New-Born Islands, Sea Level Rise and Maritime Space', in J. A. Frowein, K. Scharioth, I. Winkelmann and R. Wolfrum (eds.), *Negotiating for Peace, Liber Amicorum Tono Eitel* (Berlin, Springer, 2003), p. 581.

In light of the vagueness of the text, the interpretation and application of Article 121(3) may vary according to States. An illustrative example concerns Rockall. The United Kingdom established a continental shelf and an exclusive fishery zone around Rockall in 1974 and 1977, respectively. This action was protested by Ireland, Denmark and Iceland. As a result, the United Kingdom gave up the 200-mile fishery zone when it acceded to the LOSC in 1997.[98]

Another example may be furnished by Okinotorishima. This marine feature, which is part of Japanese territory, is located in the Pacific Ocean, around 1,700 kilometres south of Tokyo. Okinotorishima comprises two tiny islets. It is beyond doubt that Okinotorishima is not a low-tide elevation, and the Japanese government regards this maritime feature as island. Thus the Japanese government established in 1977 a 200-mile fishery zone and, in 1996, a 200-mile EEZ around Okinotorishima. In 1989, the Japanese government encased Okinotorishima in a concrete and steel bank with a view to preventing erosion. However, in 2004, the Chinese government expressed the view that Okinotorishima cannot have a 200-mile EEZ because it is a rock. In 2005, Taiwan raised the same question against the legal status of Okinotorishima.[99] Furthermore, in 2009, the Republic of Korea and China presented their compliments to the UN Secretary-General with regard to the submission made by Japan to the Commission on the Limits of the Continental Shelf, and claimed that Okinotorishima, considered as a rock under Article 121(3), is not entitled to any continental shelf extending to or beyond 200 nautical miles.[100] As shown in this example, the legal status of a maritime feature may raise particular sensitivities for the claim over the continental shelf beyond 200 nautical miles measured from a maritime feature.

Concerning the interpretation of Article 121(3), five elements must, in particular, be examined.

The first element that needs to be discussed concerns the meaning of 'rocks'. There is no clear definition of rocks in the LOSC.[101] A question that calls for particular notice concerns the relationship between paragraphs 1 and 2 of Article 121 and paragraph 3 of the same provision. As noted earlier, by distinguishing rocks from islands, Article 121(3) seeks to prevent the situation that all insular formations generate extended areas of EEZ and continental shelf. Accordingly, there appears to be a general sense that paragraph 3 of Article 121 must be read in conjunction with paragraphs 1 and 2 of

[98] D. H. Anderson, 'British Accession to the UN Convention on the Law of the Sea' (1997) 46 *ICLQ* p. 778; Churchill and Lowe, *Law of the Sea*, p. 164.

[99] Yann-huei Song, 'Okinotorishima: A "Rock" or an "Island"? Recent Maritime Boundary Controversy between Japan and Taiwan/China', in Seoung-Yong Hong and J. M. Van Dyke (eds.), *Maritime Boundary Disputes, Settlement Process, and the Law of the Sea* (Leiden and Boston, Nijhoff, 2009), p. 146 and pp. 151–154. See also by the same author, 'The Application of Article 121 of the Law of the Sea Convention to the Selected Geographical Features Situated in the Pacific Ocean', (2010) 9 *Chinese Journal of International Law*, pp. 668–674 and pp. 691–694.

[100] Republic of Korea: www.un.org/Depts/los/clcs_new/submissions_files/jpn08/kor_27feb09.pdf; the People's Republic of China: www.un.org/Depts/los/clcs_new/submissions_files/jpn08/chn_6feb09_e.pdf.

[101] There is no indication as to the size of rocks in the LOSC. No attempts to introduce specific criteria concerning size, population and location were supported at UNCLOS III. Kwiatkowska and Soons, 'Entitlement to Maritime Areas', pp. 155–159; Kolb, 'L'interprétation de l'article 121, paragraph 3', p. 904.

the same provision. There may be room for the view that 'rocks' set out in Article 121(3) are a sub-category of islands; and that they constitute an exception to the regime of islands provided in Article 121(1) and (2).[102]

A second element involves the phrase, 'rocks which *cannot sustain*'. This phrase would seem to suggest that the criterion concerns the capability or possibility of rocks to sustain human habitation or economic life, not the factual situation of sustaining human habitation. The possibility to sustain human habitation or economic life may change over time according to the development of human capacity to inhabit, or to technological innovations.

A third element pertains to the test of human habitation. As noted, it seems that Article 121(3) requires only the capability to sustain human habitation. Hence it is not necessary that human habitation on an island is permanent. Arguably, the fact that a human population has inhabited an island would prove the habitability of the island.[103] Furthermore, the interrelationship between the human habitation test and the test of 'economic life of their own' is not free of controversy. A literal interpretation seems to suggest that the text of Article 121(3) provides the alternative, 'human habitation *or* economic life of their own'. According to this interpretation, only one of these tests must be met in order to remove a marine feature from the restrictions of Article 121(3).[104] On the other hand, some argue that the phrase is a single concept.[105] In practice, it appears difficult to imagine economic life totally detached from human life. Hence it may be argued that these two elements are intimately intertwined.

Fourth, the concept of 'economic life' needs further clarification. According to one view, the concept of 'economic life' should be of a commercial or productive nature only.[106] However, this view does not seem to be entirely in conformity with practice. Considering this issue, Jan Mayen may provide an interesting example for discussion. Jan Mayen appertains to Norway. Its total area is 380 square kilometres (or 148 square miles); it is inhabited by only some twenty-five technical and other staff of the island's meteorological station, a LORAN (long-range radio navigation) station, and the coastal radio station. There is a regular service by military aircraft, which permits personnel transfers and light cargo deliveries. The landing field can also provide for search and rescue operations and for emergency evacuation and medical assistance.[107] In 1981, the Conciliation Commission on the Continental Shelf Area between Iceland and Jan Mayen stated that Jan Mayen must be considered as an island.[108]

[102] *Ibid*; Charney, 'Rocks', p. 864; Maria Silvana Fusillo, 'The Legal Régime of Uninhabited "Rocks" Lacking an Economic Life of their Own' (1978–1979) 4 *Italian Yearbook of International Law* p. 51. See also Presentation by Professor Lowe in the 2009 *Romania/Ukraine* case, Verbatim Record, CR 2008/20, 4 September 2008, p. 41, paras. 11–13.

[103] Kwiatkowska and Soons, 'Entitlement to Maritime Areas', p. 166; Kolb, 'L'interprétation de l'article 121, paragraph 3', p. 907.

[104] Charney, 'Rocks', p. 868.

[105] Kolb, 'L'interprétation de l'article 121, paragraph 3', p. 906. [106] *Ibid.*, p. 907.

[107] Counter-Memorial Submitted by the Government of the Kingdom of Norway, 11 May 1990, pp. 23–28, paras. 78–101.

[108] *Report and Recommendations to the Governments of Iceland and Norway of the Conciliation Commission on the Continental Shelf Area Between Iceland and Jan Mayen*, (1981) 20 *ILM* pp. 803–804.

Similarly, the ICJ in the 1993 *Greenland/Jan Mayen* case did not cast doubt on the legal status of Jan Mayen as an island. These two instances would seem to imply that the concept of economic life does not necessarily need to be of a commercial nature.

Finally, there is a need to examine the phrase 'of their own'. According to a restrictive interpretation, this phrase means that a State cannot create necessary conditions 'by injecting an artificial economic life, based on resources from its other land territory'.[109] However, it appears that this view does not wholly conform with precedent. In the case of Jan Mayen, for instance, bulk supplies are brought in by ship and uploaded in Hvalrossbukta (Walrus Bay) to support human life there.[110] Nonetheless, as noted, the Conciliation Commission and the ICJ regarded Jan Mayen as an island. The example of Jan Mayen seems to imply that the need for external supply does not deprive a marine formation of the legal status of an island.

3.4 Customary law nature of Article 121

The ICJ, in the 2001 *Qatar/Bahrain* case (Merits), pronounced that Article 121(2) of the LOSC reflects customary law.[111] The Conciliation Commission in the 1981 *Jan Mayen* case also considered that Article 121 of the 1980 Draft Convention on the Law of the Sea (Informal Text) reflected the present status of international law. However, it must be noted that the law applicable to this case was limited to paragraphs 1 and 2 of Article 121.[112] Thus there appears to be a general sense that the Conciliation Commission regarded only these paragraphs as customary law.

In fact, it is uncommon for coastal States to incorporate Article 121(3) in their national legislation. It would appear that the only example of incorporation of Article 121(3) into national legislation is the 1986 EEZ Federal Act of Mexico.[113] With the notable exception of Rockall, it is rare for coastal States to abandon the establishment of an EEZ or continental shelf around marine formations because they constitute rocks under Article 121(3). It is also infrequent for municipal courts to deal with Article 121(3) of the LOSC. A notable exception is the Norwegian Supreme Court Judgment of 7 May 1996. In this case, the Supreme Court held that Abel Island, which is 13.2 square kilometres in area, was too large to be a 'rock' within the meaning of Article 121(3); and that the island would be able to support a significant polar bear hunt, were such hunting not prohibited for conservation reasons.[114] Overall, it is highly difficult to find evidence to prove the existence of 'extensive and virtually uniform' State practice and *opinio juris* with

[109] D. W. Bowett, *The Legal Regime of Islands in International Law* (New York, Oceana, 1979), p. 34.

[110] Counter-Memorial Submitted by Norway (11 May 1990), p. 27, para. 96.

[111] ICJ Reports 2001, p. 97, para. 185.

[112] *Report of the Conciliation Commission*, p. 804.

[113] Article 51 of the Federal Act (1986) 25 *ILM* p. 896. Nonetheless, Mexico gave full effect to many miniscule islets generating its EEZ. Van Overbeek, 'Article 121(3) LOSC', p. 262; Kwiatkowska and Soons, 'Entitlement to Maritime Areas', p. 176; Kolb, 'L'interprétation de l'article 121, paragraph 3', pp. 896–897.

[114] R. Churchill, 'Norway: Supreme Court Judgment on Law of the Sea Issues', (1996) 11 *IJMCL* pp. 576–580 (in particular, p. 579).

regard to Article 121(3). It is doubtful, therefore, that Article 121(3) represents customary international law.

3.5 Reefs

Before UNCLOS I, little attention was given to a rule governing coral islands or islands fringed with reefs. While serious attention was, for the first time, given at UNCLOS I, no provision concerning reefs was contained in the TSC.[115] However, the LOSC contains a special rule relating to islands situated on atolls or islands having fringing reefs.

There is no definition of the term 'atoll' in the LOSC. In geographical terms, an atoll is a ring-shaped reef with or without an island situated on it surrounded by the open sea that encloses or nearly encloses a lagoon.[116] The lagoon is rich in marine life and the economic well-being of the indigenous people depends basically on the lagoon fishery.[117] The term 'reef' refers to a mass of rock or coral which either reaches close to the sea surface or is exposed at low tide. That part of a reef which is above water at low tide but submerged at high tide is called drying reef. Thus, drying reefs belong to the category of low-tide elevations.[118] The reef not only forms the lagoon that sustains the indigenous population but also protects the islands from the destructive force of waves and ocean swells.

Owing to the intimate connection between reefs, lagoons and islands, it is desirable that the waters between reefs and islands should be internal waters. Normally lagoon waters are difficult to access and are unsuitable for navigation. Accordingly, it would be difficult to apply a right of innocent passage to lagoon waters in practice.[119] In this regard, Article 6 of the LOSC provides that:

> In the case of islands situated on atolls or of islands having fringing reefs, the baseline for measuring the breadth of the territorial sea is the seaward low-water line of the reef, as shown by the appropriate symbol on charts officially recognized by the coastal State.

This provision calls for three comments with regard to its interpretation.

First, Article 6 refers to 'islands situated on atolls', not atolls alone. It would follow that unless there is an island, namely terra firma, on the atoll, the atoll cannot generate a territorial sea.[120]

[115] I. Kawaley, 'Delimitation of Islands Fringed with Reefs: Article 6 of the 1982 Law of the Sea Convention' (1992) 41 *ICLQ* pp. 154–156.

[116] UNDOALOS, *Baselines*, p. 50.

[117] R. D. Hodgson, 'Islands: Normal and Special Circumstances', in *Law of the Sea: the Emerging Regime of the Oceans, Proceedings of Law of the Sea Institute Eighth Annual Conference, June 18–21, 1973* (Cambridge, Mass., Ballinger, 1974), pp. 165–166.

[118] UNDOALOS, *Baselines*, p. 60; H. W. Jayewardene, *The Regime of Islands in International Law* (Dordrecht, Nijhoff, 1990), p. 95.

[119] P. B. Beazley, 'Reefs and the 1982 Convention on the Law of the Sea' (1991) 6 *IJECL* pp. 303–304.

[120] L. L. Herman, 'The Modern Concept of the Off-Lying Archipelago in International Law' (1985) 23 *Canadian Yearbook of International Law* p. 191.

Second, it appears that this provision does not apply to permanently submerged reef features.[121] In the 1999 *Eritrea/Yemen* Arbitration (Second Phase), Eritrea claimed that a reef called the 'Negileh Rock' could be used as part of a straight baseline system. Yemen objected to the use of the reef as part of the baseline because the reef is not above water at any state of the tide. The Arbitral Tribunal did not admit the claim of Eritrea on the basis of Articles 6 and 7(4) of the LOSC.[122]

Third, the meaning of 'fringing reef' is open to discussion. Some argue that the 'fringing reef' covers barrier reefs which are walls of coral rocks generally separated from the low-water line of the island by a deep channel, usually a lagoon.[123] According to this view, Article 6 of the LOSC can be applied to any reefs without distinction. However, other writers are more cautious about taking such a broad interpretation.[124] Considering that there is no clear limit of the distance between a fringing reef which is to be used as a baseline and an island, the broad interpretation would seem to encourage an excessive claim for baselines. It is also to be noted that Article 6 contains no rule concerning the situation where the fringing reef is incomplete and a gap exists in sections of the reef. While, in this case, it appears to be reasonable to draw a straight line across the gap, this may be questioned where the gap is extensive.[125] Where the reef fringes only a part of the island, the question will arise as to how it is possible to link the island to the reef in order to close internal waters.[126] Moreover, the meaning of the term 'seaward' low-water line is not without ambiguity. One wonders whether this term excludes reefs on the side of a lagoon as opposed to the open sea.[127]

4 LOW-TIDE ELEVATIONS

4.1 Identification of low-tide elevations

Article 13(1) of the LOSC defines low-tide elevations as follows:

> A low-tide elevation is a naturally formed area of land which is surrounded by and above water at low tide but submerged at high tide.

This provision further provides that: 'Where a low-tide elevation is situated wholly or partly at a distance not exceeding the breadth of the territorial sea from the mainland or an island, the low-water line on that elevation may be used as the baseline for measuring the breadth of the territorial sea'. Where a low-tide elevation is wholly situated outside the territorial sea, however, it has no territorial sea of its own (Article 13(2), see Figure 2.3). Considering that low-tide elevations may have an impact on identifying

121 Kawaley, 'Delimitation of Islands', p. 157; UNDOALOS, *Baselines*, p. 10.
122 (2001) 40 *ILM* p. 1007, paras. 143–145.
123 Jayewardene, *The Regime of Islands*, p. 99; UNDOALOS, *Baselines*, p. 10; Beazley, 'Reefs', p. 297.
124 Kawaley, 'Delimitation of Islands', p. 156; Churchill and Lowe, *Law of the Sea*, p. 52.
125 *Ibid.* 126 UNDOALOS, *Baselines*, p. 12.
127 Kawaley, 'Delimitation of Islands Fringed with Reefs', p. 157.

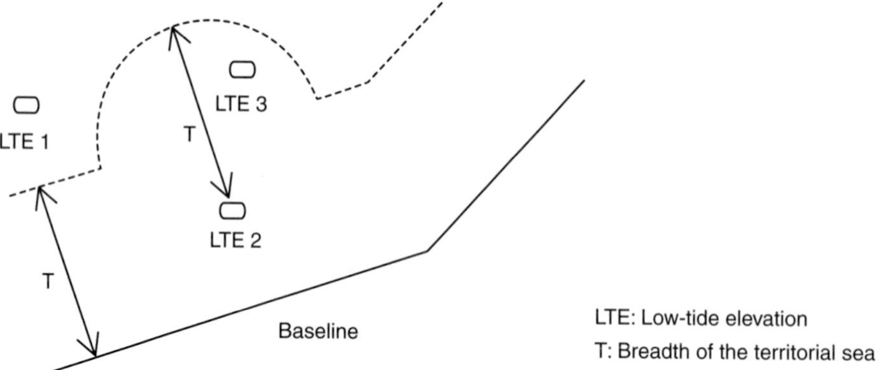

Figure 2.3. Low-tide elevations (Article 13)

the outer limits of marine spaces under national jurisdiction, such elevations have practical importance for the coastal State.

In relation to this, a question that may arise concerns the identification of low-tide elevations. As the legal status of marine features may be changeable depending on the tidal datum in borderline cases, the selection of tidal datum is of central importance. Nonetheless, no tidal datum was given in Article 11 of the TSC and Article 13 of the LOSC.[128] In the *United States v Alaska* case of 1997, the Special Master's Report indicated that 'high tide' was understood as 'mean high water' according to well-established United States practice. The Supreme Court of the United States would seem to be supportive of this view.[129] If the mean high tide is a well-established standard in the United States, this does not mean that it is an internationally accepted standard, however.

Despite attempts at international standardisation of the tidal datum, currently there is no uniformity in State practice in this matter. The situation is more complicated because States have used more than one datum along their coasts.[130] It seems, therefore, that there are no customary rules concerning the use of tidal datum. It is also inconceivable that there are 'general principles of law recognised by civilized nations' on this issue. Thus, a dispute can be raised where the States concerned use different tidal datums, and the legal status of a marine feature differs depending on the datum. In this regard, two cases call for particular attention.

4.2 Case law concerning low-tide elevations

The first case that needs to be examined is the 1977 *Anglo-French Continental Shelf* arbitration. In this case, a dispute was raised between the United Kingdom and France

[128] The United Kingdom's Court of Appeal, in the 1967 *Post Office v Estuary Radio Ltd* case, had already pointed to the problem. However, that Court refrained from entering into this issue since the Court was not obliged to and it was better that it should not. J. T. Edgerley (ed.), *The All England Law Reports 1967*, vol. 3 (London: Butterworths, 1968), p. 685.

[129] *Report of the Special Master*, J. Keith Mann, March 1996, No. 84, Original, the Supreme Court of the United States, pp. 234–236; 521 *United States Reports, Cases Adjudged in the Supreme Court at October Term 1996* (Washington DC, 2000), pp. 30–32.

[130] Nuno Sérgio Marques Antunes, 'Tidal Datum', p. 8.

with regard to the use of Eddystone Rocks as a base point in the delimitation of the English Channel.

The United Kingdom contended that Eddystone Rocks were to be regarded as islands and should accordingly be used as a base point for determining a median line in the English Channel west of the Channel Islands. Counsel for the United Kingdom argued that the Eddystone Rocks were only totally covered at high-water equinoctial springs, namely the highest tide in the year;[131] and that they were uncovered at mean high-water springs, which was the required definition of an island in the United Kingdom Territorial Waters Order in Council of 1964, and was surely also in accord with international practice. Concerning tidal datum, the United Kingdom affirmed that, whether under customary law or under Article 10 of the TSC, the relevant high-water line was the line of mean high-water spring tides. In the view of the United Kingdom, the mean high-water spring tides was the only precise one, and the use of equinoctial high tide was not acceptable as sufficiently precise in this context. According to the United Kingdom, the height of the natural rock at the base of the stump of the old Smeanton lighthouse was approximately two feet above mean high-water spring tide and 0.2 feet above the highest astronomical tide.[132] Hence the United Kingdom alleged that Eddystone Rocks were not to be ranked as a low-tide elevation.[133]

On the other hand, the French government contested the use of the Eddystone Rocks as a base point because it was not an island but a low-tide elevation.[134] France argued that the British concept of 'high-water' was very questionable and a large number of States, including France, took it as meaning the limit of the highest tides. France also claimed that, as soon as a reef did not remain uncovered continuously throughout the year, it had to be ranked as a low-tide elevation, not as an island.[135]

The Court of Arbitration made it clear that the question to be decided was not the legal status of Eddystone Rocks as an island but its relevance in the delimitation of the median line in the Channel. It then held that France had previously accepted the relevance of Eddystone Rocks as a base point for the United Kingdom's fishery limits under the 1964 European Fisheries Convention as well as in the negotiations of 1971 regarding the continental shelf. For this reason, the Court of Arbitration accepted the use of Eddystone Rocks as a base point on the basis of estoppel.[136] It may be said that the Court of Arbitration took a pragmatic approach leaving the status of Eddystone Rocks unresolved.

131 Technically speaking, equinoctial spring tide means those tides occurring near the equinoxes when the full or new moon and the sun have little or low declination and spring tides of greater range than the average occur, particularly if the moon is also nearly in perigee. IHO, *Hydrographic Dictionary*, p. 248.

132 Highest astronomical tide means the highest level of water that can be predicted to be found under any combination of astronomical factors, considering average meteorological conditions. Nuno Sérgio Marques Antunes, 'Tidal Datum', p. 28. See also IHO, *Hydrographic Dictionary*, p. 104.

133 The *Anglo-French Continental Shelf* case, 18 *Report of International Arbitral Awards* (New York, United Nations), pp. 66–70, paras. 122–130.

134 *Ibid.*, p. 72, para. 138.

135 *Ibid.*, p. 67, para. 125. See also p. 70, para. 130.

136 *Ibid.*, pp. 72–74, paras. 139–144.

A second instance relating to low-tide elevations is the 2001 *Qatar/Bahrain* case (Merits). In this case, Qatar and Bahrain disputed whether Qit'at Jaradah, a maritime feature situated northeast of Fasht al Azm, was an island or a low-tide elevation. According to Bahrain, there were strong indications that Qit'at Jaradah was an island that remained dry at high tide. By referring to a number of eyewitness reports, Bahrain asserted that it was evident that part of its sandbank had not been covered by water for some time.[137] According to the data submitted by Bahrain, at high tide, its length and breadth were about 12 by 4 metres, and its altitude was approximately 0.4 metres.[138] However, Qatar argued that Qit'at Jaradah was always indicated on nautical charts as a low-tide elevation. Qatar also insisted that, even if there were periods when it was not completely submerged at high tide, its physical status was constantly changing and thus it should be considered as no more than a shoal.[139]

Having carefully analysed the evidence submitted by the Parties and the conclusions of experts, the ICJ held that Qit'at Jaradah was an island which should be considered for the determination of the equidistance line.[140] Yet the reason why Qit'at Jaradah could be regarded an island, not a low-tide elevation, remains obscure.

5 CONCLUSIONS

On the basis of the matters considered in this chapter, six points should be highlighted.

(i) The rules governing straight baselines are abstract and lack precision in some respects. In particular, the following elements seem to create challenges to the practical application of these rules:

- lack of objective criteria which may identify deeply indented coasts,
- lack of an objective test to identify the close linkage between the land domain and the sea area lying within the straight baselines,
- lack of any limit to the maximum length of straight baselines,
- lack of an objective test to identify the existence of a 'fringe of islands',
- vagueness of the concept of the coast's 'immediate vicinity', and
- vagueness of the concept of 'economic interests peculiar to the region concerned'.

(ii) Owing to the vagueness of rules concerning straight baselines, the coastal State has an extensive discretion in drawing such baselines. In reality, the coastal States are likely to apply the straight baseline system in an excessive manner. It appears that currently the method of straight baselines is used by coastal States as a tool to expand the spatial ambit of national jurisdiction in the oceans.

137 ICJ Reports 2001, p. 98, para. 192.

138 *Ibid.*, p. 99, para. 197.

139 *Ibid.*, p. 99, para. 193.

140 *Ibid.*, p. 99, para. 195. Three Judges dissented with the majority opinion concerning the legal status of Qit'at Jaradah. Dissenting Opinion of Judges Bedjaoui, Ranjeva and Koroma, *ibid.*, pp. 207–208, para. 195. For the same reasons, Judge Vereshchetin also concluded that Qit'at Jaradah was a low-tide elevation. Declaration of Judge Vereshchetin, *ibid.*, pp. 220–221, para. 13.

(iii) Currently Article 10 of the LOSC can be regarded as general rules governing juridical bays. It is significant that the rules governing juridical bays specify the maximum length of the closing line (twenty-four nautical miles) and the geometrical test (semi-circle test). However, there are no well-established general rules governing historic bays. Accordingly, the validity of the claim to a historic bay is to be examined on a case-by-case basis.

(iv) It is argued that rocks can be considered as a sub-category of islands. Unlike islands, however, rocks which cannot sustain human habitation or economic life of their own have no EEZ or continental shelf. Hence the distinction between islands and rocks is a crucial issue. While criteria concerning the distinction are enshrined in Article 121(3), this provision is rather difficult to apply due to the vagueness of the language. In particular, socio-economic elements need further clarification. State practice is far from uniform on this particular matter. In light of the paucity of judicial practice on this subject, it appears highly difficult to clarify the interpretation of this provision.

(v) Whilst islands must be above water at high tide, low-tide elevations are submerged at high tide. Thus the distinction between islands and low-tide elevations is affected by tidal levels. In borderline cases, the difference between tidal datums may give rise to international disputes with regard to the legal status of marine features. Yet there is no established general rule of international law relating to the selection of tidal datum. Further consideration should thus be given to technical aspects in the law of the sea, including the selection of tidal datum.

(vi) In light of the infinite variety of coastal configurations, it is difficult to formulate general and specific rules respecting baselines. The same applies to rules governing maritime features, including islands, rocks and low-tide elevations. As a consequence, rules on these subjects contain many obscure elements. It may be said that the tension between generality of law and geographical diversity is a major cause of ambiguity in rules governing the limits of marine spaces.

FURTHER READING

1 General

In order to understand technical terms and concepts respecting hydrography, the following documents will be useful.

C. Carleton and C. Shofield, 'Developments in the Technical Determination of Maritime Space: Charts, Datums, Baselines, Maritime Zones and Limits', *Maritime Briefing*, vol. 3, no. 3 (Durham, International Boundaries Research Unit, 2001).

International Hydrographic Organization, *Hydrographic Dictionary, Part 1*, vol. 1, 5th edn (Monaco, 1994).

Nuno Sérgio Marques Antunes, 'The Importance of the Tidal Datum in the Definition of Maritime Limits and Boundaries', *Maritime Briefing*, vol. 2, no. 7 (Durham, International Boundaries Research Unit, 2000).

G. K. Walker and J. E. Noyes, 'Definitions for the 1982 Law of the Sea Convention: Part II', (2002–2003) 33 *California Western International Law Journal* pp. 191–324.

2 Baselines

D. D. Caron, 'Climate Change, Sea Level Rise and the Coming Uncertainty in Oceanic Boundaries: A Proposal to Avoid Conflict', in Seoung-Yong Hong and J. M. Van Dyke (eds.), *Maritime Boundary Disputes, Settlement Processes, and the Law of the Sea* (London and Boston, Nijhoff, 2009) pp. 1–17.

V. Prescott and C. Schofield, *The Maritime Political Boundaries of the World*, 2nd edn (Leiden and Boston, Nijhoff, 2005).

W. M. Reisman and G. S. Westerman, *Straight Baselines in International Maritime Boundary Delimitation* (New York, St Martin's Press, 1992).

J. A. Roach and R. W. Smith, 'Straight Baselines: The Need for a Universally Applied Norm', (2000) 31 *ODIL* pp. 47–80.

A. H. A. Soons, 'The Effects of a Rising Sea Level on Maritime Limits and Boundaries', (1990) 37 *NILR* pp. 207–232.

C. Symmons and M. W. Reed, 'Baseline Publicity and Charting Requirements: An Overlooked Issue in the UN Convention on the Law of the Sea', (2010) 41 *ODIL* pp. 77–111.

UNDOALOS, *The Law of the Sea: Baselines: An Examination of the Relevant Provisions of the United Nations Convention on the Law of the Sea* (New York, United Nations, 1989).

US Department of State, *Limits of the Seas*, available online at: www.state.gov/g/oes/ocns/opa/convention/c16065.htm.

C. H. M. Waldock, 'The Anglo-Norwegian Fisheries Case' (1951) 28 *BYIL* pp. 114–171.

3 Bays

A. Gioia, 'The Law of Multinational Bays and the Case of the Gulf of Fonseca' (1993) 24 *Netherlands Yearbook of International Law* pp. 81–137.

C. Symmons, *Historic Waters in the Law of the Sea: A Modern Re-Appraisal* (Leiden and Boston, Brill, 2008).

'The Maritime Border Areas of Ireland, North and South: An Assessment of Present Jurisdictional Ambiguities and International Precedents Relating to Delimitation of "Border Bays"' (2009) 24 *IJMCL* pp. 457–500.

Symposium on Historic Bays of the Mediterranean (1984) 11 *Syracuse Journal of International Law and Commerce* pp. 205–415.

UN Secretariat, 'Judicial Régime of Historic Waters, Including Historic Bays', Document A/CN.4/143, (1962) 2 *YILC* pp. 1–26.

G. Westerman, *The Juridical Bay* (Oxford University Press, 1987).

4 Islands

D. W. Bowett, *The Legal Regime of Islands in International Law* (New York, Oceana, 1979).

H. Dipla, *Le régime juridique des îles dans le droit international de la mer* (Paris, PUF, 1984).

H. W. Jayewardene, *The Regime of Islands in International Law* (Dordrecht, Nijhoff, 1990).

J. L. Jesus, 'Rocks, New-Born Islands, Sea Level Rise and Maritime Space', in J. A. Frowein, K. Scharioth, I. Winkelmann and R. Wolfrum (eds.), *Negotiating for Peace, Liber Amicorum Tono Eitel* (Berlin, Springer, 2003), pp. 579–603.

R. Kolb, 'L'interprétation de l'article 121, paragraph 3, de la Convention de Montego Bay sur le droit de la mer: les "roches qui ne se prêtent pas à l'habitation humaine ou à une vie économique propre ..."' (1994) 40 *AFDI* pp. 876–909.

B. Kwiatkowska and H. A. Soons, 'Entitlement to Maritime Areas of Rocks Which Cannot Sustain Human Habitation or Economic Life of their Own' (1990) 21 *NYIL* pp. 139–181.

A. G. Oude Elferink, 'Is it Either Necessary or Possible to Clarify the Provision on Rocks of Article 121(3) of the Law of the Sea Convention?' in M. Pratt and J. A. Brown (eds.), *Borderlands Under Stress* (The Hague, Kluwer, 2000), pp. 389–407.

N. Papadakis, *The International Legal Regime of Artificial Islands* (Leiden, Sijthoff, 1977).

C. Symmons, *The Maritime Zones of Islands in International Law* (The Hague, Nijhoff, 1979).

5 Reefs

P. B. Beazley, 'Reefs and the 1982 Convention on the Law of the Sea' (1991) 6 *IJECL* pp. 281–312.

I. Kawaley, 'Delimitation of Islands Fringed with Reefs: Article 6 of the 1982 Law of the Sea Convention' (1992) 41 *ICLQ* pp. 152–160.

6 Low-Tide Elevations

G. Guillaume, 'Les hauts-fonds découvrants en droit international', in *La mer et son droit, Mélanges offerts à Laurent Lucchini et Jean-Pierre Quéneudec* (Paris, Pedone, 2003), pp. 287–302.

R. Lavalle, 'Not Quite a Sure Thing: The Maritime Areas of Rocks and Low-Tide Elevations under the UN Law of the Sea Convention' (2004) 19 *IJMCL* pp. 43–69.

C. Symmons, 'Some Problems Relating to the Definition of "Insular Formations" in International Law: Islands and Low-Tide Elevations', *Maritime Briefing*, vol. 1, no. 5 (Durham: International Boundaries Research Unit, 1995), pp. 1–32.

'When Is an "Island" Not an "Island" in International Law? The Riddle of Dinkum Sands in the Case of US v. Alaska', *Maritime Briefing*, vol. 2, no. 6 (Durham: International Boundaries Research Unit, 1999).

Y. Tanaka, 'Low-Tide Elevations in International Law of the Sea: Selected Issues' (2006) 20 *Ocean Yearbook* pp. 189–219.

P. Weil, 'Les hauts-fonds découvrants dans la délimitation maritime: à propos des paragraphes 200–209 de l'arrêt de la Cour internationale de Justice du 16 mars 2001 en l'affaire de la délimitation maritime et questions territoriales entre Qatar et Bahreïn', in N. Ando et al. (eds.), *Liber Amicorum Judge Shigeru Oda* (The Hague, Kluwer, 2002), pp. 307–321.

3

Marine Spaces under National Jurisdiction I: Territorial Sovereignty

Main Issues

Internal waters, territorial seas, international straits and archipelagic waters are marine spaces under the territorial sovereignty of the coastal State. However, the use of the marine environment for sea communication necessitates the freedom of navigation through those spaces. Consequently, marine spaces under territorial sovereignty are part of the territory of the coastal State and the highway for sea communication at the same time. The dual nature of marine spaces gives rise to the fundamental question of how it is possible to reconcile the territorial sovereignty of the coastal State and the freedom of navigation. With that question as a backdrop, this chapter will examine the following issues in particular:

(i) What is the coastal State's jurisdiction over foreign vessels in internal waters?
(ii) How is it possible to reconcile the need to provide refuge for ships in distress and the protection of the offshore environment of the coastal State?
(iii) What is the right of innocent passage?
(iv) Do foreign warships enjoy the right of innocent passage through the territorial sea?
(v) What is the legal regime of international straits?
(vi) What is the legal regime of archipelagic waters?
(vii) What are the differences between the right of innocent passage, the right of transit passage and the right of archipelagic sea lane passage?

1 INTRODUCTION

This chapter will seek to examine rules of international law governing marine spaces under territorial sovereignty. In this regard, particular attention must be devoted to two issues with regard to the reconciliation between the territorial sovereignty of the coastal State and the freedom of navigation.

The first issue involves the tension between the strategic interest of naval powers and the security interest of coastal States. On the one hand, ensuring the freedom of navigation of warships through marine spaces under national jurisdiction is of paramount importance for naval powers. On the other hand, the passage of foreign warships through offshore areas may be a source of threat to the security of coastal States. Thus a question arises of how it is possible to reconcile the two contrasting interests.

A second issue concerns the reconciliation between the navigational interest of user States and the shipping industry on the one hand and the marine environmental protection of coastal States on the other hand. Nowadays the size of vessels is ever increasing, and the contents of cargoes may be highly dangerous to the marine environment of the coastal State in the event of an accident. Consequently, the protection of the marine environment from vessel-source hazards is a matter of serious concern for coastal States. A question thus arises as to how it is possible to balance the freedom of navigation and the protection of the offshore environment of coastal States.

Noting these issues, the present chapter will address rules of international law governing internal waters (section 2), the territorial sea (section 3), international straits (section 4) and archipelagic waters (section 5).

2 INTERNAL WATERS

2.1 Spatial scope of internal waters

Internal waters are 'those waters which lie landward of the baseline from which the territorial sea is measured'.[1] Specifically, internal waters in a legal sense embrace (i) parts of the sea along the coast down to the low-water mark, (ii) ports and harbours, (iii) estuaries, (iv) landward waters from the closing line of bays, and (v) waters enclosed by straight baselines. On the other hand, as noted earlier, internal waters in the law of the sea do not include waters within the land territory and land-locked waters or lakes.[2]

The seaward limit of internal waters is determined by a baseline from which the territorial sea is measured. The baseline becomes the landward limit of the territorial sea. Accordingly, internal waters are bound by the territorial sea of the coastal State. An exception is the case of archipelagic States. As will be seen, archipelagic States may draw lines limiting their internal waters across the mouths of rivers, bays and ports only within their archipelagic waters. In this case, the internal waters are bound by the archipelagic waters, not by the territorial sea.

[1] LOSC, Article 8(1).

[2] G. Gidel, *Le droit international public de la mer: le temps de paix*, vol.1, *Introduction, la haute mer* (reprint, Paris, Duchemin, 1981), pp. 40–41; P. Vincent, *Droit de la mer* (Brussels, Larcier, 2008), p. 33. See also Chapter 1, section 2.

2.2 Legal status of internal waters

Every coastal State enjoys full sovereignty over its internal waters. Article 2(1) of the LOSC provides as follows:

> The sovereignty of a coastal State extends, beyond its land territory and internal waters and, in the case of an archipelagic State, its archipelagic waters, to an adjacent belt of sea, described as the territorial sea.

Unlike the territorial sea, the right of innocent passage does not apply to internal waters. The exception to this rule is that where the internal waters have been newly enclosed by a straight baseline, the right of innocent passage shall exist in those waters by virtue of Article 5(2) of the TSC and Article 8 of the LOSC.

2.3 Jurisdiction of the coastal State over foreign vessels in internal waters

Normally the civil jurisdiction of the coastal State is not exercised in connection with disputes of a private nature arisinge between members of the crew. In relation to criminal jurisdiction, international lawyers have been accustomed to contrast the Anglo-American position with the French position.[3]

According to the Anglo-American position, the coastal State has complete jurisdiction over foreign vessels in its ports. Nonetheless, as a matter of comity, the coastal State may refrain from exercising its jurisdiction over those vessels.[4] This position was echoed by the US Supreme Court in the 1887 *Wildenhus* case.[5]

According to the French position, the coastal State has in law no jurisdiction over purely internal affairs on foreign vessels in its ports. This position derived from the opinion of the French *Conseil d'Etat* in the *Sally* and *Newton* cases in 1806. These two cases involved two American ships in French ports. In both cases, one member of the crew assaulted another. The *Conseil d'Etat* declared that local jurisdiction did not apply to matters of internal discipline or offences by members of a crew, unless the peace and good order of the port were affected, or the local authorities were asked for assistance.[6]

[3] L. Lucchini and M. Voelckel, *Droit de la mer*, vol. 1 (Paris, Pedone, 1990), pp. 157–159; I. Brownlie, *Principles of Public International Law* (Oxford University Press, 2008), p. 319.

[4] The delegation of Great Britain explained its position at the 1930 Hague Conference. S. Rosenne (ed.), *League of Nations Conference for the Codification of International Law* [1930], vol. 2 (New York, Oceana, 1975), p. 317.

[5] 120 *U.S.* 1 (1887), 11. The judgment was reproduced in K. R. Simmonds, *Cases on the Law of the Sea*, vol. 2 (Dobbs Ferry, New York, Oceana Publications, 1977), pp. 406–411 (at p. 409). This position is also confirmed in Reporter's Note of the Restatement of the Law Third, The Foreign Relations Law of the United States. The American Law Institute, *Restatement of the Law Third: The Foreign Relations Law of the United States*, vol. 2 (American Law Institute Publishers, 1990) § 512, Reporter's Note 5, p. 42.

[6] The *Sally* and the *Newton* cases were reproduced in Simmonds, *Cases*, vol. I, pp. 77–78. France explained its position at the 1930 Hague Conference. Rosenne, *League of Nations Conference*, pp. 299–300.

As aptly pointed out by Gidel, however, the opinion of the *Conseil d'Etat* of 1806 did not completely deny the territorial jurisdiction of the coastal State over offences committed on board foreign ships in French ports. The opinion merely declared that the coastal State would not exercise its jurisdiction in certain cases.[7] In fact, a French court, in the 1859 *Tempest* case, held that homicide of a fellow crew member compromised the peace of the port, and therefore brought the ship under local jurisdiction.[8] As a matter of practice, therefore, the points of difference between the two positions appear to be minimal.

In modern practice, the scope of criminal jurisdiction of the coastal State over foreign merchant ships is provided by specific consular conventions. Recent State practice seems to be generally consistent on the following matters.[9]

1. Foreign ships entering a port are subject to the sovereignty of the coastal State and that State has criminal jurisdiction over them. However, the coastal State does not exercise criminal jurisdiction over matters involving solely the internal discipline of the ship.
2. The coastal State will exercise criminal jurisdiction in the following cases:
   (i) when an offence caused on board the ship affects or is likely to affect the peace and order or the tranquillity of the port or on land, or its interests are engaged,
   (ii) when its intervention is requested by the captain, or the consul of the flag State of the vessel,
   (iii) when a non-crew member is involved,
   (iv) when an offence caused on board the ship is of a serious character, usually punishable by a sentence of imprisonment for more than a few years,
   (v) when matters which do not concern solely the 'internal economy' of a foreign ship, such as pollution and pilotage, are involved.
3. It is solely the coastal State which may determine the existence of a situation as described above.

Unlike merchant ships, warships and other government ships operated for non-commercial purposes enjoy sovereign immunity.[10] Members of the crew ashore on duty or official mission are immune from the local jurisdiction, when committing breaches of local law. Members of the crew committing breaches of local law when ashore on leave and rejoining the ship are also immune from the local jurisdiction. It is debatable whether political asylum may be granted on board in positive international law.[11] However, it seems beyond doubt that slaves on board shall be free because slavery is prohibited in international law. In this respect, Article 13 of the Geneva Convention on

[7] Gidel, *Le droit international public de la mer*, vol. 2: *Les eaux intérieures* (reprint, Paris, Douchemin, 1981), p. 87 and pp. 204–205; J. L. Brierly, *The Law of Nations: An Introduction to the International Law of Peace*, 6th edn (Oxford, Clarendon Press, 1963), p. 225.

[8] The *Tempest* case was reproduced in Simmonds, *Cases*, vol. I, pp. 448–459.

[9] M. Hayashi, 'Jurisdiction over Foreign Commercial Ships in Ports: A Gap in the Law of the Sea Codification' (2004) 18 *Ocean Yearbook* p. 505.

[10] TSC, Article 22(2); LOSC, Article 32. Warships are defined in Article 29 of the LOSC.

[11] Brownlie, *Principles*, p. 372.

the High Seas and Article 99 of the LOSC explicitly hold that: 'Any slave taking refuge on board any ship, whatever its flag, shall *ipso facto* be free'.

2.4 Access to ports

As ports are under the territorial sovereignty of the coastal State, that State may regulate foreign vessels' entry to its ports. Indeed, the ICJ, in the *Nicaragua* case, clearly stated that: 'It is also by virtue of its sovereignty that the coastal State may regulate access to its port'.[12] One can say, therefore, that there is no right of entry into ports of foreign States in customary international law.[13] In this regard, the 1958 *Aramco* award, which upheld the right of ships to access to ports under customary international law,[14] does not seem to be entirely in conformity with State practice.

In fact, it is not uncommon that nuclear-powered ships and ships carrying nuclear or other noxious substances can enter a port only with the permission of the coastal State.[15] The coastal State is empowered to establish particular requirements for the entry of foreign vessels into their ports in order to prevent pollution from vessels in accordance with Article 211(3) of the LOSC. In the case of ships proceeding to internal waters or a call at a port facility outside internal waters, the coastal State has the right to take the necessary steps to prevent any breach of the conditions to which admission of those ships to internal waters or such a call is subject (Article 25(2)). A foreign warship has no automatic right to enter into internal waters or ports of another State, without diplomatic clearance.

In practice, sea communication would be much disturbed without access to ports. Thus, many bilateral treaties of 'Friendship, Commerce and Navigation' confer rights of entry to ports for foreign merchant ships. For instance, Article XIX(2) of the 1956 Treaty of Friendship, Commerce and Navigation between the Netherlands and the United States of America stipulates that: 'Vessels of either Party shall have liberty ... to come with their cargoes to all ports, places and waters of such other Party open to foreign commerce and navigation'.[16] As for multilateral treaty provisions, Article 2 of the 1923 Geneva Convention and Statute on the International Regime of Maritime Ports provides that:[17]

> Subject to the principle of reciprocity and to the reservation set out in the first paragraph of Article 8, every Contracting State undertakes to grant the vessels of every other Contracting State equality of treatment with its own vessels, or those of any other States whatsoever, in the maritime ports situated under its sovereignty or authority, as regards freedom of access to the port, the use of the port, and the full enjoyment of the benefits as regards navigation and commercial operations which it affords to vessels, their cargoes and passengers.

[12] ICJ Reports 1986, p. 111, para. 213.

[13] This conclusion was echoed by the 1957 Amsterdam Resolution of the *Institut de droit international*. Institut de droit international, 'The Distinction Between the *Régime* of the Territorial Sea and the *Régime* of Internal Waters', Session of Amsterdam, 24 September 1957, Part II. The French text is authoritative.

[14] (1958) 27 *ILR* p. 212.

[15] V. D. Degan, 'Internal Waters' (1986) 17 *Netherlands Yearbook of International Law* pp. 3–44 (at p. 21).

[16] 285 *UNTS* p. 232.

[17] 58 *LNTS* p. 285. The text was reproduced in A. V. Lowe and S. A. G. Talmon, *Basic Documents on the Law of the Sea: The Legal Order of the Oceans* (Oxford, Hart Publishing 2009), p. 1.

It can be presumed that normally the ports of the coastal State are open to merchant vessels unless otherwise provided.

2.5 Ships in distress at sea

In light of imminent danger, particular rules apply to a ship in distress. Concerning the criteria for determining a distress situation, Lord Stowell, in the *Eleanor* case, specified four requirements. First, distress must be urgent and something of grave necessity. Second, 'there must be at least a moral necessity'. Third, 'it must not be a distress which he has created himself'. Fourth, 'the distress must be proved by the claimant in a clear and satisfactory manner'.[18] At the treaty level, the 1979 International Convention on Maritime Search and Rescue defines a 'distress phase' as: 'A situation wherein there is a reasonable certainty that a vessel or a person is threatened by grave and imminent danger and requires immediate assistance'.[19]

For humanitarian and safety reasons, it is generally recognised that any foreign vessel in distress has a right of entry to any foreign port under customary international law.[20] In the words of the 1809 *Eleanor* judgment, '[r]eal and irresistible distress must be at all times a sufficient passport for human beings under any such application of human laws'.[21] A ship in distress entering a port or a place of refuge enjoys immunity from local laws. The immunity applies to arrest of the vessel, to local health, criminal and tax laws, as well as to public charges levied for entry into port. The burden of proof to establish distress is on the party claiming exemption from local laws, namely the ship in question.[22] A ship in distress is also exempted from certain rules regulating marine pollution because such rules apply only to ships that have voluntarily entered a port or an offshore terminal.[23] However, a ship in distress enjoys immunity only where local laws are breached for reasons of *force majeure*, and the ship cannot enjoy immunity from all local laws.[24] One can also say that a ship in distress that is engaged in any activity contrary to *jus cogens*, such as slave trading, should lose its immunity if it enters a place of refuge.[25]

A contemporary issue that needs further consideration involves environmental hazards arising from ships in distress. In former times, ships were smaller in size and their cargoes were not inherently dangerous to the marine environment of coastal States. Nowadays, however, the size of ships has increased and there is growing concern that

18 The *Eleanor* case (1809) 165 *English Reports* p. 1068.

19 1405 *UNTS* p. 97. Annex Chapter 1.3.11.

20 The customary law character of the right of entry into a foreign port by ships in distress is fully supported by expert commentators, including: P. C. Jessup, *The Law of Territorial Waters and Maritime Jurisdiction* (New York, G. A. Jennings Co., 1927), p. 208; Degan, 'Internal Waters', p. 10; R. R. Churchill and A. V. Lowe, *The Law of the Sea*, 3rd edn (Manchester University Press, 1999), p. 63; J. E. Noyes, 'Ships in Distress', in *Max Planck Encyclopedia*, p. 2, para. 11; R. Barnes, 'Refugee Law at Sea' (2004) 53 *ICLQ* p. 58.

21 The *Eleanor* case, p. 1067.

22 Noyes, 'Ships in Distress', p. 4, para. 21.

23 LOSC, Articles 218(1)(3) and 220(1).

24 D. P. O'Connell (I. A. Shearer ed.), *The International Law of the Sea*, vol. 2 (Oxford, Clarendon Press, 1984), p. 857.

25 Noyes, 'Ships in Distress', p. 5, para. 24.

the contents of cargoes and fuel can threaten the offshore environment of coastal States. In the case of accidents, the economic and health interests of a coastal State's local community may be seriously damaged. It is probable, therefore, that coastal States will refuse to grant ships in distress access to a place of refuge in order to protect the environment of offshore areas, as occurred when France refused to give refuge to the *Erika* in 1999. Likewise, in 2001, several coastal States refused the damaged tanker *Castor* refuge in safer waters. In 2002, Spain ordered the oil tanker *Prestige* to be towed out to sea from the Bay of Biscay. As demonstrated in these examples, a tension arises as to how it is possible to reconcile the need to provide refuge for ships in distress and the marine environmental protection of the coastal State.

In this regard, one can detect a sign of qualifying the customary right of entry into a foreign port by vessels in distress. One might take the Irish municipal decision of the 1995 *M/V Toledo* case as an example. In this case, Barr J, in the Irish High Court of Admiralty ruled:

> In summary, therefore, I am satisfied that the right of a foreign vessel in serious distress to the benefit of a safe haven in the waters of an adjacent state is primarily humanitarian rather than economic. It is not an absolute right. If safety of life is not a factor, then there is a widely recognised practice among maritime states to have proper regard to their own interests and those of their citizens in deciding whether or not to accede to any such request.[26]

Likewise, the qualification of the right of a vessel in distress can be seen in the Guidelines on Places of Refuge for Ships in Need of Assistance adopted on 5 December 2003 by the International Maritime Organization (IMO).[27] Paragraph 3.12 of the Guidelines states that:

> Where permission to access a place of refuge is requested, there is no obligation for the coastal State to grant it, but the coastal State should weight all the factors and risks in a balanced manner and give shelter whenever reasonably possible.

However, this paragraph seems to leave some room for discussion.

First, as noted, the right of entry into foreign ports by vessels in distress is a long-established rule of customary international law. It is debatable whether there is widespread and uniform State practice, along with *opinio juris*, which may change the rule at this stage. It must also be recalled that Article 195 of the LOSC explicitly forbids

[26] *ACT Shipping (PTE) Ltd v The Minister for the Marine, Ireland and the Attorney General* (1995) 3 *The Irish Reports*, p. 426.

[27] IMO, Resolution A.949(23), 'Guidelines on Places of Refuge for Ships in Need of Assistance', A 23/Res.949, 5 March 2004. Under the Guidelines, 'ships in need of assistance' are defined as: 'a ship in a situation, apart from one requiring rescue of persons on board, that could give rise to loss of the vessel or an environmental or navigational hazard' (para. 1.18). The 2003 Guidelines were complemented by the 'Guidelines on the Control of Ships in an Emergency' adopted on 19 October 2007, MSC.1/Circ.1251.

States 'to transfer, directly or indirectly, damage or hazards from one area to another or transform one type of pollution into another'.

Second, humanitarian consideration is the primary basis of the right of vessel in distress. As implied in the *M/V Toledo* judgment, there is a good reason to argue that if safety of life is a factor, the coastal State should not refuse to provide refuge to ships in distress.

Third, where a ship in distress is sent back out to sea, very dangerous situations may arise for both the ship and the environment of coastal States. In this regard, it must be recalled that the *Erika* and the *Prestige* were eventually destroyed, causing substantial pollution to the offshore environment. Thus there appears to be a general sense that allowing a ship in distress into a place of refuge would be the best way to prevent environmental damage. In this respect, it is notable that Article 20 of Directive 2002/59/EC requires the EU Member States to draw up plans to accommodate ships in distress in the waters under their jurisdiction.[28] Likewise, the Protocol Concerning Cooperation in Preventing Pollution from Ships and, in Cases of Emergency, Combating Pollution of the Mediterranean Sea of 2002 also imposes upon the Contracting Parties a duty to define strategies concerning reception in places of refuge, including ports, of ships in distress presenting a threat to the marine environment.[29] At the same time, there is also a need for the flag State to make vigorous efforts to eliminate substandard shipping.

3 TERRITORIAL SEA

3.1 Legal status of the territorial sea

The territorial sea is a marine space under the territorial sovereignty of the coastal State up to a limit not exceeding twelve nautical miles measured from baselines.[30] The territorial sea comprises the seabed and its subsoil, the adjacent waters, and its airspace. The landward limit of the territorial sea is the baseline. In the case of archipelagic States, the inner limit of the territorial sea is the archipelagic baseline. The outer limit of the territorial sea is the line every point of which is at a distance from the nearest point of the baseline equal to the breadth of the territorial sea.

At present, some 137 States Parties to the LOSC have established a twelve-nautical-mile territorial sea, and approximately ten States have claimed, wholly or partly, a territorial sea of less than twelve nautical miles. Some twenty-four States that formerly claimed a territorial sea more than twelve nautical miles in breadth have pulled back its breadth to twelve nautical miles.[31] Only nine States, including four parties to the LOSC,

[28] Directive 2002/59/EC of the European Parliament and of the Council of 27 June 2002 establishing a Community Vessel Traffic Monitoring and Information System and Repealing Council Directive 93/75/EEC.

[29] Article 16. The text of the Convention is available at: www.internationalwildlifelaw.org/Barcelonanewemergency.pdf.

[30] LOSC, Article 3.

[31] Those States are: Albania, Angola, Argentina, Brazil, Cameroon, Cape Verde, Gabon, Germany, Ghana, Guinea, Guinea-Bissau, Haiti, Madagascar, Maldives, Mauritania, Nicaragua, Nigeria, Panama, Senegal, Sierra Leone, Syria, Tanzania, Tonga and Uruguay. Apart from Syria, these

claim a greater breadth than twelve nautical miles.[32] Nonetheless, those claims have encountered protests from other States.[33] Considering that the 200-nautical-mile EEZ is currently well-established as customary law, it may be said that the 200-nautical-mile territorial sea is contrary to international law. Overall, it seems that the twelve nautical miles maximum breadth of the territorial sea is now established in customary international law.[34] Whilst the LOSC contains no rule relating to a minimum breadth of the territorial sea, no State has claimed a territorial sea of less than three nautical miles in practice.

In addition, roadsteads which are normally used for the loading, unloading and anchoring of ships, and which would otherwise be situated wholly or partly outside the outer limit of the territorial sea, are included in the territorial sea.[35] In practice, there seem to be few areas more than twelve miles from the baseline that are suitable for the loading, unloading and anchoring of ships. Hence it appears that roadsteads have only a minor role in determining the spatial scope of the territorial sea.

Concerning the judicial character of the territorial sea, the Court of Arbitration, in the 1909 *Grisbadara* case between Norway and Sweden, stated that 'the maritime territory is an essential appurtenance of land territory', and 'an inseparable appurtenance of this land territory'.[36] According to Judge McNair, 'the possession of this territory [territorial waters] is not optional, not dependent upon the will of the State, but compulsory'.[37] There is no doubt that the territorial sea is under the territorial sovereignty of the coastal State. As explained earlier, territorial sovereignty in international law is characterised by completeness and exclusiveness.[38] Accordingly, the coastal State can exercise complete legislative and enforcement jurisdiction over all matters and all people in an exclusive manner unless international law provides otherwise. At the same time, under Article 2(3) of the LOSC, sovereignty over the territorial sea is

States have ratified the LOSC. R. R. Churchill, 'The Impact of State Practice on the Jurisdictional Framework contained in the LOS Convention', in A. G. Oude Elferink (ed.), *Stability and Change in the Law of the Sea: The Role of the LOS Convention* (Leiden and Boston, Nijhoff, 2005), p. 110; J. A. Roach and R. W. Smith, *United States Responses to Excessive Maritime Claims*, 2nd edn (The Hague, Nijhoff, 1996), pp. 152–153. The list of States which have reduced excessive claims to territorial sea may vary according to the time of research.

32 Those States are: Benin (200 nautical miles), Ecuador (200 nautical miles), El Salvador (200 nautical miles), Peru (200 nautical miles), the Philippines (beyond 12 nautical miles), Somalia (200 nautical miles), and Togo (30 nautical miles). Benin, Philippines, Somalia and Togo are parties to the LOSC. The Philippines claims as its territorial sea a rectangle defined by coordinates, which in places extends beyond twelve nautical miles from the baseline.

33 Roach and Smith, *United States Responses*, pp. 153–161.

34 T. Treves, 'Codification du droit international et pratique des Etats dans le droit de la mer' (1990-IV) 223 *RCADI* p. 66; Churchill and Lowe, *The Law of the Sea*, p. 80; S. Wolf, 'Territorial Sea', in *Max Planck Encyclopedia* p. 2, para. 4.

35 LOSC, Article 12. A roadstead means 'an area near the shore where vessels are intended to anchor in a position of safety; often situated in a shallow indentation of the coast'. 'Consolidated Glossary of Technical Terms Used in the United Nations Convention on the Law of the Sea', in UNDOALOS, *The Law of the Sea: Baselines: An Examination of the Relevant Provisions of the United Nations Convention on the Law of the Sea* (New York, United Nations, 1989), p. 60.

36 (1910) 4 *AJIL* p. 231 (an English translation). For an original text of the Award, see 11 *Reports of International Arbitral Awards (RIAA)* pp. 147–166.

37 The *Norwegian Fisheries* case, ICJ Reports 1951, p. 160.

38 See Chapter 1, section 2.2.

subject to the Convention and to other rules of international law. As will be seen next, coastal States' sovereignty over the territorial sea is restricted by the right of innocent passage for foreign vessels.

3.2 The right of innocent passage

The right of innocent passage through the territorial sea is based on the freedom of navigation as an essential means to accomplish freedom of trade. In his book published in 1758, Vattel had already accepted the existence of such a right.[39] In the *Twee Gebroeders* case of 1801, Lord Stowell ruled that 'the act of inoffensively passing over such portions of water, without any violence committed there, is not considered as any violation of territory belonging to a neutral state – permission is not usually required'.[40] It may be considered that the right of innocent passage became established in the middle of the nineteenth century.[41] In this regard, the Report Adopted by the Committee on April 10th 1930 at the Hague Conference for the Codification of International Law clearly stated that:

> This sovereignty [over the territorial sea] is, however, limited by conditions established by international law; indeed, it is precisely because the freedom of navigation is of such great importance to all States that the right of innocent passage through the territorial sea has been generally recognised.[42]

At the treaty level, the right of innocent passage was, for the first time, codified in Article 14(1) of the TSC. This provision was followed by Article 17 of the LOSC, which provides as follows:

> Subject to this Convention, ships of all States, whether coastal or land-locked, enjoy the right of innocent passage through the territorial sea.

It is important to note that the right of innocent passage does not comprise the freedom of overflight.

Under Article 18(1) of the LOSC, innocent passage comprises lateral passage and vertical passage. Lateral passage is the passage traversing the territorial sea without entering internal waters or calling at a roadstead or port facility outside internal waters. Vertical or inward/outward-bound passage concerns the passage proceeding to or from internal waters or a call at such roadstead or port facility. As will be seen, the direction of the passage is at issue in relation to the criminal jurisdiction of coastal

39 Emmerich de Vattel, *The Law of Nations; or Principles of the Law of Nature, Applied to the Conduct and Affairs of Nations and Sovereigns* (translated by Joseph Chitty, Philadelphia, T. and J. W. Johnson and Co., Law Booksellers, 1853), section 288 and section 292.

40 *The Twee Gebroeders*, in K. R. Simmonds, *Cases on the Law of the Sea*, vol. 1 (Dobbs Ferry, Oceana, 1976), p. 23.

41 O'Connell, *The International Law of the Sea*, p. 275. See also p. 19.

42 Rosenne, *League of Nations Conference* (vol. 4), p. 1412.

States over vessels of foreign States in the territorial sea. The LOSC contains several rules concerning the manner of innocent passage through the territorial sea.

First, passage shall be continuous and expeditious. This means that ships are required to proceed with due speed, having regard to safety and other relevant factors. Under Article 18(2), passage includes stopping and anchoring only in so far as the same are incidental to ordinary navigation or are rendered necessary by *force majeure* or distress or for the purpose of providing assistance to persons, ships or aircraft in danger or distress. Accordingly, the act of hovering by a foreign vessel is not normally considered innocent passage.

Second, in the territorial sea, submarines and other underwater vehicles are required to navigate on the surface and to show their flag pursuant to Article 20. This provision follows essentially from Article 14(6) of the TSC. In this respect, the question arises as to whether a breach of the requirement to navigate on the surface can be the negation of the right of innocent passage. Whilst it seems that a submerged submarine in the territorial sea is not considered as innocent passage, submergence in the territorial sea will not instantly justify the use of force against the submarine. Above all, every measure should be taken short of armed force to require the submarine to leave.[43]

Third, foreign ships exercising the right of innocent passage through the territorial sea shall comply with all such laws and regulations and all generally accepted international regulations relating to the prevention of collisions at sea in accordance with Article 21(4). The most important regulations are probably those in the 1972 Convention on the International Regulations for Preventing Collisions at Sea.[44]

Concerning *innocent* passage, the question arises as to when passage becomes prejudicial and hence non-innocent. In this respect, Article 19(1) of the LOSC, which is a replica of Article 14(4) of the TSC, provides as follows:

> Passage is innocent so long as it is not prejudicial to the peace, good order or security of the coastal State. Such passage shall take place in conformity with this Convention and with other rules of international law.

More specifically, Article 19(2) contains a catalogue of prejudicial activities: (a) any threat or use of force, (b) any exercise with weapons of any kind, (c) spying, (d) any act of propaganda, (e) the launching, landing or taking on board of any aircraft, (f) the launching, landing or taking on board of any military device, (g) the loading or unloading of any commodity, currency or person contrary to the customs, fiscal, immigration or sanitary laws of the coastal State, (h) any act of wilful and serious pollution, (i) fishing activities, (j) research or survey activities, (k) interference with coastal communications or any other facilities, and (l) any other activity not having a direct bearing on passage. The last item in the list, (l), seems to imply that the above list is non-exhaustive. Article 19 calls for four comments.

[43] O'Connell, *The International Law of the Sea*, vol. 1, p. 297.

[44] For the text of the Convention, 1050 *UNTS* p. 18. Entered into force 15 July 1977.

First, the term 'activities' under Article 19(2) seems to suggest that the prejudicial nature of innocent passage is judged on the basis of the *manner* in which the passage is carried out, not the type of ship. This approach seemed to be echoed by the ICJ in the 1949 *Corfu Channel* case. In that case, the Court relied essentially on the criterion of 'whether the *manner* in which the passage was carried out was consistent with the principle of innocent passage'.[45]

Second, some clauses of Article 19(2) are so widely drafted that disputes may arise with respect to their interpretation. For instance, Article 19(2)(a) refers to '... or in any other manner in violation of the principles of international law embodied in the Charter of the United Nations'. Arguably, this reference may provide wide discretion to the coastal State. Similarly, the coastal State may have wide discretion in the interpretation of Article 19(2)(c), 'any act aimed at collecting information to the prejudice of the defence or security of the coastal State' and (j), 'the carrying out of research or survey activities'. In response to possible disagreements concerning the interpretation of Article 19(2), for instance, paragraph 4 of the 1989 Uniform Interpretation between the United States and the USSR stated that:

> A coastal State which questions whether the particular passage of a ship through its territorial sea is innocent shall inform the ship of the reason why it questions the innocent passage, and provide the ship an opportunity to clarify its intentions or correct its conduct in a reasonably short period of time.

Third, a question arises whether paragraph 2 of Article 19 is meant to be an illustrative list of paragraph 1 of the same provision, or whether the coastal State may evaluate innocence solely on the basis of paragraph 1, independent from paragraph 2. If paragraph 2 is an illustrative list of paragraph 1, paragraph 1 would seem to be superfluous. Unlike the second paragraph, the first paragraph makes no explicit reference to 'activities'. Hence there appears to be scope to argue that the criterion for judging innocence under Article 19(1) is not limited to the manner of the passage of ships. At least, there is no clear evidence that the criteria for evaluating innocence of the passage of foreign warships in paragraphs 1 and 2 of Article 19 must be the same. If this is the case, it seems that the coastal State can regard the particular passage of a ship as non-innocent on the basis of Article 19(1), even if the passage concerned does not directly fall within the list of Article 19(2). Following this interpretation, for instance, the Japanese government takes the view that the passage of foreign warships carrying nuclear weapons through its territorial sea is not innocent, whilst Japan generally admits the right of innocent passage of foreign warships.[46]

[45] Emphasis original. ICJ Reports 1949, p. 30.

[46] A. Kanehara, 'The Japanese Legal System Concerning Innocent Passage of Foreign Vessels 1990–1998' (1999) 42 *The Japanese Annual of International Law* p. 105. The Japanese policy is based on 'Three Non-Nuclear Principles', which do not allow nuclear materials to be brought into Japanese territory.

Fourth, a question that may arise is whether a violation of a coastal State's law would *ipso facto* deprive a passage of its innocent character. Whilst the opinion of the members of the ILC was divided on this particular issue, the literal interpretation of Article 14(4) of the TSC appears to suggest that the violation of the coastal State's law does not *ipso facto* deprive a passage of its innocent character, unless such violation is prejudicial to the coastal State's interests.[47] The only exception involves Article 14(5), which provides that:

> Passage of foreign fishing vessels shall not be considered innocent if they do not observe such laws and regulations as the coastal State may make and publish in order to prevent these vessels from fishing in the territorial sea.

This provision was inserted in order to introduce an additional criterion of innocence. It seems to imply that apart from the violation of fishing law, the breach of the law of the coastal State does not *ipso facto* deprive a passage of its innocence. Likewise, there appears to be scope to argue that, under the LOSC, the violation of the law of the coastal State does not *ipso facto* deprive a passage of its innocent character, unless such violation falls within the scope of Article 19.[48]

3.3 The right of innocent passage of warships

(a) Customary law

The right of innocent passage of warships is of paramount importance for major naval powers in order to secure global naval mobility. However, the passage of foreign warships through the territorial sea may be a threat to the security of the coastal State. A difficult question thus arises as to whether or not foreign warships have the right of innocent passage in international law. In this respect, Article 11 of the Resolution adopted by the *Institut de droit international* at its 1928 Stockholm session stated that the free passage of foreign warships may be subject to special rules of the riparian State.[49] In 1929, 'Research in International Law' by Harvard Law School also stated that: 'The sovereignty of the littoral state is restricted by the right of innocent passage because of a recognition of the freedom of the seas for the commerce of all states. There is, therefore, no reason for freedom of innocent passage of vessels of war'.[50]

At the 1930 Hague Codification Conference, Articles 12 and 13 of the Legal Status of the Territorial Sea, attached to the Report Adopted by the Committee on April 10th 1930, read that:

[47] Churchill and Lowe, *The Law of the Sea*, p. 84.

[48] This interpretation is supported by writers, including: Carlos Espaliú Berdud, *Le passage inoffensive des navires de guerre étrangers dans la mer territoriale: portée du régime contenu dans la Convention des Nations Unies sur le droit de la mer* (Brussels, Bruylant, 2006), p. 54; P. Birnie, A. Boyle and C. Redgwell, *International Law and the Environment*, 3rd edn (Oxford University Press, 2008), p. 417.

[49] Institut de droit international, *Projet de règlement relatif à la mer territoriale en temps de paix*, Sessionde Stockholm, 1928. www.idi-iil.org/idiF/resolutionsF/1928_stock_03_fr.pdf.

[50] (1929) 23 *AJIL* (Special Supplement) p. 295.

> As a general rule, a coastal State will not forbid the passage of foreign warships in its territorial sea and will not require a previous authorisation or notification. The coastal State has the right to regulate the conditions of such passage. Submarines shall navigate on the surface.[51]
>
> If a foreign warship passing through the territorial sea does not comply with the regulations of the coastal State and disregards any request for compliance which may be brought to its notice, the coastal State may require the warship to leave the territorial sea.[52]

In view of those provisions, Gidel argued that the passage of foreign warships through the territorial sea is not a right, but a tolerance (*tolérance*) of the coastal State.[53]

Later, the right of innocent passage of foreign warships was at issue in the 1949 *Corfu Channel* case between the United Kingdom and Albania. In this case, Albania asserted that it could regulate the passage of foreign warships in Albanian territorial waters. By contrast, the United Kingdom maintained that warships possess a right of innocent passage through the territorial sea of another State. While the ICJ accepted the right of innocent passage of foreign warships in straits used for international navigation, it did not directly address the question whether foreign warships have the same right of innocent passage in the territorial sea.[54] Overall it may have to be accepted that customary international law is obscure on this subject.

(b) Treaty law

The TSC contains no provision relating to the right of innocent passage of foreign warships. However, Article 14(1) of the TSC stipulates that:

> Subject to the provisions of these articles, ships of all States, whether coastal or not, shall enjoy the right of innocent passage through the territorial sea.

It must be noted that this provision is under the rubric 'Rules Applicable to All Ships'. Further, Article 14(2) sets out that submarines are required to navigate on the surface, when in the territorial sea, and to show their flag. It can be presumed that this provision relates specifically, if not totally, to military submarines. Moreover, Article 23 provides that if a warship fails to comply with the regulations of the coastal State concerning passage through the territorial sea, the coastal State may require the warship to leave the territorial sea. Noting these points, some argue that warships have a right of innocent passage under the TSC.[55]

51 Article 12. Rosenne, *League of Nations Conference*, p. 1418.

52 Article 13. *Ibid.*, p. 1419.

53 Gidel, *Le droit international public de la mer*, vol. 3: *La mer territoriale et la zone contiguë* (Paris, Duchemin, 1981), p. 284. See also Jessup, *The Law of Territorial Waters*, p. 120.

54 ICJ Reports 1949, pp. 27–28. However, several members of the Court addressed this question. See Dissenting Opinion by Judge Azevedo, *ibid.*, p. 99; Dissenting Opinion by Judge Krylov, *ibid.*, p. 74; Individual Opinion by Judge Alvares, *ibid.*, pp. 46–47.

55 Sir Gerald Fitzmaurice, 'Some Results of the Geneva Conference on the Law of the Sea: Part I – The Territorial Sea and Contiguous Zone and Related Topics' (1959) 8 *ICLQ* pp. 102–103; O'Connell,

In common with the TSC, the LOSC contains no explicit provision with respect to the right of innocent passage of foreign warships in the territorial sea. However, four points must be noted.

First, like Article 14(1) of the TSC, Article 17 of the LOSC, which provides the right of innocent passage, is under the rubric 'Rules Applicable to All Ships'. It can be presumed, therefore, that Article 17 is applicable to all ships, including warships.

Second, as with Article 14(2) of the TSC, Article 20 of the LOSC requires submarines and other underwater vehicles to navigate on the surface and to show their flag in the territorial sea.

Third, as has been seen, Article 19(2) sets out a catalogue of activities which render passage non-innocent. Some of these activities, such as any exercise or practice with weapons, the take-off or landing of aircraft, and the launching or receiving of any military device, relate specifically, if not totally, to warships.

Fourth, Article 30 stipulates that if any warship does not comply with the laws and regulations of the coastal State concerning passage through the territorial sea and disregards any request for compliance therewith which is made to it, the coastal State may require it to leave the territorial sea immediately. This provision would be pointless if foreign warships had no right of innocent passage in the territorial sea.

Overall, those provisions seem to hint at the right of innocent passage of foreign warships. This interpretation seems to be supported by writers, such as Brown, Carlos Espaliú Berdud, Churchill, R.-J. Dupuy, Johnson, Keyuan, Lucchini/Voelckel, Rothwell/Stephens and Treves.[56]

(c) State practice

State practice is not uniform on this subject. In ratifying the LOSC, some States – for example, Germany and the Netherlands – explicitly declared that the Convention permits innocent passage in the territorial sea for all ships, including foreign warships. Thailand has also taken the position that all foreign ships, including warships, can exercise the right of innocent passage in the territorial sea.[57] Of particular importance is the 1989 Uniform Interpretation of Norms of International Law Governing Innocent Passage between the USA and the USSR.[58] Paragraph 2 of this bilateral document states that:

The International Law of the Sea, pp. 290–291; E. D. Brown, *The International Law of the Sea, Volume I Introductory Manual* (Aldershot, Dartmouth, 1994), p. 72.

[56] Brown, *The International Law of the Sea*, p. 66; Carlos Espaliú Berdud, *Le passage inoffensive*, pp. 14–15; Churchill, 'The Impact of State Practice', pp. 111–112; R.-J. Dupuy, 'The Sea under National Competence', in R.-J. Dupuy and D. Vignes, *A Handbook on the New Law of the Sea*, vol. 1 (Dordrecht, Nijhoff, 1991), p. 259; D. H. N. Johnson, 'Innocent Passage, Transit Passage', in R. Bernhardt (ed.), *Encyclopedia of Public International Law*, vol. 11 (Amsterdam, North-Holland, 1989), p. 152; Z. Keyuan, 'Innocent Passage for Warships: The Chinese Doctrine and Practice' (1998) 29 *ODIL* p. 211. L. Lucchini and M. Voelckel, *Droit de la mer*, vol. 2: *Navigation et Pêche* (Paris, Pedone, 1996), pp. 250–255; D. R. Rothwell and T. Stephens, *The International Law of the Sea* (Oxford and Portland, Oregon, Hart Publishing, 2010), p. 268; Treves, 'Codification du droit international', pp. 116–117.

[57] Statement of the Ministry of Foreign Affairs of Thailand (1993) 23 *Law of the Sea Bulletin* p. 108.

[58] (1989) 14 *Law of the Sea Bulletin* pp. 12–13.

All ships, including warships, regardless of cargo, armament or means of propulsion, enjoy the right of innocent passage through the territorial sea in accordance with international law, for which neither prior notification nor authorisation is required.

Whilst, at UNCLOS I, the USSR took the position that the passage of foreign warships through a territorial sea required prior authorisation, the USSR had become a leading naval power by the end of the 1960s and early 1970s. Consequently, the USSR changed its policy in order to ensure the maximum freedom of navigation of warships.[59]

However, nearly forty States, mainly developing States, require prior notification or prior authorisation of the passage of warships through their territorial sea.[60] In ratifying the LOSC, however, some States – Germany, Italy, the Netherlands and the United Kingdom – expressed the view that claims to prior authorisation and prior notification were at variance with the LOSC. The USA has also protested against most of the claims to both prior authorisation and prior notification.[61] A question thus arises whether prior notification or prior authorisation is compatible with the LOSC.

When considering this issue, a distinction must be drawn between the requirement of prior notification and that of prior authorisation. There appears to be scope to argue that the requirement of prior notification could fall within the scope of Article 21(1)(a) of the LOSC. If this is the case, the right of innocent passage of foreign warships and the requirement of prior notification of the coastal State could be compatible. However, it appears that the legality of prior authorisation remains a matter for discussion.[62]

Coastal State action against foreign warships is qualified by the sovereign immunity afforded to warships. However, the coastal State may require any warship to leave its territorial sea if the warship does not comply with the laws and regulations of the coastal State pursuant to Article 30 of the LOSC. Under Article 31, the flag State is also obliged to bear international responsibility for any loss or damage to the coastal State resulting from the non-compliance by a warship or other governmental ship operated for non-commercial purposes with the laws and regulations of the coastal State concerning passage through the territorial sea or with the provisions of the LOSC or other rules of international law.

A further question is whether a foreign warship has a right to enter into the territorial sea of another State to render assistance to persons in distress, without prior notification to the coastal State. Article 98 of the LOSC, which applies to the high seas

59 E. Franckx, 'Innocent Passage of Warships: Recent Developments in US–Soviet Relations' (1990) 14 *Marine Policy* p. 485; L. Caflisch, 'La convention des Nations Unies sur le droit de la mer adoptée le 30 avril 1982' (1983) 39 *ASDI* pp. 52–53.

60 For a list of States restricting innocent passage of foreign warships, see Roach and Smith, *United States Responses*, pp. 266–267; Churchill, 'The Impact of State Practice', pp. 112–113; W. K. Agyebeng, 'Theory in Search of Practice: The Right of Innocent Passage in the Territorial Sea' (2006) 39 *Cornell International Law Journal* pp. 396–398.

61 Roach and Smith, *United States Responses*, pp. 256–270; Churchill, 'The Impact of State Practice', p. 114.

62 *Ibid.*, pp. 113–114; Rothwell and Stephens, *The International Law of the Sea*, p. 223.

and the EEZ, places an explicit obligation upon every State to render assistance to any person found at sea in danger of being lost. Whilst the LOSC contains no duty to render assistance to any persons in distress in the territorial sea, the offer of such assistance would be consistent with the requirement of the consideration of humanity. Indeed, a temporary entrance of a foreign warship into the territorial sea for the purpose of rendering assistance to persons in distress would pose no threat to the coastal State. Hence there may be room for the view that a foreign warship can render assistance to persons in distress in the territorial sea without notification to the coastal State.

3.4 The right of innocent passage of foreign nuclear-powered ships and ships carrying inherently dangerous or noxious substances

Passage of foreign nuclear-powered ships and ships carrying hazardous cargoes has recently attracted growing attention in the international community. In particular, sea shipments of highly radioactive or radiotoxic nuclear materials are becoming a matter of serious concern to coastal States because these materials may cause widespread and long-term contamination of the marine environment in the event of an accident. In this regard, Article 23 of the LOSC provides as follows:

> Foreign nuclear-powered ships and ships carrying nuclear or other inherently dangerous or noxious substances shall, when exercising the right of innocent passage through the territorial sea, carry documents and observe special precautionary measures established for such ships by international agreements.

Examples of international agreements regulating the passage of nuclear-powered ships or ships carrying hazardous substances include the 1962 Convention on the Liability of Operators of Nuclear Ships, the 1973 International Convention for the Prevention of Pollution from Ships as modified by the 1978 Protocol (MARPOL), and the 1974 International Convention for the Safety of Life at Sea (SOLAS).[63]

It seems beyond doubt that foreign nuclear-powered ships and ships carrying hazardous cargoes enjoy the right of innocent passage through the territorial sea. This is clear from the expression of Article 23, 'when exercising the right of innocent passage'. It is also to be noted that this provision is under the rubric 'Rules Applicable to All Ships'. Furthermore, Article 22(2) allows the coastal State to require nuclear-powered ships and ships carrying nuclear or other inherently dangerous or noxious substances to confine their passage to such sea lanes as it may designate or prescribe for the regulation of the passage of ships.

In practice, some States require prior notification or prior authorisation of the passage of foreign nuclear-powered ships and ships carrying hazardous cargoes through their territorial sea.[64] However, those claims have encountered opposition from several

[63] Some of these treaties will be discussed in Chapter 8, section 6.

[64] According to Churchill, at least nine parties to the LOSC require prior authorisation: Bangladesh, Maldives, Oman, Samoa, Seychelles, Yemen, Egypt, Malaysia and Saudi Arabia. Two non-parties to

States.[65] Thus a question analogous to that of foreign warships has been raised with regard to the navigation of foreign nuclear-powered ships and ships carrying hazardous cargoes.

A requirement of prior notification is consistent with the LOSC. As noted, the coastal State may require 'tankers, nuclear-powered ships and ships carrying nuclear or other inherently dangerous or noxious substances or materials' to confine their passage to such sea lanes and traffic separation schemes as it may designate or prescribe for the regulation of the passage of ships by virtue of Article 22(1) and (2). If the coastal State is not entitled to know the passage of those ships, arguably that State cannot exercise its right set out in these provisions. On the other hand, it may be debatable whether a requirement of prior authorisation is compatible with the LOSC because such a requirement amounts to denial of the right of innocent passage of foreign nuclear-powered ships and ships carrying hazardous cargoes.[66]

In this regard, the UN General Assembly noted that States should maintain dialogue and consultation, in particular under the auspices of the International Atomic Energy Agency and the IMO, with the aim of improved mutual understanding, confidence-building and enhanced communication in relation to the safe maritime transport of radioactive materials; and that States involved in the transport of such materials are urged to continue to engage in dialogue with small island developing States and other States to address their concerns.[67]

3.5 The rights of the coastal State concerning innocent passage

Articles 21, 22 and 25 of the LOSC provide rights of the coastal State with respect to innocent passage.

First, Article 21(1) stipulates that the coastal State possesses the legislative jurisdiction relating to innocent passage through the territorial sea, with respect to all or any of the following:

(a) the safety of navigation and the regulation of maritime traffic;
(b) the protection of navigational aids and facilities and other facilities or installations;
(c) the protection of cables and pipelines;
(d) the conservation of the living resources of the sea;
(e) the prevention of infringement of the fisheries laws and regulations of the coastal State;
(f) the preservation of the environment of the coastal State and the prevention, reduction and control of pollution thereof;

the LOSC, Iran and Syria, also require prior authorisation. Further, six parties to the LOSC, namely Canada, Djibouti, Libya, Malta, Pakistan and Portugal, require prior notification, and one non-party, the United Arab Emirates, requires prior notification. Churchill, 'The Impact of State Practice', pp. 115–116. See also T. Scovazzi, 'The Evolution of International Law of the Sea: New Issues, New Challenges' (2000) 286 *RCADI* pp. 157–158.

[65] Roach and Smith, *United States Responses*, pp. 271–276.

[66] Churchill, 'The Impact of State Practice', p. 115; Hakapää and Molenaar, 'Innocent Passage', p. 144.

[67] UN General Assembly, *Oceans and the Law of the Sea*, A/RES/63/111, adopted on 5 December 2008, p. 16, para. 83.

(g) marine scientific research and hydrographic surveys;
(h) the prevention of infringement of the customs, fiscal, immigration or sanitary laws and regulations of the coastal State.

Such laws and regulations shall not apply to the design, construction, manning or equipment of foreign ships unless they are giving effect to generally accepted international rules or standards pursuant to Article 21(2).

Second, the coastal State is entitled to require foreign ships exercising the right of innocent passage through its territorial sea to use such sea lanes and traffic separation schemes as it may designate or prescribe for the regulation of the passage of ships by virtue of Article 22(1). Article 22(4) places an obligation upon the coastal State to clearly indicate such sea lanes and traffic separation schemes on charts to which due publicity shall be given.

Third, the coastal State is entitled to take the necessary steps in its territorial sea to prevent passage which is not innocent in conformity with Article 25(1). Whilst this provision does not specify the necessary steps, they could include requesting a delinquent ship to stop certain conduct, requesting a ship to leave the territorial sea, and the intervention of State authorities to board and exclude the ship from its territorial sea.[68] Concerning the preservation of the environment of the coastal State, in particular, Article 220(2) provides that where there are clear grounds for believing that a vessel navigating in the territorial sea of a State has violated laws and regulations of that State during its passage therein, the coastal State may undertake physical inspection of the vessel relating to the violation, and may, where the evidence so warrants, institute proceedings, including detention of the vessel.

In the case of ships proceeding to internal waters or a call at a port facility outside internal waters, the coastal State has the right to take the necessary steps to prevent any breach of the conditions to which admission of those ships to internal waters or such a call is subject by virtue of Article 25(2). Article 25(3) further empowers the coastal State to suspend the innocent passage of foreign vessels under five conditions:

(i) suspension must be essential for the protection of its security;
(ii) suspension must be temporal;
(iii) suspension must be limited to specific areas of its territorial sea;
(iv) suspension must be without discrimination;
(v) suspension shall take effect only after having been duly published;

As the territorial sea is under the territorial sovereignty of the coastal State, theoretically the coastal State may exercise criminal jurisdiction over foreign vessels passing through the territorial sea. In order to pay due regard to the interests of navigation, however, Article 27(1) of the LOSC provides that the criminal jurisdiction of the coastal State 'should not' be exercised on board a foreign ship passing through the territorial sea, save only in the following cases:

[68] Rothwell and Stephens, *The International Law of the Sea*, p. 218.

(a) if the consequences of the crime extend to the coastal State;
(b) if the crime is of a kind to disturb the peace of the country or the good order of the territorial sea;
(c) if the assistance of the local authorities has been requested by the master of the ship or by a diplomatic agent or consular officer of the flag State; or
(d) if such measures are necessary for the suppression of illicit traffic in narcotic drugs or psychotropic substances.

The phrase 'should not' seems to suggest that the exercise of criminal jurisdiction is not strictly prohibited in other cases. It would seem to follow that the coastal State has a discretion with regard to the exercise of criminal jurisdiction. The restriction of criminal jurisdiction under Article 27(1) does not apply to the case of inward/outward-bound navigation by virtue of Article 27(2). Where a crime has been committed before the ship entered the territorial sea and the ship is only passing through the territorial sea without entering internal waters, however, the coastal State may not exercise criminal jurisdiction over the ship under Article 27(5). This is a mandatory prohibition on the exercise of the criminal jurisdiction of the coastal State in the territorial sea.

Article 28 of the LOSC limits the exercise of civil jurisdiction of the coastal State in certain cases. Under Article 28(1), 'the coastal State should not stop or divert a foreign ship passing through the territorial sea for the purpose of exercising civil jurisdiction in relation to a person on board the ship'. The term 'should not' seems to suggest that the restriction of the civil jurisdiction is a matter of comity.[69] Under Article 28(2), the coastal State may not levy execution against or arrest the ship for the purpose of any civil proceedings, save only in respect of obligations or liabilities assumed or incurred by the ship itself in the course or for the purpose of its voyage through the waters of the coastal State. However, Article 28(2) is not applicable to inward/outward-bound navigation by virtue of Article 28(3).

3.6 The obligations of the coastal State concerning innocent passage

In light of the importance of sea communication for all States, the LOSC places certain obligations upon the coastal State to ensure the interests of navigation in its territorial sea.

First, the coastal State is obliged not to hamper the innocent passage of foreign ships pursuant to Article 24(1) of the LOSC. Specifically, Article 24(1) provides that the coastal State shall not:

(a) impose requirements on foreign ships which have the practical effect of denying or impairing the right of innocent passage; or
(b) discriminate in form or in fact against the ships of any State or against ships carrying cargoes to, from or on behalf of any State.

[69] O'Connell, *The International Law of the Sea*, vol. 2, p. 874; Fitzmaurice, 'Some Results', p. 107.

Second, the coastal State is under the obligation to give appropriate publicity to any danger to navigation under Article 24(2). This obligation follows from the *dictum* in the *Corfu Channel* judgment.[70]

Third, no charge may be levied upon foreign ships by reason only of their passage through the territorial sea pursuant to Article 26.

4 INTERNATIONAL STRAITS

4.1 Legal framework for international straits prior to 1982

In light of the paramount importance of international straits for sea communication, the freedom of navigation through straits has attracted much attention in the international community. A question is whether or not foreign vessels enjoy the right of innocent passage through international straits between one part of the high seas and another under customary law. The ICJ, in the 1949 *Corfu Channel* case, gave a positive answer to this question, by stating that:

> It is, in the opinion of the Court, generally recognized and in accordance with international custom that States in time of peace have a right to send their warships through straits used for international navigation between two parts of the high seas without the previous authorization of a coastal State, provided that the passage is *innocent*. Unless otherwise prescribed in an international convention, there is no right for a coastal State to prohibit such passage through straits in time of peace.[71]

Reflecting the *dictum* in the *Corfu Channel* judgment, Article 16(4) of the TSC provided that:

> There shall be no suspension of the innocent passage of foreign ships through straits which are used for international navigation between one part of the high seas and another part of the high seas or the territorial sea of a foreign State.

As this provision relates to the right of innocent passage in the territorial sea, it is clear that the right does not comprise the freedom of overflight. On the other hand, unlike the right of innocent passage through the territorial sea in general, the exercise of the right through international straits shall not be suspended. To this extent, the right of innocent passage through international straits is more strengthened than the right of innocent passage through the territorial sea in general. In light of the *Corfu Channel* judgment, it seems that foreign warships also possess the right of non-suspendable innocent passage set out in Article 16(4).

[70] ICJ Reports 1949, p. 22; *Virginia Commentaries*, vol. II, p. 226.
[71] Emphasis original. ICJ Reports 1949, p. 28.

TABLE 3.1. TYPOLOGY OF INTERNATIONAL STRAITS IN THE LOSC

A. Straits where Part III is applied (straits as territorial sea)	B. Straits where Part III is not applied
A.1. Straits where transit passage is applied. High seas/EEZ ↔ High seas/EEZ (Art. 37)	B.1. High seas routes or routes through EEZ through straits used for international navigation (Art. 36)
A.2. Straits where innocent passage is applied. (a) High seas/EEZ↔High seas/EEZ with islands (Arts. 38(1), 45(1)(a)) (b) High seas/EEZ↔Territorial sea (Art. 45(1)(b))	B.2. Straits in which passage is regulated in whole or in part by long-standing international conventions (Art. 35(c)) B.3. Straits within archipelagic waters

As noted earlier, the *Corfu Channel* judgment referred only to straits 'between two parts of the high seas'. By referring to straits 'between one part of the high seas and another part of the high seas or the territorial sea of a foreign State', however, Article 16(4) extended the scope of straits. Thus it may be said that Article 16(4) is a result of the development of customary law, not simple codification of the law.[72]

4.2 Typology of international straits under the LOSC

According to a survey, there are 52 international straits less than 6 nautical miles in width, 153 international straits between 6 and 24 nautical miles in width, and 60 international straits more than 24 nautical miles in width.[73] By establishing the twelve-mile territorial sea, many straits which include a strip of high seas fall within the territorial sea of the coastal States. The 'territorialisation' of international straits would compromise the freedom of overflight of (military) aircraft and navigation of foreign warships, including submerged submarines. Thus maritime States urged the introduction of a new regime relating to the right of 'transit passage', which was finally embodied in Part III of the LOSC. It is important to note that the agreement on the twelve-mile territorial sea was closely linked to ensuring the freedom of navigation and overflight through international straits. The Convention divides international straits into two main rubrics according to the applicability of Part III, namely, straits to which Part III applies and straits outside the scope of Part III.

4.3 International straits under Part III of the LOSC

First, we shall examine straits where Part III applies. In this regard, it must be noted that Part III does not affect any areas of internal waters within a strait, except where the establishment of a straight baseline in accordance with the method set forth in Article 7 has the effect of enclosing as internal waters areas which had not previously

[72] Churchill and Lowe, *The Law of the Sea*, p. 104.

[73] A. R. Thomas and J. C. Duncan (eds.), *Annotated Supplement to the Commander's Handbook on the Law of Naval Operations*, (1999) 73 *International Legal Studies (Naval War College)*, pp. 207–208, Table A2-5.

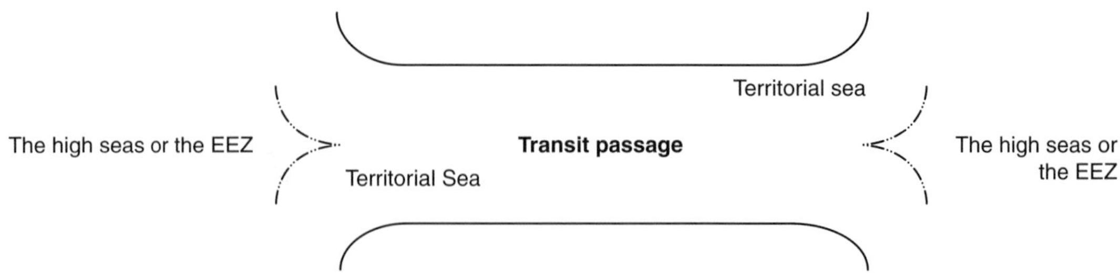

Figure 3.1. Transit passage under Article 37

been considered as such (Article 35(a)). It would seem to follow that basically Part III applies to international straits as the territorial sea. The straits under Part III of the LOSC contain two types of straits.

The first type concerns straits to which the regime of transit passage applies (type A-1, see Figure 3.1). In this regard, Article 37 provides that:

> This section applies to straits which are used for international navigation between one part of the high seas or an exclusive economic zone and another part of the high seas or an exclusive economic zone.

This provision contains two criteria for identifying international straits under Part III.

The first is the geographical criterion. Such straits are those connecting 'one part of the high seas or an exclusive economic zone and another part of the high seas or an exclusive economic zone'. The second is the functional criterion, namely 'straits used for international navigation'. Concerning the relationship between the two criteria, the ICJ, in the *Corfu Channel* case, seemed to consider that the geographical criterion provided the primary criterion. In the words of the Court,

> It may be asked whether the test is to be found in the volume of traffic passing through the Strait or in its greater or lesser importance for international navigation. But in the opinion of the Court the decisive criterion is rather its geographical situation as connecting two parts of the high seas and the fact of this *being used* for international navigation.[74]

The functional criterion raises an issue as to how it is possible to identify 'straits used for international navigation'. In this regard, it is argued that a strait must actually be being used for international navigation as a useful route for international maritime traffic in order to meet the functional criterion. Mere potential utility would be insufficient.[75]

[74] Emphasis added. ICJ Reports 1949, p. 28. See also, B. B. Jia, *The Regime of Straits in International Law* (Oxford, Clarendon Press, 1998), p. 39; H. Camios, 'The Legal Regime of Straits in the 1982 United Nations Convention on the Law of the Sea' (1987) 205 *RCADI* pp. 127–129.

[75] O'Connell, *The International Law of the Sea*, vol. 1, p. 314; T. Treves, 'Navigation', in Dupuy and Vignes, *A Handbook*, p. 951; S. N. Nandan and D. H. Anderson, 'Straits Used for International

As will be seen, transit passage applies to the strait between one part of the high seas or an EEZ and another part of the high seas or an EEZ in accordance with Article 38(1). Examples of international straits to which the regime of transit passage applies may be provided by the Dover Strait.[76] In some cases, a question arises whether or not a strait can be considered as a 'transit passage' strait. One might take the Canadian Northwest Passage through Canada's Arctic archipelago as an example. This passage is a transcontinental maritime route connecting the Atlantic and the Pacific. Recently, growing attention has been paid to the Northwest Passage because the presumed decline in sea ice in the Arctic Ocean may open a navigational route through the Northwest Passage in the future. In 1985, Canada drew straight baselines around its Arctic archipelago and, consequently, the Northwest Passage fell within Canada's internal waters. Canada thus rejected 'any suggestion that the Northwest Passage is such an international strait'.[77] However, the United States has taken the position that the Passage is a strait used for international navigation subject to the transit passage regime.[78] The disagreement was circumscribed by the 1988 Agreement on Arctic Cooperation between Canada and the United States. In this Agreement, the United States and Canada agreed to 'undertake to facilitate navigation by their icebreakers in their respective Arctic waters and to develop cooperative procedures for this purpose'.[79] A similar question arises with regard to the legal status of the Northeast Passage, north of Russia.[80]

In addition to this, some mention should be made of the Straits of Malacca and Singapore. Traffic transiting the Straits of Malacca and Singapore is heavy because they form one of the world's major choke points for international trade and commerce. The Joint Statement of the Governments of Indonesia, Malaysia and Singapore of 16 November 1971 stated that 'the Straits of Malacca and Singapore are not international straits while fully recognising their use for international shipping in accordance with the principle of innocent passage'.[81] Later, however, these three States became parties to the LOSC. As a consequence, one can say that transit passage presently applies to the Straits of Malacca and Singapore in accordance with relevant provisions of the Convention.[82]

Navigation: A Commentary on Part III of the United Nations Convention on the Law of the Sea 1982' (1989) 60 *BYIL* p. 168. See also Jia, *The Regime of Straits*, pp. 49–52.

76 The United Kingdom and France explicitly declared that unimpeded transit passage applies to the Dover Strait. Joint Declaration on Transit Passage in Straits of Dover, 2 November 1988.

77 Canadian Reply to the US Government, (1970) 9 *ILM* p. 612.

78 National Security Presidential Directive and Homeland Security Presidential Directive, NSPD-66/HSPD-25, 9 January 2009. This document is available at: www.dhs.gov/xabout/laws/gc_1267821646976.shtm#1.

79 Article 3. For the text of the Agreement, see (1989) 28 *ILM* pp. 142–143.

80 Roach and Smith, *United States Responses*, pp. 328 *et seq.*

81 Brown, *The International Law of the Sea*, vol. 2, p. 89.

82 It appears that this view can also be supported by Article 311(2) of the LOSC. According to Mahmoudi, no conflict of views has been reported with regard to transit passage through the Straits of Malacca and Singapore in recent years. S. Mahmoudi, 'Transit Passage', in *Max Planck Encyclopedia*, p. 6, para. 29. See also José A. de Yturriaga, *Straits Used for International Navigation: A Spanish Perspective* (Dordrecht, Nijhoff, 1991), p. 318.

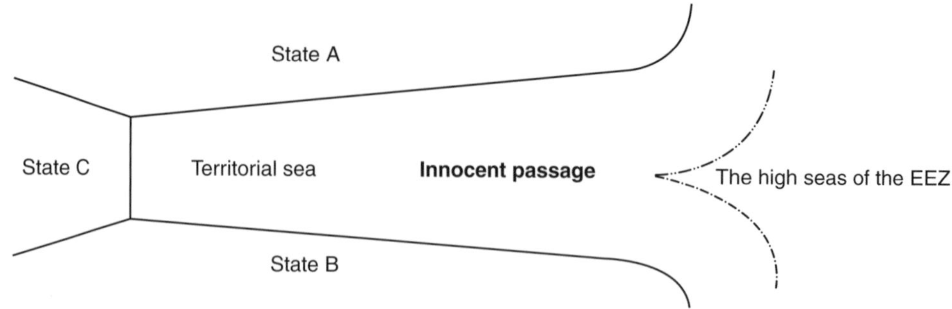

Figure 3.2. Innocent passage under Article 45(1)(b)

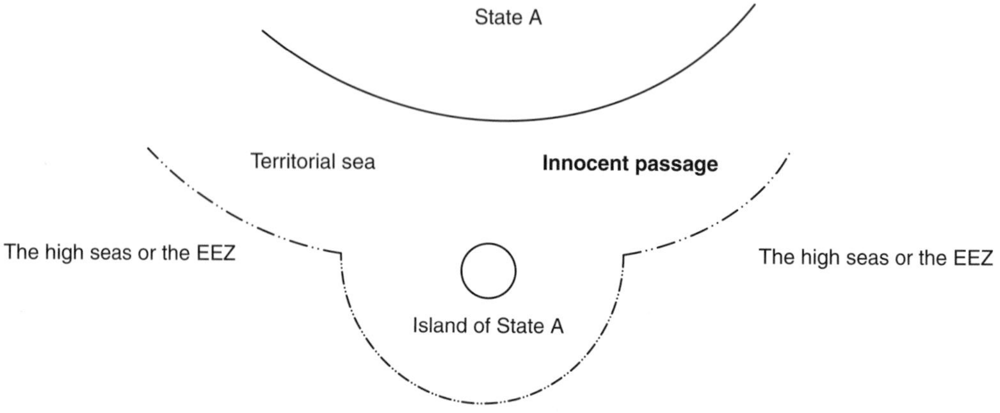

Figure 3.3. Innocent passage under Articles 38(1), 45(1)(a)

A second type relates to straits to which the right of innocent passage applies (type A-2, see Figures 3.2 and 3.3). Such straits include:

- straits which are excluded from the application of the regime of transit passage under Article 38(1) of the LOSC, and
- straits between a part of the high seas or an EEZ and the territorial sea of a foreign State.

'Straits which are excluded from Article 38(1)' are straits formed by an island of a State bordering the strait and its mainland, and there exists seaward of the island a route through the high seas or through an EEZ of similar convenience with respect to navigational and hydrographical characteristics. A good example is the Messina Strait. An example of 'straits between a part of the high seas or an EEZ and the territorial sea of a foreign State' may be provided by the Tiran Strait and the Gulf of Aquaba.

4.4 International straits outside the scope of Part III of the LOSC

The second rubric concerns straits to which Part III of the LOSC does not apply. Three types of straits are included in the rubric.

First, under Article 36 of the LOSC, Part III does not apply to straits used for international navigation which contain a route through the high seas or through an EEZ of similar convenience with respect to navigational and hydrographical characteristics (type B-1).[83] Article 36 appears to imply that if a route through the high seas or through an EEZ in the international strait is not convenient with respect to navigational and hydrographic characteristics, Part III will apply to the territorial sea within the strait. In relation to this, it is interesting to note that Japan has limited its territorial sea claim in five international straits, namely the Soya Strait, the Tsugaru Strait, the Tsushima Eastern Channel, the Tsushima Western Channel and the Osumi Strait, creating a corridor of the EEZ in the middle of these straits. As a result, these five straits pertain to a strait 'which contains a route through an EEZ of similar convenience' under Article 36 of the LOSC.[84]

Second, Part III does not apply to straits in which passage is regulated in whole or in part by long-standing international conventions in force specifically relating to such straits pursuant to Article 35(c) (type B-2). While the LOSC does not specify the straits to which Article 35(c) applies, examples may be briefly summarised as follows:

(i) *The Turkish Straits*: these straits include the Dardanelles, the Sea of Marmara, and the Bosphorus, which connect the Black Sea and the Aegean Sea. The Turkish Straits are governed by the 1936 Convention Regarding the Régime of the Straits (Montreux Convention).[85] The Convention contains a set of special rules for, *inter alia*, the free passage of warships, merchant vessels and authorisation for civil aviation.

(ii) *The Danish Belts and the Sound*: these straits comprise the Little Belt between Jutland and the island of Funen, the Great Belt between Funen and the island of Zealand, and the Öresund Sound between Zealand and Sweden. These straits are regulated by the Treaty for the Redemption of the Sound Dues between Denmark and European States of 14 March 1857 (the Treaty of Copenhagen).[86] Article I of the Convention provides for a right of passage of foreign ships through the Danish straits, by stating that: 'No vessel shall henceforth, under any pretext whatsoever, be subject in its passage of the Sound or the Belts to any detention or hindrance'.[87] The rights provided in the Copenhagen Treaty were accorded to ships of all States, including ships from third States.[88]

(iii) *The Strait of Magellan*: the Strait between Argentina and Chile connects the Pacific and the Atlantic Oceans. Article 5 of the 1881 Treaty between Argentina and Chile confirmed the neutralisation of the Strait of Magellan and free navigation to the

[83] *Ibid.* [84] Treves, 'Codification du droit international', pp. 127–128.

[85] (1937) 31 *AJIL Supplement* pp. 1–17. [86] 116 *CTS* p. 357.

[87] Original in French. Translation by the government of Denmark in the *Great Belt* case, *Counter-Memorial Submitted by Denmark*, vol. 1, May 1992, p. 227, para. 675.

[88] *Ibid.*, p. 228, para. 683. According to Bangert, while the Copenhagen Treaty in principle did not apply to warships, Danish State practice has extended the right of free passage to such ships. K. Bangert, 'Denmark and the Law of the Sea', in T. Treves (ed.), *The Law of the Sea: The European Union and its Member States* (The Hague, Nijhoff, 1997), p. 106. See also by the same writer, 'Belts and Sund', in *Max Planck Encyclopedia*, pp. 1–6.

flags of all nations.[89] This was confirmed by Article 10 of the 1984 Treaty of Peace and Friendship between Argentina and Chile.[90]

(iv) *The Strait of Gibraltar*: this strait joints the Mediterranean Sea and the Atlantic Ocean. The free passage of the Strait of Gibraltar was declared in the 1904 Anglo-French Declaration (Article 7),[91] and was confirmed by Article 6 of the 1912 Treaty between France and Spain regarding Morocco.[92]

(v) *The Åland Strait*: upon signing the LOSC, Finland and Sweden declared that Article 35(c) of the Convention is applicable to the strait between Finland (the Åland Islands) and Sweden. The applicable treaties are the 1921 Convention on the Non-Fortification and Neutrality of the Åland Islands[93] and the 1940 Agreement between Finland and the Soviet Union concerning the Åland Islands, which obliged Finland to demilitarise the Åland Islands and not to fortify them.[94]

The third category of straits to which Part III does not apply involves international straits within archipelagic waters (type B-3). Navigation in the archipelagic waters will be examined in section 5 of this chapter.

4.5 The right of transit passage

Article 38(2) defines transit passage as:

> the exercise in accordance with this Part [III] of the freedom of navigation and overflight solely for the purpose of continuous and expeditious transit of the strait between one part of the high seas or an exclusive economic zone and another part of the high seas or an exclusive economic zone.

This provision continues that: 'the requirement of continuous and expeditious transit does not preclude passage through the strait for the purpose of entering, leaving or returning from a State bordering the strait, subject to the conditions of entry to that State'. Thus the transit passage includes lateral and vertical passage. The right of transit passage in international straits differs from the right of innocent passage in the territorial sea in four respects.

First, Article 38(1) makes it clear that all ships and aircraft enjoy the right of transit passage. It is clear, therefore that warships enjoy the right of transit passage.

Second, the right of transit passage includes overflight by all aircraft, including military aircraft.

Third, concerning submarines, the LOSC provides no explicit obligation to navigate on the surface and to show their flag. Article 39(1)(c) provides that ships and aircraft, while exercising the right of transit passage, shall 'refrain from any activities other

89 The Treaty Between Argentine Republic and Chile, Establishing the Neutrality of Straits of Magellan, (1909) 3 *AJIL Supplement* pp. 121–122.

90 (1985) 24 *ILM* pp. 11–16.

91 Declaration between the United Kingdom and France Respecting Egypt and Morocco, 8 April 1904, (1907) 1 *AJIL Supplement* pp. 6–9.

92 (1913) 7 *AJIL Supplement* pp. 81–93.

93 (1923) 17 *AJIL Supplement* pp. 1–6.

94 144 *BSP* p. 395.

than those incident to their normal modes of continuous and expeditious transit unless rendered necessary by *force majeure* or by distress'. Arguably, the normal mode for submarines to transit is submerged navigation.[95] Furthermore, Article 38(2) stipulates that transit passage means the exercise 'in accordance with this Part [III]' of the freedom of navigation and overflight. It would follow that the transit passage is to be subject only to provisions in Part III. There is no cross-reference to the specific provision on innocent passage which requires on-surface navigation. It appears that this interpretation is also consistent with the *travaux préparatoires* for UNCLOS III.[96] In conclusion, there is room for the view that submarines and other underwater vehicles in transit passage are not required to navigate on the surface and to show their flag.

Fourth, unlike the right of innocent passage through the territorial sea in general, there shall be no suspension of transit passage by virtue of Article 44.

On the other hand, ships and aircraft are required to comply with three types of duties during transit passage: common duties for ships and aircraft in transit passage, duties of ships in transit passage, and duties of aircraft in transit passage.

First, ships and aircraft are commonly obliged to comply with four duties enunciated in Article 39(1) of the LOSC:

(a) proceed without delay through or over the strait;
(b) refrain from any threat or use of force against the sovereignty, territorial integrity or political independence of States bordering the strait, or in any other manner in violation of the principles of international law embodied in the Charter of the United Nations;
(c) refrain from any activities other than those incident to their normal modes of continuous and expeditious transit unless rendered necessary by *force majeure* or by distress;
(d) comply with other relevant provisions of this Part.

In essence, this provision has parallels in Article 19 of the LOSC.

Second, ships in transit passage are under duties to:

(i) comply with generally accepted international regulations, procedures, and practice for safety at sea, including the International Regulations for Preventing Collisions at Sea (Article 39(2)(a));[97]
(ii) comply with generally accepted international regulations, procedures and practices for the prevention, reduction and control of pollution from ships (Article 39(2)(b));[98]
(iii) refrain from carrying out any research or survey activities without the prior authorisation of the States bordering straits (Article 40);
(iv) respect applicable sea lanes and traffic separation schemes (Article 41 (7));

95 *Virginia Commentaries*, vol. 2, p. 342.
96 Caminos, 'The Legal Regime of Straits', pp. 155–158.
97 The 1974 International Convention for the Safety of Life at Sea (SOLAS) and 1988 Protocol relating thereto would fall within 'generally accepted international regulations'.
98 The 1973 International Convention for the Prevention of Pollution from Ships and its 1978 Protocol (MALPOL 73/78) would be included in international regulations referred to in this provision.

(v) comply with law and regulations adopted by States bordering a strait under Article 42(1) of the LOSC (Article 42(4)).[99]

Third, Article 39(3)(a) and (b) provides that aircraft in transit passage shall:

(a) observe the Rules of the Air established by the International Civil Aviation Organization as they apply to civil aircraft; state aircraft will normally comply with such safety measures and will at all times operate with due regard for the safety of navigation;
(b) at all times monitor the radio frequency assigned by the competent internationally designated air traffic control authority or the appropriate international distress radio frequency.

Concerning Article 39(3)(a), a question arises whether or not States bordering straits have a right to issue and apply their own air regulations in the airspace of the straits used for international navigation. Upon signature and ratification of the LOSC, the Spanish government claimed such a right. However, the United States objected to the Spanish interpretation.[100] Whilst opinions of writers are divided,[101] the Secretariat of ICAO took the view that the Rules of the Air as adopted by the Council of ICAO would have mandatory application over the straits and the States bordering the strait cannot file an alteration to Rules of the Air under Article 38 of the Chicago Convention with respect to the airspace over the straits.[102]

4.6 Rights and obligations of coastal States bordering straits

The coastal State has a right to adopt laws and regulations relating to transit passage through straits. Under Article 42(1), those laws and regulations involve:

(a) the safety of navigation and the regulation of maritime traffic, as provided in Article 41,
(b) the prevention, reduction and control of pollution, by giving effect to applicable international regulations regarding the discharge of oil, oily wastes and other noxious substances in the strait,
(c) with respect to fishing vessels, the prevention of fishing, including the stowage of fishing gear, and
(d) the loading or unloading of any commodity, currency or person in contravention of the customs, fiscal, immigration or sanitary laws and regulations of States bordering straits.

States bordering straits are required to give due publicity to all such laws and regulations in accordance with Article 41(3). Further, the coastal State bordering straits may

[99] See also Article 42(5).
[100] Roach and Smith, *United States Responses*, pp. 301–309.
[101] Yturriaga is supportive of the Spanish claim, but Caminos considers that the Spanish claim is inappropriate. Yturriaga, *Straits Used for International Navigation*, pp. 227–232; Caminos, 'The Legal Regime of Straits', p. 229.
[102] *Virginia Commentaries*, vol. 2, pp. 344–345. It must be noted that the Rules of the Air do not automatically apply to State aircraft, including military aircraft in the airspace over the straits.

designate sea lanes and prescribe traffic separation schemes for navigation in straits where necessary to promote the safe passage of ships pursuant to Article 41(1).

The legislative jurisdiction of the coastal State is qualified by paragraph 2 of Article 42 in two respects. The first limitation is that the laws and regulations of the coastal State bordering international straits 'shall not discriminate in form or in fact among foreign ships'.[103] The second limitation is that the application of the laws and regulations shall not 'have the practical effect of denying, hampering or impairing the right of transit passage'. In relation to this, there is the question whether, in the case of the violation of the municipal law of the State bordering straits, that State could terminate the right of transit passage unilaterally. The language of Article 42(2) seems to suggest that States bordering straits are not allowed to directly deny the right of transit passage merely on grounds of breach of their municipal law.[104] In the case of a violation of the laws and regulations referred to in Article 42(1)(a) and (b), however, Article 233 of the LOSC explicitly allows the State bordering a strait to exercise its enforcement jurisdiction.

Coastal States bordering straits shall undertake the following duties in accordance with Article 44:

(i) not to hamper transit passage,
(ii) to give appropriate publicity to any danger to navigation or overflight within or over the strait of which they have knowledge, and
(iii) not to suspend transit passage.

Moreover, Article 43 of the LOSC requires user States and States bordering a strait to cooperate '(a) in the establishment and maintenance in a strait of necessary navigational and safety aids or other improvements in aid of international navigation; and (b) for the prevention, reduction and control of pollution from ships'. By way of example, Japan has been promoting international cooperation in the Straits of Malacca and Singapore through the Malacca Strait Council in such fields as hydrographic survey, maintenance of aids to navigation, making nautical charts, transfer of technology and clearance of sunken ships.[105] From 2005, a series of Meetings on the Straits of Malacca and Singapore have been convened. The Singapore Meeting of 2007 agreed, *inter alia*, that user States, shipping industry and other stakeholders should seek to participate in the work of the cooperation mechanisms on a voluntary basis, and that the littoral States should continue their efforts towards enhancing maritime security in the Straits.[106]

103 This provision has parallels in Articles 24(1)(b), 25(3), 52(2) and 227 of the LOSC. *Virginia Commentaries*, vol. 2, p. 376.

104 *Ibid.*, p. 377; J. N. Moore, 'The Regime of Straits and the Third United Nations Conference on the Law of the Sea' (1980) 74 *AJIL* p. 103. However, it is not suggested that the State bordering straits cannot exercise its enforcement jurisdiction if the ship should enter that State's ports.

105 H. Terashima, 'Transit Passage and Users' Contributions to the Safety of the Straits of Malacca and Singapore', in M. H. Nordquist, T. T. B. Koh and J. N. Moore, *Freedom of Seas, Passage Rights and the 1982 Law of the Sea Convention* (Leiden and Boston, Nijhoff, 2009), pp. 357–368.

106 The Singapore Statement on Enhancement of Safety, Security and Environmental Protection in the Straits of Malacca and Singapore, 6 September 2007, available at: www.mpa.gov.sg/sites/pdf/spore_statement.pdf.

Finally, environmental protection of international straits should be mentioned. As international straits are often narrow, the risk of marine casualties is higher than in other marine spaces. Thus the health of waterways is a matter of serious concern for States bordering international straits. In this regard, the question arises as to whether, under Part III of the LOSC, the coastal State has a right to introduce a compulsory pilotage system in an international strait.

A case in point is the compulsory pilotage system adopted by Australia.[107] In 2006, Australia established a compulsory pilotage system for certain vessels in the Torres Strait and Great North East Channel in order to protect sensitive marine habitats. The Torres Strait is a strait used for international navigation to which the regime of transit passage applies. The depths of the Torres Strait are shallow and navigation in that strait is highly difficult. As the Torres Strait contains a highly sensitive marine habitat, it became a Particularly Sensitive Sea Area (PSSA) in 2005.

According to Marine Notice 8/2006, the compulsory pilotage system applies to merchant ships 70 metres in length and over or oil tankers, chemical tankers and liquefied gas carriers, irrespective of size, when navigating the Torres Strait and the Great North East Channel. According to Marine Notice 16/2006, the Australian authorities will not suspend or deny transit passage and will not stop, arrest, or board ships that do not take on a pilot while transiting the Strait. However, the owner, master, and/or operator of the ship may be prosecuted on the next entry into an Australian port, for both ships on voyages to Australian ports and ships transiting the Torres Strait en route to other destinations. Australia's compulsory pilotage system was protested by the United States and Singapore. The controversy relating to the compulsory pilotage system in the Torres Strait seems to signal a growing tension between the navigational interest of the user States and the environmental interest of States bordering an international strait. In this respect, Article 43 of the LOSC to merits particular attention with a view to reconciling such contrasting interests through international cooperation.[108]

4.7 Customary law character of the right of transit passage

Some States, notably the United States and Thailand, are of the view that the right of transit passage is a codification of customary law.[109] However, it must be recalled that the regime of transit passage of the LOSC is a result of compromise and significantly beyond the rules of the 1958 TSC and traditional customary law in this matter.[110] In this respect, the closing statement by the President of UNCLOS III bears quoting:

[107] Generally on this issue, see R. C. Beckman, 'PSSAs and Transit Passage: Australia's Pilotage System in the Torres Strait Challenges the IMO and UNCLOS' (2007) 38 *ODIL* pp. 325–357.

[108] Scovazzi, 'The Evolution of International Law of the Sea', p. 186.

[109] Roach and Smith, *United States Responses*, p. 312; Statement of the Ministry of Foreign Affairs of Thailand (1993) 23 *Law of the Sea Bulletin* p. 108.

[110] Caflisch, 'La convention des Nations Unies', p. 52; O. Schachter, *International Law in Theory and Practice* (Dordrecht, Nijhoff, 1991) pp. 285–286; Brownlie, *Principles*, p. 271.

> The argument that, except for Part XI, the Convention [LOSC] codifies customary law or reflects existing international practice is factually incorrect and legally insupportable. The regime of transit passage through straits used for international navigation and the regime of archipelagic sea lanes passage are only two examples of the many new concepts in the Convention.[111]

At present, there appears to be little evidence to prove that 'extensive and virtually uniform' State practice and *opinio juris* exist with regard to the right of transit passage. One can say, therefore, that the right of transit passage is a new regime established by the LOSC, and has yet to become a part of customary international law.[112]

4.8 Non-suspendable innocent passage

As noted, the right of innocent passage applies to straits used for international navigation excluded from the application of Article 38(1); or between a part of the high seas or an EEZ and the territorial sea of a foreign State (Article 45(1)). Unlike the right of innocent passage through the territorial sea, there shall be no suspension of innocent passage through international straits by virtue of Article 45(2). As with innocent passage through the territorial sea, aircraft do not enjoy the freedom of overflight. Further, submarines and other underwater vehicles are required to navigate on the surface and to show their flag in the exercise of the right of non-suspendable innocent passage.

4.9 Legality of creation of bridges in international straits

A debatable issue is the legality of the creation of bridges in international straits. This question was raised in the 1991 *Great Belt* case between Finland and Denmark before the ICJ.[113] The facts of this case can be summarised as follows: on 10 June 1987, the Danish Parliament passed a law on the construction of a fixed link across the Great Belt Strait and, in 1989, the Danish authorities adopted the final version of the form of the link. The Danish project involved the construction over the West Channel of the Great Belt of a low-level bridge for road and rail traffic, and over the East Channel of a high-level suspension bridge for road traffic, with clearance for passage of 65 metres above mean sea level. As a result, the East Channel Bridge would permanently close the Baltic Sea for deep draught vessels over 65 metres in height.

Since the early 1970s, Finland, or strictly speaking, more than ten mobile offshore drilling units (MODUs, i.e. drill ships and drill rigs) built in Finland had used the Great Belt. Some of the Finnish MODUs reached a height of close to 150 metres. Once the fixed link was created across the Great Belt, these MODUs would no longer be able to pass through the Great Belt, damaging Finnish commercial activity. Thus a dispute arose between Finland and Denmark with regard to the Danish project. On 17 May 1991,

111 A/CONF.62/SR.193, 193rd Plenary Meeting, *Closing Statement by the President*, 10 December 1982, pp. 135–136, para. 48.
112 This view seems to be the majority opinion. Jia, *The Regime of Straits*, pp. 207–208.
113 *Case Concerning Passage Through the Great Belt* (Provisional Measures), ICJ Reports 1991, p. 12.

the Finnish government filed an application instituting proceedings against Denmark before the ICJ. Further, on 23 May 1991, the Finnish government requested the Court to indicate provisional measures.

This dispute gave rise to several interesting questions in the law of the sea, such as the legal status of MODUs (e.g. whether drill rigs can be regarded as ships), the law applicable to the movement of MODUs, the right of coastal States to construct a fixed link in an international strait, the compatibility of the construction of a fixed bridge across the Great Belt with the right of free passage, the relevance of a comparison of interests on the basis of the equitable principles for the right of passage, the right of passage of reasonably foreseeable ships, and acquiescence, etc. In essence, these questions concern the balance between the navigational interest of third States and the interest of the coastal State bordering the strait.

In its Order of 29 July 1991, the Court refused to indicate provisional measures primarily because there was no urgency justifying the indication of these measures.[114] Later, on 3 September 1992, only one week before the oral hearings were to open before the Court, Denmark and Finland agreed to settle the dispute. Denmark agreed to pay a sum of 90 million Danish kroner (around 15 million US dollars), and Finland agreed to withdraw its application.[115] As a consequence, the Court did not have occasion to pronounce its view on this dispute, and the questions remain open.

5 ARCHIPELAGIC WATERS

5.1 General considerations

The key concept of archipelagic waters is that a group of islands in mid-ocean, i.e. 'mid-ocean archipelagos', should be considered as forming a unit; and that the waters enclosed by baselines joining the outermost points of the archipelago should be under territorial sovereignty. Whilst the question of a special archipelagic regime has been discussed on various occasions since the early twentieth century, neither the 1930 Hague Conference, nor UNCLOS I could resolve this question. The 1958 Geneva Conventions contain no provision with regard to mid-ocean archipelagos or archipelagic waters.

At UNCLOS III, the question of a special regime for archipelagos was taken up in the broader context of the new international economic order. A group of archipelagic States – Fiji, Indonesia, Mauritius and the Philippines – vigorously promoted the special regime for archipelagos with a view to safeguarding their interests in the oceans, on the basis of (i) political and security interests, (ii) historical factors, (iii) natural features, (iv) economic interests, (v) environmental protection, and (vi) reasonableness.[116] A legal

[114] ICJ Reports 1991, p. 20, para. 38.

[115] M. Koskenniemi, 'Case Concerning Passage Through the Great Belt' (1996) 27 *ODIL* pp. 274–279. The view of the disputing Parties differed with regard to the legal nature of the payment. While Finland considered it as 'compensation', Denmark claimed that that payment was made *ex gratia*. *Ibid.*, p. 279. See also by the same writer, 'Introductory Note' (1993) 32 *ILM* p. 103.

[116] H. W. Jayewardene, *The Regime of Islands in International Law* (Dordrecht, Nijhoff, 1990), pp. 106–110; Churchill and Lowe, *The Law of the Sea*, pp. 119–120.

regime for archipelagic States was gradually formulated, and was finally embodied in Part IV of the LOSC. It may be said that the legal regime for archipelagic waters is a result of the development of international law, not the codification of the law.[117]

5.2 Definition of an archipelago, archipelagic States and archipelagic waters

Article 46(a) of the LOSC defines an 'archipelagic State' as 'a State constituted wholly by one or more archipelagos and may include other islands'. It follows that States possessing territory in a continent, i.e. mainland States, are not archipelagic States. For example, Greece is not an archipelagic State under the LOSC. A key question is the meaning of the term 'archipelago'. Article 46(b) defines 'archipelago' as follows:

> 'Archipelago' means a group of islands, including parts of islands, interconnecting waters and other natural features which are so closely interrelated that such islands, waters and other natural features form an intrinsic geographical, economic and political entity, or which historically have been regarded as such.

The definition contains four criteria which must be present in order for an island group to constitute an archipelago: (i) the existence of a group of islands, (ii) the compactness or the adjacency of islands, (iii) the existence of an intrinsic geographical, economic and political entity, and (iv) historical practice. Yet these criteria may not be wholly unambiguous. For instance, there is no criterion with regard to the minimum number of islands. It appears that 'an economic and political entity' does not always coincide with 'a geographical entity'. The test of historicity may give rise to the question how it is possible to demonstrate evidence in this matter.[118]

Currently twenty-two States have formally claimed archipelagic status. Those States are: Antigua and Barbuda, Bahamas, Cape Verde, Comoros, Dominican Republic, Fiji, Grenada, Indonesia, Jamaica, Kiribati, Maldives, Marshall Islands, Mauritius, Papua New Guinea, Philippines, Saint Vincent and the Grenadines, São Tomé e Principe, Seychelles, Solomon Islands, Trinidad and Tobago, Tuvalu and Vanuatu. All these States are parties to the LOSC.[119]

'Archipelagic waters' mean the waters enclosed by the archipelagic baselines drawn in accordance with Article 47 regardless of their depth or distance from the coast (LOSC, Article 49(1)). The breadth of the territorial sea, the contiguous zone, the EEZ and the continental shelf is to be measured from archipelagic baselines (Article 48). Thus archipelagic waters must be distinguished from the territorial sea. Further, Article 50 stipulates that within its archipelagic waters, the archipelagic State may draw closing lines for the delimitation of internal waters in accordance with Articles

[117] *Closing Statement by the President*, 10 December 1982, pp. 135–136, para. 48; Caflisch, 'La convention des Nations Unies', p. 61.

[118] L. L. Herman, 'The Modern Concept of the Off-Lying Archipelago in International Law' (1985) 23 *Canadian Yearbook of International Law* pp. 181–185.

[119] UNDOALOS, Table of Claims to Maritime Jurisdiction as at 15 July 2011, available at: www.un.org/Depts/los/LEGISLATIONANDTREATIES/claims.htm.

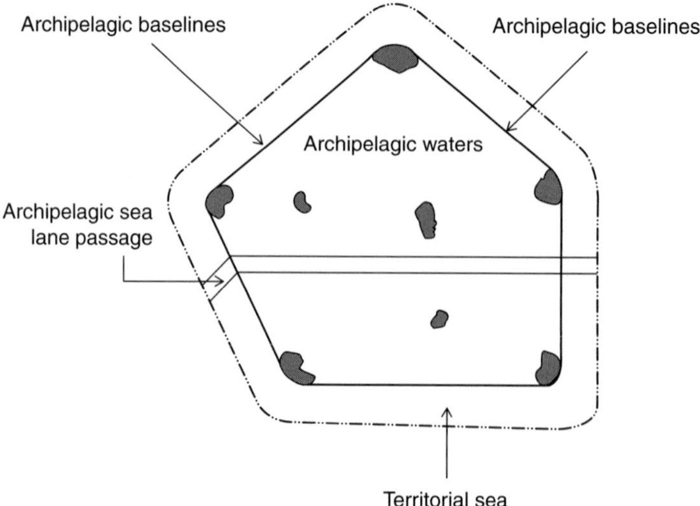

Figure 3.4. Archipelagic baselines

9, 10, and 11 (Article 50). The landward areas of these closing lines become internal waters of an archipelagic State. Hence, it must be stressed that archipelagic waters do not constitute internal waters. On ratifying the LOSC in 1984, however, the Philippines declared that the concept of archipelagic waters is similar to the concept of internal waters under the Constitution of the Philippines. Some States – Australia, Belarus, Bulgaria, Czechoslovakia, Ukraine, the USA and the USSR – protested the Philippine Declaration.[120] It appears that the declaration is at variance with the concept of archipelagic waters in the LOSC.[121]

5.3 Archipelagic baselines

The next issue that needs to be discussed concerns the manner of constructing archipelagic baselines. Article 47(1) of the LOSC provides as follows (see Figure 3.4):

> An archipelagic State may draw straight archipelagic baselines joining the outermost points of the outermost islands and drying reefs of the archipelago ...

[120] The Declaration of the Philippines is reproduced in UNDOALOS, *The Law of the Sea: Declarations and Statements with Respect to the United Nations Convention on the Law of the Sea and to the Agreement relating to the Implementation of Part XI of the United Nations Convention on the Law of the Sea of 10 December 1982* (New York, United Nations, 1997), p. 40. The objections against the Declaration were reproduced in *ibid.*, pp. 47–55. Concerning the objection by the USA, see Roach and Smith, *United States Responses*, pp. 216–222; Treves, 'Codification du droit international', pp. 142–143.

[121] On 26 October 1988, the Philippines replied to the objection made by Australia, saying that: 'The Philippine Government intends to harmonize its domestic legislation with the provisions of the Convention', (1994) 25 *Law of the Sea Bulletin* p. 49.

A key point is that the legal criteria of being an archipelago must be fulfilled in order to construct archipelagic baselines. In other words, a State which does not meet the legal definition of an archipelagic State is not entitled to draw archipelagic baselines.[122] The language of this provision also suggests that the establishment of archipelagic baselines is facultative. Article 47 sets out conditions for drawing these baselines in some detail.

(i) The archipelagic waters must include main islands, and the ratio of the area of the water to the area of the land, including atolls, is between 1 to 1 and 9 to 1 pursuant to Article 47(1). The lower ratio was designed to exclude those archipelagos which are dominated by one or two large islands or islands that are connected only by comparatively small sea areas. This requirement will not allow, for instance, Australia, Cuba, Iceland, Madagascar, New Zealand and the United Kingdom to draw archipelagic baselines. The upper ratio was intended to exclude those archipelagos which are widely dispersed, such as Tuvalu and Kiribati.[123]

(ii) The length of such baselines shall not exceed 100 nautical miles. But up to 3 per cent of the total number of baselines enclosing any archipelago may exceed that length, up to a maximum length of 125 nautical miles pursuant to Article 47(2). It is notable that unlike straight baselines, the maximum length of the archipelagic baselines is fixed. Considering that there is no restriction on the number of baseline segments that can be used in order to draw archipelagic baselines, however, it appears possible for the archipelagic State to adjust the number of segments in order to secure the necessary number of very long baselines.[124]

(iii) The drawing of such baselines shall not depart to any appreciable extent from the general configuration of the archipelago (Article 47(3)). This elusive criterion seeks to ensure a linkage between the unit or entity concept and the technique for drawing archipelagic baselines.

(iv) Archipelagic baselines shall not be drawn to and from low-tide elevations, unless lighthouses or similar installations which are permanently above sea level have been built on them or where a low-tide elevation is situated wholly or partly at a distance not exceeding the breadth of the territorial sea from the nearest island (Article 47(4)). On the other hand, as quoted earlier, Article 47(1) provides that 'an archipelagic State may draw straight archipelagic baselines joining the outermost points of the outermost island and drying reefs'. At UNCLOS III, it was understood that 'drying reefs' were above water at low tide but submerged at high tide. It would follow that 'drying reefs' are low-tide elevations.[125] If this is the case, paragraph 1 of Article 47 may seem to contradict paragraph 4 of the same provision which prohibits drawing archipelagic baselines to and from low-tide elevations. In response to this question, a possible interpretation may be to apply the condition set up in Article 47(4), 'unless lighthouses or

[122] Herman, 'The Modern Concept', p. 186.

[123] V. Prescott and C. Schofield, *The Maritime Political Boundaries of the World*, 2nd edn (Leiden, Nijhoff, 2005), p. 176.

[124] *Ibid*., p. 174; UNDOALOS, *Baselines*, p. 37.

[125] *Virginia Commentaries*, vol. 2, p. 430.

similar installations', to Article 47(1). According to this interpretation, an archipelagic State may draw straight archipelagic baselines joining the outermost points of the outermost drying reefs, provided that 'lighthouses or similar installations which are permanently above sea level have been built on them or where drying reefs are situated wholly or partly at a distance not exceeding the breadth of the territorial sea from the nearest island'.[126]

(v) The system of archipelagic baselines shall not be applied by an archipelagic State in such a manner as to cut off from the high seas or the EEZ the territorial sea of another State under Article 47(5).

(vi) Archipelagic baselines shall be shown on charts of a scale or scales adequate for ascertaining their position. Alternatively, lists of geographical coordinates of points, specifying the geodetic datum, may be substituted (Article 47(8)). Furthermore, the archipelagic State shall give due publicity to such charts or list of geographical coordinates and shall deposit a copy of each such chart or list with the UN Secretary-General in accordance with Article 47(9).

5.4 Jurisdiction of archipelagic States over archipelagic waters

As clearly stated in Article 49(1) and (2) of the LOSC, archipelagic waters are under the territorial sovereignty of the archipelagic State. On the other hand, Article 49(3) provides that this sovereignty is exercised subject to Part IV of the LOSC. Under Part IV of the LOSC, the territorial sovereignty of the archipelagic State is qualified by rights of third States in four respects.

First, the archipelagic State is required to respect the traditional fishing rights of third States pursuant to Article 51(1) of the LOSC. This provision was intended to meet the concerns of Malaysia with respect to prospective Indonesian archipelagic waters.[127] On 25 July 1982, Indonesia and Malaysia concluded a bilateral treaty on this matter.[128] Under Article 2(2) of this treaty, in return for Malaysia's recognition of Indonesia's archipelagic regime, Indonesia accepted the existing rights of Malaysia relating to: (i) the rights of access and communication of Malaysia's ships and aircraft, (ii) the traditional fishing right of Malaysian traditional fishermen in the designated area, (iii) the legitimate interest relating to submarine cables and pipelines, (iv) the legitimate interest in maintaining law and order through cooperation, (v) the legitimate interest to undertake search and rescue operations, and (vi) the legitimate interest to cooperate in marine scientific research.

Second, under Article 51(2), the archipelagic State is under the obligation to respect existing submarine cables. This provision applies only to existing cables, and no

[126] *Ibid.*, p. 431. The United Kingdom and the USA would seem to support this interpretation. See Text of a Joint Demarche Undertaken by the United Kingdom of Great Britain and Northern Ireland and the United States of America in relation to the Law of the Dominican Republic Number 66-07 of 22 May 2007, done on 18 October 2007.

[127] *Virginia Commentaries*, vol. 2, p. 452.

[128] For the text of the treaty, see UNDOALOS, *The Law of the Sea: Practice of Archipelagic States* (New York, United Nations, 1992), pp. 144–155.

mention is made of pipelines. It would seem to follow that the laying of new cables and pipelines depends on the consent of archipelagic States.

Third, Article 47(6) provides that:

> If a part of the archipelagic waters of an archipelagic State lies between two parts of an immediately adjacent neighbouring State, existing rights and all other legitimate interests which the latter State has traditionally exercised in such waters and all rights stipulated by agreement between those States shall continue and be respected.

This situation can be seen between the Malaysian mainland and Sarawak by the extension of Indonesia's archipelagic waters associated with the Kepulauan Anambas and Kepulauan Bunguran.[129]

Fourth, by establishing archipelagic waters, some important navigation channels, such as the Sunda and Lombok Straits, fall under the territorial sovereignty of the archipelagic State. If passage through archipelagic waters is not accepted, sea communication will be considerably disturbed. Hence there is a strong need to guarantee the freedom of navigation of foreign vessels in archipelagic waters. Part IV of the LOSC ensures the freedom of navigation through archipelagic waters by providing the right of innocent passage and that of archipelagic sea lanes passage. As will be seen, the territorial sovereignty of an archipelagic State is thus qualified by the rights of navigation of foreign ships in archipelagic waters.

5.5 The right of innocent passage through archipelagic waters

The right of innocent passage is applicable to archipelagic waters. In this regard, Article 52(1) of the LOSC provides as follows:

> Subject to article 53 [right of archipelagic sea lanes passage] and without prejudice to article 50 [delimitation of internal waters], ships of all States enjoy the right of innocent passage through archipelagic waters, in accordance with Part II, section 3 [the right of innocent passage in the territorial sea].

The right of innocent passage in archipelagic waters is essentially parallel to the right of innocent passage in the territorial sea. Accordingly, under Article 52(2), the archipelagic State may suspend temporarily the right of innocent passage in archipelagic waters if such suspension is essential for the protection of its security. Part IV of the LOSC holds no provision concerning submarines and other underwater vehicles. Like the right of innocent passage in the territorial sea, it seems that submarines and other underwater vehicles will be required to navigate on the surface and to show their flag in archipelagic waters. The right of innocent passage in archipelagic waters contains no freedom of overflight.

[129] UNDOALOS, *Baselines*, pp. 37–38.

5.6 The right of archipelagic sea lanes passage

In addition to the right of innocent passage, all ships and aircraft can enjoy the more extensive right of archipelagic sea lanes passage through archipelagic waters. Article 53(3) of the LOSC defines the right of archipelagic sea lanes passage as follows:

> Archipelagic sea lanes passage means the exercise in accordance with this Convention of the rights of navigation and overflight in the normal mode solely for the purpose of continuous, expeditious and unobstructed transit between one part of the high seas or an exclusive economic zone and another part of the high seas or an exclusive economic zone.

The principal elements of the right of archipelagic sea lanes passage can be summarised as follows.

(i) As with the right of transit passage, the right of archipelagic passage applies between one part of the high seas or an EEZ and another part of the high seas or an EEZ.

(ii) All ships and aircraft enjoy the right of archipelagic sea lanes passage in such sea lanes and air routes under Article 53(2). The right of archipelagic sea lanes passage contains the rights of overflight by aircraft. In common with the right of transit passage, foreign warships and military aircraft have the right of archipelagic sea lanes passage.

(iii) Like the right of transit passage, archipelagic sea lanes passage must be the exercise of the rights of navigation and overflight solely for the purpose of continuous, expeditious and unobstructed transit.

On the other hand, as Articles 39, 40, 42 and 44 of the LOSC apply *mutatis mutandis* to archipelagic sea lanes passage (Article 54), ships and aircraft during their passage are under the duties provided in those provisions. Furthermore, Article 53(5) requires that ships and aircraft in archipelagic sea lanes passage shall not deviate more than 25 nautical miles to either side of such axis lines, i.e. the centre line, during passage. At the same time, this provision holds that such ships and aircraft shall not navigate closer to the coasts than 10 per cent of the distance between the nearest points on islands bordering the sea lane. There are two different interpretations with regard to this provision.

According to the first interpretation, the phrase '10 per cent of the distance between the nearest points on islands' means the whole width of the channel between the bordering islands. If the channel is 40 nautical miles, for example, the two prohibited zones would each measure 4 nautical miles. As a consequence, the sea lane would be 32 nautical miles wide and a maximum deviation would be 16 nautical miles. According to this interpretation, only if the channel between islands is at least 62.5 nautical miles wide, will the full deviation of 25 nautical miles on either side of the axis line be permissible.

In the second interpretation, the formula set out in Article 53(5) means 10 per cent of the distance from the axis line to the nearest island. In this case, the narrowest channel, which allows ships and aircraft to deviate by 25 nautical miles from the axis of the sea lane, is 55.6 nautical miles wide. In 1996, Indonesia applied the 10 per cent rule in this way in designating its archipelagic sea lanes, and the Maritime Safety Committee of the IMO accepted the submission of Indonesia in 1998. Thus it would appear that this interpretation is supported by the IMO.[130]

The archipelagic State may designate archipelagic sea lanes and air routes under Article 53(1) of the LOSC. Article 53 sets out several conditions designating such sea lanes and air routes:

(i) The sea lanes for the archipelagic passage and air routes shall traverse the archipelagic waters and the adjacent territorial sea, and shall include normal passage routes used as routes for international navigation or overflight through or over archipelagic waters, and, within such routes, so far as ships are concerned, all normal navigational channels in accordance with Article 53(4).

(ii) Such sea lanes and air routes shall be defined by a series of continuous axis lines from the entry points of passage routes to the exit points under Article 53(5). An archipelagic State may also prescribe traffic separation schemes for the safe passage of ships through narrow channels in such sea lanes pursuant to Article 53(6). Such sea lanes and traffic separation schemes shall conform to generally accepted international regulation under Article 53(8).

(iii) In designating or substituting sea lanes or prescribing or substituting traffic separation schemes, an archipelagic State is obliged to refer proposals to the competent international organisation with a view to their adoption pursuant to Article 53(9). This provision has a parallel in Article 41(4) of the LOSC. As with Article 41(4), the competent international organisation means the IMO.[131] In 1998, an Indonesian partial proposal for archipelagic sea lanes was adopted at the 69th session of the Marine Safety Committee of the IMO.

(iv) Article 53(10) places an obligation upon the archipelagic State to clearly indicate the axis of the sea lanes and the traffic separation schemes on charts. The provisions of the LOSC concerning the designation of archipelagic sea lanes were further elaborated by IMO General Provisions on the Adoption, Designation and Substitution of Archipelagic Sea Lanes in 1998.[132]

(v) If an archipelagic State does not designate sea lanes or air routes, the right of archipelagic sea lanes passage may be exercised through the routes normally used for

[130] Prescott and Schofield, *The Maritime Political Boundaries*, pp. 179–180. See also, R. Warner, 'Implementing the Archipelagic Regime in the International Maritime Organization', in D. R. Rothwell and S. Bateman (eds.), *Navigational Rights and Freedoms and the New Law of the Sea* (The Hague, Nijhoff, 2000), pp. 179–184.

[131] Article 53(9) does not refer to air routes. It would follow that literally speaking, an archipelagic State has no duty to submit proposals of air routes. In practice, however, the involvement of the ICAO will be desirable for safety and coordination reasons. It may be noted that the ICAO's Rules of the Air are applied to archipelagic sea lanes passage by virtue of Articles 54 and 39(3) of the LOSC. *Virginia Commentaries*, vol. 2, p. 479; C. Johnson, 'A Rite of Passage: The IMO Consideration of the Indonesian Archipelagic Sea-Lanes Submission' (2000) 15 *IJMCL* p. 321.

[132] IMO Marine Safety Committee, Annex 8, Resolution MSC.71(69), Adoption of Amendments to the General Provisions on Ship's Routeing (Resolution A.572(14) as Amended), MSC 69/22/Add.1, 19 May 1998, p. 2.

international navigation by virtue of Article 53(12). It would seem to follow that even if archipelagic sea lanes or air routes not have been designated by the archipelagic State, submarines will be able to transit the routes normally used for international navigation submerged.[133] On the other hand, there is a concern that a dispute may be raised between user States and archipelagic States as to what 'the routes normally used for international navigation' are. Furthermore, non-designation of sea lanes or air routes may create confusion as to which right – the right of innocent passage or the right of archipelagic sea lanes passage – applies in the same archipelagic waters.

5.7 Rights and obligations of an archipelagic State

Article 44 of the LOSC applies *mutatis mutandis* to archipelagic sea lanes passage.[134] It follows that archipelagic States shall not hamper archipelagic sea lanes passage and shall give appropriate publicity to any danger to navigation or overflight within or over the strait of which they have knowledge. In addition to this, there shall be no suspension of archipelagic sea lanes passage.

An archipelagic State may adopt laws and regulations relating to the prevention of marine pollution in archipelagic waters by virtue of Articles 42(1) and 54 of the LOSC. Ships in archipelagic sea lanes passage are required to comply with generally accepted international regulations, procedures and practice for the prevention, reduction and control of pollution from ships under Articles 39(2)(b) and 54 of the LOSC. Although Articles 220 and 233 of the LOSC give the coastal State additional enforcement jurisdiction regulating pollution from ships in the territorial sea and the straits, these provisions contain no reference to archipelagic waters. However, Article 233 refers to Article 42 concerning laws and regulations of States bordering straits relating to transit passage; and Article 42 applies *mutatis mutandis* to archipelagic waters in accordance with Article 54. Therefore, it seems logical to argue that Article 233 is also applicable to archipelagic waters.[135]

6 CONCLUSIONS

The matters considered in this chapter lead to the following conclusions:

(i) Internal waters are under the territorial sovereignty of the coastal State and commercial vessels voluntarily navigating in internal waters are therefore subject to the jurisdiction of the coastal State. Due to the special character of ships as self-contained units, however, coastal States tend to refrain from exercising jurisdiction over the internal discipline of the ship, unless their interests are engaged. In practice, the scope of criminal jurisdiction of the coastal State over foreign merchant ships is specified in bilateral consular conventions.

[133] Churchill and Lowe, *The Law of the Sea*, p. 128. [134] Article 54.

[135] *Virginia Commentaries*, vol. 2, p. 487. See also, R. P. M. Lotilla, 'Navigational Rights in Archipelagic Waters: A Commentary from the Philippines', in Rothwell and Bateman, *Navigational Rights*, p. 156.

(ii) The right of ships in distress to enter into a foreign port is a well-established rule of customary international law. However, refuge for ships in distress creates particular sensitivities associated with the environmental protection of offshore areas of the coastal State. In reality, there have been several instances where coastal States have refused an oil tanker in distress refuge to offshore areas. With a view to achieving a sound balance between the humanitarian and security considerations and the environmental interests of the coastal State, it is desirable to create reception facilities to accommodate ships in distress in the waters under their jurisdiction.

(iii) The right of innocent passage is an important principle that seeks to reconcile territorial sovereignty and the freedom of navigation. In this regard, the most debatable issue involves the right of innocent passage of foreign warships. This is a matter of sensitive balance between the strategic interest of naval powers and the security interests of coastal States. In light of the sensitivity associated with this subject, State practice is sharply divided on this matter. Whilst, arguably, the requirement of prior notification to enter into the territorial sea may be compatible with the LOSC, the legality of the requirement of prior authorisation seems to be a matter for discussion.

(iv) The tension between the strategic interests of naval powers and the security interests of coastal States also arises with regard to sea communication through international straits. In this regard, the LOSC provides the right of transit passage which favours the freedom of navigation and overflight of all vessels and aircraft. The right of transit passage seeks to accommodate the military and strategic interests of naval powers by accepting the freedom of navigation of foreign warships and overflight by military aircraft.

(v) The territorial sovereignty of the archipelagic State extends to the archipelagic waters. However, territorial sovereignty over these waters is qualified by the following factors set out in the LOSC:

- the right of innocent passage (Article 52),
- the right of archipelagic sea lane passage (Article 53),
- existing rights and all other legitimate interests of neighbouring States (Article 47(6)),
- all rights stipulated by agreement between neighbouring States (Article 47(6)),
- existing agreements with other States (Article 51(1)),
- the traditional fishing rights and other legitimate interests of neighbouring States (Article 51(1)), and
- the obligation to respect existing submarine cables (Article 51(2)).

In particular, the right of innocent passage and archipelagic sea lane passage are of central importance in order to reconcile the territoriality of the archipelagic waters and the freedom of sea communication.

(vi) The right of transit passage and archipelagic sea lane passage differ from the traditional right of innocent passage through the territorial sea in three respects:

- the right of transit passage and archipelagic sea lane passage comprise the freedom of overflight by all aircraft, including military aircraft,

- submarines and other underwater vehicles in transit passage and archipelagic sea lane passage are not required to navigate on the surface and to show their flag, and
- the right of transit passage and archipelagic sea lane passage cannot be suspended.

(vii) Presently the protection of the offshore environment from vessel-source pollution attracts growing attention from coastal States. As shown by the introduction of the compulsory pilotage system in international straits, it is likely that coastal States will increasingly strengthen the regulation of sea communication with a view to protecting the healthy environment of waterways. Thus the reconciliation between the navigational interest of user States and the environmental interest of coastal States will be increasingly important in the law of the sea.

FURTHER READING

1 Internal Waters

A. Chircop, 'Ships in Distress, Environmental Threats to Coastal States, and Places of Refuge: New Directions for an Ancient Regime?' (2002) 33 *ODIL* pp. 207–226.

A. Chircop and O. Linden (eds.) *Places of Refuge for Ships: Emerging Environmental Concerns of a Maritime Custom* (Leiden and Baston, Nijhoff, 2006).

V. D. Degan, 'Internal Waters' (1986) 17 *Netherlands Yearbook of International Law* pp. 3–44.

L. de la Fayette, 'Access to Ports in International Law' (1996) 11 *IJMCL* pp. 1–22.

S. Hetherington, 'Places of Refuge for Ships in Need of Assistance: The Work of the Comité Maritime International' (2010) 24 *Ocean Yearbook* pp. 331–358.

A. V. Lowe, 'The Right of Entry into Maritime Ports in International Law' (1976–77) 14 *San Diego Law Review* pp. 597–622.

C. F. Murray, 'Any Port in a Storm? The Right of Entry for Reasons of Force Majeure or Distress in the Wake of the *Erika* and the *Castor*' (2002) 63 *Ohio State Law Journal* pp. 1465–1506.

M. H. Nordquist, 'International Law Governing Places of Refuge for Tankers Threatening Pollution of Coastal Environments', in T. M. Ndiaye and R. Wolfrum (eds.), *Law of the Sea, Environmental Law and Settlement of Disputes: Liber Amicorum Judge Thomas A. Mensah* (Leiden and Boston, Nijhoff, 2007), pp. 497–519.

E. Van Hooydonk, 'The Obligation to Offer a Place of Refuge to a Ship in Distress' (2004) *Lloyd's Maritime and Commercial Law Quarterly* pp. 347–374.

2 Territorial Sea

W. K. Agyebeng, 'Theory in Search of Practice: The Right of Innocent Passage in the Territorial Sea' (2006) 39 *Cornell International Law Journal* pp. 371–399.

Carlos Espaliú Berdud, *Le passage inoffensive des navires de guerre étrangers dans la mer territoriale: portée du régime contenu dans la Convention des Nations Unies sur le droit de la mer* (Brussels, Bruylant, 2006).

F. Ngantcha, *The Right of Innocent Passage and the Evolution of the International Law of the Sea* (London and New York, Pinter Publisher, 1990).

D. R. Rothwell, 'Innocent Passage in the Territorial Sea: The UNCLOS Regime and Asia Pacific State Practice', in D. R. Rothwell and S. Bateman (eds.), *Navigational Rights and Freedoms and the New Law of the Sea* (The Hague, Nijhoff, 2000) pp. 74–93.

J. M. Van Dyke, 'The Legal Regime Governing Sea Transport of Ultrahazardous Radioactive Materials' (2002) 33 *ODIL* pp. 77–108.

3 International Straits

S. Bateman and M. White 'Compulsory Pilotage in the Torres Strait: Overcoming Unacceptable Risks to a Sensitive Marine Environment' (2009) 40 *ODIL* pp. 184–203.
H. Caminos, 'The Legal Regime of Straits in the 1982 United Nations Convention on the Law of the Sea' (1987) 205 *RCADI* pp. 9–245.
M. George, 'Transit Passage and Pollution Control in Straits under the 1982 Law of the Sea Convention' (2002) 33 *ODIL* pp. 189–205.
B. B. Jia, *The Regime of Straits in International Law* (Oxford, Clarendon Press, 1998).
A. G. López Martín, *International Straits: Concept, Classification and Rules of Passage* (Heidelberg, Springer, 2010).
S. N. Nandan and D. H. Anderson, 'Straits Used for International Navigation: A Commentary on Part III of the United Nations Convention on the Law of the Sea 1982' (1989) 60 *BYIL* pp. 159–204.
P. J. Neher, 'Compulsory Pilotage in the Torres Strait', in M. H. Nordquist, T. T. B. Koh and J. N. Moore, *Freedom of Seas, Passage Rights and the 1982 Law of the Sea Convention* (Leiden and Boston, Nijhoff, 2009), pp. 339–355.
W. L. Schachte, Jr and J. P. A. Bernhardt, 'International Straits and Navigational Freedoms' (1992–93) 33 *Virginia Journal of International Law* pp. 527–556.
J. A. de Yturriaga, *Straits Used for International Navigation: A Spanish Perspective* (Dordrecht, Nijhoff, 1991).

4 Archipelagic Waters

R. Cribb and M. Ford (eds.), *Indonesia beyond the Water's Edge: Managing an Archipelagic State* (Singapore, Institute of Southeast Asian Studies, 2009).
C. Johnson, 'A Rite of Passage: The IMO Consideration of the Indonesian Archipelagic Sea-Lanes Submission' (2000) 15 *IJMCL* pp. 317–332.
S. Kopela, '2007 Archipelagic Legislation of the Dominican Republic: An Assessment' (2009) 24 *IJMCL* pp. 501–533.
M. Munavvar, *Ocean States: Archipelagic Regimes in the Law of the Sea* (Dordrecht, Nijhoff, 1995).
M. Tsamenyi, C. Schofield and B. Milligan, 'Navigation through Archipelagos: Current State Practice', in D. R. Rothwell and S. Bateman (eds.), *Navigational Rights and Freedoms and the New Law of the Sea* (The Hague, Nijhoff, 2000), pp. 413–454.
UNDOALOS, *The Law of the Sea: Practice of Archipelagic States* (New York, United Nations, 1992).

4

Marine Spaces under National Jurisdiction II: Sovereign Rights

Main Issues

This chapter will examine rules governing the contiguous zone, the EEZ and the continental shelf. In the contiguous zone, the coastal State may exercise the control necessary to prevent and punish infringement of its customs, fiscal, immigration or sanitary laws and regulations within its territory or territorial sea. Whilst the LOSC contains only succinct provisions respecting the contiguous zone, the legal nature of the coastal State jurisdiction over the zone deserves serious consideration. The *raison d'être* of the institution of the EEZ and the continental shelf involves the conservation and management of natural resources. In this sense, the EEZ and the continental shelf can be considered as a 'resource-oriented zone'. Owing to the increasing importance of marine natural resources, these zones are particularly important for coastal States. Presently the extension of the continental shelf to a limit of 200 nautical miles attracts particular attention. This chapter will discuss the following issues in particular:

(i) What is the coastal State jurisdiction over the contiguous zone?
(ii) What is the coastal State jurisdiction over the EEZ and the continental shelf?
(iii) What is the difference between territorial sovereignty and sovereign rights?
(iv) What are the freedoms that all States can enjoy in the EEZ?
(v) What residual rights are there in the EEZ?
(vi) What are the criteria for determining the outer limits of the continental shelf?

1 INTRODUCTION

The legal regimes governing the EEZ and the continental shelf are essentially a result of the aspiration of coastal States for their need to control offshore natural resources. As will be seen, the coastal State exercises sovereign rights over the EEZ and the continental shelf for the purpose of exploring and exploiting natural resources. Other States cannot explore and exploit these resources in the EEZ and the continental shelf without the consent of the coastal State. On the other hand, as the EEZ and the continental shelf are part of the ocean as a single unit, legitimate activities in these zones by third States, such as freedom of navigation, overflight and the laying of submarine cables and pipelines, must be secured.

An essential question thus arises as to how it is possible to reconcile the sovereign rights of the coastal State and the freedom of the seas exercised by other States in the EEZ and the continental shelf. With this question as a backdrop, this chapter will address rules governing the EEZ and the continental shelf. As the contiguous zone is part of the EEZ when the coastal State established it, this chapter will also examine rules governing the contiguous zone.

2 CONTIGUOUS ZONE

2.1 The concept of the contiguous zone

The contiguous zone is a marine space contiguous to the territorial sea, in which the coastal State may exercise the control necessary to prevent and punish infringement of its customs, fiscal, immigration or sanitary laws and regulations within its territory or territorial sea.[1] The development of the contiguous zone was a complicated process of concurrence of different claims by coastal States.[2] Whilst it has been considered that the origin of the concept of the contiguous zone dates back to the Hovering Acts enacted by Great Britain in the eighteenth century, it was not until 1958 that rules governing the contiguous zone were eventually agreed. The rules governing the contiguous zone were enshrined in Article 24 of the TSC. Later, this provision was, with some modifications, reproduced in Article 33 of the LOSC.

The landward limit of the contiguous zone is the seaward limit of the territorial sea. Under Article 33(2) of the LOSC, the maximum breadth of the contiguous zone is twenty-four nautical miles. Article 33 of the LOSC contains no duty corresponding to Article 16, which obliges the coastal State to give due publicity to charts. It would seem to follow that there is no specific requirement concerning notice in the establishment of the contiguous zone.[3] The contiguous zone is an area contiguous to the high seas under Article 24(1) of the TSC. Under the LOSC, the contiguous zone is part of the EEZ where the coastal State claims the zone. Where the coastal State does not claim its EEZ, the contiguous zone is part of the high seas. As of 15 July 2011, some eighty-nine States claim a contiguous zone.[4]

1 LOSC, Article 33(1); H. Caminos, 'Contiguous Zone', in *Max Planck Encyclopaedia*, p. 1, para. 1.
2 For an analysis in some detail of the historical development of the contiguous zone, see D. P. O'Connell (I. A. Shearer ed.), *The International Law of the Sea*, vol. 2 (Oxford, Clarendon Press 1984), pp. 1034 *et seq.*; A. V. Lowe, 'The Development of the Contiguous Zone' (1981) 52 *BYIL* pp. 109–169.
3 *Virginia Commentaries*, vol. II, p. 274.
4 United Nations, *Table of Claims to Maritime Jurisdiction as at 15 July 2011.*

2.2 Coastal State jurisdiction over the contiguous zone

Article 33(1), which follows Article 24(1) of the TSC, provides that:

1. In a zone contiguous to its territorial sea, described as the contiguous zone, the coastal State may exercise the control necessary to:
   (a) prevent infringement of its customs, fiscal, immigration or sanitary laws and regulations within its territory or territorial sea;
   (b) punish infringement of the above laws and regulations committed within its territory or territorial sea.

This provision requires three brief comments.

First, Article 33(1) contains no reference to internal waters. However, it would be inconceivable that the drafters of this provision had an intention to exclude the internal waters from the scope of this provision since these waters are under the territorial sovereignty of the coastal State. Thus it appears to be reasonable to consider that internal waters are also included in the scope of 'its territory or territorial sea'.

Second, Article 33(1) literally means that the coastal State may exercise only enforcement, not legislative, jurisdiction within its contiguous zone. It would follow that relevant laws and regulations of the coastal State are not extended to its contiguous zone; and that infringement of municipal laws of the coastal State within the zone is outside the scope of this provision. Considering that an incoming vessel cannot commit an offence until it crosses the limit of the territorial sea, it would appear that head (b) of Article 33(1) can apply only to an outgoing ship. By contrast, head (a) can apply only to incoming ships because prevention cannot arise with regard to an outgoing ship in the contiguous zone.

Third, Article 33(1) does not make the further specification with regard to 'control necessary to punish infringement' of municipal law of the coastal State in its contiguous zone. In this regard, Article 111(1) makes clear that the coastal State may undertake the hot pursuit of foreign ships within the contiguous zone.[5] Article 111(6), (7) and (8) further provide the coastal State's right to stop a ship, the right to arrest the ship, and the right to escort the ship to a port. One can say, therefore, that the coastal State jurisdiction to punish the infringement of its municipal laws in the contiguous zone includes these rights. On the other hand, Article 111(1) does not specify the place where the infringement of laws and regulations of the coastal State must have occurred. In view of maintaining consistency with Article 33(1), it appears reasonable to consider that the coastal State may commence the hot pursuit of a ship only where that ship has already breached the laws and regulation of that State within its territory or territorial sea.[6]

The legal nature of the coastal State jurisdiction over the contiguous zone is not free from controversy. According to a literal or restrictive view, the coastal State has only enforcement jurisdiction in its contiguous zone and, consequently, action of the coastal

[5] The right of hot pursuit will be discussed in Chapter 5, section 2.7.
[6] Lowe, 'The Contiguous Zone', p. 166.

State may only be taken concerning offences committed within the territory or territorial sea of the coastal State, not in respect of anything done within the contiguous zone itself. Sir Gerald Fitzmaurice is a leading writer supporting this view. According to Fitzmaurice, the power over the contiguous zone is 'essentially supervisory and preventative'.[7]

According to a liberal view, the coastal State may regulate the violation of its municipal law within the contiguous zone for some limited purposes. For instance, Oda argued that in the contiguous zone, the coastal State should be entitled to exercise its authority as exercisable in the territorial sea only for some limited purposes of customs or sanitary control. O'Connell and Shearer echoed this view.[8]

There appears to be little doubt that a strict reading of Article 33(1) does not allow coastal States to extend legislative jurisdiction to its contiguous zone. There is an exception, however. Concerning the protection of objects of an archaeological and historical nature found at sea, Article 303(2) of the LOSC provides that:

2. In order to control traffic in such objects, the coastal State may, in applying Article 33, presume that their removal from the seabed in the zone referred to in that article without its approval would result in an infringement within its territory or territorial sea of the laws and regulations referred to in that article.

This provision relies on a dual legal fiction. First, the removal of archaeological and historical objects is to be regarded as infringement of customs, fiscal, immigration or sanitary laws and regulations of the coastal State. Second, the removal of archaeological and historical objects within the contiguous zone is to be considered as an act within the territory or the territorial sea. By using the dual fiction, the removal of archaeological and historical objects within the contiguous zone is subject to the control of the coastal State, including hot pursuit. Thus, in so far as the prevention of the removal of archaeological and historical objects is concerned, the coastal State may exercise legislative and enforcement jurisdiction within its contiguous zone by virtue of Article 303(2).

Currently the contiguous zone is part of the EEZ when the coastal State claimed the zone. As will be seen, in the EEZ, the coastal State may exercise both legislative and enforcement jurisdiction for limited matters provided by the law of the sea. Considering that the contiguous zone is becoming important for the purpose of regulation of illegal traffic in drugs, claims to legislative jurisdiction in the zone will not cause a serious problem in reality.[9] If this is the case, as a matter of practice, it may not be unreasonable

[7] G. Fitzmaurice, 'Some Results of the Geneva Conference on the Law of the Sea' (1959) 8 *ICLQ*, p. 114.

[8] S. Oda, 'The Concept of the Contiguous Zone' (1962) 11 *ICLQ* p. 153; O'Connell, *The International Law of the Sea*, p. 1060; I. A. Shearer, 'Problems of Jurisdiction and Law Enforcement against Delinquent Vessels' (1986) 35 *ICLQ* p. 330.

[9] R. R. Churchill and A. V. Lowe, *Law of the Sea*, 3rd edn (Manchester University Press, 1999), p. 138. Some States claim both legislative and enforcement jurisdiction over the contiguous zone. Examples include: India, the Territorial Waters, Continental Shelf, Exclusive Economic Zone and Other Maritime Zones Act, 1976, article 5(5); Pakistan, Territorial Waters and Maritime Zone Act, 1976, article 4(3); Sri Lanka, Maritime Zones Law, No. 22 of 1976, section 4(2). For the text of these provisions, see UNDOALOS, *The Law of the Sea: National Legislation on the Territorial Sea, the Right*

to extend the legislative jurisdiction of the coastal State over the contiguous zone for the limited purposes provided in Article 33 of the LOSC. In any case, it must be remembered that disputes with regard to the exercise by a coastal State of its jurisdiction over the contiguous zone fall within the scope of the compulsory settlement procedure in Part XV of the LOSC.

3 EXCLUSIVE ECONOMIC ZONE

3.1 Genesis of the concept of the EEZ

The EEZ is an area beyond and adjacent to the territorial sea, not extending beyond 200 nautical miles from the baseline of the territorial sea.[10] The origin of the concept of the EEZ may go back to the practice of the Latin American States after World War II.[11] Originally the figure of 200 nautical miles appeared in 1947, when Chile, Peru and Ecuador claimed such an extent for the exercise of full sovereignty. The figure of 200 nautical miles relied on scientific facts: it would enable the Andean States to reach the Peruvian and the Humboldt Currents, which were particularly rich in living species. Furthermore, the guano birds, whose deposit is an important fertiliser, feed on anchovy. Scientific research has shown that anchovy larvae had also been located in up to a 187-mile width. The three Andean States thus inferred that a perfect unity and interdependence existed between the sea's living resources and the coastal populations. For the three countries of Latin America's Pacific coast, the claim for a 200 nautical mile zone was considered as a means to correct an inequity inflicted upon them by geography, namely the lack of a continental shelf.

Later on, the claim for a 200-mile zone spread to the majority of coastal developing States. As the Caracas session of UNCLOS III approached, however, it became apparent that the maritime powers would not accept such an extensive territorial sea which would deter economic and military interests. Thus, in 1971, Kenya proposed the concept of the EEZ in the Asian-African Legal Consultative Committee at Colombo in a spirit of compromise. In August 1972, with overwhelming support from the developing countries, Kenya formally submitted its proposal for a 200-mile EEZ to the UN Seabed Committee. According to this proposal, the natural resources of the zone would be placed under the jurisdiction of the coastal State, while freedom of navigation was to be guaranteed. Further to this, a variant of the concept of the EEZ, the notion of the 'patrimonial sea', was reflected in the Declaration of Santo Domingo, adopted by

of Innocent Passage and the Contiguous Zone (New York, United Nations, 1995), pp. 160, 257, 354, respectively. Some States claim jurisdiction for the purpose of security within the contiguous zone. But these claims have been protested by the USA. See J. A. Roach and R. W. Smith, *United States Responses to Excessive Maritime Claims*, 2nd edn (The Hague, Nijhoff, 1996), pp. 166–172.

10 LOSC, Articles 55 and 57.

11 Concerning the background of the EEZ, see R.-J. Dupuy, 'The Sea under National Competence', in R.-J. Dupuy and D. Vignes, *A Handbook on the New Law of the Sea*, vol. 1 (Dordrecht, Nijhoff, 1991), pp. 275 *et seq.*; D. Attard, *The Exclusive Economic Zone in International Law* (Oxford, Clarendon Press, 1987), pp. 1 *et seq.*; T. Scovazzi, 'The Evolution of International Law of the Sea: New Issues, New Challenges' (2000) 286 *RCADI* pp. 96 *et seq.*

the Conference of Caribbean Countries on 7 June 1972. On 2 August 1973, Colombia, Mexico and Venezuela submitted its proposal for the 'patrimonial sea' to the Seabed Committee.[12] The two concepts effectively merged at UNCLOS III. By 1975, the basic concept of the EEZ seemed to be well established.[13] Thus the legal regime governing the EEZ was embodied in Part V of the LOSC.

Unlike the continental shelf, the coastal State must claim the zone in order to establish an EEZ. The vast majority of coastal States have claimed a 200-mile EEZ.[14] In this regard, the ICJ, in the *Libya/Malta* case of 1985, stated that: '[T]he institution of the exclusive economic zone, with its rule on entitlement by reason of distance, is shown by the practice of States to have become a part of customary law'.[15]

It is said that the 200-mile EEZ amounts to some 35–36 per cent of the oceans as a whole. Seven leading beneficiaries of the EEZ are: the USA, France, Indonesia, New Zealand, Australia, Russia and Japan.[16] It is ironic that leading EEZ beneficiaries are essentially the developed States. Whilst most States which had previously claimed an exclusive fishing zone (EFZ) have replaced such a zone by an EEZ, several States still maintain an EFZ.[17] Considering that all States claiming an EFZ became parties to the LOSC, it may be argued that the relevant provisions of the EEZ respecting fisheries are applicable to the EFZ.

3.2 Legal status of the EEZ

The landward limit of the EEZ is the seaward limit of the territorial sea. The seaward limit of the EEZ is at a maximum of 200 nautical miles from the baseline of the territorial sea. Given that the maximum breadth of the territorial sea is 12 nautical miles, the maximum breadth of the EEZ is 188 nautical miles, that is to say, approximately 370 kilometres. The outer limit lines of the EEZ and the delimitation lines shall be shown on charts of a scale or scales adequate for ascertaining their position. Where appropriate, lists of geographical coordinates of points may also be substituted for such outer limit lines or

[12] The concept of the patrimonial sea can be defined as an economic zone not more than 200 nautical miles breadth from the base line of the territorial sea where the coastal State will have an exclusive right to all resources, whilst there will be freedom of navigation and overflight there. L. D. M. Nelson, 'The Patrimonial Sea' (1973) 22 *ICLQ*, p. 668.

[13] S. Oda, 'Exclusive Economic Zone', in R. Bernhardt (ed.), *Encyclopedia of Public International Law*, vol. 11 (Amsterdam, North-Holland, 1989), p. 104.

[14] According to Churchill, 100 out of the 127 coastal States Parties to the LOSC have claimed an EEZ. R. R. Churchill, 'The Impact of State Practice on the Jurisdictional Framework contained in the LOS Convention', in A. G. Oude Elferink (ed.), *Stability and Change in the Law of the Sea: The Role of the LOS Convention* (Leiden and Boston, Nijhoff, 2005), p. 126.

[15] ICJ Reports 1985, p. 33, para. 34. See also The American Law Institute, *Restatement of the Law Third: The Foreign Relations Law of the United States*, vol. 2 (American Law Institute Publishers, 1990) § 514, comment (a), p. 56.

[16] Churchill and Lowe, *Law of the Sea*, p. 178.

[17] These States are: Algeria, Belgium (coterminous with the EEZ), Croatia, Denmark (for the Faroe Islands), Finland, Gambia, Libya, Malta, Norway (Jan Mayen and Svalbard), Papua New Guinea, Spain (in the Mediterranean Sea), Tunisia and the United Kingdom. Ireland declared an EEZ in 2006, while it also declared an EFZ and a Pollution Response Zone. Department of Foreign Affairs and Trade, Ireland: www.dfa.ie/home/index.aspx?id=365. For an analysis of the EFZ, see S. Kvinikhidze, 'Contemporary Exclusive Fishery Zones or Why Some States Still Claim an EFZ' (2008) 23 *IJMCL* pp. 271–295.

delimitation lines pursuant to Article 75(1) of the LOSC. The coastal State is also obliged to give due publicity to such charts or lists of geographical coordinates and shall deposit a copy of each such chart or list with the UN Secretary-General under Article 75(2).

The concept of the EEZ comprises the seabed and its subsoil, the waters superjacent to the seabed as well as the airspace above the waters. With respect to the seabed and its subsoil, Article 56(1) provides that '*in the exclusive economic zone*' the coastal State has '(a) sovereign rights for the purpose of exploring and exploiting, conserving and managing the natural resources, whether living or non-living, of the waters superjacent to the seabed and *of the seabed and its subsoil*' (emphasis added). It would follow that the concept of the EEZ includes the seabed and its subsoil. The rights of the coastal State with respect to the seabed and subsoil are to be exercised in accordance with provisions governing the continental shelf by virtue of Article 56(3).

Article 58(1) stipulates that '*in the exclusive economic zone*', all States, whether coastal or land-locked, enjoy 'the freedoms referred to in article 87 of navigation and *overflight*' (emphasis added). Article 56(1) further provides that the coastal State has sovereign rights with respect to other activities for the economic exploitation and exploration of the zone, such as the production of energy from the water, currents and *winds*. One can say, therefore, that the concept of the EEZ also includes the airspace.

Article 55 of the LOSC makes clear that the EEZ 'is an area beyond and adjacent to the territorial sea, subject to the specific legal regime established in this Part [V]'. Thus, the EEZ is not the territorial sea. Indeed, unlike internal waters and the territorial sea, the territorial sovereignty of the coastal State does not extend to the EEZ. Article 86 of the LOSC provides that the provisions of Part VII governing the high seas 'apply to all parts of the sea that are not included in the exclusive economic zone, in the territorial sea or in the internal waters of a State, or in the archipelagic waters of an archipelagic State'. Accordingly, the EEZ is not part of the high seas. In fact, the freedoms apply to the EEZ in so far as they are not incompatible with Part V of the LOSC governing the EEZ in accordance with Article 58(2). In this sense, the quality of the freedom exercisable in the EEZ differs from that exercisable on the high seas. Overall it can be concluded that the EEZ is regarded as a *sui generis* zone, distinguished from the territorial sea and the high seas.

3.3 Sovereign rights over the EEZ

The key provision concerning coastal State jurisdiction over the EEZ is Article 56 of the LOSC. The first paragraph of Article 56 provides as follows:

1. In the exclusive economic zone, the coastal State has:
   (a) sovereign rights for the purpose of exploring and exploiting, conserving and managing the natural resources, whether living or non-living, of the waters superjacent to the seabed and of the seabed and its subsoil, and with regard to other activities for the economic exploitation and exploration of the zone, such as the production of energy from the water, currents and winds.

It is important to note that the sovereign rights of the coastal State over the EEZ are essentially limited to economic exploration and exploitation (limitation *ratione materiae*). In this respect, the concept of sovereign rights must be distinguished from territorial sovereignty, which is comprehensive unless international law provides otherwise.

The concept of sovereign rights can also be seen in the 1958 Geneva Convention on the Continental Shelf. Article 2(2) of the Geneva Convention provides that:

> The rights referred to in paragraph 1 of this Article [sovereign rights] are exclusive in the sense that if the coastal State does not explore the continental shelf or exploit its natural resources, no one may undertake these activities, or make a claim to the continental shelf, without the express consent of the coastal State.

Although Part V does not contain a similar provision, it may be argued that the sovereign rights in the EEZ are essentially exclusive in the sense that no one may undertake these activities or make a claim to the EEZ, *without the express consent of the coastal State*. It is true that third States have the right of access to natural resources in the EEZ.[18] Considering that the exercise of the right is conditional upon agreement with the coastal State, however, it does not challenge the exclusive nature of the coastal State's jurisdiction over the EEZ.[19]

With respect to matters provided by the law, the coastal State exercises both legislative and enforcement jurisdiction in the EEZ. In this respect, the key provision is Article 73(1):

> The coastal State may, in the exercise of its sovereign rights to explore, exploit, conserve and manage the living resources in the exclusive economic zone, take such measures, including boarding, inspection, arrest and judicial proceedings, as may be necessary to ensure compliance with the laws and regulations adopted by it in conformity with this Convention.

Whilst this provision provides enforcement jurisdiction for the coastal State, the reference to 'the laws and regulations by it' seems to suggest that the State also has legislative jurisdiction.

It is beyond serious doubt that the measures provided under Article 73(1) can be applied to foreign vessels within the EEZ. This is clear from Article 73(4), which provides that:

> In cases of arrest or detention of foreign vessels the coastal State shall promptly notify the flag State, through appropriate channels, of the action taken and of any penalties subsequently imposed.

[18] LOSC, Articles 62(2), 69 and 70. See also Chapter 7, section 3.2.

[19] B. Kwiatkowska, *The 200 Mile Exclusive Economic Zone in the New Law of the Sea* (Dordrecht, Nijhoff, 1989), p. 15.

Thus a coastal State jurisdiction within its EEZ contains no limit *ratione personae*. Overall the sovereign rights of the coastal State in its EEZ can be summarised as follows:

(i) The sovereign rights of the coastal State can be exercised solely within the EEZ. In this sense, such rights are spatial in nature.

(ii) The sovereign rights of the coastal State are limited to the matters defined by international law (limitation *ratione materiae*). On this point, sovereign rights must be distinguished from territorial sovereignty.

(iii) However, concerning matters defined by international law, the coastal State may exercise both legislative and enforcement jurisdiction.

(iv) The coastal State may exercise sovereign rights over all people regardless of their nationality within the EEZ. Thus the sovereign rights contain no limit *ratione personae*. In this respect, sovereign rights over the EEZ differ from personal jurisdiction.

(v) The sovereign rights of the coastal State over the EEZ are exclusive in the sense that other States cannot engage upon activities in the EEZ without consent of the coastal State.

In short, unlike territorial sovereignty, the sovereign rights of the coastal State over the EEZ lack comprehensiveness of material scope. With respect to matters accepted by international law, however, the coastal State can exercise both legislative and enforcement jurisdiction over all people within the EEZ in an exclusive manner. The essential point is that the rights of the coastal State over the EEZ are spatial in the sense that they can be exercised solely within the particular space in question regardless of the nationality of persons or vessels. Thus the coastal State jurisdiction over the EEZ can be regarded as a spatial jurisdiction. Due to the lack of comprehensiveness of material scope, this jurisdiction should be called a limited spatial jurisdiction.[20]

3.4 Jurisdiction of coastal States over the EEZ

Under Article 56(1)(b) of the LOSC, the coastal State possesses jurisdiction over matters other than the exploration and exploitation of marine natural resources, namely (i) the establishment and use of artificial islands, installations and structures, (ii) marine scientific research, and (iii) the protection and preservation of the marine environment. The coastal State also has other rights and duties provided for in this Convention (Article 56(1)(c)). The coastal State jurisdiction with regard to these matters requires some comments.

Concerning the coastal State jurisdiction over artificial islands, Article 60 stipulates that:

[20] See Chapter 1, section2.2. R.-J. Dupuy took the view that the coastal State enjoys 'power of a spatial type' in the EEZ. Dupuy, 'The Sea under National Competence', p. 293. Combacau considered the coastal State's jurisdiction over the EEZ as territorial jurisdiction. J. Combacau, *Le droit international de la mer: Que sais-je?* (Paris, PUF, 1985), p. 21. Bastid considered the continental shelf and the EEZ as maritime domain under limited territorial jurisdiction (*la compétence territoriale limitée*). S. Bastid, *Droit international public: principes fondamentaux, les Cours de droit* 1969–1970 (Université de Paris), pp. 814–815.

1. In the exclusive economic zone, the coastal State shall have the exclusive right to construct and to authorize and regulate the construction, operation and use of:
   (a) artificial islands;
   (b) installations and structures for the purposes provided for in article 56 and other economic purposes;
   (c) installations and structures which may interfere with the exercise of the rights of the coastal State in the zone.[21]
2. The coastal State shall have exclusive jurisdiction over such artificial islands, installations and structures, including jurisdiction with regard to customs, fiscal, health, safety and immigration laws and regulations.

At the same time, the rights of the coastal State on this matter are subject to certain obligations. Under Article 60(3), due notice must be given of the construction of such artificial islands, installations and structures, and permanent means for giving warning of their presence must be maintained. Any installations or structures which are abandoned or disused must be removed to ensure safety of navigation. Under Article 60(7), the coastal State may not establish artificial islands, installations and structures and the safety zones around them 'where interference may be caused to the use of recognised sea lanes essential to international navigation'.

It is clear that the coastal State has exclusive jurisdiction, including both legislative and enforcement jurisdiction, over installations and structures for economic purposes by virtue of Article 60. On the other hand, a question arises whether or not the coastal State also has the jurisdiction to authorise and to regulate the construction and use of installations and structures for non-economic purposes, such as military purposes. It appears that State practice is not uniform on this particular matter. When ratifying the LOSC, Brazil, Cape Verde and Uruguay made declarations claiming that the coastal State has the exclusive right to authorise and regulate the construction and use of all kinds of installations and structures, without exception, whatever their nature or purpose.[22] By contrast, when ratifying the LOSC, Germany, Italy, the Netherlands and the United Kingdom declared that the coastal State enjoys the right to authorise, construct, operate and use only those installations and structures which have economic purposes.[23] Whilst this is a debatable issue, the preferable view appears to be that a dispute falls within the scope of Article 59 because the LOSC does not explicitly attribute rights or jurisdiction in this matter to a coastal State or to other States.[24]

[21] Article 60(1)(c) seems to literally mean that in the exclusive economic zone, the coastal State shall have the exclusive right to construct and to authorise and regulate the construction, operation and use of installations and structures which may interfere with the exercise of the rights of the coastal State in the zone. Yet this will lead to a strange consequence.

[22] A. V. Lowe and S. A. G. Talmon (eds.), *The Legal Order of the Oceans: Basic Documents on the Law of the Sea* (Oxford, Hart Publishing 2009) pp. 915, 917 and 967.

[23] *Ibid.*, pp. 935, 941, 948–949 and 965. See also Churchill, 'The Impact of State Practice', p. 136.

[24] A. V. Lowe, 'Some Legal Problems Arising from the Use of the Seas for Military Purposes' (1986) 10 *Marine Policy* p. 180; Churchill, 'The Impact of State Practice', p. 136. It is also to be noted that freedom to construct artificial islands and other installations is not included in Article 58(1) and (2).

As noted, Article 56(1)(b)(ii) of the LOSC makes clear that the coastal State has jurisdiction with regard to marine scientific research in the EEZ. In relation to this, Article 246(1) stipulates that:

> Coastal States, in the exercise of their jurisdiction, have the right to regulate, authorise and conduct marine scientific research in their exclusive economic zone and on their continental shelf in accordance with the relevant provisions of this Convention.

Marine scientific research in the EEZ and on the continental shelf is to be conducted with the consent of the coastal State in conformity with Article 246(2).

It is clear from Article 56(1)(b)(iii) that in the EEZ, the coastal State has legislative and enforcement jurisdiction with regard to the protection and preservation of the marine environment. Further to this, Articles 210(1) and 211(5) provide legislative jurisdiction of the coastal State concerning the regulation of dumping and vessel-source pollution. Moreover, Articles 210(2) and 220 contain enforcement jurisdiction of the coastal State with regard to the regulation of dumping and ship-borne pollution.

The LOSC contains no provision with regard to the coastal State jurisdiction over archaeological and historical objects found within the EEZ beyond the contiguous zone. Thus the protection of these objects would need to be assessed by the application of Article 59. In this regard, on 2 November 2001, UNESCO adopted the Convention on the Protection of Underwater Cultural Heritage (hereafter the UNESCO Convention) in order to ensure the protection of such heritage.[25] Article 9 of the UNESCO Convention places an explicit obligation upon all States Parties to protect underwater cultural heritage in the EEZ and on the continental shelf in conformity with this Convention. Under Article 10(2) of the Convention, a State Party in whose EEZ or on whose continental shelf underwater cultural heritage is located has the right to prohibit or authorise any activity directed at such heritage to prevent interference with its sovereign rights or jurisdiction as provided for by international law, including the LOSC. Article 10(4) allows the coastal State as 'Coordinating State' to take all practical measures to prevent any immediate danger to underwater cultural heritage. These provisions would seem to provide the coastal State with grounds for exercising its jurisdiction over such heritage within the EEZ. In this regard, it is interesting to note that under Article 10(6), the 'Coordinating State' shall act 'on behalf of the States Parties as a whole and not in its own interest'.

3.5 Freedoms of third States

The next issue to be examined involves legitimate activities by third States in the EEZ.[26] In this regard, Article 58(1) of the LOSC stipulates that:

[25] Entered into force on 2 January 2009. For the text of the Convention, (2002) 48 *Law of the Sea Bulletin*, p. 29; Lowe and Talmon, *Basic Documents*, p. 721.

[26] The legality of military exercises in the EEZ of another State will be discussed in Chapter 11, section 4.

> In the exclusive economic zone, all States, whether coastal or land-locked, enjoy, subject to the relevant provisions of this Convention, the freedoms referred to in article 87 of navigation and overflight and of the laying of submarine cables and pipelines, and other internationally lawful uses of the sea related to these freedoms, such as those associated with the operation of ships, aircraft and submarine cables and pipelines, and compatible with the other provisions of this Convention.

It follows that among the six freedoms enumerated in Article 87 of the LOSC, three freedoms of the seas – freedoms of navigation, overflight and the lying of submarine cables and pipelines – apply to the EEZ. Further, Articles 88 to 115 and other pertinent rules of international law relating to the high seas apply to the EEZ in so far as they are not incompatible with this rule under Article 58(2).

However, Article 58(3) requires States to 'have due regard to the rights and duties of the coastal State and shall comply with the laws and regulations adopted by the coastal State in accordance with the provisions of this Convention and other rules of international law in so far as they are not incompatible with this Part [V]'. It would seem to follow that, unlike on the high seas, the three freedoms of the seas may be qualified by coastal State jurisdiction in the EEZ. For instance, overflight in the EEZ for the purposes of exploration and exploitation is subject to the permission of the coastal State.

Navigation of foreign vessels through an EEZ is subject to regulation of the coastal State with respect to marine pollution. Navigation of foreign vessels may also be affected by the presence of artificial islands and installations of the coastal State. In addition to this, shipping in the inner twenty-four miles of the EEZ will be subject to coastal State jurisdiction over its contiguous zone. Whilst the freedom of laying submarine cables and pipelines applies to the EEZ, the delineation of the course of a pipeline in the seabed of the EEZ is subject to the consent of the coastal State in accordance with Article 79(3). To this extent, the freedoms enjoyed by foreign States in the EEZ are not exactly the same as those enjoyed on the high seas.

3.6 Residual rights

Whilst the LOSC provides rules involving most of the obvious uses of the EEZ, there are some uses of the zone where it remains unclear whether they fall within the rights of the coastal State or other States. Here residual rights in the EEZ are at issue. In this regard, Article 59 provides as follows:

> In cases where this Convention does not attribute rights or jurisdiction to the coastal State or to other States within the exclusive economic zone, and a conflict arises between the interests of the coastal State and any other State or States, the conflict should be resolved on the basis of equity and in the light of all the relevant circumstances, taking into account the respective importance of the interests involved to the parties as well as to the international community as a whole.

Under Article 59, there is no presumption in favour of either the coastal State or other States. It would seem to follow that the possible attribution of residual rights is to be decided on a case-by-case basis.[27]

An international dispute could well arise with regard to a matter where the LOSC does not specify which States are to have jurisdiction. Such a dispute is to be settled by peaceful means of their own choice pursuant to Articles 279 and 280 of the LOSC. If this is unsuccessful, the dispute is to be referred to the compulsory procedures of dispute settlement in Part XV of the LOSC, unless the dispute relates to limitations and exceptions to the compulsory procedures. An example may be provided by the 1999 *M/V Saiga (No. 2)* case between Saint Vincent and the Grenadines and Guinea.[28] A central question in this case was whether or not Guinea was entitled to apply its customs law in its EEZ. In this regard, ITLOS held that whilst the coastal State has jurisdiction to apply customs laws and regulations in respect of artificial islands, installations and structures in the EEZ pursuant to Article 60(2) of the LOSC, the Convention does not empower a coastal State to apply its customs laws in respect of any other parts of the EEZ not mentioned in that provision.[29] In so ruling, ITLOS was wary about extending customs laws of the coastal State to its EEZ.

4 CONTINENTAL SHELF

4.1 Genesis of the concept of the continental shelf

Geologically the continental shelf is an area adjacent to a continent or around an island extending from the low-water line to the depth at which there is usually a marked increase of slope to greater depth.[30] Before World War II, natural resources in the seabed and its subsoil had attracted little interest between States.[31] However, natural resources in the seabed and its subsoil, in particular, an extensive reserve of oil and gas, have attracted growing interest since World War II because of the increased demand for petrol. Furthermore, technological progress at the turn of the twentieth century has enabled the continental shelf's hydrocarbon resources to be extracted from the surface of the sea. Against that background, on 28 September 1945, the United States took the decisive step with the Truman Proclamation to extend its jurisdiction over the natural resources of the continental shelf.[32] The Truman Proclamation declared that:

[27] Churchill and Lowe, *Law of the Sea*, p. 176. Concerning residual rights, see S. Karagiannis, 'L'article 59 de la Convention des Nations Unies sur le droit de la mer (ou les mystères de la nature juridique de la zone économique exclusive', (2004) 37 *RBDI* pp. 325–418.

[28] The *M/V Saiga (No. 2)* case (Judgment), (1999) 38 *ILM* p. 1323. In this case, ITLOS did not refer to Article 59 of the LOSC.

[29] *Ibid.*, p. 1351, para. 127.

[30] UNDOALOS, *Definition of the Continental Shelf*, p. 44.

[31] However, in 1942, the United Kingdom concluded a treaty with Venezuela dividing the seabed of the Gulf of Paria for the purpose of the exploitation of the oil field beneath the Gulf. O'Connell, *The International Law of the Sea*, p. 470.

[32] US Presidential Proclamation No. 2667, Policy of the United States with Respect to the Natural Resources of the Subsoil of the Sea Bed and the Continental Shelf. Reproduced in Lowe and Talmon, *Basic Documents*, p. 19.

> Having Concern for the urgency of conserving and prudently utilizing its natural resources, the Government of the United States regards the natural resources of the subsoil and sea bed of the continental shelf beneath the high seas but contiguous to the coasts of the United States as appertaining to the United States, subject to its jurisdiction and control.

The unilateral action of the United States created a chain reaction, and many States unilaterally extended their jurisdiction towards the high seas. The Latin American States – which have virtually no continental shelf in a geological sense – claimed their full sovereignty over all the seabed at whatever depth and over all the adjacent seas at whatever depth to a distance of 200 nautical miles. Whilst State practice was not consistent until the early 1950s, the vast majority of States were prepared to agree to create a new zone relating to the exploitation of natural resources on the continental shelf with the passage of time.[33] Thus a legal regime governing the continental shelf was, for the first time, enshrined in the 1958 Geneva Convention on the Continental Shelf. In this regard, the ICJ, in the 1969 *North Sea Continental Shelf* cases, took the view that Articles 1 to 3 of the Convention on the Continental Shelf, which included the definition of the continental shelf, were 'regarded as reflecting, or as crystallizing, received or at least emergent rules of customary international law relative to the continental shelf'.[34] Today there is no doubt that the rights of the coastal State over the continental shelf are well established in customary international law.

4.2 Spatial scope of the continental shelf

The landward limit of the continental shelf in the legal sense is the seaward limit of the territorial sea. In this respect, Article 1 of the Convention on the Continental Shelf stipulates that the continental shelf is the seabed and subsoil of the submarine areas adjacent to the coast but outside the area of the territorial sea. Similarly, Article 76(1) of the LOSC stipulates that 'the continental shelf of a coastal State comprises the seabed and subsoil of the submarine areas that extend beyond its territorial sea'. It follows that the continental shelf in a legal sense does not include the seabed of the territorial sea.

On the other hand, the seaward limit of the continental shelf needs careful consideration. Article 1(a) of the Geneva Convention on the Continental Shelf provides two criteria to locate the seaward limits of the continental shelf: the 200 metres isobath and the exploitability test.[35] However, the exploitability test gave rise to a considerable degree of uncertainty because legal interpretation of the test may change according to the development of technology. In fact, the technological development during the 1960s made it possible to exploit the seabed at depths in excess of 1000 metres. It

33 C. L. Rozakis, 'Continental Shelf', in R. Bernhardt (ed.), *Encyclopedia of Public International Law*, vol. 11 (Amsterdam, North-Holland, 1989), p. 84.

34 ICJ Reports 1969, p. 39, para. 63.

35 Simply put, 'isobath' means a line connecting points of equal water depth. International Hydrographic Organization, *Hydrographic Dictionary, Part I*, vol. I, 5th edn (Monaco, 1994), p. 118 and p. 63.

could be reasonably presumed that this capacity would progress further. In this regard, some argue that the concept of exploitability may be interpreted in relation to the most advanced standards of technology. If this is the case, according to an extreme interpretation, all the ocean floor of the world would eventually be divided among the coastal States.[36] Hence it was hardly surprising that the precise limits of the continental shelf became a significant issue at UNCLOS III.

Negotiations at the Conference resulted in Article 76 of the LOSC. Article 76(1) provides two alternative criteria determining the outer limits of the continental shelf beyond 200 nautical miles:

> The continental shelf of a coastal State comprises the seabed and subsoil of the submarine areas that extend beyond its territorial sea throughout the natural prolongation of its land territory to the outer edge of the continental margin, or to a distance of 200 nautical miles from the baselines from which the breadth of the territorial sea is measured where the outer edge of the continental margin does not extend up to that distance.

This provision provides two criteria: (i) the limit of the outer edge of the continental margin (geological criterion) or (ii) a distance of 200 nautical miles (distance criterion).

There is little doubt that the distance criterion is closely linked to the concept of the EEZ. One can say that with the emergence of the concept of the EEZ, the continental shelf within 200 nautical miles from the baseline is currently established as customary law.[37] Hence the coastal State has the continental shelf in a legal sense up to 200 nautical miles regardless of the configuration of the seabed. As a consequence, approximately 36 per cent of the total seabed is now under the national jurisdiction of coastal State.[38]

In relation to this, legal title over the continental shelf should be mentioned. Legal title can be defined as the criteria on the basis of which a State is legally empowered to exercise rights and jurisdiction over the marine areas adjacent to its coasts.[39] According to the Truman Proclamation, the continental shelf 'may be regarded as an extension of the land-mass of the coastal nation and thus naturally appurtenant to it'. Noting on this phrase, the ICJ, in the *North Sea Continental Shelf* cases, highlighted the concept of natural prolongation as a legal title over the continental shelf.[40] On the other hand, the emergence of the concept of the 200-mile EEZ inevitably affected the legal title of the continental shelf. As noted, the EEZ is based on the distance criterion. In this regard, the ICJ, in the *Libya/Malta* case, pronounced that:

[36] S. Oda, *International Control of Sea Resources* (Dordrecht, Nijhoff, 1989), p. 167.
[37] ICJ Reports 1985, p. 33, para. 34.
[38] Churchill and Lowe, *Law of the Sea*, p. 148.
[39] P. Weil, *The Law of Maritime Delimitation: Reflections* (Cambridge, Grotius, 1989), p. 48.
[40] ICJ Reports 1969, p. 31, para. 43.

Although there can be a continental shelf where there is no exclusive economic zone, there cannot be an exclusive economic zone without a corresponding continental shelf. It follows that, for juridical and practical reasons, the distance criterion must now apply to the continental shelf as well as to the exclusive economic zone.[41]

In light of the *dictum* of the Court and Article 76 of the LOSC, it may be argued that currently the distance criterion is the legal title over the continental shelf up to 200 nautical miles and the natural prolongation offers legal title over the shelf beyond 200 nautical miles.

4.3 Criteria for determining the outer limits of the continental shelf beyond 200 nautical miles

Where the outer edge of the continental margin extends beyond 200 nautical miles, the limit of the continental shelf is to be determined on the basis of the geological criteria set out by Article 76(4). This provision contains two criteria for fixing the seaward limit of the continental shelf.

The first criterion is the sedimentary thickness test enshrined in Article 76(4)(a)(i). As this criterion was introduced by Ireland, this is called the *Irish formula* or *Gardiner formula* (see Figure 4.1). According to this criterion, the outer edge of the continental margin is fixed by a line delineated by reference to the outermost fixed points at each of which the thickness of sedimentary rocks is at least 1 per cent of the shortest distance from such point to the foot of the continental slope. The sedimentary thickness test may provide a possible criterion to evaluate the presence or absence of hydrocarbon reserves. It may be said that this criterion seeks to reserve the right to exploit petrol for the coastal State.

A second criterion is the *Hedberg formula* provided in Article 76(4)(a)(ii) (see Figure 4.2). According to this formula, the outer edge of the continental margin is determined by a line delineated by reference to fixed points not more than 60 nautical miles from the foot of the continental slope. In the absence of evidence to the contrary, the foot of the continental slope shall be determined as the point of maximum change in the gradient at its base by conformity with Article 76(4)(b).

In either case, lines delineating the outer limits of the continental shelf must be straight lines not exceeding 60 nautical miles in length, connecting fixed points, defined by coordinates of latitude and longitude (Article 76(7)). The fixed points comprising the line of the outer limits of the continental shelf on the seabed shall not exceed 350 nautical miles from the baselines from which the breadth of the territorial sea is measured or shall not exceed 100 nautical miles from the 2,500-metre isobaths (Article 76(5), see Figure 4.3).

Presently the continental shelf beyond 200 nautical miles attracts many coastal States. Yet there is a concern that this regime reintroduces the inequalities between

[41] ICJ Reports 1985, p. 33, para. 34.

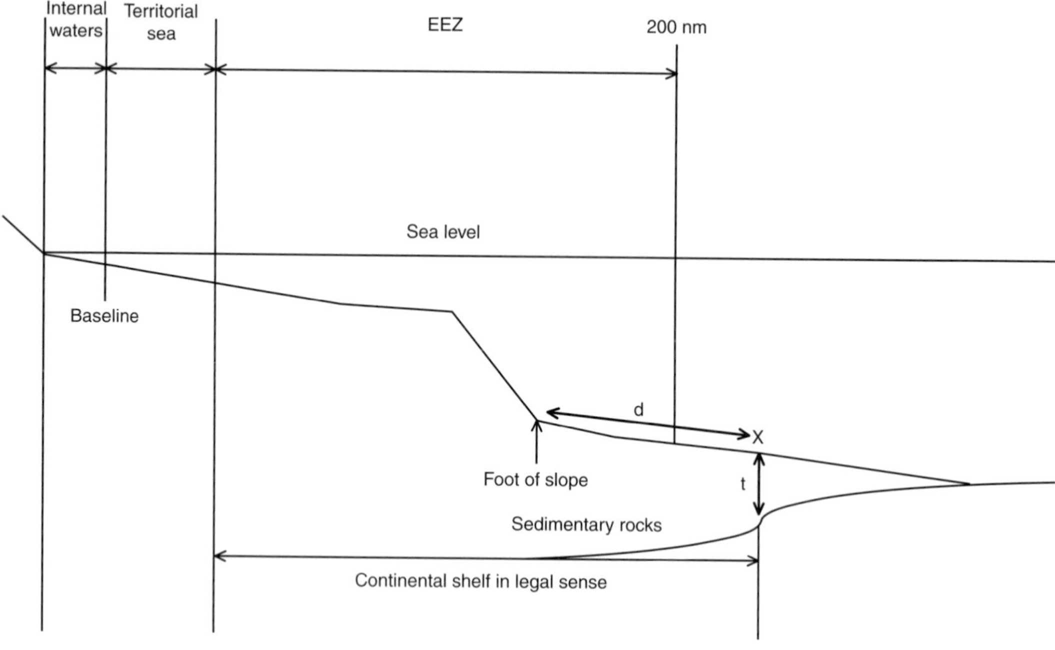

Figure 4.1. Continental shelf as defined in accordance with Article 76(4)(a)(i)

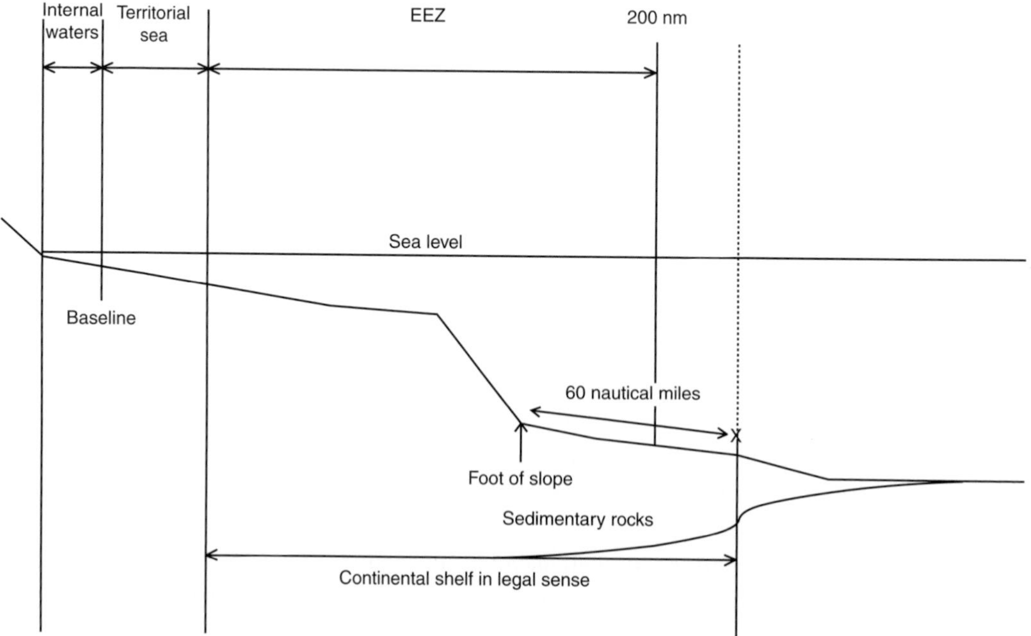

Figure 4.2. Continental shelf as defined in accordance with Article 76(4)(a)(ii)

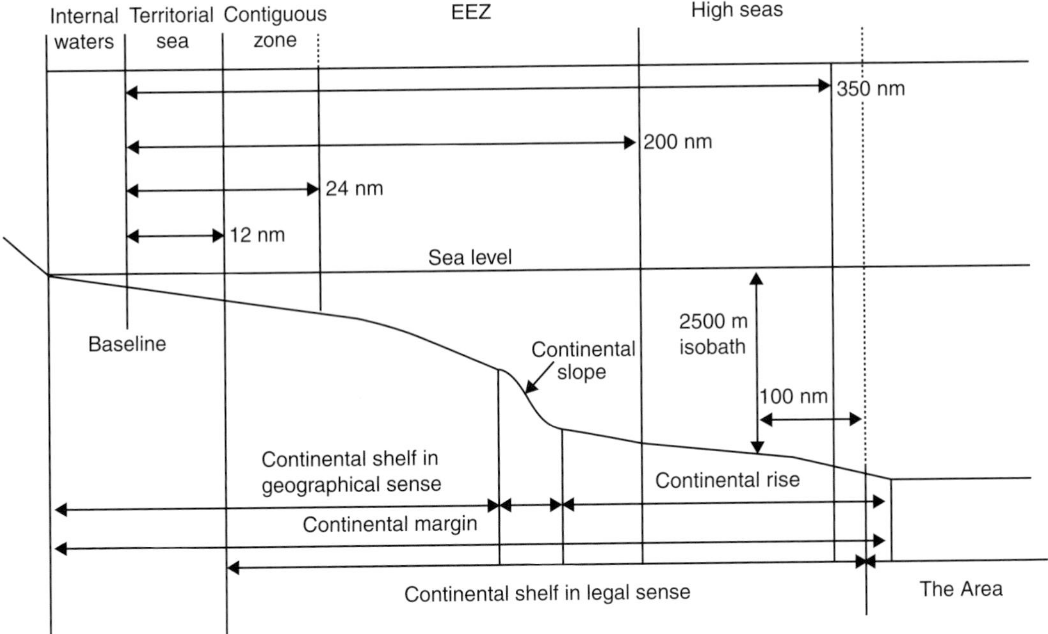

Figure 4.3. Continental shelf as defined in accordance with Article 76(5)

States which the uniform breadth of 200 nautical miles was supposed to remove. Further to this, the criteria set out in Article 76 give rise to a degree of uncertainty as to its practical application. For instance, in the application of the Irish and the Hedberg formulae, the location of the foot of the continental slope is of primary importance. However, the identification of the foot of the continental slope is not free from difficulty in practice.[42] It is also suggested that the observed sediment thickness can be in error by as much as 10 per cent. If this is the case, this will have a significant impact upon the location of the outer limits of the continental shelf.[43] The points of the 2,500-metre isobath may also be difficult to locate when isobaths are complex or repeated in multiples.[44] In light of the scientific uncertainties, the LOSC established a technical body which assesses data respecting the outer limits of the continental shelf, namely the Commission on the Limits of the Continental Shelf (hereafter CLCS or the Commission).

[42] *Scientific and Technical Guidelines of the Commission on the Limits of the Continental Shelf Adopted by the Commission on 13 May 1999 at its Fifth Session*, CLCS/11, p. 47, paras. 6.3.2 and 6.3.3; C. Carleton, 'Article 76 of the UN Convention on the Law of the Sea: Implementation Problems from the Technical Perspective' (2006) 21 *IJMCL* pp. 293–296; R. Macnab, 'The Case for Transparency in the Delimitation of the Outer Continental Shelf in Accordance with UNCLOS Article 76' (2004) 35 *ODIL* p. 5; by the same writer, 'Initial Assessment', in P. J. Cook and C. M. Carleton (eds.) *Continental Shelf Limits: The Scientific and Legal Interface* (New York, Oxford University Press, 2000), p. 258.

[43] *Ibid.*, p. 259. [44] Macnab, 'The Case for Transparency', p. 8.

4.4 The Commission on the Limits of the Continental Shelf

As we shall discuss later, the coastal State intending to claim a continental shelf beyond 200 nautical miles is required to submit information on the limits of the shelf to the Commission. The Commission consists of twenty-one members who shall be experts in the field of geology, geophysics or hydrography. The members of the Commission are to be elected by States Parties to the LOSC from among their nationals, having due regard to the need to ensure equitable geographical representation, and they shall serve in their personal capacities in accordance with Article 2(1) of Annex II. The members are to be elected for a term of five years and can be re-elected (Article 2(4) of Annex II). Whilst the tasks of the Commission are not completely separated from the legal interpretation of relevant rules of the Convention, the Commission contains no jurists. No representative of the International Seabed Authority (hereafter the Authority) is included in the membership of the Commission, while the Authority is directly affected by the recommendation of the Commission.

The Commission is conferred with two functions by Article 3(1) of Annex II. First, the Commission is to consider the data and other material submitted by coastal States and to make recommendations to the coastal States in this matter in accordance with Article 76 and the Statement of Understanding adopted on 29 August 1980 by UNCLOS III. Second, the Commission is to provide scientific and technical advice, if requested by the coastal State concerned.

It can be reasonably presumed that the extension of the continental shelf beyond 200 nautical miles will increase overlapping of continental shelves. However, delimitation of the continental shelf beyond 200 nautical miles is outside the scope of the jurisdiction of the Commission. Article 9 of Annex II, along with Article 76(10), make clear that the actions of the Commission shall not prejudice matters relating to delimitation of boundaries between States with opposite or adjacent coasts. Paragraph 2 of Annex I of the Rules of Procedure of the Commission, adopted on 11 April 2008, states that:

> In case there is a dispute in the delimitation of the continental shelf between opposite or adjacent States, or in other cases of unresolved land or maritime disputes, related to the submission, the Commission shall be:
>
> (a) Informed of such disputes by the coastal States making the submission; and
> (b) Assured by the coastal States making the submission to the extent possible that the submission will not prejudice matters relating to the delimitation of boundaries between States.[45]

In cases where a land or maritime dispute exists, the Commission shall not consider and qualify a submission made by any of the States concerned in the dispute, unless there is prior consent given by all States that are parties to such a dispute.[46] The submissions

[45] The Rules of Procedure of the Commission are available at: www.un.org/Depts/los/clcs_new/commission_documents.htm.

[46] Para. 5(a) of Annex I of the Rules of the Commission.

made before the Commission and the recommendations approved by the Commission thereon shall not prejudice the position of States which are parties to a land or maritime dispute.[47]

In order not to prejudice questions relating to the delimitation of boundaries between States, a State may make partial or joint submissions to the Commission.[48] For example, on 19 May 2006, France, Ireland, Spain and the United Kingdom made a joint submission to the Commission. On 1 December 2008, the Republic of Mauritius and the Republic of Seychelles also made a joint submission to the Commission. It appears that joint submissions may contribute to reduce the workload of the Commission and encourage cooperation between neighbouring coastal States to determine their outer limits of the continental shelf in an amicable manner.[49]

4.5 Procedures to establish the outer limits of the continental shelf

The process of establishing the outer limits of the continental shelf beyond 200 nautical miles involves four steps.[50]

(i) Step One: The coastal State is to initially delineate the outer limits of its continental shelf in conformity with criteria set out in Article 76 of the LOSC.

(ii) Step Two: The coastal State is to submit information on the limits to the CLCS within ten years of the entry into force of the LOSC for that State.[51] A submission by a coastal State is examined by a sub-commission which is composed of seven members of the Commission, and, next, the sub-commission submits its recommendation to the Commission.[52] The representatives of the coastal State which made a submission to the Commission may participate in the relevant proceedings without the right to vote pursuant to Article 5 of Annex II. Approval by the Commission of the recommendations of the sub-commission is to be by a majority of two-thirds of Commission members present and voting pursuant to Article 6(2) of Annex II. The recommendations of the Commission are to be submitted in writing to the coastal State which made the submission and to the UN Secretary-General in accordance with Article 6(3) of Annex II. The LOSC contains no rule concerning public access to the information submitted to the Commission. Nor is there any provision with regard to the public promulgation of the recommendations of the Commission. However, the executive summary of a submission to the Commission is public pursuant to Rule 50 of the Rules of Procedure, and third States have been allowed to make observations on submissions to the Commission.

(iii) Step Three: The coastal State is to establish the outer limits of its continental shelf on the basis of the recommendations of the Commission. Where the coastal State

[47] Para. 5(b) of Annex I of the Rules of the Commission.

[48] Paras. 3 and 4 of Annex I of the Rules of the Commission.

[49] H. Llewellyn, 'The Commission on the Limits of the Continental Shelf: Joint Submission by France, Ireland, Spain, and the United Kingdom' (2007) 56 *ICLQ* pp. 683–684.

[50] R. Wolfrum, 'The Delimitation of the Outer Continental Shelf: Procedural Considerations', in *Liber Amicorum Jean-Pierre Cot: Le procès international* (Brussels, Bruylant, 2009), pp. 352–353.

[51] Article 76(8); para. 4 of Annex II. Concerning the procedures for submission of information, see Rules of Procedure of the Commission on the Limits of the Continental Shelf, CLCS/40/ Rev. 1, 17 April 2008.

[52] Paras. 5 and 6(1) of Annex II.

disagrees with the recommendations of the Commission, the State is to make a revised or new submission to the Commission in accordance with Article 8 of Annex II of the LOSC. Under Article 76(8) of the LOSC, the limits of the continental shelf established by a coastal State on the basis of the recommendations of the Commission shall be final and binding. This provision requires two brief comments.

First, strictly speaking, what is final and binding is the outer limits established by a coastal State on the basis of the Commission's recommendations, not the recommendations themselves.[53] In the case of disagreement by the coastal State with the recommendations of the Commission, the coastal State is to make a revised or new submission to the Commission within a reasonable time pursuant to Article 8 of Annex II.

Second, Article 76(8), along with Article 7 of Annex II, appears to indicate that the coastal State cannot establish outer limits of the continental shelf on the basis of information that has not been considered by the Commission. Yet the Commission is not empowered to assess whether a coastal State has established the outer limits of the continental shelf on the basis of its recommendations. It seems that the outer limits of the continental shelf which have not been established on the basis of the recommendations of the Commission will not become binding on other States.[54]

(iv) Step Four: Under Article 76(9), the coastal State is to deposit with the UN Secretary-General charts and relevant information, including geodetic data, permanently describing the outer limits of its continental shelf. The Secretary-General is to give due publicity thereto. Article 84(2) requires the coastal State to give due publicity to charts or lists of geographical coordinates and deposit a copy of each such chart or list with the UN Secretary-General and, in the case of those showing the outer limit lines of the continental shelf, the Secretary-General of the International Seabed Authority.[55]

To date, fifty-one coastal States have submitted full or partial information on the outer limits of the continental shelf beyond 200 nautical miles. A question that may arise is whether or not non-States Parties to the LOSC may claim a continental shelf beyond 200 nautical miles under customary international law. It seems very difficult to find 'extensive and virtually uniform' State practice and *opinio juris* with regard to the continental shelf beyond 200 nautical miles. Hence it would be difficult to argue that the continental shelf beyond 200 nautical miles is part of customary international law.[56] In fact, in his statement at the final session of UNCLOS III, Tommy Koh, the President of the Conference, stated that 'a state which is not a party to this Convention cannot invoke the benefits of Article 76'.[57] Furthermore, Article 4 of Annex II sets

[53] L. D. M. Nelson, 'The Settlement of Disputes Arising from Conflicting Outer Continental Shelf Claims' (2009) 24 *IJMCL* p. 419.

[54] International Law Association, *The Second ILA Report (2006)* p. 15.

[55] On 21 October 2009, Mexico became the first member of the International Seabed Authority which had deposited charts and other relevant information on the limit of its continental shelf with respect to the western polygon in the Gulf of Mexico. ISBA/16/A/2, 8 March 2010, p. 20, para. 74.

[56] S. V. Suarez, *The Outer Limits of the Continental Shelf: Legal Aspects of their Establishment* (Berlin, Springer, 2008), p. 181.

[57] UNCLOS III, *Official Records*, vol. XVII, A/CONF.62/SR.193, p. 136, para. 48.

out a time limit for submissions of ten years after entry into force of the LOSC. This provision would seem to exclude the possibility of submission by a non-Party to the Convention.[58] It must also be noted that Article 76 is linked to Article 82 with regard to revenue sharing. The claim over the continental shelf beyond 200 nautical miles without the acceptance of the obligation with regard to revenue sharing should not be assumed.[59] Further to this, it is apparent that non-States Parties to the LOSC cannot use the recommendations of the CLCS. Hence there may be room for the view that the outer limits of the continental shelf unilaterally established by non-States Parties lack legitimacy because the limits have not been established through an internationally accepted procedure.

A further issue involves peaceful settlement of disputes concerning the interpretation and application of Article 76 of the LOSC. Other States Parties may be considered to have a legal interest in the outer limits of the continental shelf beyond 200 nautical miles. For instance, it may be argued that a State Party which undertakes the exploration and exploitation of resources in the Area has a legal interest in the outer limits of the continental shelf beyond 200 nautical miles.[60] Accordingly, it seems possible that other States may challenge the validity of the outer limits of the continental shelf concerned. There is no reference to such disputes under section 3 of Part XV which provides for limitations and exceptions to the compulsory procedures of dispute settlement. Thus, disputes involving the outer limits of the continental shelf beyond 200 nautical miles can, if necessary, be settled by recourse to the compulsory procedures of Part XV.[61]

4.6 Payments concerning the exploitation of the continental shelf beyond 200 nautical miles

Under Article 82 of the LOSC, the coastal State is obliged to make payments or contributions in kind in respect of the exploitation of the non-living resources of the continental shelf beyond 200 nautical miles. It is generally recognised that this provision represents a compromise between a group of States which advocated their claims over their continental shelves beyond 200 nautical miles and an opposing group which attempted to limit the continental shelves at 200 nautical miles.[62]

The payments and contributions are to be made annually with respect to all production at a site after the first five years of production of that site. For the sixth year, the rate of payment or contribution is to be 1 per cent of the value or volume of production at the site. The rate is to increase by 1 per cent for each subsequent year until the

58 T. Treves, 'Remarks on Submissions to the Commission on the Limits of the Continental Shelf in Response to Judge Marotta's Report' (2006) 21 *IJMCL* p. 364; ILA Second Report, p. 21; A. G. Oude Elferink, 'Submissions of Coastal States to the CLCS in Cases of Unresolved Land or Maritime Disputes', in M. H. Nordquist, J. N. Moore and T. H. Heider (eds.), *Legal and Scientific Aspects of Continental Shelf Limits* (Leiden and Boston, Nijhoff, 2004), p. 269.

59 *Ibid.* See also ILA Second Report, p. 21.

60 Wolfrum, 'The Delimitation of the Outer Continental Shelf', pp. 363–364; Second ILA Report, p. 26.

61 *Ibid.*, p. 25; Wolfrum, 'The Delimitation of the Outer Continental Shelf', p. 364.

62 ILA, *Report on Article 82 of the 1982 UN Convention on the Law of the Sea (UNCLOS), Rio De Janeiro Conference (2008)*, p. 2.

twelfth year and shall remain at 7 per cent thereafter in conformity with Article 82(2). However, a developing State which is a net importer of a mineral resource produced from its continental shelf is exempt from making such payments in respect of that mineral resource by virtue of Article 82(3). Under Article 82(4), the payments or contributions are to be made through the Authority. The Authority is to distribute them to States Parties to the LOSC on the basis of equitable sharing criteria, taking into account the interests and needs of developing States, particularly the least developed and the land-locked among them. It may be said that the principle of the common heritage of mankind counterbalances overexpansion of the exclusive interests of coastal States.[63]

4.7 The sovereign rights of the coastal State over the continental shelf

The coastal State exercises sovereign rights over the continental shelf for the purpose of exploring and exploiting its natural resources in accordance with Article 77(1). The principal features of the sovereign rights can be summarised in six points:

(i) The sovereign rights of the coastal State over the continental shelf are inherent rights, and do not depend on occupation, effective or notional, or on any express proclamation. Thus a continental shelf exists *ipso facto* and *ab initio*.[64]

(ii) The sovereign rights of the coastal State relate to the exploration and exploitation of natural resources on the continental shelf. Non-natural resources are not included in the ambit of sovereign rights of the coastal State even if they are found on the continental shelf. For instance, wrecks lying on the shelf do not fall within the ambit of the sovereign rights over the continental shelf.[65] The sovereign rights are thus characterised by the lack of comprehensiveness of material scope. On this point, the sovereign rights must be distinguished from territorial sovereignty.

(iii) The natural resources basically consist of the mineral and other non-living resources of the seabed and subsoil. However, exceptionally, sedentary species are also included in natural resources on the continental shelf. Under Article 77(4), the sedentary species are organisms which, at the harvestable stage, either are immobile on or under the seabed or are unable to move except in constant physical contact with the seabed or the subsoil. Examples include oysters, clams and abalone. Yet it is debatable whether crabs and lobster fall within the category of sedentary species.[66] Where the coastal State established the EEZ, that State has the sovereign rights to explore and exploit all marine living resources on the seabed in the zone.

(iv) Although there is no provision like Article 73(1), there seems to be a general sense that the sovereign rights include legislative and enforcement jurisdiction with a view to exploring and exploiting natural resources on the continental shelf. In fact, Article 111(2) stipulates that:

[63] Oda, *International Control*, p. xxxii. [64] ICJ Reports 1969, p. 22, para. 19.
[65] Churchill and Lowe, *Law of the Sea*, p. 152. [66] *Ibid.*, p. 151.

> The right of hot pursuit shall apply *mutatis mutandis* to violations in the exclusive economic zone or on the continental shelf, including safety zones around continental shelf installations, of the laws and regulations of the coastal State applicable in accordance with this Convention to the exclusive economic zone or the continental shelf, including such safety zones.

This provision appears to suggest that the coastal State has legislative and enforcement jurisdiction with respect to the continental shelf.

(v) The sovereign rights of the coastal State are exercisable over all people or vessels regardless of their nationalities. Thus there is no limit concerning personal scope.

(vi) The rights are exclusive in the sense that if the coastal State does not explore the continental shelf or exploit its natural resources, no one may undertake these activities without the express consent of the coastal State.[67] At the same time, the exercise of the rights of the coastal State over the continental shelf must not infringe or result in any unjustifiable interference with navigation and other rights and freedoms of other States as provided for in the LOSC (Article 78(2)).

Overall sovereign rights of the coastal State over the continental shelf are limited to certain matters provided by international law. With respect to matters provided by international law, however, the coastal State may exercise legislative and enforcement jurisdiction over all peoples regardless of their nationalities in an exclusive manner. In essence, rights over the continental shelf are spatial in the sense that they can be exercised solely within the particular space in question regardless of the nationality of persons or vessels. Hence, like the EEZ, the sovereign rights of the coastal State over the continental shelf can also be regarded as a limited spatial jurisdiction.

In addition to these sovereign rights, the coastal State has jurisdiction with regard to artificial islands, marine scientific research, dumping and other purposes. Relevant provisions can be summarised as follows.

First, under Article 80 of the LOSC, Article 60 concerning the coastal State's jurisdiction over artificial islands is applied *mutatis mutandis* to the continental shelf. It follows that on the continental shelf, the coastal State has exclusive rights to construct and to authorise and regulate the construction, operation and use of (a) artificial islands, (b) installations and structures for the purposes provided for in Article 56 and other economic purposes, and (c) installations and structures which may interfere with the exercise of the rights of the coastal State in the zone. The coastal State also has exclusive jurisdiction over such artificial islands, installations and structures, including jurisdiction with regard to customs, fiscal, health, safety and immigration laws and regulations.

Second, on the continental shelf, the coastal State has jurisdiction with regard to marine scientific research in accordance with Articles 56(1)(b)(ii) and 246(1) of the LOSC. Article 246(2) makes clear that marine scientific research in the EEZ and on the

[67] LOSC, Article 77(2); Article 2(2) of the Geneva Convention on the Continental Shelf. The ICJ echoed this view: ICJ Reports 1969, p. 22, para. 19.

continental shelf shall be conducted with the consent of the coastal State. However, with regard to the continental shelf beyond 200 nautical miles, the discretion of the coastal State is limited by Article 246(6), the first sentence of which provides as follows:

> Notwithstanding the provisions of paragraph 5, coastal States may not exercise their discretion to withhold consent under subparagraph (a) of that paragraph in respect of marine scientific research projects to be undertaken in accordance with the provisions of this Part on the continental shelf, beyond 200 nautical miles from the baselines from which the breadth of the territorial sea is measured, outside those specific areas which coastal States may at any time publicly designate as areas in which exploitation or detailed exploratory operations focused on those areas are occurring or will occur within a reasonable period of time.

At the same time, this provision seems to suggest that within 'those specific areas in which exploitation or detailed exploratory operations focused on those areas are occurring or will occur within a reasonable period of time', the coastal States may exercise their discretion to withhold consent if, as provided in Article 246(5)(a), a research project is of direct significance for the exploration and exploitation of natural resources. Furthermore, the restriction in Article 246(6) does not apply to the withdrawal of consent relating to marine scientific research on the basis of Article 246(5)(b)–(d).

Third, Article 210(5) of the LOSC makes clear that the coastal State has the right to permit, regulate and control dumping on the continental shelf. At the same time, the coastal State has enforcement jurisdiction with respect to pollution by dumping on the continental shelf.

Finally, Article 81 provides that: 'The coastal State shall have the exclusive rights to authorize and regulate drilling on the continental shelf for all purposes'. The phrase, 'for all purposes', seems to suggest that the exclusive rights of the coastal State concerning drilling on the continental shelf are not limited to the purposes of exploration and exploitation of natural resources.

4.8 Freedoms of third States

With respect to the freedom of use *on* the continental shelf, Article 79(1) stipulates that all States are entitled to lay submarine cables and pipelines on the continental shelf. However, the delineation of the course for the laying of such pipelines on the continental shelf is subject to the consent of the coastal State pursuant to Article 79(3). Under Article 79(2), the coastal State also has rights to take reasonable measures for the exploration of the continental shelf, the exploitation of its natural resources and the prevention, reduction and control of pollution from pipelines.

In this context, some mention should be made of the judicial nature of the superjacent waters above the continental shelf. Following Article 3 of the Convention on the Continental Shelf, Article 78(1) of the LOSC provides that the rights of the coastal State over the continental shelf do not affect the legal status of the superjacent waters or of the airspace above those waters. It follows that where the coastal State has not claimed an EEZ, the superjacent waters above the continental shelf are the high seas. Where the coastal State has established an EEZ, the superjacent waters above the continental shelf beyond 200 nautical miles are always the high seas under the LOSC. Hence all States enjoy the freedoms of navigation and fishing in the superjacent waters of the continental shelf and the freedom of overflight in the airspace above those waters. However, it must be noted that freedoms of third States may be qualified by the coastal State in the superjacent water of the continental shelf beyond 200 nautical miles.

First, the coastal State has exclusive jurisdiction over the construction of artificial islands as well as installations and structures on the continental shelf beyond 200 nautical miles by virtue of Article 80 of the LOSC. In practice, artificial islands and other installations are constructed in superjacent waters above the continental shelf. It would seem to follow that freedom to construct artificial islands may be qualified by the coastal State jurisdiction, even though literally the superjacent waters of the continental shelf beyond 200 nautical miles are the high seas.

Second, in practice, coastal States explore and exploit natural resources on the continental shelf from the superjacent waters above the continental shelf. Accordingly, it appears inescapable that the coastal State excises its jurisdiction in the superjacent waters above the continental shelf for the purpose of the exploration and exploitation of natural resources.[68] In fact, Article 111(2) of the LOSC provides the right of hot pursuit in respect of violations on the continental shelf, including safety zones around continental shelf installations, of the laws and regulations of the coastal State applicable to the continental shelf, including such safety zones. In practice, safety zones are established on the superjacent waters of the continental shelf. It would seem to follow that the coastal State jurisdiction relating to the exploration and exploitation of the continental shelf is to be exercised at least in safety zones on the superjacent waters of the shelf.

Third, as noted, the coastal State has jurisdiction with regard to marine scientific research *on* the continental shelf under Articles 56(1)(b)(ii) and 246(1) of the LOSC, and such research on the continental shelf is to be conducted with the consent of the coastal State pursuant to Article 246(2). On the other hand, Article 257 of the LOSC provides that all States have the right to conduct marine scientific research *in* the water column beyond the limits of the EEZ 'in conformity with this Convention'. A question arises whether the complete freedom of marine scientific research applies to superjacent waters of the continental shelf. According to a literal interpretation, consent under Article 246(2) seems to be required only for research physically taking place on the sea floor. Considering that normally marine scientific research is carried out from the superjacent waters or airspace above the continental shelf, however, it appears to be naïve to consider that coastal States will not exercise their jurisdiction to regulate marine scientific research there.

[68] S. Oda, 'Proposals for Revising the Convention on the Continental Shelf', in S. Oda, *Fifty Years of the Law of the Sea: With a Special Section on the International Court of Justice* (The Hague, Nijhoff), p. 275; Churchill and Lowe, *Law of the Sea*, p. 215.

In summary, it appears that in some respects the freedom of the high seas may be qualified by coastal State jurisdiction in the superjacent waters above the continental shelf and the airspace above the waters. To this extent, their legal status should be distinguished from the high seas per se.

5 CONCLUSIONS

The principal points discussed in this chapter can be summarised as follows:

(i) In the contiguous zone, the coastal State may exercise jurisdiction to prevent and punish infringement of its customs, fiscal, immigration or sanitary laws and regulations within its territory, internal waters and the territorial sea. Literally the coastal State has only enforcement jurisdiction, not prescriptive jurisdiction, in the contiguous zone. In light of the increasing importance of the prevention of illegal traffic in drugs, in particular, there appears to be scope to reconsider the question whether the coastal State cannot extend legislative jurisdiction to the contiguous zone in practice.

(ii) The coastal State exercises sovereign rights over the EEZ and the continental shelf for the purpose of exploring and exploiting the natural resources there. The sovereign rights are limited to the matters defined by international law (limitation *ratione materiae*). Thus the sovereign rights must be distinct from territorial sovereignty in the sense that such rights lack the comprehensiveness of material scope.

(iii) Concerning matters provided by international law, in the EEZ and the continental shelf, the coastal State may exercise legislative and enforcement jurisdiction over all peoples regardless of their nationalities in an exclusive manner. Furthermore, like territorial sovereignty, sovereign rights over the EEZ and the continental shelf are essentially spatial because they can be exercised only within the specific space concerned. Hence, it is argued that the sovereign rights of the coastal State can be considered as a sort of spatial jurisdiction, namely, limited spatial jurisdiction.

(iv) In the EEZ, all States enjoy freedoms of navigation, overflight and the laying of submarine cables and pipelines. In exercising these freedoms, however, States must have due regard to the rights and duties of the coastal State under Article 58(3) of the LOSC. To this extent, freedoms of the seas in the EEZ may be qualified by coastal State jurisdiction.

(v) If an international dispute arises with regard to a matter where the LOSC does not specify which States are to have jurisdiction, such a dispute should be resolved on the basis of equity and in the light of all the relevant circumstances in accordance with Article 59 of the LOSC. This provision contains no presumption in favour of either the coastal State or other States.

(vi) The outer limit of the continental shelf beyond 200 nautical miles is to be determined by the criteria enshrined in Article 76 of the LOSC, namely, the sedimentary thickness test (the *Irish formula* or *Gardiner formula*) and the fixed distance (60 nautical miles) test (the *Hedberg formula*). The coastal State is required to submit information with regard to the outer limits of the continental shelf beyond 200 nautical miles to the CLCS. On the basis of the recommendations of the CLCS, that State is to establish the outer limits of its continental shelf. Whilst the extension of the continental shelf beyond 200 nautical miles attracts growing attention between States, such a claim may create a difficult issue with regard to the delimitation of overlapping shelves between two or more coastal States.

(vii) The institution of the EEZ and the continental shelf rests on a balance between the rights of the coastal State on the basis of the principle of sovereignty and the right of other States according to the principle of freedom. Nonetheless, it is likely that the coastal State will attempt to extend its jurisdiction over matters which do not clearly fall within the rights of that State. The increasing influence of the coastal State may entail the risk of promoting 'territorialisation' of the EEZ.

FURTHER READING

1 Contiguous Zone

A. V. Lowe, 'The Development of the Contiguous Zone' (1981) 52 *BYIL* pp. 109–169.

S. Oda, 'The Concept of the Contiguous Zone' (1962) 11 *ICLQ* pp. 131–153.

A. Pazarci, 'Le concept de zone contiguë dans la convention sur le droit de la mer de 1982' (1984–85) 18 *RBDI* pp. 249–271.

2 Exclusive Economic Zone

As there are many studies with regard to the EEZ, only monographs on this subject will be listed here.

D. Attard, *The Exclusive Economic Zone in International Law* (Oxford, Clarendon Press, 1987).

E. Franckx and P. Gautier (eds.), *The Exclusive Economic Zone and the United Nations Convention on the Law of the Sea, 1982–2000: A Preliminary Assessment of State Practice* (Brussels, Bruylant, 2003).

B. Kwiatkowska, *The 200-Mile Exclusive Economic Zone in the New Law of the Sea* (Dordrecht, Nijhoff, 1989).

F. Orrego Vicuña, *The Exclusive Economic Zone* (Cambridge University Press, 1989).

The United Nations has published useful documents on the EEZ.

United Nations, *The Law of the Sea: National Legislation on the Exclusive Economic Zone and the Exclusive Fishery Zone* (New York, United Nations, 1986).

The Law of the Sea: Exclusive Economic Zone: Legislative History of Articles 56, 58 and 59 of the United Nations Convention on the Law of the Sea (New York, United Nations, 1992).

The Law of the Sea: National Legislation on the Exclusive Economic Zone and the Exclusive Fishery Zone (New York, United Nations, 1993).

3 Continental Shelf

A. Caligiuri, 'Les revendications des Etats côtiers de l'océan arctique sur le plateau continental au-delà de 200 milles marins' (2007) 12 *Annuaire du droit de la mer* pp. 273–294.

D. A. Colson, 'The Delimitation of the Outer Continental Shelf between Neighbouring States' (2003) 97 *AJIL* pp. 91–107.

M. S. T. Gau, 'Third Party Intervention in the Commission on the Limits of the Continental Shelf Regarding a Submission Involving a Dispute' (2009) 40 *ODIL* pp. 61–79.

B. Kunoy, 'Establishment of the Outer Limits of the Continental Shelf: Is Crossing Boundaries Trespassing?' (2011) 26 *IJMCL* pp. 313–334.

H. Llewellyn, 'The Commission on the Limits of the Continental Shelf: Joint Submission by France, Ireland, Spain, and the United Kingdom' (2007) 56 *ICLQ* pp. 677–694.

R. Macnab, 'The Case for Transparency in the Delimitation of the Outer Continental Shelf in Accordance with UNCLOS Article 76' (2004) 35 *ODIL* pp. 1–17.

L. D. M. Nelson, 'The Continental Shelf: Interplay of Law and Science', in N. Ando et al. (eds.), *Liber Amicorum Judge Shigeru Oda* (The Hague, Kluwer, 2002) pp. 1235–1253.

M. H. Nordquist, J. N. Moore and T. H. Heider (eds.), *Legal and Scientific Aspects of Continental Shelf Limits* (Leiden and Boston, Nijhoff, 2004).

A. G. Oude Elferink, 'Article 76 of the LOSC on the Definition of the Continental Shelf: Questions concerning its Interpretation from a Legal Perspective' (2006) 21 *IJMCL* pp. 271–272.

'"Openness" and Article 76 of the Law of the Sea Convention: The Process Does Not Need to Be Adjusted' (2009) 40 *ODIL* pp. 36–50.

'The Establishment of Outer Limits of the Continental Shelf beyond 200 Nautical Miles by the Coastal State: The Possibilities of Other States to Have an Impact on the Process' (2009) 24 *IJMCL* pp. 535–556.

D. R. Rothwell, 'Issues and Strategies for Outer Continental Shelf Claims' (2008) 23 *IJMCL* pp. 185–211.

M. Sheng-ti Gau, 'The Commission on the Limits of the Continental Shelf as a Mechanism to Prevent Encroachment upon the Area' (2011) 10 *Chinese Journal of International Law* pp. 3–33.

S. V. Suarez, *The Outer Limits of the Continental Shelf: Legal Aspects of their Establishment* (Berlin, Springer, 2008).

'Commission on the Limits of the Continental Shelf' (2010) 14 *Max Planck Yearbook of United Nations Law* pp. 131–168.

C. R. Symmons, 'The Irish Partial Submission to the Commission on the Limits of the Continental Shelf in 2005: A Precedent for Future Such Submissions in the Light of the "Disputed Areas" Procedures of the Commission?' (2006) 37 *ODIL* pp. 299–317.

UNDOALOS, *The Law of the Sea: Definition of the Continental Shelf* (New York, United Nations, 1993).

R. Wolfrum, 'The Delimitation of the Outer Continental Shelf: Procedural Considerations', in *Liber Amicorum Jean-Pierre Cot: Le procès international* (Brussels, Bruylant, 2009), pp. 349–366.

See also articles included in 'Special Issue: Symposium on the Outer Continental Shelf' (2006) 21 *IJMCL* pp. 263–372.

The outer limits of the continental shelf are a subject of discussion in the International Law Association. To date, three reports have been published. These reports are available at the website of the ILA: www.ila-hq.org/en/committees/index.cfm/cid/33.

5

Marine Spaces beyond National Jurisdiction

Main Issues

This chapter will examine rules governing marine spaces beyond the limits of national jurisdiction, namely, the high seas and the Area. The high seas are essentially characterised by the principle of freedom of the sea, and order in the high seas is ensured primarily by the flag State. Thus the principle of the exclusive jurisdiction of the flag State and its exceptions are key issues underlying international law governing the high seas. However, the Area is governed by the principle of the common heritage of mankind. This principle is innovative because it may bring new viewpoints beyond the State-to-State perspective in the law of the sea. Against that background, this chapter will discuss particularly the following issues:

(i) What is the principle of freedom of the high seas?
(ii) What is the function of the principle of the exclusive jurisdiction of the high seas?
(iii) What are the problems associated with flags of convenience and how is it possible to address them?
(iv) What are the peace-time exceptions to the principle of the exclusive jurisdiction of the flag State on the high seas?
(v) What is the *raison d'être* of the principle of the common heritage of mankind?
(vi) To what extent was the regime governing the Area in the LOSC changed by the 1994 Implementation Agreement?
(vii) Is the common heritage of mankind still a significant principle governing the Area?

1 INTRODUCTION

The high seas are governed by the principle of freedom. However, it is not suggested that there is no legal order on the high seas. The order on the high seas is essentially ensured by the principle of the exclusive jurisdiction of the flag State. Thus this principle and its exceptions become principal issues in the international law governing the high seas.

However, the Area, namely 'the seabed and ocean floor and subsoil thereof, beyond the limits of national jurisdiction',[1] is governed by the principle of the common heritage of mankind. As will be seen, this principle is an important innovation in the law of the sea in the sense that it introduces the concept of 'mankind' as an emerging actor in international law. The principle of the common heritage of mankind will provide a touchstone to consider the question whether and to what extent international law in the twenty-first century is moving toward an international law for mankind, which is beyond the State-to-State system. Against that background, this chapter focuses on legal regimes governing the high seas (section 2) and the Area (section 3).

2 THE HIGH SEAS

2.1 Spatial scope of the high seas

The LOSC devotes Part VII to the high seas. Under Article 86, the high seas are defined as 'all parts of the sea which are not included in the EEZ, in the territorial sea or in the internal waters of a State, or in the archipelagic waters of an archipelagic State'. Where a coastal State has established its EEZ, the landward limit of the high seas is the seaward limit of the EEZ. Where the coastal State has not claimed its EEZ, the landward limit of the high seas is the seaward limit of the territorial sea. In this case, the seabed of the high seas is the continental shelf of the coastal State up to the limit fixed by the international law of the sea. The seabed and subsoil beyond the outer limits of the continental shelf are the Area, which is the common heritage of mankind. The superjacent waters above the Area are always the high seas. Where the continental shelf extends beyond the limit of 200 nautical miles, the superjacent waters and the airspace above those waters are the high seas under Article 78 of the LOSC.

2.2 Principle of the freedom of the high seas[2]

The principle of the freedom of the high seas was established in the early nineteenth century.[3] This principle has two meanings.

[1] LOSC, Article 1(1).

[2] Concerning the juridical nature of the high seas, there is a classical controversy as to whether the high seas should be regarded as *res nullius* (nobody's thing) or *res communis* (thing of the entire community). Yet these Latin words seem to have been given a meaning different from the original meaning in Roman law and, consequently, created unnecessary confusion. Thus, Gidel proposed that the reference to the concept of *res nullius/res communis* should be avoided. In light of the modern development of rules governing the high seas, it would seem that currently the *res nullius/ res communis* controversy is of limited value. See G. Gidel, *Le droit international public de la mer: le temps de paix*, vol. 1: *Introduction, La haute mer* (reprint, Paris, Duchemin, 1981), pp. 213–224 (in particular, pp. 214–215). See also D. P. O'Connell (I. A. Shearer ed.), *The International Law of the Sea*, vol. 2 (Oxford, Clarendon Press, 1984), pp. 792–796.

[3] J. L. Brerly, *The Law of Nations: An Introduction to the International Law of Peace*, 6th edn (Oxford, Clarendon Press, 1963), p. 305; R. R. Churchill and A. V. Lowe, *Law of the Sea*, 3rd edn (Manchester University Press, 1999), p. 205.

First, the freedom of the high seas means that the high seas are free from national jurisdiction. In this regard, Article 89 of the LOSC makes clear that: 'No State may validly purport to subject any part of the high seas to its sovereignty'.

Second, the freedom of the high seas means the freedom of activities there. This is a corollary of the fact that the high seas are free from the national jurisdiction of any State. Consequently, each and every State has an equal right to enjoy the freedom to use the high seas in conformity with international law. In this regard, Article 87(1) provides as follows:

> The high seas are open to all States, whether coastal or land-locked. Freedom of the high seas is exercised under the conditions laid down by this Convention and by other rules of international law. It comprises, *inter alia*, both for coastal and land-locked States:
>
> (a) Freedom of navigation;
> (b) Freedom of overflight;
> (c) Freedom to lay submarine cables and pipelines, subject to Part VI;
> (d) Freedom to construct artificial islands and other installations permitted under international law, subject to Part VI;
> (e) Freedom of fishing, subject to the conditions laid down in section 2;
> (f) Freedom of scientific research, subject to Parts VI and XIII.

This provision calls for three brief comments.

First, the term '*inter alia*' suggests that the freedom of the high seas may comprise other freedoms which are not provided for in Article 87(1). Yet it is unclear what activities may fall within the category of other freedoms of the high seas. In particular, a sensitive issue arises with regard to the legality of military activities on the high seas. Whilst Article 88 of the LOSC provides that the high seas shall be reserved for peaceful purposes, it is generally considered that this provision does not prohibit naval manoeuvres and conventional weapons testing on the high seas.[4] However, Article 301 explicitly prohibits military activities which are contrary to the UN Charter, by providing that:

> In exercising their rights and performing their duties under this Convention, States Parties shall refrain from any threat or use of force against the territorial integrity or political independence of any State, or in any other manner inconsistent with the principles of international law enshrined in the Charter of the United Nations.

Second, as explained in the previous chapter, freedom to construct artificial islands and freedom of scientific research may be qualified by the coastal State jurisdiction in superjacent waters of the continental shelf beyond 200 nautical miles.[5] It would

[4] Churchill and Lowe, *Law of the Sea*, p. 206. [5] See Chapter 4, section 4.8.

follow that the six freedoms fully apply only to the high seas as superjacent waters of the Area.

Third, the freedom of the high seas is not absolute. As provided in Article 87(2), the freedom must be exercised 'with due regard for the interest of other States in their exercise of the freedom of the high seas, and also with due regard for the rights under this Convention with respect to activities in the Area'. It is also to be noted that the freedom of the high seas may be qualified by specific treaties respecting such things as conservation of marine living resources and marine environmental protection.

2.3 Principle of the exclusive jurisdiction of the flag State

The flag State, namely, the State which has granted a ship the right to sail under its flag, has the exclusive jurisdiction over vessels flying its flag. This is called the principle of the exclusive jurisdiction of the flag State. The principle is well established in customary international law. Article 92(1) of the LOSC formulates it as follows.

> Ships shall sail under the flag of one State only and, save in exceptional cases expressly provided for in international treaties or in this Convention, shall be subject to its exclusive jurisdiction on the high seas.

The flag State jurisdiction comprises both legislative and enforcement jurisdiction over its ships on the high seas. The flag State exercises enforcement jurisdiction over all peoples within its ships flying its flag regardless of their nationalities. In this regard, ITLOS stated that:

> [T]he ship, every thing on it, and every person involved or interested in its operations are treated as an entity linked to the flag State. The nationalities of these persons are not relevant.[6]

As a consequence, as stated in the Third Restatement of the Law, the flag State is entitled to make claims against other States in case of damage to its ship or injury to the seamen manning it, regardless of their nationality.[7]

The legal basis of the principle of the exclusive jurisdiction of the flag State was sometimes explained by the theory of the territoriality of the ship. According to this theory, a ship is considered as a 'floating island' or a 'detached part of the territory' of the State to which it belongs.[8] Nonetheless, the theory of the territoriality of the ship is contrary to the fact that, in certain circumstances, merchant vessels are subject to the right of visit by foreign warships, and vessels within internal waters and the territorial seas are in principle under the territorial sovereignty of the coastal State.[9] Hence the

6 The *M/V Saiga (No. 2)* case (1999) 38 *ILM* p. 1347, para. 106.

7 The American Law Institute, *Restatement of the Law Third: The Foreign Relations Law of the United States* vol. 2 (American Law Institute Publishers, 1990) §502, Comment (h), p. 21

8 The Case of the SS *Lotus*, PCIJ, 1928 Series A/10, p. 25.

9 Dissenting Opinion by Lord Finlay, the Case of the SS *Lotus*, PCIJ Series A, No. 10, p. 53.

theory of the territoriality of the ship is obsolete and indefensible for practical reasons. The principle of the exclusive jurisdiction of the flag State should be considered as a corollary of the freedom of the high seas and the requirement of the submission of the high seas to law, or, according to Gidel, the *juridicité* (or 'juridicity') of the high seas.[10] Considering that the high seas are not subject to any national jurisdiction and that there is no centralised authority governing the high seas, legal order on the high seas can be ensured primarily by the flag State.

The principle of the exclusive jurisdiction of the flag State plays a dual role. First, this principle prevents any interference by other States with vessels flying its flag on the high seas. In so doing, the principle of the exclusive jurisdiction of the flag State ensures the freedom of activity of vessels on the high seas. Second, under this principle, the flag State has responsibility to ensure compliance with national and international laws concerning activities of ships flying its flag on the high seas.

The principle of the exclusive jurisdiction of the flag State does not mean that only States are entitled to fly their flags on their vessels. As provided in Article 7 of the Geneva Convention on the High Seas and Article 93 of the LOSC, international organisations are also entitled to fly their own flag on their vessels.[11] Indeed, the International Committee of the Red Cross (ICRC) has been identifying its vessels by displaying its emblem for decades. In the UN Emergency Force (UNEF) in Egypt between 1956 and 1957, vessels were chartered by UNEF itself, and the United Nations flag was flown by certain of these vessels, on some occasions alone, and on others together with the national flag.[12]

Whilst the obligations of the flag State are diverse, Article 94 of the LOSC specifies in particular the following duties.

(i) Every State is under the duty to effectively exercise its jurisdiction and control in administrative, technical and social matters over ships flying its flag. In particular, every State is obliged to maintain a register of ships containing the names and particulars of ships flying its flags and to assume jurisdiction under its internal law over each ship flying its flag and its master, officers and crew in respect of administrative, technical and social matters respecting the ship.

(ii) Under Article 94(3), every State is obliged to take such measures for ships flying its flag as are necessary to ensure safety at sea with regard, *inter alia*, to:

(a) the construction, equipment and seaworthiness of ships;
(b) the manning of ships, labour conditions and the training of crews, taking into account the applicable international instruments;
(c) the use of signals, the maintenance of communications and the prevention of collisions.

[10] Gidel, *Le droit international public de la mer*, p. 225.

[11] Generally on this issue, see L. Savadogo, 'Les navires battant pavillon d'une organisation internationale' (2007) 53 *AFDI* pp. 640–671; V. P. Bants, *Ships Flying the Flag of International Organizations: A Study of the Maritime Flag of International Organizations*, Studies and Working Papers (Geneva, Graduate Institute of International Studies, 1999).

[12] *Ibid.*, p. 32.

(iii) In taking those measures called for in Article 94(3)(4), each State is required to conform to generally accepted international regulations, procedures and practices and to take any steps which may be necessary to secure their observance (Article 94(5)). 'Generally accepted international regulations, procedures and practices' include treaties adopted under the auspices of the IMO and the ILO as well as practices on the basis of those instruments. For example, the seaworthiness of ships is regulated by the 1974 International Convention for the Safety of Life at Sea (SOLAS),[13] the 1966 International Convention on Load Lines,[14] the 1971 Agreement on Special Trade Passenger Ships[15] and its Protocol of 1973,[16] the 1977 International Convention for the Safety of Fishing Vessels and the 1993 Torremolinos Protocol.[17] Collision at sea is governed by the 1972 Convention on the International Regulations for Preventing Collisions at Sea.[18] The quality of crews is regulated by the 1976 ILO Convention No. 147 concerning Minimum Standards in Merchant Ships,[19] the 1978 International Convention on Standards of Training, Certification and Watchkeeping for Seafarers,[20] the 1995 International Convention on Standards of Training, Certification and Watchkeeping for Fishing Vessel Personnel (STCW-F),[21] and the 2006 Maritime Labour Convention.[22] The role of the ILO is significant in this field.

(iv) Under Article 94(6), a State which has clear grounds to believe that proper jurisdiction and control with respect to a ship have not been exercised may report the facts to the flag State. Upon receiving such report, the flag State is obliged to investigate the matter, and if appropriate, take any action necessary to remedy the situation.

One issue which has arisen involves the extent of flag State jurisdiction in the situation where vessels flying the flags of different States have collided on the high seas. In this regard, the most often cited instance is the 1928 *Lotus* case. On 2 August 1926, the French mail steamer *Lotus* collided with a Turkish vessel *Boz-Kourt* on the high seas. As a result of the collision, the Turkish vessel sank and eight Turkish nationals on board lost their lives. Upon the arrival of the *Lotus* in Constantinople, the Turkish authorities instituted criminal proceedings against, among others, Lieutenant Demons, a French officer of the watch on board the *Lotus* at the time of collision. On 15 September 1926, the Criminal Court sentenced Lieutenant Demons to eighty days' imprisonment and a fine of £22. The action of the Turkish judicial authorities gave rise to a dispute between France and Turkey and, by a special agreement signed at Geneva on 12 October 1926, the two governments submitted the case to the Permanent Court of International Justice (PCIJ).

[13] 1184 *UNTS* p. 278. Entered into force 25 May 1980. This Convention has been amended many times to keep it up to date.
[14] 640 *UNTS* p. 133. Entered into force 21 July 1968.
[15] 910 *UNTS* p. 61. Entered into force 2 January 1974.
[16] 1046 *UNTS* p. 317. Entered into force 2 June 1977.
[17] The 1977 Convention was replaced by the 1993 Torremolinos Protocol.
[18] 1050 *UNTS* p. 18. Entered into force 15 July 1977.
[19] 1259 *UNTS* p. 335. Entered into force 28 November 1981.
[20] 1361 *UNTS*, p. 2. Entered into force 28 April 1984. The 1995 amendments completely revised the Convention. The amendments entered into force 1 February 1997.
[21] Not entered into force.
[22] Not entered into force. The text of the Convention is available at: www.ilo.org/.

In this case, the PCIJ took the view that 'there is no rule of international law prohibiting the State to which the ship on which the effects of the offence have taken place belongs from regarding the offence as having been committed in its territory and prosecuting, accordingly, the delinquent'.[23] The Court thus held, by the President's casting vote, that the Turkey had not acted in conflict with the principle of international law, contrary to Article 15 of the Convention of Lausanne of 24 July 1923.[24] Nonetheless, the *Lotus* judgment was much criticised because penal proceedings before foreign courts in the event of collision on the high seas may constitute an intolerable interference with international navigation.[25] As a consequence, the 1952 Brussels Convention for the Unification of Certain Rules relating to Penal Jurisdiction provided for the exclusive jurisdiction of the flag State or of the State of nationality of an offender in the event of a collision or any other incident of navigation concerning a sea-going ship.[26] This rule was echoed in Article 11 of the Geneva Convention on the High Seas and Article 97 of the LOSC. Furthermore, Article 98(1)(c) of the LOSC places a clear obligation upon every State to require the master of a ship flying its flag, after a collision, to render assistance to the other ship, its crew and its passengers.

2.4 The nationality of a ship

The flag State jurisdiction is exercised on the basis of the nationality of a ship. Thus, the nationality of a ship is of central importance in order to establish the juridical link between a State and a ship flying its flag. Under international law, each State is entitled to determine conditions for the grant of its nationality to ships. In the *M/V Saiga (No. 2)* case, ITLOS ruled that:

> Determination of the criteria and establishment of the procedures for granting and withdrawing nationality to ships are matters within the exclusive jurisdiction of the flag State.[27]

However, the right of States to grant their nationality to ships is not without limitation. It is generally recognised that a State may not grant its nationality to a ship which has already been granted the nationality of another State. This requirement follows from customary international law and Article 92(1) of the LOSC which obliges ships to sail under the flag of one State only.[28] The right of the State to grant its nationality to vessels may also be qualified by specific treaties, such as the United Nations Convention on Conditions for Registration of Ships (hereafter the UN Registration Convention).[29]

The validity of the nationality of a ship may be questioned in international adjudication. In the 2001 *Grand Prince* case between Belize and France, for example, ITLOS

23 The Case of the SS *Lotus*, Series A. No. 10, p. 25.
24 *Ibid.*, p. 32.
25 ILC, 'Report to the General Assembly covering its work of the eighth session, Articles concerning the Law of the Sea with Commentaries' (1956-II) *YILC* p. 281, Art. 35 (1).
26 439 *UNTS* p. 234, Articles 1 and 3.
27 The *M/V Saiga (No. 2)* case, p. 1340, para. 65. See also LOSC, Article 91(1).
28 D. König, 'Flags of Ships', in *Max Planck Encyclopedia*, p. 6, para. 21. See also Articles 4(4) and 11(4) of the United Nations Convention on Conditions for Registration of Ships.
29 For the text of the Convention, see (1986) 7 *Law of the Sea Bulletin* pp. 87–106.

examined the question of whether Belize could be considered as the flag State of the *Grand Prince* when the application was made. The Tribunal then concluded that Belize failed to establish that it was the flag State of the *Grand Prince*.[30] A related issue is whether the change of the ownership of a ship results in the change of the nationality of the ship. In this regard, ITLOS, in the 2007 *Tomimaru* case, took the view that ownership of a vessel and the nationality of a vessel are different issues and it cannot be assumed that a change in ownership automatically leads to the change or loss of its flag.[31] This judgment provides an important precedent on this subject.

As noted, the juridical link between a State and a ship that is entitled to fly its flag is a prerequisite for securing effective exercise of the flag State jurisdiction. With a view to securing the juridical link, Article 5(1) of the Geneva Convention on the High Seas and Article 91(1) of the LOSC provide the requirement of a 'genuine link' between the flag State and the ships flying its flag. Article 91(1) deserves quotation in full:

> Every State shall fix the conditions for the grant of its nationality to ships, for the registration of ships in its territory, and for the right to fly its flag. Ships have the nationality of the State whose flag they are entitled to fly. There must exist a genuine link between the State and the ship.

In relation to this, Article 94(1) further requires that: 'Every State shall effectively exercise its jurisdiction and control in administrative, technical and social matters over ships flying its flag'.

There is little doubt that the concept of a 'genuine link' arose from the *Nottebohm* judgment of 1955. In this judgment, the ICJ held that a State cannot claim that the municipal rules governing the grant of its own nationality are entitled to recognition by another State 'unless it has acted in conformity with this general aim of making the legal bond of nationality accord with the individual's *genuine connection* with the State which assumes the defence of its citizens by means of protection as against other States'.[32]

According to ITLOS, 'the need for a genuine link between a ship and its flag State is to secure more effective implementation of the duties of the flag State'.[33] Yet the Convention on the High Seas and the LOSC leave entirely unspecified the concept of a genuine link.[34] This situation creates at least two questions that need further consideration. The first is as to how it is possible to ensure a 'genuine link' between the flag State and the ships flying its flag in practice. It is particularly relevant to flags

[30] The *Grand Prince* case, para. 93.

[31] The *Tomimaru* case, para. 70. In the 2004 *Juno Trader* case, Judges Mensah, Wolfrum and Ndiaye took the same view: Joint Separate Opinion of Judges Mensah and Wolfrum, paras. 9–10; Separate Opinion of Judge Ndiaye, para. 28.

[32] Emphasis added. ICJ Reports 1955, p. 23.

[33] The *M/V Saiga (No. 2)* case, p. 1343, para. 83.

[34] Thus the concept of a genuine link invited strong criticisms from writers. See for instance, M. S. McDougal, W. T. Burke and I. A. Vlasio, 'The Maintenance of Public Order at Sea and the Nationality of Ships' (1960) 54 *AJIL* pp. 28–43.

of convenience. The second question concerns the consequences to be attached to the absence of a genuine link.

2.5 Problems associated with flags of convenience

Whilst there is no generally agreed definition, 'flag of convenience' or 'open registry' States refer, in essence, to States that permit foreign shipowners, having very little or virtually no real connection with those States, to register their ships under the flags of those States.[35] The flag of convenience States allow shipowners to evade national taxation and to avoid the qualifications required of the crews of their ships. In so doing, flag of convenience States give shipowners an opportunity to reduce crew costs by employing inexpensive labour, whilst these States receive a registry fee and an annual fee. As one of the few variables in shipping costs is crew costs, a highly competitive market within the international shipping industry prompts shipowners to resort to open registry States.

In relation to this, attention must also be drawn to a mechanism of 'second' or 'international' registries that allow for the use of the national flag, albeit under conditions which are different from those applicable for the first national registry. Examples include the Norwegian International Ship Register (NIS), the Danish International Register of Shipping (DIS), and the French International Register (RIF). The NIS and the RIF cater to some foreign-controlled tonnage, whilst the DIS is almost only used by Danish-controlled ships.[36] The ten largest open and international registry States that cater almost exclusively to foreign-controlled ships are: Panama, Liberia, Bahamas, Marshall Islands, Malta, Cyprus, Isle of Man, Antigua and Barbuda, Bermuda, and Saint Vincent and the Grenadines.[37]

Even though non-compliance with relevant rules is by no means peculiar to flags of convenience, there is rightly the concern that open registry States do not commit themselves to effectively enforce the observance of relevant rules and standards by vessels flying their flag with regard to, *inter alia*, safety of navigation, labour conditions of the crew, the regulation of fisheries and marine pollution, since strict law enforcement will have a negative effect on the economic policy of attracting ships to register.[38] Illegal fishing by the flags of convenience is also a matter of pressing concern.[39]

In 1986, the UN Registration Convention was adopted under the auspices of the United Nations Conference on Trade and Development (UNCTAD) with a view to tightening a genuine link between the flag State and the ships flying its flag. The UN Registration Convention elaborates several conditions with which the flag State shall comply. In particular, ownership of ships, manning of ships, and the management of

[35] Churchill and Lowe, *Law of the Sea*, p. 258. For an analysis in some detail of flags of convenience, see *OECE Study on Flags of Convenience*, reproduced in (1972–1973) 4 *Journal of Maritime Law and Commerce* pp. 231–254.

[36] UNCTAD, *Review of Maritime Transport 2008* (New York and Geneva, United Nations, 2008), p. 47.

[37] *Ibid.*, p. 45.

[38] H. W. Wefers Bettink, 'Open Registry, the Genuine Link and the 1986 Convention on Regulation Conditions for Ships' (1987) 18 *NYIL* p. 77.

[39] J.-P. Pancracio, *Droit de la mer* (Paris, Dalloz, 2010), p. 81. See also Chapter 7, section 4.1.

ships and shipowning companies constitute key elements of the tightening of a genuine link between the flag State and the ships flying its flag. However, this Convention has not entered into force. Furthermore, it appears to be questionable whether the flag of convenience States will ratify this Convention. The problem of flags of convenience seems, broadly, to derive from international competition in the shipping and fishing industry, in which case, it is debatable whether the tightening of the requirement of a genuine link would provide an effective solution.[40]

A further issue involves legal consequences arising from the absence of a genuine link between the flag State and the ship concerned. Should a foreign State be free not to recognise the nationality of a ship because of the absence of a genuine link between the ship and the flag State? Considering this question, three cases merit attention.

The first example is the *Magda Maria* case of 1986. On 1 August 1981, the *Magda Maria* flying the Panamanian flag was seized by the Dutch authorities on the high seas nine miles off the Dutch coast because of unauthorised broadcasting from the high seas. The *Magda Maria* was brought into port at Amsterdam harbour and broadcasting equipment on board was seized. Although the District Court of The Hague upheld the validity of the seizure by the Dutch authority,[41] the Supreme Court quashed the decision of the District Court and remitted the case to the Court of Appeal of The Hague for retrial and decision.[42] Before the Court of Appeal, the Procurator-General claimed that in view of the absence of a genuine link as referred to in Article 5 of the Convention on the High Seas, the *Magda Maria* had become stateless. Nonetheless, the Court of Appeal dismissed this claim. According to the Court, the concept of the genuine link obliges Panama as the flag State only to exercise its jurisdiction effectively. However, '[i]t does not imply that the Dutch Government has the right to recognise or otherwise the right to fly the Panamanian flag which was granted to the ship by Panama'.[43] Thus, the Court of Appeal held that 'it cannot be said on the basis of the examination at the sitting that the MS *Magda Maria* was stateless on account of the absence of a genuine link'.[44]

The second case involves the Advisory Opinion in the Constitution of the Maritime Safety Committee of the Inter-Governmental Maritime Consultative Organisation (IMCO) of 1960. In this case, the ICJ was asked to answer to the question with regard to the validity of the constitution of the Maritime Safety Committee of the Inter-Governmental Maritime Consultative Organisation (IMCO). Under Article 28(a) of the Convention of the IMCO, the members of the Maritime Safety Committee consisted of fourteen members elected by the Assembly which included the world's eight largest ship-owning countries. Nonetheless, Liberia and Panama were not elected to the Committee, although they ranked third and eighth on the world tonnage scale at that time. In the course of arguments, it was contended that the Assembly was entitled to

[40] McDougal et al., 'Maintenance of Public Order at Sea', p. 35.
[41] (1982) 13 *NYIL* pp. 381–391. [42] (1985) 16 *NYIL* pp. 514–518.
[43] (1989) 20 *NYIL* p. 351. [44] *Ibid.*, pp. 351–352.

take the concept of a genuine link into consideration in assessing the ship-owning size of each country. However, the ICJ ruled that the concept of the genuine link was irrelevant for the purpose of the Advisory Opinion; and that the determination of the largest ship-owning nations depends solely upon the tonnage registered in the countries in question. Hence, the Court concluded, by nine votes to five, that the Maritime Safety Committee of the IMCO was not constituted in accordance with the Convention for the Establishment of the Organisation.[45]

The third case is the 1999 *M/V Saiga (No. 2)* decision. In this case, Guinea claimed that there was no genuine link between the *Saiga* and Saint Vincent and the Grenadines, and, consequently, it was not obliged to recognise the claims of Saint Vincent and the Grenadines in relation to the ship.[46] ITLOS noted the fact that, in the legislative process of Article 5(1) of the Geneva Convention on the High Seas, the proposal that the existence of a genuine link should be a basis for the recognition of nationality was not adopted.[47] Article 91 of the LOSC followed the approach of the Convention on the High Seas. Hence ITLOS concluded that the purpose of Article 91 was *not* to establish criteria by reference to which the validity of the registration of ships in a flag State may be challenged by other States.[48]

In light of the vagueness of the concept of a genuine link, unilateral discretion of States to deny the nationality of vessels because of the absence of a genuine link may endanger the freedom of the seas.[49] Hence there may be room for the view that a third State cannot refuse to recognise the nationality of a ship on the basis of the absence of a genuine link between a flag State and a ship. It appears that the judicial practice is also supportive of this view.

2.6 Exceptions to the exclusive jurisdiction of the flag State (1): the right of visit

(a) General considerations

The principle of the exclusive jurisdiction of the flag State applies to warships as well as ships used only on government non-commercial service without any exception. This is clear from Articles 95 and 96 of the LOSC.[50] On the other hand, private ships are subject to two types of exception.

The first exception involves the right of visit. The right of visit is exercised by a warship or a military aircraft pursuant to Article 110. In essence, the right of visit seeks to reinforce an international order on the high seas.

The second exception concerns the right of hot pursuit. The hot pursuit of a foreign ship may be undertaken by the competent authorities of the coastal State by virtue of Article 111. The right of hot pursuit seeks to safeguard the interests of coastal States. It will be appropriate to commence our consideration with the right of visit.

[45] ICJ Reports 1960, p. 171. [46] The *M/V Saiga (No. 2)* case, p. 1342, paras. 75–76.
[47] *Ibid.*, p. 1343, para. 80. [48] *Ibid.*, para. 83.
[49] McDougal et al., 'Maintenance of Public Order at Sea', p. 35.
[50] Ships owned by a government may be regarded as private ships if such ships are involved in commercial activities.

The right of visit is provided in Article 110(1) of the LOSC as follows:

> 1. Except where acts of interference derive from powers conferred by treaty, a warship which encounters on the high seas a foreign ship, other than a ship entitled to complete immunity in accordance with articles 95 and 96, is not justified in boarding it unless there is reasonable ground for suspecting that:
>   (a) the ship is engaged in piracy;
>   (b) the ship is engaged in the slave trade;
>   (c) the ship is engaged in unauthorized broadcasting and the flag State of the warship has jurisdiction under article 109;
>   (d) the ship is without nationality; or
>   (e) though flying a foreign flag or refusing to show its flag, the ship is, in reality, of the same nationality as the warship.

Article 110(1) distinguishes two cases where the foreign warship or the military aircraft may exercise the right of visit.

The first is the case where acts of interference derive from powers conferred by specific treaties. In those cases, only the States Parties to relevant conventions are entitled to exercise the right of visit on vessels flying the flag of other States Parties. In fact, some fishery treaties allow a State Party to board and inspect vessels of other Parties on the high seas.[51]

The second case involves the right of visit with respect to activities of foreign vessels enumerated in Article 110(1). In this case, the warship or military aircraft may send a boat under the command of an officer to the suspected ship in order to verify the ship's right to fly its flag. If suspicion remains after the documents have been checked, it may proceed to a further examination on board the ship (Article 110(2)). If the suspicions prove to be unfounded, however, it shall be compensated for any loss or damage that may have been sustained pursuant to Article 110(3). Next, the exceptions listed in Article 110(1) must be briefly examined.

(b) Piracy

The suppression of piracy is a well-established exception to the exclusive jurisdiction of the flag State. Under customary law and Article 105 of the LOSC, every State may seize a pirate ship or aircraft and arrest suspected pirates. This exception seeks to safeguard the common interest of the international community as a whole in protecting the freedom of navigation and human life. The international law of piracy will be discussed in the context of maritime security.[52]

(c) Slave trade

From the early nineteenth century, a large number of international treaties have been concluded with regard to the abolition and suppression of the slave trade. On 2 July 1890, the General Act for the Repression of African Slave Trade was adopted by the

[51] See Chapter 7, sections 6.2 and 6.3. [52] See Chapter 11, section 2.

Anti-Slavery Conference held in Brussels. The General Act was signed and ratified by seventeen States. The General Acts provided the reciprocal right of visit, of search and of seizure of vessels whose tonnage is less than 500 tons in the limited zone, namely, the Indian Ocean and the Red Sea.[53] In 1926, the Slavery Convention was adopted by the Assembly of the League of Nations and signed by the representatives of thirty-six States.[54] In 1956, the Supplementary Convention on the Abolition of Slavery, the Slave Trade, and Institutions and Practices Similar to Slavery was adopted.[55] Unlike the 1890 General Act, those conventions do not provide the right of visit, search and seizure.

However, the right of visit was revived in Article 23 of the Convention on the High Seas and Article 110 of the LOSC. One can say that the right of visit to a ship that is engaged in the slave trade represents customary law. In the case of the suppression of the slave trade, it is generally considered that enforcement jurisdiction beyond the right of visit is limited to the flag State.[56] Under Article 99, every State is obliged to take effective measures to prevent and punish the transport of slaves in ships authorised to fly its flag and to prevent the unlawful use of its flag for that purpose. Any slave taking refuge on board any ship, whatever its flag, shall *ipso facto* be free.

(d) Unauthorised broadcasting

The Geneva Convention on the High Seas contains no rule with regard to the repression of unauthorised broadcasting. In the early 1960s, however, unauthorised broadcasting from the high seas became a matter of concern particularly in Europe. Unauthorised broadcasting may create various problems, such as electrical interference with licensed broadcasts and frequencies used for distress calls, copyright of broadcast materials, and taxation.[57] Thus, in 1965, the European Agreement for the Prevention of Broadcasting Transmitted from Stations Outside National Territories was adopted under the auspices of the European Council.[58] Under Article 3 of the 1965 Agreement, each Contracting Party shall punish their nationals who have committed or assisted unauthorised broadcasting on its territory, ships, or aircraft, or outside national territories on any ships, aircraft or any other floating or airborne object. Each Contracting Party shall also punish non-nationals who, on its territory, ships or aircraft, or on board any floating or airborne object under its jurisdiction have committed or assisted unauthorised broadcasting. Thus the 1965 Agreement did not depart from the principle of the exclusive jurisdiction of the flag State.

However, the LOSC allows non-flag States to exercise jurisdiction over unauthorised broadcasting. Under Article 109(2) of the LOSC, 'unauthorised broadcasting' means 'the transmission of sound radio or television broadcasts from a ship or installation

[53] United Nations, 'The Relation between the Articles Concerning the Law of the Sea Adopted by the International Law Commission and International Agreements Dealing With the Suppression of the Slave Trade', A/CONF.13/7, *Official Records of the United Nations Conference on the Law of the Sea*, vol. 1 (Geneva, United Nations, 1958), p. 166.

[54] 60 *LNTS* 253. Entered into force 9 March 1927.

[55] 266 *UNTS* 2. Entered into force 30 April 1957.

[56] Churchill and Lowe, *Law of the Sea*, p. 212; T. Treves, 'High Seas', in *Max Planck Encyclopedia*, p. 4, para. 19.

[57] Generally on this issue, see N. March Hunnings, 'Pirate Broadcasting in European Waters' (1965) 14 *ICLQ* pp. 410–433.

[58] 634 *UNTS* 239. Entered into force 19 October 1967.

on the high seas intended for reception by the general public contrary to international regulation, but excluding the transmission of distress calls'. All States are required to cooperate in the suppression of unauthorised broadcasting from the high seas in accordance with Article 109(1). Under Article 109(3), any person engaged in unauthorised broadcasting may be prosecuted before courts of the following:

(a) the flag State of the ship;
(b) the State of registry of the installation;
(c) the State of which the person is a national;
(d) any State where the transmissions can be received; or
(e) any State where authorised radio communication is suffering interference.

On the high seas, a State having jurisdiction in accordance with paragraph 3 may, in conformity with Article 110, arrest any person or ship engaged in unauthorised broadcasting and seize the broadcasting apparatus pursuant to Article 109(4). Thus, unlike in the case of piracy, Article 109 does not set out a universal jurisdiction with regard to the suppression of unauthorised broadcasting.

(e) Ship without nationality

Whilst the situation in which a vessel loses its nationality may be rare, stateless vessels exist in reality. At least two possible situations can be identified.

First, under Article 92(2) of the LOSC, a ship which sails under the flags of two or more States as a matter of convenience may be 'assimilated to a ship without nationality', namely a stateless ship. Such a ship may not claim any of the nationalities in question with respect to any other State.

Second, a ship may become stateless if its flag State revokes the registration of the vessel because of the continued violation of the laws of the flag State. A ship may also become stateless if the ship revokes its registration of its own accord for some reasons and does not acquire another nationality.[59]

A ship without nationality is without protection under customary law. Thus Article 110(1) and (2) of the LOSC empower a warship or a military aircraft to visit and verify the ship's right to fly its flag where there is a reasonable ground to suspect that the ship is without nationality. Yet the LOSC is silent on the legal consequences of being a stateless vessel. On the basis of the practice of the United States, O'Connell argued that when a ship loses its nationality, its status becomes a question for the municipal law of the owners, and that law is likely to regulate the ship.[60] In this regard, care should be taken in noting that the national State of the individual on the stateless vessel enjoys diplomatic protection.[61] In any case, it seems clear at least that, unlike in the case of piracy, the LOSC does not provide universal jurisdiction over a stateless vessel.

[59] T. L. McDorman, 'Stateless Fishing Vessels, International Law and the U.N. High Seas Fisheries Conference' (1994) 25 *Journal of Maritime Law and Commerce* p. 531 and pp. 533–534.
[60] O'Connell, *The International Law of the Sea*, p. 756.
[61] Churchill and Lowe, *Law of the Sea*, p. 214.

(f) Ships with suspicious nationality
Concerning ships with suspicious nationality, Article 110(1)(e) provides that a warship or a military aircraft may visit and verify the ship's right to fly its flag where there is a reasonable ground for suspecting that a ship, though flying a foreign flag or refusing to show its flag, is of the same nationality as the warship in reality. It is universally recognised that warships of every State may seize, and bring to a port of their own for punishment, any foreign vessel sailing under the same flag as the inspecting warship without any authorisation.[62]

2.7 Exceptions to the exclusive jurisdiction of the flag State (2): the right of hot pursuit

Hot pursuit is the legitimate chase of a foreign vessel on the high seas following a violation of the law of the pursuing State committed by the vessel within the marine spaces under the pursuing State's jurisdiction. The right of hot pursuit seems to be, to a considerable extent, a product of Anglo-Saxon jurisprudence.[63] Indeed, the right was clearly recognised in the *North* case of 1906.[64] Presently the right of hot pursuit is enshrined in both Article 23 of the Geneva Convention on the High Seas and Article 111 of the LOSC. The right of hot pursuit is subject to several requirements.

(i) The hot pursuit must be undertaken by warships or military aircraft, or other ships or aircraft clearly marked and identifiable as being on government service and authorised to that effect in accordance with Article 111(5).

(ii) The hot pursuit of a foreign ship may be undertaken when the competent authorities of the coastal State have good reason to believe that the ship has violated the laws and regulations of that State. It follows that the alleged illicit conduct of the foreign ship is crucial. If the foreign ship is within a contiguous zone, the pursuit may only be undertaken if there has been a violation of the rights for the protection of which the zone was established, that is to say, customs, fiscal, immigration or sanitary laws (Article 111(1)). A controversial issue is whether attempted offences give rise to a right of hot pursuit. In drafting Article 23 of the Geneva Convention on the High Seas, which is essentially equivalent to Article 111(1) of the LOSC, Brazil proposed to the ILC that the draft Article should refer to an offence which was about to be committed. In this regard, the ILC seemed to consider that the suggestion was already implied in the text.[65] Hence it can be argued that the right of hot pursuit is exercisable with regard to attempted offences.[66]

(iii) Since, in essence, hot pursuit is a temporary extension of the coastal State's jurisdiction onto the high seas, the pursuit must be commenced when the foreign ship or one of its boats is within the internal waters, the archipelagic waters, the territorial

[62] Sir Robert Jennings and Sir Arthur Watts (eds.), *Oppenheim's International Law*, 9th edn, vol. 1, *Peace* (Harlow, Longman, 1992), p. 737.
[63] O'Connell, *The International Law of the Sea*, p. 1076.
[64] *The King v The 'North'*, (1908) 2 *AJIL* pp. 688–707 (see in particular, p. 699).
[65] See (1956) *YILC*, vol. 2, p. 40; *ibid.*, vol. 1, p. 50.
[66] O'Connell, *The International Law of the Sea*, pp. 1088–1089.

sea or the contiguous zone of the pursuing State pursuant to Article 111(1).[67] The right of hot pursuit is to apply *mutatis mutandis* to violations of the laws and regulations of the coastal State in the EEZ or on the continental shelf, including safety zones around continental shelf installations (Article 111(2)).

(iv) The pursuit may only be commenced after a visual or auditory signal to stop has been given at a distance which enables it to be seen or heard by the foreign ship in conformity with Article 111(4). This requirement is a replica of Article 23(3) of the TSC. In this regard, the ILC took the view that the words 'visual or auditory signal' exclude signals given at a great distance and transmitted by wireless.[68] In this connection, the use of radio signals was at issue in the *R. v Mills and Others* case of 1995. In light of the development of modern technology, Judge Devonshire at Croydon Crown Court ruled that the transmission of the radio signals complied with the preconditions of the Convention on the High Seas concerning the right of hot pursuit.[69]

(v) The pursuit must be hot and continuous. The aircraft giving the order to stop must itself actively pursue the ship until a ship or another aircraft of the coastal State arrives to take over the pursuit, unless the aircraft is itself able to arrest the ship pursuant to Article 111(6)(b). It is also recognised that hot pursuit can be transferred between ships, although there is no explicit provision on this particular matter.[70]

(vi) The right of hot pursuit ceases as soon as the ship pursued enters the territorial sea of its own State or of a third State (Article 111(3)), since pursuit in the territorial sea of another State would violate the territorial sovereignty of that State. It would follow that hot pursuit may continue in the EEZ of a third State. Where the hot pursuit was unjustified, compensation shall be paid for any loss or damage that may have been sustained thereby (Article 111(8)). According to ITLOS, the conditions for the exercise of the right of hot pursuit under this provision are cumulative and each of them has to be satisfied for the pursuit to be legitimate under the LOSC.[71]

The right of hot pursuit raises at least three issues that need further consideration. The first issue relates to the validity of hot pursuit that involves ships in pursuit from two or more coastal States. Examples of so-called 'multilateral hot pursuit' can be found in the Southern Ocean. In 2001, the Togo-registered *South Tomi* was pursued from Australia's EEZ by the Australian-flagged *Southern Supporter.* After a fourteen-day chase covering a distance of 3,300 nautical miles, the *South Tomi* was finally apprehended by Australian personnel with the aid of two South African vessels. In 2003, after a twenty-day hot pursuit, covering 3,900 nautical miles, the Uruguayan-flagged fishing vessel *Viarsa 1* was apprehended by the *Southern Supporter* with the aid of South African- and United Kingdom-flagged vessels. Considering that these pursuits satisfied the conditions of hot pursuit and officials of the coastal State that initiated the pursuit could formally apprehend the suspected vessels, one can say that

[67] See also Article 111(4). [68] (1956) *YILC*, vol. 2, p. 285.

[69] W. C. Gilmore, 'Hot Pursuit: The Case of *R. v. Mills and Others*' (1995) 44 *ICLQ* p. 957.

[70] (1956) *YILC*, vol. 2, p. 285, para. 2(c). In fact, in the *I'm Alone* case between Canada and the United States, two United States coastguard vessels were involved in the hot pursuit: 3 *RIAA* pp. 1609 *et seq.*

[71] The *M/V Saiga (No. 2)* case, p. 1354, para. 146.

the multilateral hot pursuits in the cases of the *South Tomi* and *Viarsa 1* were not at variance with Article 111 of the LOSC.[72] Later, in 2003, Australia and France concluded a bilateral treaty which is applicable in the Southern Ocean.[73] Article 3(3) of this treaty allows each Party to request assistance from the other Party when engaged in a hot pursuit. Article 4 of the 2003 Treaty allows a vessel or other craft authorised by one of the Parties to continue hot pursuit through the territorial sea of the other Party under certain conditions.

The second issue involves the validity of the doctrine of constructive presence.[74] This doctrine allows the coastal State to arrest foreign ships which remain on the high seas but commit an offence within the territorial sea or the EEZ by using their boats. The doctrine of constructive presence may operate with the right of hot pursuit. In this regard, a classical case is the *Tenyu Maru* case of 1910.[75] The Japanese schooner, the *Tenyu Maru*, laid off from shore about 11.5 miles off the Pribilof seal islands and sent her boats out hunting seals. On 9 July 1909, the US revenue cutter discovered two boats within about a mile and a half of the shores of Otter Island. The cutter captured a boat within the three-mile limit from shore and the other after crossing the three-mile line. The *Tenyu Maru*, together with her captain and crew, was conveyed by the cutter to Dutch Harbour, Alaska. In this case, District Judge Overfield considered that: 'The schooner was therefore just as much "engaged in" killing the seals, under the statutes, when the small boat was captured within the three-mile limit on July 9th as though she had been standing within the zone at the time, in the absence of any evidence showing extenuating circumstances.'[76] Thus, the *Tenyu Maru* was forfeited to the United States.[77]

The doctrine of constructive presence seems to be implicitly recognised in Article 23(3) of the Convention on the High Seas and Article 111(4) of the LOSC. However, it appears that the validity of extensive constructive presence needs further consideration. Whilst simple constructive presence involves the case where the ship's own boats are used to establish the nexus, extensive constructive presence concerns the case where other boats are used.[78] The doctrine of extensive constructive presence was upheld in *R. v Mills and Others*.[79] The *Poseidon*, a ship registered in Saint Vincent and the Grenadines, transferred 3.25 tons of cannabis to a British-registered fishing trawler, the *Delvan*, on the high seas. The *Delvan* had set out from Cork in the Republic of Ireland for this purpose. The *Delvan* headed to the United Kingdom and, later, it

72 E. J. Molenaar, 'Multilateral Hot Pursuit and Illegal Fishing in the Southern Ocean: The Pursuits of the *Viarsa 1* and the *South Tomi*' (2004) 19 *IJMCL* pp. 19–42.

73 Treaty between the Government of Australia and the Government of the French Republic on Cooperation in the Maritime Areas Adjacent to the French Southern and Antarctic Territories (TAAF), Heard Island and the McDonald Islands. Entered into force 1 February 2005. For the text of the Treaty, (2004) 19 *IJMCL* pp. 545 *et seq.*

74 O'Connell, *The International Law of the Sea*, pp. 1092–1093; Churchill and Lowe, *Law of the Sea*, p. 215.

75 4 Alaska 129 (1910). This case was reproduced in K. R. Simmonds, *Cases on the Law of the Sea*, vol. 4 (New York, Oceana, 1984), pp. 33–46.

76 *Ibid.*, p. 41. 77 *Ibid.*, p. 46.

78 O'Connell, *The International Law of the Sea*, p. 1093.

79 Gilmore, 'Hot Pursuit', pp. 950–953.

arrived in the south-coast port of Littlehampton. The cargo was unloaded there but the shore party was arrested shortly thereafter. Next, the *Poseidon* was arrested by the British task force on the high seas. A question arose whether the relationship between the *Poseidon* and the *Delvan* was such as to satisfy the requirements set out in Article 23(3) of the Convention on the High Seas, namely team work and the existence of a mother ship relationship. On this issue, Judge Devonshire took the view that there was the existence of a mother ship relationship.[80]

The third issue to be addressed involves the use of force in the exercise of the right of hot pursuit. An often quoted case on this matter is the *I'm Alone* case.[81] The *I'm Alone*, which was a British ship of Canadian registry, engaged in smuggling liquor into the United States. The vessel was sighted within one hour's sailing time from the United States by the coastguard cutter, the *Wolcott*. As the *I'm Alone* refused to stop, the *Wolcott* pursued the vessel onto the high seas. Still in hot pursuit, another revenue cutter, the *Dexter*, joined the pursuit and, on 22 March 1929, the *I'm Alone* was sunk on the high seas in the Gulf of Mexico by the revenue cutter. The Joint Interim Report of the Commissioners of 1933 stated that:

> [I]f sinking should occur incidentally, as a result of the exercise of necessary and reasonable force for such purpose [of effecting the objects of boarding, searching, seizing and bringing into port the suspected vessel], the pursuing vessel might be entirely blameless.[82]

In light of the circumstances in this case, however, the Commissioners considered that the admittedly intentional sinking of the suspected vessel was not justified by anything in the 1924 Convention between the United States of America and Great Britain to Aid in the Prevention of the Smuggling of Intoxicating Liquors into the United States.[83] Finally, in the Joint Final Report of 1935, the Commissioners found that the sinking of the vessel was not justified by the 1924 Convention or by any principle of international law.[84]

More recently, the use of force in hot pursuit was in issue in the *M/V Saiga (No. 2)* case. In this case, ITLOS held that:

> The normal practice used to stop a ship at sea is first to give an auditory or visual signal to stop, using internationally recognized signals. Where this does not succeed, a variety of actions may be taken, including the firing of shots across the bows of the ship. It is only after the appropriate actions fail that the pursuing vessel may, as a last resort, use force.[85]

[80] *Ibid.*, p. 955. While the United Kingdom was a Party to the Convention on the High Seas, Saint Vincent and the Grenadines was not. But the judge considered that Article 23 of the Convention concerning hot pursuit constituted a codification of pre-existing customary international law. *Ibid.*, pp. 953–954.

[81] 3 *RIAA* pp. 1609–1618. [82] *Ibid.*, p. 1615.

[83] *Ibid.* [84] *Ibid.*, p. 1617.

[85] The *M/V Saiga (No. 2)* case, p. 1355, para. 156.

In this case, the Guinean officers fired at the *Saiga* with live ammunition indiscriminately. As a consequence, considerable damage was done to the ship and, more seriously, caused severe injuries to two of the persons on board. Thus ITLOS ruled that Guinea used excessive force and endangered human life before and after boarding the *Saiga*, and thereby violated the rights of Saint Vincent and the Grenadines under international law.[86]

Those precedents suggest that the use of force is a last resort and must be necessary and reasonable. In this regard, Article 22(1)(f) of the 1995 Fish Stocks Agreement requires that the inspecting State shall ensure that its duly authorised inspectors

> avoid the use of force except when and to the degree necessary to ensure the safety of the inspectors and where the inspectors are obstructed in the execution of their duties. The degree of force used shall not exceed that reasonably required in the circumstances.

Likewise, Article 9 of the 2005 SUA Convention provides that: 'Any use of force pursuant to this article shall not exceed the minimum degree of force which is necessary and reasonable in the circumstance.'[87]

2.8 Exceptional measures

In addition to the above exceptions,[88] the principle of the exclusiveness of flag State jurisdiction on the high seas may be varied in two situations. First, it is possible to depart from the principle of the exclusiveness of flag State jurisdiction by specific treaties. A particular example is the regulation of illicit traffic in narcotic drugs or psychotropic substances by sea. Second, the issue arises as to whether or not the interference with foreign vessels on the high seas can be justified by self-defence.

(a) The regulation of illicit traffic in narcotic drugs or psychotropic substances

The use of private vessels for illicit traffic in narcotic drugs has long been a serious problem. Thus Article 27(1)(d) of the LOSC provides an exception with regard to the criminal jurisdiction of the coastal State. Furthermore, Article 108 of the Convention places an obligation upon all States to cooperate in the suppression of drug smuggling at sea. At the bilateral level, the United States concluded a series of bilateral agreements with twenty-nine Latin American and Caribbean States in order to combat illicit drug and immigrant smuggling.[89] At the multilateral level, of particular importance is the 1988 United Nations Convention against Illicit Traffic in Narcotic Drugs and

86 *Ibid.*, p. 1356, paras. 158–159.
87 The 2005 SUA Convention will be discussed in Chapter 11, section 3.1.
88 Where the coastal State has not claimed its EEZ, the rights of that State in the contiguous zone constitute a further exception.
89 J. E. Kramek, 'Bilateral Maritime Counter-Drug and Immigrant Interdiction Agreements: Is This the World of the Future?' (2000) 31 *University of Miami Inter-American Law Review* p. 123 and pp. 150–151. The United States has also made a Model Agreement on this subject. This instrument is reproduced *ibid.*, pp. 152–160.

Psychotropic Substances.[90] This Convention aims to promote cooperation among the Parties in order to address more effectively the various aspects of such traffic that have an international dimension.[91]

Specifically, Article 17(1) of the 1988 Convention requires the Parties to cooperate to the fullest extent possible to suppress illicit traffic by sea, in conformity with the international law of the sea. Article 17(3) further provides that a Party which has reasonable grounds to suspect that a vessel exercising freedom of navigation flying the flag of another Party is engaged in illicit traffic may so notify the flag State, request confirmation of registry and, if confirmed, request authorisation from the flag State to take appropriate measures in regard to that vessel. In this case, pursuant to Article 17(4), the flag State may authorise the requesting State to, *inter alia*: (a) board the vessel; (b) search the vessel; and (c) if evidence of involvement in illicit traffic is found, take appropriate action with respect to the vessel, persons and cargo on board. Action under Article 17(4) is to be carried out only by warships or military aircraft, or other governmental ships in accordance with Article 17(10). A Party which has taken any action in accordance with Article 17 is under a duty to promptly inform the flag State concerned of the results of that action.

Article 17 was further amplified by the 1995 Agreement on Illicit Traffic by Sea, Implementing Article 17 of the United Nations Convention against Illicit Traffic in Narcotic Drugs and Psychotropic Substances (hereafter the Council of Europe Agreement).[92] This Agreement, which was adopted under the auspices of the Council of Europe, contains a complex text consisting of thirty-six provisions and one annex. The Council of Europe Agreement obliges the Parties to cooperate to the fullest extent possible to suppress illicit traffic in narcotic drugs and psychotropic substances by sea in conformity with the international law of the sea under Article 2(1). Where the intervening State has reasonable grounds to suspect that a vessel flying the flag of another Party is engaged in the commission of a relevant offence, the intervening State may request the authorisation of the flag State to stop and board the vessel in waters beyond the territorial sea of any Party and to take some or all of the other actions specified in this Agreement by virtue of Article 6.[93] The flag State is to communicate a decision thereon as soon as possible and, wherever practicable, within four hours of receipt of the request in accordance with Article 7. Having received the authorisation of the flag State, the intervening State may take actions specified in Article 9(1), such as stopping and boarding the vessel. Actions under Article 9(1) are to be carried out only by warships or military aircraft, or governmental ships and aircraft pursuant to Article 11(2).

[90] 1582 *UNTS* 165. Entered into force 11 November 1990. See also J. Gurulé, 'The 1988 U.N. Convention against Illicit Traffic in Narcotic Drugs and Psychotropic Substances: A Ten year Perspective: Is International Cooperation Merely Illusory?' (1998) 22 *Fordham International Law Journal* pp. 74–121.

[91] Article 2(1).

[92] 2136 *UNTS* 79. Entered into force 1 May 2000. See also W. C. Gilmore, 'Narcotics Interdiction at Sea: The 1995 Council of Europe Agreement' (1996) 20 *Marine Policy* pp. 3–14.

[93] 'Intervening State' means a State Party which has requested or proposes to request authorisation from another Party to take action under the Agreement in relation to a vessel flying the flag or displaying the marks of registry of that other State Party (Article 1(a)).

It is important to note that these measures rely on the authorisation of the flag State. In this sense, this Agreement does not change the principle of exclusive jurisdiction of the flag State. In fact, Article 3(4) makes clear that the flag State has preferential jurisdiction over any relevant offence committed on board its vessel.

Several bilateral treaties also provide prior authorisation for the boarding of ships for the purpose of the suppression of illicit drug traffic at sea. The case in point is the 1981 UK–US Exchange of Notes.[94] Under paragraph 1 of the Exchange of Notes, the United States is authorised to board a private vessel under the British flag outside the limits of the territorial sea and contiguous zone of the United States and within the areas described in paragraph 9 of the Note where the authorities of the United States reasonably believe that the vessel has on board a cargo of drugs for importation into the United States in violation of the law of the United States. Similarly, the 1990 Treaty between Spain and Italy to Combat Illicit Drug Trafficking at Sea recognises the mutual right to board and search commercial ships displaying the flag of the other State.[95] The prior authorisation to stop and board a suspected vessel located seaward of any nation's territorial sea is also provided in the 1996 Agreement between the Government of the Republic of Trinidad and Tobago and the Government of the United States of America Concerning Maritime Counter-Drug Operations.[96]

(b) Self-defence on the high seas

There is no doubt that States have the inherent right of self-defence under international law,[97] but can interference with foreign ships on the high seas be justified by the right of self-defence? After World War II, States have sometimes justified interference with foreign vessels on the high seas on the basis of the right of self-defence. During the Algerian Emergency between 1956 and 1962, for example, the French Navy undertook to visit and search a considerable number of foreign ships on the high seas with a view to stemming the flow of arms and munitions into Algeria. Nonetheless, most of the States whose ships were affected by the French naval operation protested, and, in some cases, gave rise to serious diplomatic difficulties particularly between France and the Federal Republic of Germany.[98]

Another well-known incident concerns the Cuban Quarantine in the 1962 Cuban missile crisis.[99] On 23 October 1962, the Organization of American States called for the withdrawal of missiles from Cuba, and recommended that the Member States take all

94 1285 *UNTS* p. 197. The Exchange of Notes entered into force immediately.

95 Article 5. (1995) 29 *Law of the Sea Bulletin* p. 77.

96 Paragraph 11 of the 1996 Agreement. The text of the Agreement is available at: www.caricom.org/jsp/secretariat/legal_instruments_index.jsp?menu=secretariat.

97 Article 51 of the Charter of the United Nations; J. Crawford, *The International Law Commission's Articles on State Responsibility: Introduction, Text and Commentaries* (Cambridge University Press, 2002), p. 166.

98 O'Connell, *The International Law of the Sea*, pp. 805–806; R. C. F. Reuland, 'Interference with Non-National Ships on the High Seas: Peacetime Exceptions to the Exclusive Rule on Flag-State Jurisdiction' (1989) 22 *Vanderbilt Journal of Transnational Law* pp. 1218–1219.

99 O'Connell, *The International Law of the Sea*, pp. 807–808; Reuland, 'Interference with Non-National Ships', pp. 1219–1220.

measures under the Inter-American Treaty of Reciprocal Assistance. Pursuant to this resolution, US President Kennedy immediately ordered that the United States Navy interdict the delivery of offensive weapons to Cuba and, thus, any ship proceeding towards Cuba might be ordered to submit to visit and search on the high seas. In order to justify this operation, the myriad possible justifications, including the right of self-defence under Article 51 of the UN Charter, were submitted. Nonetheless, it appears debatable whether the US operation could be fully justified on the basis of self-defence.[100]

The ILC was cautious about including a rule governing self-defence in the Geneva Convention on the High Seas 'mainly because of the vagueness of terms like "imminent danger" and "hostile acts", which leaves them open to abuse'.[101] One can say that the validity of the exercise of the right of self-defence on the high seas is to be judged on a case-by-case basis in accordance with the international law of self-defence, in particular Article 51 of the UN Charter.

3 THE AREA

3.1 General considerations

The exploration and exploitation of natural resources in the deep seabed is a new subject in the law of the sea. At the end of the nineteenth century, polymetallic nodules were discovered in the Arctic Ocean off Siberia. During the 1872–77 scientific expedition of HMS *Challenger*, they were found to occur in most oceans of the world.[102] Polymetallic nodules, which were also called manganese nodules, are small brown-black balls, usually 1 to 20 centimetres in diameter. In the 1950s, attention was drawn to the economic significance of the nodules. During the International Geophysical Year between 1957 and 1958, polymetallic nodules were collected on the Tuamotu plateau approximately 370 kilometres east of Tahiti at a depth of some 900 metres. These nodules proved to contain commercially valuable minerals, such as nickel, copper and cobalt.[103] Thus the exploration and exploitation of polymetallic nodules has attracted growing attention. As noted, the management of the deep seabed resources gave an impetus to convene UNCLOS III. The LOSC devotes Part XI to the regime governing the Area.

3.2 Spatial scope of the Area

The limits of the Area are the seaward limit of the continental shelf in the legal sense. It follows that the limits of the Area consist in at the maximum the 200 nautical miles from the baseline or the limit of the continental margin where it extends beyond 200

[100] O'Connell, *The International Law of the Sea*, p. 808; Churchill and Lowe, *Law of the Sea*, p. 426.
[101] (1956) *YILC*, vol. 2, p. 284.
[102] International Seabed Authority, *Polymetallic Nodules*, available at: www.isa.org.jm/files/documents/EN/Brochures/ENG7.pdf.
[103] P. Lévy, 'The International Sea-Bed Area', in R.-J. Dupuy and D. Vignes, *A Handbook on the New Law of the Sea* (Dordrecht, Nijhoff, 1991), vol. 1, pp. 595–602; A. M. Post, *Deepsea Mining and the Law of the Sea* (The Hague, Nijhoff, 1983), pp. 11–17.

nautical miles. As noted earlier,[104] rocks 'which cannot sustain human habitation or economic life of their own' have no EEZ nor continental shelf. Hence, in the case of a rock, the limit of the Area exceptionally is the seaward limit of the territorial sea around the rock.

The limits of the Area are determined by each Sate in conformity with international law. Under Article 134(4) of the LOSC, the International Seabed Authority (hereafter the Authority) is not entitled to affect the establishment of the outer limits of the continental shelf under Part VI or the validity of agreements relating to delimitation between States with opposite or adjacent coasts. The Authority only receives such charts or lists showing the outer limit lines of the continental shelf by virtue of Article 84(2) of the LOSC.

3.3 *Raison d'être* of the principle of the common heritage of mankind

The Area is governed by the principle of the common heritage of mankind. Whilst this principle had been already introduced into space law,[105] the LOSC established a more advanced mechanism.

Before UNCLOS III, there were three different views relating to the legal status of natural resources in the deep seabed beyond the limits of national jurisdiction.[106] According to the first interpretation, the seaward limit of coastal States' continental shelves moved into deeper waters under the 'exploitability' criterion enshrined in Article 1 of the 1958 Geneva Convention on the Continental Shelf. According to this view, ultimately the whole ocean floor would be divided among coastal States. It would seem to follow that natural resources in the deep seabed would be subject to the sovereign rights of coastal States. By contrast, in the second view, the deep seabed is *res communis* and, thus, the ocean beds as well as natural resources there would be subject to the freedom of the high seas. Consequently, whereas no State can appropriate the ocean floor, the area and its resources could be used by any State according to the freedom of the high seas. On the other hand, according to the third interpretation, the deep seabed as well as its natural resources should be treated as *res nullius*. In this view, mining States would be able to appropriate the ocean floor as well as its natural resources through occupation.

In spite of differences in opinion, arguably the practical result of those interpretations would be almost the same: only technologically developed States would be best placed to explore and exploit natural resources in the deep ocean floor. Further, unrestricted seabed mining would have negative impacts upon land-based exporters of the minerals concerned, in particular those which are developing States; such a situation would exacerbate uneven development between developed and developing countries. The consequence would not be acceptable to developing States, which called for the establishment of a New International Economic Order (NIEO). Hence it has been

[104] See Chapter 2, section 3.3.
[105] Article 11 of the 1979 Agreement Governing the Activities of States on the Moon and the Other Celestial Bodies, (1979) 18 *ILM* p. 1434. Entered into force 11 July 1984.
[106] Churchill and Lowe, *Law of the Sea*, pp. 224–225.

considered that neither the principle of sovereignty nor the principle of freedom could provide a legal framework ensuring the fair and equitable sharing of natural resources of the Area.

It is in this context that in 1967, Maltese Ambassador Dr Arvid Pardo made a historic proposal that the seabed and its natural resources beyond the limits of national jurisdiction should be the common heritage of mankind. This new proposal was to be discussed in a thirty-five State ad hoc committee, which was replaced in 1968 by the permanent Committee on the Peaceful Uses of the Sea-Bed and Ocean Floor beyond the Limits of National Jurisdiction. This Committee submitted reports to the 24th and 25th sessions of the UN General Assembly. In 1969, General Assembly Resolution 2574 D (XXIV), known as the Moratorium Resolution, declared that pending the establishment of an international regime, 'States and persons, physical or juridical, are bound to refrain from all activities of exploitation of the resources of the area of the sea-bed and ocean floor, and the subsoil thereof, beyond the limits of national jurisdiction'.

In 1970, the Declaration of Principles Governing the Sea-Bed and the Ocean Floor, and the Subsoil Thereof, Beyond the Limits of National Jurisdiction was adopted (hereafter the 1970 Declaration).[107] Principle 2 of the 1970 Declaration pronounced that: 'The area shall not be subject to appropriation by any means by States or persons, natural or judicial, and no State shall claim or exercise sovereignty or sovereign rights over any part thereof'. At the same time, the 1970 Declaration explicitly recognised that the existing legal regime of the high seas did not provide substantive rules for regulating the exploration of the seabed area beyond the limits of national jurisdiction and the exploitation of its resources. Thus, the 1970 Declaration solemnly declared that:

> The sea-bed and ocean floor, and the subsoil thereof, beyond the limits of national jurisdiction (hereafter referred to as the area), as well as the resources of the area, are the common heritage of mankind.

It is important to note that the principle of the common heritage of mankind came into existence in a situation where neither the principle of sovereignty nor that of freedom could provide a legal framework ensuring the equitable share of the benefit derived from natural resources of the Area. In fact, the application of the two traditional principles to the deep seabed was clearly negated in the 1970 Declaration.

3.4 Elements of the principle of the common heritage of mankind

Article 136 pronounces that:

> The Area and its resources are the common heritage of mankind.

[107] UN Resolution 2749 (XXV). This resolution was adopted 108 in favour, none against, with fourteen abstentions.

All rights in the resources of the Area are vested in mankind as a whole, on whose behalf the Authority shall act by virtue of Article 137(2). Under Article 133(a), 'resources' means 'all solid, liquid or gaseous mineral resources *in situ* in the Area at or beneath the sea-bed, including polymetallic nodules'. The principle of the common heritage of mankind in the LOSC is composed of three legal elements.

The first element is the non-appropriation of the Area as well as its natural resources. In this regard, Article 137(1) stipulates that:

> No State shall claim or exercise sovereignty or sovereign rights over any part of the Area or its resources, nor shall any State or natural or juridical person appropriate any part thereof. No such claim or exercise of sovereignty or sovereign rights nor such appropriation shall be recognized.

Here the appropriation of the Area on the basis of the principle of sovereignty is clearly negated. At the same time, it should be noted that the appropriation of 'its resources' is also prohibited. It follows that there is no freedom to explore and exploit natural resources in the Area. On this point, the Area must be distinguished from *res communis*. Consequently, the two traditional principles in the law of the sea are excluded in the legal framework governing the Area.

The second element concerns the benefit of mankind as a whole. Article 140(1) explicitly provides that activities in the Area shall be carried out for the benefit of mankind as a whole. Article 140(2) calls for the Authority to provide for the equitable sharing of financial and other economic benefits derived from activities in the Area through any appropriate mechanism, on a non-discriminatory basis, in accordance with Article 160(2)(f)(i). Thus the concept of the benefit of mankind as a whole and the equitable sharing of benefits are intimately intertwined. It can be said that the benefit of mankind as a whole is at the heart of the principle of the common heritage of mankind.[108]

The third element pertains to the peaceful use of the Area. In this regard, Article 141 makes it explicit that the Area shall be open to use exclusively for peaceful purposes by all States.

3.5 International Seabed Authority

The next issue to be examined involves a specific mechanism for promoting the benefit of mankind as a whole. In this regard, Article 153(1) provides that activities in the Area shall be organised, carried out and controlled by the Authority on behalf of mankind as a whole. 'Activities in the Area' means all activities of exploration for, and exploitation of, the resources of the Area.[109] More specifically, the Seabed Disputes Chamber of ITLOS made clear that 'activities in the Area' include: drilling, dredging, coring, and excavation; disposal, dumping and discharge into the marine environment of sediment, wastes or other effluents; and construction and operation or maintenance

[108] A. C. Kiss, 'La notion de patrimoine commun de l'humanité' (1982) 175 *RCADI*, pp. 229 and 231.
[109] LOSC, Article 1(1).

of installations, pipelines and other devices related to such activities.[110] However, processing, namely the process through which metals are extracted from the minerals and transportation is excluded from 'activities in the Area'.[111]

All States Parties to the LOSC are *ipso facto* members of the Authority (Article 156(2)). The Authority sits in Jamaica (Article 156(4)). The Authority comprises three principal organs, that is to say, an Assembly, a Council and a Secretariat (Article 158(1)).

The Assembly, which consists of all the members of the Authority, is the supreme organ of the Authority to which the other principal organs shall be accountable as specifically provided for in the LOSC (Articles 159(1) and 160(1)). The Assembly is entitled to establish general policies on any question or matter within the competence of the Authority (Article 160(1)).

The Council, which consists of thirty-six members of the Authority, is the executive organ of the Authority (Articles 161(1) and 162(1)). Each member of the Council shall be elected for four years (Article 161(3)). The Council is empowered to establish the specific policies to be pursued by the Authority on any question or matter within the competence of the Authority (Article 162(1)).

The Secretariat of the Authority comprises a Secretary-General and such staff as the Authority may require (Article 166(1)). In the performance of their duties, the Secretary-General and the staff shall not seek or receive instructions from any government or from any other source external to the Authority. They shall refrain from any action which might reflect on their position as international officials responsible only to the Authority. In addition, the Secretary-General and the staff shall have no financial interest in any activity relating to exploration and exploitation in the Area (Article 168(1) and (2)). Those qualifications will contribute to secure the independence and neutrality of the Secretariat.

The LOSC contains detailed provisions with regard to the jurisdiction of the Authority. Principal features of its jurisdiction can be summarised in five points.

First, the Authority's jurisdiction is limited to the Area and is limited *ratione loci*.[112] The Area comprises the seabed and ocean floor and subsoil thereof beyond the limits of national jurisdiction. Under Article 135, the Authority's jurisdiction shall not affect the legal status of the waters superjacent to the Area or that of the airspace above the waters. Accordingly, the jurisdiction is spatially limited to the seabed and its subsoil beyond the limits of national jurisdiction.

Second, the jurisdiction of the Authority is limited to matters provided by the LOSC and 1994 Implementation Agreement (limitation *ratione materiae*).[113] In this respect, Article 157(2) makes clear that the powers and functions of the Authority shall be those expressly conferred upon it by the LOSC. It is true that the Authority has such incidental powers as are implicit in and necessary for the exercise of those powers and functions

[110] *Responsibilities and Obligations of States Sponsoring Persons and Entities with Respect to Activities in the Area*, Case No. 17, 1 February 2011, p. 28, para. 87. The text is available at: www.itlos.org.
[111] *Ibid.*, p. 30, paras. 95–96.
[112] F. H. Paolillo, 'Institutional Arrangements', in Dupuy and Vignes, *A Handbook*, p. 720.
[113] *Ibid.*, p. 718.

with respect to activities in the Area by virtue of Article 157(2). However, this does not mean that the Authority's jurisdiction is of a general nature in its material scope. The task of the Authority is limited in essence to organise, carry out and control activities in the Area (Articles 153(1) and 157(1)). Thus States may carry out other activities unconnected with the exploration and exploitation of the Area's mineral resources, such as laying pipelines and cables, without the permission of the Authority.

Third, the Authority has legislative and enforcement jurisdiction with respect to activities in the Area. Concerning the legislative jurisdiction, Article 17(1) of Annex III provides that:

> The Authority shall adopt and uniformly apply rules, regulations and procedures in accordance with article 160, paragraph 2(f)(ii), and article 162, paragraph 2(o)(ii), for the exercise of its functions as set forth in Part XI on, *inter alia*, the following matters.

Such matters include: (a) administrative procedures relating to prospecting, exploration and exploitation in the Area; (b) operations; (c) financial matters; (d) implementation of decisions taken pursuant to Article 151(10) and Article 164(2)(d). The Authority is also empowered to adopt appropriate rules concerning protection of human life (Article 146), protection of the marine environment (Article 145), installations used for carrying out activities in the Area (Article 147(2)(a)), the equitable sharing of financial and other economic benefits derived from activities in the Area and the payments and contributions made pursuant to Article 82 (Article 160(2)(f)–(i)). Furthermore, it has the power to adopt rules and regulations, including regulations relating to prospecting, exploration and exploitation in the Area (Articles 160(2)(f)–(ii) and 162(2)(o)–(ii)).

Concerning enforcement jurisdiction, Article 153(5) confers on the Authority the right to take at any time any measures provided for under the Part XI with a view to ensuring compliance with its provisions and the exercise of the functions of control and regulation assigned to it thereunder or under any contract. At the same time, the Authority possesses the right to inspect all installations in the Area used in connection with activities in the Area. The Council of the Authority is empowered to supervise and coordinate the implementation of the provisions of Part XI on all questions and matters within the competence of the Authority and invite the attention of the Assembly to cases of non-compliance under Article 162(2)(a).

Further, the Authority has the power to sanction non-compliance. Article 18(1) of Annex III provides that a contractor's rights under the contract may be suspended or terminated in the cases where the contractor has conducted his activities in such a way as to result in serious, persistent and wilful violations of the fundamental terms of the contract, Part XI and the rules and regulations of the Authority; or where the contractor has failed to comply with a final binding decision of a dispute settlement body applicable to him. The Authority may also impose upon the contractor monetary penalties proportionate to the seriousness of the violation in conformity with Article 18(2) of Annex III. In addition to this, a State Party which has grossly and persistently violated the provisions of Part XI may be suspended from the exercise of the rights and privileges of membership by the Assembly upon the recommendation of the Council pursuant to Article 185. The Council may issue emergency orders, which may include orders for the suspension or adjustment of operations, to prevent serious harm to the marine environment arising out of activities in the Area under Articles 162(2)(w).

Fourth, the jurisdiction of the Authority is exercised over all natural and legal persons engaging in activities in the Area, regardless of their nationalities. In this sense, the Authority's jurisdiction is of a general nature in its personal scope. As we shall discuss later, activities in the Area are to be carried out by the Enterprise, an operational organ of the Authority, and in association with the Authority by other commercial entities in accordance with Article 153(2). In this regard, Article 4(6) of Annex III requires that every applicant other than the Enterprise must undertake:

(a) to accept as enforceable and comply with the applicable obligations created by the provisions of Part XI, the rules and regulations of the Authority, the decisions of the organs of the Authority and terms of his contracts with the Authority,
(b) to accept control by the Authority of activities in the Area, as authorized by this Convention,
(c) to provide the Authority with a written assurance that his obligations under the contract will be fulfilled in good faith, and
(d) to comply with the provision on the transfer of technology set forth in Article 5 the of Annex.

It is of particular interest to note that the jurisdiction of the Authority is directly exercisable over natural persons. In this sense, it may be said that the Authority has a supranational jurisdiction.[114]

Finally, the jurisdiction of the Authority is exclusive in the sense that no State or enterprise or natural and juridicial person can be engaged upon activities in the Area without approval of the Authority.[115] In summary, the jurisdiction of the Authority is limited to matters provided by the LOSC. Concerning those matters, however, the Authority can exercise both legislative and enforcement jurisdiction over all people and objects in the Area in an exclusive manner. Further, the jurisdiction of the Authority is essentially spatial in the sense that it can be exercised solely within a specific space, namely the Area. Thus the Authority exercises a sort of spatial jurisdiction – a limited spatial jurisdiction – over the Area.[116]

[114] J. Combacau, *Le droit international de la mer, Que sais-je?* (Paris, PUF, 1985), p. 91. See also R.-J. Dupuy, *Le droit international, Que sais-je?* (Paris, PUF, 2001), p. 30.

[115] Paolillo, 'Institutional Arrangements', p. 706.

[116] Combacau considered that the Authority's jurisdiction is similar to the territorial jurisdiction of States. Combacau, *Le droit international de la mer*, p. 88. Interestingly, Virally argued that Part XI of the LOSC conferred the Authority 'the sovereign rights' over the Area. M. Virally, 'Panorama du droit international contemporain: Cours général de droit international public' (1983-V) 183 *RCADI* pp. 348–349.

3.6 System for the exploration and exploitation of resources of the Area

Activities in the Area are to be carried out by the Enterprise and other commercial operators in accordance with Article 153(2) of the LOSC. The commercial operators include States Parties, State enterprises, natural or juridical persons which possess the nationality of States Parties or are effectively controlled by them or their nationals provided for in Article 153(2). This arrangement is called the 'parallel system'. This system represents a compromise between various interest groups. Actually the LOSC provides three operational modes for deep seabed mining.[117]

First, the Authority carries out activities in the Area directly through its operational organ, i.e. the Enterprise. As will be seen, however, the establishment of the Enterprise was postponed. It is also to be noted that the initial operations are to be carried out through joint ventures pursuant to section 2(2) of the 1994 Implementation Agreement. A contractor which has contributed a particular area to the Authority as a reserved area has the right of first refusal to enter into a joint-venture arrangement with the Enterprise for exploration and exploitation of that area (section 2(5) of the Implementation Agreement).

Second, the deep seabed operations may also be carried out in association with the Authority by States Parties or other entities specified in Article 153(2)(b). Under Article 153(3), these operators are obliged to submit, in the form of a contract with the Authority, a plan of work to the Authority. The plan is to be approved by the Council after review by the Legal and Technical Commission. The plan of work must be in the form of a contract in accordance with Article 3 of Annex III.[118] In this case, each application is required to cover a total area sufficiently large and of sufficient estimated commercial value to allow *two mining operations*. Within forty-five days of receiving such data, the Authority is to designate which part is to be reserved solely for the conduct of activities by the Authority through the Enterprise or in association with developing States pursuant to Article 8 of Annex III of the LOSC. The part not reserved for the exploitation by the Enterprise becomes the area for the exploitation of the applicant. This arrangement is called the 'banking system' or 'site-banking system'. This system is closely linked with the parallel system.

Third, activities in the Area can also be carried out by the joint arrangement between the Authority and States or other entities referred to in Article 153(2)(b) to conduct activities in the Area in accordance with Article 11 of Annex III.

In all cases the Authority is to exercise such control over activities in the Area as is necessary for the purpose of securing compliance with the relevant provisions of Part XI and the Annexes relating thereto, and other relevant rules under Article 153(4). As the Seabed Disputes Chamber of ITLOS stated in its Advisory Opinion of 2011, the sponsoring State must assist the Authority and act on its own with a view to ensure that entities under its jurisdiction conform to the rules on deep seabed mining.[119]

117 Paolillo, 'Institutional Arrangements', pp. 708–709.

118 As of 2010, there are eight contractors for exploration of polymetallic nodules in the Area. ISBA/16/A/2, 8 March 2010, p. 15, para. 60.

119 *Responsibilities and Obligations of States Sponsoring Persons and Entities with Respect to Activities in the Area*, Case No. 17, p. 65, para. 226; p. 25, para. 76. See also LOSC, Article 139.

However, one of the major concerns of some industrialised States involved the lack of protection for substantial investments already made in seabed mining prior to the adoption of the LOSC. In respond to this concern, UNCLOS III set out special rules for 'pioneer investors' in two resolutions appended to the Final Act of the Conference. Resolution I relates to the establishment of the preparatory commission for the Authority and for ITLOS. Resolution II contains detailed rules involving preparatory investment in pioneer activities relating to polymetallic nodules. This resolution referred to four States (France, Japan, India and the USSR), four multinational consortia, and pioneers from developing States which satisfied certain conditions as pioneer investors.[120] A pioneer investor registered pursuant to this resolution has the exclusive right to carry out pioneer activities in the pioneer area allocated to it from the date of registration.[121] As we shall examine next, however, original provisions set out in the LOSC were subsequently modified by the 1994 Implementation Agreement.

3.7 The 1994 Implementation Agreement

(a) General considerations

The regime established by Part XI was innovative in the sense that it provided the parallel system, production policies, the transfer of technology, financial terms of contracts, and review conference. Nonetheless, some industrialised States, including the United States, strongly objected to the framework governing the Area. On 29 January 1982, for instance, US President Regan stated that: '[W]hile most provisions of the draft convention are acceptable and consistent with US interests, some major elements of the deep seabed mining regime are not acceptable'.[122] Thus the United States voted against the Convention and did not sign it. Other industrialised States abstained and did not ratify the Convention. As a consequence, it became apparent that apart from Iceland, all States Parties to the Convention were developing States.

Later on, major industrialised States, such as the United States (1980), the United Kingdom (1981), Federal Republic of Germany (1980, amended 1982), France (1981), Japan (1982), the USSR (1982) and Italy (1985), enacted unilateral domestic legislation in relation to deep seabed mining.[123] In 1984, eight industrialised States concluded the Provisional Understanding Regarding Deep Seabed Matters in order to avoid overlapping in deep seabed operations.[124] This was called the reciprocating State regime or the 'mini-treaty' regime. However, there were growing concerns that this situation ran the serious risk of damaging the unity and universality of the deep seabed regime established in Part XI and the LOSC as a whole. The delay in the commercial exploitation of deep seabed resources and economic moves towards market-oriented approaches at the global level also encouraged States to reconsider Part XI.

[120] Paragraph 1(a) of Resolution II. [121] Paragraph 6 of Resolution II.

[122] Statement by the President, 29 January 1982, (March 1982) 82 *Department of State Bulletin*, Number 2060, p. 54.

[123] E. D. Brown, 'Neither Necessary nor Prudent at this Stage: The Regime of Seabed Mining and its Impact on the Universality of the UN Convention on the Law of the Sea' (1993) *Marine Policy* p. 93.

[124] The eight States are: Belgium, France, Federal Republic of Germany, Italy, Japan, the Netherlands, the United Kingdom and the United States. For the text, see (1984) 23 *ILM* pp. 1354–1360.

Against that background, in July 1990, the UN Secretary-General Javier Pérez de Cuéllar initiated informal consultation in order to meet the specific objections of the developed States. These informal consultations took place from 1990 to 1994 and fifteen meetings were convened.[125] As a result, on 28 July 1994, the UN General Assembly adopted the Implementation Agreement, by a vote of 121 in favour, none against, and seven abstentions.[126]

In addition to the Preamble, the Implementation Agreement is composed of ten Articles and an Annex which is divided into nine sections. The provisions of the Implementation Agreement and Part XI of the LOSC are to be interpreted and applied as a single instrument. In the event of any inconsistency between the 1994 Agreement and Part XI, the provisions of the former shall prevail (Article 2(1)). After the adoption of the 1994 Agreement, any instrument of ratification or formal confirmation of or accession to the Convention shall also represent consent to be bound by the 1994 Agreement (Article 4(1)). No State or entity may establish its consent to be bound by the 1994 Implementation Agreement unless it has previously established or establishes at the same time its consent to be bound by the Convention (Article 4(2)). Despite the title of the 'Implementation' Agreement, it modifies the original regime of Part XI of the LOSC. Four points merit highlighting in particular.

(b) Cost-effectiveness

As stated in section 1(2) of the Agreement, cost-effectiveness is a key element in the Implementation Agreement. As a corollary, the setting up and the functioning of the organs and subsidiary bodies of the Authority is to be based on an evolutionary approach (section 1(3)). For example, the Secretariat of the Authority is to perform the functions of the Enterprise until it begins to operate independently of the Secretariat (section 2(1)). Upon the approval of a plan of work for exploitation for an entity other than the Enterprise, or upon receipt by the Council of an application for a joint-venture operation with the Enterprise, the Council of the Authority is to take up the issue of the functioning of the Enterprise independently of the Secretariat of the Authority (section 2(2)).

The obligation of States Parties to fund one mine site of the Enterprise as provided for in Annex IV, Article 11(3) shall not apply in light of the delay in commercial production of mineral resources in the Area. Further to this, States Parties are not required to finance any of the operations in any mine site of the Enterprise or under its joint-venture arrangements by virtue of section 2(3). The obligations applicable to contractors shall also apply to the Enterprise under section 2(4). As a consequence, the Enterprise lost its original advantageous position.

[125] Concerning the consultations process, see UN General Assembly, *Consultations of the Secretary-General on Outstanding Issues Relating to the Deep Seabed Mining Provisions of the United Nations Convention on the Law of the Sea, Report of the Secretary-General*, A/48/950, 9 June 1994.

[126] 1836 *UNTS* p. 42; (1994) 33 *ILM* p. 1309. Entered into force 28 July 1996. As at July 2011, 141 States have ratified the Agreement.

Concerning the budget of the Authority, section 1(14) provides that until the end of the year following the year during which the Agreement enters into force, the administrative expenses of the Authority shall be met through the budget of the United Nations. Thereafter, the administrative expense of the Authority is to be met by assessed contributions of its members until the Authority has sufficient funds from other sources to meet those expenses. The Authority shall not exercise the power to borrow funds to finance its administrative budget provided in Article 174(1) of the LOSC. On the other hand, a Finance Committee, which is composed of fifteen members, was established in section 9(1).

(c) The market-oriented approaches

The following changes to Part XI, which can, essentially, be characterised by their market-oriented approaches, should be highlighted.

(i) Production policies: In order to prevent adverse effects on the economies of developing countries which produce and export the mineral to be mined from the Area, Article 151 of the LOSC provided for production limitation.[127] However, the industrialised States opposed the limitation of seabed production because it would deter the development of the exploitation of deep seabed mineral resources.[128] Thus, the production limitation was disapplied by section 6(7) of the Implementation Agreement.

(ii) The obligation to transfer technology: The transfer of technology is crucial for the developing States because the Enterprise would be unable to operate in the reserved areas if it did not acquire technology necessary to the operation. Thus, Article 5 of Annex III of the LOSC provided mandatory transfer of technology to the Enterprise. Nevertheless, this obligation was unacceptable to the industrialised States because compulsory transfer of technology was considered prejudicial to intellectual property rights and this requirement would introduce a bad precedent.[129] In response, the mandatory transfer of technology enshrined in Article 5 of Annex III of the LOSC was disapplied by section 5(2) of the Implementation Agreement.

(iii) Financial terms of contracts: Article 13(2) of Annex III of the LOSC required that a fee be levied for the administrative cost of processing an application for approval of a plan of work in the form of a contract and fixed it at an amount of US$500,000 per application. Further, Article 13(3) to (10) of Annex III imposed on a contractor detailed financial obligations, including an annual fixed fee of US$1 million from the date of entry into force of the contract. However, the industrialised countries considered that the financial terms of the contract were too onerous.[130] The Implementation

[127] It must be remembered that the product limitation was applicable only to an interim period of twenty-five years in accordance with Article 151(3) of the LOSC.

[128] See for instance, statement of special representative of the US President for UNCLOS III. J. L. Malone, *Statement before the House Foreign Affairs Committee on 23 February, 1982*, (1982) 82 *Department of State Bulletin*, No. 2062, p. 61.

[129] See for instance, J. L. Malone, *Statement before the House Foreign Affairs Committee on 12 August, 1982* (1982) 82 *Department of State Bulletin*, No. 2067, p. 49.

[130] See for instance, White House Fact Sheet, 29 January 1982, (March 1982) 82 *Department of State Bulletin*, No. 2060, p. 55.

Agreement thus halves the application fee for either the exploration or exploitation phase to US$250,000 in accordance with section 8(3). The detailed financial obligations of miners set out in Article 13(3) to (10) of Annex III were deleted by section 8(2) of the Implementation Agreement. An annual fixed fee is to be payable from the date of commencement of commercial production pursuant to section 8(1)(d). This will further reduce the burden on the contractor.

(iv) Economic assistance: In order to assist developing countries which suffer serious adverse effects on their export earnings or economies because of activities in the Area, Article 151(10) of the LOSC required the Assembly of the Authority to establish a system of compensation or take other measures of economic adjustment assistance. However, the factors necessary for gauging the adverse effects of deep seabed production on developing land-based producer States would not be known until the commencement of commercial production of mineral resources in the Area. It was also maintained that economic assistance should not be excessive. Thus section 7(1) of the Implementation Agreement provides that the Authority shall establish an economic assistance fund from a portion of the funds of the Authority which exceeds those necessary to cover the administrative expenses of the Authority; and that economic assistance to developing land-based producer States shall be provided from the fund of the Authority.

(d) Decision-making

Originally the Assembly was considered as the supreme organ of the Authority establishing general policies under Article 160(1) of the LOSC. However, the Implementation Agreement strengthened the power of the Council in policy-making (section 3(1) and (4)). Furthermore, the decision-making system in the Assembly and the Council was modified by the Implementation Agreement. Under Article 159(7) and (8) of the LOSC, decisions on questions of procedure in the Assembly were to be taken by a majority, and decisions on questions of substance in the Assembly were to be taken by a two-thirds majority of members present and voting, provided that such majority included a majority of the members participating in the session. Under Article 161(8)(b) and (c), decisions on questions of substance in the Council were to be taken by a two-thirds majority or a three-fourths majority of the members present and voting.

However, section 3(2) of the Implementation Agreement introduced a consensus procedure. If all efforts to reach a decision by consensus have been exhausted, decisions by voting in the Assembly are to be taken by a majority of members present and voting, and decisions on questions of substance are to be taken by a two-thirds majority of members present and voting, as provided for in Article 159(8) of the LOSC (section 3(3)). Moreover, Article 161(8)(b) and (c) of the Convention shall not apply. Instead, section 3(5) introduced a collective-veto system, by providing that:

> If all efforts to reach a decision by consensus have been exhausted, decisions by voting in the Council on questions of procedure are to be taken by a majority of members present and voting, and decisions on questions of substance, except where the Convention provides for decisions by

> consensus in the Council, shall be taken by a two-thirds majority of members present and voting, provided that such decisions are not opposed by a majority in any one of the chambers referred to in paragraph 9.

Paragraph 9 refers to three chambers which are composed of four members, and one chamber which consists of twenty-four States, respectively.[131] The practical effect is that three of the four members of each chamber can block substantive decisions which do not require consensus. It is to be noted that Russia and the United States are permanently to be elected as members of the chamber provided for in paragraph 15(a) of section 3.[132]

(e) Review conference

Article 155 of the LOSC provided procedures relating to the conference for the review of those provisions of Part XI and the relevant Annexes. In the consultations, however, several industrialised States, including the United States, cast doubt on the validity of this procedure.[133] Section 4 of the Implementation Agreement thus provides that Articles 155(1), (3) and (4) of the LOSC shall not apply.

3.8 Evaluation

The Implementation Agreement revised the original regime of the deep seabed under the LOSC in favour of the industrialised States. However, it must be stressed that the essential elements governing the Area, namely, the principle of the common heritage of mankind, the non-appropriation of the Area and its natural resources, the use exclusively for peaceful purposes, and the benefit of mankind as a whole, remain intact.[134] In this regard, Article 311(6) of the LOSC makes clear that:

> States Parties agree that there shall be no amendments to the basic principle relating to the common heritage of mankind set forth in article 136 and that they shall not be party to any agreement in derogation thereof.

[131] Section 9(a) stipulates that: 'Each group of States elected under paragraph 15(a) to (c) shall be treated as a chamber for the purposes of voting in the Council. The developing States elected under paragraph 15(d) and (e) shall be treated as a single chamber for the purposes of voting in the Council.' Chambers set out in paragraph 15(a) to (c) are: a major consumers group, a major investments group, and a major exporters group. The chamber provided for in paragraphs (d) and (e) is composed of six developing States and eighteen members elected according to the principle of ensuring an equitable geographical distribution.

[132] Paragraph 15(a) refers to 'one State from the Eastern European region having the largest economy in terms of gross domestic product', which implies the Russian Federation. The same paragraph also refers to 'the State, on the date of entry into force of the Convention, having the largest economy in terms of gross domestic production', which implies the United States.

[133] See for instance, White House Fact Sheet, 29 January 1982, (March 1982) 82 *Department of State Bulletin*, No. 2060, p. 55.

[134] L. D. M. Nelson, 'The New Deep Sea-Bed Mining Regime' (1995) 10 *IJMCL* p. 203.

The Preamble of the Implementation Agreement also reaffirmed that 'the seabed and ocean floor and subsoil thereof, beyond the limits of national jurisdiction ... as well as the resources of the Area, are the common heritage of mankind'. Moreover, section 4 of the Agreement affirms that the principles referred to in Article 155(2) of the LOSC shall be maintained. This provision confirms the essential elements of the principle of the common heritage of mankind.

As explained earlier, the establishment of the Enterprise was postponed. Even so, the direct exploration and exploitation of natural resources in the Area through the Enterprise was maintained because this is at the heart of the deep seabed regime. Thus it could well be said that the 'parallel system' remains unchanged. Furthermore, as the Seabed Disputes Chamber of ITLOS stated, the role of the sponsoring State is to realise the common interest of all States in the proper implementation of the principle of the common heritage of mankind by assisting the Authority and by acting on its own with a view to ensuring that entities under its jurisdiction conform to the rules on deep seabed mining.[135] Overall it may be concluded that essential elements of the principle of the common heritage of mankind remain intact.

Whilst the commercial exploitation of resources of the Area would seem to be a remote possibility,[136] the Authority is playing an important role in the elaboration of rules and regulations with regard to activities in the Area. On 13 July 2000, Regulations on Prospecting and Exploration for Polymetallic Nodules in the Area (the Mining Code) were approved by the Assembly of the Authority. On 7 May 2010, the Assembly of the Authority approved the Regulations on Prospecting and Exploration for Polymetallic Sulphides in the Area. Furthermore, the Authority is required to promote and encourage the conduct of marine scientific research in the Area and to disseminate the results of such research under Article 143 of the LOSC. In relation to this, in 2006, the Authority established the International Seabed Authority Endowment Fund for Marine Scientific Research in the Area. Moreover, the role of the Authority is increasingly important in the environmental protection of the Area.[137] Overall it may be said that the Authority is already playing a valuable role in the making of relevant rules regulating seabed activities, environmental protection and scientific research in the Area.

4 CONCLUSIONS

(i) The high seas are governed by the principle of the freedom of the seas. This principle seeks to ensure non-appropriation of the high seas and the freedom of various uses of the oceans, such as navigation, overflight, laying submarine cables and pipelines, construction of artificial islands, fishing and marine scientific research.

135 *Responsibilities and Obligations of States Sponsoring Persons and Entities with Respect to Activities in the Area*, Case No. 17, p. 65, para. 226; p. 25, para. 76. Articles 139(1), 153(4) and Article 4(4) of Annex III of the LOSC refer to the sponsoring States. *Ibid.*, pp. 32–33, para. 101.

136 M. W. Lodge, 'The International Seabed Authority's Regulations on Prospecting and Exploitation for Polymetallic Nodules in the Area' (2002) 20 *Journal of Energy and Natural Resources Law* p. 294.

137 This issue will be discussed in Chapter 9, section 8.2 of this book.

(ii) In principle, legal order on the high seas is secured by the exclusive jurisdiction of the flag State. In this sense, the principle of the exclusive jurisdiction of the flag State is the cardinal principle of international law governing the high seas. Under this principle, the flag State has responsibility to ensure compliance with relevant rules of international law concerning vessels flying its flag.

(iii) However, flag State jurisdiction is seriously undermined by the practice of flags of convenience. As shown by the UN Registration Convention, an attempt has been made to ensure a genuine link between the flag State and ships flying its flag but with only limited success. Thus the role of the coastal and port States seems to be increasingly important with a view to securing compliance with relevant rules of the law of the sea.[138]

(iv) The principle of the exclusive jurisdiction of the flag State is subject to two exceptions. The first exception involves the right of visit. Under Article 110(1) of the LOSC, the right of visit applies to: piracy, the slave trade, unauthorised broadcasting, a ship without nationality, and a ship with suspicious nationality. In essence, the right of visit seeks to safeguard the common interests of the international community as a whole. The second exception relates to the right of hot pursuit, which seeks to protect the interests of the coastal State.

(v) Neither the principle of sovereignty nor the principle of freedom could provide an equitable legal framework for governing the Area. For this reason, the common heritage of mankind has emerged as the cardinal principle governing the Area. It is argued, therefore, that the principle of the common heritage of mankind can be regarded as an antithesis to the traditional principles governing the law of the sea.

(vi) The original regime embodied in the LOSC was significantly modified by the 1994 Implementation Agreement. Major changes include: the costs to States Parties and institutional arrangements, the approval procedure for an exploration plan, the Enterprise, decision-making, the review conference, transfer of technology, production policy, the financial terms of contracts, the establishment of a finance committee, and economic assistance. Nonetheless, the principal elements of the principle of the common heritage of mankind remain intact. Hence it is argued that the common heritage of mankind continues to be the cardinal principle governing activities in the Area.

FURTHER READING

1 The High Seas

A. Ademun-Odeke, 'An Examination of Bareboat Charter Registries and Flag of Convenience Registries in International Law' (2005) 36 *ODIL* pp. 339–362.

Institut du droit économique de la mer, *Le pavillon: colloque tenu à l'Institut océanographique de Paris* (Paris, Pedone, 2008).

[138] This question will be addressed in Chapter 7, sections 6.4 and 6.5 and Chapter 8, sections 6.3 and 6.4.

A. Kanehara, 'Challenging the Fundamental Principle of the Freedom of the High Seas and the Flag State Principle Expressed by Recent Non-Flag State Measures on the High Seas' (2008) 51 *Japanese Yearbook of International Law* pp. 21–56.

F. J. M. Llácer, 'Open Registers: Past, Present and Future' (2003) 27 *Marine Policy* pp. 513–523.

J. N. K. Mansell, *Flag State Responsibility: Historical Development and Contemporary Issues* (Heidelberg, Springer, 2009).

A. J. Marcopoulos, 'Flags of Terror: An Argument for Rethinking Maritime Security Policy Regarding Flags of Convenience' (2007) 32 *Tulane Maritime Law Journal* pp. 277–312.

N. M. Poulantzas, *The Right of Hot Pursuit in International Law*, 2nd edn (The Hague, Nijhoff, 2002).

T. Treves, 'Intervention en haute mer et navires étrangers' (1995) 41 *AFDI* pp. 651–675.

'Flags of Convenience before the Law of the Sea Tribunal' (2004–2005) 6 *San Diego International Law Journal* pp. 179–189.

United Nations, *Commentary on the United Nations Convention against Illicit Traffic in Narcotic Drugs and Psychotropic Substances 1988* (New York, United Nations, 1998).

M. J. Wing, 'Rethinking the Easy Way Out: Flags of Convenience in the Post-September 11th Era' (2003–2004) 28 *Tulane Maritime Law Journal* pp. 173–190.

2 The Area

D. H. Anderson, 'Resolution and Agreement Relating to the Implementation of Part XI of the UN Convention on the Law of the Sea: General Assessment' (1995) 55 *ZaöRV* pp. 275–289.

E. D. Brown, 'The 1994 Agreement on the Implementation of Part XI of the UN Convention on the Law of the Sea: Breakthrough to Universality?' (1995) 19 *Marine Policy* pp. 5–20.

Sea-Bed Energy and Minerals: The International Legal Regime (The Hague, Kluwer, 2001).

L. Caflisch, 'A New Type of Intergovernmental Organisation: The International Seabed Authority' (1983) 9 *Philippine Yearbook of International Law* pp. 1–46.

D. French, 'From the Depths: Rich Pickings of Principles of Sustainable Development and General International Law on the Ocean floor – the Seabed Disputes Chamber's 2011 Advisory Opinion' (2011) 26 *IJMCL* pp. 525–568.

M. W. Lodge, 'International Seabed Authority: Current Legal Developments' (2009) 24 *IJMCL* pp. 185–193.

L. D. M. Nelson, 'The New Deep Sea-Bed Mining Regime' (1995) 10 *IJMCL* pp. 189–203.

A. G. Oude Elferink and E. J. Molenaar (eds.). *The International Legal Regime of Areas beyond National Jurisdiction: Current and Future Developments* (Leiden, Nijhoff, 2010).

B. H. Oxman, 'The 1994 Agreement and the Convention' (1994) 88 *AJIL* pp. 687–696.

A. M. Post, *Deepsea Mining and the Law of the Sea* (The Hague, Nijhoff, 1983).

L. B. Sohn, 'International Law Implications of the 1994 Agreement' (1994) 88 *AJIL* pp. 696–705.

United Nations, *The Law of the Sea: Concept of the Common Heritage of Mankind. Legislative History of Articles 131–150 and 311(6) of the United Nations Convention on the Law of the Sea* (New York, United Nations, 1996).

M. C. Wood, 'The International Seabed Authority: Fifth to Twelfth Sessions (1999–2006)' (2007) 11 *Max Planck Yearbook of United Nations Law* pp. 47–98.

6

Maritime Delimitation

Main Issues

As discussed in previous chapters, in the international law of the sea, human activities in the ocean are regulated according to multiple jurisdictional zones. Thus the spatial distribution of jurisdiction of States is the foundation of oceans governance. In determining the spatial extent of coastal State jurisdiction, a question that may arise is the situation where the jurisdiction of two or more coastal States overlaps. In this case, delimitation of the overlapping marine spaces is at issue. It will deal with rules of international law with regard to maritime delimitation. This chapter will focus mainly on the following issues:

(i) What is the cardinal principle applicable to maritime delimitations?
(ii) What are the basic approaches adopted by international courts and tribunals with regard to maritime delimitations?
(iii) What are the advantages and disadvantages of the basic approaches to the law of maritime delimitations?
(iv) What are the principal relevant circumstances in the law of maritime delimitation?
(v) What is the role of international courts and tribunals in the development of the law of maritime delimitations?
(vi) How is it possible to reconcile the requirement of predictability and that of flexibility in the law of maritime delimitation?

1 INTRODUCTION

The spatial ambit of coastal State jurisdiction over marine spaces in the law of the sea is, in principle, defined on the basis of distance from the coast. In this regard, a question which may arise is how it is possible to delimit marine spaces where the jurisdictions of two or more coastal States overlap. Without rules on maritime delimitation in spaces where coastal State jurisdictions overlap, coastal States cannot enjoy the legal uses of maritime spaces effectively. Hence the law of maritime delimitation is of paramount importance in the law of the sea. In this regard, particular attention must be drawn to two issues.

The first issue relates to the quest for a well-balanced legal system that reconciles predictability and flexibility in the law. In common with all types of law, the law of maritime delimitation must have a certain degree of predictability. On the other hand, as each maritime delimitation case differs, flexible consideration of various geographical and non-geographical factors is also required with a view to achieving equitable results. How then is it possible to ensure predictability, while taking into account the infinite variety of geographical and non-geographical situations in order to achieve an equitable result? While predictability versus flexibility of law is a classical dilemma in the legal field, it is of particular concern in the law of maritime delimitation.

The second issue involves change and continuity in the law of maritime delimitation. In essence, the law of maritime delimitation has been developed by international courts and tribunals. In this respect, it is important to note that international courts' approaches to maritime delimitations may change with the passage of time. Hence there is a need to analyse both change and continuity in the case law relating to maritime delimitation in order to clarify the direction of the development of the law in this field. Focusing on these issues, this chapter will present an outline of the international law of maritime delimitation.[1]

2 CONCEPT OF MARITIME DELIMITATION

2.1 Definition

Maritime delimitation may be defined as *the process of establishing lines separating the spatial ambit of coastal State jurisdiction over maritime space where the legal title overlaps with that of another State*. This definition calls for three comments.

First, a distinction must be made between maritime *limits* and maritime *delimitation*.[2] The establishment of maritime 'limits' consists of drawing lines that define the maritime spaces of a *single* State, that is to say, spaces that are not in contact with those of another coastal State. The establishment of 'limits' is by its nature a *unilateral* act. On the other hand, 'maritime delimitation' is an operation to be effected between two or more States, because its object is to separate overlapping areas where legal titles of coastal States compete and each State attempts to exercise spatial jurisdiction over the same maritime space.

Second, maritime delimitation is not a unilateral act, but must be effected by agreement between relevant States. The Chamber of the ICJ in the *Gulf of Maine* case affirmed this point, by stating that: 'No maritime delimitation between States with opposite or adjacent coasts may be effected unilaterally by one of those States'.[3] Hence, maritime delimitation is *international* by nature.

[1] The present author made a detailed examination on this subject in: Y. Tanaka, *Predictability and Flexibility in the Law of Maritime Delimitation* (Oxford, Hart Publishing, 2006). The argument of this chapter is based on the analysis made there with modifications and updating.

[2] L. Caflisch, 'The Delimitation of Marine Spaces between States with Opposite and Adjacent Coasts', in R.-J. Dupuy and D. Vignes (eds.), *A Handbook on the New Law of the Sea* (Dordrecht, Nijhoff, 1991), pp. 426–427.

[3] The *Gulf of Maine* case, ICJ Reports 1984, p. 299, para. 112.

Third, according to the definition given, the phenomenon of maritime delimitation is confined to States. Accordingly, delimitation issues among the members of federations fall outside the scope of this chapter. For the same reason, international organisations, among others the International Seabed Authority, are not subjects of maritime delimitation.

2.2 Typology of maritime delimitation

Under the 1958 Geneva Conventions and the 1982 LOSC, four types of maritime delimitation can be identified:

(i) Delimitation of the territorial sea (Article 12 of the Convention on the Territorial Sea and the Contiguous Zone (hereafter the TSC); Article 15 of the LOSC),
(ii) delimitation of the contiguous zone (TSC, Article 24),
(iii) delimitation of the continental shelf (Article 6 of the Convention on the Continental Shelf; LOSC, Article 83), and
(iv) delimitation of the EEZ (LOSC, Article 74).

These treaties contain no provision with regard to the delimitation of internal waters, although that problem may arise, for instance, in the case of a bay with several riparians. In addition to this, the single maritime boundary, which would delimit the continental shelf and the EEZ/fishery zone (FZ) by one line, is at issue. Considering that the factors to be taken into account may be different for the seabed and superjacent waters, it seems possible that the delimitation line of a continental shelf and an EEZ/FZ would differ as well.[4] A divergence of factors relevant to the seabed and the superjacent waters may entail the risk of creating two competing lines dividing coincident areas and create a situation in which part of the EEZ belonging to one State may overlap part of another State's continental shelf. Such a situation would give rise to complex problems relating to jurisdiction. The same problem arises in the application of customary law. In practice, with a few exceptions,[5] there is a clear trend that States draw a single maritime boundary for the continental shelf and the EEZ/FZ.

3 TREATY LAW CONCERNING MARITIME DELIMITATION

3.1 The 1958 Geneva Conventions

Concerning the delimitation of the territorial seas, Article 12(1) of the TSC provides the triple rule of 'agreement – equidistance (median line) – special circumstances':

[4] The concept of the FZ does not include the seabed. The institution of the EEZ comprises the seabed where the EEZ is established (LOSC, Article 56(1)). Accordingly, the seabed is no longer the continental shelf, but the seabed of the EEZ. Thus, theoretically, such a single maritime boundary becomes simply the boundary of the EEZ. Strictly speaking, the expression of 'a single maritime boundary between the continental shelf and the EEZ' might be questioned. At present, however, many writers often use the expression.

[5] There are at least three agreements drawing separate maritime boundaries for the seabed and the superjacent waters, namely the 1978 Torres Strait Treaty between Australia and Papua New Guinea, the 1997 Perth Treaty between Australia and Indonesia on the Timor and Arafra Seas, and the 1970 Agreement between Indonesia and Malaysia. Tanaka, *Predictability and Flexibility*, pp. 338–344.

> Where the coasts of two States are opposite or adjacent to each other, neither of the two States is entitled, failing agreement between them to the contrary, to extend its territorial sea beyond the median line every point of which is equidistant from the nearest points on the baselines from which the breadth of the territorial seas of each of the two States is measured. The provisions of this paragraph shall not apply, however, where it is necessary by reason of historic title or other special circumstances to delimit the territorial seas of the two States in a way which is at variance with this provision.

That triple rule can also be seen in Article 6 of the 1958 Convention on the Continental Shelf:

> 1. Where the same continental shelf is adjacent to the territories of two or more States whose coasts are opposite each other, the boundary of the continental shelf appertaining to such States shall be determined by agreement between them. In the absence of agreement, and unless another boundary line is justified by special circumstances, the boundary is the median line, every point of which is equidistant from the nearest point of the baselines from which the breadth of the territorial sea of each State is measured.
> 2. Where the same continental shelf is adjacent to the territories of two adjacent States, the boundary of the continental shelf shall be determined by agreement between them. In the absence of agreement, and unless another boundary line is justified by special circumstances, the boundary shall be determined by application of the principle of equidistance from the nearest point of the baselines from which the breadth of the territorial sea of each State is measured.

The triple rule calls for three comments.

First, one may wonder whether the reference to 'agreement' could have been omitted as self-evident. As explained earlier, however, maritime delimitation is not a unilateral act. Accordingly, the reference to 'agreement' may be at least useful to highlight the international character of maritime delimitation.

Second, a question arises with regard to the relationship between the element of 'equidistance' and that of 'special circumstances'. Provided that there is a hierarchy between these two elements, it may be possible to interpret equidistance as a principle and special circumstances as an exception, or, by contrast, special circumstances as a principle and equidistance as an exception. Should there be no hierarchy in those elements, equidistance and special circumstances can be regarded as one combined rule. As will be seen, the Court of Arbitration in the 1977 *Anglo-French Continental Shelf* case adopted this interpretation. In any case, it is difficult to find an authoritative answer in the framework of the Geneva Conventions.

The third issue concerns the concept of special circumstances. The concept of special circumstances is intended to avoid inequitable results from a mechanical application of the equidistance method. Nonetheless, the Geneva Conventions do not give a clear meaning for special circumstances. Hence, the specifics of special circumstances must be clarified through the development of jurisprudence and State practice in the field of maritime delimitation.

With regard to delimitation of the contiguous zone, Article 24(3) of the TSC provides a delimitation rule different from that governing the territorial sea and the continental shelf:

> Where the coasts of two States are opposite or adjacent to each other, neither of the two States is entitled, failing agreement between them to the contrary, to extend its contiguous zone beyond the median line every point of which is equidistant from the nearest points on the baselines from which the breadth of the territorial sea of the two States is measured.

It follows that the *pure* equidistance method is applicable to the delimitation of contiguous zones. The omission of any reference to special circumstances is likely to be explained by the limited powers attributed to coastal States in such zones.[6] However, the TSC contains no rule relating to the delimitation of internal waters. Considering that coastal States possess even more extensive powers in their internal waters than in their territorial sea, it appears to be possible to apply, by analogy or a fortiori, the same triple rule.[7]

3.2 The 1982 UN Convention on the Law of the Sea

The LOSC differs from the 1958 Geneva Conventions in three respects.

First, the law applicable to the continental shelf was separated from that of territorial sea delimitation. While, under Article 15 of the LOSC, the delimitation of the territorial sea is governed by the traditional triple rule, the delimitation of the continental shelf follows a different rule.

Second, the delimitation of the contiguous zone is no longer mentioned in the text of the LOSC. Consequently, the rule applicable to the contiguous zone became unclear.

Third, Articles 74(1) and 83(1) of the LOSC formulate identical rules for the delimitation of the continental shelf and of the EEZ:

> The delimitation of the exclusive economic zone [the continental shelf] between States with opposite and adjacent coasts shall be effected by agreement on the basis of international law, as referred to in Article 38 of the Statute of the International Court of Justice, in order to achieve an equitable solution.

[6] Caflisch, 'The Delimitation of Marine Spaces', p. 443.

[7] *Ibid.*, p. 442; L. Lucchini and M. Voelkel, *Droit de la mer*, tome 2: *Délimitation, Navigation et Pêche*, vol. 1, *Délimitation* (Paris, Pedone 1996), pp. 63–64.

In the drafting of these provisions, there was disagreement between the supporters of 'equidistance' and the supporters of 'equitable principles'.[8] The confrontation between the two groups was also linked to another difficult issue concerning peaceful settlement of disputes. Whilst the supporters of 'equidistance' were, as part of the package, in favour of establishing a compulsory, third-party system for the settlement of delimitation disputes, the supporters of 'equitable principles' generally rejected the idea of compulsory judicial procedures. Owing to the confrontation between the two schools of thought, as late as one year before the adoption of the LOSC no agreement had yet been reached with respect to the rule applicable to the delimitation of the EEZ and to the continental shelf. In order to break this deadlock, President Koh proposed a draft article which would bring about a compromise and, on 28 August 1981, the draft was incorporated into the Draft Convention.[9] With a few modifications suggested by the Drafting Committee and approved by the Plenary Conference on 24 September 1982, the texts became, finally, Articles 74(1) and 83(1) of the LOSC. These provisions require four observations.

First, Articles 74(1) and 83(1) omit any reference to a method of delimitation. In the absence of any method of delimitation, these provisions are likely to remain meaningless in specific situations. As will be seen, however, the interpretation of Articles 74(1) and 83(1) has changed through the development of jurisprudence relating to maritime delimitations. Currently international courts and tribunals take the view that the equidistance method is incorporated into these provisions.

Second, the concept of 'equitable solution' is highly obscure. Hence this reference may be too vague to be very useful.

Third, it appears that the reference to Article 38 of the Statute of the ICJ as a whole is not of much use in determining the applicable law because Article 38 simply enumerates the sources of international law. Furthermore, decisions *ex aequo et bono*, i.e. extra-legal considerations set out in Article 38(2), seem to be less relevant. There is scope to argue that the references in Articles 74 and 83 should have been limited to Article 38(1).[10]

Fourth, Article 311(1) of the LOSC stipulates that it shall prevail, as between States Parties, over the 1958 Geneva Conventions. Article 311(5) further provides that: '[t]his Article does not affect international agreements expressly permitted or preserved by other Articles of this Convention'. This provision is applicable to Article 6 of the Geneva Convention on the Continental Shelf, since Article 83 of the LOSC refers to Article 38 of the ICJ Statute. It would follow that Article 6 of the Geneva Convention applies between Parties to both the Geneva Convention and the LOSC.[11]

[8] For a detailed legislative history of these provisions, see *Virginia Commentaries*, vol. II (Dordrecht, Nijhoff, 1993), pp. 796–819, and pp. 948–985; S. P. Jagota, *Maritime Boundary* (Dordrecht, Nijhoff, 1985), pp. 219–272; G. J. Tanja, *The Legal Determination of International Maritime Boundaries* (Deventer, Kluwer, 1990), pp. 81–116; Dissenting Opinion of Judge Oda in the *Tunisia/Libya* case, ICJ Reports 1982, pp. 234–247, paras. 131–145.

[9] Doc. A/CONF.62/L.78.

[10] Caflisch, 'The Delimitation of Marine Spaces', p. 485.

[11] *Ibid.*, p. 479.

4 DEVELOPMENT OF CASE LAW RELATING TO MARITIME DELIMITATION: TWO CONTRASTING APPROACHES

A remarkable feature of the law of maritime delimitation is that the law has been developed through international courts and tribunals. Two distinct phases may be identified in the development of jurisprudence in this field.

4.1 The first phase (1969–1992)

The development of modern jurisprudence in the field of maritime delimitation commenced with the 1969 *North Sea Continental Shelf* judgment.[12] In this judgment, the ICJ held that: 'delimitation must be the object of agreement between the States concerned, and that such agreement must be arrived at in accordance with equitable principles'.[13] After the judgment, equitable principles as customary law came to be at the heart of the law of maritime delimitation. However, the Court rejected the existence of any obligatory method of continental shelf delimitation. According to the Court, 'there [is] no other single method of delimitation the use of which is in all circumstances obligatory'.[14] The Court continued that 'it is necessary to seek not one method of delimitation, but one goal'.[15] In the Court's view, it is the goal which should be stressed, and the law of maritime delimitation should be defined only by this goal, i.e. the achievement of equitable results. In this sense, one could speak of a result-oriented equity approach.[16] This approach allows international courts to decide, case-by-case, on the equitable results to be achieved without being bound by any method of maritime delimitations. Thus, the result-oriented equity approach emphasises maximum flexibility of the law of maritime delimitation.

However, the Arbitral Tribunal, in the 1977 *Anglo-French Continental Shelf* case, followed a line of argument different from that adopted in the *North Sea Continental Shelf* judgment. Unlike the ICJ in the *North Sea Continental Shelf* cases, the Court of Arbitration equated Article 6 of the 1958 Geneva Convention on the Continental Shelf, as a single combined equidistance–special circumstances rule, with the customary law of equitable principles.[17] On the basis of this interpretation, the Court of Arbitration applied the equidistance method with modification in the Atlantic region. In this regard, the Court of Arbitration made an important pronouncement:

[12] It is not suggested that prior to 1969 there was no decision with regard to maritime delimitations. For example, the 1909 *Grisbadarna* case between Norway and Sweden may provide an important case concerning the delimitation of the territorial sea.

[13] ICJ Reports 1969, p. 46, para. 85. See also p. 53, para. 101(C)(1).

[14] ICJ Reports 1969, p. 53, para. 101(B). See also p. 49, para. 90.

[15] *Ibid.*, p. 50, para. 92.

[16] The result-oriented equity approach is a concept for analysis. Basically, this approach corresponds to the concept of 'autonomous equity' presented by Weil. P. Weil, *Perspective du droit de la délimitation maritime* (Paris, Pedone 1988), pp. 179–181, 203–212.

[17] The *Anglo-French Continental Shelf* arbitration, 18 *Reports of International Arbitral Awards*, p. 45, para. 70.

> The Court notes that in a large proportion of the delimitations known to it, *where a particular geographical feature has influenced the course of a continental shelf boundary, the method of delimitation adopted has been some modification or variant of the equidistance principle rather than its total rejection.* ... it seems to the Court to be in accord not only with the legal rules governing the continental shelf but also with State practice to seek the solution in *a method modifying or varying the equidistance method rather than to have recourse to a wholly different criterion of delimitation.*[18]

The Court of Arbitration thus accepted the applicability of the equidistance method as a starting point, even where a particular geographical element exists in a situation of lateral delimitation. In so doing, the Court of Arbitration considered equity to be a corrective element. In this sense, one may call this methodology the corrective-equity approach.[19] According to this approach, the equidistance method is applied at the first stage of delimitation, and then a shift of the equidistance line may be envisaged if relevant circumstances warrant it. Equidistance is the only predictable method for ensuring predictability of results in the sense that once the base points are fixed, the delimitation line is mathematically determined. The corrective-equity approach thus highlights predictability in the law of maritime delimitation. In summary, two contrasting approaches appeared in the 1969 and 1977 decisions on the basis of equitable principles.

In the 1982 *Tunisia/Libya* case concerning continental shelf delimitation, the ICJ further promoted the result-oriented equity approach. The Court pronounced that:

> The result of the application of equitable principles must be equitable. ... It is, however, the result which is predominant; the principles are subordinate to the goal. The equitableness of a principle must be assessed in the light of its usefulness for the purpose of arriving at an equitable result.[20]

In this case, the Court accepted neither the mandatory character of equidistance, nor some privileged status of equidistance in relation to other methods.[21] According to the Court's approach, the application of equitable principles would be broken down into relevant circumstances in specific situations, ruling out any predetermined method.[22]

In the 1984 *Gulf of Maine* case relating to the delimitation of a single maritime boundary, the Chamber of the ICJ also echoed the result-oriented equity approach. In this case, the Chamber pronounced a 'fundamental norm' applicable to every maritime

[18] Emphasis added. *Ibid.*, p. 116, para. 249. The Court took into account the fact that, in the Atlantic region, Article 6 was applicable. As Article 6 is the particular expression of customary law of equitable principles, the result would be the same if customary law had been applied.

[19] The corrective-equity approach is a concept for analysis. Weil called this approach 'équité correctrice'. Weil, 'Perspectives', p. 179.

[20] ICJ Reports 1982, p. 59, para. 70.

[21] *Ibid.*, p. 79, para. 110.

[22] Judge Jiménez de Aréchaga clearly advocated this view. Separate Opinion of Judge Jiménez de Aréchaga, *ibid.*, p. 106, para. 24.

delimitation between neighbouring States. The first part of the norm is that maritime delimitation must be sought and effected by means of an agreement in good faith. The second part of the norm is:

> In either case, delimitation is to be effected by the application of equitable criteria and by the use of practical methods capable of ensuring, with regard to the geographic configuration of the area and other relevant circumstances, an equitable result.[23]

In this formulation, 'an equitable result' should be achieved by resort to 'equitable criteria' and a 'practical method'. According to the Chamber, there has been no systematic definition of equitable criteria because of their highly variable adaptability to different concrete situations. Thus, 'equitable criteria' are excluded from the legal domain.[24] The same is true regarding the 'practical method', since the latter would be selected on a case-by-case basis, relying on actual situations.[25] In the view of the Chamber, the law defines neither the equitable criteria nor the practical method, simply advancing the idea of 'an equitable result'.

The full Court, in the *Libya/Malta* case of 1985, also stressed the result to be achieved, not the means to be applied.[26] At the stage of establishing the continental shelf boundary, however, the Court applied the equidistance method as a first provisional step, and the equidistance line was adjusted in a second stage on account of relevant circumstances.[27] In so doing, the Court adopted the corrective-equity approach for the delimitation of the continental shelf between opposite coasts at the operational stage. It may be said that the *Libya/Malta* judgment has a hybrid character in the sense that two approaches were used. The result-oriented approach was echoed by the 1985 *Guinea/Guinea-Bissau* arbitration[28] and the 1992 *St Pierre and Miquelon* arbitration.[29] Overall it can be observed that between 1969 and 1992 international courts and tribunals basically took the result-oriented equity approach.

4.2 The second phase (1993–present)

However, the law of maritime delimitation was to change towards the corrective-equity approach. A turning point was the 1993 *Greenland/Jan Mayen* judgment. The *Greenland/Jan Mayen* case involved a maritime delimitation between the continental shelf and the EEZ/FZ. In this case, there was no agreement on a single maritime boundary and, thus, the law applicable to the continental shelf and to the EEZ/FZ had to be examined separately. Both Parties had ratified the Convention on the Continental Shelf. In this case, the Court attempted to achieve assimilation at three levels.

23 ICJ Reports 1984, p. 300, para. 112. 24 *Ibid.*, pp. 312–313, paras. 157–158.
25 *Ibid.*, p. 315, paras. 162–163. 26 ICJ Reports 1985, pp. 38–39, para. 45.
27 *Ibid.*, pp. 52–53, para. 73.
28 (1986) 25 *ILM* pp. 289–290, para. 89. The French text is the authentic one. Award of 14 February 1985, (1985) 89 *RGDIP* pp. 484 *et seq.* The *Guinea/Guinea-Bissau* award will be quoted from the English translation to enhance comprehension.
29 The *St Pierre and Miquelon* case, (1992) 31 *ILM* p. 1163, para. 38.

First, the Court equated Article 6 of the Convention on the Continental Shelf with customary law by relying on a passage of the 1977 award of the Court of Arbitration in the *Anglo-French Continental Shelf* case.[30] The Court ruled that:

> [I]n respect of the continental shelf boundary in the present case, even if it were appropriate to apply, not Article 6 of the 1958 Convention, but customary law concerning the continental shelf as developed in the decided cases, it is in accord with precedents to begin with the median line as a provisional line and then to ask whether 'special circumstances' require any adjustment or shifting of that line.[31]

Second, with respect to the law applicable to the Fishery Zone, the Court equated the customary law applicable to the FZ with that governing the EEZ on the basis of the agreement of the Parties.[32]

Third, quoting the *Anglo-French* Arbitral Award, the Court assimilated the law of continental shelf delimitation with that of the FZ at the customary law level. In this regard, the Court took the view that: 'It thus appears that, both for the continental shelf and for the fishery zones in this case, it is proper to begin the process of delimitation by a median line provisionally drawn'.[33] Furthermore, the Court held that:

> It cannot be surprising if an equidistance–special circumstances rule produces much the same result as an equitable principles–relevant circumstances rule in the case of opposite coasts, whether in the case of a delimitation of continental shelf, of fishery zone, or of an all-purpose single boundary.[34]

Thus, for the first time in the case law of the ICJ, the Court applied the corrective-equity approach as customary law. It is important to note that under this approach, the equidistance method is incorporated into the domain of customary law.

Later on, basically the corrective-equity approach was echoed by jurisprudence relating to maritime delimitations. In the 1999 *Eritrea/Yemen* arbitration (Second Phase), the Arbitral Tribunal applied the corrective-equity approach under Articles 74 and 83 of the LOSC.[35] In the 2001 *Qatar/Bahrain* case, the ICJ accepted the applicability of the corrective-equity approach as customary law in the delimitation between States with adjacent coasts.[36] Furthermore, the ICJ, in the 2002 *Cameroon/Nigeria* case, broke new ground by applying the corrective-equity approach under Articles 74 and 83 of the LOSC.[37] According to the Court's interpretation, a specific method, i.e. the equidistance method, should be incorporated into Articles 74 and 83. Considering that any reference to a specific delimitation method was omitted in

[30] The *Greenland/Jan Mayen* case, ICJ Reports 1993, p. 58, para. 46.
[31] *Ibid.*, p. 61, para. 51. [32] *Ibid.*, p. 59, para. 47.
[33] *Ibid.*, p. 62, para. 53. [34] *Ibid.*, para. 56.
[35] The *Eritrea/Yemen* arbitration (Second Phase), p. 1005, paras. 131–132.
[36] ICJ Reports 2001, p. 91, para. 167 and p. 111, para. 230.
[37] ICJ Reports 2002, pp. 441–442, paras. 288–290.

drafting those provisions, it may be said that this is a creative interpretation by the Court.

In the 2006 *Barbados/Trinidad and Tobago* arbitration, the Arbitral Tribunal did not admit a mandatory character of any delimitation method. Nevertheless, the Arbitral Tribunal took the view that 'the need to avoid subjective determinations requires that the method used starts with a measure of certainty that equidistance positively ensures, subject to its subsequent correction if justified'.[38] Thus the Arbitral Tribunal applied the corrective-equity approach in the operation of maritime delimitation under Articles 74 and 83 of the LOSC.[39] The Arbitral Tribunal, in the 2007 *Guyana/Suriname* arbitration, applied the corrective-equity approach more clearly under Articles 74 and 83 of the LOSC. The view of the Arbitral Tribunal deserves quoting:

> The case law of the International Court of Justice and arbitral jurisprudence as well as State practice are at one in holding that the delimitation process should, in appropriate cases, begin by positing a provisional equidistance line which may be adjusted in the light of relevant circumstances in order to achieve an equitable solution. The Tribunal will follow this method in the present case.[40]

However, the ICJ, in the 2007 *Nicaragua/Honduras* case, took the view that the application of the equidistance method at the first stage of maritime delimitation is not obligatory. Owing to the very active morphodynamism of the relevant area, the Court found itself that it could not apply the equidistance line in the *Nicaragua/Honduras* case. Accordingly, the Court established a single maritime boundary by applying the bisector method. Nonetheless, the Court prudently added that: 'equidistance remains the general rule'.[41] In fact, with respect to the delimitation around the islands in the disputed area, the Court applied, without any problem, the corrective-equity approach by referring to the *Qatar/Bahrain* case.[42] It is arguable, therefore, that the departure from the previous jurisprudence is only partial.[43]

The ICJ, in the 2009 *Romania/Ukraine* case, applied the corrective-equity approach to the delimitation of a single maritime boundary. According to the Court, the process of maritime delimitation will be divided into three stages. The first stage is to establish the provisional equidistance line. At the second stage, the Court will examine whether there are relevant circumstances calling for the adjustment of the provisional

38 The *Barbados/Trinidad and Tobago* arbitration, p. 94, para. 306. The text of the Award is available at the home page of the Permanent Court of Arbitration: www/pca-cpa.org.

39 *Ibid.*, p. 73, para. 242.

40 The *Guyana/Suriname* arbitration, p. 110, para. 342. See also pp. 108–109, para. 335. The text of the award is available at: www.pca-cpa.org.

41 ICJ Reports 2007, p. 745, para. 281.

42 *Ibid.*, pp. 751–752, paras. 303–304.

43 Y. Tanaka, 'Case Concerning the Territorial and Maritime Dispute between Nicaragua and Honduras in the Caribbean Sea (8 October 2007)' (2008) 23 *IJMCL* pp. 342–343; R. Churchill, 'Dispute Settlement under the UN Convention on the Law of the Sea: Survey for 2007' (2008) 23 *IJMCL* pp. 622–624. See also Y. Tanaka, 'Reflections on Maritime Delimitation in the *Nicaragua/Honduras* Case' (2008) 68 *ZaöRV* pp. 903–937.

equidistance line in order to achieve an equitable result. At the final and third stage, the Court will verify whether the delimitation line does not lead to an inequitable result by applying the test of disproportionality.[44] Considering that the disproportionality test aims to check for an equitable outcome to maritime delimitation, it may be argued that the three-stage approach in the *Romania/Ukraine* case can be regarded as a variation of the corrective-equity approach developed through judicial practice in the field of maritime delimitation.[45]

4.3 Commentary

Overall the history of the law of maritime delimitation shows a vacillation between two contrasting approaches to equitable principles: the result-oriented equity approach which emphasises maximum flexibility and the corrective-equity approach which highlights predictability. In this sense, it may be said that the development of the law of maritime delimitation is essentially characterised by the tension between predictability and flexibility in the law.

In a broad perspective, it may be observed that the law of maritime delimitation has developed from the coexistence of the two approaches towards the unified approach based on corrective equity. The unification of the law can be seen at four levels:

(i) The interpretation of treaties: the unification of the interpretation of Article 6 of the Geneva Convention on the Continental Shelf and that of Article 83 of the LOSC;
(ii) Sources of the law: the unification between customary law and treaty law in the field of maritime delimitation;
(iii) Maritime spaces: the unification of the law applicable to the delimitation of the territorial sea, the continental shelf and the EEZ;
(iv) The configuration of the coast: the unification of the law applicable to delimitation between States with adjacent coasts, and those with opposite coasts.

Under the result-oriented equity approach, international courts and tribunals may exercise a large measure of discretion in each case without being bound by any method. Considering that the factors to be considered vary in each case, the merit of flexibility of this approach is not negligible. However, because of its excessive subjectivity and the lack of predictability, the result-oriented equity approach runs the risk of reducing the normativity of the law of maritime delimitation.

By contrast, the important advantage of the corrective-equity approach is that it has a certain degree of predictability by incorporating a specific method of delimitation, i.e. the equidistance method, into the legal domain. According to the corrective-equity approach, a consideration of equity may come into play at a second stage, but only in cases in which equidistance lines provisionally drawn produce inequitable results. To this extent, the corrective-equity approach makes it possible to reduce the subjectivity and unpredictability of equitable principles. It may be said that the

[44] ICJ Reports 2009, pp. 101–103, paras. 115–122.
[45] Y. Tanaka, 'Reflections on Maritime Delimitation in the *Romania/Ukraine* Case before the International Court of Justice' (2009) 56 *NILR* pp. 419–420.

corrective-equity approach would provide a better framework for balancing predictability and flexibility.[46]

5 CONSIDERATION OF RELEVANT CIRCUMSTANCES (1): GEOGRAPHICAL FACTORS

Under the corrective-equity approach, the final delimitation line is determined by the consideration of relevant circumstances. It is thus necessary to identify the relevant circumstances and their legal effect on the modification of the provisional equidistance line. Relevant circumstances claimed by the parties to a maritime delimitation dispute are highly diverse, and a comprehensive exposition on those circumstances is out of place in this book.[47] Thus this section and that which follows it seek to outline the principal relevant circumstances.

5.1 Configuration of coasts

It is beyond serious argument that geographical factors play an important role in maritime delimitation. In fact, every international judgment regarding maritime delimitation has taken them into account. Three factors merit highlighting in particular.

The first factor concerns the distinction between opposite and adjacent coasts. International courts and tribunals have attached great importance to the distinction when evaluating the appropriateness of the equidistance method.[48] A reason for this distinction may be that the risks of inequity arising from the equidistance method are different between opposite and adjacent coasts.[49] Nonetheless, currently international courts and tribunals tend to apply the equidistance method at the first stage of maritime delimitation, regardless of the configuration of the coast. Hence, it appears that the distinction between opposite and adjacent coasts is of limited value in the law of maritime delimitation.

Second, it has been considered that the concavity or convexity of coasts constitutes a relevant circumstance. In particular, the ICJ, in the *North Sea Continental Shelf* cases, regarded the equidistance method as inequitable where coasts are concave on account of the distorting effect produced by that method.[50] This view was echoed by the *Libya/Malta* judgment.[51] In reality, however, it is often difficult to define concavity and convexity of the coast in practice. The difficulty was highlighted in the following paragraph of the *Guinea/Guinea-Bissau* award:

[46] Judge Gilbert Guillaume confirmed this view. Speech by His Excellency Judge Gilbert Guillaume, President of the International Court of Justice, to the Sixth Committee of the General Assembly of the United Nations, 31 October 2001.

[47] For a comprehensive analysis of relevant circumstances, see Tanaka, *Predictability and Flexibility*, pp. 151–327.

[48] The *Anglo-French Continental Shelf* case, p. 57, para. 97.

[49] *The North Sea Continental Shelf* cases, ICJ Reports 1969, p. 37, para. 58. This *dictum* was echoed in the *Libya/Malta* case. The *Libya/Malta* case, ICJ Reports 1985, p. 51, para. 70.

[50] ICJ Reports 1969, p. 17, para. 8.

[51] ICJ Reports 1985, p. 44, para. 56. See also p. 51, para. 70.

If the coasts of each country are examined separately, it can be seen that the Guinea-Bissau coastline is convex, when the Bijagos are taken into account, and that that of Guinea is concave. However, if they are considered together, it can be seen that the coastline of both countries is concave and this characteristic is accentuated if we consider the presence of Sierra Leone further south.[52]

In fact, interpretation of the configuration of the coast may vary according to the scale of the map or micro- or macrogeography, i.e. the question of whether coasts of third neighbouring States will be taken into account in appreciating the configuration of the coasts concerned.[53]

The third factor is the general direction of the coast. While the determination of the general direction of the coast was at issue in the *Tunisia/Libya*[54] and *Gulf of Maine* cases,[55] the most dramatic impact of the general direction of the coast can be seen in the *Guinea/Guinea-Bissau* case. In that case, the Arbitral Tribunal drew a line *grosso modo* perpendicular to the general direction of the coastline joining Pointe des Almadies (Senegal) and Cape Schilling (Sierra Leone), arguing that the overall configuration of the West African coastline should be taken into account. The point to be noted is that, when specifying the general direction of the coast, the Arbitral Tribunal selected two points located in third States.[56] Nonetheless, with respect, the selection of the Tribunal is open to question. In fact, the line connecting Pointe des Almadies and Cape Schilling cuts almost all the coast of Guinea-Bissau for nearly 350 kilometres and runs approximately 70 kilometres inside the latter's territory. As a consequence, the line selected by the Tribunal is clearly unfavourable to Guinea-Bissau and entails the risk of refashioning nature.[57]

5.2 Proportionality

The concept of proportionality holds an important position in the case law in the sense that the concept has been taken into account in almost every judgment on maritime delimitation. According to this concept, maritime delimitation should be effected by taking into account the ratio between the maritime spaces attributed to each Party and the lengths of their coastlines. In the context of maritime delimitation, the concept of proportionality was originally formulated by the Federal Republic of Germany in the *North Sea Continental Shelf* cases.[58] The Federal Republic of Germany contended that each State concerned should receive a 'just and equitable share' of the available continental shelf, proportionate to the length of its coastline or sea frontage.[59] Although the

[52] The *Guinea/Guinea-Bissau* case, pp. 294–95, para. 103.
[53] ICJ Reports 1982, p. 34, para. 17.
[54] *Ibid.*, p. 85, para. 120. [55] ICJ Reports 1984, p. 338, para. 225.
[56] The *Guinea/Guinea-Bissau* case, pp. 297–298, paras. 109–111.
[57] E. David, 'La sentence arbitrale du 14 février 1985 sur la délimitation de la frontière maritime Guinée-Guinée Bissau' (1985) 31 *AFDI* pp. 385–386.
[58] It is to be noted that as early as 1946, Sir Francis Vallat suggested an idea of proportionality in the context of a bay. Sir Francis Vallat, 'The Continental Shelf' (1946) 23 *BYIL* p. 336.
[59] Emphasis added. ICJ Reports 1969, p. 20, para. 15.

ICJ rejected the idea of a 'just and equitable share', it did accept the concept of proportionality as a final factor to be taken into account:

> A final factor to be taken account of is the element of a reasonable degree of proportionality which a delimitation effected according to equitable principles ought to bring about between the extent of the continental shelf appertaining to the States concerned and the lengths of their respective coastlines – these being measured according to their general direction *in order to establish the necessary balance between States with straight, and those with markedly concave or convex coasts, or to reduce very irregular coastlines to their truer proportions.*[60]

The above phrase suggests three geographical features which justified the recourse to proportionality: (i) adjacent coasts, (ii) existence of particular coastal configurations, such as concavity and convexity, (iii) quasi-equal length of the relevant coasts. In such geographical circumstances, the application of the equidistance method would have reduced the continental shelf of the Federal Republic of Germany as compared to that of its neighbours, although the coastlines were similar in length. It was in this particular geographical situation that proportionality came into play, in order to eliminate or diminish the distortions created by recourse to the equidistance method. It must also be noted that the Court regarded proportionality not as a distinct principle of delimitation, but as one of the factors ensuring delimitation in accordance with equitable principles. Moreover, proportionality remained a 'final' factor. In light of the geographical limitations and the relatively minor position of proportionality, at least in 1969, it is doubtful whether the Court was of the view that the theory of proportionality would be universally applicable to maritime delimitations.[61]

In subsequent cases, however, international courts and tribunals began to resort to proportionality in completely different geographical situations. In the *Tunisia/Libya* case, the ICJ relied on proportionality when delimiting between adjacent coasts, although there was no situation of concavity or convexity.[62] In the *Gulf of Maine* (second segment),[63] *Libya/Malta*,[64] *Greenland/Jan Mayen*[65] and *Eritrea/Yemen* (Second Phase)[66] cases, proportionality was considered in delimitation between States with opposite coasts. Proportionality was also taken into account in the *St Pierre and Miquelon* case, where it was not obvious whether the coasts were opposite or adjacent.[67] The concept of proportionality was also taken into account in the *Barbados/Trinidad and Tobago*,[68]

60 Judgment, *ibid.*, p. 52, para. 98 (emphasis added).

61 Dissenting Opinion of Judge Oda in the *Libya/Malta* case, ICJ Reports 1985, pp. 134–135, para. 18. This view was echoed by Judges Valticos and Schwebel. Separate Opinion of Judge Valticos, ICJ Reports 1985, p. 110, para. 19; Dissenting Opinion of Judge Schwebel, *ibid.*, pp. 182–185. See also D. W. Bowett, *The Legal Régime of Islands in International Law* (New York, Oceana, 1979), p. 164.

62 ICJ Reports 1982, p. 91, para. 131.

63 ICJ Reports 1984, p. 323, paras. 184–185; pp. 334–337, paras. 218–222.

64 ICJ Reports 1985, p. 50, para. 68; pp. 53–55, paras. 74–75.

65 ICJ Reports 1993, pp. 65–69, paras. 61–69.

66 The *Eritrea/Yemen* arbitration (Second Phase), pp. 1010–1011, paras. 165–168.

67 The *St Pierre and Miquelon* arbitration, p. 1162, para. 33; p. 1176, para. 93.

68 The *Barbados/Trinidad and Tobago* arbitration, pp. 102–103, paras. 337–338; pp. 111–112, paras. 376–379.

Guyana/Suriname,[69] and *Romania/Ukraine*[70] cases, where the geographical situations in these cases differ from the original situation shown in the *North Sea Continental Shelf* judgment. It thus appears that currently international courts and tribunals are ready to apply proportionality to every geographical situation.

Furthermore, the international courts and tribunal enlarged the function of proportionality. In the *Tunisia/Libya* case, proportionality was to be applied as a test of the equitableness of the suggested delimitation line. This approach was echoed in the *Libya/Malta, Guinea/Guinea-Bissau, St Pierre and Miquelon, Eritrea/Yemen, Barbados/Trinidad and Tobago, Guyana/Suriname* and *Romania/Ukraine* cases. In the *Romania/Ukraine* case, the ICJ considered this concept as the third stage of maritime delimitation, distinguishing it from other relevant circumstances.[71] In other instances, proportionality was used as a factor for shifting provisionally drawn equidistance lines. Examples include the *Gulf of Maine* (second segment), *Libya/Malta*, and *Greenland/Jan Mayen* cases. It may be said that proportionality has played a double role in the case law: as a test of equitableness and as a justification for shifting initial equidistance lines.[72] In summary, international courts and tribunals have enlarged the scope of the application of proportionality geographically and functionally. Nevertheless, the enlarged application of the concept of proportionality is not free from controversy.

The first problem is the lack of any objective criterion for calculating the coastal lengths and surfaces. In order to calculate the lengths of relevant coasts, it is necessary to define the coasts to be evaluated. Nonetheless, as had been shown in the *Gulf of Maine, St Pierre and Miquelon, Eritrea/Yemen, Barbados/Trinidad and Tobago* and *Guyana/Suriname* cases, the definition of relevant coasts is itself a disputable point; international courts and tribunals have failed to come up with any objective criterion. Nor is there any criterion for calculating the lengths of the relevant coasts. That calculation may be complicated by the presence of islands. It is also difficult to define relevant areas, especially the where legal titles of third States may be at issue.

The second obstacle is the lack of an objective criterion for evaluating differences in coastal lengths. In this regard, the Court, in the *Romania/Ukraine* case, stated that:

> The Court cannot but observe that various tribunals, and the Court itself, have drawn different conclusions over the years as to what disparity in coastal lengths would constitute a significant disproportionality which suggested the delimitation line was inequitable and still required adjustment. This remains in each case a matter for the Court's appreciation, which it will exercise by reference to the overall geography of the area.[73]

[69] The *Guyana/Suriname* arbitration, p. 127, para. 392.
[70] ICJ Reports 2009, pp. 129–130, paras. 210–216.
[71] *Ibid.*, p. 103, para. 122.
[72] However, the distinction between proportionality as a test and as a corrective factor is, in reality, obscure. Dissenting Opinion of Judge Weil in the *St Pierre and Miquelon* case, p. 1207, para. 25.
[73] ICJ Reports 2009, p. 129, para. 213.

The above passage did seem to imply that currently there is no objective criterion for evaluating 'particularly marked disparities' in coastal lengths of the disputing parties.

The third difficulty pertains to the lack of an objective criterion for evaluating the reasonable relation between coastal lengths and the maritime areas attributed to the parties. In all cases, the international courts concluded that there was no disproportion between the ratio of coastal lengths and the ratio of maritime areas appertaining to the parties. Nonetheless, it is impossible, or at least highly difficult, to extrapolate any objective criterion for judging whether there is reasonable relation between the coastal length and maritime area appertaining to each party.

Finally, it may have to be accepted that the concept of proportionality necessarily includes some aspects of apportionment, although the ICJ clearly distinguished between delimitation and apportionment.[74] In this regard, the concept of proportionality contradicts the rejection of the idea of apportionment in maritime delimitation. It must also be noted that since the number of lines capable of producing the same proportion is limitless, proportionality will not determine any concrete delimitation line.[75]

5.3 Baselines

The selection of baseline or base points is fundamental to draw a provisional equidistance line. In this regard, one question to arise is whether the same baselines or base points for measuring limits of maritime zones should be used for the purpose of maritime delimitations.[76] In this regard, Article 15 of the LOSC as well as Article 6 of the Geneva Convention on the Continental Shelf seem to suggest that when applying the equidistance method to maritime delimitations, an equidistance line should be, in principle, drawn from the baselines of the territorial sea. Nonetheless, the practice of international courts appears to demonstrate that where the use of the baseline or base points established by the parties may produce an inequitable result, international courts and tribunals may select, within their compass, relevant base points for the purpose of maritime delimitations. Four cases merit particular attention.

First, in the *Libya/Malta* case, the validity of straight baselines for Malta was at issue. Under the Territorial Waters and Contiguous Zone Act, adopted on 7 December 1971, Malta established straight baselines. Although the ICJ refrained from expressing any opinion on the legality of the Maltese baselines, the Court considered it equitable *not* to take account of Filfla in the calculation. The Court thus pronounced that: 'the baselines as determined by coastal States are not per se identical with the points chosen on a coast to make it possible to calculate the area of the continental shelf appertaining to that State'.[77]

[74] The *North Sea Continental Shelf* cases, ICJ Reports 1969, p. 22, para. 18.

[75] Dissenting Opinion of Judge Oda, ICJ Reports 1982, p. 258, para. 162; H. Thirlway, 'The Law and Procedure of the International Court of Justice, Part Five' (1994) 64 *BYIL* p. 42.

[76] On this issue, see P. Weil, 'A propos de la double fonction des lignes et points de base dans le droit de la mer', in *Écrits de droit international* (Paris, PUF, 2000), pp. 279–299.

[77] ICJ Reports 1985, p. 48, para. 64.

Second, in the *Eritrea/Yemen* case (the Second Phase), the validity of Eritrea's baseline was discussed. In Eritrean domestic law, enacted by Ethiopia in 1953, its territorial sea is defined as extending from the extremity of the seaboard at maximum annual high tide. Nevertheless, the Arbitral Tribunal took the view that the median line boundary was to be measured from the low-water line in conformity with Article 5 of the LOSC because both Parties had agreed that the Tribunal was to take into account the provisions of that Convention. Further to this, Eritrea integrated a marine feature called the 'Negileh Rock' into its straight-baselines system. However, the Arbitral Tribunal did not admit the use of this marine feature as a base point and decided that the western base points to be employed on this part of the Eritrean coast should be on the low-water line of certain of the outer Dahlak islets, Mojeidi, and an unnamed islet east of Dahret Segala.[78]

Third, in the *Qatar/Bahrain* case, Bahrain contended that, as a multiple-island State characterised by a cluster of islands off the coast of its main islands, it was entitled to draw a line connecting the outermost islands and low-tide elevations. Nonetheless, the Court ruled that Bahrain was not entitled to apply the method of straight baselines.[79]

Fourth and importantly, the ICJ, in the *Romania/Ukraine* case, clearly distinguished the baseline for measuring the seaward breadth of marine spaces from the baseline for the purpose of maritime delimitations, by stating that:

> The Court observes that the issue of determining the baseline for the purpose of measuring the breadth of the continental shelf and the exclusive economic zone and the issue of identifying base points for drawing an equidistance/median line for the purpose of delimiting the continental shelf and the exclusive economic zone between adjacent/opposite States are two different issues.[80]

The judicial examination of baselines or base points in the context of maritime delimitations may contribute to prevent an inequitable result arising from the liberal application of straight baselines.

In State practice, a question arises in cases where the validity of straight baselines established by one party is disputed by the other party. In these cases, some treaties gave only half (or partial) effect to the contested straight baselines. A case in point is the 1984 Agreement between Denmark and Sweden establishing a single maritime boundary. Both countries established straight baselines, and, as a general rule, their straight baselines were used to compute the delimitation line. In the Baltic, however, Denmark objected to Sweden's basepoint of Falsterborev. In the Southern Kattegat, Sweden objected to a Danish baseline connecting Hesselø with Sjælland. In both instances, the parties agreed to split in half the area generated by those

[78] The *Eritrea/Yemen* arbitration (Second Phase), pp. 1006–1008, paras. 133–146.

[79] ICJ Reports 2001, pp. 103–104, paras. 210–215. See also Joint Dissenting Opinion of Judges Bedjaoui, Ranjeva and Koroma, *ibid.*, p. 202, para. 183 and para. 185.

[80] ICJ Reports 2009, p. 108, para. 137. See also p. 101, para. 117.

baselines.[81] The half-effect solution concerning straight baselines was also adopted in the 1975 Agreement between Italy and Yugoslavia[82] and the 1977 Maritime Boundary Agreement between the USA and Cuba.[83] The half or partial effect given to straight baselines seems to offer a solution when the validity of these baselines is disputed.

5.4 Presence of islands

There is no serious doubt that the presence of islands may constitute a relevant circumstance in maritime delimitation. However, State practice is so diverse that it is difficult to specify a general rule with respect to the legal effect given to islands. Thus, international courts and tribunals are to decide the effect given to islands within the framework of equitable principles. In broad terms, four modes of effect given to islands can be identified in case law.

The first mode is to give full effect to an island. In the *Qatar/Bahrain* case, for instance, the ICJ gave full effect to the Hawar Islands and Janan Island when drawing an equidistance boundary line.[84] In the *Nicaragua/Honduras* case, Honduran islands in the Caribbean Sea – Bobel Cay, Port Royal Cay, Savanna Cay and South Cay – and Nicaragua's Edinburgh Cay were given full effect.[85] In relation to this, it is of particular interest to note that the Arbitral Tribunal, in the *Eritrea/Yemen* case (Second Phase), presented the 'integrity test' as a criterion for determining the effect given to islands. According to this approach, where relevant islands constitute an integral part of a mainland coast, full effect may be given to those islands. This criterion was expressed in relation to the Dahlaks, a tightly knit group of islands and islets belonging to Eritrea. The Arbitral Tribunal gave full effect to the Dahlaks because it 'is a typical example of a group of islands that forms an integral part of the general coastal configuration'.[86] For the same reason, full effect was given to the Yemeni islands of Kamaran, Uqban and Kutama.[87] To a certain extent, the integrity test would seem to present a useful criterion for determining the effect to be given to islands.

The second mode is to give no effect to an island. For instance, the ICJ, in the *Tunisia/Libya* case, neglected the island of Jerba, which is separated from the mainland by a very narrow strait, in drawing a boundary.[88] In the *Guinea/Guinea-Bissau* case, the Arbitral Tribunal gave no effect to coastal islands, the Bijagos Islands and Southern Islands. In the *Qatar/Bahrain* case, the Court gave almost no effect to Qit'at Jaradah, by drawing a delimitation line passing immediately to the east of Qit'at Jaradah.[89] Similarly, the Court decided that Fasht al Jarim should have no effect on the boundary

[81] Report by E. Franckx, in J. I. Charney and L. M. Alexander (eds.), *International Maritime Boundaries*, vol. II (Dordrecht, Nijhoff, 1993), p. 1935 (hereafter this document will be quoted as *International Maritime Boundaries*).

[82] Report by T. Scovazzi and G. Francalanci, *ibid.*, p. 1642.

[83] Report by R. W. Smith, *ibid.*, vol. I, p. 419.

[84] ICJ Reports 2001, p. 109, para. 222.

[85] ICJ Reports 2007, p. 752, paras. 304–305.

[86] The *Eritrea/Yemen* arbitration (Second Phase), p. 1007, para. 139.

[87] *Ibid.*, p. 1008, paras. 150–151.

[88] ICJ Reports 1982, p. 85, para. 120.

[89] ICJ Reports 2001, pp. 104–109, para. 219.

line in the northern sector.[90] By referring to the integrity text expressed in the 1999 *Eritrea/Yemen* award, the ICJ, in the *Romania/Ukraine* case, gave no effect to Serpents' Island belonging to Ukraine.[91]

The third mode involves the enclave solution. This method was adopted by the Court of Arbitration in the *Anglo-French Continental Shelf* case with regard to the Channel Islands. The Channel Islands, which are under British sovereignty, lie off the French coasts of Normandy and Brittany. The Court of Arbitration took the view that giving full effect to the Channel Islands would constitute a circumstance that would entail inequity.[92] Thus the Court adopted a twofold solution. First, as the primary boundary, the Court drew a median line between the mainlands of the two States. Second, it created a twelve-mile enclave to the north and west of the Channel Islands.[93] While a precedent for the enclave solution could be found in the delimitation of lakes,[94] there was no precedent in the context of maritime delimitation *before* this award. It seems, therefore, that the enclave solution is a novel creation of the Court of Arbitration.[95]

The fourth mode is to give only partial effect, such as half effect, to islands in drawing a maritime boundary. In the *Anglo-French Continental Shelf* case, the Court of Arbitration took the view that the projection westwards of the Scilly Isles constituted a special circumstance.[96] The Court thus determined to give the Scilly Isles half effect. The distance between the Scilly Isles and the mainland of the United Kingdom is twice that separating Ushant from the French mainland. For the Court, this was an indication of the suitability of the half-effect method. Accordingly, the Court drew, first, an equidistance line without using offshore islands as a base point and, next, an equidistance line using them as a base point. A boundary line was then drawn midway between those two equidistance lines.[97]

The half-effect solution was also adopted in the *Tunisia/Libya* judgment. A line drawn from the most westerly point of the Gulf of Gabes along the seaward coast of the Kerkennah Islands would run at a bearing of approximately 62° to the meridian. However, the Court considered that the line of 62° to the meridian, which runs parallel to the coastline of the islands, would give excessive weight to the Kerkennahs. For that reason, the Court decided to attribute half effect to the Kerkennah Islands. It did so by drawing a line bisecting the angle between the line of the Tunisian coast (42°) and the tangent of the seaward coast of the Kerkennah Islands (62°). Consequently, a line of 52° to the meridian was to be the boundary of the continental shelf in this area.[98]

[90] *Ibid.*, pp. 114–115, paras. 247–248.

[91] ICJ Reports 2009, pp. 109–110, para. 149. See also pp. 122–123, para. 187.

[92] The *Anglo-French Continental Shelf* case, p. 93, para. 196.

[93] *Ibid.*, pp. 94–95, paras. 201–202.

[94] L. Caflisch, 'Règles générales du droit des cours d'eau internationaux' (1989) 219 *RCADI* pp. 99–100; H. W. Jayewardene, *The Regime of Islands in International Law* (Dordrecht, Nijhoff, 1990), pp. 245–247.

[95] D. W. Bowett, 'The Arbitration between the United Kingdom and France Concerning the Continental Shelf Boundary in the English Channel and South-Western Approaches' (1978) 44 *BYIL* p. 8.

[96] The *Anglo-French Continental Shelf* case, p. 114, para. 244.

[97] *Ibid.*, p. 117, para. 251.

[98] ICJ Reports 1982, pp. 88–89, paras. 128–129.

In the *Gulf of Maine* case, the Chamber of the ICJ determined to give the Canadian territory of Seal Island half effect. Specifically, the Chamber drew Seal Island back to half its real distance from the mainland. The distance between Seal Island and Chebogue Point in Nova Scotia was 14,234 metres. Dividing this distance by two, a position of 7,117 metres from Chebogue Point would represent a notional half-effect position for Seal Island.[99] The judicial practice calls for two brief comments.

First, the legal grounds for giving half effect to an island seem to be unclear. While the half effect given to the Scilly Isles in the *Anglo-French Continental Shelf* case had geometrical grounds, there was no such reason in the *Tunisia/Libya* and *Gulf of Maine* cases.

Second, the modalities of the half-effect method have varied in each case. The half-effect techniques are not free from criticism. For instance, the validity of the method adopted in the *Tunisia/Libya* case seems to be questionable because it relies solely on the Tunisian coast and Libya's coast was completely neglected.[100] In future cases, it will be necessary for international tribunals to search for more equitable half-effect techniques.

5.5 Geological and geomorphological factors

While geology relates to the composition and structure of the seabed, geomorphology concerns its shape and form. In general, international courts and tribunals attribute limited importance to geological and geomorphological factors. A reason is that currently coastal States may claim the continental shelf as well as an EEZ/FZ of 200 miles, regardless of the geological or geomorphological characteristics of the area. As a result, geological and geomorphological factors become irrelevant in the process of delimitation. With respect to single maritime boundaries, the application of neutral criteria and geometrical methods will also contribute to disregarding geological and geomorphological factors.

State practice also shows that in the majority of agreements, the characteristics of the seabed did not have a significant effect on the location of maritime boundaries. Even when those factors are considered, they usually play only a secondary role, either for fixing terminal points of the boundary or together with other elements including economic and navigational interests.[101]

5.6 Presence of third States

In the context of maritime delimitation, the existence of third States creates a difficult question relating to the principle of *res inter alios acta*. In this regard, two possible approaches can be identified in case law.

[99] Technical Report of the *Gulf of Maine* case, ICJ Reports 1984, p. 350, para. 13.

[100] Dissenting Opinion of Judge Oda, ICJ Reports 1982, pp. 268–269, para. 179.

[101] K. Highet, 'The Use of Geophysical Factors in the Delimitation of Maritime Boundaries', in *International Maritime Boundaries*, vol. I, p. 195.

According to the first approach, international courts draw a delimitation line in an area where legal titles of third States may be involved. The Court of Arbitration, in the *Anglo-French Continental Shelf* case, took this approach. In that case, a question was raised with regard to a possible meeting of the continental shelf boundary between the parties with the boundary between Ireland and the United Kingdom. The United Kingdom questioned the Court's power to delimit the Anglo-French continental shelf boundary westward of a notional meeting point with the Anglo-Irish boundary. The Court of Arbitration did not admit this view on the basis of the principle of *res inter alios acta*.[102] Nevertheless, this approach did not survive in other instances.

A second approach is to cut off the area where claims of third States may be involved from the scope of the jurisdiction of the judgment. According to this approach, international courts simply stop the delimitation line at the point where a third State might become involved. The cut-off approach was applied in the *Tunisia/Libya*, *Libya/Malta*, *Eritrea/Yemen*, *Qatar/Bahrain*, *Barbados/Trinidad and Tobago*, *Cameroon/Nigeria*, *Nicaragua/Honduras* and *Romania/Ukraine* cases. The most dramatic example of this approach can be seen in the *Libya/Malta* case. In that case, the ICJ limited the scope of its judgment so as not to infringe upon the rights of Italy in the region. Specifically, the Court confined itself to areas where no claims by Italy existed, namely, to the area between the meridians 13° 50' E and 15° 10' E.[103] Nonetheless, with respect, the Court's approach seems to be highly controversial in the sense that the extent of the Court's jurisdiction is determined by the claim of the third State, namely Italy.[104]

The question associated with the legal rights of third States is concerned with the legal effect of Article 59 of the Statute of the ICJ. In this regard, the ICJ in the *Cameroon/Nigeria* case (Merits), made an important pronouncement.

> [I]n particular in the case of maritime delimitations where the maritime areas of several States are involved, the protection afforded by Article 59 of the Statute may not always be sufficient. In the present case, Article 59 may not sufficiently protect Equatorial Guinea or Sao Tome and Principe from the effects – even if only indirect – of a judgment affecting their legal rights. ... It follows that, in fixing the maritime boundary between Cameroon and Nigeria, the Court must ensure that it does not adopt any position which might affect the rights of Equatorial Guinea and Sao Tome and Principe.[105]

In reality, it is undeniable that the delimitation line drawn by the Court might affect the legal rights and interests of third States, creating a presumption of the finality of the boundary regardless of the formalistic protection of Article 59.[106] In this sense, it

102 The *Anglo-French Continental Shelf* case, p. 27, para. 28.

103 The *Libya/Malta* case, ICJ Reports 1985, pp. 25–26, paras. 21–22.

104 Dissenting Opinion of Judge Mosler, *ibid.*, pp. 116–117; Dissenting Opinion of Judge Schwebel, *ibid.*, p. 177.

105 ICJ Reports 2002, p. 421, para. 238.

106 Argument by Professor George Abi-Saab, Counsel of Nigeria, Verbatim Record, CR 2002/23, p. 18, paras. 3–4.

seems that, as the Court stated, Article 59 is insufficient to protect the rights of third States in maritime delimitations.

In applying the cut-off approach, how is it possible to determine such an area where legal titles of third States may be involved? In response to this question, the prima facie legal credibility test, which was contended by Nigeria in the *Cameroon/Nigeria* case, is of particular interest. According to this test, the Court verifies the credibility of potential rights of third States on the basis of the equidistance method.[107] If one applies the legal credibility test on the basis of an objective method, i.e. the equidistance method, it may be possible to a certain extent to avoid the danger of an excessive claim by a third State. Considering that international courts and tribunals tend to draw an equidistance line at the first stage of maritime delimitation, the credibility test sounds persuasive. On the other hand, the application of the credibility test becomes complex in a situation where islands of third States exist. Furthermore, according to the credibility test, the spatial extent of the Court's jurisdiction may be highly limited in a situation where several third States coexist in close proximity in the same region.[108]

6 CONSIDERATION OF RELEVANT CIRCUMSTANCES (2): NON-GEOGRAPHICAL FACTORS

6.1 Economic factors

Economic factors may include the existence of natural resources, such as oil, gas and fish, and socio-economic factors, such as States' economic dependency on natural resources and national economic wealth. In international adjudication, States often invoke these two types of economic factors jointly, for they are interrelated. In a general way the influence of economic factors remains modest in jurisprudence relating to maritime delimitation. The ICJ, in the *Cameroon/Nigeria* case, stated that:

> [I]t follows from the jurisprudence that, although the existence of an express or tacit agreement between the parties on the siting of their respective oil concessions may indicate a consensus on the maritime areas to which they are entitled, oil concessions and oil wells are not in themselves to be considered as relevant circumstances justifying the adjustment or shifting of the provisional delimitation line. Only if they are based on express or tacit agreement between the parties may they be taken into account.[109]

[107] *Ibid.*, pp. 22–23, para. 21.

[108] Y. Tanaka, 'Reflections on Maritime Delimitation in the *Cameroon/Nigeria* case' (2004) 53 *ICLQ* pp. 401–402.

[109] ICJ Reports 2002, p. 447, para. 304.

In fact, apart from the *Greenland/Jan Mayen* case,[110] no judgment concerning the delimitation of the continental shelf or single maritime boundaries has taken the presence of natural resources into account, at least at the operational stage.

In some cases, economic factors re-entered at the verification stage as a test of the equitableness of the boundaries drawn. In the *Gulf of Maine* case, for instance, the Chamber of the ICJ in effect verified whether the result would be 'radically inequitable' or entail 'catastrophic repercussions for the livelihood and economic well-being of the population of the countries concerned' and came up with negative answers.[111] The Court of Arbitration in the *St Pierre and Miquelon* case applied the 'radically inequitable' test which was formulated by the *Gulf of Maine* judgment, and concluded that the proposed delimitation line would not have a radical impact on existing fishing patterns in the area.[112] In any event, these elements played merely a secondary role in testing whether the established boundaries produced 'radically inequitable' results.

In common with the jurisprudence in this field, the actual State practice appears to show that normally economic factors have not *directly* affected the location of boundaries of either continental shelves or single maritime boundaries. Instead, in some agreements, States have resolved economic questions flexibly by inserting common deposit clauses or by establishing regimes of joint development.

The 'common deposit clause' or 'mineral deposit clause' relates to transboundary mineral resources, including petroleum. When a party exploits a single petroleum reservoir, such exploitation will interfere with the neighbouring State's right to the petroleum in the reservoir by causing it to flow from one side of the boundary to the other. The 'common deposit clause' or 'mineral deposit clause' seeks to avoid such situations. By inserting common deposit clauses into a maritime delimitation agreement, it will be possible both to create maritime boundaries and to resolve the problem of transboundary mineral resources. The validity of common mineral deposit clauses was confirmed in the 1999 *Eritrea/Yemen* arbitration (Second Phase).[113]

While the concept of 'joint development' has not been uniformly understood, this concept may be considered as an intergovernmental agreement that aims to establish joint exploration and/or exploitation of living or non-living resources in a designated zone.[114] Joint development schemes may be provisional or permanent. Joint development schemes can be divided into two categories. The first category involves areas where maritime delimitation lines are being established. In such areas, a joint development zone is to be established straddling a delimitation line. Concerning mineral resources, a typical example of a joint development zone may be the 1981 Agreement

110 In the *Greenland/Jan Mayen* case, the ICJ divided southernmost zone 1 into two parts of equal extent, so as to allow both parties to enjoy equitable access to the capelin stock. ICJ Reports 1993, pp. 79–81, para. 92.

111 ICJ Reports 1984, pp. 342–344, paras. 237–241.

112 The *St Pierre and Miquelon* arbitration, p. 1173, paras. 84–85.

113 The *Eritrea/Yemen* arbitration (Second Phase), pp. 998–999, para. 86.

114 Generally on this issue, see M. Miyoshi, 'The Joint Development of Offshore Oil and Gas in Relation to Maritime Boundary Delimitation', *Maritime Briefing*, vol. 2 (Durham, International Boundaries Research Unit, 1999).

between Norway and Iceland.[115] The joint development zone straddling the single maritime boundary between the parties was established on the basis of the recommendation of the Conciliation Commission in 1981.[116] Concerning fisheries resources, the 1978 Agreement on the Delimitation of Marine and Submarine Areas and Maritime Cooperation between the Dominican Republic and Colombia established a common scientific research and fishing zone, bisected by a single maritime boundary.[117]

The second category of joint development schemes concerns areas where delimitation was not or could not be effected. An illustrative example is the joint development zone created in the 1974 Agreement between Japan and South Korea. In the East China Sea, the claims of the parties over the continental shelf overlapped considerably. In search of a breakthrough, both parties agreed to establish a joint development zone in the overlapping area.[118] Another important example is the 1989 Agreement between Australia and Indonesia (Timor Gap), which established a zone of cooperation.[119] The Agreement provides a comprehensive system with regard to the activities of joint development. In 2000, Australia and the United Nations Transitional Administration in East Timor (UNTAET) exchanged notes concerning the continued operation of the Timor Gap Treaty. In 2001, the UNTAET and Australia adopted a Memorandum of Understanding (MOU) that provided a new Timor Sea Arrangement.[120] The 2001 MOU created the Joint Petroleum Development Area (JPDA). The 2002 Timor Sea Treaty between East Timor and Australia maintains the JPDA and regulates all resource activities there.[121] The Timor Sea Treaty is an interim agreement and provisionally gives East Timor 90 per cent of petroleum production from the JPDA (Article 4).[122] Other examples of treaties which established the second category of a joint development zone include: the 1974 Agreement between Saudi Arabia and Sudan,[123] the 1979 Memorandum of Understanding between Malaysia and Thailand in the Gulf of Thailand, the 1992 Memorandum of Understanding between Malaysia and Vietnam,[124] and the 1993 Agreement between Colombia and Jamaica.[125]

6.2 Conduct of the parties

Normally the influence of the conduct of the parties is very limited in jurisprudence and State practice relating to maritime delimitation. So far the only exception is the

115 *International Maritime Boundaries*, vol. II, pp. 1762 *et seq.* Entered into force 2 June 1982.
116 (1981) 20 *ILM* pp. 797 *et seq.*
117 *International Maritime Boundaries*, vol. I, pp. 488 *et seq.* Entered into force 2 February 1979.
118 *Ibid.*, pp. 1073 *et seq.* Entered into force 22 June 1978.
119 *Ibid.*, vol. II, pp. 1256 *et seq.* Entered into force 9 February 1991.
120 *Ibid.*, vol. IV, pp. 2769 *et seq.*
121 *Ibid.*, vol. V, pp. 3829 *et seq.* Entered into force 2 April 2003. See also Report by J. R. V. Prescott and G. Triggs, *ibid.*, pp. 3806 *et seq.*
122 In 2006, a further interim agreement, namely, Treaty between the Government of Australia and the Government of the Democratic Republic of Timor-Leste on Certain Maritime Arrangements in the Timor Sea was concluded. A. V. Lowe and S. A. G. Talmon (eds.), *The Legal Order of the Oceans: Basic Documents on the Law of the Sea* (Oxford, Hart Publishing 2009), pp. 783 *et seq.* Entered into force 23 February 2007.
123 952 *UNTS*, pp. 198 *et seq.* Entered into force in 1974.
124 *International Maritime Boundaries*, vol. III, pp. 2341 *et seq.* Entered into force 5 June 1992.
125 *Ibid.*, pp. 2200 *et seq.* Entered into force 14 March 1994.

Tunisia/Libya judgment, which clearly took such conduct into account. In that case, the ICJ attached great importance to a de facto line drawn from Ras Ajdir at an angle of some 26° east of north, which resulted from concessions for the offshore exploration and exploitation of oil and gas granted by both parties.[126] It was the de facto line which effectively governed the delimitation in the first segment to be delimited. The *Tunisia/Libya* judgment seems to suggest that only when the conduct of the parties can prove the existence of a modus vivendi or a de facto line, or an agreement to apply a particular method, may such facts be taken into account by the courts. Nonetheless, the Court's approach entails the risk of introducing the idea of effectiveness or occupation into the law of maritime delimitation. The rights over the continental shelf are attributed to the coastal State *ipso facto* and *ab initio*. Accordingly, the idea of effectiveness would be incompatible with the fundamental character of legal rights over the continental shelf. Furthermore, by giving excessive weight to the conduct of the parties, unilateral acts of occupation of the continental shelf may be encouraged. In view of these questions, it appears that the *Tunisia/Libya* judgment cannot have general application in the law of maritime delimitation.

6.3 Historic rights

The term 'historic rights' may be defined as rights over certain land or maritime areas acquired by a State through a continuous and public usage from time immemorial and acquiescence by other States, although those rights would not normally accrue to it under general international law.[127] The fact that a State has long enjoyed exclusive or particular benefits in an area without protests from third States could be a means of entitlement to that area in derogation of the standard rules.[128] Concerning the delimitation of the territorial sea, both Article 12 of the TSC and Article 15 of the LOSC explicitly include historic titles in a category of special circumstances. As regards the delimitation of the continental shelf and the EEZ, however, no mention was made of such titles in Articles 74(1) and 83(1) of the LOSC. An issue which thus arises is whether historic titles may be regarded as a relevant circumstance in the context of the continental shelf or EEZ delimitation.

The ICJ, in the *Tunisia/Libya* case, regarded historic rights as relevant, stating that: 'Historic titles must enjoy respect and be preserved as they have always been by long usage.'[129] At the operational stage of the delimitation, however, the Court did not consider it necessary to decide on the validity of Tunisian historic rights with regard to Libya because the line indicated by the Court left Tunisia in full possession of the area covered by such rights.[130] The Arbitral Tribunal, in the *Eritrea/Yemen* arbitration, did not take the traditional fishing regime into account on the grounds that free

[126] ICJ Reports 1982, p. 71, para. 96.

[127] For this concept, see, in particular, Y. Z. Blum, 'Historic Rights', in *Encyclopedia of Public International Law*, vol. 2 (Amsterdam, 1995), pp. 710–715; Charles de Visscher, *Les effectivités du droit international public* (Paris, Pedone, 1967), p. 51.

[128] D. P. O'Connell, *The International Law of the Sea*, vol. II (Oxford, Clarendon Press, 1984), p. 713.

[129] ICJ Reports 1982, p. 73, para. 100. See also p. 75, para. 102.

[130] *Ibid.*, p. 86, para. 121.

access to fishing, which is the essence of that regime, was not dependent on maritime delimitation.[131] Thus the Tribunal shows another possible solution, separating traditional fishing regimes from maritime delimitations. If, as the Tribunal indicated, free access to natural resources is to be the real interest which underlies historic rights, such interest could be protected by an agreement ensuring such access independently of maritime delimitation.

In State practice, it is notable that the 1976 Agreement between India and Sri Lanka resolved the question of historic rights, without adjusting the delimitation line by instituting a transitory period for fisheries and attributing a certain amount of fish to the other State involved. This solution seems to provide practical guidance in solving the question.

6.4 Security interests

The ICJ, in the *Libya/Malta* case, regarded security factors as a relevant circumstance. At the operational stage, however, security interests did not affect the location of the continental shelf boundary in the *Libya/Malta* judgment because the delimitation line drawn by the Court was 'not so near to the coast of either Party as to make questions of security a particular consideration in the present case'.[132] The same applied to the *Greenland/Jan Mayen* and *Romania/Ukraine* cases.[133] It is interesting to note that the Court considered security interests to be a matter of distance. Yet so far there is no predictable standard on this matter. Like case law, it can be observed that the direct influence of security factors remains somewhat unclear in State practice.

6.5 Navigational factors

In the *Eritrea/Yemen* arbitration (the Second Phase), the Arbitral Tribunal took navigational interests into account in several parts of the delimitation line dividing the territorial seas.[134] In addition to this, the Arbitral Tribunal, in the *Guyana/Suriname* case, explicitly regarded navigation as a special circumstance in the delimitation of the territorial seas under Article 15 of the LOSC.[135] Apart from these cases, usually the influence of navigational factors remains modest. State practice seems to demonstrate more concern about protection of navigation in agreements delimiting territorial seas than in agreements concerning the continental shelf or single maritime boundaries.

6.6 Environmental factors

While protection of the marine environment is a matter of important concern, the existing case law seems to pay little attention to environmental concern in the context of maritime delimitations. In the *Gulf of Maine* case, the United States relied on environmental factors to justify an equitable maritime boundary. However, the Chamber of

[131] The *Eritrea/Yemen* arbitration (Second Phase), pp. 1001–1002, paras. 103–110.
[132] ICJ Reports 1985, p. 42, para. 51.
[133] ICJ Reports 1993, pp. 74–75, para. 81; ICJ Reports 2009, p. 128, para. 204.
[134] The *Eritrea/Yemen* arbitration (Second Phase), pp. 1004–1005, paras. 125–128.
[135] The *Guyana/Suriname* arbitration, pp. 96–97, paras. 304–306.

the ICJ discarded the ecological criterion primarily because such a criterion was inconsistent with the 'neutral criteria' for drawing a single maritime boundary.[136] Usually environmental considerations have played little, if any, role in agreements concerning maritime delimitations.

7 AN EVALUATION

7.1 General trend of case law

In general, it can be observed that international courts and tribunals normally attach more importance to geographical than to non-geographical factors.[137] In particular, the configuration of the coast plays an essential role in the process of maritime delimitation. Proportionality comes into play in almost all judgments in this field. Where islands exist in the delimitation area, legal effect given to those islands will always be an important issue in the delimitation process.

By contrast, non-geographical factors play but a modest role in the process of maritime delimitation. In fact, the influence of economic factors remains modest in maritime delimitation. The conduct of the parties and historic rights have rarely been taken into account by international courts and tribunals. Navigational factors were exceptionally taken into account only in the *Eritrea/Yemen* and *Guyana/Suriname* cases. Other non-geographical factors, such as security interests and environmental factors, have never been taken into account by international courts or tribunals, although their relevance has not necessarily been denied.

Overall, it can be observed that maritime delimitation is effected by international courts and tribunals on the basis, in essence, of geographical considerations. In particular, the modest role played by economic factors appears to demonstrate that maritime delimitation relates to the conflicts over how much maritime space coastal States can obtain on account of geographical factors, regardless of their economic importance. In that sense, it may be said that in essence, maritime delimitation is of a *spatial* rather than of an *economic* nature.

7.2 Judicial creativity in the law of maritime delimitation

The above consideration appears to show that rules of law have been developed through the case law of international courts and tribunals, independently of State practice and *opinio juris*. A typical example is the concept of proportionality. The large role of proportionality as an operational rule or as a test of equitableness cannot be explained from the viewpoints of State practice and *opinio juris*. To a certain extent, the same is true of the effect to be given to islands. While international courts and tribunals have developed the 'half-effect' solution concerning offshore islands, agreements giving half effect to offshore islands are rare in State practice. It seems, therefore, that the

[136] ICJ Reports 1984, p. 327, para. 193.

[137] T. Scovazzi, 'The Evolution of International Law of the Sea: New Issues, New Challenges' (2000) 286 *RCADI* p. 200.

courts' solution of giving half effect to offshore islands in the *Anglo-French Continental Shelf*, *Tunisia/Libya* and *Gulf of Maine* cases is a novelty in this field. Such a solution can be regarded as an example of 'judicial creativity'.

Under Article 38(1) of the Statute of the ICJ, judicial decisions are merely subsidiary means for the determination of rules of law. In the context of maritime delimitation, however, it can be said that the ICJ and arbitral courts have been creating and developing the law of maritime delimitation. The significant role of judicial creativity in the nature of maritime delimitation may be explained by at least two reasons.

First, to achieve equitable results, there is a need to take various geographical and non-geographical factors into account. Since one cannot expect there to be specific rules regarding each and every factor to be considered, international courts and tribunals often face potential lacunae in the law. Accordingly, within their compass, they need to develop rules with regard to the effect to be attributed to those factors in the framework of equitable principles.

Second, the parties to a treaty seldom explain in the latter why and to what extent a certain relevant circumstance has been taken into account when drawing a maritime boundary. For this very reason, it is difficult to find evidence of *opinio juris* in State practice. Here there is an inherent difficulty in identifying customary rules in the field of maritime delimitation. Accordingly, it is hardly surprising that international courts and tribunals have to rely mainly on judge-made law in this particular field.

8 CONCLUSIONS

The above considerations can be summarised as five points.

(i) There is no doubt that equitable principles are at the heart of the law of maritime delimitation. However, there are two contrasting approaches to these principles. According to the result-oriented equity approach, no method of delimitation is prescribed by law, and equity is the sole parameter prescribed. Under the corrective-equity approach, the equidistance method is applied at the first stage and, at the second stage, a shift of the provisional equidistance line should be envisaged if relevant circumstances warrant it. While the result-oriented equity approach seeks to maintain maximum flexibility, the corrective-equity approach stresses predictability. In this sense, the history of the law of maritime delimitation vacillates between predictability and flexibility.

(ii) Currently there is a general trend, 'unless there are compelling reasons' not to do so, for international courts and tribunals to apply the corrective-equity approach to all types of maritime delimitations at the conventional and customary law levels. In broad terms, it can be said that the law of maritime delimitation is moving in a direction from the result-oriented equity approach to the corrective-equity approach.

(iii) While the result-oriented equity approach is flexible, it runs the risk of producing legal impressionism by blurring the distinction between decisions based on equitable principles and those taken *ex aequo et bono*. By contrast, the corrective-equity approach enhances predictability as a requirement of law by incorporating an objective method, namely the equidistance method, into the realm of law. Under this approach, a consideration of equity may come into play at the second stage with a view to ensuring an equitable result. It may be said that the corrective-equity approach would provide a better framework for reconciling the two requirements of law, namely predictability and flexibility.

(iv) If the equidistance method is applicable at the first stage of maritime delimitation, the final line is determined by the consideration of relevant circumstances in order to achieve an equitable result. While those circumstances are diverse, the general direction of case law and State practice appears to demonstrate a predominance of geographical over non-geographical factors. Principal geographical factors include: coastal configuration, proportionality, baselines, the presence of islands, and the presence of third States.

(v) It can be observed that in the field of maritime delimitations, the international courts and tribunals have developed special rules, which do not rely on State practice, in the framework of case law. The judicial practice in the field of maritime delimitation provides an important insight into international law-making through jurisprudence.

FURTHER READING

1 Monographs

There are a considerable number of books and articles with regard to maritime delimitations. Thus, only principal monographs on this subject will be suggested here.

F. A. Ahnish, *The International Law of Maritime Boundaries and the Practice of States in the Mediterranean Sea* (Oxford, Clarendon Press, 1993).

M. N. Antunes, *Towards the Conceptualization of Maritime Delimitation* (Leiden, Nijhoff, 2003).

D. Evans, *Relevant Circumstances and Maritime Delimitation* (Oxford, Clarendon Press, 1987).

D. M. Johnston, The Theory and History of Ocean Boundary-Making (Kingston, McGill-Queen's University Press, 1988).

M. Kamga, *Délimitation maritime sur la côte atlantique africaine* (Brussels, Bruylant, 2006).

R. Kolb, *Case Law on Equitable Maritime Delimitation: Digest and Commentaries* (The Hague, Nijhoff, 2003).

R. Lagoni and D. Vignes (eds.), *Maritime Delimitation* (Leiden, Nijhoff, 2006).

L. Lucchini and M. Voelkel, *Droit de la mer*, vol. 2: *Délimitation, Navigation et Pêche*, vol. I, *Délimitation* (Paris, Pedone, 1996).

A. G. Oude Elferink, *The Law of Maritime Boundary Delimitation: A Case Study of the Russian Federation* (Dordrecht, Nijhoff, 1994).

V. Prescott and C. Schofield, *The Maritime Political Boundaries of the World*, 2nd edn (Leiden, Nijhoff, 2005).

A. Razavi, *Continental Shelf Delimitation and Related Maritime Issues in the Persian Gulf* (The Hague, Nijhoff, 1997).

Y. Tanaka, *Predictability and Flexibility in the Law of Maritime Delimitation* (Oxford, Hart Publishing, 2006).

P. Weil, *Perspective du droit de la délimitation maritime* (Paris, Pedone, 1988) (English translation: *The Law of Maritime Delimitation: Reflections* (Cambridge, Grotius, 1989)).

2 Collection of Documents

An important source of treaties with regard to maritime delimitation is the series of *International Maritime Boundaries* by the American Society of International Law. To date, six volumes of *International Maritime Boundaries* have been published by Nijhoff in 1993 (vols. I and II), 1998 (vol. III), 2002 (vol. IV), 2005 (vol. V) and 2011 (vol. VI).

PART II

Our Common Ocean: Protection of Community Interests at Sea

OUTLINE OF PART II

7

Conservation of Marine Living Resources

Main Issues

Marine living resources are of vital importance for mankind because these resources are an essential source of protein and many human communities depend on fishing. As marine living resources are renewable, there is certainly a need to pursue conservation policies in order to secure sustainable use of these resources. Nonetheless, the depletion of these resources is a matter of more pressing concern in the international community. Thus the conservation of marine living resources is a significant issue in the law of the sea. This chapter will examine rules of international law governing the conservation of these resources focusing particularly on the following issues:

(i) What are the problems associated with the traditional approaches, namely the zonal management approach and the species specific approach, to conservation of marine living resources?
(ii) What is the role of the concept of sustainable development in the conservation of marine living resources?
(iii) What is the difference between the species specific approach and the ecosystem approach?
(iv) What are the significance of, and limitations of the precautionary approach to the conservation of these resources?
(v) How is it possible to ensure compliance with rules respecting the conservation of marine living resources?

1 INTRODUCTION

Considering that marine living resources are of vital importance for mankind because these resources constitute an increasingly important source of protein,[1] it could well be said that conservation of marine living resources can be considered as a common interest

[1] According to the FAO, in 2007 fish accounted for 15.7 per cent of the global population's intake of animal protein and 9.1 per cent of all protein consumed. FAO, *The Status of World Fisheries and Aquaculture* (Rome, FAO, 2010), p. 3.

of the international community. In this regard, it is relevant to note that the LOSC, in its Preamble, explicitly recognises its aim of promoting the conservation of marine living resources. At the same time, marine living resources are important for the international trade and industry of many countries. It may be said that conservation of marine living resources deeply involves not only community interests but also national interests at the same time. Thus the rules of international law on this subject rest on the tension between the protection of community interests and the promotion of national interests.

Whilst there is no universal definition of conservation, one can take as an example Article 2 of the 1958 Geneva Convention on Fishing and Conservation of the Living Resources of the High Seas (hereafter the High Seas Fishing Convention), which provides as follows:

> As employed in this Convention, the expression 'conservation of the living resources of the high seas' means the aggregate of the measures rendering possible the optimum sustainable yield from those resources so as to secure a maximum supply of food and other marine products. Conservation programmes should be formulated with a view to securing in the first place a supply of food for human consumption.

As shown in this provision, conservation does not directly mean a moratorium or prohibition of exploitation of marine living resources.[2] In practice, the 'supply of food for human consumption' will be determined on the basis of economic and social needs. Hence conservation is not a purely scientific or biological concept, but is qualified by economic, political and social elements.

Presently there are growing concerns that marine living resources are at serious risk due to overcapacity, overfishing, illegal, unregulated and unreported fishing (IUU fishing) and marine pollution.[3] According to the Report of the UN Secretary-General, many scientists consider that if current levels of exploitation were maintained, not only would the commercial extinction of fish stocks soon become a reality, but the long-term biological sustainability of many fish stocks would also be threatened.[4] Arguably, the failure of conservation of marine living resources is due to a lack of will on the part of States to take appropriate conservation measures. From a legal viewpoint, however, there is a need to examine the limitations of the traditional approaches to conservation of marine living resources in international law and explore new approaches which may enhance the efficiency of conservation of these resources. Thus this chapter will examine essential legal issues with regard to the conservation of marine living resources.[5]

[2] Article II(2) of the 1980 Convention on the Conservation of Antarctic Marine Living Resources explicitly states that 'the term "conservation" includes rational use'. For an analysis of the concept of conservation, see Y. Tanaka, *A Dual Approach to Ocean Governance: The Cases of the Zonal and Integrated Management in International Law of the Sea* (England, Ashgate, 2008), pp. 32 *et seq.*

[3] UN General Assembly, A/RES/58/240, adopted on 23 December 2003, para. 12 of Preamble.

[4] UN General Assembly, *Oceans and the Law of the Sea: Report of the Secretary-General*, A/59/62, 4 March 2004, p. 53, para. 206.

[5] The basic idea of the present writer on this subject is expressed in: Tanaka, *A Dual Approach*, Chapters 2 and 3; by the same author, 'The Changing Approaches to Conservation of Marine Living

2 CONSERVATION OF MARINE LIVING RESOURCES PRIOR TO 1982

The degradation of commercial species in the oceans was already a matter of concern in the second half of the nineteenth century. Whilst one may detect several treaties relating to conservation of marine species in the nineteenth century and the early twentieth century,[6] it was only after World War II that conservation of marine living resources became a subject of multilateral treaties concluded between States.

At the global level, an obligation to conserve marine living resources was, for the first time, enshrined in the 1958 High Seas Fishing Convention. This Convention obliges States to apply conservation measures to their own nationals pursuant to Articles 3 and 4. The Convention was innovative in two respects.

The first innovation involved the concept of a special interest of the coastal State. Given that the high seas fisheries may have adverse effects upon marine species in the territorial seas of the coastal State, the protection of interest of the coastal State is of particular importance in this field. The High Seas Fishing Convention thus introduced a new concept of the 'special interest' of the coastal State. Article 6(1) of the Convention explicitly provided: 'A coastal State has a special interest in the maintenance of the productivity of the living resources in any area of the high seas adjacent to its territorial sea'. However, this does not mean that the coastal State acquires exclusive or preferential rights over fisheries in the area concerned.[7] It is true that, in certain circumstances, the coastal State is empowered to take unilateral measures of conservation appropriate to any stock of fish or other marine resources in any area of the high seas adjacent to its territorial sea by virtue of Article 7. However, this provision should not be construed in such a way as to entitle the coastal State to directly apply its measures to nationals of other States. Rather, it should be interpreted to mean that fishing States are obliged to apply the measures unilaterally adopted by the coastal State to its own nationals. In this sense, Article 7(1) does not disturb the exclusivity of the flag State jurisdiction over vessels flying its flag.[8]

The second innovation involved the obligations of newcomer States. The presence of free-riders may seriously undermine the effectiveness of regulatory measures necessary for the conservation of marine species. In response, Article 5 of the High Seas Fishing Convention ensures that if, subsequent to the adoption of the conservation measures referred to in Articles 3 and 4, nationals of other States, i.e. the newcomer States, engage in fishing the same stock or stocks of fish or other living marine resources in any area or areas of the high seas, the newcomer States shall apply the measures to '*their own nationals*' not later than seven months after the date on which the measures shall have

Resources in International Law' (2011) 71 *ZaöRV* pp. 291–330. This chapter relies partly on the analysis made in these studies with modifications.

[6] L. Juda, *International Law and Ocean Use Management: The Evolution of Ocean Governance* (London and New York, Routledge, 1996), p. 20.

[7] J. H. W. Verzijl, 'The United Nations Conference on the Law of the Sea, Geneva, 1958, II' (1959) 6 *NILR* p. 125; S. Oda, *International Control of Sea Resources* (Dordrecht, Nijhoff, 1989), p. 116.

[8] S. Oda, 'Fisheries Under the United Nations Convention on the Law of the Sea' (1983) 77 *AJIL* p. 740.

been notified to the Director-General of the Food and Agriculture Organization of the United Nations. As the newcomer States are to apply the measures 'to their own nationals', this provision should not be construed as allowing the fishing State or States to exercise jurisdiction over the nationals of the newcomer States. In any case, the High Seas Fishing Convention was ratified by only thirty-eight States and achieved only limited success.

3 CONSERVATION OF MARINE LIVING RESOURCES UNDER THE LOSC (1): THE ZONAL MANAGEMENT APPROACH

The LOSC created a basic legal framework for conservation of marine living resources. The framework relies on two basic approaches, namely, the zonal management approach and the species specific approach. Sections 3 and 4 of this chapter examine these two approaches and their limitations.

3.1 General considerations

Under the zonal management approach, different rules apply to conservation of marine living resources according to each jurisdictional zone. The basic framework of the LOSC on this matter can be succinctly summarised as follows.

As explained earlier, internal waters, the territorial seas and the archipelagic waters are under territorial sovereignty.[9] As the territorial sovereignty is comprehensive and exclusive in its nature, the coastal State can exercise its exclusive jurisdiction over marine resources in these marine spaces. There is little doubt that the coastal State has jurisdiction with regard to conservation of marine living resources in those spaces in accordance with international law. Yet the LOSC contains no explicit obligation to conserve marine living resources in these marine spaces.

In the EEZ and the continental shelf, the coastal State has sovereign rights for the purpose of exploring and exploiting the natural resources pursuant to Articles 56(1) and 77(1) of the LOSC as well as customary international law. As discussed earlier, the sovereign rights are essentially exclusive in the sense that no one may undertake activities involving the exploration and exploitation of natural resources or make a claim to the EEZ, without the express consent of the coastal State.[10] The LOSC places explicit obligations upon States to conserve marine living resources in the EEZ. Whilst the natural resources on the continental shelf include sedentary species by virtue of Article 77(4), the LOSC provides no specific obligation to conserve these species.

On the high seas, all States enjoy the freedom of fishing. The freedom is not absolute, however. As will be seen, States are obliged to cooperate to conserve living resources on the high seas. Under Article 133(a), resources of the Area, which are the common heritage of mankind, involve only mineral resources, and they do not include marine living resources.

[9] See Chapter 3.
[10] See Chapter 4, section 3.3.

3.2 Conservation of marine living resources in the EEZ

Conservation of living resources in the EEZ is particularly important since approximately 90 per cent of all commercially exploitable fish stocks are caught within 200 miles of the coast.[11] In this regard, Article 61(2) of the LOSC provides an explicit obligation to ensure that the maintenance of the living resources in the EEZ is not endangered by over-exploitation. The conservation of these resources in the EEZ is based on two key concepts, namely, allowable catch and maximum sustainable yield (MSY).

First, Article 61(1) places a clear obligation upon the coastal State to determine the allowable catch of the living resources in its EEZ. Article 62(2) further obliges the coastal State to determine its capacity to harvest the living resources of the EEZ. Where the coastal State does not have the capacity to harvest the entire allowable catch, the coastal State shall, through agreements or other arrangements, give other States access to the surplus of the allowable catch. Accordingly, other consequential decisions with regard to access to the fish in the EEZ depend essentially on the amount of the allowable catch determined by the coastal States.[12]

Second, the concept of MSY, which is enshrined in Article 61(3), aims at taking the greatest quantity of fish from a self-generating stock year after year without affecting significantly its renewability. In other words, MSY seeks to maintain the productivity of the oceans by permitting the taking of only that number of fish from a stock that is replaced by the annual rate of new recruits entering the stock.[13] However, the concepts of allowable catch and MSY encounter considerable difficulty in their practical implementation.

A first difficulty involves the determination of the total allowable catch. A population of fish may occur both in the waters of the coastal State and in other areas and, consequently, harvesting can also take place in those other areas. In this case, the coastal State's determination of the allowable catch within its zone must take due account of the harvesting that takes place beyond the limits of its jurisdiction, be it within the zones of another State or on the high seas.[14] However, there is no mechanism to do so in the LOSC. Furthermore, the collection and analysis of reliable scientific data are a prerequisite to determine the total allowable catch. However, such data are frequently inadequate and costly particularly for developing States.[15] Moreover, it must

[11] P. Malanczuk, *Akehurst's Modern Introduction to International Law*, 7th rev. edn (London, Routledge, 1997), p. 183; P. G. G. Davies and C. Redgwell, 'The International Legal Regulation of Straddling Fish Stocks' (1996) 67 *BYIL* p. 200; R. R. Churchill and A. V. Lowe, *Law of the Sea*, 3rd edn (Manchester University Press, 1999), p. 162.

[12] W. T. Burke, *The New International Law of Fisheries: UNCLOS 1982 and Beyond* (Oxford University Press, 1994), p. 44.

[13] P. Birnie, A. Boyle and C. Redgwell, *International Law and the Environment*, 3rd edn (Oxford University Press, 2008), p. 591. For an analysis in some detail of the concept of MSY, see G. L. Kesteven, 'MSY Revisited: A Realistic Approach to Fisheries Management and Administration' (1997) 21 *Marine Policy* pp. 73–82.

[14] C. A. Fleischer, 'Fisheries and Biological Resources', in R.-J. Dupuy and D. Vignes (eds.), *A Handbook on the New Law of the Sea*, vol. 2 (Dordrecht, Nijhoff, 1991), p. 1073.

[15] Burke, *The New International Law of Fisheries*, p. 45; Churchill, '10 Years of the UN Convention on the Law of the Sea', p. 107.

be noted that the coastal State has a broad discretion to determine the allowable catch. Apart from the single qualification not to endanger living resources by over-exploitation, the coastal State may in fact set the allowable catch as it wishes.[16] The coastal State's capacity to harvest living resources would seem not to depend only on the capital and technology of its own national economy. If this is the case, the coastal State may always have the capacity to harvest the entire allowable catch, by introducing foreign capital and technology.[17] Thus, theoretically at least, it is possible that the coastal State emerges with a zero surplus and thereby evades its duty to allocate surpluses in its EEZ by manipulating the allowable catch.[18]

A second difficulty concerns the validity of the concept of MSY as a conservation objective. This concept is open to question because it fails to take into account not only economic objectives but also the ecological relationships of species, the qualitative status of that habitat, the limits of the given area's biomass, and factors disturbing the environment.[19] Furthermore, there is a concern that determination of MSY is rarely, if ever, correct and the administrative measures taken with a view to its adoption have been and generally still are inadequate and inappropriate.[20]

A third obstacle pertains to the lack of review process by a third party capable of examining the validity of the conservation measures of the coastal State in its EEZ. As will be seen, any disputes relating to a State's sovereign rights with respect to the living resources in the EEZ or their exercise, including its discretionary powers for determining the allowable catch, are exempted from the compulsory settlement procedure embodied in Part XV of the LOSC.[21] Whilst a dispute involving a coastal State's obligation to ensure conservation of living resources in the EEZ is to be submitted to conciliation under Annex V, the conciliation commission cannot substitute its discretion for that of the coastal State under Article 297(3)(c). In any case, the report of the conciliation commission is not binding. Overall, one is forced to conclude that the obligations to conserve living resources in the EEZ remain weak.

3.3 Conservation of marine living resources in the high seas

Traditionally, conservation of living resources in the high seas has attracted little attention in the international community. As a result of the establishment of the 200-mile EEZ, however, fishing vessels of distant fishing States increasingly go to fish in the remaining high seas, leading to exhaustion of living resources. A typical example is the 'Doughnut Hole' in the Bering Sea. This is a small pocket of approximately 50,000 square miles of high seas remaining in the central part of the Bering

16 Burke, *The New International Law of Fisheries*, pp. 47–48.

17 Oda, 'Fisheries', p. 744.

18 However, such manipulations would be contrary to the obligation of optimum utilisation as well as the obligation not to abuse rights by virtue of Article 300 of the LOSC. L. Caflisch, 'Fisheries in the Exclusive Economic Zone: An Overview', in U. Leanza (ed.), *The International Legal Regime of the Mediterranean Sea* (Milan, Giuffrè, 1987), p. 161.

19 Birnie, Boyle and Redgwell, *International Law and the Environment*, p. 591.

20 Kesteven, 'MSY Revisited', p. 73.

21 LOSC, Article 297(3)(a). See also Chapter 13, section 3.2.

Sea. Foreign trawlers, which can no longer engage upon fishing within the EEZs of the United States and Russia, intensively exploited the Doughnut Hole. As a consequence, by 1992, the pollock stock had completely collapsed.[22] As shown in this example, currently the conservation of living resources in the high seas is becoming a matter of serious concern.

The LOSC places obligations upon States to conserve marine living resources in the high seas. Under Article 87(1)(e), the freedom of fishing is subject to conditions laid down in section 2, Part VII. Article 116 provides that all States have the right for their nationals to engage in fishing on the high seas subject to: (a) their treaty obligations; (b) the rights and duties as well as the interests of coastal States provided for, *inter alia*, in Article 63, paragraph 2, and Articles 64 to 67; and (c) the provisions of section 2, Part VII. More specifically, Article 119(1) obliges States to take measures which are designed to maintain or restore populations of harvested species at levels which can produce the 'maximum sustainable yield' in determining the allowable catch and establishing other conservation measures for the living resources in the high seas. Under Article 119(2), States are also obliged to exchange available scientific information relevant to the conservation of fish stocks in the high seas.

The obligation to cooperate is a prerequisite in the conservation of living resources on the high seas. Article 117 thus imposes upon 'all States' a duty to take or to co-operate with other States in taking such measures for their respective nationals as may be necessary for the conservation of the living resources of the high seas. Article 118 places a clear obligation upon States to cooperate with each other in the 'conservation and management' of living resources in the areas of the high seas. Article 118 further obliges States whose nationals exploit identical living resources, or different living resources in the same area, to negotiate with a view to take the measures necessary for the conservation of the living resources concerned. Article 118 requires States to cooperate as appropriate to establish subregional or regional fisheries organisations to this end. Arguably participation in regional fisheries bodies is one method of fulfilling the obligation to cooperate in the conservation of the living resources of the high seas.[23]

On the other hand, Articles 117 and 118 contain no specific guidance describing how the cooperation shall be performed, and how it is possible to judge whether or not such an obligation has been breached. Even if some States reach agreement with respect to the conservation of living resources in the high seas, the accord may be at the mercy of new entrants. Overall, the normative implementation of these provisions seems to remain modest.

However, it is not suggested that the obligation has no normative force. As the ICJ ruled in the 2010 *Pulp Mills on the River Uruguay* case, 'the mechanism for co-operation

[22] D. A. Balton, 'The Bering Sea Doughnut Hole Convention: Regional Solution, Global Implications', in O. S. Stokke (ed.) *Governing High Seas Fisheries: The Interplay of Global and Regional Regimes* (Oxford University Press, 2001), pp. 144–149.

[23] UNDOALOS, *The Law of the Sea: The Regime for High-Seas Fisheries, Status and Prospects* (New York, United Nations, 1992), p. 26, para. 78.

between States is governed by the principle of good faith'.[24] Furthermore, Article 26 of the 1969 Vienna Convention on the Law of Treaties, which represents customary international law, provides that: 'Every treaty in force is binding upon the parties to it and must be performed by them in good faith.'[25] Hence one can say that an arbitral rejection to cooperate on the high seas is contrary to Articles 117 and 118 and the principle of good faith.

3.4 Limits of the zonal management approach

An essential limitation associated with the zonal management approach involves the divergence of the law and nature. In the law of the sea, as noted, the spatial ambit of coastal State jurisdiction over marine spaces is defined on the basis of distance from the coast, irrespective of the nature of the ocean and the natural resources within it. By using the distance criterion, the ecological interactions between marine species as well as the ecological conditions of the physical surroundings are to be ignored. As a consequence, the spatial scope of man-made jurisdictional zones does not always correspond to 'ecologically defined space' which comprises the area where marine ecosystems extend.[26] Nevertheless, several species, such as straddling and highly migratory species, do not respect artificial boundaries. Hence a clear-cut distinction between marine spaces under the coastal State's jurisdiction and marine spaces beyond such a jurisdiction is not always suitable for the conservation of those species.

This question was already raised in the 1893 *Bering Sea Fur-Seals* arbitration between Great Britain and the United States. In this case, the United States extended its national jurisdiction beyond the ordinary three-mile limit in order to protect fur-seals frequenting the islands of the United States in the Bering Sea, whilst Great Britain advocated the strict application of the freedom of the high seas. The Arbitral Tribunal rejected the claim of the United States on this matter. At the same time, however, the Tribunal determined regulations applicable to both parties, including the prohibition of the hunting of fur-seals within a zone of sixty miles around the Pribilov Islands.[27] In so doing, the Arbitral Tribunal attempted to reconcile the interest of the distant-water fishing States and the need for conservation of marine species. The *Bering Sea Fur-Seals* dispute seems to demonstrate the difficulty of the conservation of marine species migrating between marine spaces under and beyond national jurisdiction. Yet it appears that the situation is not improved very much in the LOSC.

[24] *Case Concerning Pulp Mills on the River Uruguay* (Argentina v Uruguay), ICJ Reports 2010, p. 47, para. 145.

[25] The ICJ regarded this provision as a rule of customary international law. *Ibid.*

[26] L. Juda, 'Considerations in Developing a Functional Approach to the Governance of Large Marine Ecosystems' (1999) 30 *ODIL* p. 93.

[27] J. B. Moore, *History and Digest of the International Arbitrations to Which the United States Has Been a Party*, vol. I (Washington DC, Government Printing Office, 1898), p. 949.

4 CONSERVATION OF MARINE LIVING RESOURCES UNDER THE LOSC (2): THE SPECIES SPECIFIC APPROACH

The LOSC specifies rules applicable to conservation of shared fish stocks (Article 63(1)), straddling fish stocks (Article 63(2)), highly migratory species (Article 64), marine mammals (Article 65), anadromous stocks (Article 66), catadromous species (Article 67) and sedentary species (Article 68).[28] According to the species specific approach, conservation measures are to be determined according to each category of marine species.

4.1 Shared and straddling fish stocks

Article 63 contains the following rules respecting conservation of shared and straddling fish stocks:

> 1. Where the same stock or stocks of associated species occur within the exclusive economic zones of two or more coastal States, these States shall seek, either directly or through appropriate subregional or regional organizations, to agree upon the measures necessary to co-ordinate and ensure the conservation and development of such stocks without prejudice to the other provisions of this Part.
> 2. Where the same stock or stocks of associated species occur both within the exclusive economic zone and in an area beyond and adjacent to the zone, the coastal State and the States fishing for such stocks in the adjacent area shall seek, either directly or through appropriate subregional or regional organisations, to agree upon the measures necessary for the conservation of these stocks in the adjacent area.[29]

This provision calls for three observations.

First, the word 'seek' seems to suggest that there is no obligation that States shall reach agreement.[30] Article 63 contains no specific recourse in the case of inability to reach agreement.[31] In the case of straddling fish stocks, a difficulty in reaching a conservation agreement will be increased where the number of potential fishing States remains indeterminate.[32] Even if the coastal States and high seas fishing States reach agreement pursuant to Article 63(2), there is a risk that the accord may be undermined by new entrants.[33]

[28] Sedentary species are discussed in Chapter 4, section 4.7.

[29] For the purpose of this chapter, fish stocks under paragraph 1 of Article 63 may be called 'shared fish stocks'.

[30] However, it has to be stressed that States 'are under an obligation so to conduct themselves that negotiations are meaningful'. The *North Sea Continental Shelf* cases, ICJ Reports 1969, p. 47, para. 85.

[31] Davies and Redgwell, 'The International Legal Regulation', p. 236.

[32] O. Thébaud, 'Transboundary Marine Fisheries Management: Recent Developments and Elements of Analysis' (1997) 21 *Marine Policy* p. 241.

[33] W. T. Burke, 'Unregulated High Seas Fishing and Ocean Governance', in J. M. Van Dyke, D. Zaelke and G. Hewison (eds.), *Freedom for the Seas in the 21st Century: Ocean Governance and Environmental Harmony* (Washington DC, Island Press, 1993), p. 240.

Second, a crucial issue in relation to the conservation of shared and straddling fish stocks involves the question as to how it is possible to allocate those stocks between the States concerned. Yet Article 63(2) contains no substantive guideline on this matter.

Third, a further issue is how it is possible to coordinate national measures with respect to conservation of the shared and straddling fish stocks. Nonetheless, Article 63 provides no substantive guidance on this matter. Article 63 also remains silent with regard to compatibility of measures between the EEZs of the neighbouring States or between the EEZ and the high seas. Overall, Article 63 seems to contain only a minimum rule relating to the conservation of shared and straddling fish stocks.

4.2 Highly migratory species

Whilst there is no definition of highly migratory fish stocks in the LOSC, these species are listed in Annex I. The list includes various species of tuna, marlin, sailfish, swordfish, dolphin, shark and cetacean. In relation to conservation of highly migratory species, Article 64(1) provides that:

> The coastal State and other States whose nationals fish in the region for the highly migratory species listed in Annex I shall cooperate directly or through appropriate international organizations with a view to ensuring conservation and promoting the objective of optimum utilization of such species throughout the region, both within and beyond the exclusive economic zone. In regions for which no appropriate international organization exists, the coastal State and other States whose nationals harvest these species in the region shall cooperate to establish such an organization and participate in its work.

Unlike Article 63, this provision places a clear obligation upon States to cooperate in conservation and promoting the objective of optimum utilisation of these species in the EEZ as well as on the high seas.[34] However, like Article 63, Article 64(1) contains no specific mechanism ensuring cooperation in this matter. Nor does this provision hold specific guidance with respect to the question how catches of highly migratory species can be allocated between the coastal State and States fishing on the high seas. Overall, it may have to be accepted that the normativity of Article 64(1) remains modest.

4.3 Marine mammals

Marine mammals are warm-blooded animals which are characterised by the production of milk in the female mammary glands and spend the majority of their lives in or close to the sea.[35] Specifically marine mammals include whales, small cetaceans, dolphins, porpoises, seals, dugongs, and marine otters. Whilst, in the LOSC, some of these species are listed as highly migratory species and thus covered by Article 64, the key provision respecting the conservation of marine mammals is Article 65:

[34] L. Lucchini and M. Vœlckel, *Droit de la mer*, vol. 2, *Navigation et Pêche* (Paris, Pedone, 1996), p. 503; R. C. Raigón, 'La pêche en haute mer', in D. Vignes, G. Cataldi, and R. C. Raigón, *Le droit international de la pêche maritime* (Brussels, Bruylant, 2000), p. 216.

[35] A. Proelß, 'Marine Mammals', in *Max Planck Encyclopedia*, p. 1, para. 1.

> Nothing in this Part restricts the right of a coastal State or the competence of an international organization, as appropriate, to prohibit, limit or regulate the exploitation of marine mammals more strictly than provided for in this Part. States shall cooperate with a view to the conservation of marine mammals and in the case of cetaceans shall in particular work through the appropriate international organizations for their conservation, management and study.

This provision also applies to the conservation and management of marine mammals in the high seas pursuant to Article 120. Article 65 calls for three brief comments.

First, this provision allows coastal States to regulate the exploitation of marine mammals more strictly than other living resources in the EEZ. However, it is not suggested that the coastal States are obliged to apply such a strict regulation. The coastal States have a discretion to determine the proper regulation respecting the exploitation of marine mammals.[36] Nor does Article 65 prohibit the exploitation of marine mammals.[37]

Second, Article 65 does not specify the appropriate international organisations. In this regard, it is notable that the second sentence of Article 65 refers to 'organisations' in the plural. Whilst undoubtedly the International Whaling Commission (IWC) is one of the organisations in the field of the conservation and management of marine mammals, it is not suggested that the IWC is the only appropriate organisation. In fact, the United Nations Division for Ocean Affairs and the Law of the Sea (UNDOALOS) lists the FAO, IWC, and UNEP as being international organisations under Article 65.[38] The North Atlantic Marine Mammal Commission (NAMMCO) may also be considered as an appropriate international organisation in this field.

Third, the obligation to 'work through' an appropriate organisation needs further clarification. On the one hand, it appears extreme to consider that coastal States must become a member of the relevant international organisation, or that they must accept the regulatory measures of a certain international organisation with regard to conservation of marine mammals.[39] On the other hand, it is equally unreasonable to argue that the 'work through' obligation in Article 65 provides a merely hortatory duty without substantive meaning.[40] Arguably it is necessary to interpret this provision so as to give it its fullest weight and effect consistent with the normal sense of the words and with other parts of the text pursuant to the principle of effectiveness.

The LOSC is not the only convention dealing with the conservation of marine mammals. At the global level, the Convention on International Trade in Endangered Species of Wild Fauna and Flora (CITES) indirectly involves this subject by controlling and preventing international commercial trade in endangered species, including many

[36] T. L. McDorman, 'Canada and Whaling: An Analysis of Article 65 of the Law of the Sea Convention' (1998) 29 *ODIL* p. 182.

[37] Birnie, Boyle and Redgwell, *International Law and the Environment*, p. 724.

[38] UNDOALOS, (1996) 31 *Law of the Sea Bulletin* p. 82; McDorman, 'Canada and Whaling', p. 185.

[39] Proelß, 'Marine Mammals', p. 4, para. 14.

[40] McDorman, 'Canada and Whaling', p. 184.

marine mammals, or their products. At the regional level, there are several treaties respecting conservation of marine mammals, including:

- The 1971 Agreement on Sealing and the Conservation of the Seal Stocks in the Northwest Atlantic,[41]
- The 1972 Convention for the Conservation of Antarctic Seals,[42]
- The 1973 Agreement on the Preservation of Polar Bears,[43]
- The 1990 Agreement on the Conservation of Seals in the Wadden Sea,[44]
- The 1992 Agreement on Cooperation in Research, Conservation and Management of Marine Mammals in the North Atlantic,[45]
- The 1992 Agreement on the Conservation of Small Cetaceans of the Baltic and North Seas,[46]
- The 1996 Agreement on the Conservation of Cetaceans of the Black Sea, Mediterranean Sea and Contiguous Atlantic Area,[47]
- The 1999 Agreement Concerning the Creation of a Marine Mammal Sanctuary in the Mediterranean.[48]

The most debatable issue in relation to the conservation of marine mammals may be whaling. The problem of overexploitation of whales was already a subject of discussion in the League of Nations. In 1930, the Economic Committee of the League of Nations convened a meeting of a Committee of Experts in Berlin. The meeting drafted an international convention relating to the regulation of whaling. On the basis of the draft, in 1931, the Convention for the Regulation of Whaling was concluded in Geneva.[49] This was the first multilateral convention regulating whaling. Since the 1931 Convention was ineffective in the protection of whales, the International Convention for the Regulation of Whaling was subsequently adopted in 1937.[50]

In the face of growing concerns over the depletion of whales, on 2 December 1946, the International Convention for the Regulation of Whaling (hereafter the 1946 Whaling Convention) was concluded.[51] In its Preamble, the 1946 Whaling Convention makes clear that it seeks to provide for 'the proper conservation of whale stocks' and 'the orderly development of the whaling industry'. The Convention applies to all waters in which whaling is prosecuted by factory ships, land stations and whale catchers

[41] 870 *UNTS* p. 85. Entered into force 22 December 1971.
[42] 1080 *UNTS* p. 175. Entered into force 11 March 1978.
[43] (1974) 12 *ILM* 13. Entered into force 26 May 1976.
[44] Entered into force 1 October 1991. The text is available at: www.cms.int/species/wadden_seals/sea_text.htm.
[45] 1945 *UNTS* 3. Entered into force 1 January 1999.
[46] 1772 *UNTS* p. 217. Entered into force 29 March 1994.
[47] 2183 *UNTS* p. 303. Entered into force 1 June 2001.
[48] 2176 *UNTS* p. 247. Entered into force 21 February 2002.
[49] 155 *League of Nations Treaty Series (LNTS)* p. 349; (1936) 30 *AJIL Supplement*, p. 167. Entered into force on 16 January 1935.
[50] 190 *LNTS* p. 79; (1940) 34 *AJIL Supplement* p. 106. Entered into force 7 May 1938.
[51] 161 *UNTS* p. 72. Entered into force on 10 November 1948. As at 2010, eighty-eight States have ratified the Convention.

pursuant to Article I(2). The Convention includes the Schedule attached thereto which forms an integral part thereof (Article I(1)). The Schedule provides specific measures relating to the conservation of whales.

The principal organ of the Convention is the IWC. The IWC is open to any States that are parties to the Convention. The Commission is entitled to make recommendations to any or all contracting governments on any matters which relate to whales or whaling and to the objectives and purposes of the Convention by virtue of Article VI. The recommendations are not binding. Under Article V(1), the IWC may amend the provisions of the Schedule by adopting regulations fixing (a) protected and unprotected species, (b) open and closed seasons, (c) open and closed waters, (d) size limits for each species, (e) time, (f) types and specifications of gear and apparatus and appliances which may be used, (g) methods of measurement, (h) catch returns and other statistical and biological records, and (i) methods of inspection. A three-fourths majority of those members voting shall be required to amend the provisions of the Schedule pursuant to Article III(2).

Amendments of the Schedule are to be effective with respect to the contracting governments ninety days following notification of the amendment by the Commission to each of the contracting governments. According to the objection procedure set out in Article V(3), however, if any government presents to the IWC an objection to any amendment within ninety days of notification, the amendment shall not become effective with respect to any of the governments for an additional ninety days. Thereupon, any other contracting governments may present an objection to the amendment at any time prior to the expiration of the additional ninety days, or before the expiration of thirty days from the date of receipt of the last objection received during such additional ninety-day period. The amendment in question is not binding upon the objecting States.

In 1982, the IWC adopted a moratorium on commercial whaling on all whale stocks from the 1985/86 whaling season.[52] The moratorium is still in force today. Although the moratorium was opposed by Japan, Norway and the USSR, these three States announced that they would cease commercial whaling after 1988.[53] The IWC established the Indian Ocean Sanctuary in 1979[54] and the Southern Ocean Sanctuary in 1994.[55] These whale sanctuaries cover an area of approximately 100 million square kilometres, which corresponds to approximately 30 per cent of the world's oceans.[56] The duration of the Indian Ocean Sanctuary was initially established for a ten-year period, and, later, was declared indefinite, while the duration of the Southern Ocean Sanctuary was *ab initio*

52 Rule 10(e) of the Schedule. However, Rule 13 of the Schedule exempts aboriginal subsistence whaling from the moratorium. As a consequence, Denmark (Greenland), Russia, the USA and Saint Vincent and the Grenadines are allowed to conduct aboriginal subsistence whaling. J. Braig, 'Whaling', in *Max Planck Encyclopaedia*, p. 4, para. 36.

53 In 1988, Japan withdrew its objection to the moratorium because of pressure from the USA. On the other hand, Norway resumed commercial whaling in 1993. Churchill and Lowe, *Law of the Sea*, pp. 317–318.

54 Rule 7(a) of the Schedule.

55 Rule 7(b) of the Schedule.

56 E. Morgera, 'Whale Sanctuaries: An Evolving Concept within the International Whaling Commission' (2004) 35 *ODIL* p. 333.

indefinite.[57] Japan objected to the Southern Ocean Sanctuary to the extent that the sanctuary applied to the Antarctic minke whales under Article V(3). As a consequence, Japan is exempted from the application of the Sanctuary respecting the harvesting of minke whales. The Russian Federation also presented an objection, but withdrew it in 1994.[58] In 1994, the Commission accepted a Revised Management Procedure (RMP) but has yet to implement it.

An issue that needs particular consideration is the validity of scientific whaling. Article VIII of the 1946 Whaling Convention allows the contracting governments to carry out scientific whaling. Japan has carried out, or claims to have carried out, scientific whaling in accordance with Article VIII. However, Japan's scientific whaling has invited criticisms with regard to, *inter alia*, (i) the lethal nature of the research programme, (ii) the size of its research catch, and (iii) the ultimate commercial sale of whale products derived from scientific hunts.[59] Thus, on 31 May 2010, Australia instituted proceedings against Japan before the ICJ that put in issue the legality of Japanese scientific whaling.[60]

4.4 Anadromous stocks

Anadromous species are species, such as salmon, shad and sturgeon, which spawn in fresh water but spend most of their life in the sea.[61] Owing to the high commercial value of anadromous stocks, Article 66 of the LOSC contains rules with regard to the conservation of these stocks in some detail. These rules can be divided into three rubrics.

(i) Conservation and management of anadromus stocks: Article 66(1) of the LOSC stipulates that the State in whose rivers such fish spawn (the State of origin) is primarily responsible for their management and shall take appropriate regulatory measures to ensure their conservation. Article 66(2) then places an obligation upon the State of origin of anadromous stocks to ensure their conservation by the establishment of appropriate regulatory measures for fishing in all waters landward of the outer limits of its EEZ and for fishing provided for in paragraph 3(b). The State of origin may establish total allowable catches for stocks originating in its rivers pursuant to Article 66(2). The word 'may' implies that this is permissive, not mandatory. In cases where anadromous stocks migrate into or through the waters landward of the outer limits of the EEZ of a State other than the State of origin, such State is obliged to cooperate with the State of origin with regard to the conservation and management of such stocks in accordance with Article 66(4).

(ii) Fishing of anadromous stocks: Under Article 66(3), fisheries for anadromous stocks must be conducted only in waters landward of the outer limits of EEZs, except where this would result in economic dislocation for a State other than the State of

[57] *Ibid.*, p. 322.
[58] IWC, 'The Schedule to the Convention'.
[59] H. S. Schiffman, 'Scientific Research Whaling in International Law: Objectives and Objections' (2001–2002) 8 *ILSA Journal of International and Comparative Law* p. 476.
[60] The case is pending.
[61] LOSC, Article 66.

origin. It follows that in principle, fishing of anadromous species beyond 200-nautical mile limits is forbidden. With respect to such fishing beyond the outer limits of the EEZ, States concerned are obliged to maintain consultations with a view to achieving agreement on terms and conditions of such fishing giving due regard to the conservation requirements and the needs of the State of origin in respect of these stocks in conformity with Article 66(3)(a). The State of origin is also required to cooperate in minimising economic dislocation in such other States fishing these stocks by virtue of Article 66(3)(b). Enforcement of regulations regarding anadromous stocks beyond the EEZ must be by agreement between the State of origin and the other State concerned under Article 66(3)(d).

(iii) Regional organisations: Article 66(5) requires the State of origin of anadromous stocks and other States fishing these stocks to make arrangements for the implementation of the provisions of Article 66, where appropriate, through regional organisations. An example of such organisations is the North Atlantic Salmon Conservation Organization (NASCO), which was established in 1984 by the 1982 Convention for the Conservation of Salmon in the North Atlantic Ocean.[62] With exceptions, fishing of salmon is prohibited not only on the high seas but also within areas of fisheries jurisdiction of coastal States beyond twelve nautical miles pursuant to Article 2 of the Convention.

Conservation of anadromous stocks is also regulated by regional treaties. The 1992 Convention for the Conservation of Anadromous Stocks in the North Pacific Ocean is an example.[63] The Parties to the Convention are Canada, Japan, Russia and the United States, which are major States of origin of North Pacific salmon. The 1992 Convention confirmed, in its Preamble, the primary interest and responsibility of the State of origin in the conservation of anadromous stocks. Article III(1)(a) prohibits directed fishing for salmon on the high seas. The Convention established the North Pacific Anadromous Fish Commission under Article VIII(1). The Commission is entitled to, *inter alia*, recommend to the Parties measures for the conservation of anadromous stocks and ecologically related species in the Convention Area, promote the exchange of information, review and evaluate enforcement actions taken by the Parties, and cooperate with relevant international organisations to obtain the best available information pursuant to Article IX.

At the bilateral level, the Treaty between the government of Canada and the government of the United States of America concerning Pacific Salmon was concluded in 1985.[64] The Treaty recognises, in its Preamble, the primary interest and responsibility of States of origin. Under Article III(1), each Party is under the obligation to conduct its fisheries and its salmon enhancement programmes so as to (a) prevent overfishing and provide for optimum production, and (b) provide for each Party to receive benefits

[62] Entered into force 1 October 1983. The text of the Convention is available at: www.nasco.int/pdf/agreements/nasco_convention.pdf. The Member Parties of NASCO are: Canada, Denmark (in respect of the Faroe Islands and Greenland), European Union, Iceland, Norway, Russian Federation and the United States.

[63] (1993) 22 *Law of the Sea Bulletin* p. 21. Entered into force 16 February 1993.

[64] Entered into force 18 March 1985. The text of the Treaty, in which Annexes were amended in 1999, 2002 and 2009, is available at: www.psc.org/pubs/Treaty.pdf.

equivalent to the production of salmon originating in its waters. The Treaty established a Pacific Salmon Commission. The Commission may make recommendations to the Parties on any matter relating to the Treaty by virtue of Article II(8). Overall the treaty practice appears to support the primary interest and responsibility of the State of origin and the prohibition of fishing of anadromous stocks on the high seas.

4.5 Catadromous species

Catadromous species are species, such as the freshwater eel, which spawn in the ocean and migrate to fresh water for most of their lives before returning to the ocean to reproduce. The life cycle of catadromous species is the opposite of the life cycle of anadromous species.[65]

Under Article 67(1) of the LOSC, a State in whose waters catadromous species spend the greater part of their life cycle (the host State) has overall management responsibility for the management of these species and is required to ensure the ingress and egress of migrating fish. Harvesting of catadromous species shall be conducted only in waters landward of the outer limits of the EEZs pursuant to Article 67(2). It follows that the fishing of catadromous species on the high seas is prohibited. Fishing of catadromous species on the high seas means the capture of juveniles, which is contrary to conservation policy. Hence, there is a good reason to prohibit fishing of these species on the high seas.

When conducted in EEZs, harvesting is to be subject to Article 67 and the other provisions of the LOSC concerning fishing in the EEZs under Article 67(2). In cases where catadromous fish migrate through the EEZ of another State, the management, including harvesting, of such fish is to be regulated by agreement between the host State and the other State concerned in accordance with Article 67(3). Such agreement must ensure the rational management of the species and take into account the responsibility of the host State for the maintenance of these species. It would follow that harvesting of catadromous species by States other than the host State is not prohibited.[66] Whilst Article 67(3) provides no guidance with respect to the situation where the host State and the other State concerned fail to reach an agreement on this matter, it seems at least arguable that Article 67(3) does not allow the host State to unilaterally exercise its jurisdiction in the EEZ of another State where catadromous fish migrate.[67]

4.6 Limits of the species specific approach

At least two limitations must be highlighted with regard to the species specific approach.

First, rules of the LOSC governing conservation of marine species do not cover all species that need particular conservation measures. For instance, the LOSC comprises no provision in relation to deep-sea species. Due to their exceptional longevity, slow

[65] *Virginia Commentaries*, vol. II, p. 681.
[66] *Ibid.*
[67] Raigón, 'La pêche en haute mer', p. 231.

growth, delayed maturity and low productivity, deep-sea species are highly vulnerable to fishing activities.[68] Hence arguably these species will need particular conservation measures. In this respect, it is to be noted that in 2008 International Guidelines for the Management of Deep-Sea Fisheries in the High Seas were adopted at the request of the Committee on Fisheries of the FAO.[69]

Second, a more fundamental limitation involves the lack of ecological consideration. The species specific approach does not adequately take account of the ecological interactions between marine species as well as the ecological conditions that support them. Whilst the LOSC contains a few provisions which take the interaction between marine species into account,[70] the interrelationship between marine species and marine ecosystems attracts little attention in the LOSC. Overall it may be concluded that the traditional approaches are inadequate to properly conserve marine living resources.

5 DEVELOPMENT AFTER THE LOSC

In response to the limits of the traditional approaches, more conservation-oriented approaches are being developed in post-LOSC treaties with regard to conservation of those resources. This part will focus on three principal elements, namely, the concept of sustainable development, the ecosystem approach and the precautionary approach. These elements are closely intertwined. Particular focus should be on the normativity of these elements as a rule of conduct and a rule for adjudication.[71]

5.1 The concept of sustainable development

Sustainable development is a key concept in the use of natural resources, including marine living resources. The concept of sustainable development was given currency by the Report of the World Commission on Environment and Development, 'Our Common Future'. In its Report, the World Commission on Environment and Development (hereafter WCED) defined this concept as 'development that meets the needs of the present without compromising the ability of future generations to meet their own needs'.[72] The concept of sustainable development seeks in essence to reconcile the need for development with environmental protection. The basic idea is echoed by the ICJ in the

[68] J. A. Koslow, et al. 'Continental Slope and Deep-Sea Fisheries: Implications for a Fragile Ecosystem' (2000) *ICES Journal of Marine Science* p. 550; L. A. Kimball, 'Deep-Sea Fisheries on the High Seas: The Management Impasse' (2004) 19 *IJMCL* pp. 261–263.

[69] The document is available at: www.southpacificrfmo.org/assets/6th-Meeting-October-2008-Canberra/DW-Subgroup-VI/SPRFMO6-SWG-INF01-FAO-Deepwater-Guidelines-Final-Sep20.pdf.

[70] Articles 61(4) and 119(1)(b).

[71] The distinction between a rule of conduct and a rule for adjudication was originally made by Eugen Ehrlich. E. Ehrlich (translated by W. L. Moll), *Fundamental Principles of the Sociology of Law* (Cambridge, Mass., Harvard University Press, 1936), p. 41 and pp. 122–123. This distinction is useful in examining the normativity of rules of international law, including the law of the sea.

[72] The World Commission on Environment and Development, *Our Common Future* (Oxford University Press, 1987), p. 43.

Gabčíkovo-Nagymaros Project case[73] as well as the Arbitral Tribunal in the *Arbitration regarding the Iron Rhine Railway* case of 2005.[74]

Currently the concept of sustainable development or 'sustainable use' is being increasingly incorporated into treaties and non-binding documents relating to the conservation of marine living resources. At the treaty level, for instance, Article 2 of the 1995 UN Fish Stocks Agreement stipulates that '[t]he objective of this Agreement is to ensure the long-term conservation and sustainable use of straddling fish stocks and highly migratory fish stocks through effective implementation of the relevant provisions of the Convention'. Article 5(a) requires coastal States and States fishing on the high seas to 'adopt measures to ensure long-term sustainability of straddling fish stocks and highly migratory fish stocks and promote the objective of their optimum utilisation'. Article 5(h) further imposes upon coastal States and States fishing on the high seas the duty to 'take measures to prevent or eliminate over-fishing and excess fishing capacity and to ensure that levels of fishing effort do not exceed those commensurate with the sustainable use of fishery resources'.

Concerning non-binding documents, the concept of sustainable development or sustainable use can be seen in Chapter 17 of Agenda 21 of 1992,[75] the 1995 Code of Conduct for Responsible Fisheries (hereafter the FAO Code of Conduct),[76] the 1999 Rome Declaration on the Implementation of the Code of Conduct for Responsible Fisheries,[77] and the 2001 Reykjavik Declaration on Responsible Fisheries in the Marine Ecosystem.[78] On the other hand, the concept of sustainable development raises uncertainties as to its normativity.[79]

First, whilst some writers attempt to enumerate relevant components of the concept, it appears that there is no uniform understanding on this matter. There remains considerable uncertainty as to the normative contents and the scope of the concept of sustainable development. The concept of sustainable development seems to be no more than a label for a set of various components of international environmental law at a high level of abstraction. However, the label is itself not law.[80] Hence it seems debatable whether and to what extent this concept can legally constrain the behaviour of States.

Second, as the WCED Report stated, the concept of sustainable development ultimately requires a change in the quality and patterns of life.[81] This is a matter of national policy of a State and, consequently, it appears difficult to *a priori* determine specific

[73] ICJ Reports 1997, p. 78, para. 140.

[74] The *Arbitration regarding the Iron Rhine Railway* case (Belgium and the Netherlands), 27 *RIAA* pp. 28–29, para. 59.

[75] Agenda 21, para. 17.46; para. 17.75, available at: www.un.org/esa/dsd/agenda21.

[76] Article 7.2.1.

[77] Paragraph 12(n). The text of the Rome Declaration is available at the homepage of the FAO.

[78] Preamble and paragraph 2. The text of the Reykjavik Declaration is available at the homepage of the FAO.

[79] Tanaka, *A Dual Approach*, pp. 71–75.

[80] A. V. Lowe, 'Sustainable Development and Unsustainable Arguments', in A. Boyle and D. Freestone (eds.), *International Law and Sustainable Development: Past Achievements and Future Challenges* (Oxford University Press, 1999), p. 26.

[81] WCED, *Our Common Future*, p. 46.

measures to achieve sustainable development in international law. If this is the case, it will be difficult for international courts and tribunals to review the validity of national action by applying the concept of sustainable development. Thus it is debatable whether the concept of sustainable development itself can be an independent rule for adjudication. Overall there may be room for the view that this concept should be regarded as a factor orienting the behaviour of States and guiding proper interpretation of relevant rules in the judicial process.[82]

5.2 The ecosystem approach

The ecosystem approach (or ecosystem-based approach) represents an important development of international law governing the conservation of marine living resources. Whilst the definition of the ecosystem approach varies according to instruments, the Biodiversity Committee of the 1992 Convention for the Protection of the Marine Environment of the North-East Atlantic defined this approach as

> the comprehensive integrated management of human activities based on the best available scientific knowledge about the ecosystem and its dynamics, in order to identify and take action on influences which are critical to the health of marine ecosystems, thereby achieving sustainable use of ecosystem goods and services and maintenance of ecosystem integrity.[83]

Unlike the traditional species specific approach, the ecosystem approach aims to conserve ecosystem structure and functioning within ecologically meaningful boundaries in an integrated manner. As the Report of the UN Secretary-General stated in 2006, '[t]he distinguishing feature of the ecosystem approach is that it is *integrated and holistic*, taking account of all the components of an ecosystem, both physical and biological, of their interaction and of all activities that could affect them'.[84] In this sense, this approach constitutes a key element of the integrated management approach.

The ecosystem approach has gained currency in various instruments relating to conservation of marine living resources. For example, the 1995 Fish Stocks Agreement clearly notes 'the need to avoid adverse impacts on the marine environment, preserve biodiversity, maintain the integrity of marine ecosystems and minimize the risk of long-term or irreversible effects of fishing operations'. Article 5(g) thus places an obligation upon coastal States and States fishing on the high seas to protect biodiversity in the marine environment. Article 4(a) of the 2006 Southern Indian Ocean Fisheries Agreement clearly provides that 'measures shall be adopted on the basis of the best scientific evidence available to ensure the long-term conservation of fishery resources, taking into account the sustainable use of such resources and implementing

[82] Tanaka, *A Dual Approach*, p. 75; Lowe, 'Sustainable Development', p. 31.

[83] Meeting of the Biodiversity Committee (BDC), Dublin, 20–24 January 2003, Summary Record BDC 2003, BDC 03/10/1-E, Annex 13, p. 1, para. 6.

[84] Emphasis added. United Nations, *Report of the Secretary-General, Oceans and the Law of the Sea*, A/61/63, 9 March 2006, p. 38, para. 136.

an ecosystem approach to their management'.[85] As for non-binding documents, the 1999 Rome Declaration on the Implementation of the Code of Conduct for Responsible Fisheries noted that 'greater consideration should be given to the development of more appropriate eco-system approaches to fisheries development and management'.[86] The need to incorporate ecosystem considerations was also stressed by the 2001 Reykjavik Declaration.[87]

It can be observed that international law concerning conservation of marine living resources has acquired a stronger ecological dimension with the emergence of the ecosystem approach. On the other hand, the ecosystem approach raises at least three issues which need further consideration.[88]

First, as the ecosystem approach itself contains no established criteria for determining specific measures to conserve marine species, there is no clarity on the normative content of the ecosystem approach. Accordingly, the ecosystem approach may be interpreted differently in different contexts.[89] If the ecosystem approach is enshrined in treaties, it seems debatable to what extent this approach will *legally* constrain States' behaviour as a rule of conduct.

Second, specific measures under the ecosystem approach are to be determined taking various scientific, political, economic and social factors into account. This is in essence a matter of national policy. Accordingly, it will be difficult, if not impossible, for international courts and tribunals to judge the violation of the obligation to apply the ecosystem approach when the application of this approach has been disputed between States. It appears questionable whether the ecosystem approach can be an independent rule for adjudication. In fact, there is no instance of the actual application of the ecosystem approach itself as a rule of international law binding upon States.

Third, a question arises with regard to compatibility of conservation measures on the basis of the ecosystem approach between marine spaces under and beyond national jurisdiction. This question is particularly at issue in relation to conservation of straddling and highly migratory species. In this respect, Article 7(2) of the 1995 Fish Stocks Agreement stipulates that:

> Conservation and management measures established for the high seas and those adopted for areas under national jurisdiction shall be compatible in order to ensure conservation and management of the straddling fish stocks and highly migratory fish stocks in their entirety. To this end, coastal States and States fishing on the high seas have a duty to cooperate for the purpose of achieving compatible measures in respect of such stocks.

[85] For the text of the Agreement, *Official Journal of European Union*, L 196/17, 18 July 2006.
[86] Paragraph 6 of the Rome Declaration.
[87] Preamble.
[88] Tanaka, *A Dual Approach*, pp. 78–82.
[89] United Nations, *Report on the Work of the United Nations Open-Ended Informal Consultative Process on Oceans and the Law of the Sea at its Seventh Meeting*, A/61/156, 17 July 2006, p. 2, para. 6.

States are thus obliged to make every effort to agree on compatible conservation and management measures within a reasonable period of time pursuant to Article 7(3). In conjunction with this, Article 7(2) enumerates various factors which need to be taken into account in determining compatible conservation and management measures in some detail. Yet it remains unclear how it is possible to balance these elements.[90]

In this regard, some argue that Article 7(2)(a) will lead to a result in favour of coastal States.[91] However, such an interpretation will considerably limit the scope of the negotiation on this subject because the validity of conservation measures in marine spaces under national jurisdiction is already presumed and the issue remaining is whether or not fishing States on the high seas accept these measures. If this is the case, the negotiation would seem to become pointless. Accordingly, there may be room for the view that Article 7(2) should be construed in such a way that conservation and management measures established for the high seas and those adopted for areas under national jurisdiction must be mutually compatible, not that measures adopted for the high seas have to be compatible with measures adopted for areas under national jurisdiction.[92]

5.3 The precautionary approach

The precautionary approach is one of the key elements which characterises a new dimension of international law with regard to the conservation of marine species.[93] Whilst the definition of the precautionary approach varies depending on the instruments, Principle 15 of the 1992 Rio Declaration on Environment and Development formulated this approach as follows:

> In order to protect the environment, the precautionary approach shall be widely applied by states according to their capabilities. Where there are threats of serious or irreversible damage, lack of full scientific certainty shall not be used as a reason for postponing cost-effective measures to prevent environmental degradation.

Whilst, on the international plane, the precautionary approach was originally adopted in order to protect the marine environment, this approach is being increasingly incorporated into instruments respecting conservation of marine living resources. For example, Article 6(1) of the 1995 Fish Stocks Agreement places a clear obligation upon States to apply 'the precautionary approach widely to conservation, management, and

[90] A. G. Oude Elferink, 'The Impact of Article 7(2) of the Fish Stocks Agreement on the Formulation of Conservation and Management Measures for Straddling Highly Migratory Fish Stocks', *FAO Legal Papers Online No. 4*, 13–18 (August 1999) available at: www.fao.org/legal/prs-ol/lpo4.pdf.

[91] See for instance H. Gherari, 'L'accord du 4 août 1995 sur les stocks chevauchants et les stocks de poissons grands migrateurs' (1996) 100 *RGDIP* p. 377; Lucchini and Vœlckel, *Droit de la mer*, p. 681; Davies and Redgwell, 'The International Legal Regulation', pp. 263–264; Francisco Orrego Vicuña, *The Changing International Law of High Seas Fisheries* (Cambridge University Press, 1999), p. 190.

[92] Oude Elferink, 'The Impact of Article 7(2)', pp. 4 and 7.

[93] It appears that the terminology of 'the precautionary approach' or 'the precautionary principle' is not unified. In this study, I use the term 'the precautionary approach'. On this issue, see Birnie, Boyle and Redgwell, *International Law and the Environment*, p. 155.

exploitation of straddling fish stocks and highly migratory fish stocks in order to protect the living marine resources and preserve the marine environment'. Annex II of the Agreement provides Guidelines for the Application of Precautionary Reference Points in Conservation and Management of Straddling Fish Stocks and Highly Migratory Fish Stocks.

Likewise, Article 4(c) of the 2006 Southern Indian Ocean Fisheries Agreement explicitly provides that 'the precautionary approach shall be applied in accordance with the Code of Conduct and the 1995 Agreement, whereby the absence of adequate scientific information shall not be used as a reason for postponing or failing to take conservation and management measures'.[94] Article 3(1)(b) of the 2009 Convention on the Conservation and Management of High Seas Fishery Resources in the South Pacific Ocean places an explicit obligation upon the Contracting Parties to 'apply the precautionary approach and an ecosystem approach'.[95]

In light of growing concerns over the depletion of marine living resources, it is hardly surprising that the precautionary approach is increasingly enshrined in international instruments respecting conservation of marine species. Furthermore, owing to the scientific uncertainty relating to the mechanisms of marine ecosystems, the application of the ecosystem approach necessitates some precautionary considerations. Thus the precautionary approach is logically linked to the ecosystem approach. In fact, international instruments adopting the ecosystem approach tend to refer to the precautionary approach at the same time.[96] However, the concept of the precautionary approach seems to leave some room for discussion with regard to its normativity.

A first issue involves a criterion for determining the existence of a risk of serious or irreversible harm, even if uncertainty exists. Due to its nature, a need for the application of the precautionary approach is to be determined on the basis of *potential* risks. However, the assessment of serious risk is often difficult to make since such risk may not be well known or discoverable through present-day science. The results of the assessment of possible serious harm may also change in accordance with the development of scientific technology.[97] A difficult question thus arises as to how it is possible to determine the existence of serious or irreversible risks which may trigger the application of the precautionary approach. The level of environmental risks which is socially acceptable must be determined considering not only scientific factors but also economic, social and political factors. Thus the evaluation of those factors essentially involves a matter of policy which can be best answered by politicians, rather than jurists or scientists.[98]

Second, the precautionary approach contains no legal guidance about how to control the environmental risks. The application of the precautionary approach itself does

[94] For the text of the Agreement, see *Official Journal of the European Union*, L 196/45, 18 July 2006.

[95] The text of the Convention is available at: www.southpacificrfmo.org/. The Convention has not entered into force.

[96] Tanaka, *A Dual Approach*, pp. 86–87.

[97] P. Martin-Bidou, 'Le principe de précaution en droit international de l'environnement' (1999) 103 *RGDIP* p. 647 and p. 651.

[98] Birnie, Boyle and Redgwell, *International Law and the Environment*, p. 161.

not automatically specify measures that should be taken. In other words, the precautionary approach can be applied in different ways in different contexts. In light of the differentiated economic and technological capacities between States, not all States can adopt the same measures with regard to the implementation of the precautionary approach.[99] Furthermore, the decision-making process of the precautionary approach is complicated because there is a need to consider not only scientific factors but also the cost-effectiveness of proposed measures, their technical capabilities, their economic and social priorities, etc.[100] This process essentially involves matters of national policy, not law. Hence there are considerable uncertainties with regard to the implementation of the precautionary approach.

Third, considering that the decision-making process of the precautionary approach essentially involves national policy, international courts and tribunals seem to encounter considerable difficulties with its application to a particular case where application of this approach is at issue. It is not surprising that international courts have been wary about applying the precautionary approach in international disputes. In the 1995 *Nuclear Tests II* and 1997 *Gabčíkovo-Nagymaros Project* cases, the ICJ made, in fact, no explicit reference to the 'precautionary principle', although the applicability of this principle was at issue in the judicial process. The judicial hesitation can also be seen in judgments of the International Tribunal for the Law of the Sea (ITLOS). Thus, no explicit mention was made of the precautionary approach in the 2001 *MOX Plant* and 2003 *Land Reclamation* cases, while the application of the 'precautionary principle' was discussed by the disputing parties. Furthermore, the WTO Appellate Body, in the *Beef Hormones* case, took the view that: 'Whether it [the precautionary principle] has been widely accepted by Members as a principle of *general* or *customary international law* appears less than clear'.[101] Thus the Panel did not make any definitive finding with regard to the legal status of this principle in international law.[102]

In summary, the normativity of the precautionary approach is modest as a rule of conduct and a rule for adjudication. It is not suggested, however, that the precautionary approach has no normative force in international adjudication. The precautionary approach can be used as an element of interpretation of existing rules of international law.[103] In the context of the conservation of marine living resources, an illustrative example on this matter may be provided by the 1999 *Southern Bluefin Tuna* case. While ITLOS did not explicitly refer to 'the precautionary principle', the Tribunal pronounced that: 'In the view of the Tribunal, the parties should in the circumstances act with prudence and caution to ensure that effective conservation measures are taken

99 F. Gonsález-Laxe, 'The Precautionary Principle in Fisheries Management' (2005) 29 *Marine Policy* p. 496.

100 Birnie, Boyle and Redgwell, *International Law and the Environment*, pp. 163–164.

101 Report of the Appellate Body, EC Measures Concerning Meat and Meat Products (Hormones), WT/DS26/AB/R, WT/DS48/AB/R, 45–46, para. 123 (16 January 1998).

102 *Ibid.*

103 Y. Tanaka, 'Rethinking *Lex Ferenda* in International Adjudication' (2008) 51 *GYIL* pp. 489–493; A. Boyle, 'Further Development of the Law of the Sea Convention: Mechanisms for Change' (2005) 54 *ICLQ* pp. 573–574.

to prevent serious harm to the stocks of southern bluefin tuna'.[104] ITLOS further stated that 'although the Tribunal cannot conclusively assess the scientific evidence presented by the parties, it finds that measures should be taken as a matter of urgency to preserve the rights of the parties and to avert further deterioration of the southern bluefin tuna stock'.[105] In so ruling, ITLOS appeared to take account of the precautionary approach as an element of the interpretation of the requirement of urgency under Article 290 of the LOSC.[106] More recently, the ICJ, in the 2010 *Pulp Mills on the River Uruguay* case, explicitly stated that 'a precautionary approach may be relevant in the interpretation and application of the provisions of the Statute [of the River Uruguay]'.[107]

6 ENSURING COMPLIANCE

The implementation of substantive rules cannot be ensured without effective compliance mechanisms. Thus it becomes necessary to explore mechanisms for ensuring effective compliance with rules concerning the conservation of marine species on the high seas. Whilst the definition of the concept of compliance in international law may vary according to writers, compliance may be defined broadly as the behaviour of a State which conforms to its international obligations.

6.1 Flag State responsibility and its limits

It is beyond serious argument that the flag State has the primary responsibility to ensure compliance with rules relating to conservation of marine species on the high seas by vessels flying its flag. However, there is a concern that the effective implementation of the flag State's jurisdiction over fishing vessels is undermined by the practice of flag of convenience States which often lack the will and the capability to properly regulate fishing activities by vessels flying its flag. Fishing vessels can also easily evade the regulation of the flag State by the simple expedient of re-flagging to another State.[108] Furthermore, the effectiveness of conservation measures taken by coastal States or regional fisheries organisations is seriously undermined by illegal, unreported and unregulated (IUU) fishing.[109] According to the FAO, IUU fishing can be defined as follows.[110]

104 The *Southern Bluefin Tuna* cases (New Zealand v Japan; Australia v Japan), Requests for Provisional Measures, (1999) 38 *ILM* p. 1634, para. 77.

105 *Ibid.*, para. 80.

106 Separate Opinion by Judge Tullio Treves, *ibid.*, p. 1645, paras. 8–9. See also Separate Opinion of Judge Laing, *ibid.*, p. 1642, para. 19; Separate Opinion of Judge ad hoc Shearer, *ibid.*, p. 1650.

107 *Case Concerning Pulp Mills on the River Uruguay* (Argentina v Uruguay), ICJ Reports 2010, p. 51, para. 164.

108 Birnie, Boyle and Redgwell, *International Law and the Environment*, p. 743.

109 For a recent study concerning IUU fishing, see T. M. Ndiaye, 'Illegal, Unreported and Unregulated Fishing: Responses in General and in West Africa' (2011) 10 *Chinese Journal of International Law* pp. 373 *et seq.*

110 Paragraph 3 of FAO, *International Plan of Action to Prevent, Deter and Eliminate Illegal, Unreported and Unregulated Fishing* (Rome, FAO, 2001). This instrument is available at: ftp.fao.org/docrep/fao/012/y1224e/y1224e00.pdf. See also W. Edeson, 'The International Plan of Action on Illegal,

3.1 Illegal fishing refers to activities:

3.1.1 conducted by national or foreign vessels in waters under the jurisdiction of a State, without the permission of that State, or in contravention of its laws and regulations;

3.1.2 conducted by vessels flying the flag of States that are Parties to a relevant regional fisheries management organization but operate in contravention of the conservation and management measures adopted by that organization and by which the States are bound, or relevant provisions of the applicable international law; or

3.1.3 in violation of national laws or international obligations, including those undertaken by cooperating States to a relevant regional fisheries management organization.

3.2 Unreported fishing refers to fishing activities:

3.2.1 which have not been reported, or have been misreported, to the relevant national authority, in contravention of national laws and regulations; or

3.2.2 undertaken in the area of competence of a relevant regional fisheries management organization which have not been reported or have been misreported, in contravention of the reporting procedures of that organization.

3.3 Unregulated fishing refers to fishing activities:

3.3.1 in the area of application of a relevant regional fisheries management organization that are conducted by vessels without nationality, or by those flying the flag of a State not party to that organization, or by a fishing entity, in a manner that is not consistent with or contravenes the conservation and management measures of that organization; or

3.3.2 in areas or for fish stocks in relation to which there are no applicable conservation or management measures and where such fishing activities are conducted in a manner inconsistent with State responsibilities for the conservation of living marine resources under international law.

In response, various treaties and non-binding instruments attempt to strengthen the flag State's responsibility. An example is provided by the 1993 Agreement to Promote Compliance with International Conservation and Management Measures (hereafter the FAO Compliance Agreement).[111] Article III of the Compliance Agreement provides flag State responsibility in some detail. For instance, Article III(3) prohibits each Party from authorising any fishing vessel entitled to fly its flag to be used for fishing on the high seas unless the Party is satisfied that it is able to exercise effectively its responsibilities under this Agreement. Article III(5) further prohibits any Party from authorising 'any fishing vessel, previously registered in the territory of another Party that has undermined the effectiveness of international conservation measures, to be used for fishing on the high seas' unless certain conditions are satisfied. The 1995 UN Fish Stocks

Unreported and Unregulated Fishing: The Legal Context of a Non-Legally Binding Instrument' (2001) 16 *IJMCL* pp. 603–623.

111 Paragraph 10 of Preamble. The FAO Compliance Agreement entered into force on 24 April 2003. Text in (1994) 33 *ILM* pp. 968.

Agreement also attempts to strengthen 'the effective control' by the flag State as well as international cooperation in this matter.[112]

However, it appears doubtful whether States often involved with IUU fisheries as well as flags of convenience will ratify the FAO Compliance Agreement or the UN Fish Stocks Agreement in the near future.[113] It must also be noted that many developing States are facing financial and human resources constraints in preventing illegal fishing by foreign fleets.[114]

Overall it may have to be accepted that the flag State jurisdiction alone is inadequate to ensure effective compliance with rules relating to conservation of marine living resources. Hence there will be a need to explore more concerted mechanisms for ensuring effective compliance. In this respect, it is of particular interest to note that non-flag measures are increasingly taken by regional fisheries bodies. Such measures may be divided into two categories: inspection at sea and inspection in port. Each category is further divided into two sub-categories: inspection of the Contracting Party vessels and inspection of non-Contracting Party vessels.[115]

6.2 At-sea inspection of vessels of the Contracting Parties

An example of at-sea inspection of Contracting Party vessels is to be found in the 1995 Fish Stocks Agreement. Article 21(1) of the Agreement provides that:

> In any high seas area covered by a subregional or regional fisheries management organization or arrangement, a state Party which is a member of, or a participant in, such organization or arrangement may, through its duly authorized inspectors, board and inspect, in accordance with paragraph 2, fishing vessels flying the flag of another State Party to this Agreement, whether or not such State Party is also a member of, or a participant in, the organization or arrangement, for the purpose of ensuring compliance with conservation and management measures for straddling fish stocks and highly migratory fish stocks established by that organization or arrangement.[116]

Thus States are required to establish procedures for boarding and inspection through subregional or regional fisheries management organisations or arrangements pursuant to Article 21(2). If, within two years of the adoption of this Agreement, any organisation or arrangement has not established such procedures, boarding and inspection shall, pending the establishment of such procedures, be conducted in accordance with Article 21 and the basic procedures set out in Article 22.[117]

Where there are clear grounds for believing that a vessel has breached the conservation measures referred to in Article 21(1), the inspecting State is to promptly notify the

[112] See Articles 18, 19 and 20.

[113] As at June 2010, the number of Parties to the FAO Compliance Agreement is thirty-nine.

[114] Hayashi, 'IUU Fishing', p. 96.

[115] For a recent analysis in some detail of non-flag State measures, see Tanaka, 'The Changing Approaches', pp. 318 *et seq.*

[116] However, Article 21(15) contains an exception to Article 21(1).

[117] Article 21(3).

flag State of the alleged violation under Article 21(5). The flag State is obliged either to fulfil its obligation to investigate and take enforcement action with respect to the vessel, or to authorise the inspecting State to investigate pursuant to Article 21(6). Where the flag State has failed to respond or failed to take action, the inspectors may require the master to assist in further investigation including, where appropriate, bringing the vessel to the nearest appropriate port by virtue of Article 21(8).

However, the flag State may, at any time, take action to fulfil its obligations under Article 19 with respect to an alleged violation. Where the vessel is under the direction of the inspecting State, the inspecting State shall, at the request of the flag State, release the vessel to the flag State in accordance with Article 21(12). At-sea inspection of Contracting Party vessels is echoed by some regional fisheries organisations, such as the North Pacific Anadromous Fish Commission (NPAFC),[118] Commission for the Conservation of Antarctic Marine Living Resources (CCAMLR Commission),[119] Northwest Atlantic Fisheries Organization (NAFO),[120] Northeast Atlantic Fisheries Commission (NEAFC),[121] and the Central Bering Sea Observer Programme.[122] At-sea inspection calls for three brief observations.

First, at-sea inspection of Contracting Party vessels rests on the consent of the Party. Furthermore, the ultimate discretion respecting prosecution and sanction is always left to the flag State.[123] Hence at-sea inspection of Contracting Party vessels cannot be considered as an exception to the principle of the exclusive jurisdiction of the flag State.

Second, the inspection schemes do not seek to establish a regime applicable to high seas fisheries in general. Indeed, the Fish Stocks Agreement regulates only straddling and highly migratory fish stocks and, consequently, the Agreement does not apply to fish stocks found on the high seas alone. The scope of jurisdiction of regional fisheries organisations is also limited to certain regions and specific species.

Third, the at-sea inspection schemes are costly. Furthermore, such inspections should be undertaken with caution, since they may run the risk of creating disputes relating to participation, cost recovery, objectivity of inspections, interference with

118 Article V of the 1992 Convention for the Conservation of Anadromous Stocks in the North Pacific Ocean.

119 The CCAMLR System of Inspection. This document was appended to the Schedule of Conservation Measures in Force 2010/11 Season. The document is available at: www.ccamlr.org/pu/E/e_pubs/cm/10-11/all.pdf.

120 Chapter IV of the Northwest Atlantic Fisheries Organization, *Conservation and Enforcement Measures*, NAFO/FC Doc. 11/1 (updated 3 December 2010).

121 Chapter IV of the NEAFC, Scheme of Control and Enforcement (London, February 2010). Entered into Force on 6 February 2010.

122 Article XI(5) of the 1999 Convention on the Conservation and Management of Pollock Resources in the Central Bering Sea. Entered into force on 8 December 1995. The text of the Convention is available at: www.afsc.noaa.gov/REFM/CBS/Docs/Convention%20on%20Conservation%20of%20Pollock%20in%20Central%20Bering%20Sea.pdf.

123 See Article XI(7)(c) of the 1994 Convention on the Conservation and Management of Pollock Resources in the Central Bering Sea; Article V(2)(d) of the 1992 Convention for the Conservation of Anadromous Stocks in the North Pacific Ocean; Article XI of the CCAMLR System of Inspection; Articles 38, 39, 40 of the Northwest Atlantic Fisheries Organization, *Conservation and Enforcement Measures*, NAFO/FC Doc. 10/1 (updated 17 December 2009); Articles 30 and 31 of the NEAFC

fishing activity, economic loss, and the evidentiary value of surveillance information as well as inspection reports.[124]

6.3 At-sea inspection of non-Contracting Party vessels

At-sea inspection of vessels of non-Contracting Parties is undertaken by some regional fisheries organisations. For instance, Chapter VI of the 2010 NAFO Conservation and Enforcement Measures provides the Scheme to Promote Compliance by non-Contracting Party Vessels with Recommendations established by NAFO (hereafter the 2010 NAFO Scheme). Under Article 53(1) of the NAFO Scheme, NAFO inspectors shall request permission to board non-Contracting Party vessels that are sighted engaging in fishing activities in the Regulatory Area. If the vessel consents to be boarded, the inspectors' findings are to be transmitted to the Secretariat without delay. The Secretariat is required to transmit this information to all Contracting Parties and other relevant Regional Fisheries Management Organisations within one business day of receiving this information, and to the flag State as soon as possible. Under Article 53(2), where evidence so warrants, a Contracting Party may take such action as may be appropriate in accordance with international law. Similar procedures for inspecting non-Contracting Party vessels can be seen in the 2010 NEAFC Scheme of Control and Enforcement (hereafter the 2010 NEAFC Scheme).[125]

At-sea inspection of non-Contracting Party vessels needs careful consideration with regard to its legitimacy. In this respect, an issue that needs particular attention involves the presumption of undermining conservation and enforcement measures by regional fisheries organisations. For instance, Article 37(2) of the 2010 NEAFC Scheme provides that the non-Contracting Party vessel that has been sighted or by other means identified as engaging in fishing activities in the Convention Area is presumed to be undermining the Recommendations established under the Convention.[126] The presumption is provided in regulatory measures of other fisheries organisations,[127] such as NAFO,[128] the Indian Ocean Tuna Commission (IOTC),[129] the International Commission for the Conservation of Atlantic Tunas (ICCAT),[130] and the CCAMLR Commission.[131]

Scheme of Control and Enforcement. See also, R. Rayfuse, *Non-Flag State Enforcement in High Seas Fisheries* (Leiden, Nijhoff, 2004), p. 329.

124 R. Rayfuse, 'To our Children's Children's Children: From Promoting to Achieving Compliance in High Seas Fisheries', (2005) 20 *IJMCL* p. 520.

125 NEAFC, Scheme of Control and Enforcement (London, February 2010).

126 See also Article 37(3). However, vessels of the cooperating non-Contracting Parties under Article 34 are exempted from the presumption.

127 R. Rayfuse, 'Regulation and Enforcement in the Law of the Sea: Emerging Assertions of a Right to Non-Flag State Enforcement in the High Seas Fisheries and Disarmament Contexts' (2005) 24 *Australian Yearbook of International Law* p. 188.

128 Article 52 of the 2010 NAFO Scheme.

129 Paragraph 2 of Resolution 01/03 Establishing a Scheme to Promote Compliance by Non-Contracting Party Vessels with Resolutions Established by IOTC, 2001.

130 Paragraph 1 of the Recommendation by ICCAT Concerning the Ban on Landings and Transshipments of Vessels from Non-Contracting Parties Identified as Having Committed a Serious Infringement, entered into force 21 June 1999. This recommendation is available at: www.iccat.int/Documents/Recs/compendiopdf-e/1998-11-e.pdf.

131 Paragraph 4 of the CCAMLR Conservation Measure 10-07 (2009).

In essence, the presumption of undermining the effectiveness in the regulatory areas shifts the burden of proving innocence to vessels of non-Contracting Parties. Nonetheless, there may be scope to consider the question whether the reversal of the burden of proof is not contrary to the principle of freedom of fishing. With some exceptions, such as high seas fishing for anadromous and catadromous species, high seas fishing is, prima facie, lawful in international law. In accordance with the principle *pacta tertiis nec nocent nec prosunt*, the regional treaty is not binding upon non-Contracting Parties unless rules of the treaty become part of customary law. In positive international law, there is no obligation upon the non-Contracting Parties to *automatically* accept regulatory measures of regional fisheries organisations on the high seas. Furthermore, some fisheries organisations affirm that a State Party which is opposed to a regulatory measure adopted by a fisheries organisation is exempted from the application of the measure.[132] It appears unreasonable to argue that vessels of third States are automatically bound to the regulatory measures of the regional fisheries organs, while Member States may be released from such regulations by opposition. Overall there is a concern that the presumption of undermining the effectiveness of conservation measures may entail the risk of de facto applying these measures to non-Contracting Party vessels on the high seas without their explicit consent.

6.4 Port inspection of Contracting Party vessels

At the regional level, port inspection of vessels of the Contracting Parties was, for the first time, embodied in the 1994 Federal States of Micronesia Arrangement for Regional Fisheries Access.[133] At the global level, this mechanism was enshrined in the FAO Compliance Agreement[134] and the 1995 Fish Stocks Agreement. Article 23 of the Fish Stocks Agreement provides that:

1. A port State has the right and the duty to take measures, in accordance with international law, to promote the effectiveness of subregional, regional and global conservation and management measures. When taking such measures a port State shall not discriminate in form or in fact against the vessels of any State.
2. A port State may, *inter alia*, inspect documents, fishing gear and catch on board fishing vessels, when such vessels are voluntarily in its ports or at its offshore terminals.

With respect to action after inspection, Article 23(3) specifies that the port State may prohibit landings and transshipment where it has been established that the catch has been taken in a manner which undermines the effectiveness of subregional, regional,

[132] For instance, Article 12(2)(b)(c) of the NEAFC Convention; Article XII(1) and (3) of the 1978 Convention on Future Multilateral Cooperation in the Northwest Atlantic Fisheries; Article VIII(3)(c) and (e) of the 1966 International Convention for the Conservation of Atlantic Tunas.

[133] Entered into force on 23 September 1995. The text of this Arrangement was reproduced in T. Aqorau and A. Bergin, 'The Federal States of Micronesia Arrangement for Regional Fisheries Access' (1997) 12 *IJMCL* pp. 57–80.

[134] Article V(2).

or global conservation and management measures on the high seas. Port State inspection of Contracting Party vessels is also undertaken by regional fisheries organisations, such as the ICCAT,[135] IOTC,[136] NAFO,[137] and NEAFC.[138]

In 2009, the Agreement on Port State Measures to Prevent, Deter and Eliminate Illegal, Unreported and Unregulated Fishing (hereafter the 2009 Agreement) was adopted under the auspices of the FAO.[139] The 2009 Agreement recognises, in its Preamble, that 'port State measures provide a powerful and cost-effective means of preventing, deterring and eliminating illegal, unreported and unregulated fishing'. This Agreement is global in scope and applies to all ports under Article 3(5). Under Article 3(3), this Agreement applies to fishing conducted in marine areas that is illegal, unreported or unregulated and to fishing related activities in support of such fishing. When a Party has sufficient proof that a vessel seeking entry into its port has engaged in IUU fishing or fishing related activities in support of such fishing, the Party shall deny that vessel entry into its ports pursuant to Article 9(4).

In relation to this, it is notable that several regional fisheries organs adopted a mandatory certification requirement. The case in point may be the CCAMLR Catch Documentation Scheme for *Dissostichus* spp. (toothfish), which became binding on all members on 7 May 2000.[140] Under this Scheme, each Contracting Party shall require that each master or authorised representative of its flag vessels authorised to engage in harvesting of *Dissostichus eleginoides* (Patagonian toothfish) and/or *Dissostichus mawsoni* (Antarctic toothfish) complete a *Dissostichus* catch document (DCD) for the catch landed or transshipped on each occasion that it lands or tranships *Dissostichus* spp. Each Contracting Party shall require that each landing of *Dissostichus* spp. at its port and each transshipment of *Dissostichus* spp. to its vessels be accompanied by a completed DCD. The landing of *Dissostichus* spp. without a catch document is prohibited. This is a sort of market-related measure and the consistency with WTO law, in particular, Article XX of the 1994 General Agreement on Tariffs and Trade, may be at issue. Thus such measures should be adopted and implemented in accordance with principles, rights and obligations established in WTO Agreements, and implemented in a fair, transparent and non-discriminatory manner.[141]

135 Recommendation by ICCAT for a Revised Port Inspection Scheme, available at: www.iccat.int/Documents/Recs/ACT_COMP_2007_ENG.pdf. Entered into force on 13 June 1998.

136 Resolution 05/03 Relating to the Establishment of an IOTC Programme of Inspection in Port. This document is available at: www.iotc.org/files/proceedings/misc/ComReportsTexts/resolutions_E.pdf.

137 Chapter V of the Northwest Atlantic Fisheries Organization, *Conservation and Enforcement Measures*, NAFO/FC Doc. 11/1 (updated 3 December 2010).

138 Chapter V of the NEAFC, Scheme of Control and Enforcement (London, February 2010).

139 The text of the Agreement is available at: www.fao.org/Legal/treaties/037t-e.pdf. Not yet in force.

140 Catch Documentation Scheme for *Dissostichus* spp. was embodied in Conservation Measure 10-05 (2009).

141 The 2001 International Plan of Action to Prevent, Deter and Eliminate Illegal, Unreported and Unregulated Fishing, para. 66.

6.5 Port inspection of non-Contracting Party vessels

Some regional fisheries organisations apply port inspection of non-Contracting Party vessels. One might take the 2010 NAFO Scheme as an example. Article 54(1) of the Scheme obliges masters of non-Contracting Party vessels intending 'to call into a port [to] notify the competent authority of the port State Contracting Party in accordance with the provisions of Article 48'. The port State Contracting Party is required to forward without delay this information to the flag State of the vessel and to the Executive Secretary. Article 54(2) further provides that: 'The port State Contracting Party shall prohibit the entry into its ports of vessels that have not given the required prior notice and provided the information referred to in paragraph 1'. When a non-Contracting Party vessel enters a port of any Contracting Party, the vessel is to be inspected by authorised Contracting Party officials pursuant to Article 54(3). This provision ensures that the vessel will not be allowed to land or tranship until this inspection has taken place; and that such inspections shall include the vessel's documents, log books, fishing gear, catch on board and any other matter relating to the vessel's activities in the Regulatory Area. Inspections of non-Contracting Party vessels in port are also provided for in the IOTC,[142] ICCAT,[143] CCAMLR Commission[144] and NEAFC.[145]

Given that the port is part of the internal waters which are under the territorial sovereignty of the coastal State, it is arguable that the State is entitled to regulate access to its ports and landings and transshipments, without discrimination among vessels. However, at least two issues need further consideration.

First, port inspection seems to shift the burden of proving innocence to non-Contracting Party vessels. However, it seems difficult to establish evidence that fish on board were caught outside the Convention Area in practice. A question thus arises as to whether unilateral prohibition in port is equivalent to de facto application of regulatory measures of the coastal State towards the high seas. In this regard, as demonstrated by the *EU – Chile Swordfish* dispute,[146] the unilateral prohibition of access, landing and transshipments in the port may run the risk of producing a dispute between the port State and the fishing State.

Second, a concern is voiced that the current system of port inspections is not very effective due to insufficient vessel information and lack of compliance among port States.[147] Furthermore, vessels of non-Contracting Parties can avoid the port State inspection simply by using ports in non-Contracting Party States which will accept

[142] Paragraphs 4 and 5 of IOTC Resolution 05/03 Relating to the Establishment of an IOTC Programme of Inspection in Port.

[143] Paragraph 2 of the Recommendation by ICCAT Concerning the Ban on Landings and Transshipments.

[144] Paragraph 5 of the CCAMLR Conservation Measure 10-07 (2009).

[145] Articles 39 and 40 of the 2010 NEAFC Scheme.

[146] WTO, *Chile – Measures Affecting the Transit and Importation of Swordfish*, Request for the Establishment of a Panel by the European Communities, WT/DS193/2, 7 November 2000; International Tribunal for the Law of the Sea, *Case Concerning the Conservation and Sustainable Exploitation of Swordfish Stocks in the South-Eastern Pacific Ocean*, 20 December 2000.

[147] S. Flothmann et al., 'Closing Loopholes: Getting Illegal Fishing Under Control' (2010) 328 *Science* pp. 1235–1236.

their landings.[148] Thus there is a risk that the effectiveness of port inspection may be undermined by the practice of using a 'port of convenience'.

7 CONCLUSIONS

The matters considered in this chapter can be summarised under six points.

(i) Traditionally international law with regard to the conservation of marine living resources was dominated by the zonal management approach and the species specific approach. However, it has became apparent that the traditional approaches to conservation of marine living resources comprise limitations in three respects particularly:

- the lack of ecological consideration,
- difficulties with regard to the conservation of migratory species,
- weakness of obligations to conserve living resources in the EEZ and high seas.

In response, new concepts and approaches are increasingly enshrined in binding and non-binding international instruments. In this respect, the concept of sustainable development, the ecosystem approach and the precautionary approach are of particular importance.

(ii) The concept of sustainable development seeks in essence to reconcile the need for development with environmental protection. This concept is increasingly enshrined in various instruments respecting the conservation of marine living resources. However, the normative contents of the concept of sustainable development remain uncertain. Considering that eventually the concept of sustainable development requires a change in the quality and patterns of human life, it appears difficult for international courts and tribunals to review the validity of national action by applying the concept of sustainable development. Thus it is argued that the concept of sustainable development should be regarded as a factor guiding the behaviour of States and the proper interpretation of relevant rules in the judicial process.

(iii) Unlike the traditional species specific approach, the ecosystem approach seeks to protect marine ecosystems and the ecological conditions surrounding them within ecologically meaningful boundaries as a whole. In so doing, this approach can be considered as a useful means to enhance the effectiveness of conservation of marine species. However, this approach contains considerable uncertainties with regard to its specific contents. Thus the extent to which the ecosystem approach can legally direct the conduct of States is debatable. For the same reason, it may be difficult to determine a breach of a treaty obligation to apply this approach in international adjudication. Overall it is argued that the normativity of the ecosystem approach remains modest as a rule of conduct and a rule of adjudication.

(iv) The essence of the precautionary approach is that once a risk has been identified, the lack of scientific proof of cause and effect shall not be used as a reason for not taking action to protect the environment. The application of this approach strengthens

[148] Rayfuse, *Non-Flag State Enforcement*, p. 223; Flothmann et al., 'Closing Loopholes', p. 1236.

the environmental dimension of international law governing conservation of marine living resources. However, the decision-making process of the precautionary approach is closely linked to national policy. Accordingly, it appears difficult for international courts and tribunals to judge the conformity of the conduct of a State to treaty obligations respecting the implementation of the precautionary approach. Like the ecosystem approach, it may have to be accepted that the normativity of the precautionary approach remains modest as a rule of conduct and a rule of adjudication.

(v) The flag State has the primary responsibility to ensure compliance with rules with regard to the conservation of marine living resources on the high seas by vessels flying its flag. In reality, however, the effectiveness of the flag State responsibility is seriously undermined by the practice of flags of convenience, re-flagging and IUU fishing. In response, non-flag State measures are adopted by some regional fisheries organs. Such measures comprise at-sea inspection and port inspection of Contracting and non-Contracting Party vessels. However, inspection of non-Contracting Party vessels is not free from controversy because regulatory measures adopted by regional fisheries bodies are not *a priori* binding on third States. In this regard, there will be a need to enhance the legitimacy of conservation measures. A possible solution may be that regional fisheries organs invite all non-Contracting Parties which have interests in the regulatory areas to participate at meetings to adopt conservation measures as a cooperating Party.

(vi) Overall, it may have to be admited that the existing rules of international law concerning the conservation of marine living resources comprise many limitations. In broad terms, however, it can be observed that the development of international law in this field represents a paradigm shift from the laissez-faire system of the freedom of fishing to conservation of marine living resources. In this regard, it must be recalled that, as early as 1974, the ICJ in the *Fisheries Jurisdiction* case had already stated that: 'the former laissez-faire treatment of the living resources of the sea in the high seas has been replaced by a recognition of a duty to have due regard to the rights of other States and *the need of conservation for the benefit of all*'.[149]

FURTHER READING

There are many books and articles with regard to the conservation of marine living resources. Only recent monographs on this subject will be listed here.

R. J. Baird, *Aspects of Illegal, Unreported and Unregulated Fishing in the Southern Ocean* (Dordrecht, Springer, 2006).

R. R. Churchill and D. Owen, *The EC Common Fisheries Policy* (Oxford University Press, 2010).

Guifang Xue, *China and International Fisheries Law and Policy* (Leiden, Nijhoff, 2005).

[149] Emphasis added. ICJ Reports 1974, p. 31, para. 72 of the judgment between the United Kingdom and Iceland.

T. Henriksen, G. Hønneland and A. Sydes, *Law and Politics in Ocean Governance: The UN Fish Stocks Agreement and Regional Fisheries Management Regimes* (Leiden, Nijhoff, 2006).

E. Hey (ed.), *Developments in International Fisheries Law* (The Hague, Kluwer, 1999).

G. Hønneland, *Russian Fisheries Management: The Precautionary Approach in Theory and Practice* (Leiden, Nijhoff, 2004).

S. B. Kaye, *International Fisheries Management* (The Hague, Kluwer, 2001).

M. Markowski, *The International Law of EEZ Fisheries: Principles and Implementation* (Groningen, Europa Law Publishing, 2010).

S. Marr, *The Precautionary Principle in the Law of the Sea: Modern Decision Making in International Law* (The Hague, Nijhoff, 2003).

M. H. Nordquist and J. N. Moore (eds.), *Current Fisheries Issues and the Food and Agriculture Organization of the United Nations* (The Hague, Kluwer, 2000).

F. Orrego-Vicuña, *The Changing Law of High Seas Fisheries* (Cambridge University Press, 1999).

M. A. Palma, M. Tsamenyi and W. Edeson, *Promoting Sustainable Fisheries: The International Legal and Policy Framework to Combat Illegal, Unreported and Unregulated Fishing* (Leiden, Nijhoff, 2010).

R. G. Rayfuse, *Non-Flag State Enforcement in High Seas Fisheries* (Leiden, Nijhoff, 2004).

O. V. Stokke, *Governing High Seas Fisheries: The Interplay of Global and Regional Regimes* (Oxford University Press, 2001).

Y. Tanaka, *A Dual Approach to Ocean Governance: The Cases of Zonal and Integrated Management in International Law of the Sea* (Surrey, England, Ashgate, 2008) (Chapters 2 and 3).

D. Vignes, G. Cataldi, and R. C. Raigón, *Le droit international de la pêche maritime* (Brussels, Bruylant, 2000).

M. Young, *Trading Fish, Saving Fish: The Interaction between Regimes in International Law* (Cambridge University Press, 2011).

8

Protection of the Marine Environment

Main Issues

Given that a healthy marine environment provides a foundation for all life, marine environmental protection is an issue of considerable importance in the law of the sea. In principle, the law regulates marine pollution according to its sources, such as land-based pollution, vessel-source pollution, dumping, pollution from seabed activities under national jurisdiction, pollution from activities in the Area, and pollution through the atmosphere. Accordingly, this chapter will seek to examine the rules of international law regulating marine pollution arising from these sources. Particular focus will be on the following issues:

(i) What is the significance of the LOSC in marine environmental protection?
(ii) Why do rules regulating land-based marine pollution remain weak at the global level?
(iii) What are the new elements to regional treaties in the regulation of land-based pollution?
(iv) What are the mechanisms for regulating vessel-source marine pollution?
(v) How is it possible to ensure compliance with relevant rules governing marine environmental protection?

1 INTRODUCTION

Currently marine pollution is an increasing threat to a healthy marine environment. Indeed, marine pollution may severely damage the environment, including ecosystems, and human health. It is common knowledge that mercury emissions from a factory at Minamata in Japan had poisoned fish and caused serious disease endangering the lives of coastal communities. It would be no exaggeration to say that the welfare of coastal populations relies essentially on a sound marine environment. Thus there appears to be a general sense that the protection of the marine environment is considered as a common interest of the international community as a whole.

Despite its vital importance, the regulation of marine pollution has attracted little attention until recently because of low awareness of environmental protection. It is only since World War II that international regulation of marine pollution has begun to develop. In the 1950s, the development of treaties regulating marine pollution was still slow moving. While the first multilateral treaty regulating oil pollution, i.e. the International Convention for the Prevention of Pollution of the Sea by Oil, was adopted in 1954,[1] the effect of this Convention was only limited. The 1958 Convention on the Territorial Seas and the Contiguous Zone (the TSC) and the 1958 Convention on the Continental Shelf contained no provision dealing directly with the protection of the marine environment. The Convention on the High Seas covered only a few sources of marine pollution, namely the discharge of oil from ships or pipelines or resulting from the exploitation and exploration of the seabed and its subsoil (Article 24), and the dumping of radioactive waste (Article 25). The result was that, subject only to the few limitations imposed by customary international law, States had a wide discretion to pollute the oceans.

By the late 1960s, however, awareness of the serious threat of oil spilling into the marine environment posed by large oil tankers had become widespread. In particular, the 1967 *Torrey Canyon* disaster exemplified the scale of oil pollution from a modern tanker.[2] This incident raised public awareness of the risk of accidental vessel-source pollution and, as a consequence, the International Convention Relating to Intervention on the High Seas in Cases of Oil Pollution Casualities was adopted in 1969.[3] In the same year, the International Convention on Civil Liability for Oil Pollution Damage was also adopted.[4]

In the 1970s and the 1980s, treaties regulating marine pollution were increasingly concluded. In particular, it is notable that the International Convention for the Prevention of Pollution from Ships was concluded under the auspices of the IMO in 1973.[5] This Convention was subsequently modified by the Protocol of 1978 relating thereto. This Convention, as modified by the 1978 Protocol, is known as, in short form, 'MARPOL 73/78' (hereafter MARPOL).[6] As will be seen, MARPOL provides the key instrument regulating pollution from ships. In this period, the scope of treaties was further extended to cover the regulation of dumping and land-based marine pollution. Furthermore, many treaties were concluded to protect certain marine areas at the regional level. There is little doubt that the protection of the marine environment is currently one of the most important issues in the law of the sea. Considering this subject, particular attention must be devoted to three points.

[1] 327 *UNTS* p. 3. Entered into force on 26 July 1958.

[2] The *Torrey Canyon* was an American-owned super-tanker under the Liberian flag. Because of the wreck, 80,000 tons of oil escaped into the sea and polluted large areas of the coasts of England and France.

[3] 970 *UNTS* p. 212; (1970) 9 *ILM* p. 25. Entered into force on 6 May 1975.

[4] (1970) 9 *ILM* p. 45. Entered into force on 19 June 1975. This Convention was replaced by the 1992 Protocol.

[5] This Convention replaced the 1954 Oil Pollution Convention.

[6] The 1978 Protocol entered into force in 1983. For the text of the Convention see IMO, *MARPOL 73/78: Consolidated Edition 2006* (London, IMO, 2006); A. V. Lowe and S. A. G. Talmon (eds.), *The Legal Order of the Oceans: Basic Documents on the Law of the Sea* (Oxford, Hart Publishing 2009), p. 105. The MARPOL Convention will be discussed in section 6.1 of this chapter.

First, marine pollution may be transported beyond man-made limits and boundaries through currents and winds. As shipping moves freely between the different jurisdictional zones, pollution from vessels may easily spread beyond maritime delimitation lines. Thus international collaboration between States becomes a prerequisite to regulate marine pollution.

Second, the ecological and physical conditions of the oceans may change with the passage of time. The degradation of the healthy marine environment may also be accelerated by human activities in the oceans. Hence there is a need to flexibly adapt the rules and standards regulating marine pollution to new environmental situations.

Third, traditionally, compliance with rules of international law has been ensured by self-regulation on the basis of reciprocity, and the same applies to the law of the sea. In essence, the principle of reciprocity seeks to secure the national interests of each State on the basis of the symmetry of rights and obligations.[7] Nonetheless, like human rights treaties, treaties concerning marine environmental protection do not seek to ensure reciprocal engagements and advantages for the mutual benefit of the Contracting Parties. The effectiveness of marine environmental protection cannot be supported by relying exclusively on self-regulation based on the principle of reciprocity. Hence there is a need to explore more institutionalised compliance mechanisms. Noting these issues, this chapter will explore the rules applicable to the protection of the marine environment in the law.

2 TYPOLOGY OF MARINE POLLUTION

2.1 General considerations

Article 1(1)(4) of the LOSC defines 'marine pollution' as:

> the introduction by man, directly or indirectly, of substances or energy into the marine environment, including estuaries, which results or is likely to result in such deleterious effects as harm to living resources and marine life, hazards to human health, hindrance to marine activities, including fishing and other legitimate uses of the sea, impairment of quality for use of sea water and reduction of amenities.

This provision calls for three brief comments. First, this is an open definition which may include all sources – the existing and new sources – of marine pollution. Second, the definition covers substances or energy which 'is likely to result' in deleterious effects. It would follow that potentially harmful effects on the marine environment

[7] The concept of reciprocity may be defined as the relationship between two or more states according each other identical or equivalent treatment. B. Simma, 'Reciprocity', in R. Bernhardt (ed.), *Encyclopedia of Public International Law*, vol. 4 (Amsterdam, Elsevier, 2000), pp. 29–30; H. Bull, *The Anarchical Society: A Study of Order in World Politics*, 3rd edn (New York, Palgrave, 2002), p. 134; M. Virally, 'Le principe de réciprocité dans le droit international contemporain' (1967-III) 122 *RCADI* p. 19.

can also become the object of regulation. Third, as shown in the reference to 'living resources and marine life', this definition makes clear that 'the marine environment' encompasses marine living organisms. Hence the protection of the marine environment also involves the protection of marine species.

Specifically, the LOSC identifies six sources of marine pollution:

(i) pollution from land-based sources,
(ii) pollution from seabed activities subject to national jurisdiction,
(iii) pollution from activities in the Area,
(iv) pollution by dumping,
(v) pollution from vessels, and
(vi) pollution from or through the atmosphere.

In broad terms, these sources of marine pollution can be divided into four principal categories: (i) land-based marine pollution, (ii) vessel-source marine pollution, (iii) dumping, and (iv) pollution from seabed activities. The nature of the problem associated with each type of pollution can be outlined as follows.

2.2 Land-based marine pollution

Land-based marine pollution includes pollution from land-based activities and pollution from or through the atmosphere. It is estimated that land-based pollution and air pollution contribute approximately 80 per cent of marine pollution.[8] While land-based sources vary, such sources include municipal, industrial or agricultural sources, both fixed and mobile, discharges from which reach the marine environment, in particular: (i) from the coast, including from outfalls discharging directly into the marine environment and through run-off, (ii) through rivers, canals or other watercourses, including underground watercourses, (iii) via the atmosphere, and (iv) from activities conducted on offshore fixed or mobile facilities within the limits of national jurisdiction.[9]

Pollutants resulting from land-based activities include sewage, industrial discharges and agricultural run-off. Some of the contaminants produce eutrophication and oxygen depletion, resulting in loss of marine life and biological diversity. Other substances are directly toxic to humans.

Air pollution from land-based activities is another source of land-based pollution which contaminates the oceans with dissolved copper, nickel, cadmium, mercury, lead, zinc and synthetic organic compounds. Once emitted, these compounds stay in the air for weeks or more, and they finally reach the oceans.[10]

In a broad context, land-based marine pollution is a result of the imbalance between human populations and industrial activities and the limited capacity of the marine

[8] UN General Assembly, *Oceans and the Law of the Sea: Report of the Secretary-General*, 18 August 2004, A/59/62/Add.1, p. 29, para. 97.

[9] Paragraph 1(b) of the 1985 Montreal Guidelines for the Protection of the Marine Environment against Pollution from Land-Based Sources. Reproduced in H. Hohmann (ed.), *Basic Documents of International Environmental Law*, vol. 1 (London, Graham and Trotman, 1992), pp. 130–147.

[10] GESAMP, *A Sea of Troubles*, Reports and Studies, No. 70, 2001, p. 21.

environment to absorb the wastes they produce. Considering that approximately 40 per cent of the world's population live within 100 km of the coast, it is foreseeable that with rapid population growth, marine pollution from land-based activities will become more problematic.

2.3 Vessel-source marine pollution

Vessel-source pollution is of two kinds: operational and accidental.[11] Operational vessel-source pollution is produced by the normal operation of ships. Vessels with oil-burning diesel engines discharge some oil with their bilge water, and the fumes discharged through their funnels into the atmosphere will eventually return to the sea. In the early days of tanker operation, it was common practice that oil tankers washed their oil tanks by means of jets spraying seawater and disposed of the oily residue at sea. As a consequence, a considerable amount of oil was discharged into the sea, causing oil pollution. Currently this problem has been virtually eliminated by 'load on top' and 'crude oil washing' methods.[12]

However, more rules and higher standards are needed for the prevention of vessel-source pollution. As will be seen, the LOSC and MARPOL provide the principal legal framework for the regulation of vessel-source pollution. Marine pollution can also be caused through accidents involving vessels. Disasters caused by oil tankers, such as the *Torrey Canyon* (1967), *Amoco Cadiz* (1978), *Exxon Valdez* (1989), *Erika* (1999) and *Prestige* (2002), exemplify the scale and severity of the damage that has been caused to marine ecosystems as well as to coastal communities.[13]

Furthermore, growing attention is paid to the introduction of alien species through discharge of ballast water. A vessel needs to take on ballast water to stabilise it, especially when the vessel is unladen. However, discharge of ballast water into the sea may introduce invasive alien species which may produce negative impacts on marine ecosystems and damage economic activities in the oceans, such as fisheries, aquaculture, tourism and marine infrastructure. Most of the ballast water is taken from sea areas near the coast or ports and such areas are likely to be contaminated by human presence. Where ballast water is taken from a contaminated area, discharge of the water into another place may lead to the introduction of bacteria or viruses into the coastal waters of other States. In response to this problem, the International Convention for the

[11] P. Birnie, A. Boyle and C. Redgwell, *International Law and the Environment*, 3rd edn (Oxford University Press, 2009), p. 399.

[12] According to the 'load on top' method, tanks are to be cleaned by high-pressure hot-water cleaning machines, and the resulting oily mixtures pumped into a special slop tank. As oil is lighter than water, oil gradually floats to the surface. Later, only the water at the bottom is pumped into the sea, leaving only crude oil in the tank. Under the crude oil washing method, the tank is cleaned by using crude oil, i.e. the cargo itself. By spraying the oil onto the sediments clinging to the tank walls, the oil can turn them back into usable oil that can be pumped off with the rest of the cargo. This method became mandatory for new crude oil tankers of 20,000 tons and above by Annex I of MARPOL 73/78 (Regulation 13(6)). Concerning these methods, see www5.imo.org/SharePoint/mainframe.asp?topic_id=306.

[13] Data concerning major oil spill incidents at sea is available at: www.cedre.fr/en/cedre/index.php.

Control and Management of Ship's Ballast Water and Sediments was adopted under the auspices of the IMO in 2004.[14]

Invasive alien species are also introduced via vessels' external structures, such as the hulls, and internal piping. In response, the application of anti-fouling compounds to ships' hull is widely used. Yet anti-fouling substances can be harmful to the marine environment.[15] For instance, tributyltin (TBT), which is the most common and effective anti-fouling substance used to date, has proved to have adverse effects on marine life. In this regard, in October 2001, the International Convention on the Control of Harmful Anti-Fouling Systems on Ships was adopted.[16] This Convention places an obligation upon each Party to prohibit the application, re-application, installation, or use of harmful anti-fouling systems on ships in accordance with Article 4.[17]

In addition, there are growing concerns that high levels of man-made noise may have harmful effects upon marine living organisms, including marine mammals.[18] Significant levels of noise may be created by ships, marine dredging and construction activities as well as the oil and gas industry. The deployment of sonar for naval and scientific purposes is also a controversial source of acoustic marine pollution. On 31 August 2004, the European Parliament adopted a Resolution on the Environmental Effects of High-Intensity Active Naval Sonar. This resolution called upon the European Union and its Member States to adopt a moratorium on the deployment of high-intensity active naval sonars until a global assessment of their cumulative environmental impact on marine mammals, fish and other marine life has been completed.[19] Acoustic noise has also been discussed in the framework of the International Whaling Commission, the Convention on the Conservation of Migratory Species of Wild Animals, the Agreement on the Conservation of Small Cetaceans of the Baltic and North Seas and the Agreement on the Conservation of Cetaceans of the Black Sea, Mediterranean Sea and Contiguous Atlantic Area.[20]

2.4 Dumping at sea

The second type of ocean-based pollution involves dumping at sea. Article 1(5)(a) of the LOSC defines 'dumping' as:

[14] For an analysis in some detail of this Convention, see M. Tsimplis, 'Alien Species Stay Home: The International Convention for the Control and Management of Ships' Ballast Water and Sediments 2004' (2005) 19 *IJMCL* pp. 411–482. The text of the Convention was reproduced in this article.

[15] Generally on this issue, see J. Roberts and M. Tsamenyi, 'International Legal Options for the Control of Biofouling on International Vessels' (2008) 32 *Marine Policy* pp. 559–569.

[16] For the text of the Convention, IMO, AFS/CONF/26, 18 October 2001. Entered into force on 17 September 2008.

[17] Under Article 2(2), 'anti-fouling system' means 'a coating, paint, surface treatment, surface, or device that is used on a ship to control or prevent attachment of unwanted organisms'.

[18] Generally on this issue, see K. N. Scott, 'International Regulation of Undersea Noise' (2004) 53 *ICLQ* pp. 287–324; J. M. Van Dyke, E. A. Gardner and J. R. Morgan, 'Whales, Submarines, and Active Sonar' (2004) 18 *Ocean Yearbook* pp. 330–363.

[19] Resolution of 28 October 2004 (P6_TA(2004)0047), *Official Journal of the European Union*, C 174 E/186, 14 July 2005.

[20] I. Papanicolopulu, 'Underwater Noise' (2008) 23 *IJMCL* pp. 365–376.

(i) any deliberate disposal of wastes or other matter from vessels, aircraft, platforms or other man-made structures at sea;
(ii) any deliberate disposal of vessels, aircraft, platforms or other man-made structures at sea.[21]

However, under Article 1(5)(b), 'dumping' does not include:

(i) the disposal of wastes or other matter incidental to, or derived from the normal operations of vessels, aircraft, platforms or other man-made structures at sea and their equipment, other than wastes or other matter transported by or to vessels, aircraft, platforms or other man-made structures at sea, operating for the purpose of disposal of such matter or derived from the treatment of such wastes or other matter on such vessels, aircraft, platforms or structures;
(ii) placement of matter for a purpose other than the mere disposal thereof, provided that such placement is not contrary to the aims of this Convention.

In the 1950s and 1960s, dumping had been a popular way of disposing of waste resulting from land-based activities. Such wastes include radioactive matter, military materials including obsolete weapons and explosives, dredged materials, sewage sludge and industrial waste. In particular, dredged materials account for about 80 to 90 per cent of all dumping.[22] At the global level, dumping is regulated primarily by the 1972 International Convention on the Prevention of Marine Pollution by Dumping of Wastes and Other Matter (hereafter the 1972 London Dumping Convention),[23] which is to be superseded by the 1996 London Protocol.[24]

2.5 Pollution from seabed activities

Marine pollution can be caused by seabed activities. In reality, the accidental oil pollution from the BP oil rig blast in April 2010 exemplified the risk of environmental disaster arising from oil exploitation in the seabed. Marine pollution may also be caused by drilling operations which produce drilling mud, drill cuttings and produced waters.

[21] The 1996 Protocol to the Convention on the Prevention of Marine Pollution by Dumping of Wastes and Other Matter defines dumping as: '(i) any deliberate disposal into the sea of wastes or other matter from vessels, aircraft, platforms or other man-made structures at sea; (ii) any deliberate disposal into the sea of vessels, aircraft, platforms or other man-made structures at sea; (iii) any storage of wastes or other matter in the seabed and the subsoil thereof from vessels, aircraft, platforms or other man-made structures at sea; and (iv) any abandonment or toppling at site of platforms or other man-made structures at sea, for the sole purpose of deliberate disposal' (Article 1 (4)(a)). The 1996 Protocol will be discussed in section 7.2 of this chapter.

[22] R. R. Churchill and A. V. Lowe, *The Law of the Sea*, 3rd edn (Manchester University Press, 1999) p. 329.

[23] 1046 *UNTS* p. 138; (1972) 11 *ILM* p. 1294. Entered into force on 30 August 1975.

[24] Protocol to the Convention on the Prevention of Marine Pollution by Dumping of Wastes and Other Matter. Entered into force on 24 March 2006. This Protocol supersedes the 1972 London Dumping Convention in accordance with Article 23. The text of the Protocol was amended on 2 November 2006. The amendment entered into force on 10 February 2007. For the consolidated version of the text of the 1996 Protocol, see Lowe and Talmon, *Basic Documents*, p. 84.

The drilling mud includes some known toxic pollutants such as hydrocarbons as well as concentrations of heavy metals, including chromium, cadmium, copper, zinc, lead, mercury and nickel.[25] Furthermore, there is an increasing need to regulate seabed activities in the Area in order to protect the environment there. In this respect, the role of the International Seabed Authority (hereafter the Authority) is increasingly important.

3 LEGAL FRAMEWORK FOR MARINE ENVIRONMENTAL PROTECTION PRIOR TO 1982

3.1 Customary law

Traditionally, the principal focus of the law of the sea has been on the use of the oceans, not on the protection of the oceans. Owing to the paucity of State practice in the field of marine environmental protection, customary law contains only general rules relevant to the question of marine pollution. Probably the most important rule on this issue would be that no State has the right to use or permit the use of its territory in such a manner as to cause injury in or to the territory of another State. The customary rule of *sic utere tuo ut alienum non laedas* (use your own property so as not to injure that of another) was upheld in the *Trail Smelter* arbitration (1938–41) and, later, it was reflected in Principle 21 of the Stockholm Declaration of 1972. Principle 21 stated that:

> States have ... the responsibility to ensure that activities within their jurisdiction or control do not cause damage to the environment of other States or of areas beyond the limits of national jurisdiction.[26]

Furthermore, the ICJ, in the *Advisory Opinion concerning Legality of the Threat or Use of Nuclear Weapons* of 1996, stressed that:

> The existence of the general obligation of States to ensure that activities within their jurisdiction and control respect the environment of other States or of areas beyond national control is now part of the corpus of international law relating to the environment.[27]

This view was confirmed by the Court in the *Gabčíkovo-Nagymaros Project* case of 1997.[28] Similarly, the ICJ, in the *Corfu Channel* case of 1949, made clear 'every State's obligation not to allow knowingly its territory to be used for acts contrary to the rights of other States'.[29] Nonetheless, it appears that the function of the rule of *sic utere tuo ut alienum non laedas* is a limited one for the following reasons.

[25] H. Esmaeili, *The Legal Regime of Offshore Oil Rigs in International Law* (Aldershot, Ashgate, 2001), pp. 148–149.
[26] Reproduced in H. Hohmann (ed.), *Basic Documents of International Environmental Law*, vol. 1, p. 26.
[27] ICJ Reports 1996, pp. 241–242, para. 29.
[28] ICJ Reports 1997, p. 41, para. 53.
[29] ICJ Reports 1949, p. 22.

First, this rule provides merely an obligation to pay 'due diligence' not to cause trans-frontier damages. This means that a State is not responsible if that State paid such 'due diligence'. Yet it appears difficult to prove the omission of due diligence.

Second, in accordance with this rule, an injured State must prove the serious consequence arising from an act in question as well as clear and convincing evidence of damage in order to establish State responsibility. With respect to long distance pollution and pollution that produces damage with a long time span, however, it is difficult for the injured State(s) to prove the cause and effect relationship concerning the act in question and the damage.

Third, the rule of *sic utere tuo ut alienum non laedas* obliges States neither to protect the environment nor to regulate sources of pollution. This rule essentially functions only *after* damage has been caused in the other State's territory, with a view to establishing State responsibility. In other words, the rule relates to the law of State responsibility concerning damage that has already been produced, and does not impose an obligation to take preventive measures *before* the damage is caused. Nonetheless, damage to the environment may be irreversible. Thus, it appears that the State-responsibility-oriented approach is of limited value where environmental protection is concerned. As the ICJ in the *Gabčíkovo-Nagymaros Project* case pointed out, vigilance and prevention are required in the field of environmental protection.[30]

Finally, as the rule of *sic utere tuo ut alienum non laedas* is based on the dichotomy between spaces under and beyond national jurisdiction, this rule is not relevant to the protection of areas beyond national jurisdiction, such as the high seas and airspace above the high seas as well as extra-terrestrial space. In this sense, this rule cannot deal with the prevention of marine pollution which is beyond the national jurisdiction of the coastal State.

Another relevant rule may involve the obligation regarding abuse of rights. This rule is explicitly embodied in Article 300 of the LOSC:

> States Parties shall fulfil in good faith the obligations assumed under this Convention and shall exercise the rights, jurisdiction and freedoms recognised in this Convention in a manner which would not constitute an abuse of right.

In accordance with this obligation, marine pollution is illegal if it is so excessive that the interests of other States are disproportionately affected. However, it appears difficult to establish an objective criterion to identify the presence of an abuse of rights. In any case, the concept of abuse of rights is not a substantive rule of environmental protection. Hence more specific rules regulating marine pollution are required at the treaty level.

30 ICJ Reports 1997, p. 78, para. 140.

3.2 Treaty law

To date, many treaties regulating marine pollution have been concluded. Concerning treaty practice, three basic approaches can be identified.

The first approach is the source-specific approach. This approach seeks to regulate and control a specified source or substance of marine pollution, such as vessel-source pollution, or a specific substance, such as oil. State practice has shown that from the 1960s to the 1970s, the majority of global conventions adopted a source- or substance-specific approach. A typical example may be provided by MARPOL. This instrument seeks to achieve the complete elimination of international pollution of the marine environment from a specific source, that is to say, a vessel.[31] Another important example in this category is the 1972 London Dumping Convention. The 1972 London Dumping Convention, as amended in 1978, 1980, 1989, 1993 and 1996, seeks to prevent marine pollution caused by a specific source, that is to say, dumping at the global level.[32]

The second approach is the regional approach which aims to regulate marine pollution in a certain region.[33] The regional treaties (see Table 8.1) adopting this approach cover: the Baltic Sea, the North-East Atlantic, the Mediterranean Sea, the South-East Pacific, the South Pacific, the Caribbean Sea, the West and Central African Region, the Red Sea and Gulf of Aden, the Indian Ocean, and the Arabian/Persian Gulf. These treaties seek to regulate various sources of marine pollution in a (quasi-) comprehensive manner.

The third approach is the regional source-specific approach, which combines the source-specific approach with the regional approach. A case in point is the 1974 Convention for the Prevention of Marine Pollution from Land-Based Sources. This Convention sought to prevent marine pollution from a specific, land-based source, in the North-East Atlantic area.[34] In addition to this, there are several Protocols for the regulation of land-based marine pollution in certain regions.[35]

4 PROTECTION OF THE MARINE ENVIRONMENT IN THE LOSC

At the global level, a comprehensive legal framework for the protection of the marine environment was, for the first time, established in the LOSC. Part XII of the Convention is devoted to the protection and preservation of the marine environment. The legal

31 Preamble of MARPOL 73/78.

32 The 1972 London Convention was replaced entirely by a new protocol adopted in 1996.

33 For an analysis of the regional approach, see T. Treves, 'L'approche régionale en matière de protection de l'environnement marin', in *La mer et son droit: Mélanges offerts à Laurent Lucchini et Jean Pierre Quéneudec* (Paris, Pedone, 2003), pp. 591–610; D. M. Dzidzornu, 'Marine Environment Protection under Regional Conventions: Limits to the Contribution of Procedural Norms' (2002) 22 *ODIL* pp. 263–316.

34 (1974) 13 *ILM* p. 352. This Convention was replaced by the 1992 OSPAR Convention.

35 These Protocols will be examined in section 5.2 of this chapter.

TABLE 8.1. EXAMPLES OF TREATIES WHICH ADOPT THE REGIONAL APPROACH

Year	Title of Treaty
1974	Convention on the Protection of the Environment of the Baltic Sea Area
1976	Convention for the Protection of the Mediterranean Sea against Pollution
1978	Kuwait Regional Convention for Cooperation on the Protection of the Marine Environment from Pollution
1981	Convention for the Protection of the Marine Environment and Coastal Area of the South-East Pacific
1981	Convention for Cooperation in the Protection and Development of the Marine and Coastal Environment of the West and Central African Region
1982	Regional Convention for the Conservation of the Red Sea and Gulf of Aden Environment
1983	Convention for the Protection and Development of the Marine Environment of the Wider Caribbean Region
1985	Convention for the Protection, Management and Development of the Marine and Coastal Environment of the Eastern African Region
1986	Convention for the Protection of the Natural Resources and Environment of the South Pacific Region
1992	Convention for the Protection of the Marine Environment of the North-East Atlantic (OSPAR).
1992	Convention on the Protection of the Marine Environment of the Baltic Sea Area

framework for marine environmental protection under the LOSC may be characterised by three elements.

4.1 Generality and comprehensiveness

The LOSC established a general and comprehensive framework for marine environmental protection. It is general in its nature because the Convention provides an obligation on all States to prevent marine pollution. Article 192 explicitly states that: 'States have the obligation to protect and preserve the marine environment'. This obligation contains no qualification. According to the ordinary meaning, the term 'marine environment' includes the ocean as a whole, without distinguishing marine spaces under and beyond national jurisdiction. It follows that the general obligation embodied in Article 192 covers the ocean as a whole, including the high seas. To this extent, it may be said that Article 192 goes beyond the customary rule of *sic utere tuo ut alienum non laedas*, which applies only to spaces under national jurisdiction.

The framework set out in the LOSC is comprehensive in the sense that it covers all sources of marine pollution. Indeed, Article 194(1) obliges States to take all measures consistent with this Convention that are necessary to prevent, reduce and control pollution of the marine environment from *any source*, using for this purpose the best practicable means at their disposal and in accordance with their capabilities. Article 194(3) further provides that the measures taken pursuant to Part XII shall deal with *all sources* of pollution of the marine environment. Thus the LOSC marks an important advance over the earlier Geneva Conventions, which cover only limited sources of marine pollution.

Overall the LOSC seems to reflect a paradigm shift in the international law of the marine environment from the freedom to pollute to an obligation to prevent pollution. Under the LOSC, the primary focus is *not* on obligations of responsibility for damage, but on general and comprehensive regulation to prevent marine pollution. In this sense, it may be said that the cardinal principle of the legal regime for the protection of the marine environment changed from the discretion of States to the duty of protection by States. Owing to the wide ratification of the Convention as well as the degree of acceptance of various treaties on the protection of the marine environment, there may be room for the view that obligations for the protection of the marine environment embodied in the LOSC have become part of customary law.[36]

4.2 Uniformity of rules

The second innovative element in the LOSC concerns the uniformity of rules relating to the regulation of marine pollution. It is desirable that the rules and standards protecting the marine environment should maintain an international minimum harmonisation. In this regard, particular attention must be devoted to the 'rules of reference'.

The LOSC often incorporate a 'no less effective' standard or 'at least have the same effect obligation' into its relevant provisions.[37] With respect to the prevention of pollution arising from seabed activities subject to national jurisdiction, for instance, Article 208(3) requires coastal States to adopt seabed operations laws which 'shall be no less effective than international rules, standards and recommended practices and procedures'. Such international rules include the 1990 International Convention on Oil Pollution Preparedness, Response, and Cooperation (hereafter the OPRC)[38] and the 2000 Protocol to the Convention. Article 210(6) obliges States to adopt dumping regulations which 'shall be no less effective in preventing, reducing and controlling such pollution than the global rules and standards'. It is generally considered that such global rules and standards are set out by the 1972 London Dumping Convention and its 1996 Protocol.[39]

Similarly, Article 211(2) stipulates that flag State regulation of vessel pollution must 'at least have the same effect as that of generally accepted international rules and standards established through the competent international organization or general diplomatic conference'. Such international rules are embodied in MARPOL. The reference to internationally agreed rules and standards was also made in relation to

[36] *Virginia Commentaries*, vol. IV pp. 36 *et seq.*; Birnie, Boyle and Redgwell, *International Law and the Environment*. p. 387; P. Sands, *Principles of International Environmental Law* (Cambridge University Press, 2003), p. 396.

[37] The list of legal instruments corresponding to 'generally accepted international rules and standards' is available in: IMO, *Circular letter No. 2456, Implication of UNCLOS for the Organization*, 17 February 2003, Annex II.

[38] (1991) 30 *ILM* p. 735. Entered into force on 13 May 1995.

[39] L. A. De La Fayette, 'The London Convention 1972: Preparing for the Future' (1998) 13 *IJMCL* p. 516.

atmospheric and land-based pollution under Articles 207(1) and 212(1), though only in a weaker manner.

The legal technique of 'rules of reference' contributes to maintain uniformity of national and international regulation with regard to marine environmental protection. Furthermore, by updating 'generally accepted international rules and standards', it becomes possible to adapt relevant rules of the LOSC to a new situation. Thus 'rules of reference' can be considered as a useful tool to take the new demands of the international community into account in the interpretation and application of existing rules and standards.

In relation to this, it is to be noted that international organisations have a valuable role in the formulation of internationally agreed rules and standards. In fact, the LOSC contains many provisions referring to the 'competent international organization'. Corresponding to these provisions, a number of agreements, regulations and standards have been adopted under the auspices of the IMO. The international instruments adopted under the auspices of the IMO have become more important since the entering into force of the LOSC because Parties to the Convention shall follow the international standards created through the IMO by virtue of 'rules of reference'. In this regard, some argue that to the extent that these rules are 'applicable' or 'generally accepted' they may be invoked by port States or by coastal States to legitimise action against ships of third States. According to this view, the power to invoke rules and standards does not depend upon whether the flag State of that particular ship is a party to the relevant conventions due to their widespread adoption.[40]

4.3 Obligation to cooperate in the protection of the marine environment

As marine pollution may easily spread beyond man-made delimitation lines, the protection of the marine environment from pollution can hardly be achieved by a single State. Thus the International Tribunal for the Law of the Sea (ITLOS), in the 2001 *MOX Plant* case, highlighted the importance of international cooperation, stating that:

> [T]he duty to cooperate is a fundamental principle in the prevention of pollution of the marine environment under Part XII of the Convention and general international law ...[41]

It is notable that the LOSC provides explicit obligations of cooperation in order to prevent marine pollution. For instance, Article 197 stipulates that States shall cooperate 'on a global basis and, as appropriate, on a regional basis, directly or through competent international organizations, in formulating and elaborating international rules, standards and recommended practices and procedures consistent with this Convention,

[40] R. Wolfrum, 'IMO Interface with the Law of the Sea Convention', in M. H. Nordquist and J. N. Moore, *Current Maritime Issues and the International Maritime Organization* (The Hague, Nijhoff, 1999), p. 231; Birnie, Boyle and Redgwell, *International Law and the Environment*, p. 389; D. Rothwell and T. Stephens, *The International Law of the Sea* (Oxford and Portland, Oregon, Hart Publishing, 2010), p. 344.

[41] The *MOX Plant* case (Request for provisional measures), (2002) 41 *ILM* p. 415, para. 82.

for the protection and preservation of the marine environment, taking into account characteristic regional features'.[42] The terms 'on a global basis' and 'on a regional basis' appear to suggest that the scope of this provision is not limited to marine spaces under national jurisdiction.

Article 198 obliges a State to immediately notify other States it deems likely to be affected by such damage, as well as the competent international organisations, when a State becomes aware of cases in which the marine environment is in imminent danger of being damaged or has been damaged by pollution. It is arguable that this obligation already represents customary international law.[43] Where imminent danger exists, the State in the area affected as well as the competent international organisations shall 'cooperate, to the extent possible, in eliminating the effects of pollution and preventing or minimizing the damage' and 'jointly develop and promote contingency plans for responding to pollution incidents in the marine environment' (Article 199). Obligations of cooperation are also provided in provisions relating to the physical investigation of foreign vessels (Article 226(2)), and responsibility and liability (Article 235(3)).

Further to this, the obligation to cooperate in the establishment of relevant rules is indirectly enshrined in provisions concerning land-based pollution (Article 207(4)), pollution from seabed activities subject to national jurisdiction (Article 208(5)), pollution from dumping (Article 210(4)), pollution from vessels (Article 211(1)), and pollution from or through the atmosphere (Article 212(3)). Overall it may be concluded that the LOSC steps forward to a comprehensive regulation of marine pollution in the oceans as a whole.

5 REGULATION OF LAND-BASED MARINE POLLUTION[44]

5.1 Limits of the global legal framework

The LOSC is the only treaty which provides general obligations to prevent land-based pollution at the global level. It is clear that land-based pollution is covered by Article 194(1). Article 194(2) imposes a duty upon States to take all measures necessary to ensure that activities under their jurisdiction or control are so conducted as not to cause damage by pollution to other States and their environment; and that pollution arising from incidents or activities under their jurisdiction or control does not spread beyond the areas where they exercise sovereign rights in accordance with the LOSC. Article 194(3)(a) stipulates that measures taken pursuant to Part XII shall include, *inter alia*, those designed to minimise to the fullest possible extent 'the release of toxic, harmful or noxious substances, especially those which are persistent, from land-based sources, from or through the atmosphere or by dumping'.

More specifically, the LOSC provides prescriptive and enforcement jurisdiction with regard to the regulation of land-based pollution. With respect to prescriptive

[42] The OSPAR Convention states in its preamble that Article 197 reflects customary international law.

[43] A. Boyle, 'Marine Pollution under the Law of the Sea Convention' (1985) 79 *AJIL* p. 369.

[44] The argument of this section is based partly on the analysis, with modifications, in Y. Tanaka, 'Regulation of Land-Based Marine Pollution in International Law: A Comparative Analysis between Global and Regional Legal Frameworks' (2006) 66 *ZaöRV* pp. 535–574.

jurisdiction, Article 207(1) calls upon States to adopt laws and regulations to prevent, reduce and control pollution of the marine environment from land-based sources, 'taking into account internationally agreed rules, standards and recommended practices and procedures'. Concerning the enforcement jurisdiction, Article 213 requires States to enforce their laws and regulations adopted under Article 207 and to take other measures necessary to implement applicable international rules and regulations. States are also under a duty to take other measures as may be necessary to prevent, reduce and control such pollution under Article 207(2).

Nonetheless, these provisions are too general to be very useful. Hence further specification would be needed with regard to, *inter alia*, the identification of harmful substances. It must also be noted that unlike pollution from seabed activities subject to national jurisdiction, pollution from dumping as well as pollution from vessels,[45] States are required only to 'take into account' internationally agreed rules etc. when adopting relevant laws and regulations concerning pollution from land-based sources (Article 207(1)). It would seem to follow that States may adopt measures which are either more or less stringent than those embodied in international law. To this extent, control by internationally agreed criteria over national standards remains modest. Thus, under the LOSC, the balance between national and international laws on this matter is in favour of national laws.

In response to the weakness of the global legal framework, attempts have been made to develop a global instrument respecting land-based pollution, in particular under the auspices of the United Nations Environment Programme (UNEP). An important outcome was the adoption of the Montreal Guidelines for the Protection of the Marine Environment against Pollution from Land-Based Sources in 1985. Whilst the Montreal Guidelines are of a voluntary nature, they specify various measures which should be taken by each State.

Later, a need for the prevention of degradation of the marine environment by land-based activities was stressed by Agenda 21 of 1992. Agenda 21 required that the UNEP Governing Council should be invited to convene, as soon as practicable, an intergovernmental meeting on the protection of the marine environment from land-based activities.[46] The global conference envisaged in Agenda 21 was held in Washington DC, from 23 October to 3 November 1995. In this conference, two instruments were adopted: the Washington Declaration on the Protection of the Marine Environment from Land-Based Activities (hereafter the 1995 Washington Declaration) and the Global Programme of Action for the Protection of the Marine Environment from Land-Based Activities (hereafter the 1995 GPA). The 1995 GPA explicitly ensures the application of the precautionary approach to this issue.[47] The need to improve and accelerate the implementation of the 1995 GPA was confirmed in the 2001 Montreal Declaration on the Protection of the Marine Environment from Land-Based Activities.[48]

45 LOSC, Articles 208(3), 210(6) and 211(2).
46 Paragraph 17.26 available at: www.un.org/esa/dsd/agenda21.
47 Paragraphs 23(h)(i) and 24, UNEP (OCA)/LBA/IG.2/7, 5 December 1995.
48 (2002) 48 *Law of the Sea Bulletin* pp. 58–61.

Overall it can be observed that attempts to address land-based marine pollution at the global level have been made only in the form of less formal instruments. In this sense, regulation at the global level remains weak. In this regard, four comments can be made.

First, in essence, the activities which may cause land-based pollution are within the territorial sovereignty of each State, and such activities are closely bound up with crucial national programmes for economic, industrial and social development of those countries. The economic costs of measures to regulate land-based pollution are seen as high and inevitably affect economic development. Hence States are often reluctant to approve any attempts at restricting their economic developments by legally binding instruments.

Second, the regulation of land-based pollution is more complex than that of pollution from other sources. In the case of vessel-source pollution, for instance, sources and substances to be regulated – mainly oil and oily mixtures – can be clearly identified. However, the regulation of land-based pollution involves more substances than oil and oily mixtures. Land-based sources are variable in their nature over time, and each source requires different measures to prevent environmental damage.[49] This requirement makes regulatory measures complex. In the case of vessel-source pollution, ships are the only actor, and the shipping industry is the major economic sector to be regulated. By contrast, many actors and activities, such as pollution-generating industrial, agricultural and municipal activities, are involved in pollution from land-based activities. The regulation of land-based marine pollution at the global level is therefore more problematic than in the case of vessel-source pollution because, in the former case, it is more difficult to balance the regulation of such pollution with various national economic policies.[50]

Third, attention should be drawn to geographical and ecological divergences in the oceans. The ocean environment is not homogeneous. The movements of ocean currents and winds are complex and different and, consequently, the degree of marine pollution varies in each coastal region. Considering that the effects of land-based pollution are more serious in shallow enclosed or semi-enclosed coastal sea areas than open oceanic areas, more stringent regulation of land-based pollution in the former than in other marine areas will be needed. In fact, almost all regional agreements governing this issue are essentially concerned with enclosed or semi-enclosed seas.[51]

Finally, it is important to note that the protection of the marine environment from land-based pollution is closely linked to widespread poverty in developing countries. In fact, the 1995 Washington Declaration clearly recognises that the alleviation of poverty is an essential factor in addressing the impacts of land-based activities on

[49] A. L. Dahl, 'Land-Based Pollution and Integrated Coastal Management' (1993) 17 *Marine Policy* p. 567.

[50] Meng Quing-Nan, *Land-Based Marine Pollution: International Law Development* (London, Nijhoff, 1987), p. 16.

[51] Birnie, Boyle and Redgwell, *International Law and the Environment*, p. 455. It is to be noted that States bordering an enclosed or semi-enclosed sea are required to endeavour to coordinate the implementation of their rights and duties with respect to the protection of the marine environment (Article 123(b)).

coastal and marine areas.[52] Likewise, the 2001 Montreal Declaration on the Protection of the Marine Environment from Land-Based Activities makes clear that poverty, particularly in coastal communities of developing countries, contributes to marine pollution through lack of basic sanitation. Marine degradation generates poverty by depleting the very basis for social and economic development.[53] This is a vicious circle. Hence the regulation of land-based pollution should be considered in the context of combating poverty in developing countries.

5.2 Development of regional treaties

Owing to economic, technological and geographical divergences in the world, it appears difficult, if not impossible, to establish at the global level uniform and detailed rules regulating land-based pollution. It would seem to follow that regional agreement which contains more specific rules will assume considerable importance to combat land-based pollution. In fact, treaties regulating marine pollution, including pollution from land-based sources, are increasingly concluded at the regional level. In particular, it is noteworthy that specific Protocols on land-based marine pollution are concluded. Examples include:

(i) the 1980 Protocol for the Protection of the Mediterranean Sea against Pollution from Land-Based Sources (the Athens Protocol),[54]
(ii) the 1983 Protocol for the Protection of the South-East Pacific against Pollution from Land-Based Sources (the 1983 Quito Protocol),[55]
(iii) the 1990 Protocol to the Kuwait Regional Convention for the Protection of the Marine Environment against Pollution from Land-Based Sources (the 1990 Kuwait Protocol),[56]
(iv) the 1992 Protocol on Protection of the Black Sea Marine Environment against Pollution from Land-Based Sources (the 1992 Bucharest Protocol),[57]
(v) the 1992 Convention on the Protection of the Marine Environment of the Baltic Sea (the 1992 Helsinki Convention),[58]
(vi) the 1992 Convention for the Protection of the Marine Environment of the North-East Atlantic (the 1992 OSPAR Convention),[59]
(vii) the 1996 Protocol for the Protection of the Mediterranean Sea against Pollution from Land-Based Sources and Activities (the 1996 Syracuse Protocol),[60]

52 Paragraph 5 of its Preamble.
53 (2002) 48 *Law of the Sea Bulletin* p. 58.
54 (1980) 19 *ILM* p. 869. Entered into force 17 June 1983. In 1996, this Protocol was amended and recorded as the Protocol for the Protection of the Mediterranean Sea against Pollution from Land-Based Sources and Activities.
55 Entered into force in 1986. For the text of the Protocol: http://sedac.ciesin.org/entri/texts/pollution.land-based.south-east.pacific.1983.html.
56 Entered into force 2 January 1993. For the text of the Protocol: http://sedac.ciesin.columbia.edu/entri/texts/acrc/kuwaitprot.txt.html.
57 (1993) 32 *ILM* p. 1122. Entered into force on 15 January 1994.
58 Entered into force 17 January 2000. The text of the agreement is available at: www.helcom.fi/.
59 Entered into force 25 March 1998. The text of the Convention is available at: www.ospar.org/eng/html/welcome.html.
60 Not yet in force. For the text of the Protocol, http://faolex.fao.org/docs/pdf/mul38141.pdf.

(viii) the 1999 Protocol Concerning Pollution from Land-Based Sources and Activities to the Convention for the Protection and Development of the Marine Environment of the Wider Caribbean Region (the 1999 Aruba Protocol),[61]

(ix) the 2005 Protocol Concerning the Protection of the Marine Environment from Land-Based Activities in the Red Sea and Gulf of Aden (the 2005 Jeddah Protocol).[62]

Concerning those treaties, it is relevant to note that internal waters are covered in the conventions' application.[63] Owing to the importance of a sound environment of coastal areas for human health and biological diversity, regulation of land-based marine pollution in internal waters is particularly important. It is also to be noted that all documents listed above regard pollution through the atmosphere as land-based marine pollution.[64] While the detailed examination of each and every regional treaty is beyond the scope of this chapter, some innovative elements must be highlighted.

5.3 Identification of harmful substances

Identification of harmful substances is the starting point in the regulation of land-based marine pollution. In this regard, treaties regulating land-based pollution traditionally adopted the black/grey lists approach. Under this approach, harmful substances are divided into two categories. With respect to the substances listed in a black list, in principle, States Parties are obliged to eliminate pollution by such substances.[65] Concerning materials enumerated in the grey list, the obligation of States is relaxed, and States are merely required to limit pollution by these materials. The black/grey list approach was adopted by the 1974 Convention for the Prevention of Marine Pollution from Land-Based Sources (hereafter the 1974 Paris Convention, Article 4), the 1974 Convention on the Protection of the Marine Environment of the Baltic Sea Area (hereafter the 1974 Helsinki Convention, Articles 5 and 6), the 1980 Athens Protocol (Articles 5 and 6), the 1983 Quito Protocol (Articles IV and V), and the 1992 Bucharest Protocol (Article 4). However, the black/grey approach is not free from controversy.

First, it seems problematic that regulatory measures applicable to the same substances vary depending on agreements. For instance, mercury and cadmium were in Annex II (the grey list) in the 1974 Helsinki Convention, whilst these materials were categorised in the black list in the 1974 Paris Convention, the 1980 Athens Protocol, the 1983 Quito Protocol, and the 1992 Bucharest Protocol. While radioactive

[61] Not yet in force. The text of the Protocol is available at: http://cep.unep.org/repcar/lbs-protocol-en.pdf.

[62] The original text is written in Arabic. English translation is available at: http://faculty.kfupm.edu.sa/CHEM/thukair/ENVS%20590/Hand%20out/Protocols/lba_protocol_persga_english.pdf.

[63] Article 3 of the 1980 Athens Protocol; Article I of the 1983 Quito Protocol; Article II of the 1990 Kuwait Protocol; Article 1(a) of the OSPAR Convention; Article 1 of the Helsinki Convention; Article 3 of the 1992 Bucharest Protocol; Article 3(c) of the 1996 Syracuse Protocol.

[64] Article 4(1)(b) of the 1980 Athens Protocol; Article II(c) of the 1983 Quito Protocol; Article III(d) of the 1990 Kuwait Protocol; Article 1 of the 1992 Bucharest Protocol; Article 2 of the 1992 Helsinki Convention; Article 1(e) of the 1992 OSPAR Convention; Article 4(1)(b) of the 1996 Syracuse Protocol; Article I(4) of the 1999 Aruba Protocol; Article 4(1)(b) of the 2005 Jeddah Protocol.

[65] In some cases, however, the discharge of harmful substances which are enumerated in the black list is not completely prohibited.

substances were in Annex I (the black list) in the 1980 Athens Protocol as well as the 1983 Quito Protocol, such substances were listed in Annex II (the grey list) in the 1974 Helsinki Convention.

Second and more importantly, the black/grey list approach is contrary to the fundamental goal of preventing all marine pollution since, according to this approach, States are merely under a relaxed obligation with respect to 'grey list' substances.

In response to these problems, an attempt was made to replace the black/grey list approach by a uniform approach, which seeks to regulate harmful substances of land-based pollution without any differentiation of obligations according to the category of harmful substances. The best example on this matter may be the 1992 OSPAR Convention. Article 3 of this Convention places an explicit obligation upon the Contracting Parties to take, individually and jointly, all possible steps to prevent and eliminate pollution from land-based sources in accordance with the provisions of the Convention, in particular as provided for in Annex I. To this end, the OSPAR Convention provides a single list of priority pollutants in Appendix 2.[66] This list is in essence a combination of the 'black and grey lists' laid down in the Annexes of the 1974 Paris Convention. It follows that the 'grey list' substances under the 1974 Paris Convention are also covered by the same obligation of preventing and eliminating these pollutants embodied in the OSPAR Convention.[67]

However, Article 2(1) of Annex I stipulates that: 'Point source discharges to the maritime area, and releases into water or air which reach and may affect the maritime area, shall be strictly subject to authorisation or regulation by the competent authorities of the Contracting Parties'. It would seem to follow that point source discharges would be possible with the authorisation of or regulation by relevant authorities. At the same time, Article 2(1) of Annex I makes it clear that '[s]uch authorisation or regulation shall, in particular, implement relevant decisions of the Commission which bind the relevant Contracting Party'. As will be seen, the OSPAR Commission, made up of representatives of each of the Contracting Parties, is under an obligation to draw up plans for the reduction and phasing out of hazardous substances in accordance with Article 3(a) of Annex I. Thus, the authorisation or regulation by the Contracting Parties with respect to emissions of such substances is subject to the control of the OSPAR Commission.

Like the OSPAR Convention, the 1992 Helsinki Convention, the 1996 Syracuse Protocol, which replaced the 1980 Athens Protocol, the 1999 Aruba Protocol and the 2005 Jeddah Protocol also make no differentiation between obligations on this matter. The uniform approach seems to reflect this paradigm shift in marine environmental protection from the principle of freedom to pollute to an obligation to prevent

[66] See also Article 1(2) of Annex I of the OSPAR Convention.

[67] M. Pallemaerts, 'The North Sea and Baltic Sea Land-Based Sources Regimes: Reducing Toxics or Rehashing Rhetoric?' (1998) 13 *IJMCL* pp. 438–439; E. Hey, T. Ijlstra and A. Nollkaemper, 'The 1992 Paris Convention for the Protection of the Marine Environment of the North-East Atlantic: A Critical Analysis' (1993) 8 *IJMCL* pp. 19–20.

pollution. In this sense, it may be said that the replacement of the black/grey approach by the uniform approach is an important development in this field.

5.4 Precautionary approach

As with the conservation of marine living resources, the precautionary approach is enshrined in some regional agreements respecting marine environmental protection. For instance, Article 2(2)(a) of the OSPAR Convention places an explicit obligation upon the Contracting Parties to apply 'the precautionary principle'. As the 'precautionary principle' is considered a general obligation, it is also applicable to land-based pollution. Likewise, Article 3(2) of the 1992 Helsinki Convention explicitly obliges the Contracting Parties to apply the 'precautionary principle' as one of the fundamental principles and obligations of the 1992 Helsinki Convention. Thus the Contracting Parties are under a duty to apply this principle to the regulation of land-based pollution. In addition, the 1996 Syracuse Protocol refers to the 'precautionary principle' in its Preamble. The application of the precautionary approach strengthens the environmental dimension of international law in this field.

On the other hand, the application of this approach may entail the risk of restricting economic and industrial activities by States, and this is particularly true of the regulation of land-based activities. A difficult question thus arises as to how it is possible to reconcile environmental protection with economic interests. In response, there will be a need to take into account not only scientific factors but also economic, social and political factors, including cost-effectiveness. Considering that the evaluation of those factors amounts in essence to policy-making by States, the application of the precautionary approach will depend on the political determination of each State. Hence, as discussed earlier, it may have to be accepted that the normativity of this approach will remain modest both as a rule of conduct and as a rule for adjudication.[68] In order to minimise inconsistency between national policies concerning the precautionary approach, it is desirable that the application of the precautionary approach should be decided by an international forum, such as the Conference of the Parties in relevant treaties.

5.5 Environmental impact assessment

In the implementation of relevant rules regulating harmful substances discharged from land-based sources, there is a need to examine the impact of planned activities upon the marine environment as well as the effectiveness of regulatory measures. Here environmental impact assessment comes into play.

According to the 'Goals and Principles of Environmental Impact Assessment', which was adopted by the UNEP in 1987, environmental impact assessment means 'an examination, analysis and assessment of planned activities with a view to ensuring

[68] See Chapter 7, section 5.3.

environmentally sound and sustainable development'.[69] The LOSC provides an obligation to undertake environmental impact assessments. Article 206 holds that:

> When States have reasonable grounds for believing that planned activities under their jurisdiction or control may cause substantial pollution of or significant and harmful changes to the marine environment, they shall, as far as practicable, assess the potential effects of such activities on the marine environment and shall communicate reports of the results of such assessments in the manner provided in article 205.

This formulation is basically reflected in Article VII(2) of the 1999 Aruba Protocol. A similar obligation is also provided in Article VIII(1) of the 1990 Kuwait Protocol.

Furthermore, it is of particular interest to note that the 1992 Helsinki Convention sets out a dual obligation relating to environmental impact assessment, namely, the obligation to undertake such an assessment as well as the obligation to cooperate on this matter. Article 7(1) of the 1992 Helsinki Convention calls upon the Contracting Parties to undertake an environmental impact assessment in the Baltic Sea Area. Article 7(3) then requires that: 'Where two or more Contracting Parties share transboundary waters within the catchment area of the Baltic Sea, these Parties shall cooperate to ensure that potential impacts on the marine environment of the Baltic Sea Area are fully investigated within the environmental impact assessment referred to in paragraph 1 of this article'.

Likewise, the 1992 OSPAR Convention directly obliges the Contracting Parties to 'undertake and publish at regular intervals joint assessments of the quality status of the marine environment and of its development, for the maritime area or for regions or sub-regions thereof' in accordance with Article 6(a). Such assessments include both an evaluation of the effectiveness of the measures taken and planned for the protection of the marine environment and the identification of priorities for action under Article 6(b). Owing to the transboundary nature of marine pollution, international collaboration in environmental assessment is significant in order to secure credible data.

Once environmental impact assessment is set out as a legal obligation in a treaty, it is arguable that a Contracting Party to the treaty whose activities cause serious land-based marine pollution can no longer deny responsibility on grounds of non-foreseeability if it has not conducted such an assessment.[70] In this sense, environmental impact assessments may limit the margin of discretion of States Parties in their environmental policy-making. Furthermore, environmental impact assessments, coupled with monitoring activities, can be a tool to assess the existence of risks which may trigger the application of this principle. To this extent, environmental impact assessment may stimulate the application of the precautionary approach.

[69] Preamble. For the text, P. Birnie and A. Boyle, *Basic Documents on International Law and the Environment* (Oxford University Press, 1995), pp. 27–30.

[70] Boyle, 'Land-Based Sources of Marine Pollution', p. 23.

5.6 International control

Like other branches of international law, the establishment of effective compliance procedures is of paramount importance in the law of the sea. In this regard, international control through international institutions is increasingly important in order to secure compliance with treaties. International control is a concept with more than one meaning, but this concept may be defined as procedures through multilateral international institutions for supervising compliance with objective obligations in a treaty.

International control seeks to supervise compliance with treaties by a variety of procedures, such as reporting from States Parties, verification, and decisions, as well as recommendations. Such an international control mechanism has been developed particularly in international human rights law, and currently many agreements with regard to environmental protection are adopting a similar mechanism. International control may provide a useful means to ensure compliance with rules of international law, where such rules do not rely exclusively on the traditional principle of reciprocity. In particular, two methods of international control merit highlighting.

(a) The reporting system

One means involves the reporting system.[71] The reporting system has been introduced into several regional conventions with regard to the regulation of land-based marine pollution. For instance, Article 13(1) of the 1996 Syracuse Protocol requires the Parties to submit reports every two years to the meetings of the Contracting Parties of measures taken, results achieved and, if the case arises, of difficulties encountered in the application of the Protocol. The Reports submitted by the Parties are to be considered by the meetings of the Parties in accordance with Article 14(2)(f). A similar reporting system or an obligation to exchange information through the organisation established by the regional treaty is provided in the 1980 Athens Protocol (Article 13), the 1983 Quito Protocol (Article IX), the 1992 Bucharest Protocol (Article 7), the 1990 Kuwait Protocol (Article XII), and the 1999 Aruba Protocol (Article XII).

Furthermore, the Helsinki Convention provides detailed reporting obligations. Article 16(1) of the Convention places an obligation upon the Contracting Parties to report to the Baltic Marine Environment Protection Commission (hereafter the Helsinki Commission) at regular intervals on:

> (a) the legal, regulatory, or other measures taken for the implementation of the provisions of this Convention, of its Annexes and of recommendations adopted thereunder;
> (b) the effectiveness of the measures taken to implement the provisions referred to in subparagraph (a) of this paragraph; and
> (c) problems encountered in the implementation of the provisions referred to in subparagraph (a) of this paragraph.

[71] For an analysis in some detail of the reporting system, see Y. Tanaka, 'Reflections on Reporting Systems in Treaties Concerning the Protection of the Marine Environment' (2009) 40 *ODIL* pp. 146–170.

Article 16(2) further requires that on the request of a Contracting Party or of the Helsinki Commission, Contracting Parties shall provide information on discharges permits, emission data or data on environmental quality as far as possible. Moreover, Annex III of the Convention calls upon the operator of an industrial plant to submit data and information to the appropriate national authority using a form of application. In this regard, at least the following data and information shall be included in the application form: general information, actual situation and/or planned activities, alternatives and their various impacts concerning ecological, economic and safety aspects.[72] On the basis of the reports submitted by the Contracting Parties, the Helsinki Commission is to keep the implementation of the Convention under continuous observation.[73] A comparable reporting system also exists in the OSPAR Convention.[74] These detailed reporting systems are useful in precluding Contracting Parties from failing to fulfil the reporting obligation or from reporting superficially to the relevant international institutions. The reporting systems have a valuable role in enhancing compliance with treaties in this field for at least three reasons.

First, the reports submitted by the Contracting Parties provide the primary source of information with regard to compliance with the relevant treaties. Reporting systems thus provide a useful means to check their implementation.

Second, information provided by the Contracting Parties may be useful in order to assess the effectiveness of the measures taken by them and/or by a treaty commission. On the basis of scientific data submitted by the Contracting Parties, it may be possible to flexibly adjust the measures necessary for the protection of the marine environment.

Third, the reporting systems provide Contracting Parties with an opportunity for self-examination of their performance.

In general, the effectiveness of reporting systems relies primarily on three elements: (i) due diligence by national authorities to submit reports; (ii) accuracy of data; and (iii) transparency of information. However, there are growing concerns that many States, including both developed and developing countries, fail to fulfil the reporting obligation, or report merely superficially to the relevant international institutions. With a view to enhancing diligence by States to submit reports, treaties provide various measures, including: publicising those states that are not reporting, providing financial and technical assistance, imposing penalties for non-reporting, where appropriate, and harmonising reporting systems.

In order to improve accuracy of information, several treaties establish mechanisms relating to:

- specification of contents of reports,
- collection and verification of data by independent bodies, and
- the participation of NGOs in compliance and information review procedures.

In addition to this, some treaties place a clear obligation upon the Contracting Parties to ensure the public availability of information.[75] It seems arguable that increased

[72] Regulation 3(1) of Annex III.
[73] Article 20(1)(a).
[74] Articles 22 and 23 of the OSPAR Convention.
[75] The Helsinki Convention (Article 17); the OSPAR Convention (Article 9).

public availability of information creates an incentive or a community pressure to comply with a reporting obligation. Publication of information may also contribute to enhance the quality of information by allowing a third party to verify the accuracy of information. It may be said that transparency of information is an important element with a view to strengthening compliance procedure, including reporting systems.

(b) Supervision through treaty commissions

Another means of international control involves the supervision through a commission established by a treaty. In the context of the regulation of land-based marine pollution, such a compliance procedure is reflected in the 1992 OSPAR Convention. Article 10 of this Convention stipulates that the OSPAR Commission has duties (a) to *supervise* the implementation of the Convention and (b) generally to review the condition of the maritime area, the effectiveness of the measures being adopted, the priorities and the need for any additional or different measures. To this end, Article 23 provides for the compliance procedure by which:

The Commission shall:

> (a) on the basis of the periodical reports referred to in Article 22 and any other report submitted by the Contracting Parties, assess their compliance with the Convention and the decisions and recommendations adopted thereunder;
> (b) when appropriate, decide upon and call for steps to bring about full compliance with the Convention, and decisions adopted thereunder, and promote the implementation of recommendations, including measures to assist a Contracting Party to carry out its obligations.

On the basis of those mechanisms, compliance with the OSPAR Convention, including rules governing land-based marine pollution, is to be supervised and controlled by the OSPAR Commission. Yet it is not suggested that the OSPAR Commission possesses enforcement jurisdiction against Contracting Parties which do not comply with their obligations under the Convention. Article 13 suggests that a Contracting Party which has voted against a decision is not bound by it.[76] Despite this limitation, it is significant that an international body possessing supervisory and control power has appeared in the field of marine environmental protection.

6 REGULATION OF VESSEL-SOURCE MARINE POLLUTION

6.1 MARPOL

Unlike the regulation of land-based marine pollution, vessel-source marine pollution is regulated primarily by global legal instruments. As noted earlier, the key

[76] R. Lagoni, 'Monitoring Compliance and Enforcement of Compliance through the OSPAR Commission' in P. Ehlers, E. Mann-Borgese and R. Wolfrum (eds.), *Marine Issues* (The Hague, Kluwer, 2002), pp. 161–162.

instruments on this subject are MARPOL and the LOSC. Chronologically, MARPOL should be examined first.

MARPOL seeks to achieve the complete elimination of international pollution of the marine environment by oil and other harmful substances and the minimisation of accidental discharge of such substances.[77] In addition to the text of the 1973 Convention and the 1978 Protocol, MARPOL contains two Protocols and six Annexes. Annexes I and II are mandatory for all Contracting Parties, whilst the remaining Annexes are optional.[78] Under Article 3(1) of the 1973 Convention, MARPOL applies to ships entitled to fly the flag of a Party to the Convention and to ships not entitled to fly the flag of a Party but which operate under the authority of a Party. However, MARPOL does not apply to any warship, naval auxiliary or other ship owned or operated by a State and used only on government non-commercial service pursuant to Article 3(3).

Under Article 4(1) of the 1973 Convention, any violation of the requirements of the Convention shall be prohibited and sanctions are to be established under the law of the Administration of the ship concerned wherever the violation occurs.[79] While in the ports or offshore terminals under the jurisdiction of a Party, a ship required to hold a certificate in accordance with MARPOL is subject to inspection by officers duly authorised by that Party pursuant to Article 5.

Each Annex to MARPOL contains detailed provisions regulating specific categories of vessel-source pollution. These provisions are highly technical and only a brief outline can be given here.[80]

Annex I, which was revised in 2004, regulates oil pollution from ships.[81] The revised Annex sets limits on discharge into the sea of oil or oily mixtures from ships to which the Annex applies (Regulation 15). Annex I also obliges oil tankers to comply with the double-hull and double-bottom requirements (Regulations 19 and 20). These requirements are important to phase out single-hull oil tankers. Annex I was amended in 2009, adding a new Chapter 8 with a view to preventing pollution during transfer of oil cargo between oil tankers at sea.[82] In 2010, Annex I acquired a new Chapter 9 respecting special requirements for the use or carriage of oils in the Antarctic area.[83]

Annex II deals with sea pollution by noxious liquid substances in bulk. Annex II was revised in 2004.[84] The revised Annex II specifies requirements with regard to the

[77] Preamble of the 1973 Convention.

[78] As at 31 May 2011, 150 states representing 99.14 per cent of the world's shipping tonnage were parties to Annexes I and II of MARPOL 73/78. IMO, *Status of Multilateral Conventions and Instruments in Respect of Which the International Maritime Organization or its Secretary-General Performs Depositary or Other Functions*, p. 101.

[79] Under Article 2(5) of the 1973 Convention, 'Administration' means the government of the State under whose authority the ship is operating. With respect to a ship entitled to fly a flag of any State, the Administration is the government of that State. Concerning fixed or floating platforms engaged in exploration and exploitation of the sea-bed and subsoil thereof adjacent to the coast, the Administration is the government of the coastal State.

[80] Annexes of MARPOL have been frequently amended. Further amendments may be made in the near future. In this case, the regulation numbers might be subject to change.

[81] Resolution MEPC.117(52) adopted on 15 October 2004. Entered into force on 1 January 2007.

[82] Resolution MEPC.186(59) adopted on 17 July 2009. Entered into force on 1 January 2011.

[83] Resolution MEPC.189(60) adopted on 26 March 2010. Entered into force on 1 August 2011.

[84] Resolution MEPC.118(52) adopted on 15 October 2004. Entered into force on 1 January 2007.

control of discharges of residues of noxious liquid substances or ballast water, tank washings or other mixtures containing such substances in some detail (Regulation 13). Noxious liquid substances are divided into four categories, namely, categories X, Y, Z and other substances. The discharge of the most hazardous noxious substances of category X into the marine environment is prohibited, whilst the discharge of substances listed in categories Y and Z into the sea is limited. At present, other substances may be discharged in the case of tank cleaning or deballasting operations (Regulation 6). In the Antarctic area, i.e. the sea area south of latitude 60° south, any discharge into the sea of noxious liquid substances or mixtures containing such substances is prohibited (Regulation 13(8)).

Annex III, which was revised in 2006,[85] aims to prevent pollution by harmful substances carried by sea in packaged form. The revised Annex III contains detailed provisions with regard to packing of a harmful substance, marking and labelling, documentation and stowage.

Annex IV, which was revised in 2004, regulates pollution by sewage from ships.[86] The revised Annex IV contains detailed regulations with regard to equipment and control of discharge of sewage into the sea. In 2006, a new regulation 13 was added with a view to introducing port State control over operational requirements.[87]

Annex V regulates disposal of garbage from ships.[88] Garbage under Annex V means all kinds of victual, domestic and operational waste excluding fresh fish and parts thereof (Regulation 1(1)). The disposal into the sea of all plastics is prohibited (Regulation 3(1)(a)). The disposal of garbage in special areas is tightened by Regulation 5.[89] However, regulation 6(a) allows a ship to dispose of garbage for the purpose of securing the safety of a ship or saving life at sea. The escape of garbage resulting from damage to a ship or its equipment is also permitted as long as all reasonable precaution has been taken by virtue of Regulation 6(b). The accidental loss of synthetic fishing nets is not prohibited, provided that all reasonable precautions have been taken to prevent such loss (Regulation 6(c)).

Revised Annex VI, which was adopted in 2008, involves regulations for the prevention of air pollution from ships.[90] The revised Annex VI limits ozone-depleting substances, sulphur oxide (SO_x) and nitrogen oxide (NO_x) emissions from ships. Furthermore, Regulation 16 prohibits shipboard incineration of certain products. The revised Annex VI also introduces an Emission Control Area where the emission of NO_x as well as SO_x and particulate matter is further restricted (Regulation 14).[91]

85 Resolution MEPC.156(55) adopted on 13 October 2006. Entered into force on 1 January 2010.
86 Resolution MEPC.115 (51) adopted on 1 April 2004. Entered into force on 1 August 2005.
87 Regulation 13 entered into force on 1 August 2007.
88 Entered into force on 31 December 1988. Annex V has been subject to subsequent amendments.
89 Under Regulation 5(1), such areas are: the Mediterranean Sea area, the Baltic Sea area, the Black Sea area, the Red Sea area, the 'Gulfs area', the North Sea area, the Antarctic area and the Wider Caribbean Region, including the Gulf of Mexico and the Caribbean Sea.
90 Resolution MEPC.176(58) adopted on 10 October 2008. Revised Annex VI entered into force on 1 July 2010.
91 Regulations 13(6) and 14(3) were amended by Resolution MEPC.190(60) on 26 March 2010. Entry into force 1 August 2011. As a consequence, the Emission Control Area includes the Baltic Sea area, the

Overall MARPOL continues to develop in response to new needs concerning the regulation of vessel-borne pollution. In this regard, three comments can be made.

First, the development of the regulation of vessel-source pollution under MARPOL is essentially characterised by the opposition between environmental interests and shipping and industry interests. On the one hand, stringent regulation of vessel-source pollution will contribute to protect the marine environment. On the other hand, it is not infrequent that the oil and shipping industry oppose new requirements for existing tankers, such as the double-hull requirement. Broadly, it can be said that the relevant provisions of MARPOL are the result of bargaining between environmental interests and shipping and industry interests.

Second, the revisions or amendments of the Annexes to MARPOL were often made in response to intense pressure arising from marine environmental disasters. For example, the *Exxon Valdez* incident in March 1989 prompted States to introduce the double-hull requirement, incorporated in Annex I in 1992. The *Erica* incident of 1999 further intensified demands for more stringent action for the phasing out of single-hull tankers. Under intense EU pressure, Annex I was amended with a view to accelerating the phase out of single-hull tankers. The *Prestige* incident of 2002 led to calls for further revision of Annex I. It may be said that serious marine disasters were a catalyst for tighter regulation under MARPOL.[92]

Third, all annexes require the Contracting Parties to undertake to ensure relevant reception facilities. However, concerns have been voiced that oil-exporting States have little incentive to bear the costs of providing reception facilities in their ports.[93] It has also been pointed out that many developing States do not consider the obligation concerning reception facilities as legally binding.[94] In the case where a port facility authority fails to handle discharged hazardous substances properly, serious problems will arise. One can take the *Probo Koala* affair as an example. In 2006, the cargo ship, *Probo Koala*, owned by a Dutch-based oil-trading company, Trafigura, tried to unload toxic waste in Amsterdam for treatment, but it decided not to do so because of the high price. Thus the *Probo Koala* was sent to Africa and discharged 500 tons of hazardous waste at a port reception facility in Abidjan, Ivory Coast, at a much lower price. An Ivorian operator, who did not have toxic waste treatment facilities, disposed of the waste in local landfills. The toxic fumes were alleged to have caused 15 deaths and hospitalisation of 69 people, and over 100,000 others sought medical treatment after the incident.[95] This incident seemed to demonstrate that in the absence of

North Sea, the North American area and any other sea area, including port areas, designated by the IMO. New appendix VII was also added to Revised Annex VI.

[92] A. K. J. Tan, *Vessel-Source Marine Pollution: The Law and Politics of International Regulation* (Cambridge University Press, 2006), pp. 139–155; G. Mattson, 'MARPOL 73/78 and Annex I: An Assessment of its Effectiveness' (2006) 9 *Journal of International Wildlife Law and Policy* pp. 185–188.

[93] Tan, *Vessel-Source Marine Pollution*, pp. 264–265.

[94] M. S. Karim, 'Implementation of the MARPOL Convention in Developing Countries' (2010) 79 *NJIL* pp. 319–320. See also Tan, *Vessel-Source Marine Pollution*, p. 267.

[95] UNEP, *UNEP Yearbook 2010*, p. 28; UN News Service, 'Toxic Wastes Caused Deaths, Illness in Côte d'Ivoire – UN Expert', 16 September 2009. In 2010, a Dutch court fined Trafigura 1 million euros

any comparable regulation of discharge of hazardous wastes on land, MARPOL merely shifts discharge of such wastes from sea to land.

6.2 The LOSC regime (1): regulation by flag States

Part XII of the LOSC contains the most detailed provisions with regard to the regulation of vessel-source pollution. Article 211(1) places a general obligation upon States to establish international rules and standards to prevent, reduce and control pollution of the marine environment from vessels and promote the adoption of routeing systems designed to minimise the threat of accidents which might cause pollution of the marine environment through the competent international organisation or general diplomatic conference. While the competent international organisation involves the IMO, it may include other international organs. Under the LOSC, vessel-source pollution is regulated by flag States, coastal States and port States.

The flag State has the primary responsibility to regulate vessel-source marine pollution. This is a corollary of the principle of the exclusive jurisdiction of the flag State. Concerning legislative jurisdiction, Article 211(2) obliges the flag State to adopt laws to regulate pollution from their vessels which 'at least have the same effect as that of generally accepted international rules and standards established through the competent international organization or general diplomatic conference'. 'The competent international organization' means the IMO. While there is no clear definition of 'generally accepted international rules', it can reasonably be presumed that those rules include the first two annexes to MARPOL because these instruments are widely ratified.[96] Penalties provided for by the laws and regulations of flag States shall be adequate in severity to discourage violations wherever they occur (Article 217(8)).

Article 217 provides enforcement jurisdiction of flag States. Under Article 217(1), flag States are required to ensure compliance by their vessels with applicable international rules and standards and with their laws concerning regulation of vessel-source pollution. Flag States are also obliged to provide for the effective enforcement of such laws and regulations, irrespective of where a violation occurs. Article 217(2) places an obligation upon flag States to take appropriate measures in order to ensure that their vessels are prohibited from sailing, until they can proceed to sea in compliance with the requirements of the international rules and standards. In relation to this, Article 217(3) imposes on flag States a duty to ensure that their vessels carry on board certificates required by and issued pursuant to international rules and standards; and that their vessels are periodically inspected in order to verify such certificates.

If a vessel commits a violation of rules and standards, the flag State is under the obligation to provide for immediate investigation and where appropriate institute proceedings in respect of the alleged violation, irrespective of where the violation occurred or where the pollution caused by such violation has occurred or has been spotted (Article

for illegally exporting waste to Ivory Coast and concealing the nature of the cargo: www.guardian.co.uk, 23 July 2010.

[96] Churchill and Lowe, *Law of the Sea*, pp. 346–347.

217(4)). At the written request of any State, flag States are obliged to investigate any violation alleged to have been committed by their vessels. If satisfied that sufficient evidence is available to enable proceedings to be brought in respect of the alleged violation, flag States shall without delay institute such proceedings in accordance with their laws (Article 217(6)). Flag States are also required to promptly inform the requesting State and the competent international organisation of the action taken and its outcome. Such information shall be available to all States by virtue of Article 217(7).

6.3 The LOSC regime (2): regulation by coastal States

With a view to complementing the flag State's responsibility over ships, the LOSC allows coastal States to exercise legislative and enforcement jurisdiction to regulate vessel-source pollution.

Concerning legislative jurisdiction, Article 211(4) empowers coastal States, in the exercise of their sovereignty within their territorial sea, to adopt laws to regulate vessel-source pollution. Such laws and regulations must not hamper innocent passage of foreign vessels. Article 21(1)(f) also allows the coastal State to adopt laws and regulations to protect the marine environment from vessels exercising the right of innocent passage through the territorial sea. However, such laws and regulations shall not apply to the design, construction, manning or equipment of foreign ships unless they are giving effect to generally accepted international rules and standards pursuant to Article 21(2). The coastal State is obliged to give due publicity to all such laws and regulations under Article 21(3). Such laws and regulations must be non-discriminatory (Article 24(1)(b)).

The establishment of the 200-nm EEZ enlarged the spatial scope of coastal State jurisdiction relating to the regulation of vessel-source pollution. Article 211(5) provides that coastal States may in respect of their EEZs adopt laws and regulations for the prevention, reduction and control of pollution from vessels conforming to and giving effect to generally accepted international rules and standards. Further to this, in a 'particular, clearly defined area' of their EEZs, Article 211(6) allows coastal States to adopt additional laws and regulations for the prevention, reduction and control of pollution from vessels implementing such international rules and standards or navigational practices for special areas after appropriate consultations through the competent international organisation. These laws and regulations apply to foreign vessels fifteen months after the submission of the communication to the organisation, provided that the organisation agrees within twelve months after the submission.

With regard to the enforcement jurisdiction of coastal States, Article 220(1) holds that when a vessel is voluntarily within a port or at an offshore terminal of a State, that State may institute proceedings in respect of any violation of the laws and regulations of that State concerning vessel-source pollution 'when the violation has occurred within the territorial sea or the exclusive economic zone of that State'. Article 220(2) further stipulates that where there are clear grounds for believing that a vessel navigating in the territorial sea of a State has, during its passage therein, violated laws and regulations of that State relating to vessel-source pollution, that State may undertake physical inspection of the vessel relating to the violation and may institute proceedings, including detention of the vessel.

Article 220(3)–(6) contains provisions concerning a violation of relevant rules committed by a foreign vessel in the EEZ of a coastal State. Where there are clear grounds for believing that a vessel navigating in the EEZ or the territorial sea of a State has, in the EEZ, committed a violation of applicable international rules and standards for the regulation of vessel-source pollution, that State may require the vessel to give relevant information pursuant to Article 220(3). Under Article 220(5), the coastal State is allowed to undertake physical inspection of vessels where there are clear grounds for believing that a vessel navigating in the EEZ or the territorial sea of a State has, in the EEZ, committed a violation referred to in Article 220(3) resulting in 'a substantial discharge causing or threatening significant pollution of the marine environment' and the vessel has refused to give information or if the information supplied by the vessel is manifestly at variance with the evident factual situation and if the circumstances of the case justify such inspection. Article 220(6) further provides that where there is clear objective evidence that a vessel navigating in the EEZ or the territorial sea of a State has, in the EEZ, committed a violation referred to in paragraph 3 resulting in 'a discharge causing major damage or threat of major damage' to the coastline or related interests of the coastal State, or to any resources of its territorial sea or EEZ, that State may institute proceedings, including detention of the vessel, in accordance with its laws.

It would follow that the detention of the foreign vessel is allowed only where its violation in the EEZ results in 'discharge causing major damage or threat of major damage'. Where the violation by the foreign vessel in the EEZ results in 'a substantial discharge causing or threatening significant pollution of the marine environment', the coastal State power is limited to undertaking physical inspection of the vessel. However, the distinction between 'a substantial discharge causing or threatening significant pollution of the marine environment' referred to in Article 220(3) and 'a discharge causing major damage or threat of major damage' provided in Article 220(6) seems to be obscure. The effect may be that the coastal States are likely to categorise any significant discharge under the rubric of 'a discharge causing major damage or threat of major damage' with a view to exercising greater enforcement jurisdiction.[97]

However, it must be noted that the coastal State enforcement is subject to several safeguards set out in section 7 of Part XII. For instance, the powers of enforcement against foreign vessels may only be exercised by governmental ships and aircraft under Article 224. States shall not endanger the safety of navigation in accordance with Article 225. Under Article 227, States are under the obligation not to discriminate in form or in fact against vessels of any other State. Furthermore, Article 226 ensures that States shall not delay a foreign vessel longer than is essential for the purposes of the investigation.

[97] *Ibid.*, p. 349.

Whenever appropriate procedures have been established whereby compliance with requirements for bonding or other appropriate financial security has been assured, the coastal State, if bound by such procedures, is required to allow the vessel to proceed pursuant to Article 220(7). Under Article 228, proceedings to impose penalties in respect of any violations of applicable laws or international rules committed by a foreign State are to be suspended where the flag State imposes penalties in respect of corresponding charges within six months. But this restriction does not apply where those proceedings relate to a case of major damage to the coastal State or the flag State in question has repeatedly disregarded its obligation to enforce effectively the applicable international rules and standards. Normally the penalties imposed for a violation must be limited to monetary ones by virtue of Article 230. Where measures against vessels are unlawful or exceed those reasonably required, States are to be liable for damage or loss attributable to them arising from such measures (Article 232).

6.4 The LOSC regime (3): regulation by port States

Under customary international law, a port State has no jurisdiction over activities of a foreign vessel on the high seas. However, the LOSC has introduced a new mode of regulation of vessel-source pollution by port States. Article 218(1) provides as follows:

> When a vessel is voluntarily within a port or at an off-shore terminal of a State, that State may undertake investigations and, where the evidence so warrants, institute proceedings in respect of any discharge from that vessel outside the internal waters, territorial sea or exclusive economic zone of that State in violation of applicable international rules and standards established through the competent international organization or general diplomatic conference.

The port State jurisdiction is innovative in the sense that the port State is entitled to take enforcement action against the vessel even where a violation was committed on the high seas or marine spaces under other States' jurisdiction, regardless of direct damage. The legal ground of port State jurisdiction rests on the treaty provision, not customary law. The port State jurisdiction must be distinct from the universal jurisdiction under customary law.

Under Article 218, the port State would assume the role of an organ of the international community in the protection of the marine environment and safety at sea. In this sense, the port State jurisdiction may provide an interesting example with regard to the individual application of the law of '*dédoublement fonctionnel*' presented by Georges Scelle.[98] According to Scelle, the realisation of law in every society must rest on three functions, namely, legislative, judicial and enforcement functions. As there is no centralised organ to perform the three social functions in international society, however, these functions are to be performed by State organs in the inter-State

[98] D. Vignes, 'Le navire et les utilisations pacifiques de la mer: la jurisdiction de l'Etat du port et le navire en droit international', in Société française pour le droit international, *Colloque de Toulon: Le Navire en Droit International* (Paris, Pedone, 1992), pp. 149–150.

order. Where State organs perform their functions in the municipal legal order, they are considered as national organs. Where State organs perform their functions in the international legal order, they are regarded as international organs. Thus, in the view of Scelle, State organs perform a dual role. The dual role is called the law of *dédoublement fonctionnel*,[99] which has a valuable part to play in the protection of community interests in international law, including the law of the sea. However, the enforcement of port State jurisdiction is not free from difficulty in practice.

First, the power to exercise port State jurisdiction is permissive, not an obligation. The LOSC contains no mechanism to supervise the implementation of port State jurisdiction. Accordingly, it appears questionable whether the port State has good incentives to exercise its jurisdiction effectively.[100]

Second, it would be very difficult if not impossible to detect evidence of a specific discharge violation in marine spaces beyond the limits of national jurisdiction. There may also be logistical problems for ports which receive many ship visits annually.[101]

Third, port State jurisdiction is subject to substantive and procedural restrictions. Concerning substantive restrictions, port State jurisdiction deals only with the violation of international rules with regard to vessel-source pollution. Thus, any breach of international rules relating to construction, design, equipment, crewing and other vessel standards falls outside the scope of Article 218. Further to this, the port State can enforce only 'international rules and standards established through the competent international organization or general diplomatic conference'. In practice, these rules and standards are considered to be established by MARPOL.[102] Accordingly, it can be said that the port State is not free to create and enforce its own discharge rules and standards.

With regard to procedural restrictions, Article 218(2) prohibits the port State from instituting proceedings where a discharge violation occurred in the internal waters, territorial sea or EEZ of another State unless that State, or the flag State, or a State damaged or threatened by the discharge violation so requests, or where the violation has caused or is likely to cause pollution in the internal waters, territorial sea or EEZ of the

99 With respect to the law of *dédoublement fonctionnel*, see G. Scelle, 'Le phénomène juridique du dédoublement fonctionnel', in *Rechtsfragen der internationalen Organisation: Festschrift für Hans Wehberg zu seinem Geburtstag* (Frankfurt am Main, Vittorio Klostermann, 1956), pp. 324–342; A. Cassese, 'Remarks on Scelle's Theory of "Role Splitting" (*dédoublement fonctionnel)* in International Law' (1990) 1 *EJIL* pp. 210–231. For an analysis of the law of *dédoublement fonctionnel* in the context of the law of the sea, see Y. Tanaka, 'Protection of Community Interests in International Law: The Case of the Law of the Sea' (2011) 15 *Max Planck Yearbook of United Nations Law* pp. 350 *et seq*.

100 In fact, Ho-Sam Bang indicated that there have been no court cases where port States have prosecuted foreign vessels for unlawful discharges in accordance with Article 218 of the LOSC. Ho-Sam Bang, 'Port State Jurisdiction and Article 218 of the UN Convention on the Law of the Sea' (2009) 40 *Journal of Maritime Law and Commerce* p. 312.

101 T. Keselj, 'Port State Jurisdiction in Respect of Pollution from Ships: The 1982 United Nations Convention on the Law of the Sea and the Memoranda of Understanding' (1999) 30 *ODIL* p. 138; Tan, *Vessel-Source Marine Pollution*, p. 220.

102 T. L. McDorman, 'Port State Enforcement: A Comment on Article 218 of the 1982 Law of the Sea Convention' (1997) 28 *Journal of Maritime Law and Commerce* p. 316.

port State. Port State jurisdiction is further qualified by Article 226. Article 226(1)(a) requires that States shall not delay a foreign vessel longer than is essential for the purposes of the investigations. Under the same provision, any physical inspection of a foreign vessel shall be limited to documentary examination. Further physical inspection of the vessel may be undertaken only when:

- there are clear grounds for believing that the documents do not correspondent substantially with the condition of the vessel;
- the documents are insufficient to confirm or verify a suspected violation; or
- the vessel is not carrying valid certificates and records.

If the investigation indicates a violation of applicable laws or international rules and standards for the protection of the marine environment, release is to be made promptly subject to reasonable procedures such as bonding or other appropriate financial security pursuant to Article 226(1)(b).

Under Article 218(4), the records of the investigation carried out by a port State pursuant to this Article are to be transmitted upon request to the flag State or to the coastal State. Any proceedings instituted by the port State on the basis of such an investigation may, subject to section 7, be suspended at the request of the coastal State when the violation has occurred within its internal waters, territorial sea or EEZ. Further to this, the flag State may force a suspension of the proceedings being undertaken by the port State for an alleged discharge violation where the flag State takes proceedings to impose penalties in respect of corresponding charges within six months pursuant to Article 228(1).

6.5 Port State Control

One of the essential limitations of the regulation of vessel-borne pollution by individual States involves the lack of coordination. In response, there is a need to institutionalise compliance mechanisms for such regulation. In this respect, it is important to note that many IMO treaties respecting the regulation of marine pollution, marine safety and seafarers working conditions have introduced port State control. This is a mechanism for verifying whether a foreign vessel itself and its documentation comply with international rules and standards relating to the safety of ships, living and working conditions on board ships and protection of the marine environment set out by relevant treaties. Unlike port State jurisdiction under Article 218 of the LOSC, port State control does not prosecute the vessel for an alleged breach of relevant international rules and standards. It is limited to taking an administrative measure of verification, including detention of a vessel. In this respect, port State control must be distinct from port State jurisdiction under Article 218 of the LOSC.[103]

Many global treaties in the field of pollution regulation and marine safety provide port State control. Examples include: the 1974 International Convention for the Safety

[103] *Ibid.*, p. 320; Ho-Sam Bang, 'Is Port State Control an Effective Means to Combat Vessel-Source Pollution? An Empirical Survey of the Practical Exercise by Port States of Their Powers of Control' (2008) 23 *IJMCL* p. 717.

of Life at Sea (SOLAS),[104] MARPOL,[105] the 1976 ILO Convention No. 147 concerning Minimum Standards in Merchant Ships,[106] the 1966 International Convention on Load Lines,[107] the 1978 International Convention on Standards of Training, Certification and Watchkeeping for Seafarers,[108] and the 2006 Maritime Labour Convention.[109]

In order to enhance the efficiency of port State control set out by these treaties, it is desirable to coordinate the action between port States. The concerted action will also be useful to eliminate so-called 'port shopping' and to reduce the burden of repetitive inspections of foreign ships. Thus port States have formulated regional institutions effectuating port State control through Memorandums of Understanding (MOUs).[110] To date, nine MOUs on regional port State control have been established: the 1982 Paris Memorandum of Understanding on Port State Control (hereafter the Paris MOU),[111] the 1992 Viña del Mar (or Latin-American Agreement), the 1993 Tokyo MOU on Port State Control (the Asia-Pacific region), the 1996 Caribbean MOU, the 1997 Mediterranean MOU, the 1998 Indian Ocean MOU, the 1999 Abuja (the West and Central African Region) MOU, the 2000 Black Sea MOU, and the 2004 Riyadh (the Arab States of the Gulf) MOU. In addition, on 19 June 1995, EC Council Directive 95/21/EC on Port State Control was adopted.[112]

Port State control enables States Parties to MOUs to carry out inspections in order to verify compliance with relevant treaties concerning safety at sea and the regulation of vessel-source pollution which are legally binding on them in a uniform manner. In so doing, port State control contributes to protect community interests. It may be argued that port State control can be considered as an institutional application of the law of *dédoublement fonctionnel.*

On the other hand, it should be noted that considerable differences in practice exist between States that are party to MOUs. In the case of the Indian Ocean MOU, for instance, in 2010, Mauritius carried out only four inspections, whilst Australia carried out 3127 inspections.[113] Such a difference in practice may create a port of convenience. There are also differences in the inspection rate between MOUs. In 2009, for example, the inspection rate in the Tokyo MOU was approximately 61 per cent[114] and that in the

[104] Annex Chapter 1, Regulation 19. 1184 *UNTS*, 278. Entered into force on 25 May 1980.

[105] Regulation 11 of Annex I, Regulation 16(9) of Annex II, Regulation 8 of Annex III, Regulation 8 of Annex V, and Regulation 10 of Annex VI.

[106] Article 4. Entered into force on 28 November 1981. The text of the Convention is available at: www.ilo.org/.

[107] Article 21. 640 *UNTS* p. 133. Entered into force on 21 July 1968.

[108] Article X and Regulation I/4. 1361 *UNTS*, p. 2. Entered into force on 28 April 1984.

[109] Regulation 5.2. Not entered into force. The text of the Convention is available at: www.ilo.org/.

[110] Whatever the need for caution, normally an MOU is considered as an instrument which is not legally binding. A. Aust, *Modern Treaty Law and Practice* (Cambridge University Press, 2007), p. 32. In this regard, it is to be noted that the Paris MOU used a less mandatory term, namely 'will'.

[111] The Paris MOU has been amended several times since 1982. On 11 May 2010, the 32nd amendment was adopted and entered into force on 1 January 2011.

[112] For an analysis of this Directive, along with the text, see E. J. Molenaar, 'The EC Directive on Port State Control in Context: The European Union' (1996) 11 *IJMCL* pp. 241–288. This Directive was amended by Directive 2001/106/EC on 19 December 2001.

[113] Indian Ocean Memorandum of Understanding on Port State Control, Annual Report 2010, p. 10.

[114] *Annual Report on Port State Control in the Asia-Pacific Region 2009*, 11.

Black Sea MOU was 58.6 per cent.[115] In the same year, the inspection rate in the Paris MOU was 29.93 per cent.[116] Furthermore, differences exist with regard to the status of ratifications of relevant instruments between Member States to MOUs. In addition, relevant instruments applied by port State authorities vary according to the MOUs. In order to enhance the efficiency of port State control, there is a need to increase coordination and cooperation between regional MOUs.

6.6 Intervention by coastal States in the case of pollution casualties

The next issue that needs to be addressed involves relevant measures *after* pollution or the threat of pollution is caused by vessels. There is little doubt that coastal States are entitled to exercise jurisdiction to prevent and control marine pollution in marine spaces under their territorial sovereignty. However, a question arises as to whether these States can exercise jurisdiction on this matter in marine spaces beyond their territorial sovereignty, in particular on the high seas. As noted earlier, this question was vividly raised in the context of the 1967 *Torrey Canyon* incident. After exhausting all other possibilities, the British government decided to bomb the wreck, although on the high seas. Whilst neither the owner nor Liberia made a protest against this action,[117] doubts were raised with regard to the legality of the action of the British government.

In response to this question, the IMO adopted the International Convention Relating to Intervention on the High Seas in Cases of Oil Pollution Casualties in 1969 (hereafter the High Seas Intervention Convention).[118] Article I(1) of this Convention explicitly allows the Parties 'to take such measures on the high seas as may be necessary to prevent, mitigate or eliminate grave and imminent danger to their coastline or related interests from pollution or threat of pollution of the sea by oil, following upon a maritime casualty or acts related to such a casualty, which may reasonably be expected to result in major harmful consequences'. However, no measures shall be taken against any warship or other ship owned or operated by a State under Article I(2). 'Maritime casualty' as referred to in this provision means 'a collision of ships, stranding or other incident of navigation, or other occurrence on board a ship or external to it resulting in material damage or imminent threat of material damage to a ship or cargo' (Article II(1)). It would follow that the coastal State cannot exercise the right of intervention in the case of operational pollution or dumping at sea.

Articles III and V specify the conditions to take measures necessary to prevent pollution or threat of pollution of the sea by oil. It is notable that 'before taking any

[115] *Port State Control in the Black Sea Region, Annual Report 2009*, 5.

[116] Paris MOU, *Annual Report 2009*, 18.

[117] The owners and time charterers agreed to pay the sum of £3 million in full and final settlement of the claims of the governments of the United Kingdom and France, between whom this sum was to be shared equally. The owners also agreed to make available sums up to £25,000 for the purpose of compensating individual claimants in both States. If the cost of settling claims exceeded this sum the two governments agreed to indemnify the owners against any excess in their respective countries. 'Remarks by U.K. Attorney General on "Torrey Canyon" Settlement' (1970) 9 *ILM* pp. 633–635.

[118] 970 *UNTS* p. 212. Entered into force on 6 May 1975.

measures', a coastal State is required to proceed to consultations with other States affected by the maritime casualty, particularly with the flag State or States pursuant to Article III(a). In the cases of extreme urgency requiring measures to be taken immediately, however, the coastal State may take measures without prior notification or consultation by virtue of Article III(d). Measures taken by the coastal State in accordance with Article I shall be proportionate to the damage actual or threatened to it (Article V(1)). Such measures must not go beyond what is reasonably necessary to achieve the end mentioned in Article I and shall cease as soon as the end has been achieved. These measures shall not unnecessarily interfere with the rights and interests of the flag State, third States and of any persons, physical or corporate, concerned (Article V(2)).

The scope of the 1969 High Seas Intervention Convention was further extended by the 1973 Protocol.[119] Whilst the 1969 Convention applies only to intervention in the case of pollution by oil, the Protocol extended the scope of a coastal State's intervention to casualties caused by substances other than oil.[120] 'Substances other than oil' means those substances enumerated in a list which was established by an appropriate body designated by the IMO and annexed to the Protocol and those other substances which are liable to create hazards to human health, to harm living resources and marine life, to damage amenities or to interfere with other legitimate uses of the sea.[121]

Under the LOSC, the coastal State rights of intervention are indirectly provided by Article 221. Paragraph 1 of this provision stipulates that:

> Nothing in this Part shall prejudice the right of States, pursuant to international law, both customary and conventional, to take and enforce measures beyond the territorial sea proportionate to the actual or threatened damage to protect their coastline or related interests, including fishing, from pollution or threat of pollution following upon a maritime casualty or acts relating to such a casualty, which may reasonably be expected to result in major harmful consequences.[122]

It is to be noted that intervention under this provision is assumed to take place where there is 'actual or threatened damage' which may 'reasonably be expected to result in major harmful consequences', whilst the 1969 Intervention Convention and its Protocol set out a high threshold referring to 'grave and imminent danger' of damage to the coastline as a condition for intervention.[123] To this extent, a condition to exercise the right of intervention seems to be mitigated under the LOSC.[124] Article 221(2) makes

[119] Protocol Relating to Intervention on the High Seas in Cases of Pollution by Substances Other than Oil. 1313 *UNTS* p. 4. Entered into force on 30 March 1983.

[120] Article I(1).

[121] Article I(2).

[122] This provision does not apply to any warship, naval auxiliary, or other governmental vessels used for non-commercial service pursuant to Article 236 of the LOSC.

[123] Article I(1) of the 1969 High Seas Intervention Convention; Article I(1) of the 1973 Protocol.

[124] Following the *Amoco Cadiz* disaster, some States, notably France, suggested that the threshold of the 1969 Convention was too restrictive and intervention should be permitted at an early stage. Thus the wording of Article 211 was modified during negotiations to omit any reference to 'grave and imminent danger'. Birnie, Boyle and Redgwell, *International Law and Environment*, p. 427.

clear that 'marine casualty' does not include a pollution incident resulting from dumping or operational pollution. Accordingly, the coastal State may invoke the rights of intervention only in the event of a collision of vessels.

6.7 Pollution emergencies at sea

In the event of maritime disasters, a question arises as to how it is possible to respond to pollution emergencies. The LOSC specifies three obligations on this matter.

First, when a State becomes aware of cases in which the marine environment is in imminent danger of being damaged or has been damaged by pollution, Article 198 obliges the State to immediately notify other States it deems likely to be affected by such damage, as well as the competent international organisations.[125] The obligation to notify imminent damage is supplemented by Article 8 of MARPOL 73/78 and its Protocol I. A similar obligation to report any marine pollution incident is also enshrined in regional treaties respecting pollution emergencies at sea.[126] Considering that coastal States can only take effective measures if information of impending disasters has been submitted to them in a timely manner, prompt notification is particularly important in response to pollution emergencies.

Second, Article 199 requires States in the area affected by pollution to cooperate, to the extent possible, in eliminating the effects of pollution and preventing or minimising the damage. To this end, States are obliged to jointly develop and promote contingency plans for responding to pollution incidents in the marine environment.

Third, where a pollution emergency occurred within the jurisdiction or control of a State, that State is obliged to take all measures necessary to ensure that that pollution does not spread beyond the areas where they exercise sovereign rights (Article 194(2)).

These obligations under the LOSC are amplified by the 1990 OPRC. This Convention aims to provide a global framework for international cooperation in response to oil pollution incidents. Article 3 obliges each Party to require that ships entitled to fly its flag have on board a shipboard oil pollution emergency plan in accordance with provisions adopted by the IMO for this purpose. Article 4(1) places a clear obligation upon each Party to require masters or other persons having charge of ships flying its flag to report without delay any event on their ship involving a discharge or probable discharge of oil to the nearest coastal State. Whenever a Party receives a report referred to in Article 4 or pollution information provided by other sources, it shall assess the event, the nature, extent and possible consequences of the oil pollution incident.

[125] See also Article 211(7).

[126] Examples include: the 1982 Protocol concerning Regional Cooperation in Combating Pollution by Oil and Other Harmful Substances in Cases of Emergency (Article 7); the 1985 Protocol Concerning Cooperation in Combating Marine Pollution in Cases of Emergency in the Eastern African Region (Article 5); the 2002 Protocol Concerning Cooperation in Preventing Pollution from Ships and, in Cases of Emergency, Combating Pollution of the Mediterranean Sea (Articles 9 and 10); the 1992 Convention on the Protection of the Marine Environment of the Baltic Sea Area (Annex VII); the 2006 Protocol on Hazardous and Noxious Substances Pollution, Preparedness, Response and Cooperation in the Pacific Region (Article 5).

Next, the Party is required, without delay, to inform all States whose interests are affected or likely to be affected by such oil pollution incident together with details of its assessments and any action it has taken (Article 5(1)). Article 6(1) further imposes on each Party to establish a national system for responding promptly and effectively to oil pollution incidents. When the severity of the incident so justifies, Parties agree to cooperate and provide advisory services, technical support and equipment for the purpose of responding to an oil pollution incident upon the request of any Party affected or likely to be affected (Article 7(1)).

In 2000, the Protocol on Preparedness, Response and Co-operation to Pollution Incidents by Hazardous and Noxious Substances was adopted by States who were party to the OPRC Convention (hereafter the HNS Protocol).[127] Like the OPRC Convention, the HNS Protocol aims to establish a global framework for international cooperation in response to pollution incidents by hazardous and noxious substances other than oil. Under Article 2(2), 'hazardous and noxious substances' means any substance other than oil which, if introduced into the marine environment is likely to create hazards to human health, to harm living resources and marine life, to damage amenities or to interfere with other legitimate uses of the sea. Under the HNS Protocol, each Party is obliged to apply rules similar to those in the OPRC to these substances.

In relation to pollution emergencies at sea, some mention should be made of salvage because it also involves control of such emergencies.[128] Under Article 1 of the 1989 International Convention on Salvage (hereafter the Salvage Convention),[129] salvage operation means 'any act or activity undertaken to assist a vessel or any other property in danger in navigable waters or in any other waters whatsoever'. Traditionally salvage is based on the 'no cure no pay' principle. According to this principle, a salvor who failed to save the ship or the cargo received no reward. The 'no cure no pay' principle was enshrined in the 1910 Convention for the Unification of Certain Rules of Law respecting Assistance and Salvage at Sea,[130] and was regarded as customary maritime law. In light of growing environmental awareness, however, it became apparent that salvage law on the basis of the 'no cure no pay' principle cannot adequately respond to large-scale pollution emergencies at sea for at least two reasons.

First, this traditional principle does not take environmental protection into account. It provides salvors with no reward for work carried out preventing marine pollution by oil or other hazardous substances.[131] As a consequence, salvors would have little incentive to provide salvage services where there is no or little prospect of saving the

[127] Entered into force on 14 June 2007. For the text of the Protocol, see IMO, *OPRC-HNS Protocol: Protocol on Preparedness, Response and Co-operation to Pollution Incidents by Hazardous and Noxious Substances, 2000* (London, IMO, 2002).

[128] Whilst legal literature is not in agreement on the legal nature of salvage law, the better view may be that the law is more a part of maritime law applicable to individuals than to States. R. Garabello, 'Salvage', in *Max Planck Encyclopaedia*, p. 2, para. 10. A detailed analysis of salvage law is beyond the scope of this chapter.

[129] (1990) 14 *Law of the Sea Bulletin* p. 77. Entered into force on 14 July 1996.

[130] Article 2 of the 1910 Convention. The Convention entered into force on 1 March 1913. The text of the Convention is available at www.admiraltylawguide.com/conven/salvage1910.html.

[131] Birnie, Boyle and Redgwell, *International Law and Environment*, p. 429.

endangered property, even though major salvage operations are needed with a view to preventing environmental disaster.[132]

Second, the traditional principle presupposes that are only two parties to the salvage service are involved, namely, the salvor and the salved (ship, cargo and freight) and their insurers. Due to the increasing transportation of hazardous cargoes by sea and growth in the size of vessels, however, the protection of the environmental interests of the coastal State is currently stressed in pollution emergencies at sea.[133]

The *Amoco Cadiz* disaster of 1978 triggered a call for re-evaluation of existing salvage law, which resulted in the adoption of the 1989 Salvage Convention. The 1989 Salvage Convention seeks to remedy the limits of traditional salvage law. Article 13 of the Convention thus introduced 'the skill and efforts of the salvors in preventing or minimising damage to the environment' as one of the criteria for fixing the reward. Furthermore, Article 14 of the Convention introduced special compensation in order to enhance the incentive for the salvor. In accordance with this provision, salvors are entitled to receive special compensation for salvage operations which have prevented or minimised damage to the marine environment. In addition to this, Article 8 obliges the salvor and the owner and master of the vessel or the owner of other property in danger to exercise due care to prevent or minimise damage to the environment.

6.8 Liability for oil pollution damage

Marine pollution incidents raise issues with regard to liability for pollution damage. In this regard, Article 235(1) of the LOSC provides that States are responsible for the fulfilment of their international obligations concerning the protection and preservation of the marine environment. States are obliged to ensure that recourse is available in accordance with their legal systems for prompt and adequate compensation or other relief in respect of damage caused by pollution of the marine environment by natural or juridical persons under their jurisdiction pursuant to Article 235(2). With the objective of assuring prompt and adequate compensation in respect of all damage caused by pollution of the marine environment, Article 235(3) obliges States to cooperate in the implementation of existing international law and the further development of international law relating to liability in this field.

Liability treaties can be divided into two categories: treaties concerning liability for oil pollution damage and those relating to liability for other pollution damage. Legal frameworks of civil liability for pollution are complex and only an outline can be provided here. This section will address civil liability for oil pollution damage. Broadly, the development of liability and compensation regimes for oil pollution damage can be divided into three stages.

[132] C. Redgwell, 'The Greening of Salvage Law' (1990) *Marine Policy* pp. 142–143.

[133] *Ibid.*, p. 144; E. Gold, 'Marine Salvage: Towards a New Regime' (1989) 20 *Journal of Maritime Law and Commerce* p. 489.

(a) The first stage

The first form of compensation regime was established by the 1969 International Convention on Civil Liability for Oil Pollution Damage (the 1969 Civil Liability Convention)[134] and the 1971 International Convention on the Establishment of an International Fund for Compensation for Oil Pollution Damage (the 1971 Fund Convention).[135] Subject to several exceptions, the 1969 Civil Liability Convention places strict liability on the shipowner for oil pollution damage caused in the territory, including the territorial sea of a contracting State, as a result of an incident (Article III). Under Article V, however, the shipowner may limit his liability in respect of any one incident to an aggregate amount of 2,000 Poincaré francs for each ton of the ship's tonnage, except where the incident occurred as a result of the actual fault or privity of the shipowner. This aggregate amount shall not in any event exceed 210 million francs.

The Civil Liability Convention was supplemented by the 1971 Fund Convention. It establishes 'the International Oil Pollution Compensation Fund' (hereafter the Fund) with a view to providing compensation for pollution damage to the extent that the protection afforded by the Liability Convention is inadequate (Article 2). Contributions to the Fund shall be made in respect of each Contracting State by any person who, in the calendar year referred to in Article 11(1), has received in total quantities exceeding 150,000 tons of oil by sea in the territory of that State (Article 10). Under Article 4(4), the aggregate amount of compensation payable by the Fund shall in respect of any one incident be limited, so that the total sum of that amount and the amount of compensation actually paid under the Civil Liability Convention for pollution damage shall not exceed 450 million francs.

In summary, the civil liability regime established by the 1969 Civil Liability Convention and the 1971 Fund Convention is based on the two-tiered system, namely, strict liability of the shipowner and the Fund financed by oil-importing persons. Under this system, compensation costs are shared by the shipowner and oil importers. Here one can detect a prototype of civil liability regime for marine pollution. Later, it became apparent that the limits of liability under the 1969 Civil Liability Convention were too low to provide adequate compensation. In fact, due to the gravity of the damage, the *Amoco Cadiz* accident of 1978 highlighted the need to reconsider compensation ceilings for oil spills. Thus, in 1984, two Protocols were adopted in order to amend the Civil Liability and Fund Conventions. Whilst the two Protocols set increased limits of liability, neither Protocol came into force because of the reluctance of the United States, a major oil importer, to accept the Protocol.

(b) The second stage

The second form of regime for civil liability and compensation was created by two Protocols adopted in 1992 which superseded the 1984 Protocols.[136] They created

[134] 973 *UNTS* p. 3. Entered into force on 19 June 1975.

[135] 1953 *UNTS* p. 373. Entered into force on 16 October 1978.

[136] Protocol of 1992 to Amend the International Convention on Civil Liability for Oil Pollution Damage 1969, with Annex and Final Act. 1956 *UNTS* p. 285. Protocol of 1992 to Amend the International

new conventions known as the 1992 Civil Liability Convention and the 1992 Fund Convention.[137] Basic elements of the 1992 Civil Liability Convention can be summarised as follows.

First, concerning the conventional scope, the 1992 Civil Liability Convention applies exclusively to pollution damage caused in the territory, including the territorial sea, and in the EEZ or equivalent area of a Contracting State (Article II). It would follow that pollution damage on the high seas is excluded from the scope of the Convention. Where an incident has caused pollution damage in these marine spaces of one or more Contracting States, actions for compensation may only be brought in the courts of any such Contracting State or States in accordance with Article IX(1).

Second, 'pollution damage' comprises loss or damage caused by contamination resulting from the escape or discharge of oil from the ship and the costs of preventive measures and further loss or damage caused by preventive measures. Notably, compensation for impairment of the environment other than loss of profit from such impairment shall be recoverable. However, it is limited to 'costs of reasonable measures of reinstatement actually undertaken or to be undertaken' (Article I(6)).[138]

Third, the 1992 Civil Liability Convention provides strict liability for shipowners.[139] In this regard, Article III(1) makes clear that except as provided in paragraphs 2 and 3 of this Article, the owner of a ship at the time of an incident shall be liable for any pollution damage caused by the ship as a result of the incident.[140]

Fourth, under Article VII, the owner of a ship registered in a Contracting State and carrying more than 2,000 tons of oil in bulk as cargo shall be required to maintain insurance or other financial security, in the sums fixed by applying the limits of liability prescribed in Article V(1) to cover his liability for pollution damage under the Convention. This is a system of compulsory liability insurance.

Convention on the Establishment of an International Fund for Compensation for Oil Pollution Damage. 1953 *UNTS* p. 330. The two Protocols entered into force on 30 May 1996. The 1971 Fund Convention ceased to be in force on 24 May 2002.

137 The texts of the 1992 Civil Liability Convention and the 1992 Fund Convention are reproduced in International Oil Pollution Compensation Funds, *Liability and Compensation for Oil Pollution Damage: Texts of the 1992 Conventions and the Supplementary Fund Protocol, 2005 Edition.* From 16 May 1998, Parties to the 1992 Protocol ceased to be Parties to the 1969 Civil Liability Convention. Equally, from 16 May 1998, Parties to the 1992 Protocol ceased to be Parties to the 1971 Fund Convention. As at 1 May 2011, 123 States became Parties to the 1992 Civil Liability Convention and 105 States became Parties to the 1992 Fund Convention.

138 Concerning the concept of environmental damage, see Birnie, Boyle and Redgwell, *International Law and the Environment*, pp. 437–438.

139 'Owner' means the person or persons registered as the owner of the ship or, in the absence of registration, the person or persons owning the ship. However, in the case of a ship owned by a State and operated by a company which in that State is registered as the ship's operator, 'owner' shall mean such company (Article I (3)).

140 These exceptions provided in Article III(2) are where damage: (a) resulted from an act of war or an inevitable natural phenomenon, (b) was wholly caused by an act or omission done with intent to cause damage by a third party, or (c) was wholly caused by the negligence or other wrongful act of any government or other authority responsible for the maintenance of lights or other navigational aids in the exercise of that function.

Fifth, the compensation limits were those originally agreed in 1984. Later, the 2000 amendments raised the limits by some 50.37 per cent as follows:[141]

- For a ship not exceeding 5,000 gross tonnage: liability is limited to 4.51 million Special Drawing Rights (SDR) as defined by the International Monetary Fund,
- For a ship 5,000 to 140,000 gross tonnage: liability is limited to 4.51 million SDR plus 631 SDR for each additional gross tonne over 5,000,
- For a ship over 140,000 gross tonnage: liability is limited to 89.77 million SDR.[142]

The 1992 Fund Convention established the International Oil Pollution Compensation Fund 1992 (IOPC or 1992 Fund). Under Article 4 of the Convention, the 1992 Fund is to pay compensation to any person suffering pollution damage if such person has been unable to obtain full and adequate compensation for the damage under the terms of the 1992 Liability Convention because of three reasons:

- no liability for damage arises under the 1992 Liability Convention,
- the shipowner liable for the damage under the 1992 Liability Convention is financially incapable of meeting his obligation in full, and
- the damage exceeds the shipowner's liability under the 1992 Liability Convention as limited pursuant to Article V(1).

However, the fund shall pay no compensation if the pollution damage resulted from an act of war or was caused by oil which has escaped from a warship or other governmental ship used for non-commercial service, or the claimant cannot prove that the damage resulted from an incident involving one or more ships by virtue of Article 4(2). Like the 1992 Civil Liability Convention, the 1992 Fund Convention does not apply to pollution damage on the high seas (Article 3).

Annual contributions to the Fund are to be made in respect of each Contracting State by any person who has received in total quantities exceeding 150,000 tons of oil by sea in a calendar year (Article 10). The aggregate amount of compensation payable by the Fund for any one incident was limited to 135 million SDR, including the sum actually paid by the shipowner or his insurer under the 1992 Civil Liability Convention. However, the amendments in 2000 raised the maximum amount of compensation payable from the Fund for a single incident, including the limit established under the 2000 Civil Liability Convention amendments, to 203 million SDR.[143]

141 Amendments of the Limitation Amounts in the Protocol of 1992 to Amend the International Convention on Civil Liability for Oil Pollution Damage, 1969. Adopted on 18 October 2000. Entered into force on 1 November 2003 (under tacit acceptance).

142 The SDR is an international reserve asset, created by the International Monetary Fund in 1969. The daily conversion rates for SDRs can be found at: www.imf.org/external/np/fin/data/rms_sdrv.aspx.

143 Amendments of the Limits of Compensation in the Protocol of 1992 to Amend the International Convention on the Establishment of an International Fund for Compensation for Oil Pollution Damage, 1971. Entered into force on 1 November 2003.

(c) The third stage

The third form of compensation regime was created by the 2003 Protocol establishing an International Oil Pollution Compensation Supplementary Fund.[144] The 2003 Protocol seeks to supplement the compensation available under the 1992 Civil Liability and Fund Conventions. The Protocol is optional and is open only to Contracting States to the 1992 Fund Convention by virtue of Article 19(3). The 2003 Protocol established 'the International Oil Pollution Compensation Supplementary Fund 2003' (hereinafter the Supplementary Fund) pursuant to Article 2. Under Article 4(2)(a), the aggregate amount of compensation payable by the Supplementary Fund for any one incident is to be limited to 750 million SDR including the amount of compensation paid under the existing 1992 Civil Liability and Fund Conventions.

In summary, first, compensation for oil pollution damage is to be paid by a shipowner under the 1992 Civil Liability Convention. Second, the 1992 Fund provides compensation for pollution damage to the extent that the protection afforded by the 1992 Civil Liability Convention is inadequate. Third, the Supplementary Fund provides compensation where the maximum compensation afforded by the 1992 Fund Convention is insufficient to meet compensation needs in certain circumstances.

In addition to this, the International Convention on Civil Liability for Bunker Oil Pollution Damage was concluded in 2001 (hereafter Bunker Oil Convention).[145] This Convention seeks to ensure the payment of adequate, prompt and effective compensation for damage caused by pollution resulting from the escape or discharge of bunker oil from ships.[146] Like the 1992 Civil Liability Convention, the 2001 Bunker Oil Convention limits 'environmental damage' to costs of reasonable measures of reinstatement actually undertaken or to be undertaken.[147] Article 3 of the Convention provides strict liability of the shipowner. Furthermore, Article 7(1) obliges the shipowner having a gross tonnage greater than 1000 registered in a State Party to maintain compulsory insurance or other financial security to cover the liability of the registered owner for pollution damage in an amount equal to the limit provided in Article 6.

6.9 Liability for other pollution damage

(a) The 1996 HNS Convention

Vessel-source marine pollution may be caused by substances other than oil. In this regard, in 1996, the International Convention on Liability and Compensation for Damage in Connection with the Carriage of Hazardous and Noxious Substances by

144 Protocol of 2003 to the International Convention on the Establishment of an International Fund for Compensation for Oil Pollution Damage, 1992. Entered into force on 3 March 2005. The text of the Protocol is reproduced in *Liability and Compensation for Oil Pollution Damage*.

145 Cm 6693. Entered into force on 21 November 2008.

146 Preamble. Under Article 1(5), 'bunker oil' means 'any hydrocarbon mineral oil, including lubricating oil, used or intended to be used for the operation or propulsion of the ship, and any residues of such oil'.

147 Article 1(9)(a).

Sea (the HNS Convention) was adopted by the IMO.[148] This Convention seeks to ensure adequate, prompt and effective compensation for damage caused by incidents in connection with the carriage by sea of hazardous and noxious substances, such as chemicals.[149] Article 1(6) of the HNS Convention defines 'damage' as including:

- loss of life or personal injury,
- loss of or damage to property outside the ship,
- loss or damage by contamination of the environment caused by the hazardous and noxious substances, and
- the costs of preventive measures and further loss or damage caused by preventive measures.

The HNS Convention does not apply to oil pollution damage as defined in the 1969 Civil Liability Convention, as amended, and loss or damage caused by radioactive materials. Nonetheless, oil carried in bulk listed in appendix I of Annex I to MARPOL are included. In accordance with Article 3, the HNS Convention applies exclusively

- to any damage caused in the territory, including the territorial sea of a State Party,
- to damage by contamination of the environment caused in the EEZ of a State Party,
- to damage, other than damage by contamination of the environment, caused outside the territory, including the territorial sea, of any State,
- to preventive measures, wherever taken.

Article 3 applies to damage anywhere at sea, including the high seas, if it is not 'damage by contamination of the environment'. However, it would appear that environmental reinstatement of the high seas is ruled out.[150]

As with the regime of civil liability for oil pollution, the HNS Convention is based on a two-tier system, namely, shipowner liability and the HNS Fund, financed by cargo interests. The first tier of compensation will be paid by the shipowner. In this regard, the HNS Convention provides strict liability for the shipowner and a system of compulsory insurance.[151] Under Article 9, the shipowner is entitled to limit its liability to an amount between 10 million and 100 million SDR, depending on the gross tonnage of the ship. In those cases where the insurance does not cover an incident, or is insufficient to satisfy the claim, the second tier of the compensation system, the International Hazardous and Noxious Substances Fund (HNS Fund), comes into play. The Fund is to be financed by contributions from receivers of HNS or titleholders for liquefied natural gases (LNG) cargo pursuant to Articles 18 and 19. The aggregate amount of compensation payable by the HNS Fund shall not exceed 250 million SDR in respect of any one incident in accordance with Article 14(5)(a).

The HNS Convention has not entered into force because of an insufficient number of ratifications. Thus, in April 2010, the Protocol to the HNS Convention was adopted

148 (1996) 35 *ILM* p. 1415.

149 Hazardous and noxious substances are defined in some detail in Article 1(5) of this Convention.

150 Birnie, Boyle and Redgwell, *International Law and the Environment*, p. 440.

151 Articles 7 and 12.

in order to bring the 1996 HNS Convention into effect.[152] Once the 2010 HNS Protocol enters into force, the 1996 Convention, as amended by the 2010 Protocol, will be called the 2010 HNS Convention. Yet the 2010 Protocol has not yet entered into force.[153] Under the 2010 HNS Protocol, hazardous or noxious substance cargoes are divided into two categories, namely, bulk hazardous or noxious substances and packaged hazardous or noxious substances. If damage is caused by bulk HNS, the shipowner is entitled to limit liability to an aggregate amount between 10 million SDR and 100 million SDR depending on the tonnage of the ship. Where damage is caused by packaged HNS or by both bulk HNS and packaged HNS, the maximum liability for the shipowner is 115 million SDR. Once this limit is reached, the HNS Fund will provide an additional tier of compensation up to a maximum of 250 million SDR, including compensation paid under the first tier.

(b) Civil liability for nuclear damage

Currently there are growing concerns that the use of nuclear energy may cause the risk of nuclear damage to the marine environment. A civil liability regime for nuclear damage is based mainly on the following instruments:

- the 1960 Paris Convention on Third Party Liability in the Field of Nuclear Damage,[154] as amended by the Protocols of 1964, 1982 and 2004 (the Paris Convention),
- the 1962 Convention on the Liability of Operators of Nuclear Ships (Brussels Convention on Nuclear Ships),[155]
- the 1963 Vienna Convention on Civil Liability for Nuclear Damage as Amended by the Protocol of 12 September 1997 (the 1997 Vienna Convention),[156]
- the 1971 Convention relating to Civil Liability in the Field of Maritime Carriage of Nuclear Material,[157]
- the 1988 Joint Protocol Relating to the Application of the Vienna Convention and the Paris Convention,[158] and
- the 1997 Convention on Supplementary Compensation for Nuclear Damage (the CSC).[159]

Whilst a full examination of the above treaties is not possible here, at least four commonalities between these instruments can be identified:[160]

152 IMO, International Conference on the Revision of the HNS Convention, LEG/CONF.17/DC/1, 29 April 2010. For a brief overview of the 2010 HNS Protocol, see *IMO News*, Issue 2, 2010, p. 6; International Oil Pollution Compensation Funds, the HNS Convention as modified by the 2010 HNS Protocol, September 2010, available at: www.iopcfund.org/npdf/HNS%202010_e.pdf.

153 Denmark has become the first country to sign the 2010 HNS Protocol in 2011.

154 (1961) 55 *AJIL* p. 1082. Entered into force on 1 April 1968.

155 (1963) 57 *AJIL* p. 268. Not in force.

156 (1997) 36 *ILM* p. 1462. Entered into force on 4 October 2003.

157 Entered into force on 15 July 1975. The text is available at www.admiraltylawguide.com/conven/protooilpolfund1992.html.

158 1672 *UNTS* p. 301. Entered into force on 27 April 1992.

159 (1997) 36 *ILM* p. 1473. Not yet entered into force.

160 For an analysis in some detail of this issue, see Birnie, Boyle and Redgwell, *International Law and the Environment*, pp. 520 *et seq.*

(i) The operator of a nuclear installation or a ship shall be liable whereever the nuclear incident occurred.[161]

(ii) The liability is strict and no proof of fault or negligence is needed as a condition of liability.[162]

(iii) The operator is obliged to maintain insurance or security for compensation.[163]

(iv) In principle, the courts of the Contracting Party within whose territory the nuclear incident occurred has jurisdiction over nuclear damage from a nuclear incident.[164]

In light of the recent development of the law of the sea with regard to the EEZ, the 1997 Protocol and 1997 CSC both provide that where a nuclear incident occurs within the area of the EEZ of a Contracting Party, jurisdiction over actions respecting nuclear damage from that nuclear incident shall lie only with the courts of that Party.[165]

7 DUMPING AT SEA

7.1 Regulation of dumping at sea under the LOSC

Dumping of wastes at sea imposes pollution risks on many other States for the benefit of a small number of industrialised States. In this regard, the LOSC provides prescriptive and enforcement jurisdiction regulating dumping at sea.

Concerning prescriptive jurisdiction, Article 210(1) requires States to adopt laws and regulations to prevent, reduce and control pollution of the marine environment by dumping. Such laws and regulations shall ensure that dumping is not carried out without the permission of the competent authorities of States (Article 210(3)). Article 210(5) further provides that dumping within the territorial sea and the EEZ or onto the continental shelf shall not be carried out without the express prior approval of the coastal State. There is no reference to internal waters in this provision. However, it is clear that no dumping may be carried out in these waters without consent of the coastal State. In addition, Article 210(6) ensures that national laws and regulations shall be no less effective in preventing, reducing and controlling such pollution than the global rules and standards. As noted earlier, such global rules are embodied in the 1972 London Dumping Convention and the 1996 Protocol.[166]

In relation to enforcement jurisdiction, Article 216(1)(a) requires the coastal State to enforce laws and regulations and applicable international rules and standards for the prevention of marine pollution by dumping within its territorial sea or its EEZ or onto its continental shelf. With regard to vessels flying its flag or vessels or aircraft of its

[161] 1997 Vienna Convention (Article II); the Paris Convention (Articles 3 and 6), as amended in 2004; Brussels Convention on Nuclear Ships (Article II); 1971 Convention relating to Maritime Carriage (Article I).

[162] 1997 Vienna Convention (Article IV); Paris Convention (Article 3), as amended 2004; Brussels Convention on Nuclear Ships (Article II).

[163] 1997 Vienna Convention (Article VII); Paris Convention (Article 10), as amended 2004; Brussels Convention on Nuclear Ships (Article III).

[164] 1997 Vienna Convention (Article XI); 1997 CSC (Article XIII); Paris Convention (Article 13).

[165] Article XI (1)*bis* of the 1997 Vienna Convention; Article XIII(2) of the 1997 CSC.

[166] See section 4.2 of this chapter.

registry, the flag State is required to enforce laws and international rules to prevent pollution by dumping (Article 216(1)(b)). Concerning acts of loading of wastes or other matter occurring within its territory or at its offshore terminals, any State shall enforce laws and international rules to prevent pollution by dumping (Article 216(1)(c)). In summary, the LOSC does not prohibit dumping, while requiring States to regulate and control marine pollution by dumping at sea.

7.2 The 1972 London Dumping Convention and the 1996 Protocol

Post-LOSC development of regulation of dumping at sea can be essentially characterised by a paradigm shift in the regulatory approach 'from permission to prohibition'. At the global level, the shift is clearly reflected in the 1972 London Dumping Convention and the 1996 Protocol.

The 1972 London Dumping Convention adopted the black/grey list approach. According to this approach, waste materials are divided into three categories. On the one hand, the dumping of wastes or other matter listed in Annex I (the black list) is prohibited pursuant to Article IV(1). These wastes include organohalogen compounds, mercury, cadmium, persistent plastics, crude oil and its wastes, radioactive wastes and materials produced for biological and chemical warfare.[167] However, the dumping of wastes or other matter listed in Annex II (the grey list) and all other wastes is permitted with a prior special permit under Article IV(1)(b) and (c).

By contrast, the 1996 Protocol to the London Convention replaced the black/grey list approach by the so-called 'reverse listing' approach. In this regard, Article 4(1) of the Protocol stipulates that:

> 1(a) Contracting Parties shall prohibit the dumping of any wastes or other matter with the exception of those listed in Annex 1.[168]
>
> (b) The dumping of wastes or other matter listed in Annex 1 shall require a permit. Contracting Parties shall adopt administrative or legislative measures to ensure that issuance of permits and permit conditions comply with the provisions of Annex 2. Particular attention shall be paid to opportunities to avoid dumping in favour of environmentally preferable alternatives.

According to the reverse listing approach, the dumping of wastes is in principle prohibited, and exceptions must be clearly listed in paragraph 1 of Annex 1. Incineration at sea of wastes or other matter is also banned by Article 5. Furthermore, Article 6

[167] Concerning radioactive wastes, the 1972 London Convention prohibited the dumping only of high-level radioactive matter defined by IAEA as unsuitable for this form of disposal. As a consequence, the dumping of low-level radioactive wastes was permitted under the Convention (Annex I, paragraph 6; Annex II, paragraph (d)).

[168] The wastes listed in Annex 1 include dredged material, sewage sludge, fish waste, or material resulting from industrial fish processing operations, vessels and platforms or other man-made structures at sea, inert, organic geological material, organic material of natural origin and bulky items primarily comprising iron, steel, concrete and similarly unharmful materials, carbon dioxide streams from carbon dioxide capture processes for sequestration. Nonetheless, these materials containing levels of radioactivity greater than *de minimis* (exempt) concentrations as defined by the IAEA and adopted by Contracting Parties shall not be considered eligible for dumping (Annex 1, paragraph 3).

prohibits Contracting Parties from exporting wastes or other matter to other countries for dumping or incineration at sea.

The reverse listing approach of the 1996 Protocol seems to contrast with the black/grey list approach in the 1972 London Dumping Convention. Under the 1972 London Dumping Convention, anything may be dumped at sea unless it is prohibited. By contrast, nothing may be dumped unless it is permitted in the 1996 Protocol. The reverse listing approach in the Protocol seems to signify a significant reversal of the burden of proof.

However, the 1996 Protocol contains some exceptions. Under Article 8(1), the prohibition of the dumping and incineration at sea shall not apply in the case of *force majeure*. Furthermore, by virtue of Article 8(2), a Contracting Party may issue a permit as an exception to the above prohibition in emergencies posing an unacceptable threat to human health, safety, or the marine environment and admitting of no other feasible solution. Before doing so, however, the Contracting Party shall consult any other countries that are likely to be affected. In relation to this, it is notable that even where dumping is permitted, the 1996 Protocol provides strict procedures for controlling the dumping. In this regard, Article 9(1) obliges each Contracting Party to designate an appropriate authority to: (a) issue permits, (b) keep records of the nature and quantities of all wastes or other matter for which dumping permits have been issued, and (c) monitor the conditions of the sea. Each Contracting Party is required to report to the IMO and where appropriate to other Contracting Parties the information concerning (b) and (c) in accordance with Article 9(4)(a). Furthermore, Annex 2 to the Protocol contains assessment of wastes that may be considered for dumping.

7.3 Regional treaties

Dumping is likely to cause special problems particularly in enclosed or semi-enclosed seas owing to their natural integrity. In fact, regional conventions and protocols regulating dumping at sea apply in mostly enclosed or semi-enclosed seas areas such as the North-East Atlantic including the North Sea,[169] the Baltic,[170] the Mediterranean,[171] the Black Sea,[172] the Red Sea[173] and the South Pacific.[174]

[169] 1992 OSPAR Convention. [170] 1992 Helsinki Convention.

[171] 1995 Convention for the Protection of the Marine Environment and the Coastal Region of the Mediterranean (Barcelona Convention). Entered into force on 9 July 2004. The text is available at: www.unepmap.org/. 1976 Protocol for the Prevention and Elimination of Pollution of the Mediterranean Sea by Dumping from Ships and Aircraft. Entered into force on 12 February 1978 and revised in 1995 as the Protocol for the Prevention and Elimination of Pollution of the Mediterranean Sea by Dumping from Ships and Aircraft or Incineration at Sea. Not in force. The text of the 1995 Protocol is reproduced in the UNEP Mediterranean Action Plan, *Convention for the Protection of the Marine Environment and the Coastal Region of the Mediterranean and its Protocols* (Athens, 2005).

[172] 1992 Convention on the Protection of the Black Sea against Pollution. (1993) 32 *ILM*, p. 1110; (1993) 22 *Law of the Sea Bulletin* p. 31. 1992 Protocol on Protection of the Black Sea Marine Environment against Pollution by Dumping. All in force in 1994. (1993) 32 *ILM* p. 1129; (1993) 22 *Law of the Sea Bulletin* p. 47. Entered into force in 1994.

[173] 1982 Regional Convention for the Conservation of the Red Sea and Gulf of Aden Environment. The text is available at: www.persga.org/Documents/Doc_62_20090211112825.pdf. Entered into force on 20 August 1985.

[174] 1986 Protocol for the Prevention of Pollution of the South Pacific Region by Dumping. (1987) 26 *ILM* p. 65. Entered into force on 22 August 1990.

Notably, the paradigm shift from permission to prohibition of dumping at sea can also be detected in regional treaties. A case in point is treaties with regard to the North-East Atlantic. Dumping in the North-East Atlantic has been regulated by the 1972 Oslo Convention for the Prevention of Marine Pollution by Dumping from Ships and Aircraft (hereafter the Oslo Convention).[175] The Oslo Convention adopted the black/grey list approach. Substances listed in Annex I (black list) are prohibited under Article 5. However, Article 6 stipulates that no waste containing such quantities of the substances and materials listed in Annex II (grey list) shall be dumped without a specific permit in each case from the appropriate national authority or authorities.

In 1992, however, the Oslo Convention was replaced by the OSPAR Convention. The OSPAR Convention prohibited the dumping of all wastes or other matter, except those wastes or other matter listed in Article 3(2)(3) of Annex II.[176] It can be said that the OSPAR Convention adopts the reverse listing approach.

A similar shift of approach can be seen in instruments with regard to the protection of the Mediterranean Sea. The 1976 Protocol for the Prevention of Pollution of the Mediterranean Sea by Dumping from Ships and Aircraft took the black/grey list approach.[177] Later, the black/grey list approach was replaced by the reverse listing approach in the 1995 Protocol for the Prevention and Elimination of Pollution of the Mediterranean Sea by Dumping from Ships and Aircraft or Incineration at Sea, which modified the 1976 Protocol.[178]

7.4 Ocean sequestration and fertilisation

In addition to traditional dumping, currently the legality of ocean sequestration and fertilisation is at issue. These are two distinct techniques to reduce anthropogenic emissions and atmospheric concentrations of CO_2.

Ocean sequestration involves the injection of CO_2 directly into the water column (typically below 1,000 metres) via a fixed pipeline or a moving ship or onto the sea floor at depths below 3,000 metres, where CO_2 is denser than water and is expected to form a 'lake', via a fixed pipeline or an offshore platform.[179] On 2 November 2006, the Resolution adopted by the First Meeting of Contracting Parties to the London Protocol recognised that carbon dioxide capture and sequestration represents an important interim solution. Thus the 1996 London Protocol was amended so as to permit the storage of carbon dioxide under the seabed.[180] On 30 October 2009, Article 6 of the London Protocol was amended with a view to permitting the export of carbon dioxide streams for disposal in accordance with Annex 1.[181]

175 Terminated on 25 March 1998.

176 Article 3(1) of Annex II.

177 Articles 4, 5 and 6. (1976) 15 *ILM* p. 300. Entered into force on 12 February 1998.

178 Article 4. Not yet in force. The text of the 1995 Protocol is available at: www.cevreorman.gov.tr/COB/Files/EN/ConventionsProtocol/BARCELONA.pdf.

179 B. Mets et al., (eds.), *IPCC Special Report on Carbon Dioxide Capture and Storage* (Cambridge University Press, 2005), p. 7.

180 Resolution LP.1(1) on the Amendment to Include CO_2 Sequestration in Sub-Seabed Geological Formations in Annex 1 to the London Protocol. The amendment entered into force in 2007.

181 Resolution LP.3(4) on the Amendment to Article 6 of the London Protocol.

Ocean fertilisation is an environmental modification technique which fertilises the ocean with nutrients such as iron, nitrogen or phosphorus in an attempt to produce massive phytoplankton blooms which may increase absorption of CO_2 from the atmosphere.[182] The Resolution adopted by the Contracting Parties to the London Convention and the London Protocol on 31 October 2008 agreed that 'the scope of the London Convention and Protocol includes ocean fertilization activities'.[183] The Resolution of 2008 further agreed that 'given the present state of knowledge, ocean fertilization activities other than legitimate scientific research should not be allowed'.[184] Likewise, in 2008, the Conference of the Parties to the Convention on Biological Diversity requested Parties and urged other governments to ensure that ocean fertilisation activities do not take place until there is an adequate scientific basis in accordance with the precautionary approach.[185]

8 REGULATION OF POLLUTION FROM SEABED ACTIVITIES

8.1 Marine pollution arising from seabed activities under national jurisdiction

The Geneva Conventions paid little attention to the regulation of marine pollution arising from seabed activities. Article 24 of the 1958 Geneva Convention on the High Seas merely places a general obligation upon every State to 'draw up regulations to prevent pollution of the seas by the discharge of oil from ships or pipelines or resulting from the exploitation and exploration of the seabed and its subsoil, taking account of existing treaty provisions on the subject'. Likewise, Article 5 of the 1958 Geneva Convention on the Continental Shelf provides a general obligation which requires the coastal State to undertake, in the safety zones around continental shelf installations, all appropriate measures for the protection of the living resources of the sea from harmful agents.

These obligations under the Geneva Conventions were slightly amplified by the LOSC. Article 208(1) obliges coastal States to adopt laws and regulations to prevent, reduce and control pollution of the marine environment arising from or in connection with seabed activities subject to their jurisdiction and from artificial islands, installations and structures under their jurisdiction pursuant to Articles 60 and 80. Such laws and regulations shall be no less effective than international rules, standards and recommended practices and procedures under Article 208(3). Such international rules are embodied in the 1990 OPRC and its Protocol.[186] Furthermore, Regulation 39 of Annex I of MARPOL 73/78 provides special requirements for fixed or floating platforms engaged

[182] Generally on this issue, see R. Rayfuse, M. G. Lawrence and K. M. Gjerde, 'Ocean Fertilization and Climate Change: The Need to Regulate Emerging High Seas Uses' (2008) 23 *IJMCL* pp. 297–326; A. Strong, S. Chisholm, C. Miller and J. Cullen, 'Ocean Fertilization: Time to Move On' (2009) 461 *Nature* pp. 347–348.

[183] Paragraph 1, Resolution LC-LP.1 on the Regulation of Ocean Fertilization.

[184] *Ibid.*, paragraph 8.

[185] C(4) of the Decision IX/16, UNEP/CBD/COP/DEC/IX/16, 30 May 2008.

[186] IMO, Circular Letter No. 2456, Implication of UNCLOS for the Organization, 17 February 2003, Annex II.

in seabed activities, while the MARPOL Convention does not apply to the release of harmful substances directly arising from the exploration, exploitation and associated offshore processing of seabed mineral resources under Article 2(3)(b)(ii).

Article 214 of the LOSC requires States to enforce their laws and regulations adopted in accordance with Article 208 and shall adopt laws and regulations and take other measures necessary to implement applicable international rules and standards to prevent, reduce and control pollution of the marine environment arising from seabed activities subject to their jurisdiction. Furthermore, under Article 208(4), States shall endeavour to harmonise their policies on the regulation of pollution from seabed activities at the appropriate regional level.

Regional conventions hold obligations to prevent and eliminate pollution from seabed activities in more detail. One can take the Helsinki Convention as an example. Article 12 of the Convention places an explicit obligation upon each Contracting Party to take all measures to prevent pollution of the Baltic Sea area resulting from exploration or exploitation of its part of the seabed and the subsoil thereof. The obligation is further amplified by Annex VI. Regulation 2 requires the Contracting Parties to use the best available technology and best environmental practice in order to prevent and eliminate pollution from offshore activities. Regulation 3 further requires that an environmental impact assessment shall be made before an offshore activity is permitted to start. In addition to this, Regulations 4 and 5 provide requirements with regard to discharges during the exploration and exploitation phases in some detail.

On the other hand, to date, there are only a few treaties with regard to liability for pollution by seabed activities under national jurisdiction. An example is the 1977 Convention on Civil Liability for Oil Pollution Damage Resulting from Exploration for and Exploitation of Seabed Mineral Resources.[187] This Convention seeks to adopt uniform rules and procedures for determining questions of liability and providing adequate compensation to persons who suffer damage caused by oil pollution posed by the exploration for and exploitation of seabed mineral resources. Article 3 makes clear that with some exceptions set out in this provision, the operator of the installation at the time of an incident shall be liable for any pollution damage resulting from the incident. Another treaty which involves liability is the 1994 Mediterranean Protocol. Article 27(1) of this Protocol requires the Parties to cooperate as soon as possible in formulating and adopting appropriate rules and procedures for determining liability and compensation for damage resulting from the seabed activities. Neither instrument has yet entered into force.

8.2 Marine pollution arising from seabed activities in the Area

The environmental protection of the Area is essentially governed by Part XI of the LOSC. Article 209(1) of the LOSC provides that: 'International rules, regulations and procedures shall be established in accordance with Part XI to prevent, reduce and

[187] Not yet in force. The text of the Convention is available at http://folk.uio.no/erikro/WWW/HNS/Civil%20Liability%20offshore.pdf.

control pollution of the marine environment from activities in the Area'. Article 209(2) then obliges States to adopt laws and regulations to prevent, reduce and control pollution of the marine environment from activities in the Area undertaken by vessels, installations, structures and other devices flying their flag or of their registry or operating under their authority. The requirements of such laws and regulations shall be no less effective than the international rules, regulations and procedures referred to in Article 209(1). Under Article 215 of the LOSC, enforcement of such international rules and regulations is to be governed by Part XI.

In addition to States, the Authority has a valuable role in the environmental protection of the Area.[188] In this regard, Article 145 requires the Authority to adopt appropriate rules, regulations and procedures for, *inter alia*:

> (a) the prevention, reduction and control of pollution and other hazards to the marine environment, including the coastline, and of interference with the ecological balance of the marine environment, particular attention being paid to the need for protection from harmful effects of such activities as drilling, dredging, excavation, disposal of waste, construction and operation or maintenance of installations, pipelines and other devices related to such activities;
> (b) the protection and conservation of the natural resources of the Area and the prevention of damage to the flora and fauna of the marine environment.[189]

It is notable that Article 145(b) explicitly refers to 'the ecological balance of the marine environment' as well as 'the flora and fauna of the marine environment'. The prescriptive jurisdiction of the Authority is also provided by the 1994 Implementation Agreement.[190] Furthermore, Regulation 31(1) of the 2000 Mining Code calls upon the Authority, in accordance with the Convention and the Agreement, to establish and keep under periodic review environmental rules, regulations and procedures to ensure effective protection for the marine environment from harmful effects which may arise from activities in the Area.

The Authority also has enforcement jurisdiction over the environmental protection of the Area. Indeed, the Council of the Authority has a jurisdiction to 'supervise and co-ordinate the implementation of the provisions of this Part [XI] on *all questions and matters within the competence of the Authority* and invite the attention of the Assembly to cases of non-compliance'.[191] It follows that the environmental protection of the Area is supervised by the Council of the Authority. Furthermore, under Article 185(1) of the LOSC, the Authority is empowered to suspend the exercise of the rights and privileges of membership of a State Party which has grossly and persistently violated the

188 T. Scovazzi, 'Mining, Protection of the Environment, Scientific Research and Bioprospecting: Some Considerations on the Role of the International Sea-Bed Authority' (2004) 19 *IJMCL* pp. 392–396; Y. Tanaka, 'Reflections on the Conservation and Sustainable Use of Genetic Resources in the Deep Seabed Beyond the Limits of National Jurisdiction' (2008) *ODIL* pp. 133–136.

189 See also Article 17(1)(b)(ix) and (xii) of Annex III of the LOSC.

190 Section 1(5)(g) and (7) of Annex. See also Section 1(5)(k) of Annex.

191 Emphasis added. Article 162(2)(a).

provisions of Part XI of the LOSC. Article 162(2)(w) of the 1982 LOSC further obliges the Council of the Authority to 'issue emergency orders, which may include orders for the suspension or adjustment of operations, to prevent serious harm to the marine environment arising out of activities in the Area'. This obligation is confirmed by Regulation 32(5) of the 2000 Mining Code. It should also be noted that the Council of the Authority is to disapprove areas for exploitation by contractors or the Enterprise in cases where substantial evidence indicates the risk of serious harm to the marine environment (Article 162(2)(x) of the LOSC).

Moreover, the Mining Code places an explicit obligation upon the Authority as well as sponsoring States to apply the precautionary approach.[192] Given the dearth of scientific knowledge about the environment of the Area as well as its marine ecosystems, it appears that the application of the precautionary approach is needed with a view to protecting the environment of the Area. In this respect, the Seabed Disputes Chamber of ITLOS has stated that: 'the precautionary approach is also an integral part of the general obligation of due diligence of sponsoring States'.[193]

9 ENVIRONMENTAL PROTECTION OF ICE-COVERED AREAS

Article 234 of the LOSC provides a special rule with regard to ice-covered areas within the EEZ.[194] This provision confers on coastal States the right to adopt and enforce non-discriminatory laws and regulations in relation to vessel-source pollution in ice-covered areas within the EEZ. Such laws and regulations shall have due regard to navigation and the protection and preservation of the marine environment based on the best available scientific evidence. Unlike Article 220, however, no qualifications are attached to the enforcement jurisdiction of coastal States under Article 234.

Whilst Article 234 contains no definition with regard to 'ice-covered areas', it is generally agreed that the Arctic can be regarded as an 'ice-covered area'. If the 'ice-covered areas' are within the limits of the EEZ, the coastal State has sovereign rights and jurisdiction there as provided in Article 56 of the LOSC. This provision already empowers the coastal State to exercise jurisdiction with regard to the protection and preservation of the marine environment. Articles 211(5) and 220(3), (5) and (6) provide the prescriptive and enforcement jurisdiction of coastal States concerning the regulation of vessel-source pollution in the EEZ. Article 194(5) provides that the measures taken under Part XII shall include those necessary to protect and preserve rare or fragile ecosystems as well as the habitat of depleted, threatened or endangered species and other forms of marine life. Hence Article 234 would seem to add little if anything to the coastal State's jurisdiction with regard to environmental protection in ice-covered areas within its EEZ.

192 Regulation 31(2).

193 *Responsibilities and Obligations of States Sponsoring Persons and Entities with Respect to Activities in the Area*, Case No. 17, 1 February 2011, p. 40, para. 131.

194 This provision was a result of direct negotiation between the States concerned, namely Canada, the USSR and the United States. *Virginia Commentaries*, vol. IV, p. 393.

Growing attention is being paid at present to the environmental protection of the Arctic Ocean. It is suggested that the rate of global warming in the Arctic region is much higher than in the rest of the world, with an increase of 2°C in the last hundred years compared to an average of 0.6°C in the rest of the world. Accordingly, climate change may have adverse effects on vulnerable marine ecosystems, the livelihood of indigenous people in the Arctic region.[195] Furthermore, increasing shipping in the Arctic Ocean may enhance the risk of marine pollution from vessels.

Unlike the Antarctic, which is governed by the 1959 Antarctic Treaty, there is no framework treaty governing the Arctic Ocean. While some global environmental treaties apply to the Arctic Ocean, they do not establish a comprehensive regime. Special attention must also be devoted to environmental interdependence in the Arctic region. Accordingly, there is a need to promote more enhanced cooperative measures on Arctic environmental protection. In this regard, two initiatives merit particular attention.

The first is the Arctic Environmental Protection Strategy (AEPS) adopted by the eight Arctic States in 1991.[196] Its strategy is to achieve five objectives: (i) protection of the Arctic ecosystem including humans, (ii) protection, enhancement and restoration of environmental quality and the sustainable utilisation of natural resources, (iii) accommodation of the traditional and cultural needs, values and practices of the indigenous people, (iv) review of the state of the Arctic environment, and (v) identification and elimination of pollution.[197] AEPS specifies response actions for six major environmental problems in the Arctic, namely, persistent organic contaminants, oil pollution, heavy metals, noise, radioactivity and acidification.

The second is the Arctic Council Initiative. The Arctic Council, which was established by the 1996 Ottawa Declaration, is a high-level intergovernmental forum for promoting cooperation and coordination between the Arctic States with regard to common Arctic issues, in particular sustainable development and environmental protection in the Arctic.[198] Members States of the Council are: Canada, Denmark (including Greenland and the Faroe Islands,) Finland, Iceland, Norway, the Russian Federation, Sweden and the United States. The scientific work of the Arctic Council is carried out in six expert working groups: Arctic Contaminant Action Program, Arctic Monitoring and Assessment Program, Conservation of Arctic Flora and Fauna, Emergency Prevention, Preparedness and Response, Protection of the Arctic Marine Environment and Sustainable Development. The Arctic Council has made an important contribution in the sponsoring of many scientific studies.[199] On 12 May 2011, the Arctic Council

[195] *European Parliament Resolution on Arctic Governance* (Brussels, 9 October 2008). See also ACIA, *Arctic Climate Impact Assessment* (Cambridge University Press, 2005). Online electronic version is available at www.acia.uaf.edu/pages/scientific.html.

[196] These States are: Canada, Denmark, Finland, Iceland, Norway, Sweden, USSR and United States. For the text of the strategy, see (1991) 30 *ILM* p. 1624.

[197] Paragraph 2.1.

[198] For the text of the Declaration, see (1996) 35 *ILM* p. 1382. The Arctic Council is not an international organisation.

[199] For an analysis in some detail of the Arctic Council, see T. Koivurova and D. Vanderzwaag, 'The Arctic Council at 10 Years: Retrospect and Prospects' (2007) 40 *UBC Law Review* pp. 121–194. Information on the activities of the Arctic Council is available at: www.arctic-council.org/.

adopted the Nuuk Declaration.[200] The Declaration decided to establish a task force to develop an international instrument on Arctic marine oil pollution preparedness and response.

10 CONCLUSIONS

The matters considered in this chapter allow the following conclusions.

(i) The LOSC represents a paradigm shift from the principle of freedom to pollute to an obligation to prevent pollution. In fact, the LOSC established a general and comprehensive legal framework for the regulation of marine pollution. It is argued that the controlling principle was changed from the discretion of States to the duty of States to protect the marine environment. In broad terms, it can be observed that the international law of the sea is increasingly strengthening its environmental dimension by limiting the margin of discretion of States in the regulation of marine pollution.

(ii) Land-based pollution is the most serious source of marine pollution. Nevertheless, the global legal framework for the regulation of land-based marine pollution remains a weak one. The reasons for this include:

- reluctance to restrict economic and industrial activities,
- complexity of sources, substances and actors involved in land-based marine pollution,
- geographical and ecological divergences in the oceans,
- limited capability of developing countries.

(iii) As a consequence, land-based marine pollution is regulated primarily by regional treaties. It is notable that new approaches and techniques are increasingly enshrined in these treaties with a view to tightening the regulation of land-based pollution. Such approaches and techniques include:

- the replacement of the black/grey list approach by the uniform approach,
- the precautionary approach,
- environmental impact assessment, and
- international control for ensuring compliance with relevant rules.

However, it must be noted that the development of regional treaties is not uniform, and the normative strength of the regulation also varies according to these treaties.

(iv) The flag State has primary responsibility for regulating vessel-source pollution. Nonetheless, compliance with relevant rules of international law on this matter cannot be effectively ensured by the flag State alone. Thus, under the LOSC, the coastal State and port State may also exercise jurisdiction to regulate vessel-source pollution. In particular, the port State jurisdiction set out in Article 218 of the LOSC is innovative in the sense that the port State is entitled to take enforcement action against the vessel even where a violation was committed on the high seas or marine spaces under other States' jurisdiction, regardless of direct damage to the port State. Port State control also

[200] This instrument is available at www.arctic-council.org/.

provides a useful means to ensure compliance with relevant rules regulating vessel-source pollution. It can be said that the port State assumes the role of an advocate for the international community in marine environmental protection.

(v) Ensuring compliance with treaties concerning marine environmental protection necessitates more institutionalised procedures, without relying on the principle of reciprocity. In this regard, three mechanisms merit highlighting. The first is international supervision. It is noteworthy here that treaties in this field tend to set out mechanisms for international supervision, such as a reporting system and supervision by a treaty commission. The second is port State jurisdiction and port State control. They provide an interesting example of marine environmental protection on the basis of the law of *dédoublement fonctionnel*. The third mechanism involves marine environmental protection through an international organisation. In this regard, it is of particular interest to note that the Authority is empowered to exercise prescriptive and enforcement jurisdiction over the environmental protection of the Area. Examination of the practice of the Authority provides a useful insight into the protection of community interests with regard to marine environmental protection through an international organisation.

FURTHER READING

1 General

P. Birnie, A. Boyle and C. Redgwell, *International Law and the Environment*, 3rd edn (Oxford University Press, 2009), Chapters 7 and 8.

A. Boyle, 'Marine Pollution under the Law of the Sea Convention' (1985) 79 *AJIL* pp. 347–372.

J. I. Charney, 'The Marine Environment and the 1982 United Nations Convention on the Law of the Sea' (1994) 28 *The International Lawyer* pp. 879–901.

P.-M. Dupuy, 'The Preservation of the Marine Environment', in R.-J. Dupuy and D. Vignes, *A Handbook on the New Law of the Sea*, vol. 2 (Dordrecht, Nijhoff, 1991), pp. 1151–1232.

D. M. Dzidzornu, 'Four Principles in Marine Environmental Protection: A Comparative Analysis' (1998) 29 *ODIL* pp. 91–123.

A. Kirchner (ed.), *International Marine Environmental Law: Institutions, Implementation and Innovations* (The Hague, Kluwer, 2003).

C. Redgwell, 'From Permission to Prohibition: The 1982 Convention on the Law of the Sea and Protection of the Marine Environment', in D. Freestone, R. Barnes and D. Ong (eds.), *The Law of the Sea: Progress and Prospects* (Oxford University Press, 2006), pp. 180–191.

P. Sand, *Principles of International Environmental Law* (Cambridge University Press, 2003), Chapter 9.

B. Smith, *State Responsibility and the Marine Environment: The Rules of Decision* (Oxford University Press, 1988).

R. Warner, *Protecting the Oceans beyond National Jurisdiction: Strengthening the International Law Framework* (Leiden, Nijhoff, 2009).

2 Land-Based Marine Pollution

A. Boyle, 'Land-Based Sources of Marine Pollution: Current Legal Regime' (1992) 16 *Marine Policy* pp. 20–35.

K. Elizabeth, 'Noncompliance and the Development of Regimes Addressing Marine Pollution from Land-Based Activities' (2008) 39 *ODIL* pp. 235–256.

D. Hassan, 'International Conventions Relating to Land-Based Sources of Marine Pollution Control: Applications and Shortcomings' (2004) 16 *Georgetown International Environmental Law Review* pp. 657–677.

Protecting the Marine Environment from Land-Based Sources of Pollution: Towards Effective International Cooperation (Aldershot, Ashgate, 2006).

L. A. Kimball, 'An International Regime for Managing Land-Based Activities that Degrade Marine and Coastal Environments' (1995) 29 *Ocean and Coastal Management* pp. 187–206.

T. A. Mensah, 'The International Legal Regime for the Protection and Preservation of the Marine Environment from Land-Based Sources of Pollution', in A. Boyle and D. Freestone (eds.), *International Law and Sustainable Development: Past Achievements and Future Challenges* (Oxford University Press, 1999), pp. 297–324.

A. Nollkaemper, 'Balancing the Protection of Marine Ecosystems with Economic Benefits from Land-Based Activities: The Quest for International Legal Barriers' (1996) 27 *ODIL* pp. 153–179.

Y. Tanaka, 'Regulation of Land-Based Marine Pollution in International Law: A Comparative Analysis between Global and Regional Legal Frameworks' (2006) 66 *ZaöRV* pp. 535–574.

D. L. Vanderzwaag and A. Powers, 'The Protection of the Marine Environment from Land-Based Pollution and Activities: Gauging the Tides of Global and Regional Governance' (2008) 23 *IJMCL* pp. 423–452.

C. Williams and B. Davis, 'Land-Based Activities: What Remains to Be Done' (1995) 29 *Ocean and Coastal Management* pp. 207–222.

3 Vessel-Source Marine Pollution

E. Franckx and A. Pauwels (eds.), *Vessel-Source Pollution and Coastal State Jurisdiction in the South-Eastern Baltic Sea* (Antwerp, Maklu, 2006).

V. Frank, 'Consequences of the *Prestige* Sinking for European and International Law' (2005) 20 *IJMCL* pp. 1–64.

Ho-Sam Bang, 'Is Port State Control an Effective Means to Combat Vessel-Source Pollution? An Empirical Survey of the Practical Exercise by Port States of their Powers of Control' (2008) 23 *IJMCL* pp. 715–759.

'Port State Jurisdiction and Article 218 of the UN Convention on the Law of the Sea' (2009) 40 *Journal of Maritime Law and Commerce* pp. 291–313.

Md Saiful Karim 'Implementation of the MARPOL Convention in Developing Countries' (2010) 79 *Nordic Journal of International Law* pp. 303–337.

T. Keselj, 'Port State Jurisdiction in Respect of Pollution from Ships: The 1982 United Nations Convention on the Law of the Sea and the Memoranda of Understanding' (1999) 30 *ODIL* pp. 127–160.

G. Mattson, 'MARPOL 73/78 and Annex I: An Assessment of its Effectiveness' (2006) 9 *Journal of International Wildlife Law and Policy* pp. 175–194.

T. L. McDorman, 'Port State Enforcement: A Comment on Article 218 of the 1982 Law of the Sea Convention' (1997) 28 *Journal of Maritime Law and Commerce* pp. 305–322.

E. J. Molennar, *Coastal State Jurisdiction over Vessel-Source Pollution* (The Hague, Kluwer, 1998).

'Port State Jurisdiction: Toward Comprehensive, Mandatory and Global Coverage' (2007) 28 *ODIL* pp. 225–257.

A. K.-J. Tan, *Vessel-Source Marine Pollution* (Cambridge University Press, 2006).

4 Dumping

L. A. De La Fayette, 'The London Convention 1972: Preparing for the Future' (1998) 13 *IJMCL* pp. 515–536.

M. Mackintosh, 'The Development of International Law in Relation to the Dumping and Disposal of Radioactive Waste at Sea' (2003) 9 *The Journal of International Maritime Law* pp. 354–368.

E. J. Molennar, 'The 1996 Protocol to the 1972 London Convention' (1997) 12 *IJMCL* pp. 396–403.

Zou Keyuan, 'Regulation of the Dumping of Wastes at Sea: The Chinese Practice', in T. L. McDorman, S. J. Rolston and A. Chircop (eds.), *The Future of Ocean Regime Building: Essays in Tribute to Douglas M. Johnston* (Leiden, Nijhoff, 2009), pp. 551–571.

5 Pollution from Seabed Activities

M. W. Lodge, 'Environmental Regulation of Deep Seabed Mining', in A. Kirchner (ed.), *International Marine Environmental Law: Institutions, Implementation and Innovations* (The Hague, Kluwer, 2003), pp. 49–59.

M. H. Rahman, 'Deep Seabed Mining and Marine Environment' (2007) 47 *Indian Journal of International Law* pp. 400–431.

6 Liability and Compensation

L. A. De La Fayette, 'Compensation for Environmental Damage in Maritime Liability Regimes', in A. Kirchner (ed.), *International Marine Environmental Law: Institutions, Implementation and Innovations* (The Hague, Kluwer, 2003), pp. 231–265.

M. Faure and J. Hu (eds.), *Prevention and Compensation of Marine Pollution Damage: Recent Developments in Europe, China and the US* (Alphen aan den Rijn, Kluwer, 2006).

D. M. Gunasekera, *Civil Liability for Bunker Oil Pollution Damage* (Frankfurt am Main, Peter Lang, 2010).

José Juste-Ruíz, 'Compensation for Pollution Damage Caused by Oil Tanker Accidents: From "Erica" to "Prestige"' (2010) 1 *Aegean Review of the Law of the Sea and Maritime Law* pp. 37–60.

N. A. Martínez Gutiérrez, *Limitation of Liability in International Maritime Conventions: The Relationship between Global Limitation Conventions and Particular Liability Regimes* (New York, Routledge, 2011).

T. A. Mensah, 'Civil Liability and Compensation for Vessel-Source Pollution of the Marine Environment and the United Nations Convention on the Law of the Sea (1982)' in N. Ando, E. W. MacWhinney and R. Wolfrum (eds.), *Liber Amicorum Judge Shigeru Oda*, vol. 2 (The Hague, Kluwer, 2002), pp. 1391–1434.

I. Zovko, 'The International Liability and Compensation Regimes Relating to Vessel-Sourced Pollution of the Marine Environment: Case Study of the Southern Ocean' (2005) 2 *New Zealand Yearbook of International Law* pp. 281–326.

7 Arctic

L. A. De La Fayette, 'Oceans Governance in the Arctic' (2008) 23 *IJMCL* pp. 531–566.

M. H. Nordquist, T. H. Heider and J. N. Moore (eds.), *Changes in the Arctic Environment and the Law of the Sea* (Leiden, Nijhoff, 2010).

T. Potts and C. Schofield, 'The Arctic: An Arctic Scramble? Opportunities and Threats in the (Formerly) Frozen North' (2008) 23 *IJMCL* pp. 151–176.

A. Proelss and T. Müller, 'The Legal Regime of the Arctic Ocean' (2008) 68 *ZaöRV* pp. 651–687.

J. A. Roach, 'International Law and the Arctic: A Guide to Understanding the Issue' (2009) 15 *Southwestern Journal of International Law* pp. 301–326.

D. R. Rothwell, 'International Law and Protection of the Arctic Environment' (1995) 44 *ICLQ* pp. 280–312.

O. S. Stokke, 'A Legal Regime for the Arctic? Interplay with the Law of the Sea Convention' (2007) 31 *Marine Policy* pp. 402–408.

G. Witschel, I. Winkelmann, K. Tiroch and R. Wolfrum (eds.), *New Chances and New Responsibilities in the Arctic Region* (Berlin, BWV Berliner Wissenschafts-Verlag, 2010).

O. R. Young, 'The Arctic in Play: Governance in a Time of Rapid Change' (2009) 24 *IJMCL* pp. 423–442.

See also *The Yearbook of Polar Law* from 2009.

9

Conservation of Marine Biological Diversity

Main Issues

Biological diversity, including marine biological diversity, is essential for human life. However, there are serious concerns that biological diversity on land and in the oceans is rapidly declining. Thus there is a strong need to establish legal frameworks for the conservation of marine biological diversity. In this regard, growing attention is being paid to the establishment of marine protected areas (MPAs). This chapter will explore emergent principles on this subject. In particular, the following issues will be examined:

(i) What are the principal approaches to conservation of marine biological diversity?
(ii) What are the limits of the LOSC with regard to the conservation of marine biological diversity?
(iii) What is the significance of, and the limitations associated with the Convention on Biological Diversity in the context of the conservation of marine biological diversity?
(iv) What is the significance of MPAs and what are their limitations?
(v) Is it possible to create MPAs on the high seas in positive international law?

1 INTRODUCTION

Biological diversity means the variability of life in all its forms, levels and combinations.[1] Biological diversity is fundamental for human life because it provides essential services for the maintenance of the biosphere in a condition which supports human and other life. Furthermore, biological diversity has a considerable scientific value because all living species are genetic libraries which record evolutionary events on the earth. It may also be noted that biological diversity has its own ethical and aesthetic

[1] P. Birnie, A. Boyle and C. Redgwell, *International Law and the Environment* (Oxford University Press, 2009), p. 588. Article 2 of the Convention on Biological Diversity defines 'biological diversity' as: 'the variability among living organisms from all sources including, *inter alia*, terrestrial, marine and other aquatic ecosystems and the ecological complexes of which they are part; this includes diversity within species, between species and of ecosystems'.

values.[2] Given its vital importance for the survival of mankind, it could be said that conservation of (marine) biological diversity is considered as a community interest of the international community as a whole.

Despite its vital importance, biological diversity is now rapidly declining in the world,[3] and marine biological diversity is no exception. According to a report of the millennium ecosystem assessment, 20 per cent of the world's coral reefs were lost and an additional 20 per cent degraded in the last several decades of the twentieth century.[4] Marine biological diversity is seriously damaged by human activities, including: over-exploitation of biological diversity; impacts of extraction methods, such as bottom trawling; sedimentation arising from activities on adjacent land; physical changes to the marine environment, such as infilling of estuaries; water pollution; the impact of tourists and divers; climate change; alien-species invasions; subdivision and development on the coast; and fragmentation of habitats.[5]

Currently particular concern is raised with regard to the adverse impact of climate change on diversity. The oceans have a vital role in generating oxygen, absorbing carbon dioxide from the atmosphere, and regulating climate and temperature. In this regard, there are growing concerns that climate change can affect marine ecosystems in many ways, modifying ecosystem structure and functioning.[6] For instance, it is suggested that coral reefs would be seriously damaged if sea surface temperatures were to increase by more than 1°C above the seasonal maximum temperature.[7] The impacts of ocean acidification on marine biological diversity are also a matter of concern.[8] Should biological diversity be lost, this diversity becomes irreplaceable. Modern technology cannot reproduce biological diversity artificially.[9] Hence conservation of marine biological diversity deserves serious consideration in the law of the sea.[10]

[2] P. Sands, 'International Law in the Field of Sustainable Development' (1994) 65 *BYIL* p. 333; M. Bowman, 'The Nature, Development and Philosophical Foundations of the Biodiversity Concept in International Law', in C. Redgwell and M. Bowman (eds.), *International Law and the Conservation of Biological Diversity* (The Hague, Kluwer, 1996), pp. 15–21.

[3] According to IUCN, current extinction rates of threatened species are 50 to 500 times higher than extinction rates in the fossil record. J. E. M. Baillie, C. Hilton-Taylor and S. N. Stuart (eds.), *2004 IUCN Red List of Threatened Species. A Global Species Assessment* (Gland, IUCN, 2004), p. xxi.

[4] *Ecosystems and Human Well-Being: Synthesis, A Report of the Millennium Ecosystem Assessment* (Washington DC, Island Press, 2005), p. 26.

[5] The Convention on Biological Diversity, Ad Hoc Technical Expert Group on Protected Areas, *Report of the Ad Hoc Technical Expert Group on Marine and Coastal Protected Areas*, UNEP/CBD/AHTEG-PA/1/INF/5, 6 June 2003, pp. 7–8, paras. 11–12; United Nations, *Report of the Secretary-General, Oceans and the Law of the Sea*, A/59/62/Add.1, 18 August 2004, pp. 54–61, paras. 205–236.

[6] Convention on Biological Diversity, SBSTTA, *Biological Diversity and Climate Change, Report of the Ad Hoc Technical Expert Group on Biodiversity and Climate Change*, UNEP/CBD/SBSTTA/9/INF12, 30 September 2003, pp. 27–43, paras. 37–72.

[7] *Ibid.*, p. 37, para. 63.

[8] United Nations, *Report of the Secretary-General, Oceans and the Law of the Sea Addendum*, A/66/70/Add.1, 11 April 2011, p. 46, para. 194.

[9] Birnie, Boyle and Redgwell, *International Law and the Environment*, p. 584.

[10] Generally on this subject, see Y. Tanaka, *A Dual Approach to Ocean Governance: The Cases of Zonal and Integrated Management in International Law of the Sea* (Surrey, England, Ashgate, 2008), Chapters 4 and 5. This chapter is based partly on the analysis made there, with modifications.

2 PRINCIPAL APPROACHES TO CONSERVATION OF MARINE BIOLOGICAL DIVERSITY

2.1 General considerations

Conservation of biological diversity has until recently attracted little attention in international law. In light of the paucity of State practice, customary international law contains few rules on this subject. Accordingly, rules respecting conservation of marine biological diversity should be sought primarily in treaties.

It was only after World War II that the conservation of biological diversity attracted attention in the international community. The 1972 Stockholm Declaration marked a milestone towards the development of treaties focusing on conservation of biological diversity.[11] Principle 2 of the Declaration made the following important statement:

> The natural resources of the earth including the air, water, land, flora and fauna and especially representative samples of natural ecosystems must be safeguarded for the benefit of present and future generations through careful planning or management, as appropriate.

Principle 4 further stated that: 'Man has a special responsibility to safeguard and wisely manage the heritage of wildlife and its habitat which are now gravely imperilled by a combination of adverse factors'. These statements seem to make clear the *raison d'être* of international law in governing the conservation of biological diversity.

Twenty years later, the UN Conference on Environment and Development adopted the Rio Declaration and Agenda 21. Agenda 21 highlighted that: 'Coastal States, with the support of international organizations, upon request, should undertake measures to maintain biological diversity and productivity of marine species and habitats under national jurisdiction' (paragraph 17.7). Agenda 21 thus required States 'to identify marine ecosystems exhibiting high levels of biodiversity and productivity and other critical habitat areas and provide necessary limitations on use in these areas, through, inter alia, designation of protected areas' (paragraph 17.86). Whilst the Rio Declaration and Agenda 21 are not binding, they can potentially guide the behaviour of States. At the same time, the UN Conference adopted the Convention on Biological Diversity (hereafter the Rio Convention).[12] This Convention is the first global treaty regarding conservation of biological diversity. The Rio Convention will be examined later.

2.2 Three approaches

Whilst the LOSC is the key instrument for examining marine issues, it seems appropriate to briefly overview relevant instruments concerning the conservation of (marine)

[11] For the text of the Declaration, see P. W. Birnie and A. Boyle, *Basic Documents on International Law and Environment* (Oxford University Press, 1995), p. 1.

[12] (1992) 31 *ILM* p. 818. Entered into force on 29 December 1993. At the present time 193 States have become Parties to the Convention. The list of the Parties is available at: www.cbd.int/convention/parties/list/.

biological diversity before the adoption of the LOSC. In this regard, three principal approaches can be identified: (i) the regional approach, (ii) the species specific approach, and (iii) the activity specific approach.

The regional approach seeks to conserve marine ecosystems in a specific marine space or a habitat. An illustrative example is the 1980 Convention on the Conservation of Antarctic Marine Living Resources (CCAMLR).[13] The CCAMLR applies to the Antarctic marine living resources of the area south of 60° south latitude and to these resources of the area between that latitude and the Antarctic Convergence which form part of the Antarctic marine ecosystem.[14] Article II(3)(a) requires the Parties to prevent a decrease in the size of any harvested population to levels below those which ensure its stable recruitment. Article II(3)(c) places a clear obligation on the Parties to prevent changes or minimise the risk of changes in the marine ecosystem which are not potentially reversible over two or three decades. The regional approach is important in the tailoring of rules that take specific environmental and ecological elements in the particular region into account.

The species specific approach seeks to conserve a certain category of species. Several treaties adopt this approach. One notable example is the 1979 Convention on the Conservation of Migratory Species of Wild Animals (CMS/Bonn Convention).[15] The Bonn Convention aims to protect migratory species of wild animals that live within or pass through one or more national jurisdictional boundaries. Appendix I specifies migratory species which are endangered, while Appendix II lists migratory species which have an unfavourable conservation status and which require international agreements for their conservation and management.[16] With several exceptions, Parties that are Range States of a migratory species listed in Appendix I shall prohibit the taking of animals belonging to such species by virtue of Article III(5). Concerning species listed in Appendix II, the Bonn Convention provides for two kinds of agreement, i.e. AGREEMENTS (Article IV(3)) and agreements (Article IV(4)). Under Article IV(3), Parties that are Range States of migratory species listed in Appendix II shall endeavour to conclude AGREEMENTS where these would benefit the species. These Parties are also encouraged to conclude agreements for any population or any geographically separate part of the population of any species or lower taxon of wild animals, members of which periodically cross one or more national jurisdictional boundaries in conformity with Article IV(4).

The activity specific approach focuses on the regulation of activities threatening the survival of endangered species. A typical example may be the 1973 Convention on International Trade in Endangered Species of Wild Flora and Fauna (CITES/1973 Washington Convention).[17] The Washington Convention aims to control international

[13] Entered into force on 7 April 1982. For the text of the Convention, see Birnie and Boyle, *Basic Documents*, p. 628.

[14] The scope of the Antarctic Convergence is defined in Article II(4) of CCAMLR. The map of the Convergence is available at: www.ccamlr.org/pu/E/conv/map.htm.

[15] (1980) 19 *ILM* p. 15. Entered into force on 1 November 1983.

[16] Articles III and IV of the Bonn Convention.

[17] 993 *UNTS* p. 243; Entered into force on 1 July 1975.

commercial trade in endangered species or their products, but it is not designed directly to conserve biological diversity. 'Trade' means 'export, re-export, import and introduction from the sea' (Article I(c)). The level of regulation of trade in endangered species differs according to the Appendix. Appendix I comprises all species threatened with extinction which are or may be affected by trade. Trade in specimens of species listed in Appendix I is subject to particularly strict regulation in order not to endanger further their survival and must only be authorised in exceptional circumstances in accordance with Article II(1). Appendix I includes marine species, such as minke and Bryde's whales, in its list. Appendix II includes all species which may be threatened with extinction unless trade in specimens of such species is subject to strict regulation in order to avoid utilisation incompatible with their survival (Article II(2)(a)). Appendix III includes all species which any Party identifies as being subject to regulation within its jurisdiction for the purposes of preventing or restricting exploitation, and as needing the cooperation of other Parties in the control of trade (Article II(3)).

It is arguable that these three approaches contribute to conserve diversity only in a piecemeal fashion. In order to deal with possible lacunae, there is a need to establish a global legal framework for conservation of (marine) biological diversity. Such a global framework is also important to provide a basis for the development of rules of customary international law in this field. At the same time, the global legal framework must be amplified by regional treaties taking particular needs and circumstances of specific regions into account. Therefore, the interaction between the global and regional legal frameworks seems to be increasingly important. Against that background, the next section will examine global legal frameworks with regard to conservation of marine biological diversity.

3 GLOBAL LEGAL FRAMEWORKS FOR THE CONSERVATION OF MARINE BIOLOGICAL DIVERSITY

3.1 The 1982 UN Convention on the Law of the Sea

The LOSC contains only two general provisions relating directly to this issue. First, Article 194(5) provides a general obligation to protect rare or fragile ecosystems:

> The measures taken in accordance with this Part [XII] shall include those necessary to protect and preserve rare or fragile ecosystems as well as the habitat of depleted, threatened or endangered species and other forms of marine life.

Arguably the 'marine environment' includes the ocean as a whole including the high seas. It follows that States are under an obligation to protect and preserve rare or fragile ecosystems in marine spaces under and beyond national jurisdiction. Second, Article 196(1) places an obligation upon States to take all measures necessary to prevent, reduce and control pollution of the marine environment resulting from the use of technologies under their jurisdiction or control, or the intentional or accidental introduction of species, alien or new, to a particular part of the marine environment, which may cause significant and harmful changes thereto. Later, Article 196 was amplified in the 2004 International Convention for the Control and Management of Ships' Ballast Water and Sediments.[18] Apart from these provisions, the LOSC made little reference to the conservation of marine biological diversity. As a consequence, basically the traditional zonal management approach applies to conservation of marine biological diversity.

The LOSC provides no distinct obligation to conserve marine biological diversity in marine spaces under territorial sovereignty, namely internal waters, the territorial sea and archipelagic waters. It follows that the coastal State is subject only to the general obligations in Articles 192, 194(5) and 196 of the LOSC. Similarly, there is no explicit provision concerning conservation of marine biological diversity in the EEZ.

However, it may not be far-fetched to argue that marine biological diversity can be included in the scope of the 'natural resources' in Article 56(1)(a) and the 'living resources' in Article 61 because such diversity concerns variability among marine living organisms. Furthermore, the coastal State is obliged to protect and preserve rare or fragile ecosystems as well as the habitat of depleted, threatened or endangered species and other forms of marine life in its EEZ under Articles 194 and 196. The coastal State is also under a general obligation to protect and preserve the marine environment under Article 192. The duty to protect the marine environment is further supplemented by Article 193. Article 56(1)(b)(iii) confers on the coastal State jurisdiction with regard to the protection and preservation of the marine environment. Article 234 provides coastal States with the right to adopt and enforce non-discriminatory laws and regulations for the prevention, reduction and control of marine pollution from vessels in ice-covered areas within the limits of the EEZ, where pollution of the marine environment could cause major harm to or irreversible disturbance of the ecological balance. The cumulative effect of these provisions seems to be that the coastal State can arguably exercise jurisdiction over conservation of marine biological diversity in its EEZ.

However, a question arises with regard to the reconciliation between the conservation of marine biological diversity and other legitimate uses of the ocean, such as navigation and laying submarine cables and pipelines, in the EEZ. In the EEZ, all States enjoy the freedom of navigation and overflight by virtue of Article 58(1) of the LOSC. In relation to this, Article 211(1) of the LOSC requires States to promote the adoption of routeing systems designed to minimise the threat of accidents which might cause pollution of the marine environment. Articles 211(5) and 220 confer on the coastal States powers to prevent vessel-source pollution. It would seem to follow that a coastal State may regulate navigation in the form of routeing measures in order to protect the environment of its EEZ, including its biological diversity. Concerning submarine cables, all States enjoy the freedom to lay such cables and pipelines in the EEZ under Article 58(1). Under Article 79(3) of the LOSC, however, the delineation

[18] (2004) 19 *IJMCL* p. 446.

of the course for the laying of such pipelines on the continental shelf is subject to the consent of the coastal State. Thus, the coastal State can regulate the course for laying cables and pipelines for the purpose of the conservation of marine biological diversity in the EEZ.

Concerning the continental shelf, a particular issue arises with regard to the conservation of cold-water coral.[19] Under Article 77(4), the only living components of natural resources falling within the continental shelf regime are sedentary species. Thus, literally interpreted, the coastal State cannot exercise its jurisdiction over marine organisms other than sedentary species on its continental shelf; and cold-water coral is beyond the scope of the natural resources on the continental shelf.

On the other hand, it must be remembered that the coastal State is under the general obligation to protect and preserve 'rare or fragile ecosystems' pursuant to Article 194(5). As there is no geographical limit in this provision, Article 194(5) arguably covers the continental shelf. In order to implement this obligation, it appears inevitable that the coastal State exercises jurisdiction over marine biological diversity on its continental shelf. Furthermore, Article 81 of the LOSC stipulates that the coastal State shall have the exclusive right to authorise and regulate drilling on the continental shelf 'for all purposes'. Thus the coastal State may regulate drilling on the continental shelf in order to prevent adverse impact on ecosystems there. Yet there will be a need to regulate fishing activities in the adjacent water to the continental shelf in order to prevent adverse impacts arising from trawl fishing on cold-water coral.

The LOSC contains no explicit provision relating to conservation of marine biological diversity in the high seas and the Area.[20] Currently there are growing concerns that the increased demand for genetic resources in the deep seabed may result in their unsustainable collection or even in the extinction of species.[21] In fact, it is becoming apparent that marine ecosystems in the deep ocean floors are threatened by various human activities, such as marine scientific research, bioprospecting, deep seabed mining and fishing activities. Yet the 1982 LOSC contains no provision on this matter. In this respect, it must be highlighted that, as discussed earlier, the International Seabed Authority (hereafter the Authority) has responsibility to protect the environment of the Area.[22] Obviously environmental protection of the Area is a prerequisite to conserving

[19] Generally on this issue, see R. Long and A. Grehan, 'Marine Habitat Protection in Sea Areas under the Jurisdiction of a Coastal Member State of the European Union: The Case of Deep-Water Coral Conservation in Ireland' (2002) 17 *IJMCL* pp. 235–261.

[20] Conservation of marine biological diversity on the high seas will be considered in conjunction with marine protected areas. See section 4.3 of this chapter.

[21] Species living in the deep seabed, in particular micro-organisms, present great interest for the marine biotechnological industry and marine science. For instance, hydrothermal organisms may yield useful medicines, enzymes, nutritional additives, and improved chemical, energy and agricultural products. L. Glowka, 'The Deepest of Ironies: Genetic Resources, Marine Scientific Research, and the Area' (1996) 12 *Ocean Yearbook* pp. 159–161; W. T. Burke, 'State Practice, New Ocean Uses, and Ocean Governance under UNCLOS', in T. A. Mensah (ed.), *Ocean Governance: Strategies and Approaches for the 21st Century: Proceedings of The Law of the Sea Institute Twenty-Eighth Annual Conference* (Honolulu, The Law of the Sea Institute, University of Hawaii 1996), p. 229. Generally on this subject, see D. K. Leary, *International Law and the Genetic Resources of the Deep Sea* (Leiden, Nijhoff, 2008).

[22] See Chapter 8, section 8.2.

biological resources there. Hence the role of the Authority will also be increasingly important in this field.[23]

3.2 The 1992 Convention on Biological Diversity

(a) Outline of the Rio Convention

The 1992 Rio Convention provides a global legal framework for conservation of biological diversity. Article 1 of the Convention specifies that it seeks three objectives:

- the conservation of biological diversity,
- the sustainable use of its components, and
- the fair and equitable sharing of the benefits arising out of the utilisation of genetic resources.

In this regard, it is relevant to note that provisions of the Rio Convention apply both to terrestrial and marine biological diversity.[24] In this regard, the Jakarta Ministerial Statement adopted in November 1995 reaffirmed the critical need for the Conference of the Parties (COP) to address the conservation and sustainable use of marine and coastal biological diversity.[25] The principal rules of the Rio Convention can be divided into six categories.

(i) General rules of international environmental law: Article 3 confirms that States have the sovereign right to exploit their own resources pursuant to their own environmental policies. The authority to determine access to genetic resources rests with national governments and is subject to national legislation.[26] However, the sovereign rights are balanced by the general duty to ensure that activities within their jurisdiction or control do not cause damage to the environment of other States or areas beyond the limits of national jurisdiction. In relation to this, it is to be noted that in its Preamble, the Rio Convention regards the conservation of biological diversity as 'a common concern of humankind'. This suggests that the management of biological diversity under a State's jurisdiction is no longer an internal matter for a State but is a matter of concern of the international community as a whole.[27] Further to this, the Rio Convention obliges each Contracting Party to promote the sustainable use of components of biological diversity.[28]

23 Generally on this issue, see Y. Tanaka, 'Reflections on the Conservation and Sustainable Use of Genetic Resources in the Deep Seabed beyond the Limits of National Jurisdiction' (2008) *ODIL* pp. 129–149.

24 Birnie, Boyle and Redgwell, *International Law and the Environment*, p. 745; M.-A. Hermitte, 'La convention sur la diversité biologique' (1992) 38 *AFDI*, p. 861.

25 Jakarta Ministerial Statement on the Implementation of the Convention on Biological Diversity, para. 14.

26 Article 15(1) of the Rio Convention.

27 R. Wolfrum, 'The Protection and Management of Biological Diversity', in F. L. Morrison, and R. Wolfrum (eds.), *International, Regional and National Environmental Law* (The Hague, Kluwer, 2000), p. 362; A. Boyle, 'The Rio Convention on Biological Diversity', in C. Redgwell and M. Bowman (eds.), *International Law and the Conservation of Biological Diversity* (The Hague, Kluwer, 1996), p. 40.

28 Articles 6 and 10.

(ii) Conservation of biological diversity: the Rio Convention provides *in situ* conservation and *ex situ* conservation. '*In situ* conservation' means 'the conservation of ecosystems and natural habitats and the maintenance and recovery of viable populations of species in their natural surroundings and, in the case of domesticated or cultivated species, in the surroundings where they have developed their distinctive properties'.[29] Specifically each Contracting Party is, *inter alia*, obliged to adopt measures concerning the following matters: regulation of important biological resources; promotion of environmentally sound and sustainable development in areas adjacent to protected areas; rehabilitation of degraded ecosystems and promotion of the recovery of threatened species; establishment of means to regulate the risks associated with the use and release of living modified organisms; prevention of the introduction of those alien species which threaten ecosystems, habitats or species; providing the conditions needed for compatibility between present uses and the conservation of biological diversity; preservation of knowledge, innovations and practices of indigenous and local communities; development of necessary legislation; regulation of the relevant processes and categories of activities; and cooperation in providing financial and other support particularly to developing countries.[30] Although the Rio Convention does not explicitly refer to the term 'the ecosystem approach', these measures seem to reflect this approach.[31]

'*Ex situ* conservation' means the conservation of components of biological diversity outside their natural habitats.[32] Article 9 obliges each Contracting Party to take the following measures: adoption of measures for the *ex situ* conservation of components of biological diversity; establishment and maintenance of facilities for such conservation; adoption of measures for the recovery and rehabilitation of threatened species; regulation and management of collection of biological resources; and cooperation in providing financial and other support for *ex situ* conservation. Historically, most *ex situ* conservation has been undertaken in developed countries; and most collections of genetic materials have been carried out without the approval of the country of origin, which is often a developing country. It is not surprising that developing countries were against the argument emphasising *ex situ* conservation as a principal measure. Thus Article 9 makes clear that *ex situ* conservation should serve as a complement to *in situ* measures. In the Rio Convention, the reference to the precautionary approach is made only in its Preamble. However, the application of this approach is set out as guidance for all activities affecting marine biological diversity in Decision IV/5 of the COP.[33]

(iii) Procedural rules intended to minimise adverse impacts upon biological diversity: Article 14(1)(a) obliges each Contracting Party to introduce, 'as far as possible and as

[29] Article 2. [30] Article 8.

[31] Birnie, Boyle and Redgwell, *International Law and the Environment*, p. 639. The application of the ecosystem approach has been discussed in the COP of the Rio Convention. See for instance, COP, Decision V/6, *Ecosystem Approach*, 2000.

[32] Article 2.

[33] The Convention on Biological Diversity, COP Decision IV/5, *Conservation and Sustainable Use of Marine and Coastal Biological Diversity, Including a Programme of Work*, Annex, section B-2, para. 4.

appropriate', procedures requiring environmental impact assessment of its proposed projects that are likely to have significant adverse effects on biological diversity, with a view to avoiding or minimising such effects. Article 14(1)(c) requires each Contracting Party, 'as far as possible and as appropriate', to 'promote, on the basis of reciprocity, notification, exchange of information and consultation on activities under their jurisdiction or control which are likely to significantly affect adversely the biological diversity of other States or areas beyond the limits of national jurisdiction, by encouraging the conclusion of bilateral, regional or multilateral arrangements, as appropriate'. In the case of imminent or great danger or damage, originating under its jurisdiction or control, to biological diversity within the area under the jurisdiction of other States or in areas beyond the limits of national jurisdiction, each Contracting Party is required to notify immediately the potentially affected States of such danger or damage, as well as initiate action to prevent or minimise such danger or damage (Article 14(1)(d)). To this end, Article 14(1)(e) provides an obligation to promote national arrangements for emergency responses to activities or events.

(iv) Fair and equitable sharing of benefits: in this regard, a key provision is Article 15. Article 15(2) requires each Contracting Party to endeavour to create conditions to facilitate access to genetic resources for environmentally sound uses by other Contracting Parties. Under Article 15(3), the genetic resources being provided by a Contracting Party are only those that are provided by Contracting Parties that are countries of origin of such resources or by Parties that have acquired the genetic resources in accordance with the Rio Convention. Access to genetic resources must be on mutually agreed terms and be subject to the prior informed consent of the Contracting Party providing such resources (Article 15(4) and (5)). Article 15(7) further obliges each Contracting Party to take legislative, administrative or policy measures with a view to sharing in a fair and equitable way the results of research and development and the benefits arising from the commercial and other utilisation of genetic resources with the Contracting Party providing such resources. These obligations are amplified by the Nagoya Protocol on Access to Genetic Resources and the Fair and Equitable Sharing of Benefits Arising from their Utilization to the Convention on Biological Diversity adopted on 29 October 2010.[34]

(v) Assistance to developing countries: in general, States situated in the lower latitudes have more abundant biological diversity than those of higher latitude. The deterioration of biological diversity is closely linked to the widespread poverty in developing countries. In this regard, Article 20(4) of the Rio Convention clearly recognises the fact that 'economic and social development and eradication of poverty are the first and overriding priorities of the developing country Parties'. In this sense, conservation of biological diversity can be characterised by a North–South axis.[35] Given that many habitats to be protected are located in the territories of developing States, the

[34] The text of the Protocol is available at: www.cbd.int/abs/. As of July 2011, the Protocol has not entered into force.

[35] A. A. Yusuf, 'International Law and Sustainable Development: The Convention on Biological Diversity' (1994) 2 *African Yearbook of International Law* p. 112.

allocation of economic benefits and transfer of technology to developing countries are particularly important. Thus Article 20(2) places an explicit obligation upon the developed country to provide 'new and additional financial resources to enable developing country Parties to meet the agreed full incremental costs to them of implementing measures'. Furthermore, Article 16(1) calls for each Contracting Party to provide and/or facilitate access for and transfer to other Contracting Parties of technologies that are relevant to the conservation and sustainable use of biological diversity. Such access to and transfer of technology is to be provided under fair and most favourable terms in accordance with Article 16(2). This provision makes clear that in the case of technology subject to patents and other intellectual property rights, such access and transfer must be provided on terms which recognise and are consistent with the adequate and effective protection of intellectual property rights. Yet the transfer of technology set out in Article 16 is not mandatory.[36] The scope of intellectual property rights also remains unresolved.

(vi) Compliance and dispute settlement: the Rio Convention does not contain a non-compliance procedure comparable to the one created by Article 8 of the 1987 Montreal Protocol to the Ozone Convention,[37] but provides for a reporting system. In this regard, Article 26 places an obligation upon each Contracting Party to present to the Conference of the Parties reports on measures which it has taken for the implementation of the provisions of the Rio Convention and their effectiveness in meeting the objectives of the Convention. Such information submitted in accordance with Article 26 is to be considered by the Conference of the Parties.[38] The reports provided by the Contracting Parties are the principal source of ecological and statistical data. The reporting system has a valuable role to play in assessing the effectiveness of the measures taken by the Contracting Parties.[39]

Article 27 provides procedures for dispute settlement with regard to the interpretation and application of the Rio Convention. Article 27(1) and (2) provides diplomatic methods of dispute settlement, namely negotiation, good offices and mediation. Under Article 27(3), a State or regional economic integration organisation may declare that it accepts the arbitration set out in Part 1 of Annex II and/or the ICJ as the compulsory means of dispute settlement. If the Parties to the dispute have not accepted the same or any procedure, the dispute is to be submitted to conciliation in accordance with Part 2 of Annex II unless the Parties otherwise agree pursuant to Article 27(4).

Finally, the relationship between the Rio Convention and other conventions, in particular the LOSC, should be mentioned. Article 22 of the Rio Convention provides that:

1. The provisions of this Convention shall not affect the rights and obligations of any Contracting Party deriving from any existing international agreement, *except where the*

[36] Wolfrum, 'The Protection and Management of Biological Diversity', p. 367.

[37] (1987) 26 *ILM* p. 1550. [38] Article 23(4)(a).

[39] Yet the Conference of the Parties expressed its concern over the delay in the submission of national reports by some Parties. Resolution VII/25. National Reporting, UNEP/CBD/COP/DEC/VII/25, 13 April 2004, para. 2.

exercise of those rights and obligations would cause a serious damage or threat to biological diversity.

2. Contracting Parties shall implement this Convention with respect to the marine environment consistently with the rights and obligations of States under the law of the sea.[40]

It appears that normally the effect of Article 22 is to ensure the predominance of the LOSC. This interpretation is also supported by Article 311(3) of the LOSC. However, it seems that this is not the case if there is 'a serious damage or threat to biological diversity'. For instance, there appears to be scope to argue that States Parties to the Rio Convention cannot justify fishing which may cause 'a serious damage or threat to biological diversity' on the basis of the LOSC.[41]

(b) Commentary

The Rio Convention calls for four comments. First, in essence, the Rio Convention is based on the zonal management approach which distinguishes between the spaces under and beyond national jurisdiction. Concerning transboundary damage on biological diversity, the Rio Convention merely places on Contracting Parties the obligation to exchange information and the obligation to consult one another. It would seem that the Rio Convention did not advance existing international law on this matter.

Second, the provisions of the Rio Convention relating to conservation apply solely to components of biological diversity in areas within the limits of a State's national jurisdiction. In areas beyond national jurisdiction, each Contracting Party is only obliged to cooperate with other Parties for the conservation and sustainable use of biological diversity in accordance with Article 5. It would seem to follow that Contracting Parties have no direct obligation relating to the conservation of specific components of biological diversity in marine spaces beyond the limits of national jurisdiction.[42]

Third, the wording of the principal Articles is heavily qualified by the words 'as far as possible' and 'as appropriate'. This qualification will leave much discretion to the Contracting Parties.

Fourth, there is a wide variety of different ecosystems in the oceans. As a consequence, the need for conservation of marine biological diversity may vary depending on the marine area. It is difficult if not impossible to establish uniform and detailed rules relating to the conservation of marine biological diversity at the global level. In light of economic and technological difficulties in developing countries, it will also be difficult to place the same obligations upon them to conserve marine biological diversity. Hence the global framework set out by the Rio Convention needs to be further amplified by regional treaties relating to conservation of marine biological diversity.

[40] Emphasis added.

[41] Birnie, Boyle and Redgwell, *International Law and the Environment*, p. 750.

[42] SBSTTA of the Rio Convention also takes the same interpretation. UNEP/CBD/SBSTTA/8/INF/3/Rev. 1, 22 February 2003, p. 19, para. 70. See also Glowka, 'The Deepest of Ironies', p. 168.

In this regard, a good example may be furnished by the OSPAR Convention.[43] The original text of the OSPAR Convention did not contain detailed provisions with regard to the conservation of marine biological diversity. Later, the scope of the Convention was expanded to cover this subject. Currently the obligation to conserve marine biological diversity is provided in Annex V as well as Appendix 3 of the Convention in some detail. In particular, Article 2(a) of Annex V obliges Contracting Parties to 'take the necessary measures to protect and conserve the ecosystems and the biological diversity of the maritime area, and to restore, where practicable, marine areas which have been adversely affected'. The OSPAR Commission is required to draw up programmes and measures for the control of human activities which have adverse effects on specific marine species, habitats and ecological processes.[44] To this end, the OSPAR Commission is to develop means for instituting protective or precautionary measures related to specific areas or particular species or habitats.[45] Furthermore, as will be seen next, the role of regional treaties is increasingly important in the creations of MPAs.

4 MARINE PROTECTED AREAS

4.1 General considerations

Marine protected areas (MPAs) seek to protect marine ecosystems of a certain area as a whole. While there is no universally established definition in international law,[46] the Biodiversity Committee of the OSPAR Convention defines an MPA as:

> An area within the maritime area for which protective, conservation, restorative or precautionary measures, consistent with international law have been instituted for the purpose of protecting and conserving species, habitats, ecosystems or ecological processes of the marine environment.[47]

While treaties creating MPAs may date back to the 1940s,[48] it was not until the 1970s that legal attention was devoted to MPA-related concepts. The 1971 Convention on Wetlands of International Importance (Ramsar Convention) is an example. Article 2(1) of the Ramsar Convention imposes on each Contracting Party an obligation to designate suitable wetland within its territory for inclusion in a List of Wetlands of

[43] For an analysis of the OSPAR Convention, see Tanaka, *A Dual Approach*, pp. 148–159.
[44] Article 3(1)(a) of Annex V.
[45] Article 3(1)(b)(ii) of Annex V.
[46] A frequently quoted definition is provided by IUCN: 'Any area of intertidal or subtidal terrain, together with its overlying water and associated flora, fauna, historical and cultural features, which has been reserved by law or other effective means to protect part or all of the enclosed environment'. G. Kelleher (ed.), *Guidelines for Marine Protected Areas* (Gland, IUCN–The World Conservation Union, 1999), p. xviii and p. 98.
[47] OSPAR Recommendation 2003/3 adopted by OSPAR 2003 (OSPAR 03/17/1, Annex 9), amended by OSPAR Recommendation 2010/2 (OSPAR 10/23/1, Annex 7), para. 1.1.
[48] Cf. the 1940 Convention on Nature Protection and Wildlife Preservation in the Western Hemisphere (Article 2). 161 *UNTS* p. 193. Entered into force in 1942.

International Importance.[49] The Contracting Parties are under the obligation to formulate and implement their planning so as to promote the conservation of the wetlands included in the List, and as far as possible the wise use of wetlands in their territory in accordance with Article 3(1). Such wetlands may cover offshore areas pursuant to Article 1(1) and Article 2(1). Some 48 per cent of the designated Ramsar sites include coastline and these sites may contain marine components.[50]

An MPA-related concept can also be detected in the 1972 Convention for the Protection of the World Cultural and Natural Heritage (hereafter the World Heritage Convention).[51] This Convention aims to protect cultural and natural heritage, including habitats of 'threatened species of animals and plants of outstanding universal value from the point of view of science or conservation'.[52] Under Article 11(1), every State Party is obliged to submit to the World Heritage Committee an inventory of property forming part of the cultural and natural heritage, which is situated in its territory and is of outstanding universal value. The Committee shall then establish a list of properties forming part of the cultural heritage and natural heritage under the title of the 'World Heritage List'. Several World Heritage sites include involve a marine site. Examples include: the Great Barrier Reef (Australia), the Belize Barrier Reef (Belize), the Wadden Sea (Germany and the Netherlands), the Whale Sanctuary of El Vizcaino (Mexico) and the Tubbataha Reef (Philippines).[53]

In the 1980s, MPAs were increasingly being incorporated into various treaties. While most MPAs were set in place in territorial seas near to coastal areas in the 1970s, the geographical scope of MPAs tended to be extended to the EEZ in the 1980s and later. Furthermore, as we shall discuss later, the need to establish MPAs in marine spaces beyond the limits of national jurisdiction is also being discussed in various forums.

4.2 Typology of MPAs in international law

MPA-related concepts can be divided into two principal categories. The first category involves MPAs intended to protect the marine environment (category 1). At least five MPA-related concepts must be noted:

- 'clearly defined area' in Article 211(6) of the LOSC,
- 'ice-covered areas' in Article 234 of the LOSC,
- 'special areas' under MARPOL 73/78,
- 'particularly sensitive sea areas' (PSSA) in IMO Guidelines, and
- 'specially protected areas' in the 1985 Montreal Guidelines.

The last item relates to the protection of marine spaces from land-based marine pollution. Other MPA-related concepts in this category are meant to protect the marine environment from vessel-source pollution. Although these MPA-related concepts do

[49] 996 *UNTS* p. 245; (1972) 11 *ILM* p. 963. Entered into force on 21 December 1975.
[50] Kelleher, *Guidelines for Marine Protected Areas*, p. 4.
[51] (1972) 11 *ILM* p. 1358. Entered into force on 17 December 1975.
[52] See Article 2.
[53] The World Heritage list which includes marine components is available at: http://whc.unesco.org/en/activities/13/.

not directly involve conservation of marine biological diversity, they will indirectly contribute to preserve diversity by protecting the marine environment.

The second category pertains to MPAs relating directly to conservation of marine biological diversity (category 2). These MPAs can be divided into two sub-categories.

The first sub-category concerns a species-specific MPA (category 2–1). This type of MPA seeks to protect specific marine life, such as marine mammals, in a particular region. MPAs in this sub-category are basically in line with the traditional species-specific approach. Examples are furnished by:

- the 1990 Agreement on the Conservation of Seals in the Wadden Sea,[54]
- the 1993 Déclaration conjointe relative à l'institution d'un sanctuaire méditerranéen pour les mammifères marins,[55]
- the Agreement on the Conservation of Cetaceans of the Black Sea, Mediterranean Sea and Contiguous Atlantic Area (ACCOBAMS),[56]
- the 1999 Agreement Establishing a Sanctuary for Marine Mammals,[57] and
- the Inter-American Convention for the Protection and Conservation of Sea Turtles.[58]

A second sub-category involves MPAs which seek to protect rare or fragile ecosystems and the habitat of depleted or endangered species and other marine life in a particular region (category 2–2). As shown in Table 9.1, there are a significant number of treaties creating this category of MPAs. One might take the Rio Convention as an example.

The Rio Convention provides the establishment of the 'protected area'. Under Article 2, the 'protected area' means 'a geographically defined area which is designated or regulated and managed to achieve specific conservation objectives'. As the geographical scope of the Rio Convention includes marine spaces, 'protected areas' can be created in marine spaces. In fact, the COP to the Rio Convention agreed that MPAs were one of the essential tools and approaches in the conservation and sustainable use of marine and coastal biological diversity.[59]

Article 8(a) of the Rio Convention provides that each Contracting Party shall, 'as far as possible and as appropriate', establish a system of protected areas or areas where special measures need to be taken to conserve biological diversity. The cumulative effect of Articles 4, 8(a) and 22(2) suggests that the protected area in the Rio Convention can be established only within the marine spaces under coastal State jurisdiction.[60]

[54] The text of the Agreement is available at: www.cms.int/species/wadden_seals/sea_text.htm.

[55] The text of the Protocol is reproduced in T. Scovazzi (ed.), *Marine Specially Protected Areas: The General Aspects and the Mediterranean Regional System* (The Hague, Kluwer, 1999), pp. 243–245.

[56] (1997) 36 *ILM*, p. 777.

[57] With respect to the 1999 Sanctuary Agreement, see T. Scovazzi, 'The Mediterranean Marine Mammals Sanctuary' (2001) 16 *IJMCL* pp. 132–141. The text of the Agreement is reproduced *ibid.*, pp. 142–145.

[58] For the text of the Convention, see www.lclark.edu/org/ielp/objects/interamerican.pdf.

[59] The Convention on Biological Diversity, COP Decision VII/5, *Marine and Coastal Biological Diversity*, UNEP/CBD/COP/DEC/VII/5, 13 April 2004, para. 16.

[60] D. K. Anton, 'Law of the Sea's Biological Diversity', in J. I. Charney, D. K. Anton, and M. E. O'Connell (eds.), *Politics, Values and Functions: International Law in the 21st Century, Essays in Honour of Professor Louis Henkin* (The Hague, Nijhoff, 1997), p. 341.

TABLE 9.1. EXAMPLES OF TREATIES WHICH ESTABLISH MPAS IN CATEGORY 2–2

Year	Title	Relevant Provision
1976	Convention on Conservation of Nature in the South Pacific	Article II
1980	Convention on the Conservation of Antarctic Marine Living Resources	Article 9(2)(g)
1981	Convention for Co-operation in the Protection and Development of the Marine and Coastal Environment of the West and Central African Region	Article 11
1982	Protocol Concerning Mediterranean Specially Protected Areas	Article 3(1)
1985	Convention for the Protection, Management and Development of the Marine and Coastal Environment of the Eastern African Region	Article 10
1985	Protocol Concerning Protected Areas and Wild Fauna and Flora in the Eastern African Region	Article 8
1985	ASEAN Agreement on the Conservation of Nature and Natural Resources	Article 3(3)(a)
1986	Convention for the Protection of the Natural Resources and Environment of the South Pacific Region	Article 14
1989	Protocol for the Conservation and Management of Protected Marine and Coastal Areas of the South-East Pacific	Articles 2 and 3
1990	Protocol Concerning Specially Protected Areas and Wildlife in the Wider Caribbean Region	Article 4
1991	Protocol to the Antarctic Treaty on Environmental Protection	Annex V
1992	Convention on Biological Diversity	Article 8(a)
1992	Convention for the Protection of the Marine Environment of the North-East Atlantic (OSPAR Convention)	See note
1992	Convention on the Protection of the Marine Environment of the Baltic Sea Area	See note
1995	Protocol Concerning Specially Protected Areas and Biological Diversity in the Mediterranean	Articles 8, 9 Annex I

Note: The list is not exhaustive. Although there is no explicit provision relating to MPAs in the OSPAR Convention, the institution of MPAs is developing through the OSPAR Commission. Likewise, Baltic Sea Protected Areas (BSPAs) are developing through the Helsinki Commission, although the Helsinki Convention did not refer to BSPAs.

Article 8(b) of the Rio Convention requires each Contracting Party to develop 'where necessary, guidelines for the selection, establishment and management of protected areas or areas where special measures need to be taken to conserve biological diversity'; Article 8(c) imposes on each Contracting Party an obligation to 'regulate or manage biological resources important for the conservation of biological diversity whether within or outside protected areas, with a view to ensuring their conservation and sustainable use'. Similarly, each Contracting Party is obliged to 'promote environmentally sound and sustainable development in areas adjacent to protected areas with a view to furthering protection of these areas' in conformity with Article 8(e). As noted, these provisions apply to the creation of the protected area in the oceans. In this case, a question that may arise is the compatibility between MPAs and other legitimate use of the oceans, in particular, the freedom of navigation. As discussed earlier, the LOSC carefully safeguards the right of navigation in each jurisdictional zone.[61] Thus, MPAs in the Rio Convention should be balanced against the freedom of navigation under the LOSC as well as customary law.

4.3 MPAs in the high seas

In recent times the need to establish MPAs in the high seas has been increasingly voiced in various forums. For example, the COP of the Rio Convention stated that: 'marine protected areas are one of the essential tools to help achieve conservation and sustainable use of biodiversity in marine areas beyond the limits of national jurisdiction'.[62] Is there a legal ground for creating MPAs in the high seas in positive international law? In considering this issue, a distinction must be made between MPAs located within the potential EEZ of the coastal State (the high seas in a broad sense) and MPAs located in the high seas beyond 200 nautical miles (the high seas in a strict sense).

(a) MPAs on the high seas in a broad sense

MPAs on the high seas in a broad sense mean MPAs which are located in the high seas which are the potential EEZ of the coastal State. The best example is MPAs in the Mediterranean Sea. Currently large expanses of waters located beyond the twelve-nautical-mile limit remain the high seas as the Mediterranean States have not yet established EEZs. Should coastal States establish their EEZs in the Mediterranean Sea, however, the whole area will fall into the EEZs of these States. In this sense, high seas areas in the Mediterranean Sea can be regarded as a *potential* EEZ of the coastal State.

In the Mediterranean Sea, two treaties provide for the establishment of MPAs on the high seas.[63] The first treaty is the 1995 Protocol Concerning Specially Protected Areas and Biological Diversity in the Mediterranean (hereafter the 1995 Protocol).[64] This Protocol aims to protect areas of particular natural or cultural value, notably by the establishment of specially protected areas, and to protect threatened or endangered species of flora and fauna under Article 3(1). The 1995 Protocol is applicable to all the marine waters of the Mediterranean Sea, the seabed and its subsoil, as well as the terrestrial coastal areas designated by each of the Parties, including wetlands.[65]

61 See for instance, LOSC, Articles 17, 24(1), 25(3), 38, 44, 52(2), 53(2) and 58(1).

62 Convention on Biological Diversity, COP Decision VIII/24, *Protected Area*, UNEP/CBD/COP/DEC/VIII/24, 15 June 2006, para. 38.

63 For an analysis of MPAs in the Mediterranean Sea, see T. Scovazzi, 'New International Instruments for Marine Protected Areas in the Mediterranean Sea', in A. Strati, *Unresolved Issues and New Challenges to the Law of the Sea: Time Before and Time After* (Leiden and Boston, Nijhoff, 2006), pp. 109–120.

64 The text of the 1995 Protocol is reproduced in Scovazzi, *Marine Specially Protected Areas*, p. 163.

65 Article 2(1) of the 1995 Protocol.

The Protocol establishes two types of MPAs in the Mediterranean Sea: 'specially protected areas' (SPAs) and 'specially protected areas of mediterranean importance' (SPAMIs). SPAs may be established in the marine and coastal zones subject to its sovereignty or jurisdiction pursuant to Article 5(1) of the 1995 Protocol. Under Article 9(1) of the Protocol, SPAMIs may be established in: '(a) the marine and coastal zones subject to the sovereignty or jurisdiction of the Parties; (b) *zones partly or wholly on the high seas*'.[66] Under Article 8(1), the Parties are required to draw up a 'List of specially protected areas of mediterranean importance' (SPAMI List) in order to promote cooperation in the management and conservation of natural areas, as well as in the protection of threatened species and their habitats. In 2001, the first twelve SPAMIs have been inscribed in the List, and the French-Italian-Monégasque Sanctuary, which was jointly proposed by the three States concerned, covers areas of the high seas.[67]

The French-Italian-Monégasque Sanctuary relies on the 1999 Agreement on the Creation in the Mediterranean Sea of a Sanctuary for Marine Mammals (hereafter the 1999 Sanctuary Agreement).[68] This is the second treaty establishing MPAs on the high seas in the broad sense. Article 2 of the Agreement calls for the Parties to establish a marine sanctuary within the area of the Mediterranean Sea as defined in Article 3, whose biological diversity and richness represent an indispensable attribute for the protection of marine mammals and their habitats. Under Article 3, the sanctuary is composed of marine areas situated within the internal waters and territorial seas of the French Republic, Italian Republic and the Principality of Monaco, as well as portions of the adjacent high seas. The Sanctuary extends over 96,000 square kilometres and is in-habited by the eight cetacean species regularly found in the Mediterranean.[69] Within the Sanctuary, the Parties shall prohibit any deliberate taking or intentional disturbance of marine mammals.

Furthermore, Article 14(2) provides that:

> In the other parts of the sanctuary [on the high seas], each of the State Parties is responsible for the application of the provisions of the present Agreement with respect to ships flying its flag as well as, within the limits provided for by the rules of international law, with respect to ships flying the flag of third States.

This provision appears to empower the States Parties to enforce the provisions of the 1999 Sanctuary Agreement on vessels of third States 'within the limits established by the rules of international law'. A question thus arises whether this provision might not be contrary to the fundamental rule of treaty law, *res inter alios acta*. In this regard, it

66 Emphasis added.

67 Scovazzi, 'New International Instruments', pp. 114–115.

68 Entered into force on 21 February 2002. For an analysis of this Agreement, along with the text, see Scovazzi, 'The Mediterranean Marine Mammals Sanctuary', pp. 132–145.

69 These species are: the fin whale, the sperm whale, Cuvier's beaked whale, the long-finned pilot whale, the striped dolphin, the common dolphin, the bottlenose dolphin and Risso's dolphin. Scovazzi, 'New International Instruments', p. 115.

must be recalled that even though the areas covered by these agreements remain high seas, they will fall under the *potential* EEZ of either of the Parties to the Convention. Consequently, the coastal States have *potential* jurisdiction over living resources, although technically those areas remain the high seas. By ratifying the Convention, it may be considered that the States Parties are declaring an exercise of their jurisdiction over conservation of living resources in the areas concerned. In this case, the coastal States are only exercising jurisdiction to a lesser degree than in an EEZ.

Those who can do more can also do less.[70] A case in point is the exclusive fishery zone. The concept of an exclusive fishery zone is more limited than that of an EEZ in the sense that an exclusive fishery zone relates only to fisheries, whereas the concept of the EEZ also includes activities in the seabed. While several States have created 200-nautical-mile exclusive fishery zones, the validity of such a zone has not been disputed. By analogy, there appears to be scope to argue that a coastal State may exercise the same jurisdiction which is exercisable in an EEZ, i.e. jurisdiction with regard to the conservation of marine biological diversity, in the marine spaces within 200 nautical miles even if technically the spaces remain the high seas. Following this interpretation, arguably at least, the coastal State may be entitled to establish MPAs on the high seas in the broad sense.

(b) MPAs on the high seas in a strict sense

The establishment of MPAs on the high seas in a strict sense remains very rare in practice. A possible instance is the 1986 Convention for the Protection of the Natural Resources and Environment of the South Pacific Region (the 1986 Noumea Convention). Article 14 of the Convention provides that:

> The Parties shall, individually or jointly, take all appropriate measures to protect and preserve rare or fragile ecosystems and depleted, threatened or endangered flora and fauna as well as their habitat in the Convention Area. To this end, the Parties shall, as appropriate, establish protected areas, such as parks and reserves, and prohibit or regulate any activity likely to have adverse effects on the species, ecosystems or biological processes that such areas are designed to protect.

In accordance with Article 2(a), the Convention Area comprises:

> (ii) those areas of high seas which are enclosed from all sides by the 200 nautical mile zones referred to in sub-paragraph (i); (iii) areas of the Pacific Ocean which have been included in the Convention Area pursuant to Article 3.

[70] T. Scovazzi, 'Marine Protected Areas on the High Seas: Some Legal and Policy Considerations' (2004) 19 *IJMCL* p. 15.

It would seem to follow that textually the Parties establish protected areas in the Convention Area, which contains part of the high seas in a strict sense. However, Article 14 immediately adds that: 'The establishment of such areas shall not affect the rights of other Parties or third States under international law'. Hence regulatory measures of the coastal State are applicable only to its nationals. Furthermore, six high seas MPAs that together cover 286,200 square kilometres of the North-East Atlantic were established by the OSPAR Ministerial Meeting in September 2010.[71]

The establishment of MPAs on the high seas in a strict sense needs careful consideration. Due to their nature, high seas MPAs close a part of the marine spaces of the high seas. Given that no State can claim territorial sovereignty or sovereign rights over parts of the high seas in a strict sense, however, no State can unilaterally establish MPAs in the high seas.[72] It is true that States are obliged to protect and preserve the marine environment, including rare or fragile ecosystems, under Articles 192 and 194(5) of the LOSC. States are also under the obligation to cooperate with each other in the conservation and management of living resources in the areas of the high seas under Articles 117 and 118. However, it is debatable whether these general obligations directly provide for any right of States with regard to the establishment of MPAs on the high seas in a strict sense.[73]

Even if some States agreed to conserve marine biological diversity on the high seas by establishing MPAs, such an agreement could not be applicable to ships flying the flag of non-parties. Furthermore, the establishment of MPAs on the high seas in a strict sense may entail the risk of limiting freedoms of the high seas, such as the freedom of navigation, freedom to lay submarine cables and pipelines, freedom of fishing and of scientific research. Should MPAs on the high seas affect the navigation of vessels including submarines, for instance, the creation of such MPAs will encounter strong opposition from naval powers.[74]

Considering that the creation of such MPAs may restrict the traditional freedoms of the high seas, the procedural legitimacy of creating those MPAs is of central importance. In order to ensure such legitimacy, much consideration will need to be given to the formulation of objective criteria identifying the need to establish MPAs on the high seas in a strict sense. It is also necessary to examine a possible organ which is legitimately entitled to identify the location of MPAs on the high seas. Overall, at the present stage, the creation of MPAs on the high seas in a strict sense seems to leave some room for discussion in positive international law.

[71] OSPAR Commission, *2010 Status Report on the OSPAR Network of Marine Protected Areas* (2011), pp. 16–24

[72] Scovazzi, 'Marine Protected Areas on the High Seas', p. 5. United Nations Open-Ended Informal Consultative Process on Oceans and the Law of the Sea, *Protection and Conservation of Vulnerable Marine Ecosystems in Areas Beyond National Jurisdiction, Submitted by the Delegation of Norway*, A/AC.259/10, 4 June 2003, p. 2, paras. 3–4 (Norway).

[73] The Ad Hoc Technical Expert Group on Protected Areas (AHTEG) has considered that high-seas areas presented a special situation in which existing legal instruments, including the Rio Convention, did not necessarily provide an adequate basis for the establishment of protected areas. Convention on Biological Diversity, AHTEG, *The Role of Protected Areas within the Convention on Biological Diversity*, UNEP/CBD/AHTEG-PA/1/INF/1, 6 June 2003, para. 57.

[74] S. Kaye, 'Implementing High Seas Biodiversity Conservation: Global Geopolitical Considerations' (2004) 28 *Marine Policy* pp. 223–224.

4.4 Limits of MPAs

Whilst MPAs are increasingly incorporated into treaties respecting conservation of marine biological diversity, the effectiveness of MPAs is not free from controversy. From a legal viewpoint, at least three obstacles must be identified.[75]

The first obstacle involves the lack of interlinkage between the MPAs for the conservation of marine biological diversity and the regulation of marine pollution. The protection of the environment from pollution is a prerequisite for the conservation of marine biological diversity. The regulation of land-based pollution is particularly important because it mainly affects coastal waters, which are sites of high biological diversity.[76] However, the establishment of MPAs intended to conserve marine biological diversity cannot of itself protect marine biological diversity from marine pollution. [77] Accordingly, MPAs for the conservation of marine biological diversity must be combined with the regulation of marine pollution in an integrated manner. Usually, however, the regulation of marine pollution is beyond the scope of the MPAs.

The second difficulty concerns the adverse impact of climate change on marine biological diversity. The marine environment is sensitive to climate and atmospheric changes. Nonetheless, MPAs cannot, in themselves, prevent adverse impacts upon marine biological diversity by climate change. Accordingly, prevention of climate change is also needed in order to halt the degradation of marine biological diversity.

Third, there is little doubt that fishing activities are one of the major threats to marine biological diversity. With few exceptions,[78] however, the regulation of fisheries falls outside the scope of treaties relating to the conservation of marine biological diversity; conversely, fisheries treaties do not focus on the conservation of marine biological diversity. As a consequence, there is a disjunction between the two legal fields. Positive coordination between MPAs and the regulation of fisheries will be increasingly important in order to effectively conserve marine biological diversity.[79]

5 CONCLUSIONS

The matters considered in this chapter can be summarised under five points.

(i) In examining treaties respecting conservation of (marine) biological diversity, at least three approaches can be identified: the regional approach, the species specific

[75] Tanaka, *A Dual Approach*, pp. 191–197.

[76] S. Kuwabara, *The Legal Regime of Protection of the Mediterranean against Pollution from Land-Based Sources* (Dublin, Tycooly, 1984), p. xvii.

[77] D. Freestone, 'The Conservation of Marine Ecosystems under International Law', in C. Redgwell and M. J. Bowman (eds.), *International Law and the Conservation of Biological Diversity* (The Hague, Kluwer, 1996), p. 94.

[78] Article 5(2)(d) of the 1990 Protocol Concerning Specially Protected Areas and Wildlife to the Convention for the Protection and Development of the Marine Environment of the Wider Caribbean Region; Article 10(d) of the 1985 Protocol Concerning Protected Areas and Wild Fauna and Flora in the Eastern African Region.

[79] UN General Assembly Resolution 59/25, adopted on 17 November 2004, calls upon regional fisheries management organisations to adopt appropriate conservation measures to address the impact of destructive fishing practices, including bottom trawling that has adverse impacts on vulnerable marine ecosystems. A/RES/59/25, p. 13, para. 67.

approach and the activity specific approach. Further to this, the establishment of a global framework is needed in order to fill possible legal lacunae in the field of conservation of (marine) biological diversity.

(ii) Although the LOSC provides for a global legal framework for conservation of marine species, it contains only a few provisions involving marine biological diversity. Arguably the traditional approaches of the LOSC, namely, the zonal management approach and the species specific approach, are inadequate to conserve marine biological diversity because they pay little attention to ecological interactions between marine species.

(iii) The Rio Convention represents the key instrument for establishing a global legal framework for conservation of biological diversity. Significantly, the rules of the Convention apply not only to conservation of terrestrial biological diversity but also to that of marine biological diversity. On the other hand, the effectiveness of the Rio Convention seems to be qualified by three points:

- weak obligations with regard to transboundary damage to biological diversity,
- weak obligations concerning conservation of biological diversity in areas beyond the limits of national jurisdiction,
- wide discretion of Contracting Parties.

Furthermore, due to economic, technological and ecological divergence in the world, regional treaties which tailor more specific rules to meet the needs of States in a certain region have a valuable role in this field.

(iv) The establishment of MPAs is increasingly being incorporated into treaties relating to conservation of biological diversity. There appears to be general agreement that MPAs have a valuable role to play in conservation of marine biological diversity. However, in view of enhancing the efficacy of MPAs, there will be a need to enhance the interlinkage between MPAs on the one hand and the protection of the marine environment, prevention of climate change and the regulation of fisheries on the other hand.

(v) The legality of MPAs on the high seas should be examined by dividing such MPAs into two categories. On the one hand, it may be possible to establish MPAs on the high seas in a broad sense because they are located in the *potential* EEZ of the coastal State. On the other hand, the legality of the creation of MPAs on the high seas in a strict sense needs careful consideration with regard to the legitimacy of procedures for selecting the location and compatibility with the freedom of the seas.

FURTHER READING

1 General

F. Francioni and T. Scovazzi (eds.), *Biotechnology and International Law* (Oxford and Portland, Oregon, Hart Publishing, 2006).

S. Iudicello and M. Lytle, 'Marine Biodiversity and International Law: Instruments and Institutions that Can Be Used to Conserve Marine Biological Diversity Internationally' (1994) 8 *Tulane Environmental Law Journal* pp. 123–161.

C. C. Joyner, 'Biodiversity in the Marine Environment: Resource Implications for the Law of the Sea' (1995) 28 *Vanderbilt Journal of Transnational Law* pp. 635–687.

Y. Tanaka, *A Dual Approach to Ocean Governance: The Cases of Zonal and Integrated Management in International Law of the Sea* (Surrey, England, Ashgate, 2008) (Chapters 4 and 5).

R. Wolfrum, 'The Protection and Management of Biological Diversity', in F. L. Morrison and R. Wolfrum (eds.), *International, Regional and National Environmental Law* (The Hague, Kluwer, 2000), pp. 355–372.

2 Convention on Biological Diversity

A. Boyle, 'The Rio Convention on Biological Diversity', in C. Redgwell and M. Bowman (eds.), *International Law and the Conservation of Biological Diversity* (The Hague, Kluwer, 1995), pp. 33–49.

M.-A. Hermitte, 'La convention sur la diversité biologique' (1992) 38 *AFDI* pp. 844–870.

V. Koester, 'The Nature of the Convention on Biological Diversity and its Application of Components of the Concept of Sustainable Development' (2007) 16 *Italian Yearbook of International Law* pp. 57–84.

R. Wolfrum and N. Mats, 'The Interplay of the United Nations Convention on the Law of the Sea and the Convention on Biological Diversity' (2000) 4 *Max Planck Yearbook of United Nations Law* pp. 445–480.

A. A. Yusuf, 'International Law and Sustainable Development: The Conservation of Biological Diversity' (1995) 2 *African Yearbook of International Law* pp. 109–137.

3 Marine Protected Areas

K. M. Gjerde, 'High Seas Marine Protected Areas' (2001) 16 *IJMCL* pp. 515–528.

G. Kelleher (ed.), *Guidelines for Marine Protected Areas* (Gland, IUCN–The World Conservation Union, 1999).

National Research Council, *Marine Protected Areas: Tools for Sustaining Ocean Ecosystems* (Washington DC, National Academy Press, 2001).

J. Roberts, *Marine Environment Protection and Biodiversity Conservation: The Application and Future Development of the IMO's Particularly Sensitive Sea Area Concept* (Berlin, Springer, 2007).

R. V. Salm, J. Clark and E. Siirila, *Marine and Coastal Protected Areas: A Guide for Planners and Managers*, 3rd edn (Gland, IUCN, 2000).

T. Scovazzi (ed.), *Marine Specially Protected Areas: The General Aspects and the Mediterranean Regional System* (The Hague, Kluwer, 1999).

'Marine Protected Areas on the High Seas: Some Legal and Policy Considerations' (2004) 19 *IJMCL* pp. 1–17.

H. Thiel, 'Approaches to the Establishment of Protected Areas on the High Seas', in A. Kirchner (ed.), *International Marine Environmental Law* (The Hague, Kluwer, 2003), pp. 169–192.

10

Marine Scientific Research

Main Issues

Ocean governance must be based on a sound scientific understanding of the marine environment. Thus it may be argued that the freedom of marine scientific research is a prerequisite of ocean governance. However, marine scientific research or other survey activities in the offshore areas may affect economic and security interests of coastal States. In particular, military survey activities in the EEZ of another State have raised highly sensitive issues between surveying and coastal States. Hence there is a need to achieve a balance between the freedom of marine scientific research and the protection of interests of coastal States. Against that background, this chapter will address particularly the following issues.

(i) What is marine scientific research?
(ii) How is it possible to reconcile the freedom of marine scientific research with the protection of interests of coastal States?
(iii) Is it possible to carry out hydrographic and military survey activities in the EEZ of another State?
(iv) How is it possible to ensure international cooperation in marine scientific research?
(v) Why should the transfer of technology be promoted in oceans governance?

1 INTRODUCTION

Marine scientific research is a foundation of ocean governance in the sense that rules governing the use of the ocean must be based on the sound scientific understanding of the marine environment. Furthermore, marine science can make an important contribution to eliminating poverty, ensuring food security, supporting human economic activity, conserving marine living resources and environment and helping predict natural disasters.[1] Thus marine scientific research is a significant issue in the law of the sea. Indeed, the development of marine science and the law of the sea are intimately intertwined. In this regard, three patterns can be identified.

[1] United Nations, *Report of the Secretary-General, Oceans and the Law of the Sea Addendum*, A/66/70/Add.1, 11 April 2011, pp. 49–50, para. 208.

First, marine scientific research is one of the catalysts for the development of the law of the sea. This is highlighted by the discovery of manganese nodules in the deep seabed and the establishment of the legal regime governing the Area.[2]

Second, marine scientific research provides essential data for the implementation of rules of the law of the sea. For instance, the best available scientific data relating to marine species is a prerequisite in order to determine maximum sustainable yield (MSY) and total allowable catch (TAC).[3] Marine scientific research is also crucial in the application of the ecosystem and precautionary approaches since the application of those approaches must be based on reliable scientific data.

Third, the law of the sea may give an impetus to develop marine scientific research. An example can be found in the recent progress of seabed research with a view to collecting geological and geomorphological data necessary for the identification of the outer limits of the continental shelf beyond 200 nautical miles.[4] The claim over the continental shelf beyond 200 nautical miles encourages coastal States to investigate the seabed and subsoil of the continental margin.

International law regulating marine scientific research rests on the tension between the freedom of such research and the protection of interests of coastal States. On the one hand, freedom is a prerequisite to developing marine scientific research. On the other hand, marine scientific research may raise particular sensitivities associated with the economic, social and security interests of coastal States. A key question thus arises as to how it is possible to reconcile the freedom of marine scientific research with the safeguarding of the interests of coastal States. With this question as a backdrop, this chapter will examine the principal legal issues with regard to marine scientific research.

2 THE CONCEPT OF MARINE SCIENTIFIC RESEARCH

As a preliminary consideration, the concept of marine scientific research must be examined. The LOSC contains no definition of marine scientific research. In general, 'marine scientific research' may be defined as any scientific study or related experimental work having *the marine environment as its object* which is designed to increase knowledge of the oceans.[5] As the marine environment contains marine life, the concept of marine scientific research covers any scientific investigation, however and wherever performed, which concerns the marine environment as well as its organisms. However, scientific research not concerning the marine environment as its object, such as astronomical observations carried out at sea, is not considered as marine scientific research by the law of the sea.[6] Scientific research undertaken outside

[2] See Chapter 5, section 3.1. [3] See Chapter 7, section 3.2. [4] See Chapter 4, section 4.3.

[5] A. H. A. Soons, *Marine Scientific Research and the Law of the Sea* (Antwerp, Kluwer, 1982), pp. 6–7 and p. 124; T. Treves, 'Marine Research', in R. Bernhardt (ed.), *Encyclopedia of Public International Law* (Amsterdam, Elsevier, 1997), p. 295.

[6] A. H. A. Soons, 'Marine Scientific Research Provisions in the Convention on the Law of the Sea: Issues of Interpretation', in E. D. Brown and R. R. Churchill (eds.), *The UN Convention on the Law of*

the surface, water column, seabed or subsoil of the oceans, such as remote sensing from satellites, is not addressed by the LOSC.[7]

The concept of marine scientific research usually covers two types of research, namely, 'fundamental' or 'pure' research, and 'applied' or 'resource-oriented' research.[8] This distinction dates back to the 1958 Geneva Convention on the Continental Shelf. Article 5(1) of the Convention forbids the coastal State 'any interference with fundamental oceanographic or other scientific research carried out with the intention of open publication', whilst Article 5(8) stipulates that the consent of the coastal State is required in respect of 'any research concerning the continental shelf and undertaken there'. Article 5(8) further provides that the coastal State shall not normally withhold its consent 'if the request is submitted by a qualified institution with a view to purely scientific research into the physical or biological characteristics of the continental shelf'. The distinction is maintained in the LOSC.

Whilst the Convention on the Continental Shelf and the LOSC contain no precise definition of the two types of research, 'fundamental research' may be defined as research which is carried out 'exclusively for peaceful purposes and in order to increase scientific knowledge of the marine environment for the benefit of all mankind'.[9] 'Applied research' can be considered that which is of 'direct significance for the exploration and exploitation of natural resources'.[10] Examples of applied research include chemical oceanographic investigations conducted for the purpose of the regulation of marine pollution, physical oceanographic investigations carried out for the purpose of enhancing long-range weather forecasting, and marine biological investigations for the purpose of the management of marine living resources.[11] The difference between pure research and applied research can be ascertained by examining whether or not the results of the research project are intended to be openly published. Applied research will not meet the test of open publication, for the results of such research will necessarily remain secret.[12] In the law of the sea, normally the concept of marine scientific research covers both kinds of research. The reference to 'marine scientific research' in this chapter also refers to the two types of research.

Marine scientific research must be distinguished from the exploration of marine natural resources, because the latter is governed by a legal framework different from that regulating marine scientific research. Whilst exploration in the EEZ is regulated only by the coastal State pursuant to Article 56(1)(a), marine scientific research in the

the Sea: Impact and Implementation, Proceedings of The Law of the Sea Institute Nineteenth Annual Conference (Honolulu, University of Hawaii, 1987), pp. 366–367.

7 D. R. Rothwell and T. Stephens, *The International Law of the Sea* (Oxford and Portland, Oregon, Hart Publishing, 2010), p. 321.

8 L. Caflisch and J. Piccard, 'The Legal Régime of Marine Scientific Research and the Third United Nations Conference on the Law of the Sea' (1978) 38 *ZaöRV*, pp. 848–853; Soon, *Marine Scientific Research*, pp. 6–7.

9 LOSC, Article 246(3).

10 R. R. Churchill and A. V. Lowe, *The Law of the Sea*, 3rd edn (Manchester University Press, 1999), pp. 405–406.

11 Soons, *Marine Scientific Research*, p. 7.

12 Caflisch and Piccard, 'The Legal Régime of Marine Scientific Research', pp. 850–851.

EEZ is regulated by the coastal State in accordance with the provisions of Part XIII. 'Exploration' means 'data-collecting activities (scientific research) concerning natural resources, whether living or non-living, conducted specifically in view of the exploitation (i.e. economic utilisation) of those natural resources'.[13] The main difference between marine scientific research and exploration lies in the purpose of the data-collecting activities. Whilst marine scientific research seeks to obtain data for scientific purposes, exploration aims to collect data for the purpose of locating areas where natural resources of possible importance occur. In practice, however, it appears difficult to make this distinction because the techniques used may sometimes be identical.[14]

It appears that the LOSC differentiates marine scientific research from other surveys. In fact, Articles 19(2)(j) and 40 refer to 'any research or survey activities'.[15] Article 21(1)(g) uses the term 'marine scientific research and hydrographic surveys'. Whilst the LOSC contains no definition of a hydrographic survey, the International Hydrographic Dictionary defines it as:

> A survey having for its principal purpose the determination of data relating to bodies of water. A hydrographic survey may consist of the determination of one or several of the following classes of data: depth of water; configuration and nature of the bottom; directions and force of currents; heights and times of tides and water stages; and location of topographic features and fixed objects for survey and navigation purposes.[16]

The data collected by hydrographic surveys is primarily used to compile nautical charts and other documents in order to ensure the safety of navigation and facilitate other maritime activities. Whilst normally hydrographic surveys are carried out for peaceful purposes, data collected by such surveys can also be used for military purposes. Thus the distinction between marine scientific research, hydrographic survey and military survey is not always clear-cut.

3 REGULATION OF MARINE SCIENTIFIC RESEARCH IN THE LOSC

3.1 General considerations

The LOSC devoted Part XIII of the Convention to marine scientific research. The opening provision, i.e. Article 238, provides that:

> All States, irrespective of their geographical location, and competent international organizations have the right to conduct marine scientific research subject to the rights and duties of other States as provided for in this Convention.

13 Soons, 'Marine Scientific Research Provisions', p. 367.

14 Soons, *Marine Scientific Research*, pp. 6–7.

15 Article 40 applies *mutatis mutandis* to archipelagic sea lanes passage by virtue of Article 54. According to the *Virginia Commentaries*, 'research and survey activities' include all kinds of research and survey activities. *Virginia Commentaries*, vol. II, p. 176.

16 International Hydrographic Organization, *Hydrographic Dictionary, Part I*, vol. I, 5th edn (Monaco, 1994), p. 237.

This provision makes clear that 'all States', including land-locked and geographically disadvantaged States as well as non-Party States to the LOSC, have the right to conduct marine scientific research.

Furthermore, Article 238 makes it explicit that international organisations have the right to carry out marine scientific research. In fact, various international organisations are engaged upon marine scientific research. Examples of marine science organisations include: the International Council for the Exploration of the Sea (ICES),[17] the Intergovernmental Oceanographic Commission of UNESCO (IOC),[18] and the International Hydrographic Organization (IHO).[19] The FAO also undertakes fishery research. The IMO promotes scientific research with regard to marine pollution. Moreover, several bodies under the UN system involve coordination of marine scientific research. Examples include the Group of Experts on the Scientific Aspects of Marine Environmental Protection (GESAMP) and the Intersecretariat Committee on Scientific Programmes relating to Oceanography. In addition, many regional fisheries organisations undertake their own scientific research or promote cooperation and coordination of marine scientific research of their Member States.

Article 238 is further amplified by Article 240, dealing with general principles for the conduct of marine scientific research. Those principles comprise: the principle of peaceful purposes, use of appropriate scientific methods, non-interference with other legitimate uses of the sea, and compliance with all relevant regulations in the LOSC. Article 241 further makes it explicit that marine scientific research activities shall not constitute the legal basis for any claim to any part of the marine environment or its resources.

3.2 Marine scientific research in marine spaces under national jurisdiction

The LOSC regulates marine scientific research according to the legal category of ocean spaces. As discussed earlier, internal waters and the territorial sea are under the territorial sovereignty of the coastal State. Hence the coastal State has the exclusive right to regulate marine scientific research there. In this regard, Article 245 further provides that:

> Coastal States, in the exercise of their sovereignty, have the exclusive right to regulate, authorize and conduct marine scientific research in their territorial sea. Marine scientific research therein

[17] ICES, established in 1902, seeks to coordinate and promote marine research on oceanography, the marine environment, the marine ecosystem, and on living marine resources in the North Atlantic. There are twenty Member States. See www.ices.dk/aboutus/aboutus.asp.

[18] The IOC was established in 1960. The principal focus of the IOC is on: coordination of oceanographic research programme, global ocean observing system and data management, mitigation of marine natural hazards, and support to capacity development. See http://ioc-unesco.org/.

[19] The IHO was established in 1921. The objectives of the IHO involve the coordination of the activities of national hydrographic offices, the greatest possible uniformity in nautical charts and documents, the adoption of reliable and efficient methods of carrying out and exploiting hydrographic surveys, and the development of the sciences in the field of hydrography and techniques employed in descriptive oceanography. See www.iho-ohi.net/english/home/.

shall be conducted only with the express consent of and under the conditions set forth by the coastal State.

Thus any research to be conducted in internal waters or the territorial sea by foreign States or by international organisations requires the express consent of the coastal State. Furthermore, Article 21(1)(g) of the LOSC makes clear that the coastal State is entitled to adopt laws and regulations relating to innocent passage through the territorial sea in respect of marine scientific research and hydrographic survey. Article 19(2)(j) of the LOSC stipulates that the carrying out of research or survey activities in the territorial sea of foreign States is regarded as non-innocent. On the other hand, the collection of data by a ship in passage which are required for the safety of navigation, such as observation of water depth, wind speed and direction, cannot be regarded as either marine scientific research or a survey activity.[20] Likewise, the conduct of marine scientific research in archipelagic waters calls for the authorisation of the archipelagic States because archipelagic waters are under the territorial sovereignty of the archipelagic States.

In summary, in marine spaces under territorial sovereignty, coastal States enjoy decisive powers over marine scientific research. In enclosed or semi-enclosed seas, however, bordering States should cooperate to coordinate their scientific research policies and undertake where appropriate joint programmes of scientific research in the area in accordance with Article 123(c).

In the EEZ and on the continental shelf, marine scientific research shall also be conducted with the consent of the coastal State. However, coastal States shall, 'in normal circumstances', grant their consent for marine scientific research projects by other States or competent international organisations, which are 'exclusively for peaceful purposes and in order to increase scientific knowledge of the marine environment for the benefit of all mankind'.[21] Where a marine scientific research project is carried out by an international organisation of which a coastal State is a member, consent is implied, unless that State has expressed any objections within four months of notification of the project by virtue of Article 247. Likewise, consent is implied, where the coastal State has not responded to a marine scientific research project within four months of the receipt of the information concerning the project under Article 252.

Article 249(1) specifies certain conditions that shall be complied with by foreign States or international organisations in undertaking marine scientific research with the approval of the coastal State. Such conditions include:

- ensuring the right of the coastal State to participate in the marine scientific project,
- providing the coastal State with the final results and conclusions,

[20] Soons, *Marine Scientific Research*, p. 149.

[21] Article 246(3). Under Article 297(2)(a)(i), however, the coastal State is not obliged to accept the submission to the compulsory procedures embodied in Part XV of any disputes arising out of the exercise by the coastal State of a right or discretion in accordance with Article 246.

- providing access for the coastal State to all data and samples derived from the marine scientific research project,
- providing the coastal State with an assessment of such data, samples and research results, and
- ensuring that the research results are made internationally available.

These conditions are an essential element of balancing the interests of the coastal State and the interests of the international marine scientific community.[22] At the same time, to some extent, these conditions may contribute to enhancing international cooperation by ensuring the participation of coastal States as well as the publication of results.[23]

Under Article 246(5), coastal States may in their discretion withhold their consent to the conduct of a marine scientific research project of another State or competent international organisation in the EEZ or on the continental shelf of the coastal State if that project:

(a) is of direct significance for the exploration and exploitation of natural resources, whether living or non-living;
(b) involves drilling into the continental shelf, the use of explosives or the introduction of harmful substances into the marine environment;
(c) involves the construction, operation or use of artificial islands, installations and structures referred to in articles 60 and 80;
(d) contains information communicated pursuant to article 248 regarding the nature and objectives of the project which is inaccurate or if the researching State or competent international organization has outstanding obligations to the coastal State from a prior research project.

However, Article 246(6) provides that coastal States may not exercise their discretion to withhold consent under Article 246(5)(a) in respect of marine scientific research projects to be undertaken on the continental shelf beyond 200 nautical miles, outside those specific areas which coastal States may at any time publicly designate as areas in which exploitation or detailed exploratory operations focused on those areas are occurring or will occur within a reasonable period of time. In other words, within the specific areas, coastal States may exercise their discretion to withhold consent concerning marine scientific research.

3.3 Marine scientific research in marine spaces beyond national jurisdiction

On the high seas, all States enjoy freedom of scientific research. At the same time, States are required to promote the exchange of marine scientific data on the high seas. In this regard, Article 119(2) of the LOSC stipulates that available scientific information relevant to the conservation of fish stocks shall be contributed and exchanged on a regular basis through competent international organisations. Scientific information

[22] *Virginia Commentaries*, vol. IV, p. 540.
[23] It should be noted that the coastal State enjoys full discretion to grant or withhold consent to publication of the research results (LOSC, Articles 246(5) and 249(2)).

should include biological data, the migratory habitats of the species in question, the fishing gear and methods utilised in harvesting those species, and the landing of each species, including incidental catches.[24] Considering that statistics on high seas fisheries are still sporadic at best, the exchange of data is an important condition for the conservation of marine living resources.

In the Area, all States, irrespective of their geographical location, and competent international organisations have the right to conduct marine scientific research in conformity with Part XIII.[25] Marine scientific research in the Area must be carried out exclusively for peaceful purposes and for the benefit of mankind as a whole in conformity with Article 143(1) of the LOSC. Article 143(3) requires States Parties to promote international cooperation in marine scientific research in the Area by: (a) participating in international programmes and encouraging cooperation in marine scientific research by personnel of different countries and of the Authority; (b) ensuring that programmes are developed through the Authority or other international organisations as appropriate for the benefit of developing States and technologically less developed States; and (c) effectively disseminating the results of research and analysis when available, through the Authority or other international channels when appropriate. Under Article 143(2), the Authority is also required to promote and encourage the conduct of marine scientific research in the Area and to coordinate and disseminate the results of such research and analysis when available.

In relation to this, growing attention is drawn to marine scientific research with regard to genetic resources in the Area. Evidence suggests that communities surrounding the deep sea benthic ecosystems, in particular hydrothermal vent ecosystems, are threatened primarily by marine scientific research as well as bioprospecting.[26] Thus, further consideration must be given to the regulation of marine scientific research in the Area in order to minimise any impact on the deep seabed ecosystems from scientific investigation.

3.4 Regulation of scientific research installations

Whilst marine scientific research is often carried out on ships, such research is also undertaken by means of scientific research installations. Thus section 4 of Part XIII is devoted to the regulation of scientific research installations. The scientific research installations or equipment do not possess the status of islands. As a consequence, they have no territorial sea of their own, and their presence does not affect maritime delimitations.[27]

The basic principle is that the deployment and use of any type of scientific research installation or equipment in any area of the marine environment are to be subject to the same conditions as are prescribed in the LOSC for the conduct of marine scientific

[24] *Virginia Commentaries*, vol. III, p. 312.
[25] LOSC, Article 256.
[26] UN General Assembly, *Oceans and the Law of the Sea: Report of the Secretary-General*, A/59/62, 4 March 2004, p. 62, para. 245.
[27] LOSC, Article 259.

research in any such area (Article 258). As a consequence, the deployment and use of scientific research installations or equipment in the territorial sea and the archipelagic waters require the consent of the coastal or archipelagic State. Those installations are subject to the coastal or archipelagic State in the territorial sea or the archipelagic waters. The deployment of scientific installations in the EEZ or the continental shelf will also require consent of the coastal State.

In this regard, a distinction should be made between scientific equipment which is not fixed to the seabed, such as floating buoys and artificial islands, and installations that are fixed to the ocean floor. Where the scientific research being proposed involves the construction or use of artificial islands and installations, the coastal State may withhold its consent regardless of the purpose or nature of the research by virtue of Article 246(5)(c). On the other hand, coastal States shall normally grant their consent for the deployment and use of scientific installations which are not fixed to the ocean floor for the purposes of pure research. Coastal States may withhold their consent for the deployment of floating scientific installations for the purposes of applied research (Article 246(5)(a)).

A related issue involves the legal regulation of unmanned instruments, particularly self-floating floats and gliders, for marine scientific research. According to the IOC Advisory Body of Experts on the Law of the Sea, a float means

> an autonomous instrument used for collection of oceanographic data, which, when deployed descends to a programmable depth where it remains until, at programmed intervals it rises to the ocean surface where its position is determined using satellite technologies and, as may be the case, any oceanographic data collected are transmitted via satellite to a data processing centre for dissemination to users.[28]

Autonomous underwater vehicles with a buoyancy engine are often called a glider. Today the use of these devices attracts growing attention. One can take the Argo project as an example. This project seeks to obtain a systematic and complete set of data of the oceans and climate change by means of profiling self-floating floats. Under the Argo project, 3,000 free-driving profiling floats were deployed between 2000 and 2007. Argo floats are launched from ships or aircraft, and periodically sink to, and rise from determined depths (2000 metres) to collect and transmit data to national centres via satellite in near real time.[29]

It appears that the strict application of the provisions of Part XIII of the LOSC to floats raises practical difficulties. Provided that the deployment of floats and gliders can be considered as pure research, the coastal State is obliged to consent to research projects in normal circumstances. Conversely, the coastal State may withhold its consent if the

[28] Intergovernmental Oceanographic Commission, *Reports of Meetings of Experts and Equivalent Bodies, Advisory Body of Experts on the Law of the Sea (IOC/ABE-LOS) 7th Session*, Libreville, Gabon, 19–23 March 2007, p. 5.

[29] Concerning the Argo project, see www.argo.ucsd.edu/index.html.

deployment of those devices falls within one of the Article 246(5) exceptions. In any case, once these devices are deployed, they are difficult to control. It is unpredictable when and where those devices might enter into the EEZs or territorial seas of foreign States by currents. Hence it appears impractical to obtain prior consent of all potential coastal States before such a situation occurs. The legal regime governing marine scientific research under the LOSC seems to presuppose that marine scientific research will be carried out in a specific place, within a limited time frame and according to advance planning. However, research by means of self-floating floats is inconsistent with the presumption. Accordingly, the provisions of the LOSC seem not to fit marine scientific research by means of floats and gliders.[30]

4 LEGALITY OF MILITARY AND HYDROGRAPHIC SURVEYS IN THE EEZ

The legality of military and hydrographic surveys in another State's EEZ without its authorisation remains a highly debatable issue in theory and practice. Military surveys mean activities undertaken in the ocean and coastal waters involving marine data collection for military purposes. Such surveys may include oceanographic, marine geological, geophysical, chemical, biological and acoustic data.[31] Military surveys raise particular sensitivities associated with the national security of coastal States.

Likewise, a hydrographic survey in another State's EEZ also raises sensitive issues because such a survey may have economic and commercial value. Indeed, the production of up-to-date charts may contribute to stimulate fishing, tourism, exploration and exploitation of marine natural resources. Such charts may be used for the regulation of marine pollution, coastal management, the modernisation of port facilities and coastal engineering.[32] Before the 1990s, it was difficult to conduct a hydrographic survey without the support of adjacent coastal State(s). After the introduction of the Navstar Global Positioning System (GPS) in 1994 and the later Differential GPS (DGPS), however, it became possible to carry out hydrographic surveys without relying on shore stations in the vicinity of the survey area. Accordingly, it is not a coincidence that hydrographic surveys in the EEZ have raised controversial issues over the last decade.[33]

The position of the United States and the United Kingdom is that hydrographic and military surveys may be freely carried out in the EEZ without the authorisation of coastal States. Indeed, the LOSC distinguishes marine scientific research from 'hydrographic surveys' and 'survey activities', and it does not provide the coastal State jurisdiction to regulate survey activities outside the territorial sea or archipelagic waters. According to this view, hydrographic and military survey activities are freedoms captured by the

[30] K. Bork, J. Karstensen, M. Visbeck and A. Zimmermann, 'The Legal Regulation of Floats and Gliders – In Quest of a New Regime?' (2008) 39 *ODIL* pp. 311–312. The IOC is drafting 'Draft Guidelines, within the context of UNCLOS, for the collection of oceanographic data by specific means'.

[31] J. A. Roach and R. W. Smith, *United States Responses to Excessive Maritime Claims*, 2nd edn (The Hague, Nijhoff, 1996), p. 427.

[32] *Ibid.*, pp. 426–427; Bateman, 'Hydrographic Surveying in the EEZ', p. 169.

[33] *Ibid.*, p. 168.

expressions 'other internationally lawful uses of the sea' related to navigation and overflight under Article 58(1) and reference to '*inter alia*' in Article 87(1) of the LOSC.[34]

By contrast, some coastal States take the position that hydrographic and military survey activities in the EEZ are subject to the regulation of coastal States. China is the leading country advocating this position. According to this position, 'freedom of navigation and overflight' in the EEZ and the term 'other internationally lawful uses of the sea' do not include the freedom to conduct military and reconnaissance activities in the EEZ of another State. Furthermore, the line of the distinction between marine scientific research and a military survey may be difficult to determine because the means of data collection used in marine scientific research and military surveys may sometimes be the same and the difference consists only in the motivation for the survey.[35] As noted, hydrographic surveying in the EEZ has relevance to the economic development of the coastal State.[36]

In reality, the difference of positions between China and the United States has created a series of incidents on this particular issue. For instance, on 23 March 2001, the hydrographic survey ship USNS *Bowditch* (T-AGS 62) carried out military survey operations in China's claimed EEZ in the Yellow Sea. However, the *Bowditch* was ordered to leave the EEZ by a Chinese frigate. On 8 March 2009, USNS *Impeccable* (T-AGOS 23), which was undertaking military survey activities in China's EEZ approximately seventy-five nautical miles south of Hainan Island in the South China Sea, was surrounded and its route blocked by five Chinese vessels. In those incidents, the US government filed a strong protest with the Chinese government.[37]

In 2002, China enacted legislation which explicitly requires that all survey and mapping activities in the territorial air, land or waters, as well as other sea areas under the jurisdiction of the People's Republic of China shall be subject to approval by the Chinese authorities.[38] Some national laws also seem to require prior consent of the coastal State to carry out 'any research'. For example, the Territorial Waters, Continental Shelf, Exclusive Economic Zone and Other Maritime Zones Act, 1976 of India provides that without an agreement or a licence, no person, including a foreign government, shall

[34] *Ibid.*, pp. 163–165; Roach and Smith, *United States Responses*, pp. 448–449.

[35] It appears that both the United States and the United Kingdom accept this point. Roach and Smith, *ibid.*, p. 427. In fact, the United Kingdom's definition of military data gathering states that 'the means of data collection used in MDG [military data gathering] may sometimes be the same as that used in Marine Scientific Research'. This document was reproduced in Bateman, 'Hydrographic Surveying in the EEZ', p. 173.

[36] Thus Bateman has argued that hydrographic surveying in an EEZ should come within the jurisdiction of the coastal State. *Ibid.*, p. 169.

[37] R. Pedrozo, 'Close Encounters at Sea: The USNS Impeccable Incident' (2009) 62 *Naval War College Review* pp. 101–102; S. Bateman, 'Hydrographic Surveying in the EEZ: Differences and Overlaps with Marine Scientific Research' (2005) 29 *Marine Policy* p. 167.

[38] Articles 2 and 7 of Surveying and Mapping Law of the People's Republic of China (Order of the President No. 75), available at: www.gov.cn/english/laws/2005-10/09/content_75314.htm. See also, Ren Xiaofeng, 'A Chinese Perspective' (2005) 29 *Marine Policy* pp. 139–146; Zhang Haiwen, 'Is It Safeguarding the Freedom of Navigation or Maritime Hegemony of the United States? Comments on Paul (Pete) Pedrozo's Article on Military Activities in the EEZ' (2010) 9 *Chinese Journal of International Law* pp. 31–47.

conduct 'any research' within the EEZ.[39] Likewise, the Territorial Sea and Exclusive Economic Zone Act, 1989, of the United Republic of Tanzania provides that without an agreement, no person shall conduct 'any research' within its EEZ.[40] The Exclusive Economic Zone Act 1984 of Malaysia stipulates that without authorisation no person shall in the EEZ or on the continental shelf carry out 'any search' or conduct 'any marine scientific research'.[41] In addition to this, Guidelines for Navigation and Overflight in the Exclusive Economic Zone provide that: 'Hydrographic surveying should only be conducted in the EEZ of another State with the consent of the coastal State'.[42]

Hydrographic and military survey activities in the EEZ of another State strongly affect interests of naval and coastal States. Due to their highly political nature, it seems unlikely that disputes on this subject will be settled by international courts and tribunals.[43] It also seems that this question will not be solved in the near future.[44]

5 INTERNATIONAL COOPERATION IN MARINE SCIENTIFIC RESEARCH

Due to the highly complex nature of the ocean, no State would be able to clarify the mechanisms of the oceans alone. Accordingly, it is natural that international cooperation is required in marine scientific research. The LOSC devotes section 2 of Part XIII to international cooperation in marine scientific research. Article 242(1) places a general obligation upon States and international organisations to cooperate in marine scientific research. More specifically, Article 243 requires States and competent international organisations to cooperate 'to create favourable conditions for the conduct of marine scientific research in the marine environment and to integrate the efforts of scientists in studying the essence of phenomena and processes occurring in the marine environment and the interrelations between them'. Such cooperation is to be undertaken through the conclusion of international agreements. The need for cooperation in marine scientific research is further amplified in Article 255, which requires States to adopt reasonable rules and procedures to promote marine scientific research.[45] Article 244 further provides an obligation to publish and disseminate information and knowledge resulting from marine scientific research. This obligation is also reflected in Annex VI of the Final Act of UNCLOS III.[46]

[39] Article 7(5). This Act is reproduced in UNDOALOS, *The Law of the Sea: National Legislation on the Exclusive Economic Zone* (New York, United Nations, 1993), p. 135.

[40] Article 10(1)(c). *Ibid.*, p. 385.

[41] Article 5(b) and (c). *Ibid.*, p. 186.

[42] EEZ Group 21, *Guidelines for Navigation and Overflight in the Exclusive Economic Zone*, Ocean Policy Research Foundation, 16 September 2005, IX(a).

[43] In its Declaration under Article 298 of the LOSC, China excluded all categories of disputes referred to in Article 298(1)(a)(b) and (c) from compulsory procedures of dispute settlement. A. V. Lowe and S. A. G. Talmon (eds.), *The Legal Order of the Oceans: Basic Documents on the Law of the Sea* (Oxford, Hart Publishing 2009), p. 921.

[44] E. Franckx, 'American and Chinese Views on Navigational Rights of Warships' (2011) 11 *Chinese Journal of International Law* pp. 187–206 (in particular p. 199).

[45] *Virginia Commentaries*, vol. IV, p. 477.

[46] Annex VI is entitled 'Resolution on Development of National Marine Science, Technology and Ocean Service Infrastructures'.

In this regard, particular attention must be paid to technical and financial assistance to developing countries. Considering that marine scientific facilities in developing countries remain insufficient, technical and financial assistance to these countries is imperative for promoting marine scientific research. In this regard, Annex VI of the Final Act of UNCLOS III explicitly states that 'unless urgent measures are taken, the marine scientific and technological gap between the developed and the developing countries will widen further and thus endanger the very foundations of the new régime'.[47] Accordingly, Annex VI urges industrialised countries to assist developing countries in the preparation and implementation of their marine science, technology and ocean service development programmes.[48]

Article 202 of the LOSC explicitly enunciates an obligation respecting scientific and technical assistance to developing States in the context of the protection of the marine environment. Such assistance shall include, *inter alia*: (i) training of their scientific and technical personnel; (ii) facilitating their participation in relevant international programmes; (iii) supplying them with necessary equipment and facilities; (iv) enhancing their capacity to manufacture such equipment; and (v) giving advice on and developing facilities for research, monitoring, educational and other programmes.

In practice, international cooperation in marine scientific research is being promoted by various international institutions. For example, the United Nations Educational, Scientific and Cultural Organization (UNESCO), through the Intergovernmental Oceanographic Commission (IOC), is the competent international organisation in the field of marine scientific research and transfer of marine technology under the LOSC. The IOC has developed many programmes in marine science and technology with a view to empowering developing countries to sustainably use their marine resources.[49] The FAO has also provided technical assistance and training to strengthen both national capacity in fisheries science and the knowledge base for implementation of the ecosystem approach to fisheries in developing countries.[50] The Authority established the International Seabed Authority Endowment Fund for Marine Scientific Research in the Area. This Fund has facilitated the development of capacity through training and technical assistance to developing countries.[51]

6 TRANSFER OF TECHNOLOGY

6.1 Transfer of technology under the LOSC

The transfer of marine scientific technology occupies an important place in scientific and technical assistance to developing States. In fact, limitations in capacity hinder States, in particular developing States, not only from benefiting from oceans and their resources but also from effectively implementing the LOSC and other relevant treaties.

[47] Preamble of Annex VI of the Final Act. [48] *Ibid.*, para. 3.

[49] UN General Assembly, *Oceans and the Law of the Sea: Report of the Secretary-General*, A/65/69, 29 March 2010, p. 26, para. 100. [50] *Ibid.*, p. 30, para. 112.

[51] *Ibid.*, p. 27, para. 104.

Accordingly, the UN General Assembly reiterated 'the essential need for cooperation, including through capacity-building and transfer of marine technology, to ensure that all States, especially developing countries, in particular the least developed countries and small island developing States, as well as coastal African States, are able both to implement the Convention and to benefit from the sustainable development of the oceans and seas, as well as to participate fully in global and regional forums and processes dealing with oceans and the law of the sea issues'.[52]

Part XIV of the Convention provides rules with regard to the transfer of technology in a general manner. Part XIV opens with Article 266 which provides a general obligation to promote the development and transfer of marine technology. Article 266(1) places an obligation upon States to cooperate in accordance with their capabilities actively to promote the development and transfer of marine science and marine technology on fair and reasonable terms and conditions. Article 266(2) obliges States to promote the development of the marine scientific and technological capacity of States which may need and request technical assistance in this field, particularly developing States. Article 266(3) requires States to endeavour to foster favourable economic and legal conditions for the transfer of marine technology for the benefit of all parties concerned on an equitable basis. At the same time, Article 267 requires States to have due regard for all legitimate interests including, *inter alia*, the rights and duties of holders, suppliers and recipients of maritime technology. This provision seeks to achieve a balance between the interests of the suppliers and those of the recipients of technology.[53] Furthermore, as provided in Article 268(d), the development of human resources through the training and education of nationals of developing States is also important. To this end, the IMO has established two educational organs, namely, the World Maritime University (1983) and the IMO International Maritime Law Institute (1989).

Section 2 of Part XIV provides various duties concerning international cooperation in the transfer of marine technology, such as international cooperation through existing bilateral or multilateral programmes (Article 270), the establishment of generally accepted guidelines (Article 271), and coordination of international programmes through competent international organisations (Article 272), cooperation between international organisations and the Authority (Article 273), and obligations of the Authority in respect of technical assistance in the field of marine technology (Article 274).

Section 3 of Part XIV contains several provisions with regard to national and regional marine scientific and technological centres. Specifically, Article 275 requires States to promote the establishment, particularly in developing coastal States, of national marine scientific and technological research centres and the strengthening of existing national centres in order to advance the conduct of marine scientific research by developing coastal States. Further to this, Article 276 places an obligation upon States to promote the establishment of regional marine scientific and technological research centres, particularly in developing States, in order to stimulate the conduct of marine

[52] UN General Assembly Resolution, *Oceans and the Law of the Sea*, A/RES/64/71, adopted on 4 December 2009, seventh preambular paragraph.

[53] *Virginia Commentaries*, vol. IV, p. 681.

scientific research by developing States and foster the transfer of marine technology. Finally, section 4, which contains Article 278, provides for cooperation among international organisations referred to in Part XIV and in Part XIII.

In addition to Part XIV, the transfer of technology is required in relation to deep seabed activities. Thus Article 144(1) requires the Authority to promote and encourage the transfer to developing States of such technology and scientific knowledge relating to activities in the Area so that all States Parties benefit therefrom. To this end, Article 144(2) obliges the Authority and States Parties to cooperate in promoting the transfer of such technology and scientific knowledge. Further to this, Article 274 requires the Authority to train nationals of developing States, to ensure that technical documentation on seabed mining is made available to all States, and to assist such States in the acquisition of technology. As noted earlier, the mandatory transfer of technology under 5 of Annex III of the LOSC was disapplied by section 5(2) of the 1994 Implementation Agreement. Instead, section 5(1)(b) of the Agreement allows the Authority to request all or any of the contractors and their respective sponsoring State(s) to cooperate with it in facilitating the acquisition of deep seabed mining technology by the Enterprise or by a developing State(s). Such technology must be acquired 'on fair and reasonable commercial terms and conditions, consistent with the effective protection of intellectual property rights'. As a general rule, section 5(1)(c) of the Agreement requires States Parties to promote international technical and scientific cooperation with regard to activities in the Area.

Furthermore, the transfer of technology is needed for the conservation of marine living resources. In this regard, Article 62(4)(j) obliges nationals of other States fishing in the EEZ to comply with the laws and regulations of the coastal State with regard to 'requirements for the training of personnel and the transfer of fisheries technology, including enhancement of the coastal State's capability of undertaking fisheries research'. Moreover, Article 202(1) places an obligation upon States, directly or through competent international organisations, to promote programmes of scientific, educational, technical and other assistance to developing States for the protection and preservation of the marine environment. Such assistance includes, *inter alia*, training of their scientific and technical personnel and supplying them with necessary equipment and facilities.

6.2 IOC criteria and guidelines on the transfer of marine technology

In 2003, the Assembly of the IOC adopted criteria and guidelines on the transfer of marine technology. According to the guidelines, marine technology includes: information on marine sciences, manuals, sampling and methodology equipment, observation facilities and equipment, equipment for *in situ* and laboratory observations, computer and computer software, and expertise and analytical methods related to marine scientific research and observation.[54]

[54] IOC Guidelines, A.2.

The key criterion is that the transfer of marine technology should enable all parties concerned to benefit on an equitable basis from developments in marine science related activities, in particular those aimed at stimulating the social and economic contexts in developing States. In conducting a transfer of marine technology, due regard should be given to, *inter alia*, the needs and interests of developing countries, particularly land-locked and geographically disadvantaged States as well as other developing States which have not been able to establish or develop their own capabilities in marine sciences.[55]

As for implementation of the guidelines, the IOC should establish and coordinate a clearing-house mechanism for the transfer of marine technology in order to provide interested users in Member States with direct and rapid access to relevant sources of information and scientific and technical expertise in the transfer of marine technology, as well as to facilitate effective scientific, technical and financial cooperation to that end.[56] Any Member State may submit to the IOC Secretariat a transfer of marine technology application.[57] The IOC Secretariat will examine the application and forward it to the identified donor or donors. Furthermore, the IOC Secretariat facilitates contracts between the identified donor or donors and the recipient Member State.[58]

7 CONCLUSIONS

From the matter considered in this chapter the following conclusions can be drawn.

(i) On the one hand, marine scientific research may contribute to promote scientific knowledge of the oceans and to the benefit of mankind. On the other hand, such research may affect the economic and security interests of States at the same time. Thus tension arises between coastal States which seek to regulate research activities and researching States which attempt to ensure the maximum freedom of marine scientific research and other surveys.

(ii) The legal framework established in the LOSC relies on a sensitive balance between the freedom of marine scientific research and the protection of interests of the coastal State. Yet the scope of marine scientific research under the Convention is not free from controversy. For instance, it is often difficult to distinguish marine scientific research from exploration of natural resources in practice. The distinction between marine scientific research and other surveys also remains obscure. The ambiguity of the concept of marine scientific research may be a source of dispute with regard to coastal State jurisdiction over survey activities in the EEZ.

(iii) The legality of hydrographic and military survey activity in the EEZ of another State is a particularly debatable issue. Whilst naval powers advocate the freedom of such surveys in the EEZ of a third State, some coastal States take the position that they are entitled to regulate these activities. So far, the question remains open.

[55] *Ibid.*, B.(c)(i). [56] *Ibid.*, C.1(a). [57] *Ibid.*, C.2.
[58] *Ibid.*, C.3 and C.4(a) and (b).

(iv) Even the strongest countries with the most developed marine scientific technologies are not able to clarify the mechanisms of the ocean alone. Thus international cooperation is needed in order to promote such research. Given that marine scientific research may contribute to the benefit of mankind as a whole, international scientific cooperation is increasingly important. As noted, the LOSC contains many provisions involving international cooperation in the field of marine scientific research. Such cooperation is also being promoted through international organisations, such as UNESCO, the IOC, the FAO and the Authority.

(v) Limitations in technological capacity create a serious challenge to developing countries being able to implement the LOSC and benefit from ocean development. Accordingly, as explained earlier, the LOSC provides various obligations for the transfer of technology to developing countries. The development of marine science is particularly important with a view to ensuring food and environmental security and eradicating poverty. Thus, further efforts are needed to develop capacity-building of developing States in this field.

FURTHER READING

1 General

M. Gorina-Ysern, *An International Regime for Marine Scientific Research* (New York, Transnational Publishers, 2003).

M. H. Nordquist, J. N. Moore and R. Long (eds.), *Law, Science and Ocean Management* (Leiden, Nijhoff, 2007).

J. A. Roach, 'Marine Scientific Research and the New Law of the Sea' (1996) 27 *ODIL* pp. 59–72.

'Defining Scientific Research: Marine Data Collection', in M. H. Nordquist, J. N. Moore and R. Long (eds.), *Law, Science and Ocean Management* (Leiden, Nijhoff, 2007), pp. 541–573.

'Marine Data Collection: Methods and the Law', in M. H. Nordquist, T. T. B. Koh and J. N. Moore, *Freedom of Seas, Passage Rights and the 1982 Law of the Sea Convention* (Leiden and Boston, Nijhoff, 2009), pp. 171–208.

A. H. A. Soons, *Marine Scientific Research and the Law of the Sea* (Antwerp, Kluwer Law and Taxation Publishers, 1982).

United Nations, *The Law of the Sea: Marine Scientific Research, A Guide to the Implementation of the Relevant Provisions of the United Nations Convention on the Law of the Sea* (New York, United Nations, 1991).

F. H. T. Wegelein, *Marine Scientific Research: The Operation and Status of Research Vessels and Other Platforms in International Law* (Leiden and Boston, Nijhoff, 2005).

2 Special Issues

D. Ball, 'Intelligence Collection Operations and EEZs: The Implications of New Technology' (2004) 28 *Marine Policy* pp. 67–82.

S. Bateman, 'Hydrographic Surveying in the EEZ: Differences and Overlaps with Marine Scientific Research' (2005) 29 *Marine Policy* pp. 163–174.

K. Bork, J. Karstensen, M. Visbeck and A. Zimmermann, 'The Legal Regulation of Floats and Gliders – In Quest of a New Regime?' (2008) 39 *ODIL* pp. 298–328.

S. Dromgoole, 'Revisiting the Relationship between Marine Scientific Research and the Underwater Cultural Heritage' (2010) 25 *IJMCL* pp. 33–61.

A. Kanehara, 'Marine Scientific Research in the Waters Where Claims of the Exclusive Economic Zones Overlap Between Japan and the Republic of Korea: Incidents Between the Two States in 2006' (2007) 49 *The Japanese Annual of International Law* pp. 98–122.

K. N. Scott, 'Marine Scientific Research and the Southern Ocean: Balancing Rights and Obligations in a Security-Related Context' (2008) 6 *New Zealand Yearbook of International Law* pp. 111–134.

Y. Tanaka, 'Obligation to Co-operate in Marine Scientific Research and the Conservation of Marine Living Resources' (2005) 65 *ZaöRV* pp. 937–965.

11

Maintenance of International Peace and Security at Sea

Main Issues

International peace and security on the oceans are currently faced with a variety of threats. For instance, piracy and armed robbery against ships are serious problems endangering the welfare of seafarers and the security of sea communication. The proliferation of weapons of mass destruction through marine transport is a matter of pressing concern. Furthermore, military uses of the oceans raise international tension between interests of the coastal State and interests of the naval State. Thus this chapter will address the maintenance of international peace and security at sea. Principal focus will be on the following issues:

(i) What are the rules applicable to the suppression of piracy and its limitations?
(ii) What are the rules applicable to the prevention and suppression of maritime terrorism and other unlawful offences at sea?
(iii) Are military exercises in the EEZ of a foreign State permissible in the law of the sea?
(iv) What is the significance of nuclear weapon-free zones in the maintenance of international peace and security at sea?

1 INTRODUCTION

The maintenance of international peace and security is a fundamental issue underlying international law and the international law of the sea is no exception. In this regard, Article 301 of the LOSC provides a clear obligation with regard to peaceful uses of the sea:

> In exercising their rights and performing their duties under this Convention, States Parties shall refrain from any threat or use of force against the territorial integrity or political independence of any State, or in any other manner inconsistent with the principles of international law embodied in the Charter of the United Nations.

Further to this, several provisions of the LOSC reserve the use of the oceans for peaceful purposes.[1]

The law of the sea does not completely prohibit military uses of the oceans. However, military activities in the oceans, such as military exercises in the EEZ of a third State, raise particular sensitivities associated with the security of coastal States. Furthermore, the prevention and suppression of maritime terrorism and other unlawful offences at sea are a matter of pressing current concern. In relation to this, non-proliferation of weapons of mass destruction at sea attracts growing attention in the international community. In general, it appears that disarmament and arms control at sea can be considered as an important element in the protection of community interests with regard to the maintenance of international peace and security.

Piracy and armed robbery are also a serious threat to human life and sea communication. According to the IMO, in 2009, there were a total of 406 reports of piracy and armed robbery at sea alleged to have been committed or attempted, of which 222 occurred off the coast of East Africa.[2] Modern piracy is changing from sporadic 'smash-and-grab' crime to highly developed organised crime. As a consequence, piracy is increasingly dangerous quantitatively and qualitatively. Traditionally pirates have been considered outlaws, *hostes humani generis* or 'enemies of all mankind'. The suppression of piracy can therefore be considered as a common interest of the international community.

Against that background, this chapter will address the principal legal issues concerning military uses of the oceans and various threats to human life as well as sea communication in the broad context of the maintenance of international peace and security. It will be appropriate to commence our discussion with piracy because this issue has long been addressed by the international law of the sea.

2 THE SUPPRESSION OF PIRACY

2.1 Concept of piracy

The concept of piracy has left room for confusion partly because the municipal laws punish as 'piracy' acts which do not constitute 'piracy' in international law.[3] Currently a modern definition of piracy can be seen in Article 101 of the LOSC:

Piracy consists of any of the following acts:

(a) any illegal acts of violence or detention, or any act of depredation, committed for private ends by the crew or the passengers of a private ship or a private aircraft, and directed:

[1] See for instance, LOSC, Articles 88, 141, 240(a). See also B. A. Boczek, 'Peaceful Purposes Provisions of the United Nations Convention on the Law of the Sea' (1989) 20 *ODIL* pp. 359–389.

[2] IMO, *Reports on Acts of Piracy and Armed Robbery against Ships: Annual Report 2009, Annex 2*, MSC4/Circ. 152, 29 March 2010. The distinction between piracy and armed robbery at sea will be discussed later.

[3] Dissenting Opinion of Mr Moore, the *Case of the S.S. 'Lotus'*, PCIJ 1928 Series A/10, p. 70.

(i) on the high seas, against another ship or aircraft, or against persons or property on board such ship or aircraft;
(ii) against a ship, aircraft, persons or property in a place outside the jurisdiction of any State;
(b) any act of voluntary participation in the operation of a ship or of an aircraft with knowledge of facts making it a pirate ship or aircraft;
(c) any act of inciting or of intentionally facilitating an act described in subparagraph (a) or (b).

It may be said that this definition represents the existing customary law.[4] This definition comprises five elements to identify piracy.

(i) There must be 'any illegal acts of violence or detention, or any act of depredation'. Whilst the existence of violence constitutes an essential element, Article 101 does not provide further precision with regard to the types of violence which constitute piracy. Violence may be committed against persons or property on board. It may be argued that one murder alone would suffice to be regarded as a piratical act.[5] However, attempts to commit illegal acts are not included in the definition of piracy.[6]

(ii) Unlawful offences must be committed for 'private ends' (the private ends requirement). It follows that piracy cannot be committed by vessels or aircrafts on military or government service or by insurgents. Yet the meaning of private ends is not wholly unambiguous. Two different views can be identified on this matter. According to the first view, any illegal acts of violence for political reasons are automatically excluded from the definition of piracy.[7] According to this view, acts are tested on the basis of the motives of an offender. However, the interpretation of private ends will rely primarily on the subjective appreciation of the offender. In the second view, all acts of violence that lack State sanction or authority are acts undertaken for private ends.[8] According to this view, in essence, the private ends requirement seems to overlap with the private ship requirement. In practice, however, lack of State status may not automatically make the actors pirates.[9] The *Santa Maria* affair sheds some light on this matter.

In 1961, the Portuguese liner, the *Santa Maria*, was taken over by offenders on board under the leadership of a Portuguese political dissident, Captain Galvão. He declared that the seizure was the first step to overthrowing the Dictator Salazar of Portugal.

4 I. Brownlie, *Principles of Public International Law* (Oxford University Press, 2008), p. 229. Article 101 is virtually the same as Article 15 of the Geneva Convention on the High Seas.

5 D. P. O'Connell (I. A. Shearer ed.), *The International Law of the Sea*, vol. 2 (Oxford, Clarendon Press, 1984), pp. 969–970; G. Gidel, *Le droit international public de la mer: le temps de paix*, vol. 1, Introduction, *La haute mer* (reprint, Paris, Duchemin, 1981), p. 309.

6 At UNCLOS I, a British proposal to include attempts in the definition of piracy was defeated by twenty-two votes to thirteen, with seventeen abstentions. United Nations Conference on the Law of the Sea, *Official Records*, vol. I, A/CONF.13/40, (1958), p. 84.

7 M. Shaw, *International Law*, 6th edn (Cambridge University Press, 2010), p. 615.

8 D. Guilfoyle, *Shipping Interdiction and the Law of the Sea* (Cambridge University Press 2009), p. 37.

9 O'Connell, *The International Law of the Sea*, pp. 975–976. Indeed, the Harvard Research Draft did not regard insurgents against a foreign government as pirates. Harvard Law School, 'Codification of International Law, Part IV: Piracy' (1932) 26 *AJIL Supplement* p. 798.

The flag State, namely Portugal, designated the seizure of the vessel as piracy. Later, the ship was taken by the offenders to Brazil, and Captain Galvão and his followers were given asylum in Brazil.[10] In the light of the attitude of the Portuguese government, it seemed clear that Captain Galvão and his party lacked any State authority. Considering that they were granted asylum, however, there is room for the view that this seizure was not made for private purposes.[11] It seems that illicit acts by organised groups for the sole purpose of achieving some political end cannot be characterised as piracy.[12] The private ends requirement should be examined by taking various factors into account, such as motives, ends, specific acts of offenders, the relationship between offenders and victims, the relationship between the offenders and the legitimate government, and reactions of third States.

A further issue involves the question as to whether or not certain conduct of environmental activists on the high seas should be regarded as a piratical act. A case in point is the *Castle John v NV Babeco* case of 1986. In this case, members of the environmental group 'Greenpeace' took action on the high seas against two Dutch vessels engaged in the discharge of noxious waste with a view to alerting public opinion. The action included boarding, occupying and causing damage to the two ships. In this case, the Belgian Court of Cassation ruled that the acts were committed for personal ends and consequently, Greenpeace had committed piracy.[13]

(iii) Piracy is committed by the crew or the passengers of a private ship or a private aircraft against another ship or aircraft, or against persons or property on board such ships or aircraft (the private ship requirement). Under Article 102 of the LOSC, the acts of piracy committed by a warship, government ship or government aircraft whose crew has mutinied and taken control of the ship or aircraft are also assimilated to acts committed by a private ship or aircraft. Under Article 103, a ship or aircraft is considered a pirate ship or aircraft if it is intended by the persons in dominant control to be used for the purpose of committing one of the acts referred to in Article 101.

(iv) Piracy involves two ships or aircraft, that is to say, pirate and victim (the two vessels requirement). In accordance with this requirement, hijacking a ship on the high seas by its own crew or passengers (internal hijacking) is not regarded as a piratical act. The case in point is the *Achille Lauro* affair. On 7 October 1985, four members of a Palestinian group, the PLF, aboard the Italian passenger ship, the *Achille Lauro*, hijacked

[10] P. W. Birnie, 'Piracy: Past, Present and Future' (1987) 11 *Marine Policy* p. 175.

[11] L. C. Green, 'The *Santa Maria*: Rebels or Pirates' (1961) 37 *BYIL* p. 503; The American Law Institute, *Restatement of the Law Third: The Foreign Relations Law of the United States*, vol. 2 (American Law Institute Publishers, 1990), § 522, Reporter's Note 2, p. 85.

[12] Brownlie, *Principles*, pp. 231–232; A. R. Thomas and J. C. Duncan (eds.), *Annotated Supplement to the Commander's Handbook on the Law of Naval Operations* (1999) 73 *International Legal Studies* (US Naval War College), p. 224; R. Wolfrum, 'Fighting Terrorism at Sea: Options and Limitations under International Law', in M. H. Nordquist, R. Wolfrum, J. N. Moore and R. Long (eds.), *Legal Challenges in Maritime Security* (Leiden and Boston, Nijhoff, 2008), p. 8.

[13] (1988) 77 *ILR* pp. 537–541. See also, S. P. Menefee, 'The Case of the Castle John, or Greenbeard the Pirate?: Environmentalism, Piracy, and the Development of International Law' (1993) 24 *California Western International Law Journal* pp. 1–16.

the ship. They demanded the release of Palestinian prisoners.[14] As the offenders had already boarded the ship, this affair involved hijacking of the ship, not piracy. For the same reason, the *Santa Maria* affair cannot be considered as an act of piracy.

(v) Piracy must be directed on the high seas or in a place outside the jurisdiction of any State, such as Antarctica. While Article 101 contains no reference to the EEZ, it seems that illegal acts of violence committed in the EEZ may also be qualified as piracy owing to a corresponding cross-reference under Article 58(2) of the LOSC.

On the other hand, illegal acts of violence committed in the territorial sea or internal waters of a coastal State cannot be regarded as acts of piracy. Those acts are often called 'armed robbery'. According to the IMO Code of Practice for the Investigation of the Crimes of Piracy and Armed Robbery against Ships adopted on 2 December 2009, 'armed robbery against ships' means any of the following acts:[15]

1. any illegal act of violence or detention or any act of depredation, or threat thereof, other than an act of piracy, committed for private ends and directed against a ship or against persons or property on board such a ship, within a State's internal waters, archipelagic waters and territorial sea;
2. any act of inciting or of intentionally facilitating an act described above.

In reality, many illicit acts of violence occur in the territorial sea. This is particularly problematic if the coastal State concerned is unable to effectively prevent and suppress such acts in its territorial sea.

2.2 Seizure of pirates

As pirates are treated as outlaws, they are denied the protection of the flag State. Thus any State may capture and punish them.[16] In this regard, Article 105 of the LOSC makes clear that on the high seas, or in any other place outside the jurisdiction of any State, every State may seize a pirate ship or aircraft, or a ship or aircraft taken by piracy and under the control of pirates, and arrest the persons and seize the property on board. The courts of the State which carried out the seizure may decide upon the penalties to be imposed, and may also determine the action to be taken with regard to the ships, aircraft or property, subject to the rights of third parties acting in good faith. Where the seizure of a ship or aircraft on suspicion of piracy has been effected without adequate grounds, however, the State making the seizure is to be liable to the State the nationality of which is possessed by the ship or aircraft for any loss or damage caused by the seizure pursuant to Article 106.

[14] On 11 October 1985, the hijackers and an alleged mastermind of the operation, Mr Abbas, were on board an Egyptian airliner bound for Tunis, but the Tunisian government did not allow it to land. While the airliner was returning to Egypt, United States military aircraft intercepted the airliner and forced it to land in Sicily. While Italy took the four hijackers into custody and eventually prosecuted and convicted them, Italy allowed Mr Abbas to escape to Yugoslavia. It is reported that the *Achille Lauro* sank off the coast of Somalia in December 1994. *The New York Times*, 3 December 1994, p. 5 of the New York edition.

[15] Paragraph 2.2. This document is annexed to IMO Resolution A.1025(26), A 26/Res.1025, 18 January 2010.

[16] Dissenting Opinion of Mr Moore, the *Case of the S.S. 'Lotus'*, PCIJ 1928 Series A/10, p. 70.

The seizure of piracy is the oldest and the most well-attested example of universal jurisdiction.[17] In this respect, Judge Guillaume, in his Separate Opinion in the *Arrest of Warrant of 11 April 2000* case, stated that: 'Traditionally, customary international law did ... recognize one case of universal jurisdiction, that of piracy'.[18] Furthermore, the UN Security Council, in its resolution of 11 April 2011, explicitly recognised that 'piracy is a crime subject to universal jurisdiction'.[19] By exercising universal jurisdiction, each State would contribute to safeguard community interests as an organ of the international community. In this sense, universal jurisdiction over piracy seems to provide an example of the law of *dédoublement fonctionnel*.[20]

Nonetheless, the suppression of piracy is not free from difficulty in practice. The language of Article 105 suggests that the power to seize and prosecute a pirate ship or aircraft is facultative, not an obligation. Accordingly, there is no guarantee that action against pirates will be effectively taken.[21] In fact, it is not uncommon that seizing States are reluctant to prosecute pirates owing to the lack of domestic legislation, legal complexities in criminal proceedings, and the expense involved.[22] In this regard, the UN Security Council urged all States 'to criminalize piracy under their domestic law, emphasizing the importance of criminalizing incitement, facilitation, conspiracy and attempts to commit acts of piracy'.[23] The Security Council also invited States to 'examine their domestic legal frameworks for detention at sea of suspected pirates to ensure that their laws provide reasonable procedures, consistent with applicable international human rights law'.[24]

State practice shows that piracy suspects are being transferred for trial to relevant States. Whilst Somali piracy suspects are standing trial in various countries, including Somalia (Puntland), France, Yemen and the Netherlands, Kenya seems to remain the preferable venue of choice.[25] In relation to this, the Kenyan government has concluded agreements on prosecuting suspected pirates with the United Kingdom, the

[17] M. D. Evans, 'The Law of the Sea', in M. D. Evans (ed.) *International Law*, 2nd edn (Oxford University Press, 2006), p. 637; Shaw, *International Law*, p. 397; P.-M. Dupuy, *Droit international public*, 8th edn (Paris, Dalloz, 2006), pp. 782–783; American Law Institute, *Restatement of the Law Third, The Foreign Relations Law of the United States*, vol. 1 (Student Edition, Washington DC, American Law Institute Publishers 1990), § 404, pp. 254–255.

[18] ICJ Reports 2002, p. 37, para. 5. See also Joint Separate Opinion of Judges Higgins, Kooijmans and Buergenthal, *ibid.*, p. 81, paras. 60–61.

[19] Resolution 1976 (2011), para. 14.

[20] Concerning Georges Scelle's theory of the law of *dédoublement fonctionnel*, see Chapter 8, section 6.4.

[21] T. Treves, 'Piracy, Law of the Sea, and Use of Force: Developments off the Coast of Somalia' (2009) 20 *EJIL* p. 402. In the period from 1998 to 2009, the incidence of universal jurisdiction over piracies was just under 1.5 per cent of reported cases: E. Kontorovich and S. Art, 'An Empirical Examination of Universal Jurisdiction of Piracy' (2010) 44 *AJIL* p. 444.

[22] UN Doc. S/PV. 6046 (16 December 2008), p. 28 (Denmark). See also Treves, 'Piracy', pp. 408–410; M. D. Fink and R. J. Galvin, 'Combating Pirates off the Coast of Somalia: Current Legal Challenges' (2009) 56 *NILR* pp. 389–391. In Singapore, the *Comité Maritime International* adopted the 'Model National Law on Acts of Piracy or Maritime Violence' in 2001.

[23] S/RES/1976 (2011), para. 13.

[24] *Ibid.*, para. 16.

[25] D. Guilfoyle, 'Counter-Piracy Law Enforcement and Human Rights' (2010) 59 *ICLQ* p. 142.

USA, the EU and Denmark.[26] Furthermore, in 2010, the Kenyan government, with the aid of international funds, opened a special court to try piracy suspects operating from Somalia in the Gulf of Aden.[27]

In dealing with piracy suspects, States cannot be released from obligations arising under applicable human rights treaties, such as the Convention against Torture, the European Convention on Human Rights and the International Covenant on Civil and Political Rights. The human rights obligations that may be at issue include: (i) the right to be brought promptly before a judge, (ii) *non refoulement*, (iii) fair trial guarantees, and (iv) the right to an effective remedy.[28] Hence careful consideration should be given to the protection of the human rights of piracy suspects.

It is beyond serious argument that international cooperation is a prerequisite to effectively suppress piratical activity. Thus Article 100 of the LOSC places an explicit obligation upon all States 'to cooperate to the fullest possible extent in the repression of piracy on the high seas in any other place outside the jurisdiction of any State'. In this respect, two approaches can be identified.

The first approach seeks to develop international cooperation in counter-piracy operations at the regional level. For instance, in 2004, the Regional Co-operation Agreement on Combating Piracy and Armed Robbery against Ships in Asia was concluded.[29] This Agreement aims to prevent and suppress piracy and armed robbery against ships at the same time. It is notable that Article 4 of the 2004 Agreement established an Information Sharing Centre in Singapore with a view to managing and maintaining the expeditious flow of information relating to piracy and armed robbery against ships among the Contracting Parties. In 2009, the Code of Conduct Concerning the Repression of Piracy and Armed Robbery against Ships in the Western Indian Ocean and the Gulf of Aden (the Djibouti Code of Conduct) was adopted by twenty-one governments.[30] Under Article 8, the Participants to the Djibouti Code of Conduct agree to use piracy information exchange centres in Kenya, Tanzania and Yemen in order to ensure coordinated information flow. In 2009, following the initiative of Japan, the IMO Djibouti Code of Conduct Trust Fund – a multi-donor voluntary fund – was established.[31]

The second approach concerns counter-piracy operations through international institutions. Various international institutions, such as the IMO, NATO, the European Union and the United Nations, are currently engaged in the prevention and suppression of piracy. For example, the European Union launched Operation Atlanta off the

26 J. T. Gathii, 'Kenya's Piracy Prosecutions' (2010) 104 *AJIL* pp. 416–417. As of 31 August 2009, at least ten cases against seventy-six suspected pirates had been brought in the Mombasa law courts. *Ibid.*, p. 417.

27 D. Akande, 'Anti-Piracy Court Opens in Kenya', *EJIL: Talk*, 28 June 2010. www.ejiltalk.org/anti-piracy-court-opens-in-kenya/.

28 Guilfoyle, 'Counter-Piracy Law Enforcement', pp. 141–169 (in particular pp. 152–167).

29 (2006) 2398 *UNTS* p. 199. Entered into force on 4 September 2006.

30 Effective as from 29 January 2009. The document was reproduced in A. V. Lowe and S. A. G. Talmon (eds.), *The Legal Order of the Oceans: Basic Documents on the Law of the Sea* (Oxford, Hart Publishing 2009), p. 896.

31 In addition, in 2010, the Trust Fund Supporting the Initiatives of States Countering Piracy off the Coast of Somalia was established by UN Secretary-General, Ban Ki Moon.

Somali coast on 8 December 2008.[32] NATO also commenced a counter-piracy mission, Operation Ocean Shield, on 17 August 2009.[33] Furthermore, in 2009, the IMO adopted two documents, namely 'Guidance to Shipowners and Ship Operators, Shipmasters and Crews on Preventing and Suppressing Acts of Piracy and Armed Robbery against Ships'[34] and 'Recommendations to Governments for Preventing and Suppressing Piracy and Armed Robbery against Ships'.[35] The UNDOALOS also provides assistance to States in the uniform application of the provisions of the LOSC concerning the repression of piracy.[36] Concerning counter-piracy operations through international institutions, as will be seen next, particular attention must be devoted to the role of the UN Security Council.

2.3 The role of the UN Security Council in counter-piracy operations

Under Chapter VII of the UN Charter, the UN Security Council adopted a series of resolutions dealing with piracy and related issues. In June 2008, the UN Security Council adopted Resolution 1816 on combating acts of piracy and armed robbery off Somalia's coast.[37] In this resolution, the UN Security Council determined that 'the incidents of piracy and armed robbery against vessels in the territorial waters of Somalia and the high seas off the coast of Somalia exacerbate the situation in Somalia which continues to constitute a threat to international peace and security in the region'.[38] Thus the resolution decided, under Chapter VII of the UN Charter, that for a period of six months from the date of the resolution, States cooperating with the Transitional Federal Government (TFG) in the fight against piracy and armed robbery at sea off the coast of Somalia may:

(a) Enter the territorial waters of Somalia for the purpose of repressing acts of piracy and armed robbery at sea, in a manner consistent with such action permitted on the high seas with respect to piracy under relevant international law; and
(b) Use, within the territorial waters of Somalia, in a manner consistent with action permitted on the high seas with respect to piracy under relevant international law, all necessary means to repress acts of piracy and armed robbery.[39]

At the same time, Resolution 1816 cautiously went on to add that 'the authorization provided in this resolution applies only with respect to the situation in Somalia' and 'it shall not be considered as establishing customary international law'.[40] The resolution further requested that the activities undertaken pursuant to the authorisation in paragraph 7 do not have the practical effect of denying or impairing the right of innocent passage to the ships of any third States.[41]

[32] See the homepage of EU NAVFOR Somalia, www.eunavfor.eu/.
[33] www.manw.nato.int/page_operation_ocean_shield.aspx.
[34] MSC.1/Circ. 1334, 23 June 2009. [35] MSC.1/Circ. 1333, 26 June 2009.
[36] Report of the Secretary-General, *Oceans and the Law of the Sea*, A/65/69, 29 March 2010, p. 66, para. 245.
[37] S/RES/1816 (2008), 2 June 2008. [38] S/RES/1816 (2008), Preamble.
[39] *Ibid.*, paragraph 7 of the operative part. [40] *Ibid.*, paragraph 9.
[41] *Ibid.*, paragraph 8.

Subsequently, the Security Council adopted a series of resolutions on this particular matter, and called upon States to take part actively in the fight against piracy and armed robbery off the coast of Somalia under Chapter VII of the UN Charter.[42] Further, Resolution 1851 decided, in paragraph 6 of the operative part, that States and regional organisations cooperating in the fight against piracy and armed robbery at sea off the coast of Somalia for which advance notification had been provided by the TFG to the Secretary-General might undertake all necessary measures that were appropriate *in Somalia*. Thus the geographical scope of the necessary measures was extended to the land of Somalia. This is an important development because counter-piracy operations at sea are inadequate and there is a need to pursue pirates into their place of operation on land.[43]

3 REGULATION OF UNLAWFUL OFFENCES AND WEAPONS OF MASS DESTRUCTION AT SEA

3.1 The 2005 SUA Convention

As noted, piracy in international law is narrowly defined and it does not cover all threats to human life and the security of navigation and commerce at sea. Thus there is a need to fill the legal vacuum in this field. In this regard, of particular importance is the 1988 Convention for the Suppression of Unlawful Acts against the Safety of Maritime Navigation (the SUA Convention).[44] This Convention was concluded under the auspices of the IMO in direct response to the *Achille Lauro* incident. The SUA Convention provides a multilateral framework for the suppression of unlawful offences at sea which are not regulated by the international law of piracy. After September 11, 2001, the 1988 SUA Convention was revised by the Protocol of 2005 to the Convention for the Suppression of Unlawful Acts against the Safety of Maritime Navigation (hereafter the 2005 SUA Convention).[45] Four main features of the Convention merit highlighting, namely, the geographical scope, a broad range of offences, ship-boarding procedures and jurisdictional criteria.

Concerning the geographical scope, the SUA Convention applies if the ship is navigating or is scheduled to navigate into, through or from waters beyond the outer limit of the territorial sea of a single State, or the lateral limits of its territorial sea with adjacent States (Article 4(1)). It would follow that the Convention covers acts of unlawful

[42] S/RES/1838 (2008), 7 October 2008, S/RES/1846 (2008), 2 December 2008, S/RES/1851 (2008), 16 December 2008.

[43] UN Doc. S/PV. 6046 (16 December 2008), p. 9 (USA).

[44] 1678 *UNTS* p. 201. Entered into force on 1 March 1992. At the same time, the Protocol for the Suppression of Unlawful Acts against the Safety of Fixed Platforms Located on the Continental Shelf was adopted.

[45] Article 15(2) of the 2005 Protocol provides that: 'Articles 1 to 16 of the Convention, as revised by this Protocol, together with articles 17 to 24 of this Protocol and the Annex thereto, shall constitute and be called the Convention for the Suppression of Unlawful Acts against the Safety of Maritime Navigation, 2005 (2005 SUA Convention)'. The text of a consolidated version of the SUA Convention as amended by the 2005 Protocol was reproduced in Lowe and Talmon, *Basic Documents*, p. 837. The Revised 2005 SUA Convention entered into force on 28 July 2010.

offences committed in the territorial seas, the archipelagic waters, international straits and the EEZ. However, the Convention is not applicable to the situation where a ship would navigate from one point of the coast of a State to another point of the coast of the same State without leaving the territorial sea or international waters.[46] Even in this case, the Convention 'nevertheless applies when the offender or the alleged offender is found in the territory of a State Party other than the State referred to in paragraph 1' (Article 4(2)).

The SUA Convention applies to persons who seek to: seize a ship, perform acts of violence against a person on board, destroy a ship, place on a ship a device or substance which is likely to destroy that ship, destroy or seriously damage maritime navigational facilities, or communicate false information endangering the safe navigation of a ship (Article 3(1)). In 2005, the scope of offences was further widened. Article 3*bis* criminalised, *inter alia*,

- using against or on a ship or discharging from a ship any explosive, radioactive material or biological, chemical, and nuclear (BCN) weapons in a manner that causes or is likely to cause death or serious injury or damage,
- discharging, from a ship, oil, liquefied natural gas, or other hazardous or noxious substance in such quantity or concentration that causes or is likely to cause death or serious injury or damage,
- using a ship in a manner that causes death or serious injury or damage,
- transporting any explosive or radioactive material, knowing that it is intended to be used to cause death or serious injury or damage for the purpose of intimidating a population, or compelling a government or an international organisation to do or to abstain from doing any act, and
- transporting biological, chemical and nuclear weapons.

It is to be noted that offences under the 2005 SUA Convention are not limited to an act against another ship. Furthermore, Article 11*bis* stipulates that: 'None of the offences set forth in these articles shall be regarded for the purposes of extradition or mutual legal assistance as a political offence'. On the other hand, the 2005 SUA Convention does not apply to a warship or a ship owned or operated by a State by virtue of Article 2. It follows that unlawful offences and transports of BCN weapons at sea that may be carried out by States fall outside the Convention.

Concerning specific measures to apprehend offenders, it is of particular interest to note that the 2005 SUA Convention adopts ship-boarding procedures by non-flag States. Clearly, ship-boarding procedures seek to effectively apprehend offenders. Under certain conditions, Article 8*bis* (5) of the Convention allows a State Party to take appropriate measures, including boarding a foreign ship located seaward of any State's territorial sea if authorised by the flag State to do so. Article 8*bis*(6) further provides that when evidence of conduct described in Article 3, 3*bis*, 3*ter*, or 3*quater* is found as the result of any boarding conducted under Article 8*bis*, the flag State may authorise

[46] F. Francioni, 'Maritime Terrorism and International Law: The Rome Convention of 1988' (1988) 31 *GYIL* pp. 273–274.

the requesting Party to detain the ship, cargo and persons on board pending receipt of disposition instructions from the flag State.

At the same time, Article 8*bis*(8) makes clear that for all boarding pursuant to this Article, the flag State has the right to exercise jurisdiction over a detained ship, cargo or other items and persons on board, including seizure, forfeiture, arrest and prosecution. Under the same provision, the flag State may, subject to its constitution and laws, consent to the exercise of jurisdiction by another State having jurisdiction under Article 6. The ship-boarding procedures are particularly important in order to reconcile the exclusive jurisdiction of the flag State and the need for the effective apprehension of offenders. Where offences have been committed, there is a need to establish jurisdiction to prosecute offenders in an effective manner. In this regard, Article 6 sets out a two-tier system.

The first involves compulsory jurisdiction. Article 6(1) obliges each State Party to establish its jurisdiction over the offences set forth in Article 3 when the offence is committed:

(a) against or on board a ship flying the flag of the State at the time the offence is committed; or
(b) in the territory of that State, including its territorial sea; or
(c) by a national of that State.

The second is an optional jurisdiction. In this regard, Article 6(2) stipulates that a State Party may establish its jurisdiction over any such offence when:

(a) it is committed by a stateless person whose habitual residence is in that State; or
(b) during its commission a national of that State is seized, threatened, injured or killed; or
(c) it is committed in an attempt to compel that State to do or abstain from doing any act.

The adoption of such a broad range of jurisdictional criteria aims to close possible jurisdictional gaps concerning unlawful marine offences. On the other hand, a question that remains involves the competing claims of jurisdiction. In this regard, two possible solutions may be envisaged.

First, where the competing claims arise between a State entitled to jurisdiction under Article 6(1), namely compulsory jurisdiction, and a State invoking jurisdiction on the basis of Article 6(2) providing optional jurisdiction, it is reasonable to consider that the former should be given priority.

Second, where the competing claims arise within the same group of jurisdictional criteria, the Convention does not provide a criterion of precedence. Accordingly, the solution seems to be a matter of discretion for the State actually detaining the alleged offender. At the same time, it is to be noted that Article 11(5) provides as follows:

A State Party which receives more than one request for extradition from States which have established jurisdiction in accordance with article 6 and which decides not to prosecute shall, in selecting the State to which the offender or alleged offender is to be extradited, pay due regard

> to the interests and responsibilities of the State Party whose flag the ship was flying at the time of the commission of the offence.

This provision seems to imply that the flag State enjoys special favour when the competing claims involve that State.[47]

The SUA Convention does not provide for universal jurisdiction. However, the Convention attempts to close any possible jurisdictional gap by providing that the duty to extradite or prosecute (*aut dedere aut iudicare*) is on the State in whose territory the alleged offender is present. In this regard, Article 6(4) holds that:

> Each State Party shall take such measures as may be necessary to establish its jurisdiction over the offences set forth in articles 3, 3*bis*, 3*ter* and 3*quater* in cases where the alleged offender is present in its territory and it does not extradite the alleged offender to any of the States Parties which have established their jurisdiction in accordance with paragraphs 1 and 2 of this article.

This obligation is further amplified by Article 10(1):

> The State Party in the territory of which the offender or the alleged offender is found shall, in cases to which article 6 applies, if it does not extradite him, be obliged, without exception whatsoever and whether or not the offence was committed in its territory, to submit the case without delay to its competent authorities for the purpose of prosecution, through proceedings in accordance with the laws of that State. Those authorities shall take their decision in the same manner as in the case of any other offence of a grave nature under the law of that State.

Where the State Party on whose territory the offender is found is to proceed to extradition, '[t]he offences set forth in articles 3, 3*bis*, 3*ter* and 3*quater* shall be deemed to be included as extraditable offences in any extradition treaty existing between any of the State Parties' (Article 11(1)). If an extradition treaty does not exist between States Parties, the requested State Party 'may, at its option', consider the SUA Convention as a legal basis for extradition in respect of the offences set forth in Articles 3, 3*bis*, 3*ter* and 3*quater* (Article 11(2)). Yet the phrase, 'may, at its option', seems to suggest that the SUA Convention does not impose a strict obligation to extradite on the State Party in whose territory the alleged offender is present. Considering that acts of unlawful maritime offences may involve States which do not have extradition treaties, arguably this seems to be a defect of the Convention. It must also be noted that the Convention falls short of laying down a duty to punish.[48]

[47] Francioni, 'Maritime Terrorism', pp. 277–278.
[48] *Ibid.*, pp. 283–285.

3.2 Proliferation security initiative

The proliferation of weapons of mass destruction, including nuclear weapons, constitutes a serious threat to the maintenance of international peace and security. Several attempts have been made to deter the spread of such weapons. The proliferation security initiative (PSI) is an example.

The PSI is a political initiative launched by US President George W. Bush in Krakow, Poland on 31 May 2003 as a response to the proliferation of weapons of mass destruction (WMD), their delivery systems and related materials worldwide.[49] According to the US Department of State, the PSI 'is a global effort that aims to stop trafficking of WMD, their delivery systems, and related materials to and from states and non-state actors of proliferation concern'.[50] Notably, members of the PSI include Russia, but not China, although its influence on the North Korea, which is an obvious target of the PSI, is crucial. It is generally considered that the commitments of the participants to the initiative are not legally binding.[51]

According to the US Department of State, Bureau of International Security and Nonproliferation, the PSI works in three primary ways. First, the PSI channels international commitment to stopping WMD-related proliferation by focusing on interdiction as a key component of a global counter-proliferation strategy. Second, the PSI provides participating countries with opportunities to improve national capabilities and for authorities to conduct interdiction. Third, the PSI provides a basis for cooperation among partners on specific actions when the need arises.[52]

On 4 September 2003, the 'Interdiction Principles for the Proliferation Security Initiative' (hereafter the Interdiction Principles) were agreed at Paris.[53] Paragraph 1 calls on the PSI participants to undertake effective measures for interdicting the transfer or transport of WMD, their delivery systems, and related materials to and from States and non-State actors of proliferation concern. Paragraph 2 commits the PSI participants to adopt streamlined procedures for rapid exchange of relevant information concerning suspected proliferation activity and the protection of the confidential character of classified information provided by other States as part of the initiative. Furthermore, Paragraph 4(d) of the Interdiction Principles calls on the PSI participants:

> To take appropriate actions to (1) stop and/or search in their internal waters, territorial seas, or contiguous zones (when declared) vessels that are reasonably suspected of carrying such

49 The White House, Remarks by the President to the People of Poland. http://georgewbush-whitehouse.archives.gov/news/releases/2003/05.

50 US Department of State, Bureau of International Security and Nonproliferation, 'Fact Sheet: Proliferation Security Initiative', Washington DC, 26 May 2008. The document is available at: http://merln.ndu.edu/archivepdf/wmd/State/105217.pdf. As of 10 September 2010, ninety-eight States were participating in the Initiative. Bureau of International Security and Nonproliferation, 'Proliferation Security Initiative Participants', Washington DC, available at: www.state.gov/t/isn/c27732.htm.

51 US Department of State states that the PSI relies on 'voluntary actions by states'.

52 US Department of State, 'Fact Sheet'.

53 This instrument is available at: www.state.gov/t/isn/c27726.htm.

cargoes [of WMD] to or from states or non-state actors of proliferation concern and to seize such cargoes that are identified; and (2) to enforce conditions on vessels entering or leaving their ports, internal waters or territorial seas that are reasonably suspected of carrying such cargoes, such as requiring that such vessels be subject to boarding, search, and seizure of such cargoes prior to entry.

However, the requirement in paragraph 4(d)(1) would seem to leave some room for discussion. Under international law, every State has the right of innocent passage through the territorial sea. While activities which are not innocent are listed in Article 19(2) of the LOSC, the transport of WMD is not mentioned in this provision.[54] It is also debatable whether the transport of WMD can be regarded as an action which is 'prejudicial to the peace, good order or security of the coastal State' under Article 19(1) of the LOSC.[55] Moreover, it appears to be questionable whether the coastal State may stop and search suspected vessels passing its contiguous zone without entering into its territorial sea.[56] In any case, the PSI does not empower States to conduct interdiction operations on the high seas.[57] It should also be noted that the PSI applies only to commercial, not governmental, transactions.[58]

With a view to promoting its initiatives for the non-proliferation of WMD, the United States began to conclude bilateral treaties with flags of convenience, such as Belize, Croatia, Cyprus, Liberia, Malta, the Marshall Islands, Mongolia and Panama. These agreements commonly seek to promote cooperation between the two Parties in the prevention of the transportation by ships of WMD, their delivery systems and related materials. The bilateral treaties concluded by the United States seem to provide a legal basis for the boarding and search of the suspect vessel, cargo and the persons on board by the requested State, i.e. non-flag State.[59] However, the main limitation with this approach is that these treaties are binding only upon the two States Parties. Accordingly, there will be a need to create a multilateral framework for ensuring international cooperation on this subject. In this respect, the UN Security Council merits particular attention.

[54] In the 1989 Uniform Interpretation of Norms of International Law Governing Innocent Passage between the USA and the USSR, the USA itself stated that Article 19(2) is an exhaustive list of activities that would render passage not innocent (paragraph 2).

[55] Wolfrum, 'Fighting Terrorism at Sea', pp. 23–26.

[56] S. Kaye, 'The Proliferation Security Initiative in the Maritime Domain' (2005) 35 *Israel Yearbook of Human Rights* p. 217.

[57] M. Malirsch and F. Prill, 'The Proliferation Security Initiative and the 2005 Protocol to the SUA Convention' (2007) 67 *ZaöRV* p. 234.

[58] M. B. Nikitin, 'Proliferation Security Initiative (PSI)' Congressional Research Service, 18 January 2011, p. 4. Available at: http://fas.org/sgp/crs/nuke/RL34327.pdf.

[59] For an analysis of ship-boarding procedure in those agreements, see N. Klein, *Maritime Security and the Law of the Sea* (Oxford University Press, 2010), pp. 184–190.

3.3 United Nations interdictions at sea

The UN Security Council may have a significant role in the non-proliferation of WMD at sea. One can take the case of the Democratic People's Republic of Korea (hereafter North Korea) as an example. On 9 October 2006, North Korea carried out a test of a nuclear weapon. Following the test, UN Security Council Resolution 1718 determined that there was a clear threat to international peace and security. Acting under Chapter VII of the UN Charter and taking measures under its Article 41, the Security Council thus decided that all Member States should prevent the direct or indirect supply, sale or transfer to North Korea, through their territories or by their nationals, or using their flag vessels or aircraft, weapons, materials and technology, which could contribute to DPRK's nuclear-related or WMD-related programmes.[60]

Further to this, under Chapter VII of the UN Charter and its Article 41, Security Council Resolution 1874 called upon all States to inspect, in accordance with their national authorities and legislation, and consistent with international law, all cargo to and from North Korea, in their territory, including seaports and airports, if there were reasonable grounds to believe that the cargo contained prohibited items.[61] The resolution further called upon all Member States to inspect vessels, 'with the consent of the flag State, on the high seas', if there were reasonable grounds to believe that the cargo of such vessels contained prohibited items. If the flag State did not consent to inspection on the high seas, the flag State was obliged to direct the vessel to proceed to an appropriate and convenient port for the required inspection by the local authorities.[62] In summary, the UN Security Council allowed UN Member States to inspect vessels on the high seas *on the basis of consent of the flag State.*

Whilst maritime terrorism is becoming a matter of serious concern in the international community, there is a concern that such a unilateral interdiction at sea may be used to promote the strategic interests of a particular State on the pretext of the prevention of maritime terrorism and the transfer of WMD-related materials at sea. Collective problems, such as terrorism and the proliferation of WMD, should be settled by using collective means within an international framework. Hence the UN Security Council seems to provide a more legitimate means for the prevention of both terrorism and the transfer of WMD at sea than reliance on unilateral interdiction.

4 MILITARY EXERCISES IN THE EEZ

The legality of military exercises in the EEZ of a third State is one of the most contentious issues in the law of the sea. The EP-3 incident provides an illustration.[63] In April

[60] S/RES/1718 (2006), para. 8. [61] S/RES/1874 (2009), para. 11.

[62] *Ibid.*, paras. 12–13.

[63] Yann-Huey Song, 'The EP-3 Collision Incident, International Law and its Implications on the U.S.-China Relations' (2001) 19 *Chinese (Taiwan) Yearbook of International Law and Affairs* pp. 1-15; E. Donnelly, 'The United States-China EP-3 Incident: Legality and Realpolitik' (2004) 9 *Journal of Conflict and Security Law* pp. 25–42.

2001, Chinese F-8 fighters flew up to greet US EP-3 planes intercepting communications and monitoring coastal and offshore activities along the Chinese coast, and one of them collided with an EP-3 at a location about seventy nautical miles south-east of Hainan Island. As a result, the Chinese plane was destroyed, while the EP-3 was also damaged and landed at Lingshui Airport on Hainan Island in China. China subsequently claimed that the US planes had violated the LOSC which 'stipulates that any flight in airspace above another nation's exclusive economic zone should respect the rights of the country concerned', and that 'the US plane's actions posed a serious threat to the national security of China'.[64] Similar incidents occurred in 2002.[65]

With regard to the legality of military exercises in the EEZ of a third State, State practice is sharply divided into two opposing groups. On the one hand, not a few developing States have taken the position that the LOSC does not allow States to carry out military exercises or manoeuvres in the EEZ without the permission of the coastal State. When ratifying UNCLOS in 2001, for instance, Bangladesh made the following declaration:

> The Government of the People's Republic of Bangladesh understands that the provisions of the Convention do not authorize other States to carry out in the exclusive economic zone and on the continental shelf military exercises or manoeuvres, in particular, those involving the use of weapons or explosives, without the consent of the coastal State.[66]

Brazil, Cape Verde, India, Malaysia, Pakistan and Uruguay also made a similar declaration when ratifying the Convention,[67] and Iran adopted the same position in its legislation.[68]

On the other hand, developed States, such as Germany, Italy, the Netherlands, the United Kingdom and the United States, have objected to the claim of the developing States.[69] In a declaration of 8 March 1983, the United States pronounced that:

> Military operations, exercises and activities have always been regarded as internationally lawful uses of the sea. The right to conduct such activities will continue to be enjoyed by all States in the exclusive economic zone. This is the import of article 58 of the Convention. Moreover, Parts XII and XIII of the Convention have no bearing on such activities.[70]

[64] Ministry of Foreign Affairs of the People's Republic of China, 'Spokesman Zhu Bangzao Gives Full Account of the Collision between US and Chinese Military Planes', 4 April 2001.

[65] J. M. Van Dyke, 'Military Ships and Planes Operating in the Exclusive Economic Zone of Another Country' (2004) 28 *Marine Policy* p. 33.

[66] Reproduced in Lowe and Talmon, *Basic Documents*, p. 911.

[67] *Ibid.*, pp. 915, 917, 939–940, 944, 952, 967.

[68] Article 16 of the 1993 Act of the Marine Areas of the Islamic Republic of Iran in the Persian Gulf and Oman. The text of the Act is available at: www.un.org/Depts/los/LEGISLATIONANDTREATIES/index.htm.

[69] Lowe and Talmon, *Basic Documents*, pp. 935, 941, 948, 965.

[70] A/CONF.62/WS/37 and Add. 1–2, *Official Records of the Third United Nations Conference on the Law of the Sea*, vol. XVII, p. 244.

The LOSC provides no specific right for the coastal State to prohibit or regulate military activities within their EEZs. Nor is there any explicit provision which confers on States a right to carry out such activities within foreign EEZs. Thus one has to accept that the legality of military activities in the EEZ of a third State is not clear-cut under the LOSC.[71] In this regard, three different views can be identified.

In the first view, States have the right to carry out military activities in the EEZ of another State.[72] This interpretation relies mainly on the text and legislative history of Article 58. According to this view, military exercises are included in 'other internationally lawful uses of the sea related to these freedoms, such as those associated with the operation of ships, aircraft and submarine cables and pipelines' provided in Article 58(1).

By contrast, in the second view, the term 'other internationally lawful uses of the sea' does not include the freedom to conduct military activities in the EEZ. According to this view, coastal States have the right to restrict or prohibit foreign military activities in their EEZs.[73]

According to the third view, this question should be considered as a matter of residual rights, and any dispute over military activities in the EEZ is to be settled by reference to Article 59 of the LOSC.[74] While this view is arguable, it must be noted that international disputes concerning military activities may be exempted from compulsory procedures for dispute settlement by virtue of Article 298(1)(b). Furthermore, warships enjoy sovereign immunity. Hence it may be difficult to settle an international dispute on this subject by international adjudication.

In light of the high degree of political sensitivity involved in this subject, it appears difficult, if not impossible, to give a definitive answer to this question. Thus only tentative comments can be made here.

[71] EEZ Group 21, which was a group of senior officials and scholars primarily from the Asia-Pacific countries, adopted 'Guidelines for Navigation and Overflight in the Exclusive Economic Zone' in 2005. This document is available at: www.sof.or.jp/en/report/pdf/200509_20051205_e.pdf.

[72] This view is supported by writers, including: H. B. Robertson, 'Navigation in the Exclusive Economic Zone' (1984) 24 *Virginia Journal of International Law* pp. 885–888; B. Kwiatkowska, 'Military Uses in the EEZ: A Reply' (1987) *Marine Policy* p. 249; G. V. Galdorisi and A. G. Kaufman, 'Military Activities in the Exclusive Economic Zone: Preventing Uncertainty and Defusing Conflict' (2001–2002) 32 *California Western International Law Journal* p. 272; R. P. Pedrozo, 'Preserving Navigational Rights and Freedoms: The Right to Conduct Military Activities in China's Exclusive Economic Zone' (2010) 9 *Chinese Journal of International Law* pp. 9–29; B. H. Oxman, 'The Regime of Warships Under the United Nations Convention on the Law of the Sea' (1984) 24 *Virginia Journal of International Law* p. 838, but his view is nuanced.

[73] R. Xiaofeng and C. Xizhong, 'A Chinese Perspective' (2005) 29 *Marine Policy* p. 142; Zhang Haiwen, 'Is It Safeguarding the Freedom of Navigation or Maritime Hegemony of the United States? Comments on Paul (Pete) Pedrozo's Article on Military Activities in the EEZ' (2010) 9 *Chinese Journal of International Law* pp. 31–47.

[74] This view is supported by writers, including: R. R. Churchill, 'The Impact of State Practice on the Jurisdictional Framework Contained in the LOS Convention' in A. G. Oude Elferink (ed.), *Stability and Change in the Law of the Sea: The Role of the LOS Convention* (Leiden and Boston, Nijhoff, 2005), p. 135; A. V. Lowe, 'Some Legal Problems Arising from the Use of the Seas for Military Purposes' (1986) 10 *Marine Policy* p. 180; T. Scovazzi, 'The Evolution of International Law of the Sea: New Issues, New Challenges' (2000) 286 *RCADI* pp. 166–167.

First, the military exercises must have 'due regard to the rights and duties of the coastal States' in the EEZ pursuant to Article 58(3). It seems arguable, therefore, that military activities in the EEZ are not permissible where they prevent the lawful enjoyment of the rights and jurisdiction of the coastal State, such as exploration and exploitation of marine resources, navigation, and marine environmental protection.[75]

Second, if fishing vessels and installations exist within an EEZ, there will be a need to take safety measures to protect human life and installations against risks arising from military exercises and manoeuvres. Moreover, particular caution must be taken where a 'clearly defined area of special mandatory measures' (Article 211(6)(a)) or other marine protected areas are established in the EEZ.[76] It can reasonably be presumed that normally the coastal State is in the best position to specify areas of the EEZ which require particular caution. Hence it will be desirable that a State intending to carry out military exercises should consult with the coastal State, in light of humanitarian and environmental considerations.

5 REGULATION OF NUCLEAR WEAPONS AT SEA

As the UN Security Council has affirmed, it is beyond doubt that the proliferation of nuclear weapons constitutes a threat to international peace and security.[77] After World War II, nuclear weapon tests on the high seas raised particularly sensitive issues with regard to their legality. One can take the *Daigo Fukuryumaru* incident as an example. On 1 March 1954, the United States undertook hydrogen bomb tests. At the time of the explosion, a Japanese fishing vessel, *Daigo Fukuryumaru*, was contaminated by the fallout from the test. After six months, a crew member died because of the radioactivity. Fish caught by the *Daigo Fukuryumaru* and other fishing vessels engaged in fisheries around Bikini Atoll were also affected by the radioactivity. On 4 January 1955, the United States and Japan agreed that the USA should pay *ex gratia* compensation of 2 million US dollars, regardless of the responsibility in international law.

Currently the testing and deployment of nuclear weapons at sea is regulated by several treaties. Apart from disarmament treaties limiting the number of and armament of nuclear weapons, treaties concerning the regulation of nuclear weapons at sea can be divided into two main categories.

The first set of treaties prohibit the test and emplacement of nuclear weapons in the oceans at the global level. The 1963 Treaty Banning Nuclear Weapon Tests in the Atmosphere, in Outer Space and Under Water prohibits any nuclear weapon test explosion at any place under its jurisdiction or control: in the atmosphere; beyond its limits, including outer space; or under water, including territorial waters or high seas.[78] The emplacement of nuclear weapons in the seabed beyond the outer limit of a seabed zone

[75] Oxman, 'The Regime of Warships', p. 838.
[76] Cf. EEZ Group 21, 'Guidelines', V(g); D. Attard, *The Exclusive Economic Zone in International Law* (Oxford, Clarendon Press, 1987), p. 68.
[77] S/RES/1718 (2006), Preamble; S/RES/1874 (2009), Preamble.
[78] Article I(1)(a). 480 *UNTS* p. 43. Entered into force on 10 October 1963.

is prohibited by the 1971 Treaty on the Prohibition of the Emplacement of Nuclear Weapons and Other Weapons of Mass Destruction on the Seabed and the Ocean Floor and in the Subsoil Thereof.[79]

A second set of treaties seeks to prohibit the testing and use of nuclear weapons at the regional level, by establishing a nuclear-free zone. The UN General Assembly Resolution of 2 December 2009 affirmed its conviction of the important role of nuclear-weapon-free zones in strengthening the nuclear non-proliferation regime.[80] Five principal instances can be highlighted.

The 1967 Treaty of Tlatelolco for the Prohibition of Nuclear Weapons in Latin America imposes upon the Contracting Parties an obligation to prohibit and prevent in their respective territories the testing, use and deployment of nuclear weapons.[81] Under Article 3, the term 'territory' includes the territorial sea, airspace and any other space over which the State exercises sovereignty. Article 3 of Additional Protocol II of the 1967 Treaty provides that 'the Governments represented by the undersigned Plenipotentiaries undertake not to use or threaten to use nuclear weapons against the Contracting Parties of the Treaty'. The Additional Protocol II was ratified by all five permanent members of the UN Security Council.

The 1985 Treaty of Rarotonga Establishing a South Pacific Nuclear-Free Zone (the Rarotonga Treaty) obliges each Party to prevent the stationing and the testing of any nuclear explosive device in internal waters, the territorial sea and archipelagic waters, the seabed and subsoil beneath, the land territory and the airspace above them.[82] Article 1 of Protocol II to the Rarotonga Treaty calls on five nuclear-weapon States – France, China, the USSR, the United Kingdom, and the USA – not to use or threaten to use any nuclear explosive device against Parties to the Treaty or any territory within the South Pacific Nuclear Free Zone. Under Article 1 of Protocol III to the Rarotonga Treaty, five nuclear-weapon States are bound to undertake not to test any nuclear explosive device anywhere within the South Pacific Nuclear Free Zone, including the high seas.

Similarly, the 1996 African Nuclear-Weapon-Free Zone Treaty (the Pelindaba Treaty) prohibits the stationing and testing of nuclear explosive devices in the territory of each Party, namely, the land territory, internal waters, territorial seas and archipelagic waters and the airspace above them as well as the seabed and subsoil beneath.[83] Article 1 of Protocol I calls on the Parties to the Protocol, namely, nuclear-weapon States, not

[79] Article I (1971) 10 *ILM* p. 145. Entered into force on 18 May 1972. For the purpose of this Treaty, the outer limit of the seabed zone shall be coterminous with the twelve-mile outer limit of the zone referred to in Part II of the 1958 Convention on the Territorial Sea and the Contiguous Zone.

[80] *Nuclear-Weapon-Free Southern Hemisphere and Adjacent Areas*, A/RES/64/44, para. 8.

[81] Article 1. 634 *UNTS* p. 325. Entered into force on 22 April 1968.

[82] Articles 1, 5 and 6 (1985) 24 *ILM* p. 1440. Entered into force on 11 December 1986. Protocol I is open for signature by France, the United Kingdom and the United States. As of May 2011, France and the United Kingdom have ratified all three Protocols. China and the Russian Federation have ratified Protocols II and III. US ratification of all three Protocols is pending.

[83] Articles 4 and 5. (1996) 35 *ILM* p. 705. Entered into force on 15 July 2009. As of May 2011, China, France, the Russian Federation and the United Kingdom have ratified Protocols I and II. The United States has not ratified these Protocols. In addition, Protocol III is open for signature by France and Spain, and only France has ratified this Protocol.

to use or threaten to use a nuclear explosive device against any Party to the Treaty or any territory within the African nuclear-weapon-free zone. Article 1 of Protocol II calls on the nuclear-weapon States not to test or assist or encourage the testing of any nuclear explosive device anywhere within the African nuclear-weapon-free zone.

Furthermore, the 1995 Treaty on the Southeast Asia Nuclear-Weapon-Free Zone (the Treaty of Bangkok) requires that each State Party undertake not to develop, station, transport, test or use nuclear weapons anywhere inside or outside the Southeast Asia Nuclear-Weapon-Free Zone.[84] The Zone comprises the territories of all States in Southeast Asia, namely, Brunei Darussalam, Cambodia, Indonesia, Laos, Malaysia, Myanmar, the Philippines, Singapore, Thailand and Vietnam and their respective continental shelves and EEZs (Article1(a)). Article 3(2) of the Treaty further provides that each State Party undertakes not to allow any other States to develop, station or test nuclear weapons in its land territory, internal waters, territorial sea, archipelagic waters, the seabed and the subsoil thereof and the airspace above them. Whilst Article 2 of the Protocol to the Treaty of Bangkok calls on the five permanent members of the UN Security Council not to use or threaten to use nuclear weapons against any State Party to the Treaty, these nuclear-weapon States have not ratified the Protocol partly because they object to the inclusion of continental shelves and EEZs within the scope of the nuclear-free zone.[85]

In addition, it may be noted that the 1959 Antarctic Treaty, which applies to the area south of the 60° south latitude, prohibits any measures of a military nature as well as the testing of any type of weapons under Article I.[86] Under Article V, any nuclear explosions in Antarctica and the disposal there of radioactive waste material are prohibited.

6 CONCLUSIONS

The discussion in this chapter can be summarised under four points.

(i) Customary international law allows any State to seize and prosecute a pirate within its territory as an exercise of universal jurisdiction. However, it is becoming apparent that an individual exercise of universal jurisdiction is inadequate to suppress piracy. In response, there is a need to create more institutionalised mechanisms for ensuring international cooperation in this matter. One approach is to create a framework for such cooperation at the regional level. Another approach is to promote concerted counter-piracy operations to be carried out through international institutions, including the United Nations and the European Union. In this regard, it is important to note that the international response to piracy should also be multifaceted since the rise in piracy correlates with various political, economic and social factors.

84 Article 3(1). (1996) 35 *ILM* p. 639. Entered into force on 28 March 1997.

85 M. C. Abard, Jr, 'A Nuclear Weapon-Free Southeast Asia and its Continuing Strategic Significance' (2005) 27 *Contemporary Southeast Asia* p. 180.

86 Entered into force on 23 June 1961. For the text of the Treaty, see 402 *UNTS* p. 71.

(ii) The definition of piracy in international law does not cover other illicit acts against the welfare of seafarers and the security of sea communication. In response, the 2005 SUA Convention seeks to establish a multilateral framework for the suppression of a wide range of unlawful acts at sea that are not covered by the definition of piracy. It is noteworthy that under certain conditions, this Convention adopted shipboarding procedures by non-flag States in order to effectively apprehend offenders. Furthermore, in order to prosecute offenders in an effective manner, the Convention sets out a two-tier system which consists of compulsory and optional jurisdiction. Moreover, it holds that the duty to extradite or prosecute (*aut dedere aut iudicare*) is on the State in whose territory the alleged offender is present, with a view to closing any possible jurisdictional gap.

(iii) Military exercises in the EEZ of a foreign State create a strong tension between the security interests of the coastal State and the strategic interests of the naval State. Owing to the divergence between State practice and the opinions of legal commentators, the legality of such exercises in the EEZ of a third State remains a matter of extensive debate. The highly political nature of this issue may make it very difficult to resolve at the normative level. It needs careful consideration, taking the interests of humanity and protection of the marine environment into account.

(iv) The protocols of treaties establishing nuclear-weapon-free zones require nuclear-weapon States not to use or threaten to use nuclear weapons against any State Party to the treaties. Where these protocols have entered into force, negative security assurances will contribute to remove a threat of nuclear weapons in certain regions. Furthermore, the establishment of nuclear-weapon-free zones can contribute to confidence-building and the maintenance of peace and security in certain regions. Moreover, it is notable that several treaties establishing nuclear-weapon-free zones prohibit the dumping of any radioactive wastes.[87] Thus these treaties will also contribute to marine environmental protection.

FURTHER READING

1 General

D. D. Caron and H. N. Scheiber (eds.), *The Oceans in the Nuclear Age: Legacies and Risks* (Leiden, Nijhoff, 2010).

D. Guilfoyle, 'Interdicting Vessels to Enforce the Common Interest: Maritime Countermeasures and the Use of Force' (2007) 56 *ICLQ* pp. 69–82.

W. Heintschel von Heinegg, 'The United Nations Convention on the Law of the Sea and Maritime Security Operations' (2005) 48 *GYIL* pp. 151–185.

N. Klein, *Maritime Security and the Law of the Sea* (Oxford University Press, 2010).

N. Klein, J. Mossop and D. R. Rothwell (eds.), *Maritime Security: International Law and Policy Perspectives from Australia and New Zealand* (London and New York, Routledge, 2010).

[87] Article 7 of the Rarotonga Treaty, Article 3(3) of the Treaty of Bangkok and Article 7 of the Pelindaba Treaty.

P. J. Kwast, 'Maritime Law Enforcement and the Use of Force: Reflections on the Categorisation of Forcible Action at Sea in the Light of the *Guyana/Suriname* Award' (2008) 13 *Journal of Conflict and Security Law*, pp. 49–91.

R. McLaughlin, *United Nations Naval Peace Operations in the Territorial Sea* (Leiden, Nijhoff, 2009).

M. H. Nordquist, R. Wolfrum, J. N. Moore and R. Long (eds.), *Legal Challenges in Maritime Security* (Leiden and Boston, Nijhoff, 2008).

J. M. Van Dyke, 'Military Ships and Planes Operating in the Exclusive Economic Zone of Another Country' (2004) 28 *Marine Policy* pp. 29–39.

P. Wendel, *State Responsibility for Interferences with the Freedom of Navigation in Public International Law* (Heidelberg, Springer, 2007).

2 Piracy

Among the many books and articles relating to piracy, the following studies are of particular interest.

M. D. Fink and R. J. Galvin, 'Combating Pirates off the Coast of Somalia: Current Legal Challenges' (2009) 56 *NILR* pp. 367–395.

A. Fischer-Lescano and L. Kreck, 'Piracy and Human Rights: Legal Issues in the Fight against Piracy within the Context of the European "Operation Atlanta"' (2009) 52 *GYIL* pp. 525–561.

J. T. Gathii, 'Kenya's Piracy Prosecution' (2010) 104 *AJIL* pp. 416–436.

R. Geiss and A. Terig, *Piracy and Armed Robbery at Sea: The Legal Framework for Counter-Piracy Operations in Somalia and the Gulf of Aden* (Oxford University Press, 2011).

D. Guilfoyle, 'Piracy off Somalia: UN Security Council Resolution 1816 and IMO Regional Counter-Piracy Efforts' (2008) 57 *ICLQ* pp. 690–699.

'Counter-Piracy Law Enforcement and Human Rights' (2010) 59 *ICLQ* pp. 141–169.

D. Heller-Roazen, *The Enemy of All: Piracy and the Law of Nations* (New York, Zone Books, 2009).

J. M. Isanga, 'Countering Persistent Contemporary Sea Piracy: Expanding Jurisdictional Regimes' (2009–2010) 59 *American University Law Review* pp. 1267–1319.

P. Leher (ed.), *Violence at Sea: Piracy in an Age of Global Terrorism* (New York, Routledge, 2007).

A. Morita, 'Piracy *Jure Gentium* Revisited: For Japan's Future Contribution' (2008) 51 *Japanese Yearbook of International Law* pp. 76–97.

J. A. Roach, 'Countering Piracy off Somalia: International Law and International Institutions' (2010) 104 *AJIL* pp. 397–416.

T. Treves, 'Piracy, Law of the Sea, and Use of Force: Developments off the Coast of Somalia' (2009) 20 *EJIL* pp. 399–414.

Zou Keyuan, 'New Developments in the International Law of Piracy' (2009) 8 *Chinese Journal of International Law* pp. 323–345.

Zou Keyuan, 'Piracy and the Security Council' (2009) 24 *IJMCL* pp. 583–595.

National legislation on piracy is available at: www.un.org/Depts/los/piracy/piracy.htm.

3 The 2005 SUA Convention

N. Klein, 'The Right of Visit and the 2005 Protocol on the Suppression of Unlawful Acts against the Safety of Maritime Navigation' (2007) 35 *Denver Journal of International Law and Policy* pp. 287–332.

M. Malirsch and F. Prill, 'The Proliferation Security Initiative and the 2005 Protocol to the SUA Convention' (2007) 67 *ZaöRV* pp. 229–240.

M. Meija and P. K. Mukherjee, 'The SUA Convention 2005: A Critical Evaluation of its Effectiveness in Suppressing Maritime Criminal Acts' (2006) 12 *The Journal of International Maritime Law* pp. 170–191.

J. A. Roach, 'PSI and SUA: An Update', in M. H. Nordquist, R. Wolfrum, J. N. Moore and R. Long (eds.), *Legal Challenges in Maritime Security* (Leiden and Boston, Nijhoff, 2008), pp. 281–325.

4 Proliferation Security Initiative

A. Bergin, 'The Proliferation Security Initiative: Implications for the Indian Ocean' (2005) 20 *IJMCL* pp. 85–95.

M. Byers, 'Policing the High Seas: The Proliferation Security Initiative' (2004) 98 *AJIL* pp. 526–545.

D. Guilfoyle, 'The Proliferation Security Initiative: Interdicting Vessels in International Waters to Prevent the Spread of Weapons of Mass Destruction?' (2005) 29 *Melbourne University Law Review* pp. 733–764.

W. Heintschel von Heinegg, 'The Proliferation Security Initiative: Security vs. Freedom of Navigation?' (2005) 35 *Israel Yearbook of Human Rights* pp. 151–203.

D. H. Joyner, 'The Proliferation Security Initiative: Nonproliferation, Counterproliferation, and International Law' (2005) 30 *Yale Journal of International Law* pp. 507–548.

S. Kaye, 'The Proliferation Security Initiative in the Maritime Domain' (2005) 35 *Israel Yearbook of Human Rights* pp. 205–229.

T. C. Perry, 'Blurring the Ocean Zones: The Effect of the Proliferation Security Initiative on the Customary International Law of the Sea' (2006) 37 *ODIL* pp. 33–53.

J. A. Roach, 'Proliferation Security Initiative (PSI): Countering Proliferation by Sea', in M. H. Nordquist, J. N. Moore and K. Fu (eds.), *Recent Developments in the Law of the Sea and China* (Leiden, Nijhoff, 2006), pp. 351–424.

M. R. Shulman, 'The Proliferation Security Initiative and the Evolution of the Law on the Use of Force' (2006) 28 *Houston Journal of International Law* pp. 771–828.

Y.-H. Song, 'The US-Led Proliferation Security Initiative and UNCLOS: Legality, Implementation, and an Assessment' (2007) 38 *ODIL* pp. 101–145.

T. V. Thomas, 'The Proliferation Security Initiative: Towards Relegation of Navigational Freedom in UNCLOS?: An Indian Perspective' (2009) 8 *Chinese Journal of International Law* pp. 657–680.

M. J. Valencia, *The Proliferation Security Initiative: Making Waves in Asia* (Routledge, Oxford, 2005).

A. C. Winner, 'The Proliferation Security Initiative: The New Face of Interdiction' (2005) 28 *Washington Quarterly* pp. 129–143.

5 Naval Interdiction

D. Guilfoyle, 'Maritime Interdiction of Weapons of Mass Destruction' (2007) 12 *Journal of Conflict and Security Law* pp. 1–36.

R. McLaughlin, 'United Nations Mandated Naval Interdiction Operations in the Territorial Sea?' (2002) 51 *ICLQ* pp. 249–278.

Zou Keyuan, 'Maritime Enforcement of United Nations Security Council Resolutions: Use of Force and Coercive Measures' (2011) 26 *IJMCL* pp. 235–261.

12

Land-Locked and Geographically Disadvantaged States

Main Issues

By reason of their geography, land-locked and geographically disadvantaged States cannot fully use the oceans and it is thus not surprising that these States have sought to safeguard their special interests. As a consequence, the LOSC provides specific rules with regard to the rights of land-locked and geographically disadvantaged States. As these States are also members of the international community, it is important to secure their right to engage in marine activities. Thus this chapter will address particularly the following issues:

(i) What are land-locked and geographically disadvantaged States?
(ii) Do land-locked States have the right of access to and from the sea?
(iii) Do land-locked States have navigational rights?
(iv) To what extent can land-locked and geographically disadvantaged States participate in the exploitation of natural resources and marine scientific research in the EEZ of another State?

1 INTRODUCTION

'Land-locked State' means a State which has no sea coast.[1] Land-locked States are distinct from other States in one decisive fact: they lack access to and from the sea. As of January 2011, there are forty-five such States which, in an international community of approximately two hundred States, makes a significant group (see Table 12.1). As for other States, the oceans are important for land-locked States as a means of communication and a reservoir of marine natural resources. From economic and strategic viewpoints, it would be no exaggeration to say that the survival and prosperity of land-locked States rely on their freedom to communicate and to trade.[2] Thus the

[1] LOSC, Article 124(1).
[2] L. Caflisch, 'Land-Locked States and their Access to and from the Sea' (1978) 49 *BYIL* p. 74.

TABLE 12.1. LIST OF LAND-LOCKED STATES

*Afghanistan	The Former Yugoslav Republic of Macedonia
*Andorra	Malawi
Armenia	Mali
Austria	Moldova
*Azerbaijan	Mongolia
Belarus	Nepal
*Bhutan	*Niger
Bolivia	Paraguay
Botswana	*Rwanda
Burkina Faso	*San Marino
*Burundi	*Serbia
*Central African Republic	Slovakia
Chad	*South Sudan
Czech Republic	*Swaziland
*Ethiopia	Switzerland
Hungary	*Tajikistan
*Kazakhstan	*Turkmenistan
*Kosovo	Uganda
*Kyrgyzstan	*Uzbekistan
Laos	*Vatican City
Lesotho	Zambia
*Liechtenstein	Zimbabwe
Luxembourg	

* *Land-locked States not Parties to the LOSC*

safeguarding of the interests of land-locked States becomes a significant issue in the law of the sea. Indeed, the Preamble of the LOSC explicitly refers to 'the interests and needs of mankind as a whole and, in particular, the special interests and needs of developing countries, *whether coastal or land-locked*'.

In addition to land-locked States, there is another category of States which requires special consideration: geographically disadvantaged States. The concept of geographically disadvantaged States has evolved from that of self-locked States, namely States, as was the case with the Federal Republic of Germany, whose continental shelves are enclosed by those of other States.[3] With the development of the 200-nautical-mile EEZ, the concept of self-locked States was transformed into that of geographically disadvantaged States.

[3] L. Caflisch, 'What Is a Geographically Disadvantaged State?' (1987) 18 *ODIL* p. 643.

Whilst there is no generally accepted definition of geographically disadvantaged States in the law of the sea,[4] it can be argued that these States are essentially characterised by geographical and economic factors. As shown in the term '*geographically* disadvantaged States', it seems obvious that geographical elements are a key criterion in defining those States. In fact, as is the case for Iraq and the Democratic Republic of Congo, some States can generate only limited maritime zones due to a short coastline. As is the case for Germany, Singapore and Togo, the presence of neighbouring States also prevents the generation of maritime zones, in particular, the continental shelf and the EEZ. Furthermore, as in the case of Jamaica, some States can have an EEZ which is poor in natural resources.[5] Hence it is arguable that economic factors should also be considered. In order to correct inequalities resulting from nature, geographically disadvantaged States, along with land-locked States, have attempted to safeguard their special interests in the oceans.[6] In the law of the sea, land-locked and geographically disadvantaged States raise three principal issues.

First, the uses of the oceans by land-locked States can only be effective if such States enjoy a right of access to and from the sea. This right depends on freedom of transit through the States by whose territories they are separated from the sea. The right of transit of land-locked States is crucial.

Second, owing to the importance of freedom to communicate and trade, the navigational rights of land-locked States merit particular consideration.

Third, land-locked and geographically disadvantaged States have legitimate interests in various uses of the oceans, such as sea communication, the exploration and exploitation of marine resources, and marine scientific research. However, the claims of coastal States over a 200-nautical-mile EEZ significantly reduce the size of the high seas where the principle of freedom applies. The extension of the coastal State jurisdiction over the high seas has placed land-locked and geographically disadvantaged States in a difficult position. Thus a third issue to be examined involves the safeguarding of their interests in using the oceans.

2 LAND-LOCKED STATES AND ACCESS TO THE SEA

2.1 Legal regime prior to the LOSC

Whilst it is uncertain whether a general right of transit exists in customary international law,[7] several treaties after World War I provided for transit rights in general. For

[4] For an analysis of the definition of geographically disadvantaged States, see S. C. Vasciannie, *Land-Locked and Geographically Disadvantaged States in the International Law of the Sea* (Oxford, Clarendon Press, 1990), pp. 7–16.

[5] Caflisch, 'What Is a Geographically Disadvantaged State?', pp. 648–650.

[6] At UNCLOS III, twenty-six States considered themselves as geographically disadvantaged States. These States were: Algeria, Bahrain, Belgium, Bulgaria, Cameroon, Ethiopia, Finland, Gambia, German Democratic Republic, Federal Republic of Germany, Greece, Iraq, Jamaica, Jordan, Kuwait, Netherlands, Poland, Qatar, Romania, Singapore, Sudan, Sweden, Syria, Turkey, United Arab Emirates, and Zaire. Caflisch, 'What Is a Geographically Disadvantaged State?', p. 658.

[7] It appears that writers are cautious about the existence of the right of transit at the customary law level. See for instance, Caflisch, 'Land-Locked States', pp. 77–79; R. R. Churchill and A. V. Lowe, *The Law of the Sea*, 3rd edn (Manchester University Press, 1999), pp. 440–441.

example, the Convention and Statute on Freedom of Transit of 1921 provided free and non-discriminatory transit across the territory of contracting States by rail or waterway on routes in use convenient for international transit.[8] However, this Convention aimed at specifying the right of freedom of transit in general and did not address special issues respecting transit for land-locked States. Article V(2) of the 1947 General Agreement on Tariffs and Trade (GATT) also provided the freedom of transit through the territory of each Contracting Party, via the routes most convenient for international transit, without explicit reference to land-locked States.[9]

The first specific rule with regard to the right of transit for land-locked States to and from the sea was embodied in the 1958 Convention on the High Seas. Article 3 of the Convention reads as follows:

> 1. In order to enjoy the freedom of the seas on equal terms with coastal States, States having no sea coast should have free access to the sea. To this end States situated between the sea and a State having no sea coast shall by common agreement with the latter, and in conformity with existing international conventions, accord:
>   (a) to the State having no sea coast, on a basis of reciprocity, free transit through their territory; and
>   (b) to ships flying the flag of that State treatment equal to that accorded to their own ships, or to the ships of any other States, as regards access to seaports and the use of such ports.
> 2. States situated between the sea and a State having no sea coast shall settle, by mutual agreement with the latter, and taking into account the rights of the coastal State or State of transit and the special conditions of the State having no sea coast, all matters relating to freedom of transit and equal treatment in ports, in case such States are not already parties to existing international conventions.

As shown by the term 'should', this provision does not provide the *right* of the land-locked States to access to and from the sea. Further to this, the transit relies on agreement between the States concerned on the basis of the principle of reciprocity.[10] It follows that the transit of land-locked States to and from the sea depends on the goodwill of the coastal States concerned.

The number of land-locked States has increased particularly in Africa owing to decolonisation in the early 1960s. The growing demands of newly-independent land-locked States led to the adoption of the 1965 New York Convention on Transit Trade of Land-Locked States (hereafter 1965 New York Convention).[11] This was the first multilateral treaty devoted exclusively to the right of transit of land-locked States. The Preamble of the Convention reaffirmed, *inter alia*, that the recognition of the right

[8] Article 2 of the Statute. 7 *LNTS* p. 13. Entered into force on 31 October 1922.
[9] 55 *UNTS* p. 187. Entered into force on 1 January 1948.
[10] The requirement of reciprocity in this context seems to be questionable. As a land-locked State lacks a sea coast by definition, that State is incapable of giving anyone the right of access to the sea. Caflisch, 'Land-Locked States', p. 89.
[11] 597 *UNTS* p. 3. Entered into force in 1967.

of each land-locked State of free access to the sea is an essential principle for the expansion of international trade and economic development. Article 2(1) makes clear that freedom of transit is to be granted under the terms of this Convention for traffic in transit and means of transport. However, the rules governing the use of means of transport shall be established by common agreement among the contracting States concerned pursuant to Article 2(2). Under Article 15, the provision of this Convention shall be applied on the basis of reciprocity. Article 11 also reserves the right of the transit State to prohibit transit 'on the grounds of public morals, public health or security or as a precaution against diseases of animals or plants or against petss' and to take 'any action necessary for the protection of its essential security interests'.[12]

The 1965 New York Convention was ratified only by a relatively small number of States, and major transit States, such as France and Pakistan, remained outside the Convention. Although the New York Convention achieved only limited success, this Convention was later to provide a good basis for negotiations at UNCLOS III.[13]

2.2 Legal regime of the LOSC

The LOSC devotes Part X to the right of access of land-locked States to and from the sea and of freedom of transit. The key provision concerning the right of transit is Article 125:

1. Land-locked States shall have the right of access to and from the sea for the purpose of exercising the rights provided for in this Convention including those relating to the freedom of the high seas and the common heritage of mankind. To this end, land-locked States shall enjoy freedom of transit through the territory of transit States by all means of transport.
2. The terms and modalities for exercising freedom of transit shall be agreed between the land-locked States and transit States concerned through bilateral, subregional or regional agreements.
3. Transit States, in the exercise of their full sovereignty over their territory, shall have the right to take all measures necessary to ensure that the rights and facilities provided for in this Part for land-locked States shall in no way infringe their legitimate interests.

Overall these provisions are intended to achieve a balance between the rights of both a land-locked State and a transit State or States.[14]

It is significant that Article 125(1) unequivocally recognises the land-locked State's right of access to and from the sea and freedom of transit. It may be said that unlike Article 3 of the Geneva Convention, the LOSC provides a *pactum de contrahendo* on this matter.[15] It is true that the right of access to and from the sea is qualified by the

[12] The term 'transit State' means any Contracting State with or without a sea coast, situated between a land-locked State and the sea, through whose territory 'traffic in transit' passes (Article 1(c).)
[13] H. Tuerk, 'The Land-Locked States and the Law of the Sea' (2007) *Revue belge de droit international* p. 98.
[14] *Virginia Commentaries*, vol. III, p. 418.
[15] Caflisch, 'La convention des Nations Unies', p. 97.

second paragraph which provides that 'terms and modalities for exercising freedom of transit' shall be a matter of special agreement with the transit State or States.[16] Even so, it must be emphasised that freedom of transit does not depend for its exercise on the conclusion of special agreements, nor is it granted 'on the basis of reciprocity'.[17] The deletion of the requirement of reciprocity seems to be fully justified.[18]

Article 125(3) allows transit States to take 'all measures necessary' to safeguard their legitimate interests. However, it would be unacceptable for the transit States to take measures which totally denied the freedom of transit of the land-locked States in light of the principle of good faith and the prohibition of an abuse of right provided in Article 300 of the LOSC. It should also be noted that Article 130(1) obliges transit States to take all appropriate measures to avoid delays or other difficulties of a technical nature in traffic in transit.

Article 126 provides for exclusion of the application of the most-favoured-nation clause to the provisions of the LOSC and special agreements relating to the exercise of the right of access to and from the sea. Under Article 127, traffic in transit shall not be subject to any customs duties, taxes or other charges except charges levied for specific service rendered in connection with such traffic. Furthermore, means of transport in transit and other facilities provided for and used by land-locked States shall not be subject to taxes or charges higher than those levied for the use of means of transport of the transit State.[19]

An example in relation to the right of transit of land-locked States may be provided by the 1985 Northern Corridor Transit Agreement.[20] 'The Northern Corridor' means '[t]he transport infrastructure and facilities in East Africa served by the port of Mombasa in the Republic of Kenya' (Article 2). The Northern Corridor is the main artery for transport facilities linking land-locked and geographically disadvantaged States in the Great Lakes region of East and Central Africa, namely Burundi, Democratic Republic of Congo, Rwanda and Uganda, to the sea port of Mombasa in Kenya. The Preamble of the Agreement highlights 'the importance of adequate transit traffic arrangements for the international trade and for the economic progress of land-locked States'. Thus, Article 1 of the Agreement provides that: 'The Contracting Parties agree to grant each other the right of transit in order to facilitate movement of goods through their respective territories and to provide all possible facilities for traffic in transit between them, in accordance with the provisions of this Agreement, its Annex and Protocols'. Article 3 then requires each Contracting Party to grant to the other Contracting Parties the

[16] 'Transit State' means a State, with or without a sea coast, situated between a land-locked State and the sea, through whose territory traffic in transit passes (LOSC, Article 124(1)(b)).

[17] *Virginia Commentaries*, vol. III, p. 418.

[18] J. Monnier, 'Right of Access to the Sea and Freedom of Transit', in R.-J. Dupuy and D. Vignes, *A Handbook on the New Law of the Sea*, vol. 1 (Dordrecht, Nijhoff, 1991), p. 519.

[19] 'Means of transport' means: (i) railway rolling stock, sea, lake and river craft and road vehicles; (ii) where local conditions so require, porters and pack animals (Article 124(1)(d)).

[20] Entered into force in 1986. The text of the Agreement is available at: www.ttcanc.org/latest/about/ncta.asp. The Contracting Parties to the Agreement are: Burundi, Kenya, Rwanda, Uganda and the Democratic Republic of the Congo (the DRC). The DRC is considered a geographically disadvantaged State.

right of transit through its territory, under the conditions specified in this Agreement and the provisions of its Protocols. Furthermore, Article 3 of Protocol No. 1 (Maritime Port Facilities) to the Agreement provides that the government of Kenya agrees to the use of her maritime port facilities by the other Contracting Parties for the movement of goods in transit to and from the Northern Corridor States, and to make available warehouses, sheds, open space and other appropriate facilities, to the extent possible, and under the terms and conditions noted in this Protocol.

Another example is the 1996 SADC Protocol on Transport, Communications and Meteorology in the Southern African Development Community (SADC) Region.[21] The Protocol obliges the Member States to apply 'the right of land-locked Member States to unimpeded access to and from the sea'.[22] At the same time, the Protocol makes clear that: 'Member States shall, in the exercise of their full sovereignty over their territory, have the right to take all measures necessary to ensure that the application of the principles contemplated in paragraph 2 shall in no way infringe their legitimate interests'.[23]

3 THE NAVIGATIONAL RIGHTS OF LAND-LOCKED STATES

In the nineteenth century, Switzerland raised an issue in relation to the navigational rights of land-locked States. In 1864, the Swiss government obtained from the Swiss Parliament permission to form a merchant marine under the Swiss flag. Subsequently, however, the Swiss government abandoned its plan and ships belonging to Swiss nationals were obliged to sail under the flag of foreign States. It was not until new land-locked States – Austria, Hungary, Czechoslovakia – appeared on the map of Europe at the end of World War I that the right of ships of land-locked States to fly a national flag was recognised. This right was recognised by the Treaty of Versailles of 1919,[24] and was confirmed by the Declaration of Barcelona of 1921.[25]

Today it is beyond doubt that land-locked States have rights of navigation. In this regard, Article 2 of the 1958 Convention on the High Seas makes clear that the high seas is open to all nations, and both coastal and non-coastal States enjoy freedom of navigation. Article 4 of the Convention clearly provides that: 'Every State, whether coastal or not, has the right to sail ships under its flag on the high seas'. Furthermore, Article 14(1) of the Convention on the Territorial Sea and the Contiguous Zone stipulates that ships of all States, whether coastal or not, shall enjoy the right of innocent passage through the territorial sea.

Article 87 of the LOSC reaffirms that both coastal and land-locked States enjoy freedom of navigation on the high seas. Article 90 explicitly confirms the rights of navigation of every State, whether coastal or land-locked. As a corollary, Article 131 holds that

[21] The text of the Protocol is available at: www.sadc.int/index/browse/page/162. The Parties to the Protocol include six land-locked States, namely, Botswana, Lesotho, Malawi, Swaziland, Zambia and Zimbabwe.

[22] Article 3.2(2)(b). [23] Article 3.2(3). [24] Article 273.

[25] Declaration Recognising the Right to a Flag of States Having no Sea Coast, 7 *LNTS* p. 73.

ships flying the flag of land-locked States shall enjoy treatment equal to that accorded to other foreign ships in maritime ports. Furthermore, Article 17 affirms the right of innocent passage of all States, whether coastal or land-locked. The same applies to the right of transit passage (Article 38(1)), the right of innocent passage through archipelagic waters (Article 52(1)) and the right of archipelagic sea lanes passage (Article 53(2)).

4 LAND-LOCKED AND GEOGRAPHICALLY DISADVANTAGED STATES AND USES OF THE OCEANS

4.1 Fishing Rights

Like other States, land-locked and geographically disadvantaged States have the freedom to fish on the high seas. In this regard, an issue to be examined involves the right of such States to participate in the fisheries of the EEZ of foreign States. The LOSC contains detailed provisions on this subject in Articles 69 to 72.

Article 69 provides for the fishing rights of land-locked States. Article 69(1) stipulates that land-locked States shall have the right to participate, on an equitable basis, in the exploitation of an appropriate part of the surplus of the living resources of the EEZ of coastal States of the same subregion or region. Under Article 69(2), however, the terms and modalities of such participation must be established by the States concerned through special agreements taking into account, *inter alia*, the following factors:

- the need to avoid effects detrimental to fishing communities or industries of the coastal State,
- the extent to which the land-locked State is participating in existing agreements in the exploitation of living resources of the EEZ of other coastal States,
- the need to avoid a particular burden for any single coastal State, and
- the nutritional needs of the populations of the respective States.

Whilst the participatory right of developed land-locked States is limited to the surplus of the living resources, this limitation does not apply to developing land-locked States by virtue of Article 69(3). Under Article 69(4), developed land-locked States can participate in the exploitation of living resources only in the EEZ of developed coastal States of the same subregion or region. It follows that the participatory right of developed land-locked States is more restricted than that of developing land-locked States.

Under Article 70, similar rules apply to geographically disadvantaged States. For the purpose of Part V dealing with the EEZ, geographically disadvantaged States are defined as:

> coastal States, including States bordering enclosed or semi-enclosed seas, whose geographical situation makes them dependent upon the exploitation of the living resources of the exclusive economic zones of other States in the subregion or region for adequate supplies of fish for the nutritional purposes of their populations or parts thereof, and coastal States which can claim no exclusive economic zones of their own.

However, it should be noted that the above definition is valid only within the framework the EEZ.[26]

Article 70(1) provides that geographically disadvantaged States shall have the right to participate, on an equitable basis, in the exploitation of an appropriate part of the surplus of the living resources of the EEZ of the same subregion or region. The terms and modalities of such participation must be established by the States concerned through special agreement taking into account similar factors already enumerated in connection with land-locked States (Article 70(3)). Whilst the participatory rights of developed geographically disadvantaged States are limited to the surpluses, this limitation does not seem to apply to developing States falling into the same category by virtue of Article 70(4). Under Article 70(5), developed geographically disadvantaged States can participate in the exploitation of living resources in the EEZ of the developed coastal States of the same subregion or region.

The above rules are supplemented by two provisions applicable to both land-locked and geographically disadvantaged States. Under Article 71, Articles 69 and 70 do not apply in the case of a coastal State whose economy is overwhelmingly dependent on the exploitation of the living resources of its EEZ. A typical example is Iceland. Article 72 further provides that the rights derived from Articles 69 and 70 may not be transferred to third States without consent of the coastal States concerned. The rules concerning the right of participation call for a number of comments.[27]

First, the exercise of the right of participation relies on the 'terms and modalities' of special agreements to be concluded with the coastal State. It would seem to follow that the right of participation depends on the goodwill of the coastal State concerned. The term 'equitable basis' referred to in Articles 69(1) and 70(1) also remains obscure. It is true that in the case of refusals on the part of the coastal State to allocate to any States the whole or part of a surplus in conformity with Articles 62, 69 and 70, Article 297(3)(b)(iii) of the LOSC provides a remedy by way of the compulsory conciliation procedure. However, in no case shall the conciliation commission substitute its discretion for that of the coastal State as provided in Article 297(3)(c). Furthermore, the report of the conciliation commission is not binding.

Second, as discussed earlier, the coastal State has a wide discretion for determining the existence of a surplus of marine living resources.[28] Accordingly, the coastal State may nullify the right of participation by manipulating the determination of the allowable catch and harvesting capacity so as to avoid any surplus. It is true that the situation seems to be different for developing land-locked and geographically disadvantaged States because the surplus rules set out in Articles 69(1) and 70(1) do not seem to apply to those States by virtue of Articles 69(3) and 70(4). Yet the fact remains that

[26] Caflisch, 'What Is a Geographically Disadvantaged State?', pp. 655–656.

[27] For critical comments on this subject, see L. Caflisch, 'The Fishing Rights of Land-Locked and Geographically Disadvantaged States in the Exclusive Economic Zone', in B. Conforti (ed.), *La zone economica esclusiva* (Milan, Giuffrè, 1983), pp. 40 *et seq.*

[28] See Chapter 7, section 3.2.

the exercise of the right of participation depends on the 'terms and modalities' of special agreements to be concluded with the coastal State.

Third, the words 'region' and 'subregion' are not defined in Articles 69 and 70 and the meaning of these words therefore remains obscure. The wider the definition given to these terms, the wider the circle of the land-locked and geographically disadvantaged States entitled to share surpluses of marine living resources and, as a result, the smaller the share allocated to each of them.

Fourth, the validity of the discriminatory application of the participatory right between developed land-locked and geographically disadvantaged States and developing States belonging to these categories needs further consideration. As noted, the developing land-locked and geographically disadvantaged States are entitled to participate in the exploitation of living resources of the EEZ of their region or subregion, regardless of the existence of a surplus. Developing countries belonging to these categories are generally situated in the neighbourhood of developing coastal States. As a consequence, developing coastal States will have to share their living resources with their neighbouring land-locked and geographically disadvantaged States. By contrast, developed land-locked and geographically disadvantaged States are entitled to surpluses only within the EEZ of developed neighbouring coastal States of the same subregion or region. In general, developed States falling within these categories are located in the vicinity of developed coastal States. Yet developed coastal States have no obligation to share their living resources of the EEZ where there is no surplus. It would seem to follow that the developed coastal States can be considered as the main beneficiaries of the rules.

Fifth, the term 'overwhelming dependence' in Article 71 remains obscure. Thus there is a concern that the abstract formulation might induce countries other than Iceland to plead 'overwhelming dependence' and contribute to undermining the participatory rights of land-locked and geographically disadvantaged States.

Finally, in light of the paucity of State practice on this subject,[29] it remains uncertain whether and to what extent Articles 69–72 of the LOSC have become customary international law.

4.2 Exploitation of non-living resources in the oceans

The land-locked States have no right to participate in the exploration and exploitation of natural resources on the continental shelf. The only counterbalance is Article 82 of the LOSC, which sets out obligations in payments and contributions with regard to the exploitation of the continental shelf beyond 200 nautical miles.[30] In this regard, it must be recalled that payments or contributions shall be made through the International

[29] In 1994, UNDOALOS indicated that: 'Morocco and Togo are the only coastal States which indicate their readiness to allow neighbouring land-locked States access to the living resources of their exclusive economic zones'. UNDOALOS, *The Law of the Sea: Practice of States at the Time of Entry into Force of the United Nations Convention on the Law of the Sea* (New York, United Nations, 1994), p. 41. See also, S. Vasciannie, 'Land-Locked and Geographically Disadvantaged States' (2005) 31 *Commonwealth Law Bulletin* p. 66.

[30] See Chapter 4, section 4.6.

Seabed Authority 'on the basis of equitable sharing criteria, taking into account the interests and needs of developing States, particularly the least developed and the land-locked among them'.

Whilst the legal regime governing the Area does not directly address special issues in relation to land-locked and geographically disadvantaged States, several provisions in Part XI of the LOSC refer to those States. For instance, Article 140 provides that activities in the Area shall be carried out for the benefit of mankind as a whole, 'irrespective of the geographical location of States, whether coastal or land-locked'. Article 141 stipulates that the Area shall be open to use exclusively for peaceful purposes by all States, whether coastal or land-locked, without discrimination. Article 148 ensures the effective participation of developing States in activities in the Area, having due regard 'in particular to the special need of the land-locked and geographically disadvantaged among them to overcome obstacles arising from their disadvantaged location, including remoteness from the Area and difficulty of access to and from it'.

Article 152(1) obliges the Authority to avoid discrimination in the exercise of its powers and function. However, Article 152(2) goes on to state that the special consideration for developing States, including particular consideration for the land-locked and geographically disadvantaged among them, specifically provided for in Part XI shall be permitted. The Council of the Authority consists of thirty-six members of the Authority elected by the Assembly. Six members must be elected from among developing States Parties, representing special interests. The special interests to be represented include those of land-locked or geographically disadvantaged States.[31] Article 160(2)(k) empowers the Assembly of the Authority to consider problems of a general nature in connection with activities in the Area arising in particular for developing States, 'particularly for land-locked and geographically disadvantaged States'. Notably, these provisions apply only to developing land-locked and geographically disadvantaged States. While overall the above provisions seek to avoid excluding land-locked and geographically disadvantaged States from the benefits to be derived from the activities in the Area, the effect of those provisions does not give those States any preferential treatment over other States.[32]

4.3 Marine scientific research

Like other States, land-locked and geographically disadvantaged States have interests in marine scientific research. In fact, Austria and Switzerland have been engaged in marine scientific research for many years and have also been members of the Intergovernmental Oceanographic Commission.[33]

Land-locked and geographically disadvantaged States also enjoy the freedom of marine scientific research on the high seas. In this regard, the LOSC contains a special

[31] Section 3(15)(d) of the 1994 Implementation Agreement on Part XI of the UN Convention on the Law of the Sea. See also LOSC, Article 161(1)(d) and (2)(a). As of 2010, Czech Republic has been elected as a member of the Council.

[32] Tuerk, 'The Land-locked States', p. 104.

[33] *Ibid.*, p. 92.

provision, namely Article 254, dealing with the rights of neighbouring land-locked and geographically disadvantaged States. Under Article 254(1), (2) and (4), land-locked and geographically disadvantaged States are entitled to be informed of any proposed marine scientific research project. The neighbouring land-locked and geographically disadvantaged States shall, at their request, be given the opportunity to participate in the proposed marine scientific research project through qualified experts appointed by them and not objected to by the coastal State. The participation of those States in the project relies on the conditions agreed between the coastal State concerned and the State or competent international organisations conducting the marine scientific research pursuant to Article 254(3).

The development of technology is of particular importance with a view to promoting marine scientific research.[34] Article 266 thus requires States to promote the development of the marine scientific and technological capacity of States which may need and request technical assistance in this field, particularly developing States, including land-locked and geographically disadvantaged States, with regard to the exploration and exploitation of marine resources, marine environmental protection and marine scientific research. Article 269(a) requires States to establish programmes of technical cooperation for the effective transfer of all kinds of marine technology to States which may need technical assistance in this field, particularly the developing land-locked and geographically disadvantaged States. Furthermore, Article 272 places an obligation upon States to endeavour to ensure that competent international organisations coordinate their activities, 'taking into account the interests and needs of developing States, particularly land-locked and geographically disadvantaged States'.

5 CONCLUSIONS

The matters considered in this chapter can be summarised as follows.

(i) In comparison with the 1958 Geneva Convention on the High Seas, the LOSC makes clear that land-locked States have a right of access to and from the sea under Article 125(1). It is true that the terms and modalities for exercising freedom of transit rely on special agreements to be concluded with the transit States concerned. However, it is not suggested that the transit State is in a position to paralyse freedom of transit by refusing to enter into a special agreement.

(ii) The navigational rights of land-locked States have been affirmed by various treaties, including the LOSC. The navigational rights of those States can reasonably be considered as part of customary international law.

(iii) Under the LOSC, land-locked and geographically disadvantaged States are entitled to participate in the exploitation of living resources in the EEZ. However, the participatory rights remain uncertain for the following reasons:

[34] See Chapter 10, section 5.

- Their exercise depends on special agreements to be concluded with the coastal State.
- The coastal State has a wide discretion in setting the surplus of marine living resources.
- The coastal State may attempt to plead overwhelming dependence on fisheries in its EEZ.
- The scope of 'region' and 'subregion' remains obscure.

(iv) Land-locked States have no right to participate in the exploration and exploitation of natural resources on the continental shelf. Whilst Part XI of the LOSC governing the Area pays special attention to land-locked States, it is not suggested that they should receive preferential treatment in relation to seabed activities.

(v) Concerning marine scientific research in the EEZ, the neighbouring land-locked and geographically disadvantaged States are entitled to be given relevant information and the opportunity to participate, whenever feasible, in proposed marine scientific research by virtue of Article 254 of the LOSC. On the high seas, like other States, land-locked and geographically disadvantaged States enjoy the freedom of marine scientific research.

FURTHER READING

L. Caflisch, 'Land-Locked States and their Access to and from the Sea' (1978) 49 *BYIL* pp. 71–100.

'The Fishing Rights of Land-Locked and Geographically Disadvantaged States in the Exclusive Economic Zone', in B. Conforti (ed.), *La zone economica esclusiva* (Milan, Giuffrè, 1983), pp. 29–48.

'What Is a Geographically Disadvantaged State?' (1987) 18 *ODIL*, pp. 641–663.

J. L. Kateka, 'Land-Locked Developing Countries and the Law of the Sea', in I. Buffard, J. Crawford, A. Pellet and S. Wittich (eds.), *International Law Between Universalism and Fragmentation: Festschrift in Honour of Gerhard Hafner* (Leiden and Boston, Nijhoff, 2008), pp. 769–782.

S. P. Menefee, 'The "Oar of Odysseus": Land-Locked and Geographically Disadvantaged States in Historical Perspective' (1992) 23 *California Western International Law Journal* pp. 1–65.

J. Monnier, 'Right of Access to the Sea and Freedom of Transit', in R.-J. Dupuy and D. Vignes, *A Handbook on the New Law of the Sea*, vol. 1 (Dordrecht, Nijhoff, 1991), pp. 501–523.

A. M. Puñal, 'The Right of Land-Locked and Geographically Disadvantaged States in Exclusive Economic Zones' (1992) 23 *JMLC* pp. 429–459.

L. Savadogo, *Essai sur une théorie générale des Etats sans littoral: l'expérience africaine* (Paris, L.G.D.J., 1997).

J. Symonides, 'Geographically Disadvantaged States under the 1982 Convention on the Law of the Sea' (1988-I) 208 *RCADI* pp. 287–406.

P. Tavernier, 'Les nouveaux Etats sans littoral d'Europe et d'Asie et l'accès à la mer' (1993) 97 *RGDIP* pp. 727–744.

H. Tuerk, 'The Land-Locked States and the Law of the Sea' (2007) *Revue belge de droit international* pp. 91–112.

H. Tuerk and G. Hafner, 'The Land-Locked Countries and the United Nations Convention on the Law of the Sea', in B. Vukas (ed.), *Essays on the New Law of the Sea* (Zagreb, Sveucilisna Naklada Liber, 1985), pp. 58–70.

UNDOALOS, *The Law of the Sea: Rights of Access of Land-Locked States to and from the Sea and Freedom of Transit: Legislative History of Part X, Articles 124 to 132 of the United Nations Convention on the Law of the Sea* (New York, United Nations, 1987).

K. Uprety, *The Transit Regime for Land-Locked States: International Law and Development Perspectives* (Washington DC, World Bank, 2005).

S. C. Vasciannie, 'Land-Locked and Geographically Disadvantaged States and the Question of the Outer Limit of the Continental Shelf' (1988) 58 *BYIL* pp. 271–302.

Land-Locked and Geographically Disadvantaged States in the International Law of the Sea (Oxford, Clarendon Press, 1990).

'Land-Locked and Geographically Disadvantaged States' (2005) 31 *Commonwealth Law Bulletin* pp. 59–68.

13

Peaceful Settlement of International Disputes

Main Issues

Peaceful settlement of international disputes occupies an important place in international law in general and the law of the sea is no exception. In this respect, the LOSC establishes a unique mechanism combining the voluntary and compulsory procedures for dispute settlement. It is particularly significant that the LOSC sets out the compulsory dispute settlement procedures as an integrated part of the Convention. Furthermore, it is of particular interest to note that a new permanent international tribunal, namely, the International Tribunal for the Law of the Sea (ITLOS), was established. The dispute settlement procedures of the LOSC provide an interesting insight into the development of dispute settlement in international law. Thus this chapter will address the dispute settlement procedures under the Convention with particular reference to the following issues:

(i) What are the principal features of the dispute settlement procedures of the LOSC?
(ii) What is the significance of and limitations associated with the compulsory procedures for dispute settlement under the LOSC?
(iii) What is ITLOS, and what is the role of the variety of chambers?
(iv) What is the role of ITLOS in the development of the law of the sea?
(v) Does the establishment of ITLOS create a risk of fragmentation of international law?

1 INTRODUCTION

Since rules of international law, customary or conventional, are interpreted and applied by States individually (auto-interpretation/auto-application), it is not uncommon that the same rule may be interpreted and applied differently by different States. Experience demonstrates that different interpretations of a rule may become a source of international disputes. Hence it can be argued that the efficacy of rules of international law relies essentially on the existence of an effective mechanism of international dispute settlement,[1] and this is particularly true of the LOSC. Indeed, as many provisions of the LOSC represent a complex balance of the interests of various actors, they are not free from uncertainty in their interpretation and application. Accordingly, the establishment of mechanisms for international dispute settlement is crucial with a view to ensuring the stability and integrity of the Convention. In response, the LOSC establishes unique procedures for international dispute settlement. Such procedures have at least four principal features which merit particular attention.

First, at UNCLOS I, only an Optional Protocol Concerning Compulsory Settlement of Dispute was adopted as a distinct treaty.[2] By contrast, the LOSC establishes dispute settlement procedures, including compulsory procedures, as an integrated part of the Convention. The built-in procedures for dispute settlement can be considered as an important tool for securing the integrity of the interpretation of the Convention.

Second, the LOSC sets out compulsory procedures for dispute settlement entailing decisions that bind the Parties to the Convention. Compulsory dispute settlement also contributes to secure the uniform interpretation of the LOSC.

The third feature concerns the establishment of a new permanent judicial body, namely ITLOS. Whilst ITLOS is largely modelled on the ICJ, it has, as will be seen, some innovations, such as a wide range of *locus standi* before the Tribunal. It is conceivable that the ITLOS jurisprudence will come to have a valuable role in the clarification of relevant rules of the LOSC as well as the law of the sea in general.

Finally, it is noteworthy that the LOSC creates a flexible system allowing the States Parties to choose one or more of the different procedures for compulsory settlement set out in Part XV of the Convention. This is a unique mechanism for reconciling the principle of free choice of means with compulsory procedures for dispute settlement.

The dispute settlement procedures are complex, and a full treatment of this subject is beyond the scope of this chapter, which has the more modest purpose of providing an outline of the procedures for international dispute settlement in the LOSC.

2 BASIC STRUCTURE OF DISPUTE SETTLEMENT PROCEDURES IN THE LOSC

2.1 General considerations

The LOSC devotes Part XV to the settlement of disputes. This part is composed of three sections. Section 1 contains general provisions which basically involve voluntary dispute settlement procedures. Section 2 provides compulsory procedures for dispute settlement. Section 3 sets out limitations and optional exceptions to the compulsory procedures.

In addition to this, the LOSC contains provisions respecting dispute settlement in various other parts. Section 5 of Part XI is devoted to dispute settlement and advisory

[1] L. Caflisch, 'Cent ans de règlement pacifique des différends interétatiques' (2001) 288 *RCADI* pp. 257–261.

[2] See Chapter 1, section 5. 2.

opinions by the Seabed Chamber of ITLOS. Dispute settlement procedures are also embodied in Annex V (Conciliation), Annex VI (ITLOS), Annex VII (Arbitration) and Annex VIII (Special Arbitration).

Notably, in some cases, the dispute settlement procedures of the LOSC may be extended beyond Parties to the Convention itself. In this regard, Article 30(1) of the 1995 Fish Stocks Agreement makes clear that the procedures for dispute settlement in Part XV of the LOSC apply *mutatis mutandis* to any dispute between States Parties to the Agreement. In accordance with this provision, States Parties to the Agreement, which are not Parties the LOSC, may also have recourse to the dispute settlement procedures of the Convention. This mechanism is unique in the sense that a State Party to one treaty can use the dispute settlement procedures of another treaty to which is not a Party. Article 30(2) of the Fish Stocks Agreement further provides that:

> The provisions relating to the settlement of disputes set out in Part XV of the Convention apply *mutatis mutandis* to any dispute between States Parties to this Agreement concerning the interpretation or application of a subregional, regional or global fisheries agreement relating to straddling fish stocks or highly migratory fish stocks to which they are parties, including any dispute concerning the conservation and management of such stocks, whether or not they are also Parties to the Convention.

The effect of this provision seems to be that as between Parties to the Fish Stocks Agreement, the dispute settlement machinery of the LOSC is incorporated into existing treaties with regard to straddling or highly migratory fish stocks.[3] Moreover, the 2006 Southern Indian Ocean Fisheries Agreement provides for the application of the compulsory procedures under section 2, Part XV of the LOSC to a dispute between Contracting Parties.[4] In addition, considering that the LOSC and the 1999 Implementation Agreement are to be read as a single instrument, it appears logical to argue that the dispute settlement procedures of Part XI of the LOSC would apply to disputes concerning the interpretation and the application of that Agreement.[5]

Articles 279 and 280 of the LOSC provide two cardinal principles on this subject. The first is the principle of peaceful settlement of international disputes. As stressed in various instruments,[6] the obligation of peaceful settlement of international disputes is the corollary of the prohibition of the use of force. This principle is reinforced by Article 279 of the LOSC, which provides that:

[3] A. Boyle, 'Problems of Compulsory Jurisdiction and the Settlement of Disputes Relating to Straddling Fish Stocks' (1999) 14 *IJMCL* p. 16.

[4] Article 20(1). For the text of the Agreement, see TRE/Multilateral/En/TRE144077.pdf.

[5] Boyle, 'Problems of Compulsory Jurisdiction', p. 23.

[6] Article 2(3) and (4) of the Charter of the United Nations, 892 *UNTS* p. 119; the Manila Declaration on the Peaceful Settlement of International Disputes, UN General Assembly Resolution 37/10, 15 November 1982. See Preamble and section I, paragraph 13.

> States Parties shall settle any dispute between them concerning the interpretation or application of this Convention by peaceful means in accordance with Article 2, paragraph 3, of the Charter of the United Nations and, to this end, shall seek a solution by the means indicated in Article 33, paragraph 1, of the Charter.

The second principle concerns free choice of means in dispute settlement. This principle has been confirmed by various instruments. For example, Article 33(1) of the UN Charter makes clear that:

> The parties to any dispute, the continuance of which is likely to endanger the maintenance of international peace and security, shall, first of all, seek a solution by negotiation, enquiry, mediation, conciliation, arbitration, judicial settlement, resort to regional agencies or arrangements, or other peaceful means of *their own choice*.[7]

Likewise, the second Principle of the 1970 Friendly Relations Declaration explicitly states that:

> International disputes shall be settled on the basis of the sovereign equality of States and in accordance with *the principle of free choice of means*.[8]

The principle of free choice of means is echoed by Article 280 of the LOSC, by providing that:

> Nothing in this Part [XV] impairs the right of any States Parties to agree at any time to settle a dispute between them concerning the interpretation or application of this Convention by any peaceful means of their own choice.

It would follow that peaceful settlement means chosen by the Parties prevail over dispute settlement procedures embodied in Part XV of the LOSC.

2.2 The interlinkage between voluntary and compulsory procedures for dispute settlement

In general, international dispute settlement in international law rests on the balance between the principle of free choice of means and the need to establish compulsory procedures for dispute settlement. With a view to reconciling these two elements, the LOSC sets out a two-tier system. According to this system, as the first step, States Parties must settle any dispute between them concerning the interpretation or application of

[7] Emphasis added.
[8] Emphasis added. UN General Assembly Resolution 2625 (XXV) of 24 October 1970.

the LOSC by peaceful means of their own choice.[9] Where the disputing Parties cannot settle a dispute through non-compulsory procedures, that dispute must be settled in accordance with the compulsory procedures set out in section 2 of Part XV. In this sense, the compulsory procedures are essentially residual under the Convention.

The key provision which links non-compulsory procedures to compulsory procedures for dispute settlement is Article 286:

> Subject to section 3, any dispute concerning the interpretation or application of this Convention shall, where no settlement has been reached by recourse to section 1, be submitted at the request of any party to the dispute to the court or tribunal having jurisdiction under this section.

By combining the voluntary procedures with the compulsory procedures, the LOSC seeks to ensure an effective solution of international disputes. Section 1 of Part XV sets out several conditions to set in motion the compulsory procedures for dispute settlement. In this regard, Articles 281, 282 and 283 are relevant.

First, mention should be made of an obligation to exchange views set out in Article 283. As noted, parties to a dispute can freely agree on the most suitable method to settle the dispute on their own. Nothing compels them to have recourse to international courts and tribunals. Accordingly, Article 283 obliges disputing parties to proceed expeditiously to an exchange of views as a preliminary to any further steps. This obligation was at issue in the 2001 *MOX Plant* case (provisional measures) between the Republic of Ireland and the United Kingdom. In this case, the United Kingdom contended that the correspondence between Ireland and the United Kingdom did not amount to an exchange of views on the dispute said to arise under the LOSC. The United Kingdom also argued that its request for an exchange of views under Article 283 of the Convention was not accepted by Ireland.[10] However, ITLOS held that: '[A] State Party is not obliged to continue with an exchange of views when it concludes that the possibilities of reaching agreement have been exhausted'.[11]

The second provision that needs to be examined is Article 281. Article 281(1) holds that if the States Parties to a dispute concerning the interpretation or application of the LOSC have agreed to seek settlement of the dispute by a peaceful means of their own choice, the procedures under Part XV of the Convention apply only where no settlement has been reached by recourse to such means and the agreement between the Parties does not exclude any further procedure. Article 281(2) further provides that if the Parties have agreed on a time limit, paragraph 1 of Article 281 applies only upon the expiration of that time limit.

Article 281(1) contains two requirements, namely,

(i) the disputing Parties must have exhausted dispute settlement procedures on the basis of mutual agreement, and

[9] LOSC, Article 279.

[10] The *MOX Plant* case (provisional measures), (2002) 41 *ILM* p. 413, paras. 56–57.

[11] *Ibid.*, p. 414, para. 60.

(ii) that agreement does not exclude resort to the procedures provided in the LOSC.

If one of the requirements has not been met, the procedures under Part XV of the LOSC do not apply.

The legal effect of Article 281 was tested in the 1999 *Southern Bluefin Tuna* dispute between New Zealand, Australia and Japan. Concerning the first requirement of Article 281(1), Japan asserted that Australia and New Zealand had not exhausted the procedures for amicable dispute settlement under Part XV, section 1 of the LOSC, in particular Article 281.[12] Nonetheless, ITLOS held that: '[A] State Party is not obliged to pursue procedures under Part XV, section 1, of the Convention when it concludes that the possibilities of settlement have been exhausted'.[13] In the Award on Jurisdiction and Admissibility of 2000, the Annex VII Arbitral Tribunal also took the same view on this particular matter.[14]

However, the second requirement of Article 281(1) was more controversial. The key question was whether or not Article 16 of the 1993 Convention for the Conservation of Southern Bluefin Tuna (hereafter the 1993 Convention) excludes the application of compulsory procedures in the LOSC. Japan contended that recourse to the Arbitral Tribunal was excluded because the 1993 Convention provides for a dispute settlement procedure. However, Australia and New Zealand maintained that they were not precluded from having recourse to the Arbitral Tribunal since the 1993 Convention does not provide for a compulsory dispute settlement procedure entailing a binding decision as required under Article 282 of the LOSC.[15]

In this regard, ITLOS ruled that the fact that the 1993 Convention applies between the Parties 'does not preclude recourse to the procedures in Part XV, section 2, of the Convention on the Law of the Sea'.[16] Therefore, it held that the requirements for invoking those procedures had been fulfilled, and that the Arbitral Tribunal would prima facie have jurisdiction over the disputes.[17]

However, the Annex VII Arbitral Tribunal took a different view on this issue. It is true that Article 16 of the 1993 Convention does not expressly exclude the applicability of any procedure, including the compulsory procedures of section 2 of Part XV of the LOSC. In the view of the Arbitral Tribunal, however, Article 16 makes clear that the dispute is not referable to adjudication by the ICJ or ITLOS or to arbitration 'at the request of any party to the dispute'. The Arbitral Tribunal also pointed out that the wording of Article 16(1) and (2) of the 1993 Convention has its essential origins in the terms of Article XI of the Antarctic Treaty. According to the Arbitral Tribunal, 'it is obvious that these provisions are meant to exclude compulsory jurisdiction'.[18] It thus concluded that Article 16 of the 1993 Convention excludes any further procedure within the

[12] The *Southern Bluefin Tuna* cases (requests for provisional measures), (1999) 38 *ILM* p. 1633, para. 56.
[13] *Ibid.*, para. 60.
[14] The *Southern Bluefin Tuna* case (Award on Jurisdiction and Admissibility) (2000) 39 *ILM* p. 1389, para. 55 (hereafter *Southern Bluefin Tuna* award).
[15] The *Southern Bluefin Tuna* cases (requests for provisional measures), pp. 1632–1633, paras. 53–54.
[16] *Ibid.*, para. 55.
[17] *Ibid.*, paras. 61–62.
[18] *Southern Bluefin Tuna* award, p. 1390, para. 58.

contemplation of Article 281(1) of the LOSC;[19] and that the Annex VII Tribunal lacked jurisdiction to entertain the merits of the dispute.[20]

According to this interpretation, a regional agreement which simply contains no provision for compulsory procedures for dispute settlement could exclude resort to the compulsory procedures of Part XV of the LOSC. Thus a concern is voiced that the effectiveness of the compulsory procedures may be seriously undermined by the liberal application of Article 281.[21]

Third, Article 282 of the LOSC may also restrict the compulsory procedures of the Convention. This provision holds that if the disputing Parties have agreed, through a general, regional or bilateral agreement or otherwise, that such dispute shall, at the request of any party to the dispute, be submitted to a procedure that entails a binding decision, that procedure shall apply in lieu of the procedures provided for in Part XV, unless the parties to the dispute otherwise agree.

The legal effect of Article 282 was discussed in the 2001 *MOX Plant* case between the Republic of Ireland and the United Kingdom. In this case, the United Kingdom asserted that the main elements of the dispute submitted to the Annex VII Arbitral Tribunal were governed by the compulsory procedures for dispute settlement in the OSPAR Convention or the EC Treaty or the Euratom Treaty. It thus argued that the Arbitral Tribunal would not have jurisdiction.[22]

However, ITLOS took the view that the dispute settlement procedures under the OSPAR Convention, the EC Treaty and the Euratom Treaty deal with disputes with regard to the interpretation and application of those agreements, and do not deal with disputes arising under the LOSC. In the view of ITLOS, since the dispute before the Annex VII Arbitral Tribunal concerned the interpretation or application of the LOSC, only the dispute settlement procedure under that Convention was relevant to the dispute. Hence it concluded that for the purpose of determining prima facie jurisdiction of the Annex VII Arbitral Tribunal, Article 282 was not applicable to the dispute submitted to the Tribunal.[23]

Later, the legal effect of Article 282 was tested again by the Annex VII Arbitral Tribunal in the *MOX Plant* case of 2003.[24] The key question involved the exclusive jurisdiction of the European Court of Justice under European Community law. According to the Tribunal, if the interpretation of the LOSC fell within the exclusive competence of the European Court of Justice, it would preclude the jurisdiction of the Tribunal entirely by virtue of Article 282 of the Convention. Thus the determination of the Tribunal's jurisdiction relied essentially on the resolution of this question. In the view

[19] *Ibid.*, p. 1390, para. 59. [20] *Ibid.*, p. 1391, para. 65.

[21] Judge Keith took the view that clear wording is needed in order to exclude the compulsory procedures provided for in the LOSC. Separate Opinion of Justice Sir Kenneth Keith, *ibid.*, pp. 1398–1399, paras. 18–22. See also Separate Opinion of Judge Wolfrum in the *MOX Plant* case (provisional measures), (2002) 41 *ILM* p. 427; A. Boyle, 'The Southern Bluefin Tuna Arbitration' (2001) 50 *ICLQ* p. 449.

[22] The *MOX Plant* case (provisional measures), p. 412, paras. 43–44.

[23] *Ibid.*, paras. 49–53.

[24] The *MOX Plant* case, Order No. 3, 24 June 2003. The order is available at: www.pca-cpa.org.

of the Arbitral Tribunal, the question is to be decided within the institutions of the European Community, particularly by the European Court of Justice. Further to this, the European Commission has indicated that it is examining the question whether to institute proceedings under Article 226 of the European Community Treaty. Hence, 'bearing in mind considerations of mutual respect and comity', the Arbitral Tribunal decided that further proceedings on both jurisdiction and the merits in this arbitration would be suspended.[25] Thus the Arbitral Award demonstrated that Article 282 may take effect to prevent recourse to compulsory procedures for dispute settlement.

A related issue may be the interrelationship between the optional clause of the ICJ and Article 282. There appears to be little doubt that the optional clause under Article 36(2) of the Statue of the ICJ is 'a procedure that entails a binding decision' set out in Article 282. It would seem to follow that between two States which have accepted the optional clause, the jurisdiction of the ICJ prevails over procedures under Part XV of the LOSC by virtue of Article 282.[26]

2.3 Voluntary conciliation

Conciliation is a diplomatic means of dispute settlement carried out by a commission composed of conciliators who are independent and impartial. The LOSC contains two types, namely voluntary conciliation and mandatory conciliation. This subsection reviews the voluntary conciliation set out in section 1 of Part XV. In this regard, Article 284(1) provides that:

> A State Party which is a party to a dispute concerning the interpretation or application of this Convention may invite the other party or parties to submit the dispute to conciliation in accordance with the procedure under Annex V, section 1, or another conciliation procedure.

As this is a *voluntary* conciliation, the consent of the disputing parties is a prerequisite to the submission of the dispute to conciliation. Indeed, Article 284(2) and (3) makes clear that:

> 2. If the invitation is accepted and if the parties agree upon the conciliation procedure to be applied, any party may submit the dispute to that procedure.
> 3. If the invitation is not accepted or the parties do not agree upon the procedure, the conciliation proceedings shall be deemed to be terminated.

When a dispute has been submitted to conciliation, the proceedings may be terminated only in accordance with the agreed conciliation procedure, unless the parties otherwise agree pursuant to Article 284(4).

[25] *Ibid*., pp. 7–9, paras. 22–29.
[26] Boyle, 'Problems of Compulsory Jurisdiction', p. 7.

The procedure for voluntary conciliation is embodied in section 1 of Annex V of the LOSC in some detail. In accordance with Article 3 of Annex V, the conciliation commission shall consist of five members. Two conciliators are appointed by each party and a fifth conciliator, who shall be chairperson, is appointed by the parties to the dispute. In case of disagreement between the parties, the UN Secretary-General shall make the necessary appointment.

After examining claims and objections by the parties, the Commission makes proposals to the parties with a view to reaching an amicable settlement pursuant to Article 6 of Annex V. The Commission is required to report within twelve months of its constitution. Its report shall record any agreements reached and, failing agreement, its conclusions on all questions of fact or law relevant to the matter in dispute and recommendations appropriate for an amicable settlement. The report is to be deposited with the UN Secretary-General and shall immediately be transmitted by him to the disputing parties. The report of the Commission shall not be binding upon the parties.[27] The fees and expenses of the Commission are to be borne by the parties to the dispute.[28]

Under Article 8 of Annex V, the conciliation proceedings are terminated when a settlement has been reached, when the parties have accepted or one party has rejected the recommendations of the report by written notification addressed to the UN Secretary-General, or when a period of three months has expired from the date of transmission of the report to the parties. Accordingly, a dispute remains unsettled if one of the disputing parties has rejected the recommendations of the conciliation report. In this case, the dispute is to be transferred to the compulsory procedures for the settlement of dispute.

3 COMPULSORY PROCEDURES FOR DISPUTE SETTLEMENT

3.1 Multiplicity of forums

Where no settlement has been reached by recourse to section 1 of Part XV, subject to section 3, any dispute concerning the interpretation or application of the LOSC shall be submitted at the request of any party to the dispute to the court or tribunal having jurisdiction under section 2.[29] A question then arises as to which court or tribunal has jurisdiction over the dispute.

The negotiations at UNCLOS III revealed disagreements with regard to forums for compulsory procedures. In a broad context, while a good number of developing States supported the creation of a new Tribunal for the Law of the Sea, many European States – apart from France – and some Latin American States were supportive of recourse to the ICJ. For the formerly Socialist States of Eastern Europe and France, 'Special Arbitration' was the only third-party procedure that they found acceptable. In order to achieve a compromise, Article 287 of the LOSC holds the formula for flexibly choosing one or more of the four different forums for compulsory procedures. This is called the

[27] LOSC, Annex V, Article 7. [28] *Ibid.*, Article 9. [29] LOSC, Article 286.

'Montreux formula' because it was suggested by the Working Group's weekend meeting in Montreux at the 1975 Geneva session.[30] The four procedures are:

- ITLOS,
- ICJ,
- an arbitral tribunal constituted in accordance with Annex VII, and
- a special arbitral tribunal constituted in accordance with Annex VIII.

An Arbitral tribunal constituted under Annex VII to the LOSC consists of five members.[31] Arbitrators must be 'persons experienced in maritime affairs', but they need not be lawyers.

A special arbitral tribunal constituted under Annex VIII consists of five members, and they are experts in the particular fields of (1) fisheries, (2) protection and preservation of the marine environment, (3) marine scientific research, and (4) navigation, including pollution from vessels and by dumping. Accordingly, special arbitrators do not need to be lawyers. The jurisdiction of special arbitral tribunals is restricted to disputes in the four particular fields.[32]

Notably, a special arbitral tribunal under Annex VIII is empowered to carry out an inquiry in accordance with the agreement between the parties to a dispute. The findings of fact of such a tribunal are considered to be conclusive as between the parties.[33] The fact-finding of the special arbitral tribunal seems to provide an interesting example of 'binding inquiry'. Furthermore, if all the disputing parties so request, the special arbitral tribunal may formulate non-binding recommendations for a review by the parties of the questions giving rise to the dispute.[34] In this case, arguably, the function of such a tribunal is equivalent to conciliation.

Under Article 287(1), when signing, ratifying or acceding to the LOSC or at any time thereafter, a State is to be free to choose, by means of a written declaration, one or more of these four means for the settlement of disputes concerning the interpretation or application of the Convention.[35] If the parties to a dispute have accepted the same procedure for dispute settlement, it may be submitted only to that procedure, unless the parties otherwise agree under Article 287(4). If no declaration is made, a State Party shall be deemed to have accepted arbitration in accordance with Annex VII.[36] If the disputing parties have not accepted the same procedure for dispute settlement, it may be submitted only to arbitration in accordance with Annex VII, unless the parties otherwise agree pursuant to Article 287(5). In this sense, the Annex VII arbitration

[30] A. O. Adede, *The System of Settlement of Disputes under the United Nations Convention on the Law of the Sea: A Drafting History and a Commentary* (Dordrecht, Nijhoff, 1987), p. 243; by the same writer, 'The Basic Structure of the Dispute Settlement Part of the Law of the Sea Convention' (1982) 11 *ODIL* pp. 130–131.

[31] LOSC, Annex VII, Articles 1 and 3. [32] LOSC, Annex VIII, Articles 1 and 2.

[33] *Ibid.*, Article 5(1) and (2). [34] *Ibid.*, Article 5(3).

[35] An updated list of choice of procedure under Article 287 is available at the website of UNDOALOS: www.un.org/Depts/los/settlement_of_disputes/choice_procedure.htm.

[36] LOSC, Article 287(3).

has residual jurisdiction. Given that many States have made no declarations on the choice of a means of dispute settlement, the role of the Annex VII arbitral tribunal is significant.[37]

Three further points about multiple forums should be noted. First, where a State has chosen more than one forum, collaboration between the disputing States will be needed in order to identify a relevant forum even in the compulsory procedures. For instance, Mexico has chosen ITLOS, the ICJ and a special arbitral tribunal without any order. Portugal has chosen all four forums without any order. If a dispute were raised between the two States, it would be necessary to exchange views to identify a relevant forum in accordance with Article 283(2) of the LOSC.

Second, in the event of a dispute as to whether a court or tribunal has jurisdiction, the matter shall be settled by decision of that court or tribunal pursuant to Article 288(4). In connection with this, Article 294(1) holds that a court or tribunal provided for in Article 287 to which an application is made in respect of a dispute referred to in Article 297 shall determine at the request of a party, or may determine *proprio motu*, whether the claim constitutes an abuse of legal process or whether prima facie it is well founded. If the court or tribunal determines that the claim constitutes an abuse of legal process or is prima facie unfounded, it shall take no further action in the case. This provision seeks to address the concerns expressed by some developing coastal States that they might be exposed to frequent legal actions by shipping States and would have to be involved in costly procedures in international courts and tribunals.[38] Preliminary proceedings must be distinguished from preliminary objections. In fact, Article 294(3) makes clear that nothing in this Article affects the right of any party to a dispute to make preliminary objections in accordance with the applicable rules of procedure.

Third, it is to be noted that even if no declaration is made under Article 287, ITLOS has compulsory jurisdiction over a request for the prompt release of vessels and crews (Article 292) and a request for provisional measures (Article 290(5)), unless the parties otherwise agree.

3.2 Limitations to the compulsory procedures

It is significant that the LOSC creates compulsory procedures for dispute settlement. However, such procedures are subject to two important limitations.

First, under Article 297(2)(a), the coastal State shall not be obliged to accept the submission to such settlement of any dispute arising out of (i) the exercise by the coastal

[37] To date, nine disputes have been submitted to Annex VII arbitration: the *Saiga* case (discontinued 1998); the *Southern Bluefin Tuna* case (2000, Australia and New Zealand v Japan) (jurisdiction and admissibility); the *MOX Plant* case (2003, Ireland v UK) (suspension of proceedings on jurisdiction and merits and request for further provisional measures) (case withdrawn 2008); the *Land Reclamation by Singapore in and around the Straits of Johor* case (Malaysia v Singapore) (case settled 2005); the *Barbados/Trinidad and Tobago* case (2006); the *Guyana/Suriname* case (2007); *Dispute concerning the Maritime Boundary between Bangladesh and Myanmar in the Bay of Bengal* (discontinued 2009); the *Bangladesh/India* case (pending); the *Mauritius/United Kingdom* case (pending).

[38] G. Jaenicke, 'Dispute Settlement under the Convention on the Law of the Sea' (1983) 43 *ZaöRV* p. 817.

State of a right or discretion in accordance with Article 246 relating to marine scientific research in the EEZ and on the continental shelf, or (ii) a decision by the coastal State to order suspension or cessation of a research project in accordance with Article 253.

Second, under Article 297(3)(a), the coastal State shall not be obliged to accept the submission to such settlement of any dispute relating to its sovereign rights with respect to the *living resources* in the EEZ or their exercise, including its discretionary powers for determining the allowable catch, its harvesting capacity, the allocation of surpluses to other States and the terms and conditions established in its conservation and management laws and regulations.

In summary, there is no compulsory dispute settlement for EEZ disputes with regard to the exercise of discretionary powers by the coastal State over fishing and marine scientific research. This limitation reflects the reality that fishing and marine scientific research in the EEZ raise particular sensitivities for the coastal State and the State has wide discretion on these subjects.

However, a dispute concerning the exercise of the coastal State's discretionary powers over marine scientific research in the EEZ is to be submitted, at the request of either party, to compulsory conciliation under Annex V, section 2. Nonetheless, the conciliation commission shall not call in question the exercise by the coastal State of its discretion to designate specific areas as referred to in Article 246(6), or of its discretion to withhold consent in accordance with Article 246(5).[39]

Similarly, where no settlement has been reached by recourse to section 1 of Part XV, namely, non-compulsory procedures, a dispute relating to fisheries excluded from the compulsory settlement procedures shall be submitted to conciliation under Annex V, section 2, at the request of any party to the dispute, when it is alleged that:

(i) a coastal State has manifestly failed to comply with its obligations to ensure through proper conservation and management measures that the maintenance of the living resources in the exclusive economic zone is not seriously endangered;
(ii) a coastal State has arbitrarily refused to determine, at the request of another State, the allowable catch and its capacity to harvest living resources with respect to stocks which that other State is interested in fishing; or
(iii) a coastal State has arbitrarily refused to allocate to any State, under Articles 62, 69 and 70 and under the terms and conditions established by the coastal State consistent with this Convention, the whole or part of the surplus it has declared to exist.[40]

It would follow that fishing disputes which are exempted from the compulsory procedure by Article 297(3)(a) are not automatically submitted to the compulsory conciliation by Article 297(3)(b). Furthermore, the discretionary powers of the coastal State over fishing in the EEZ are safeguarded by Article 297(3)(c), which provides that: 'In no case shall the conciliation commission substitute its discretion for that of the coastal State'.

[39] LOSC, Article 297(2)(b). [40] *Ibid.*, Article 297(3)(b).

It may also be noted that the report of the conciliation commission is not binding upon the disputing parties.[41]

The limitations to the compulsory procedures for dispute settlement raise at least two issues. The first issue pertains to the categorisation of a dispute. Suppose that a dispute was raised with regard to a claim over an EEZ around a disputed island or rock and the exercise of a coastal State's jurisdiction over living resources within this EEZ. If this dispute involves the exercise of sovereign rights with respect to living resources in the EEZ, the dispute will be exempted from the compulsory procedures by virtue of Article 297. If this is a dispute concerning entitlement to an EEZ under Part V and Articles 121(3), it is not excluded from compulsory procedures in the Convention. Thus the scope of compulsory procedures may change according to the formulation of a dispute.[42] In this regard, it should be noted that whether a particular dispute falls within the scope of Article 297 is not a matter to be unilaterally decided by the disputing State, but is an issue for the court or tribunal whose jurisdiction is in question.[43]

The second issue relates to the distinction between disputes susceptible to the compulsory procedures and disputes which are exempted from these procedures. For instance, disputes over high seas fisheries fall within the scope of the compulsory procedures for dispute settlement in the LOSC. As demonstrated in the *Fishery Jurisdiction* dispute between Spain and Canada, however, a fisheries dispute may be raised with regard to fish stocks straddling the EEZ and the high seas. Whilst the question of high seas fisheries is subject to compulsory procedures for dispute settlement, the question of the management of fish stocks in the EEZ does not seem to be susceptible to the compulsory procedures. However, it makes little sense to separate the question concerning high seas fisheries from the management of fish stocks in the adjacent EEZ.[44]

3.3 Optional exceptions to the compulsory procedures

Compulsory procedures for dispute settlement under the LOSC may also be qualified by optional exceptions set out in Article 298. Article 298(1) holds that when signing, ratifying or acceding to this Convention or at any time thereafter, a State may declare in writing that it does not accept any one or more of the compulsory procedures with respect to one or more of the following categories of disputes:[45]

- disputes concerning the interpretation or application of Articles 15, 74 and 83 relating to maritime delimitations or those involving historic bays or title,

[41] LOSC, Annex V, Articles 7(2) and 14.

[42] A. Boyle, 'Dispute Settlement and the Law of the Sea Convention: Problems of Fragmentation and Jurisdiction' (1997) 46 *ICLQ* pp. 44–45.

[43] LOSC, Articles 288(4) and 294.

[44] Boyle, 'Dispute Settlement', p. 43.

[45] Actually ten States declared that they do not accept the compulsory procedures for dispute settlement with respect to all three categories of disputes in conformity with Article 298 of the LOSC. These States are: Argentina, Canada, Chile, China, France, Nicaragua, Portugal, Republic of Korea, Russian Federation and Tunisia. Declaration under Article 298 of the LOSC is available at: www.un.org/Depts/los/settlement_of_disputes/choice_procedure.htm.

- disputes concerning military activities and disputes concerning law enforcement activities in regard to the exercise of sovereign rights or jurisdiction excluded from the jurisdiction of a court or tribunal under Article 297(2) or (3),
- disputes in respect of which the UN Security Council is exercising the functions assigned to it by the UN Charter, unless the Security Council decides to remove the matter from its agenda or calls upon the parties to settle it by the means provided for in the LOSC.

Under Article 298(4), a State Party which has made a declaration under paragraph 1 shall not be entitled to submit any dispute falling within the excepted category of disputes to any procedure in this Convention as against another State Party, without the consent of that Party. Declarations and notices of withdrawal of declarations under Article 298 shall be deposited with the Secretary-General of the United Nations in accordance with Article 298(6). A new declaration, or the withdrawal of a declaration, does not in any way affect proceedings pending before a court or tribunal in accordance with Article 298, unless the parties otherwise agree, by virtue of paragraph 5.

Whilst maritime delimitation disputes or those involving historic bays or title may be exempted from the compulsory procedures entailing binding decisions, they are subject to the compulsory conciliation under section 2, Annex V to the LOSC, where no agreement is reached in negotiations between the parties. But any dispute that necessarily involves the concurrent consideration of any unsettled dispute concerning sovereignty or other rights over continental or insular land territory shall be excluded from such submission.[46] The parties shall negotiate an agreement on the basis of the report of the conciliation commission. If these negotiations do not result in an agreement, the parties shall, by mutual consent, submit the question to one of the compulsory procedures provided for in section 2 of Part XV, unless the parties otherwise agree.[47] However, this subparagraph does not apply to any sea boundary dispute finally settled by an arrangement between the parties, or to any such dispute which is to be settled in accordance with a bilateral or multilateral agreement binding upon those parties.[48]

Concerning exceptions to compulsory procedures, two further points should be noted. First, as Article 299 provides, the disputing parties may submit a dispute in an excluded category to the compulsory procedures by agreement. It would follow that the effect of Articles 297 and 298 is to prevent the unilateral submission of a dispute in an excluded category to the compulsory procedures.

Second, where a dispute is submitted to the ICJ, the scope of the Court's jurisdiction may change according to the mode of referral of the dispute. For example, where a dispute is submitted in accordance with the compulsory procedures in the LOSC, the Court's jurisdiction is subject to the limitations and exceptions set out in Articles 297 and 298. However, if a party to a dispute submits the dispute to the ICJ on the basis of the optional clause, the scope of the Court's jurisdiction is subject to

[46] LOSC, Article 298(1)(a)(i). [47] *Ibid.*, Article 298(1)(a)(ii).
[48] *Ibid.*, Article 298(1)(a)(iii).

reservations to the clause. Provided that the disputing parties accept the optional clause of the ICJ and no reservation involving fisheries disputes is made to that clause, for example, it seems that a dispute relating to fishing in the EEZ is subject to the ICJ's jurisdiction. In this case, the procedure of the ICJ is to apply in lieu of the procedures provided for in Part XV of the LOSC by virtue of Article 282.[49]

4 THE INTERNATIONAL TRIBUNAL FOR THE LAW OF THE SEA (1): ORGANISATION

4.1 Members of ITLOS

ITLOS is a permanent judicial body established in accordance with Annex VI to the LOSC (hereafter the ITLOS Statute).[50] Whilst the ICJ is the principal judicial organ of the United Nations,[51] ITLOS is not an organ of the United Nations.[52] Indeed, the expenses of ITLOS are to be borne by the States Parties and by the Authority rather than the UN.[53] The seat of ITLOS is in the Free and Hanseatic City of Hamburg in the Federal Republic of Germany.[54] Like the ICJ, the official languages of ITLOS are English and French.[55] The official inauguration of ITLOS took place on 18 October 1996. As summarised in Table 13.1, to date, nineteen cases have been submitted to ITLOS.

ITLOS is a body composed of twenty-one independent members, elected from among persons enjoying the highest reputation for fairness and integrity and of recognised competence in the field of the law of the sea. The representation of the principal legal systems of the world and equitable geographical distribution shall be assured.[56] No two members of ITLOS may be nationals of the same State.[57] There shall be no fewer than three members from each geographical group as established by the UN General Assembly. The geographical distribution was decided by the fifth Meeting of States Parties in 1996 and was rearranged by the nineteenth Meeting in 2009 (SPLOS/201 of 26 June 2009). Whilst the numbers of judges from African, Asian and Western European and other States Groups may vary, the current composition of ITLOS is summarised in Table 13.2.

The procedure for electing the members of ITLOS is provided in Article 4 of the ITLOS Statute. Each State Party may nominate not more than two persons having the qualifications prescribed in Article 2 of this Statute. The members of ITLOS are to be elected from the list of persons thus nominated. Elections are to be held at a meeting of the States Parties to the LOSC, and the members of ITLOS are to be elected by secret ballot. The persons elected to ITLOS shall be those nominees who obtain the largest

[49] Boyle, 'Problems of Compulsory Jurisdiction', p. 7.
[50] LOSC, Article 287(1)(a).
[51] Article 92 of the UN Charter; ICJ Statute, Article 1.
[52] The general relations between ITLOS and the United Nations are regulated by the 1997 Agreement on Co-operation and Relationship between the United Nations and the International Tribunal for the Law of the Sea. Entered into force on 8 September 1998. The text is available at:www.itlos.org/start2_en.html.
[53] ITLOS Statute, Article 19. [54] *Ibid.*, Article 1(1).
[55] Article 43 of the Rules of the International Tribunal for the Law of the Sea (hereafter ITLOS Rules).
[56] ITLOS Statute, Article 2. [57] *Ibid.*, Article 3.

TABLE 13.1. LIST OF CASES BEFORE ITLOS

Case Number	Year of decision	Case
Case No. 1	1997	The M/V 'Saiga' Case (Saint Vincent and the Grenadines v Guinea), Prompt Release
Case No. 2	1998	The M/V 'Saiga' (No. 2) Case (Saint Vincent and the Grenadines v Guinea), Provisional Measures
	1999	Merits
Case Nos. 3, 4	1999	Southern Bluefin Tuna Cases (New Zealand v Japan; Australia v Japan), Provisional Measures
Case No. 5	2000	The 'Camouco' Case (Panama v France), Prompt Release
Case No. 6	2000	The 'Monte Confurco' Case (Seychelles v France), Prompt Release
Case No. 7		Case Concerning the Conservation and Sustainable Exploitation of Swordfish Stocks in the South-Eastern Pacific Ocean (Chile v European Community), Proceedings discontinued
Case No. 8	2001	The 'Grand Prince' Case (Belize v France), Prompt Release
Case No. 9		The 'Chaisiri Reefer 2' Case (Panama v Yemen), Prompt Release, Proceedings discontinued
Case No. 10	2001	The MOX Plant Case (Ireland v United Kingdom), Provisional Measures
Case No. 11	2002	The 'Volga' Case (Russian Federation v Australia), Prompt Release
Case No. 12	2003	Case Concerning Land Reclamation by Singapore in and around the Straits of Johor (Malaysia v Singapore), Provisional Measures
Case No. 13	2004	The 'Juno Trader' Case (Saint Vincent and the Grenadines v Guinea-Bissau), Prompt Release
Case No. 14	2007	The 'Hoshinmaru' Case (Japan v Russian Federation), Prompt Release
Case No. 15	2007	The 'Tomimaru' Case (Japan v Russian Federation), Prompt Release
Case No. 16		Case Concerning Delimitation of the Maritime Boundary between Bangladesh and Myanmar in the Bay of Bengal, Merits (pending)
Case No. 17	2010	Responsibility and Obligations of States Sponsoring Persons and Entities with respect to Activities in the International Seabed Area, Advisory Opinion
Case No. 18	2010	The M/V 'Louisa' Case (Saint Vincent and the Grenadines v Spain), Provisional Measures
Case No. 19		The M/V 'Virginia G' Case (Panama v Guinea-Bissau, pending)

number of votes and a two-thirds majority of the States Parties present and voting, provided that such majority includes a majority of the States Parties.[58]

The members of ITLOS are elected for nine years and may be re-elected.[59] The President and the Vice-President are elected for three years and they may be re-elected.[60] Article 7(1) of the ITLOS Statute sets out the status of judges of ITLOS as follows:

[58] The first election took place on 1 August 1996. For an examination in more detail of elections to ITLOS, see G. Eiriksson, *The International Tribunal for the Law of the Sea* (The Hague, Nijhoff, 2000), pp. 33 *et seq*.

[59] ITLOS Statute, Article 5(1). [60] *Ibid*, Article 12.

TABLE 13.2. CURRENT GEOGRAPHICAL DISTRIBUTION OF THE MEMBERS OF ITLOS AND THE ICJ

	ITLOS	ICJ
Africa	5	3
Asia	5	3
Latin America and Caribbean States	4	2
Western European and other States	4	5
Eastern Europe	3	2
Total	21	15

No member of the Tribunal may exercise any political or administrative function, or associate actively with or be financially interested in any of the operations of any enterprise concerned with the exploration for or exploitation of the resources of the sea or the seabed or other commercial use of the sea or the seabed.

This paragraph appears to signify that the members of ITLOS may engage in any other function which is not prohibited by provision. This point represents a sharp contrast to Article 16(1) of the ICJ Statute, which forbids members of the Court to 'exercise any political or administrative function, or engage in any other occupation of a professional nature'.

The difference in status between the members of ITLOS and those of the ICJ is also reflected in their remuneration. Whilst each member of the ICJ receives 'an annual salary' under Article 32(1) of the Statute of the Court, the members of ITLOS receive 'an annual allowance' and, for each day on which he exercises his functions, 'a special allowance' in accordance with Article 18(1) of the ITLOS Statute. This system seems to suggest that members of ITLOS are not expected to be engaged on a full-time basis on the work of ITLOS, and judges are assumed to have some other sources of income.[61]

When engaged on the business of ITLOS, its members are to enjoy diplomatic privileges and immunities by virtue of Article 10 of the ITLOS Statute. These privileges and immunities are defined in the 1997 Agreement on the Privileges and Immunities of ITLOS.[62]

Members of ITLOS of the nationality of any of the parties to a dispute shall retain their right to participate as members of the Tribunal. As with the ICJ, a judge ad hoc may be appointed by a party or parties to a dispute currently unrepresented in accordance with Article 17(2) and (3) of the ITLOS Statute. The provisions concerning national

[61] Eiriksson, *The International Tribunal*, p. 103.

[62] Entered into force on 30 December 2001. The text of the 1997 Agreement is available at: www.itlos.org/fileadmin/itlos/documents/basic_texts/agr_priv_imm_en.pdf.

judges and judges ad hoc apply to the Seabed Disputes Chamber and Special Chambers by virtue of Article 17(4) of the Statute. Judges ad hoc shall fulfil the conditions required by Articles 2 (composition), 8 (conditions to participate in a particular case) and 11 (solemn declaration) of the ITLOS Statute.[63]

4.2 The Seabed Disputes Chamber

A Seabed Disputes Chamber was established on 20 February 1997 in accordance with section 5, Part XI of the LOSC and Article 14 of the ITLOS Statute. The Seabed Disputes Chamber is composed of eleven members, selected by a majority of the elected members of ITLOS from among them for a three-year term and may be selected for a second term.[64] As stated in Article 35(2) of the Statute, the representation of the principal legal systems of the world and equitable geographical distribution must be assured in electing the Chamber.

The Chamber is empowered to form an ad hoc chamber which is composed of three members in order to deal with particular disputes submitted to it under Article 188(b) of the LOSC. The establishment of this 'chamber of a chamber' can be considered as a result of compromise between States which supported the Seabed Disputes Chamber as appropriate for dealing with disputes relating to Part XI of the LOSC and those which would have preferred arbitration. The composition of the ad hoc chamber is to be determined by the Seabed Disputes Chamber 'with the approval of the parties'.[65]

If the parties do not agree on the composition of an ad hoc chamber, each party to the dispute is to appoint one member, and the third member is to be appointed by them in agreement. If they disagree, or if any party fails to make an appointment, the President of the Seabed Disputes Chamber shall promptly make the appointment or appointments from among its members, 'after consultation with the parties'.[66] By emphasising the consent of the parties in the composition of the ad hoc chamber, some argue that this chamber is akin to a sort of 'arbitration within the Tribunal'.[67] However, it is to be remembered that the members of the ad hoc chamber must not be in the service of, or nationals of, any of the parties to the dispute pursuant to Article 36(3) of the ITLOS Statute.

As provided in Article 187 of the LOSC, the Seabed Disputes Chamber has jurisdiction over disputes with regard to activities in the Area. Specifically the Seabed Disputes Chamber exercises jurisdiction over disputes (i) between States, (ii) between a State and the Authority, (iii) between the parties to a contract, including States, a State enterprise, the Authority or the Enterprise, and natural or juridical persons, and (iv) between the Authority and a prospective contractor. It is of particular interest to note

[63] ITLOS Statute, Article 17(6). [64] *Ibid.*, Article 35(1) and (3).
[65] *Ibid.*, Article 36(1).
[66] *Ibid.*, Article 36(2).
[67] R. Wolfrum, 'The Settlement of Disputes before the International Tribunal for the Law of the Sea: A Progressive Development of International Law or Relying on Traditional Mechanisms?' (2008) 51 *Japanese Yearbook of International Law* pp. 161–162.

that the Seabed Disputes Chamber is open to entities other than States, such as the Authority or the Enterprise, State enterprises and natural or juridical persons.[68]

However, the Seabed Disputes Chamber has no jurisdiction with regard to the exercise by the Authority of its discretionary powers. In no case shall it substitute its discretion for that of the Authority. Furthermore, the Chamber is not allowed to pronounce on the question of whether any rules and regulations of the Authority are in conformity with the LOSC, nor declare invalid any such rules and regulations.[69] A judgment given by the Seabed Disputes Chamber is considered to be rendered by ITLOS.[70] The decisions of the Chamber shall be enforceable in the territories of the States Parties in the same manner as judgments or orders of the highest court of the State Party in whose territory the enforcement is sought by virtue of Article 39 of the ITLOS Statute. Furthermore, as will be seen, the Chamber also has jurisdiction to give advisory opinions.[71]

4.3 Special chambers

ITLOS may form three types of special chamber in accordance with Article 15 of the ITLOS Statute. Ad hoc judges may be appointed in special chambers pursuant to Article 17(4) of the Statute. A judgment given by any of the chambers is considered to be rendered by ITLOS under Article 15(5) of the Statute.

(i) Chamber dealing with particular categories of disputes: on the model of Article 26(1) of the ICJ Statute, Article 15(1) of the ITLOS Statute merely provides that ITLOS may form this type of chamber, composed of three or more of its selected members. In this case, it shall determine the particular category of disputes for which it is formed, the number of its members, the period for which they will serve, the date when they will enter upon their duties and the quorum for meetings. The members of the chamber are selected by ITLOS upon the proposal of its President from among the members, having regard to any special knowledge, experience or previous experience in relation to the category of disputes the chamber deals with.[72] Accordingly, the expertise of members is secured in this type of chamber.

In 1997, ITLOS formed two chambers of this type, namely, the Chamber for Fisheries Disputes, composed of seven members, and the Chamber for Marine Environment Disputes, which is also composed of seven members. In 2007, the Chamber for Maritime Delimitation Disputes, composed of eight members, was established.

(ii) Chamber dealing with a particular dispute: this chamber is known as an ad hoc chamber. On the model of Article 26(2) of the ICJ Statute, Article 15(2) of the ITLOS Statute obliges ITLOS to form the chamber if the parties so request. The composition of an ad hoc chamber is determined by ITLOS with the approval of the parties. A request for the formation of an ad hoc chamber must be made within two months from the date

[68] See ITLOS Statute, Article 37. [69] LOSC, Article 189.
[70] ITLOS Statute, Article 15(5). [71] See section 5.6. of this chapter.
[72] ITLOS Rules, Article 29.

of the institution of proceedings.[73] The ad hoc chamber was formed in the *Swordfish Stocks* case between Chile and the European Community in 2000.

(iii) Chamber of Summary Procedure: the establishment of this chamber is mandatory and it is formed annually with a view to the speedy dispatch of business.[74] It is composed of the President and the Vice-President of ITLOS, acting *ex officio*, and three other members. In addition, two members are to be selected to act as alternates. The members and alternates of the chamber are to be selected by ITLOS upon the proposal of its President.[75] The Chamber of Summary Procedure can deal with applications for prompt release if the applicant has so requested in the application.[76]

5 THE INTERNATIONAL TRIBUNAL FOR THE LAW OF THE SEA (2): PROCEDURE

5.1 Jurisdiction of ITLOS

The jurisdiction of ITLOS is provided in Article 288 of the LOSC and Articles 21 and 22 of the Statute. Concerning jurisdiction *ratione materiae*, Article 288 holds that ITLOS has jurisdiction over any dispute concerning the interpretation and application of the LOSC, which is submitted to it in accordance with Part XV. It also has jurisdiction over any dispute concerning the interpretation and application of an international agreement related to the purposes of the LOSC, which is submitted to it in accordance with the agreement. Furthermore, ITLOS has jurisdiction over all disputes and all applications submitted to it in accordance with the LOSC and all matters specifically provided for in any other agreement which confers jurisdiction on the Tribunal.[77] If all the parties to a treaty or convention already in force and concerning the subject matter covered by the LOSC so agree, any disputes concerning the interpretation or application of such treaty or convention may, in accordance with such agreement, be submitted to ITLOS.[78]

With regard to jurisdiction *ratione personae*, ITLOS is open to States Parties to the LOSC. It is also open to entities other than States Parties, but only as specifically provided for in the Convention.[79] In this regard, Article 20(2) of the ITLOS Statute holds that the Tribunal shall be open to entities other than States Parties in any case expressly provided for in Part XI or in any case submitted pursuant to any other agreement conferring jurisdiction on the Tribunal which is accepted by all the parties to that case. In fact, Article 37 of the ITLOS Statute makes clear that the Seabed Disputes Chamber is to be open to the States Parties, the Authority and the other entities referred to in Part XI, Section 5. Such entities would comprise the Enterprise, State enterprises and natural or juridical persons.[80] To this extent, ITLOS seems to open up the possibility of potential parties other than States coming before the Tribunal.[81]

[73] *Ibid.*, Article 30(1). [74] ITLOS Statute, Article 15(3). [75] ITLOS Rules, Article 28.
[76] *Ibid.*, Article 112. [77] ITLOS Statute, Article 21. [78] *Ibid.*, Article 22.
[79] LOSC, Article 291. [80] *Ibid.*, Article 187.
[81] Wolfrum, 'The Settlement of Disputes', pp. 143–145; Eiriksson, *The International Tribunal*, p. 115.

5.2 Applicable law

The applicable law of ITLOS consists of the LOSC and other rules of international law not incompatible with this Convention. ITLOS may also decide a case *ex aequo et bono* if the parties so agree.[82] Furthermore, the Seabed Disputes Chamber shall apply the rules, regulations and procedures of the Authority and the terms of contracts concerning activities in the Area in accordance with Article 38 of the ITLOS Statute.

5.3 Proceedings before ITLOS

As stated in Article 24 of the ITLOS Statute, disputes are submitted to ITLOS either by notification of a special agreement or by written application, addressed to the Registrar. In either case, the subject of the dispute and the parties shall be indicated.

Article 54(2) of the ITLOS Rules requires that the application shall specify as far as possible the legal grounds upon which the jurisdiction of ITLOS is said to be based; it shall also specify the precise nature of the claim, together with a succinct statement of the facts and grounds on which the claim is based. In relation to this, Article 295 stipulates that any dispute between States Parties concerning the interpretation or application of the LOSC may be submitted to the compulsory procedures provided for in section 2, Part XV of the Convention only after local remedies have been exhausted where this is required by international law. The applicability of the exhaustion of local remedies was at issue in the *M/V Saiga (No. 2)* case, where Guinea objected to the admissibility of the case because Saint Vincent and the Grenadines had failed to exhaust local remedies available in Guinea. However, ITLOS held that the rule on the exhaustion of local remedies did not apply because the claims advanced by Saint Vincent and the Grenadines all involved direct violations of the rights of that State.[83]

5.4 Incidental proceedings

(a) Preliminary objections

As stated in Article 288(4) of the LOSC, in the event of a dispute as to whether a court or tribunal has jurisdiction, the matter is to be settled by the decision of that court or tribunal. The procedure for preliminary objections is amplified by Article 97 of the ITLOS Rules. Under Article 97(1), any objection to ITLOS's jurisdiction or to the admissibility of the application, or other objection the decision upon which is requested before any further proceedings on the merits, must be made in writing within ninety days from the institution of proceedings. The preliminary objection must set out the facts and the law on which the objection is based, as well as the submissions in accordance with Article 97(2). As provided in Article 97(3), the submission of the preliminary objection suspends the proceedings on the merits. Finally, Article 97(6) makes clear that ITLOS gives its decision in the form of a judgment.

[82] LOSC, Article 293.

[83] The *M/V Saiga (No. 2)* case, (1999) 38 *ILM* pp. 1344–1346, paras. 89–102.

(b) Provisional measures

In order to ensure the effectiveness of the court judgment, it is necessary to prevent either or both parties from aggravating the situation and to preserve the respective rights of the disputing parties pending the final decision of the court. Article 290(1) thus provides as follows:

> If a dispute has been duly submitted to a court or tribunal which considers that *prima facie* it has jurisdiction under this Part or Part XI, section 5, the court or tribunal may prescribe any provisional measures which it considers appropriate under the circumstances to preserve the respective rights of the parties to the dispute or to prevent serious harm to the marine environment, pending the final decision.

Article 25(1) of the ITLOS Statute makes clear that ITLOS and its Seabed Disputes Chamber are empowered to prescribe provisional measures in accordance with Article 290. As stated in Article 25(2) of the Statute, the Chamber of Summary Procedure shall prescribe provisional measures if ITLOS is not in session or a sufficient number of members are not available to constitute a quorum. Such provisional measures are subject to review or revision of ITLOS at the written request of a party within fifteen days of the prescription of the measures. ITLOS may also at any time decide *proprio motu* to review or revise the measures.[84] While there is no explicit provision in the ITLOS Statute, special chambers dealing with a particular category of disputes or a particular dispute may also prescribe provisional measures since such chambers act as an organ of ITLOS.[85]

Furthermore, under Article 290(5), ITLOS or, with respect to activities in the Area, the Seabed Disputes Chamber, has residual jurisdiction to prescribe provisional measures concerning a dispute that has been submitted to an arbitral tribunal, provided that two conditions are satisfied.[86] First, a request for provisional measures has been communicated by one of the disputing parties to the other party or parties, and they could not agree, within a period of two weeks after the request was made, on a court or tribunal to which the request has been submitted. Second, ITLOS concludes that prima facie the arbitral tribunal to which the dispute is being submitted on the merits would have jurisdiction over the merits of the dispute.

Article 290 requires three brief observations. First, Article 290(1) states that the court or tribunal may 'prescribe' provisional measures, whereas Article 41(1) of the Statute of the ICJ uses the term 'indicate'. Further to this, Article 290(6) makes clear that: 'The parties to the dispute shall comply promptly with any provisional measures prescribed under this article'. These provisions signify that provisional measures prescribed by ITLOS are binding upon the disputing parties.[87] In relation to this, Article

[84] ITLOS Rules, Article 91(2).

[85] Wolfrum, 'The Settlement of Disputes', p. 153.

[86] T. A. Mensah, 'Provisional Measures in the International Law of the Sea (ITLOS)' (2002) 62 *ZaöRV* p. 46.

[87] However, the legal effects of provisional measures indicated by the ICJ have been the subject of extensive controversy in the literature. The ICJ, in the *LaGran* case of 2001, ended the

95(1) of the ITLOS Rules obliges each party to inform ITLOS as soon as possible as to its compliance with any provisional measures the tribunal has prescribed.

Second, concerning the duration of the effect of provisional measures, Article 290(5) provides that, once constituted, the arbitral tribunal to which the dispute has been submitted may modify, revoke or affirm those provisional measures. It follows that where a dispute has been submitted to an arbitral tribunal, the provisional measures are to be binding pending a decision of the arbitral tribunal.[88] Where ITLOS considers a request for provisional measures under Article 290(1), these measures will be in force pending its own final decision.

Third, unlike Article 41(1) of the ICJ Statute, Article 290(1) refers to the prevention of 'serious harm to the marine environment'. Reference to marine environmental protection, which is not directly linked to the interests of the disputing parties, as a justification for provisional measures appears to highlight the importance of marine environmental protection as a community interest.[89]

In order to prescribe provisional measures under the LOSC, the following conditions must be satisfied.

(i) Request for provisional measures: Article 290(3) holds that provisional measures may be prescribed, modified or revoked under this Article only at the request of a party to the dispute and after the parties have been given an opportunity to be heard.[90] Thus there must be a request from a disputing party to prescribe provisional measures. Unlike the ICJ,[91] ITLOS does not possess the power to prescribe provisional measures *proprio motu*.

(ii) Prima facie jurisdiction: Article 290(1) makes clear that it is necessary that the court or tribunal seised of a request for provisional measures has, prima facie, i.e. presumptively, jurisdiction under Part XV or Part XI, Section 5 of the LOSC. This is a key requirement in the prescription of provisional measures. In this regard, two cases must be distinguished.

First, where a dispute has been submitted to ITLOS and a party to the dispute requests the tribunal to prescribe provisional measures, ITLOS has to verify its own prima facie jurisdiction.

Second, as explained earlier, pending the constitution of an arbitral tribunal, ITLOS or, with respect to activities in the Area, the Seabed Disputes Chamber, may prescribe provisional measures in accordance with Article 290(5). In this case, ITLOS or the Seabed Disputes Chamber is required to determine whether the arbitral tribunal to which a dispute is being submitted would have prima facie jurisdiction.

long debate in this matter by accepting the binding force of provisional measures. ICJ Reports 2001, p. 503, para. 102.

88 In fact, ITLOS, in the *Southern Bluefin Tuna* cases, clearly stated that it prescribed the provisional measures 'pending a decision of the arbitral tribunal'. The *Southern Bluefin Tuna* cases, p. 1635, para. 90. According to Judge Treves, this expression should be read as meaning up to the moment in which a judgment on the merits has been rendered. Separate Opinion of Judge Treves, *ibid.*, p. 1644, para. 4. See also the *MOX Plant* case, p. 416, para. 89.

89 Wolfrum, 'The Settlement of Disputes', p. 155.

90 See also ITLOS Statute, Article 25(2).

91 Rules of the ICJ, Article 75(1).

(iii) Urgency: Urgency is an essential requirement of the prescription of provisional measures.[92] Article 290(5) clarifies this condition, by providing that 'the urgency of situation so requires'. Article 89(4) of the ITLOS Rules also requires that a request for the prescription of provisional measures must indicate 'the urgency of the situation'. Where a dispute has been submitted to ITLOS, it is to examine the question whether urgency exists pending its own final decision. Where a dispute has been submitted to an arbitral tribunal, ITLOS is required to determine whether the urgency of the situation requires provisional measures pending the constitution of the arbitral tribunal (Article 290(5)).[93]

The case law of the ICJ appears to show that the situation of urgency is closely linked to a risk of irreparable damage to rights of one or other of the parties.[94] In the 2001 *MOX Plant* case, ITLOS also ruled that provisional measures may be prescribed 'if the Tribunal considered that the urgency of the situation so requires in the sense that action prejudicial to the rights of either party or causing serious harm to the marine environment is likely to be taken before the constitution of the Annex VII arbitral tribunal'.[95] ITLOS took a similar approach in the *Malaysia/Singapore* case of 2003.[96] ITLOS, in the 2010 *M/V Louisa* case between Saint Vincent and the Grenadines and Spain, focused on the question of whether or not there existed a real and imminent risk that irreparable prejudice would be caused to the rights of the parties, without directly referring to urgency.[97]

Interestingly, in some cases, ITLOS has ordered provisional measures even where there was no situation of urgency. In the *MOX Plant* case, for instance, ITLOS did not find that the urgency of the situation required the prescription of the provisional measures requested by Ireland.[98] Nonetheless, ITLOS ordered provisional measures. Likewise, ITLOS, in the *Land Reclamation* case, prescribed provisional measures, while finding that there was no situation of urgency.[99]

(iv) Interlinkage between provisional measures and the application made: As the prescription of provisional measures is intended to preserve rights that are in dispute, such measures must be ancillary to the main claim. Accordingly, provisional measures cannot be used to deal with issues which are not the subject of the main dispute and must not go beyond what is required to preserve the parties' respective rights in relation to the case.

ITLOS may prescribe provisional measures different in whole or in part from those requested. This is clear from Article 89(5) of the ITLOS Rules. In fact, it exercised

[92] Separate Opinion of Judge Treves in the *Southern Bluefin Tuna* cases (provisional measures), (1999) 38 *ILM*, p. 1644, para. 2.
[93] *Ibid.*, paras. 3–4.
[94] See for instance, the *Belgium/Senegal* case, Provisional Measures, Order of 28 May 2009, ICJ Reports 2009, p. 152, para. 62.
[95] The *MOX Plant* case, (2002) 41 *ILM*, p. 414, para. 64.
[96] *Case Concerning Land Declamation by Singapore in and around the Straits of Johor* (request for provisional measures, electronic text), 8 October 2003, Case No. 12, para. 72.
[97] The *M/V 'Louisa'* case (request for Provisional Measures), Order of 23 December 2010, p. 15, para. 72.
[98] The *MOX Plant* case, p. 415, para. 81.
[99] *Case Concerning Land Reclamation by Singapore in and around the Straits of Johor*, p. 16, para. 72.

this power in the *M/V Saiga (No. 2)*, *Southern Bluefin Tuna*, *MOX Plant* and *Land Reclamation* cases. It must also be noted that provisional measures should not be an interim judgment concerning the application made.

(c) Intervention

The ITLOS Statute provides two types of third party intervention. First, Article 31 of the Statute deals with requests to intervene. Article 31(1) provides that a State Party to the LOSC that has an interest of a legal nature which may be affected by the decision in any dispute, may submit a request to ITLOS to be permitted to intervene. If a request to intervene is granted, the decision of ITLOS in respect of the dispute is binding upon the intervening State Party in so far as it relates to matters in respect of which that State Party intervened.[100]

Second, Article 32 provides a right to intervene in the case of interpretation or application of the LOSC as well as other international agreements. Under Article 32(1), wherever the interpretation and application of the LOSC are in question, the Registrar notifies all States Parties forthwith. Furthermore, whenever the interpretation or application of an international agreement is in question, the Registrar also notifies all the parties to the agreement pursuant to Article 32(2). In this case, every party has the right to intervene in the proceedings. If it uses this right, the interpretation given by the judgment will be equally binding upon it (Article 32(3)).[101]

5.5 Judgment

All questions must be decided by a majority of the members of ITLOS. In the event of an equality of votes, the President or the member of ITLOS who acts in his place shall have a casting vote.[102] Like the ICJ, any member shall be entitled to deliver a separate opinion.[103] Article 33 of the ITLOS Statute holds that the decision of ITLOS is final and shall be complied with by all the parties to the dispute. The decision shall have no binding force except between the parties in respect of that particular case.[104] Unless otherwise decided by ITLOS, each party shall bear its own costs.[105]

Unlike the ICJ,[106] there is no procedure to ensure the implementation of a judgment of ITLOS. On the other hand, the LOSC contains provisions with regard to measures to be taken to implement a decision by the Seabed Disputes Chamber. Where the Council of the Authority institutes proceedings on behalf of the Authority before the Seabed Disputes Chamber, the Legal and Technical Commission of the Authority is entitled to make recommendations to the Council with respect to measures to be taken upon a decision by the Seabed Disputes Chamber (Article 165(2)(j)). Pursuant to Article 162(2)(v),

100 ITLOS Statute, Article 31(3). See also ITLOS Rules, Article 99.

101 See also, *ibid.*, Article 100.

102 ITLOS Statute, Article 29.

103 *Ibid.*, Article 30(3).

104 See also LOSC, Article 296.

105 ITLOS Statute, Article 34. In order to assist developing States which are parties to a dispute before ITLOS, the International Tribunal for the Law of the Sea Trust Fund was established in 2000. The terms of reference of the Fund are annexed to UN General Assembly Resolution 55/7 of 30 October 2000 (Annex I).

106 Article 94 of the UN Charter.

the Council is to notify the Assembly upon a decision by the Seabed Disputes Chamber and make any recommendations which it may find appropriate with respect to measures to be taken. Furthermore, as noted, Article 39 of the ITLOS Statute requires that the decisions of the Chamber shall be enforceable in the territories of the States Parties in the same manner as judgments or orders of the highest court of the State Party in whose territory the enforcement is sought.

Article 33(3) of the ITLOS Statute stipulates that in the event of dispute as to the meaning or scope of *the decision*, ITLOS shall construe it upon the request of any party. Whilst the term 'the decision' appears to include both a judgment and an order, Article 126 of the ITLOS Rules makes clear that in the event of dispute as to the meaning or scope of *a judgment*, any party may make a request for its interpretation.

Article 127 of the ITLOS Rules provides for revision of the judgment. Under this provision, a request for revision of a judgment may be made only when it is based upon the discovery of some fact of such a nature as to be a decisive factor, which fact was unknown to ITLOS and also to the party requesting revision when the judgment was given. However, such ignorance must not be due to negligence. Such request must be made at the latest within six months of the discovery of the new fact and before the lapse of ten years from the date of the judgment.

5.6 Advisory Proceedings

Like the ICJ, ITLOS is empowered to give advisory opinions. The advisory jurisdiction is exercised by the Seabed Disputes Chamber as well as the ITLOS full court.

(a) The advisory jurisdiction of the Seabed Disputes Chamber

The Assembly and the Council of the Authority are empowered to request an advisory opinion from the Seabed Disputes Chamber. This means that the advisory jurisdiction is connected with the activities of the two principal organs of the Authority. The underlying reason for the advisory jurisdiction of the Chamber is that the Authority may require the assistance of an independent and impartial judicial body in order to exercise its function properly.[107]

Article 159(10) holds that upon a written request addressed to the President and sponsored by at least one-fourth of the members of the Authority for an advisory opinion on the conformity with ITLOS of a proposal before the Assembly on any matter, the Assembly is to request the Seabed Disputes Chamber to give an advisory opinion. The Council of the Authority is also allowed to request an advisory opinion from the Seabed Disputes Chamber.[108]

The key provision in relation to the advisory jurisdiction of the Chamber is Article 191 of the LOSC:

[107] *Responsibilities and Obligations of States Sponsoring Persons and Entities with Respect to Activities in the Area* (electronic text), Case No. 17, 1 February 2011, p. 14, para. 26.

[108] LOSC, Article 191.

> The Seabed Disputes Chamber shall give advisory opinions at the request of the Assembly or the Council on legal questions arising within the scope of their activities. Such opinions shall be given as a matter of urgency.

This provision contains three conditions for the giving of give an advisory opinion:

(i) There is a request from the Assembly or Council,
(ii) The request concerns legal questions, and
(iii) These legal questions have arisen within the scope of the Assembly's or Council's activities.

Where these conditions are met, the Seabed Disputes Chamber is obliged to give an advisory opinion. Unlike Article 65(1) of the ICJ Statute which states that the Court 'may give' an advisory opinion, Article 191 provides that the Chamber 'shall give' advisory opinions. In light of this difference, some argue that once the Chamber has established its jurisdiction, the Chamber has no discretion to decline a request for an advisory opinion. Yet the Chamber, in its first advisory opinion of 2011, did not pronounce on the consequences of that difference.[109]

In the exercise of its functions relating to advisory opinions, the Seabed Disputes Chamber shall consider whether the request for an advisory opinion relates to a legal question pending between two or more parties. When the Chamber so determines, Article 17 of the ITLOS Statute applies, as well as the provisions of the ITLOS Rules concerning the application of that Article.[110] Any judge may attach a separate or dissenting opinion to the advisory opinion of the Chamber.[111] The advisory opinions of the Chamber have no binding effect.

(b) The advisory jurisdiction of the ITLOS full court

Originally there was no express provision for the advisory jurisdiction of ITLOS under either the LOSC or the ITLOS Statute. However, Article 138 of the ITLOS Rules confers advisory jurisdiction on ITLOS itself, by providing that:

> 1. The Tribunal may give an advisory opinion on a legal question if an international agreement related to the purposes of the Convention specifically provides for the submission to the Tribunal of a request for such an opinion.
> 2. A request for an advisory opinion shall be transmitted to the Tribunal by whatever body is authorized by or in accordance with the agreement to make the request to the Tribunal.
> 3. The Tribunal shall apply *mutatis mutandis* articles 130 to 137.[112]

[109] *Responsibilities and Obligations of States Sponsoring Persons*, pp. 18–19, paras. 47–48.

[110] ITLOS Rules, Article 130. Article 17 of the ITLOS Statute relates to nationality of members, including judges ad hoc.

[111] ITLOS Rules, Article 135(3).

[112] For an analysis in some detail of this provision, see Ki-Jun You, 'Advisory Opinions of the International Tribunal for the Law of the Sea: Article 138 of the Rules of the Tribunal, Revisited', (2008) 39 *ODIL* pp. 360 *et seq.*

Article 138 contains strict requirements for the request of an advisory opinion from the ITLOS full Court.

First, 'an international agreement' must exist. It is reasonable to argue that such an agreement means a treaty within the meaning of Article 1(1)(a) of the Vienna Convention on the Law of Treaties.

Second, such an international agreement must relate to the purpose of the LOSC.

Third, a request for an advisory opinion must involve 'a legal question'. In theory, if a question is not legal, but political, that question could not be the subject of an advisory opinion. Considering that a political question may involve some legal elements, however, the distinction between a legal question and one that is political seems to be narrow in practice.

Fourth, as explained above, the Seabed Disputes Chamber is to deal with questions with regard to activities in the Area. Accordingly, it appears logical to consider that a legal question must be unrelated to such activities, though this condition is not expressly stated.

Finally, an international agreement must specifically provide for the submission to ITLOS of a request for such an opinion. To date, there has been no request for an advisory opinion before the full court of ITLOS.

5.7 Prompt release procedure

(a) General considerations

The prompt release procedure set out in Article 292 of the LOSC plays an important part in the ITLOS jurisprudence. According to the procedure, if a vessel is detained by a coastal State for a violation of its regulations with regard to, for instance, fisheries or marine pollution, the vessel shall be promptly released upon posting a bond or other financial security in order to protect the economic and humanitarian interests of the flag State. At the same time, it is necessary for the detaining State to ensure that the master or other relevant persons on the vessel will appear in its domestic courts. Thus, in the words of ITLOS, the prompt release procedure seeks to 'reconcile the interest of the flag State to have its vessel and its crew released promptly with the interest of the detaining State to secure appearance in its court of the Master and the payment of penalties'.[113]

The jurisdiction of ITLOS under Article 292 is compulsory between all States Parties to the LOSC irrespective of whether they have accepted that jurisdiction under Article 287 of the Convention. The prompt release procedure is not incidental in nature but independent from any other proceedings in ITLOS.[114] This procedure is not a form of appeal against a decision of a national court.[115] ITLOS can deal only with the question of release, without prejudice to the merits of the case before the appropriate domestic forum.

[113] The *Monte Confurco* case (electronic text), Case No. 6, 18 December 2000, para. 71.

[114] The *M/V Saiga* case, Case No. 1, 4 December 1997, (1998) 37 *ILM* p. 370, para. 50.

[115] The *Monte Confurco* case, para. 72; the *Hoshinmaru* case (electronic text), 6 August 2007, Case No. 14, para. 89.

Article 292(2) makes clear that: 'The application for prompt release may be made only by or on behalf of the flag State of the vessel.' The phrase 'on behalf of the flag State' appears to suggest that applications could be made not only by a government official, including a consular or diplomatic agent, but also by a private person not part of the government of the flag State if that person is authorised to do so by the flag State. In either case, the detained vessel must be flying the flag of the applicant and, thus, the validity of the registration of a vessel is of particular importance.

(b) Substantive requirements

Article 292 specifies substantive and procedural requirements to be fulfilled in order to bring before ITLOS a dispute regarding prompt release. Two substantive requirements exist.

First, the prompt release procedure applies only to alleged violations of the provisions of the Convention on the prompt release of a vessel or its crew upon the posting of a reasonable bond or other financial security (LOSC, Article 292(1)). Views of commentators do not coincide as to which relevant provisions are subject to the prompt release procedure. ITLOS, in the *M/V Saiga (No. 1)* case of 1997, pointed to three provisions that correspond expressly to the above description: Articles 73(2), 220(6) and (7), and, at least to a certain extent, 226(1)(c).[116] There may also be scope for considering that to some extent, the prompt release procedure applies to Articles 216, 218, 219, 220(2), and 226(1)(b).[117] To date, all prompt release disputes have concerned the violation of Article 73(2), which relates to enforcement of laws and regulations of the coastal State with respect to living resources. The fact seems to highlight the seriousness of illegal fishing.

Second, a vessel flying the flag of a State Party to the Convention and/or its crew must have been detained by the authorities of another State Party. As shown in the *Camouco*, *Monte Confurco* and *Hoshinmaru* cases, disputes may arise with regard to the legal situation of the crew of a vessel staying in the State which detained the vessel. Whilst the situation of a crew member must be judged on a case-by-case basis, a key factor may be the seizure of the crew member's passport by a coastal State authority. In the *Camouco* and *Monte Confurco* cases, ITLOS ordered the release of the master in accordance with Article 292(1) of the LOSC in light of the fact that the master's passport had been seized by the coastal State authorities.[118]

(c) Procedural requirements

The first procedural requirement for submitting a prompt release dispute to ITLOS is that the parties have failed to agree on submitting the case to a court or tribunal

[116] The *M/V Saiga (No. 1)* case, p. 371, para. 52.

[117] Y. Tanaka, 'Prompt Release in the United Nations Convention on the Law of the Sea: Some Reflections on the ITLOS Jurisprudence' (2004) 51 *NILR* pp. 241–246; R. Lagoni, 'The International Tribunal for the Law of the Sea: Establishment and "Prompt Release" Procedures' (1996) 11 *IJMCL* pp. 153–158; D. H. Anderson, 'Investigation, Detention and Release of Foreign Vessels under the UN Convention on the Law of the Sea of 1982 and Other International Agreements' (1996) *IJMCL* pp. 170–176.

[118] The *Camouco* case, 7 February 2000, Case No. 5, (2000) 39 *ILM*, p. 680, para. 71; the *Monte Confurco* case, para. 90.

within ten days from the detention. Once the ten-day period has expired, the question of release may be brought before any court or tribunal accepted by the detaining State under Article 287, or such a question may be directly brought before ITLOS, unless the Parties have agreed otherwise. The ten-day time limit ensures prompt action on this matter. At the same time, it allows the detaining State to release the detained vessel and/or its crew before the matter is brought before a court or tribunal.

The second procedural requirement is that the flag State has not decided to submit the application for prompt release to 'a court or tribunal accepted by the detaining State under Article 287'. Owing to the urgency of the prompt release procedure, it is hardly conceivable, in reality, that a flag State will bring a dispute relating to prompt release before an arbitral tribunal since it would run the risk of delaying the proceedings by the need to select arbitrators. For the same reason, it appears unlikely, if not impossible, that such a dispute will be submitted to the ICJ unless the Court adopts rules regarding prompt-release proceedings.[119]

Third, Article 292(1) inserts another condition by reserving the case where the parties otherwise agree. This represents a fundamental principle of freedom of choice. Thus, if there is such an agreement, it is possible to extend the time limit for negotiation by agreement and not to use the prompt release procedure.[120]

However, the deposit of a bond or other financial security is not a requirement for invoking Article 292. This is clear from Article 111(2)(c) of the ITLOS Rules, which provides that the application 'shall specify the amount, nature and terms of the bond or other financial security that *may have been imposed* by the detaining State'.[121] ITLOS confirmed this view in the *M/V Saiga* and the *Camouco* judgments.[122] Furthermore, it is generally recognised that the exhaustion of local remedies rule is not applicable to proceedings regarding prompt release.[123]

Is it possible to bring the case before ITLOS if a municipal court of the detaining State has already rendered a judgment? A leading case on this particular matter is the *Tomimaru* case between Japan and the Russian Federation. The arrested vessel flying the flag of Japan, the *Tomimaru*, was confiscated in accordance with a judgment of the Petropavlovsk-Kamchatsky City Court before the dispute was submitted to ITLOS. After the closure of the hearing before ITLOS, the Supreme Court of the Russian Federation dismissed the complaint concerning the review of the decision on the confiscation of the *Tomimaru*. ITLOS ruled that a decision to confiscate eliminates the provisional character of the detention of the vessel rendering the prompt release procedure without object.[124] Therefore, ITLOS concluded that the application of Japan no longer had any object.[125] At the same time, it stressed that confiscation of a fishing vessel must not be used in such a manner as to prevent the flag State from resorting to the prompt release procedure set out in the LOSC.[126]

119 Treves, 'The Proceedings', p. 188. 120 *Ibid.*
121 Emphasis added. 122 The *M/V Saiga* case, p. 375, para. 76; the *Camouco* case, p. 679, para. 63.
123 *Virginia Commentaries*, vol. V, p. 81.
124 The *Tomimaru* case (electronic text), 6 August 2007, Case No. 15, para. 76.
125 *Ibid.*, para. 82. 126 *Ibid.*, paras. 75–76.

(d) Reasonable bond

A crucial issue in relation to prompt release involves the reasonableness of the bonds to be posted. In the *Camouco*, *Monte Confurco*, *Grand Prince* and *Hoshinmaru* cases, the Applicants alleged that the bonds required by the domestic courts of the detaining States were not 'reasonable'. A number of relevant factors need to be considered when determining the reasonableness of the bond. In this regard, ITLOS, in the *Camouco* case, indicated four factors:[127]

- the gravity of the alleged offences,
- the penalties imposed or imposable under the laws of the detaining State,
- the value of the detained vessel,[128]
- the value of the cargo seized, and
- the amount of the bond imposed by the detaining State and its form.

As the *Monte Confurco* judgment stressed, however, the list was by no means complete. Nor did ITLOS lay down rigid rules on the exact weight to be attached to each factor.[129] In this regard, it stressed that: 'The assessment of the relevant factors must be an objective one, taking into account all information provided to ITLOS by the parties'.[130] However, the evaluation of those elements is not an easy task in practice. For instance, the ITLOS jurisprudence shows that the value of a vessel cannot always be easily determined. In fact, in the *Camouco* case, the parties differed on the value of the ship.[131] Likewise, in the *Monte Confurco* case, the parties' valuations of the vessel differed greatly.[132] The same was true in the *Juno Trader* case.[133] In the *Hoshinmaru* case, ITLOS did not take the value of the vessel into account in determining the amount of the bond. It would seem, with respect, that there is a certain degree of inconsistency on this particular matter in the ITLOS jurisprudence.[134]

6 CONCLUSIONS

The matters considered in this chapter can be summarised as follows.

(i) The dispute settlement mechanism under the LOSC rests on a balance between the voluntary and compulsory procedures. In this regard, the multiple forms of judicial settlement set out in Part XV of the Convention are noteworthy because they seek to strike a balance between the compulsory procedures and the flexibility of the selection of an appropriate forum on the basis of the consent of the disputing parties.

(ii) While the establishment of the compulsory procedures for dispute settlement is a key step forward, two important categories of disputes, namely, fisheries and marine scientific research in the EEZ, are exempted from the compulsory procedures for dispute settlement. Furthermore, certain categories of disputes – disputes concerning

127 The *Camouco* case, p. 679, para. 67. 128 See also ITLOS Rules, Article 111(2)(b) and (c).
129 The *Monte Confurco* case, para. 76.
130 The *Juno Trader* case, 18 December 2004, Case No. 13, (2005) 44 *ILM* p. 514, para. 85.
131 The *Camouco* case, p. 680, para. 69. 132 The *Monte Confurco* case, para. 84.
133 The *Juno Trader* case, p. 514, para. 92.
134 Declaration of Judge Kolodk in the *Hoshinmaru* case.

maritime delimitations or those involving historic bays or title, disputes concerning military activities, and disputes in respect of which the UN Security Council is exercising its functions – may also be exempt from such procedures. Moreover, the compulsory procedures may be qualified by the application of Articles 281 and 282 of the Convention.

(iii) ITLOS is a permanent judicial organ and it comprises a variety of chambers. In so doing, ITLOS seems to deal with various types of disputes in the law of the sea. In relation to this, it is noteworthy that with regard to particular disputes, ITLOS is open to a broad range of entities other than States. It appears that the wide scope of *locus standi* of ITLOS reflects the diversity of actors involved in marine affairs.

(iv) The ITLOS jurisprudence has a valuable role in the identification, clarification and formulation of rules of the law of the sea. To date, the majority of disputes referred to ITLOS involve either provisional measures or the prompt release of vessels and crews. The accumulation of ITLOS jurisprudence will contribute to develop rules on these subjects. Moreover, advisory opinions of the Seabed Disputes Chamber and ITLOS can be considered as an important tool to clarify relevant rules of the law of the sea.

(v) Concerning the establishment of ITLOS, a concern was voiced that the creation of a new tribunal specialised in law of the sea disputes would run the risk of separating the development of the law of the sea from the general rules of international law.[135] This question relates to wider issues with regard to the proliferation of international courts and the fragmentation of international law.[136] So far, the number of disputes referred to ITLOS remains modest, and it is too early to give a definitive answer to this question. All that can be said here is that ITLOS has endeavoured to secure consistency with the jurisprudence of the ICJ as well as the development of the rules of international law in general. Thus it would be wrong to lay too great an emphasis on the risk of the fragmentation of international law in the ITLOS jurisprudence.

FURTHER READING

1 General

A. O. Adede, 'The Basic Structure of the Dispute Settlement Part of the Law of the Sea Convention' (1982) 11 *ODIL* pp. 125–148.

The System of Settlement of Disputes under the United Nations Convention on the Law of the Sea: A Drafting History and a Commentary (Dordrecht, Nijhoff, 1987).

A. Boyle, 'Dispute Settlement and the Law of the Sea Convention: Problems of Fragmentation and Jurisdiction' (1997) 46 *ICLQ*, pp. 37–54.

J. Charney, 'The Implications of Expanding International Dispute Settlement Systems: The 1982 Convention on the Law of the Sea' (1996) 90 *AJIL* pp. 69–75.

R. Churchill, 'Trends in Dispute Settlement in the Law of the Sea: Towards the Increasing Availability of Compulsory Means', in D. French, M. Saul and N. D. White (eds.),

[135] S. Oda, 'Dispute Settlement Prospects in the Law of the Sea' (1995) 44 *ICLQ* p. 864.

[136] The fragmentation of international law is a subject of discussion in the ILC.

International Law and Dispute Settlement: New Problems and Techniques (Oxford and Portland, Oregon, Hart Publishing, 2010), pp. 143–171.

M. P. Gaertner, 'The Dispute Settlement Provisions of the Convention on the Law of the Sea: Critique and Alternatives to the International Tribunal for the Law of the Sea' (1982) 19 *San Diego Law Review* pp. 577–597.

G. Jaenicke, 'Dispute Settlement under the Convention on the Law of the Sea' (1983) 43 *ZaöRV* pp. 813–827.

N. Klein, *Dispute Settlement in the UN Convention on the Law of the Sea* (Cambridge University Press, 2005).

D. König (ed.), *Symposium to Mark the Tenth Anniversary of ITLOS: The Jurisprudence of the International Tribunal of the Law of the Sea: Assessment and Prospects* (2007) 22 *IJMCL* pp. 347–462.

T. A. Mensah, 'The Dispute Settlement Regime of the 1982 United Nations Convention on the Law of the Sea' (1998) 2 *Max Planck Yearbook of United Nations Law* pp. 307–323.

J. G. Merrills, *International Dispute Settlement* (Cambridge University Press, 2011) (Chapter 8).

S. Oda, 'Dispute Settlement Prospects in the Law of the Sea' (1995) 44 *ICLQ* pp. 863–872.

S. P. Sharma, 'Framework of Likely Disputes under the Law of the Sea Convention – Some Thoughts' (1985) 45 *ZaöRV* pp. 465–496.

L. B. Sohn, 'Settlement of Law of the Sea Disputes' (1995) 10 *IJMCL* pp. 205–217.

2 ITLOS

P. Chandrasekhara Rao, 'ITLOS: The First Six Years' (2002) 6 *Max Planck Yearbook of United Nations Law* pp. 183–300.

P. Chandrasekhara Rao and P. Gautier (eds.), *The Rules of the International Tribunal for the Law of the Sea: A Commentary* (Leiden, Nijhoff, 2006).

G. Eiriksson, *The International Tribunal for the Law of the Sea* (The Hague, Nijhoff, 2000).

M. Kamto, 'Regard sur la jurisprudence du Tribunal international du droit de la mer depuis son entrée en fonctionnement (1997–2004)' (2005) 109 *RGDIP* pp. 769–828.

M. M. Marsit, *Le Tribunal du droit de la mer: présentation et texts officiels* (Paris, Pedone, 1999).

T. M. Ndiaye, 'Proceedings on the Merits before the International Tribunal for the Law of the Sea' (2008) 48 *Indian Journal of International Law* pp. 169–187.

T. Treves, 'The Law of the Sea Tribunal: Its Status and Scope of Jurisdiction after November 16, 1994' (1995) 55 *ZaöRV* pp. 421–451.

R. Wolfrum, 'The Settlement of Disputes before the International Tribunal for the Law of the Sea: A Progressive Development of International Law or Relying on Traditional Mechanisms?' (2008) 51 *Japanese Yearbook of International Law* pp. 140–163.

3 Provisional Measures

P. Gautier, 'Mesures conservatoire, préjudice irréparable et protection de l'environnement', in *Liber amicorum Jean-Pierre Cot: le procès international* (Brussels, Bruyant, 2009), pp. 131–154.

J.-G. Mahinga, 'Les procedures en prescription de measures conservatoires devant le Tribunal international du droit de la mer' (2004) 9 *Annuaire du droit de la mer*, pp. 65–113.

T. A. Mensah, 'Provisional Measures in the International Law of the Sea (ITLOS)' (2002) 62 *ZaöRV* pp. 43–54.

F. Orrego Vicuña, 'The International Tribunal for the Law of the Sea and Provisional Measures: Settled Issues and Pending Problems' (2007) 22 *IJMCL*, pp. 451–462.

S. Rosenne, *Provisional Measures in International Law: The International Court of Justice and the International Tribunal for the Law of the Sea* (Oxford University Press, 2005).

T. Treves, 'Les mesures conservatoires au Tribunal de droit de la mer et à la Cour internationale de justice: Contribution au dialogue entre cours et tribunaux internationaux', in *Liber amicorum Jean-Pierre Cot: le procès international* (Brussels, Bruyant, 2009), pp. 341–348.

P. Weckel, 'Les premières applications de l'article 290 de la Convention sur le droit de la mer relative à la prescription de mesures conservatoires' (2005) 109 *RGDIP* pp. 829–858.

R. Wolfrum, 'Provisional Measures of the International Tribunal for the Law of the Sea', in P. C. Rao and R. Khan (eds.), *The International Tribunal for the Law of the Sea* (The Hague, Kluwer, 2001), pp. 173–186.

4 Prompt Release

For an overview of the prompt release procedure, the following articles are of particular interest.

R. Lagoni, 'The International Tribunal for the Law of the Sea: Establishment and "Prompt Release" Procedures' (1996) 11 *IJMCL* pp. 137–231.

T. A. Mensah, 'The Tribunal and the Prompt Release of Vessels' (2007) 22 *IJMCL* pp. 425–450.

Y. Tanaka, 'Prompt Release in the United Nations Convention on the Law of the Sea: Some Reflections on the ITLOS Jurisprudence' (2004) 51 *NILR* pp. 237–271.

T. Treves, 'The Proceedings Concerning Prompt Release of Vessels and Crews before the International Tribunal for the Law of the Sea' (1996) 11 *IJMCL* pp. 179–200.

M. White, 'Prompt Release Cases in ITLOS', in T. M. Ndiaye, R. Wolfrum and C. Kojima (eds.), *Law of the Sea, Environmental Law and Settlement of Disputes: Liber Amicorum Judge Thomas A. Mensah* (Leiden, Nijhoff, 2007), pp. 1025–1052.

5 Advisory Opinion

Ki-Jun You, 'Advisory Opinions of the International Tribunal for the Law of the Sea: Article 138 of the Rules of the Tribunal, Revisited' (2008) 39 *ODIL* pp. 360–371.

T. M. Ndiaye, 'The Advisory Function of the International Tribunal for the Law of the Sea' (2010) 9(3) *Chinese Journal of International Law* pp. 565–587.

L. B. Sohn, 'Advisory Opinions by the International Tribunal for the Law of the Sea or its Seabed Disputes Chamber', in M. H. Nordquist and J. N. Moore (eds.), *Ocean Policy: New Institutions, Challenges and Opportunities* (The Hague, Nijhoff, 1999), pp. 61–72.

T. Treves, 'Advisory Opinions Under the Law of the Sea Convention', in M. H. Nordquist and J. N. Moore (eds.), *Current Marine Environmental Issues and the International Tribunal for the Law of the Sea* (The Hague, Nijhoff, 2001), pp. 81–93.

Index

11, 30, 33, 34, 39, 49, 50–2, 56, 58, 60
62

156

396
400